アイエル

STONEBOT
MANGA

TITAN
MANGA

**Translation:** Motoko Tamamuro & Jonathan Clements
**Lettering:** Ayoub Bensidi

**ALL KIND BOT LLC / TITAN COMICS**
**Managing Director & Acquisitions** Diego Barassi - All Kind Bot LLC
**Assistant Editor** Louis Yamani / **Designer** David Colderley
**Group Editor** Jake Devine / **Senior Creative Editor** David Manley-Leach
**Editor** Phoebe Hedges / **Editorial Assistant** Ibraheem Kazi
**Art Director** Oz Browne / **Head of Production** Kevin Wooff
**Production Manager** Jackie Flook / **Production Controllers** Caterina Falqui & Kelly Fenlon
**Publicity Manager** Will O'Mullane / **Publicist** Caitlin Storer
**Publicity & Sales Coordinator** Alexandra Iciek
**Digital & Marketing Manager** Jo Teather / **Marketing Coordinator** Lauren Noding
**Sales & Circulation Manager** Steve Tothill
**Head Of Rights** Rosanna Anness / **Rights Executive** Pauline Savouré
**Head of Creative & Business Development** Duncan Baizley
**Publishing Directors** Ricky Claydon & John Dziewiatkowski
**Chief Operating Officer** Andrew Sumner / **Publishers** Vivian Cheung & Nick Landau

## I.L

I.L. of the works by Osamu Tezuka
©2024 by Tezuka Productions
All Rights Reserved
First publication in Japan in 1969
English translation rights arranged with Tezuka Productions
through Toutlemonde Productions.

10 9 8 7 6 5 4 3 2 1

First edition: December 2024
Printed in the UK
ISBN: 9781787744400

A CIP catalogue record for this title is available from the British Library.

This book is a work of fiction. It contains content and language that may be offensive or distressing to
some readers. The publisher and copyright holder do not endorse the views or depictions presented.

Please note: Image quality may vary depending on the artwork received from the original
Japanese manga. Every effort has been made to preserve the condition of the original artwork to
ensure our readers can fully appreciate the story as it was intended.

To the readers,

The works in the Osamu Tezuka Manga Collection include depictions of many non-Japanese people, including Africans and South-East Asians. Some of them are shown quite differently from today's norm, with an emphasis on a primitive appearance or an outdated form of exaggerated caricature. Such imagery has been called out as racist towards some non-Japanese people. As people feel uncomfortable or offended by such imagery, we need to acknowledge it and take it seriously.

Exaggerated caricature and comical depictions have been some of the most important elements for humor in the graphic arts. They are particularly prominent in the works of Tezuka, who parodied people from many different countries in his work. Not only humans, but even plants and animals, or things from fantasy worlds were lampooned in his creations. He didn't even spare himself, depicting his own nose as far larger than it was in real life. His stories always had a strong undercurrent of love for all humanity, and he always strongly believed that hatred and antipathy were evil, as was the stand-off between civilized and uncivilized, developed versus developing countries, the powerful versus the powerless, the rich versus the poor and the able-bodied versus the disabled.

We continue to publish the Osamu Tezuka Manga Collection in its original format. Alteration is impossible now that the author is no longer with us, as allowing a third party to retroactively redact the imagery feels like an inappropriate means of dealing with this issue, and would also be an infringement of the author's moral rights. Furthermore, we have a duty to protect works that are recognised as part of Japan's cultural heritage. From the start, we have been opposed to discrimination of all kinds on Earth, and we will continue our efforts to challenge bigotry. We believe that this is all part of our responsibility as publishers. We hope that this Tezuka work will be an opportunity for you to acknowledge the fact that various forms of discrimination exist, and deepen your understanding of the issue.

Tezuka Productions/Kodansha

# CONTENTS
PART 1

# EPISODE 1
# The Woman in the Box

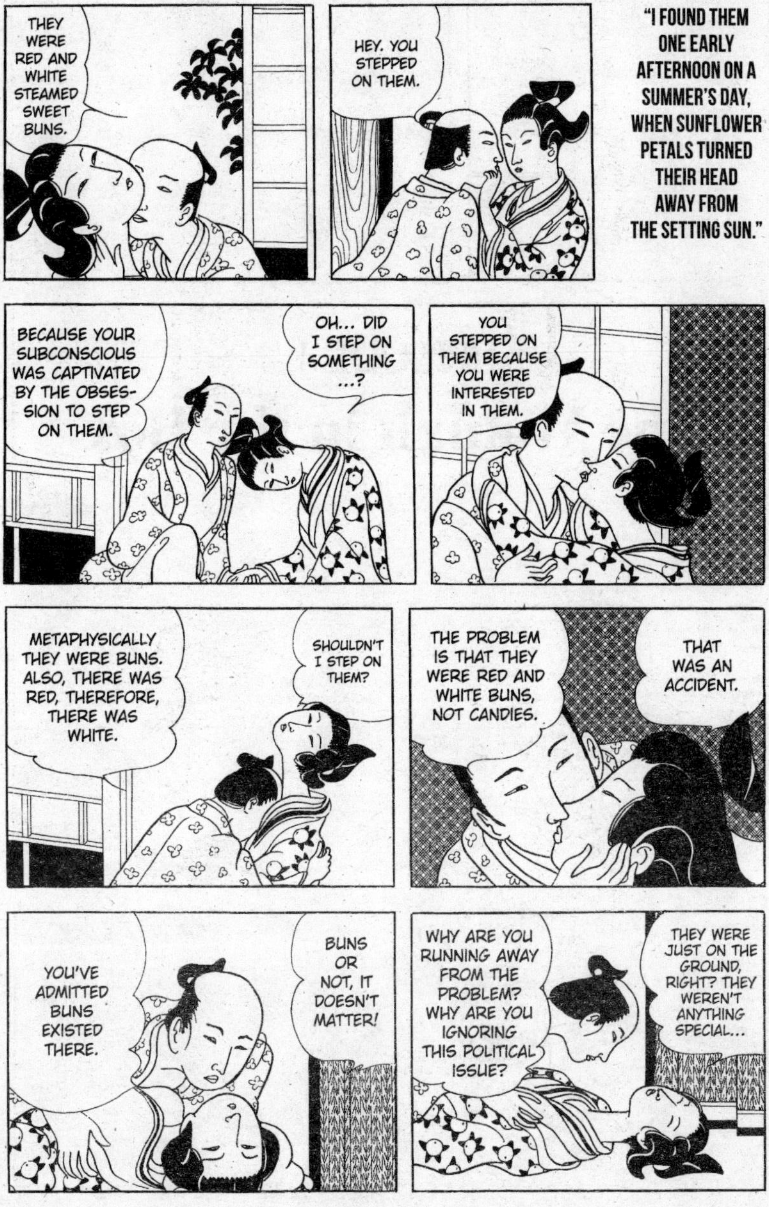
"I FOUND THEM ONE EARLY AFTERNOON ON A SUMMER'S DAY, WHEN SUNFLOWER PETALS TURNED THEIR HEAD AWAY FROM THE SETTING SUN."
HEY. YOU STEPPED ON THEM.
THEY WERE RED AND WHITE STEAMED SWEET BUNS.
YOU STEPPED ON THEM BECAUSE YOU WERE INTERESTED IN THEM.
OH... DID I STEP ON SOMETHING ...?
BECAUSE YOUR SUBCONSCIOUS WAS CAPTIVATED BY THE OBSESSION TO STEP ON THEM.
THAT WAS AN ACCIDENT.
THE PROBLEM IS THAT THEY WERE RED AND WHITE BUNS, NOT CANDIES.
SHOULDN'T I STEP ON THEM?
METAPHYSICALLY THEY WERE BUNS. ALSO, THERE WAS RED, THEREFORE, THERE WAS WHITE.
THEY WERE JUST ON THE GROUND, RIGHT? THEY WEREN'T ANYTHING SPECIAL...
WHY ARE YOU RUNNING AWAY FROM THE PROBLEM? WHY ARE YOU IGNORING THIS POLITICAL ISSUE?
BUNS OR NOT, IT DOESN'T MATTER!
YOU'VE ADMITTED BUNS EXISTED THERE.

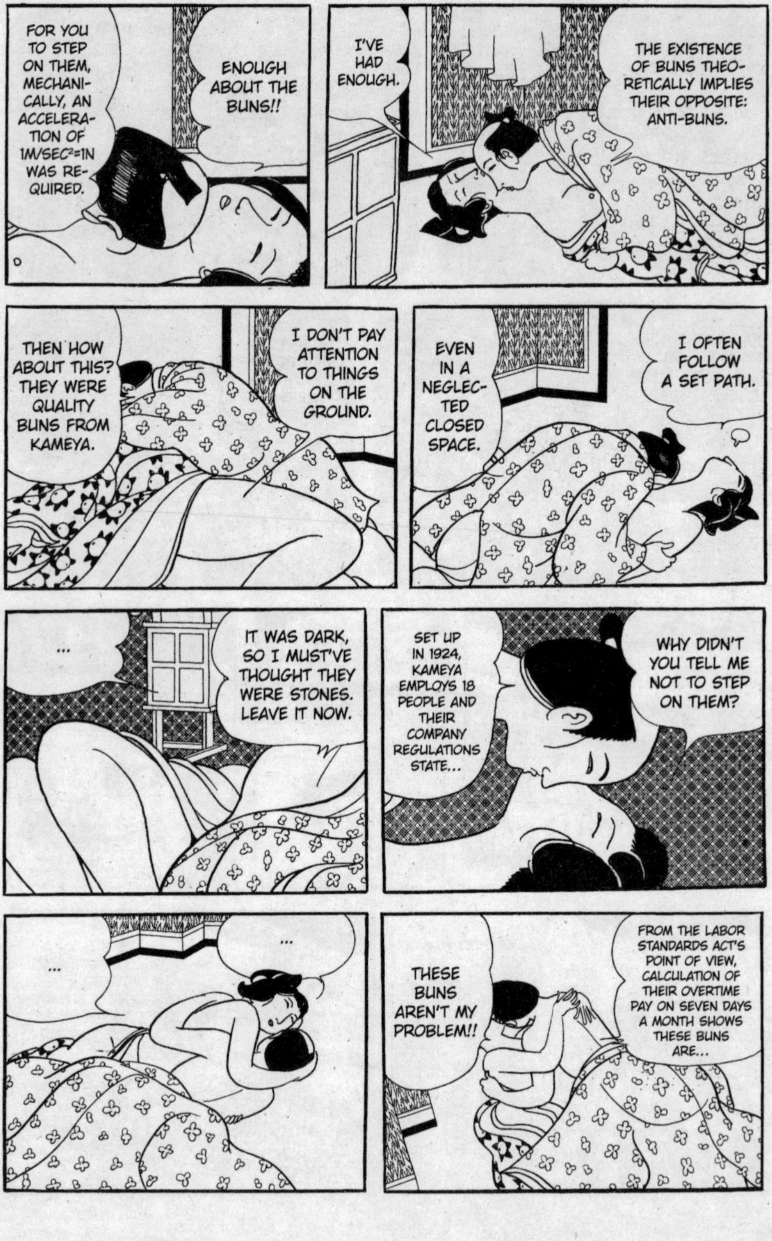
THE EXISTENCE OF BUNS THEORETICALLY IMPLIES THEIR OPPOSITE: ANTI-BUNS.
I'VE HAD ENOUGH.
ENOUGH ABOUT THE BUNS!!
FOR YOU TO STEP ON THEM, MECHANICALLY, AN ACCELERATION OF $1M/SEC^2=1N$ WAS REQUIRED.
I OFTEN FOLLOW A SET PATH.
EVEN IN A NEGLECTED CLOSED SPACE.
I DON'T PAY ATTENTION TO THINGS ON THE GROUND.
THEN HOW ABOUT THIS? THEY WERE QUALITY BUNS FROM KAMEYA.
WHY DIDN'T YOU TELL ME NOT TO STEP ON THEM?
SET UP IN 1924, KAMEYA EMPLOYS 18 PEOPLE AND THEIR COMPANY REGULATIONS STATE...
IT WAS DARK, SO I MUST'VE THOUGHT THEY WERE STONES. LEAVE IT NOW.
...
FROM THE LABOR STANDARDS ACT'S POINT OF VIEW, CALCULATION OF THEIR OVERTIME PAY ON SEVEN DAYS A MONTH SHOWS THESE BUNS ARE...
THESE BUNS AREN'T MY PROBLEM!!
...
...

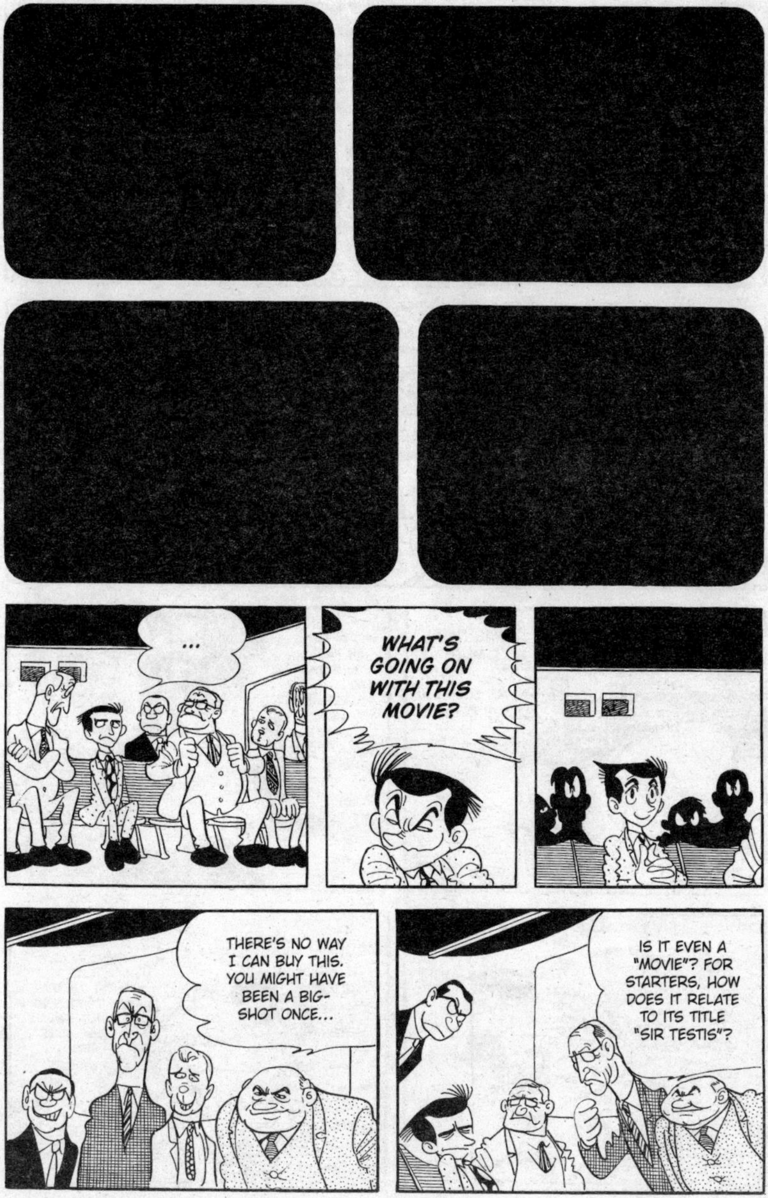
WHAT'S GOING ON WITH THIS MOVIE?
...
IS IT EVEN A "MOVIE"? FOR STARTERS, HOW DOES IT RELATE TO ITS TITLE "SIR TESTIS"?
THERE'S NO WAY I CAN BUY THIS. YOU MIGHT HAVE BEEN A BIG-SHOT ONCE...

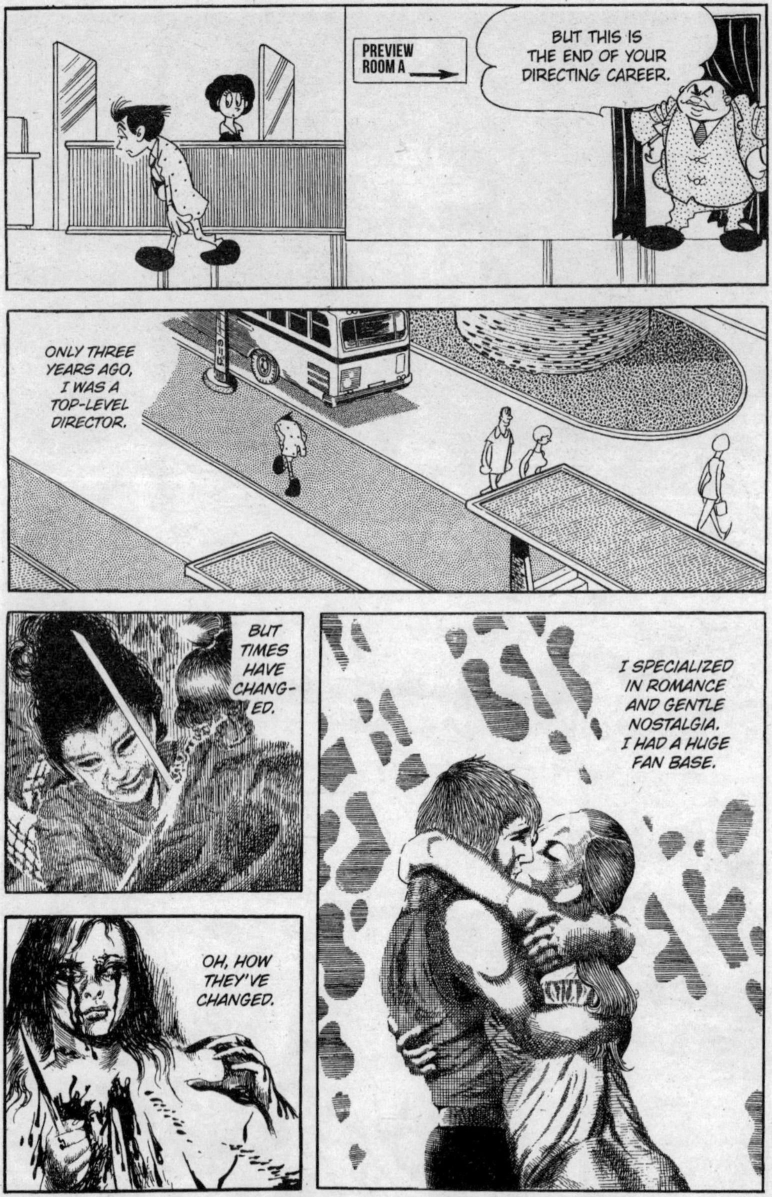
BUT THIS IS THE END OF YOUR DIRECTING CAREER.
PREVIEW ROOM A
ONLY THREE YEARS AGO, I WAS A TOP-LEVEL DIRECTOR.
I SPECIALIZED IN ROMANCE AND GENTLE NOSTALGIA. I HAD A HUGE FAN BASE.
BUT TIMES HAVE CHANG-ED.
OH, HOW THEY'VE CHANGED.

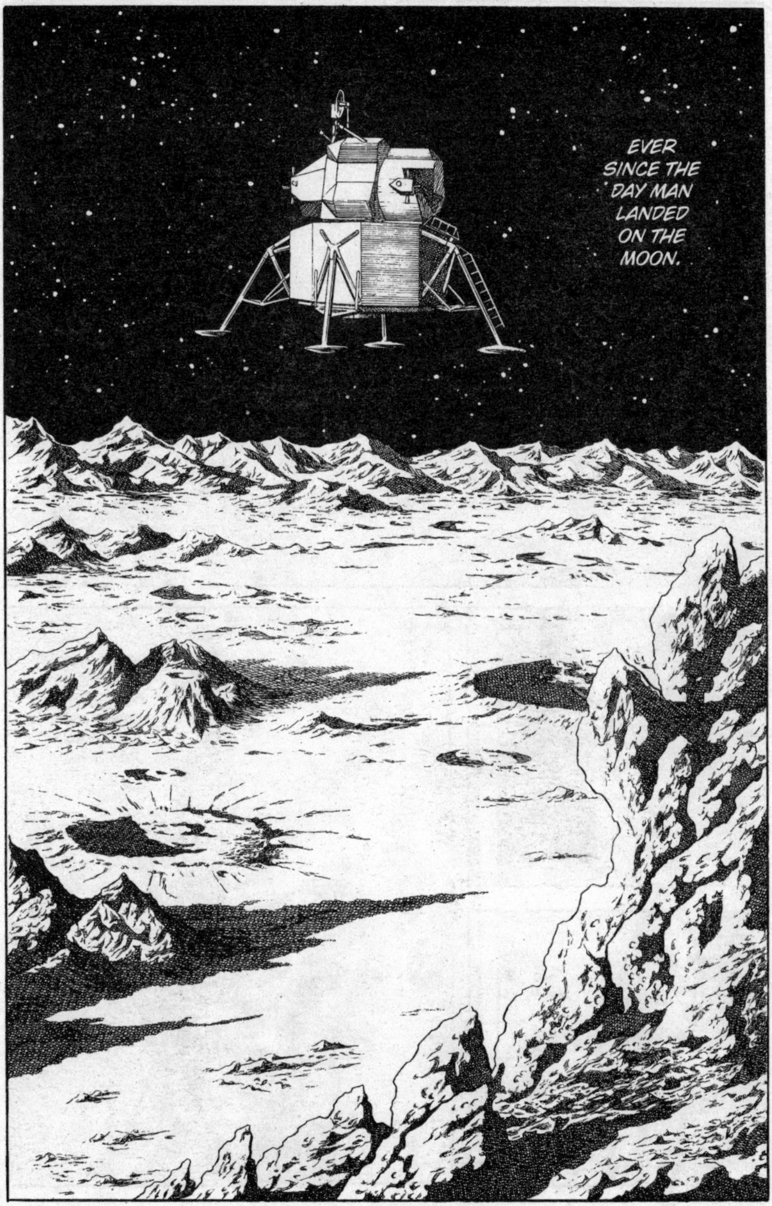
EVER SINCE THE DAY MAN LANDED ON THE MOON.

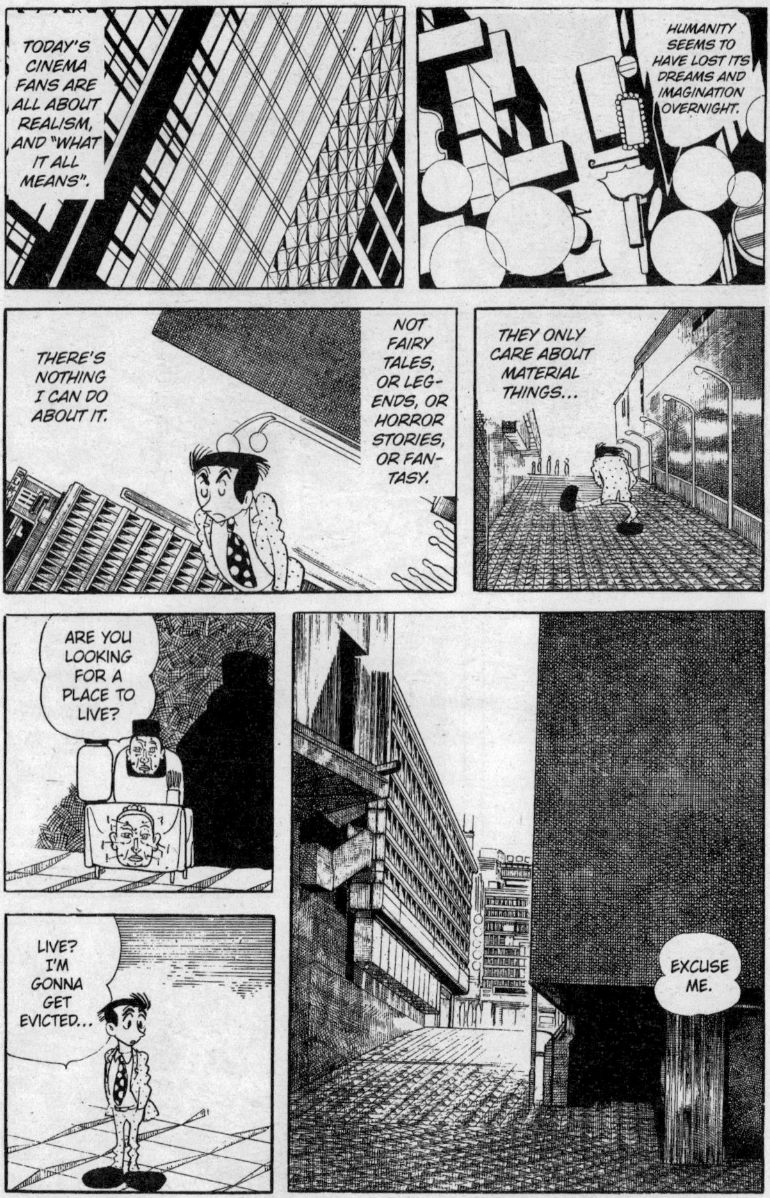
HUMANITY SEEMS TO HAVE LOST ITS DREAMS AND IMAGINATION OVERNIGHT.
TODAY'S CINEMA FANS ARE ALL ABOUT REALISM, AND "WHAT IT ALL MEANS".
THEY ONLY CARE ABOUT MATERIAL THINGS...
NOT FAIRY TALES, OR LEG-ENDS, OR HORROR STORIES, OR FAN-TASY.
THERE'S NOTHING I CAN DO ABOUT IT.
EXCUSE ME.
ARE YOU LOOKING FOR A PLACE TO LIVE?
LIVE? I'M GONNA GET EVICTED...

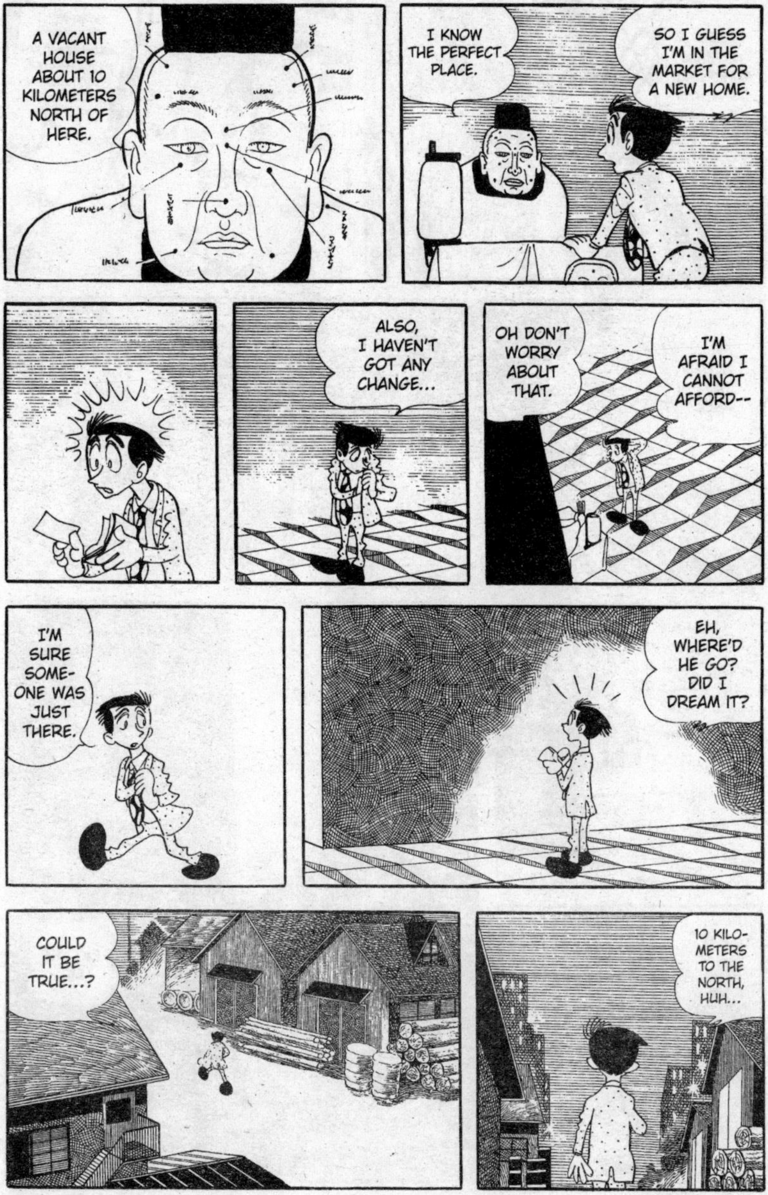
SO I GUESS I'M IN THE MARKET FOR A NEW HOME.
I KNOW THE PERFECT PLACE.
A VACANT HOUSE ABOUT 10 KILOMETERS NORTH OF HERE.
I'M AFRAID I CANNOT AFFORD--
OH DON'T WORRY ABOUT THAT.
ALSO, I HAVEN'T GOT ANY CHANGE...
EH, WHERE'D HE GO? DID I DREAM IT?
I'M SURE SOMEONE WAS JUST THERE.
10 KILOMETERS TO THE NORTH, HUH...
COULD IT BE TRUE...?

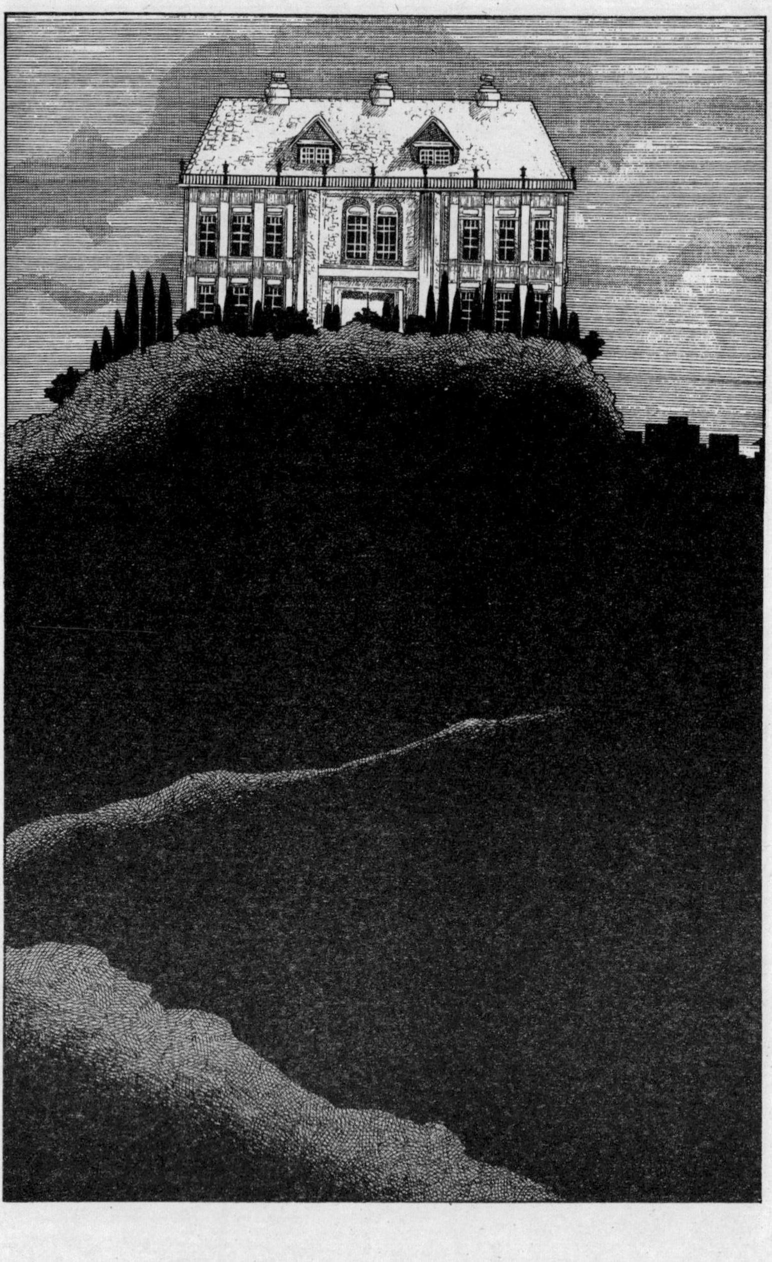

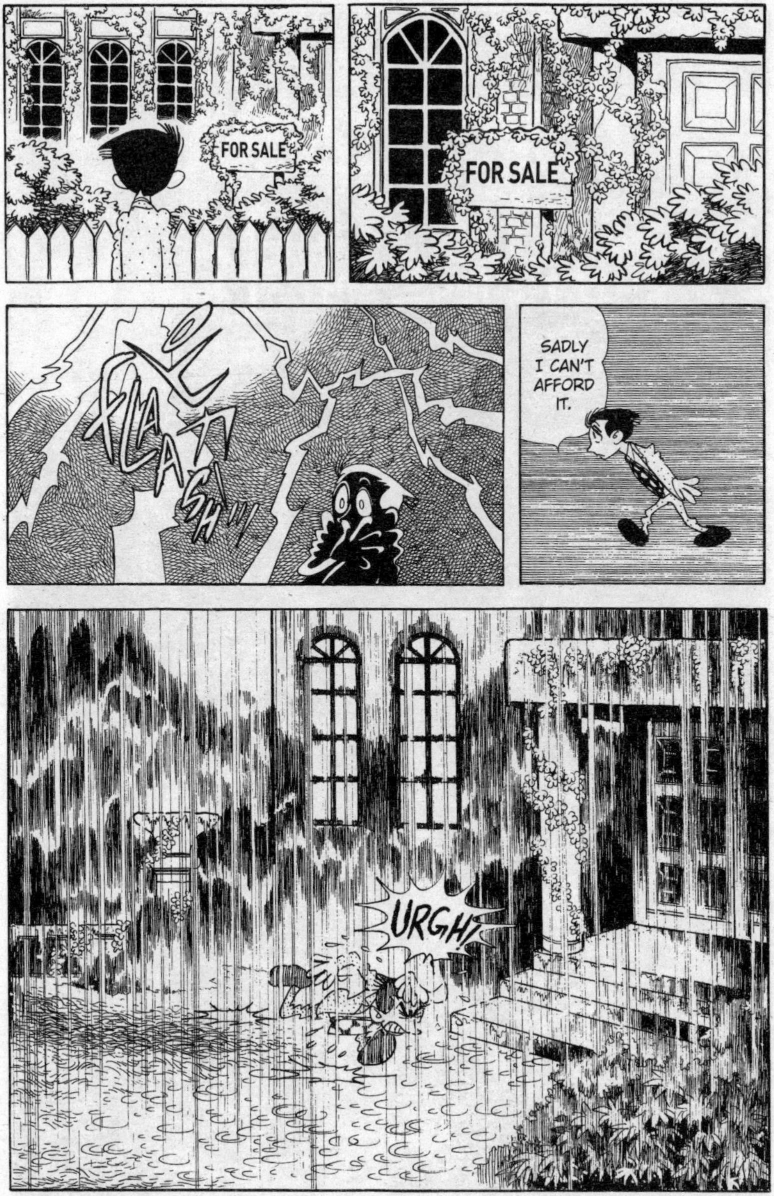
FOR SALE
FOR SALE
SADLY I CAN'T AFFORD IT.
FLASH!!!
URGH!

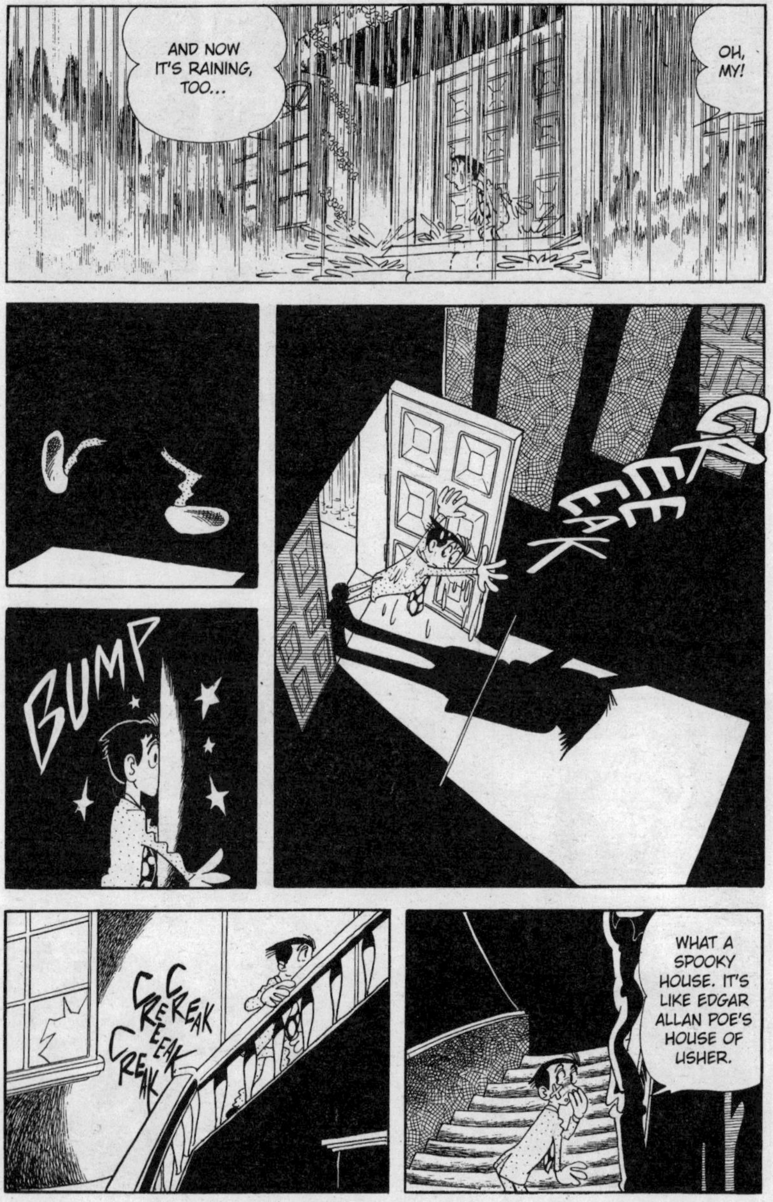
OH, MY!
AND NOW IT'S RAINING, TOO...
CREEEAK
BUMP
WHAT A SPOOKY HOUSE. IT'S LIKE EDGAR ALLAN POE'S HOUSE OF USHER.
CREAK
CREEEAK
CREAK

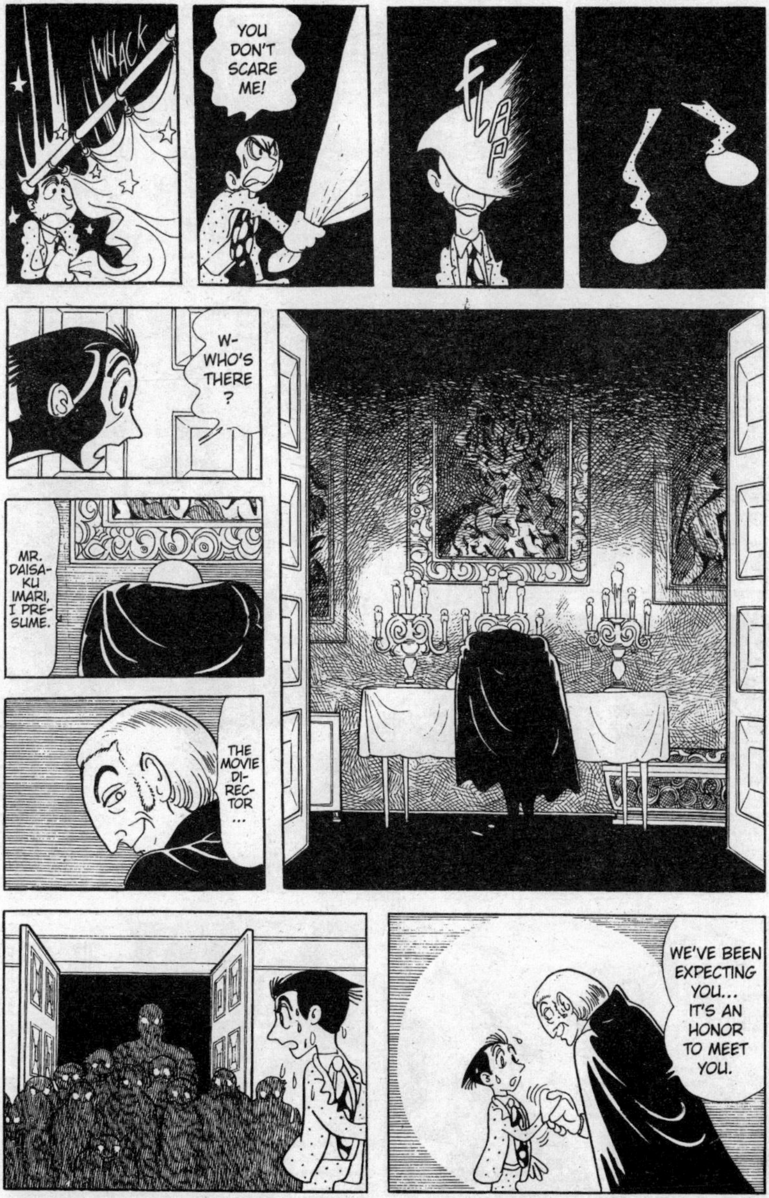
FLAP
YOU DON'T SCARE ME!
WHACK
W-WHO'S THERE?
MR. DAISAKU IMARI, I PRESUME.
THE MOVIE DIRECTOR...
WE'VE BEEN EXPECTING YOU... IT'S AN HONOR TO MEET YOU.

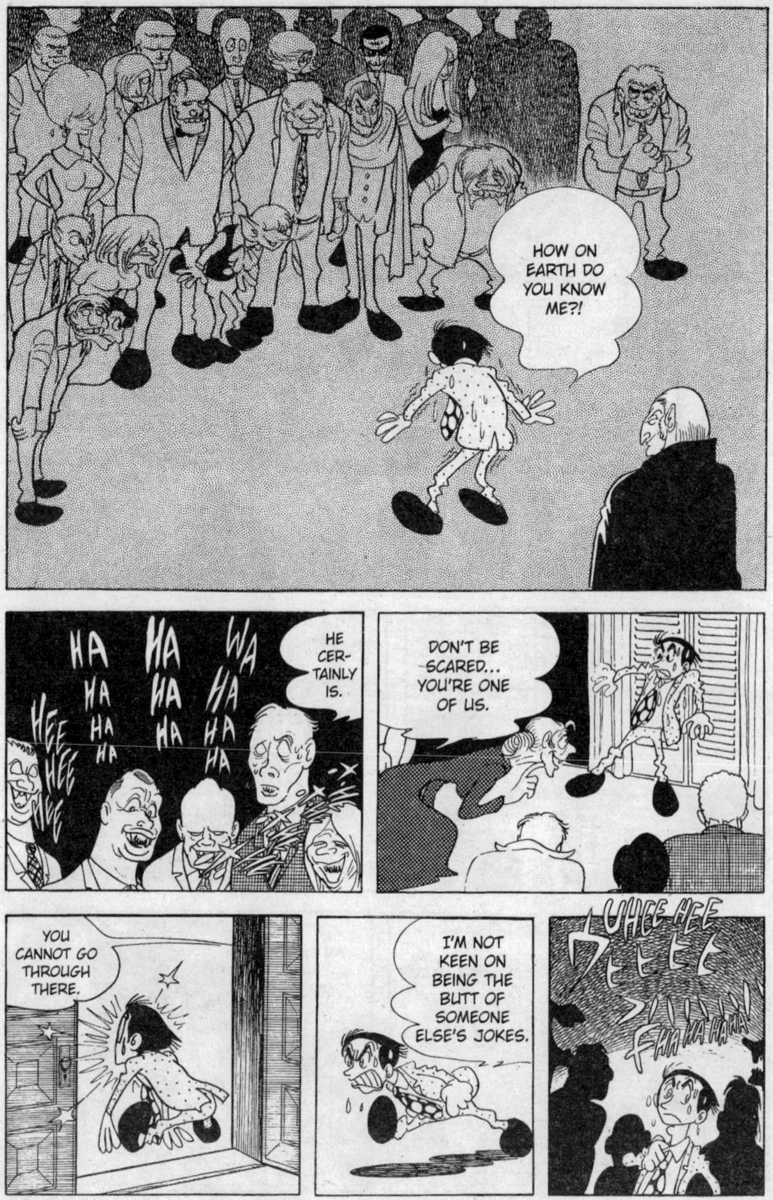
HOW ON EARTH DO YOU KNOW ME?!
DON'T BE SCARED... YOU'RE ONE OF US.
HE CER-TAINLY IS.
HA HA HA HA
HA HA HA HA
WA HA HA HA HA
HEE HEE HEE
UHEE HEE
FHA HA HA HA!
I'M NOT KEEN ON BEING THE BUTT OF SOMEONE ELSE'S JOKES.
YOU CANNOT GO THROUGH THERE.

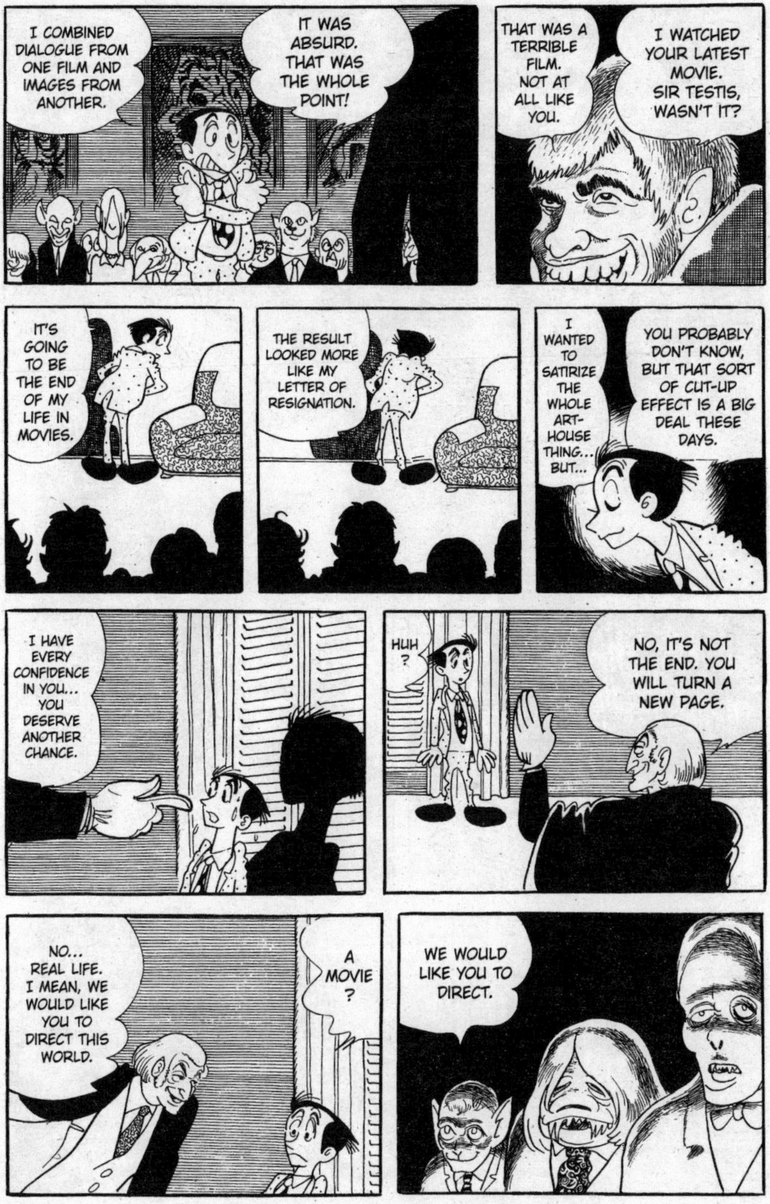
I WATCHED YOUR LATEST MOVIE. SIR TESTIS, WASN'T IT?
THAT WAS A TERRIBLE FILM. NOT AT ALL LIKE YOU.
IT WAS ABSURD. THAT WAS THE WHOLE POINT!
I COMBINED DIALOGUE FROM ONE FILM AND IMAGES FROM ANOTHER.
YOU PROBABLY DON'T KNOW, BUT THAT SORT OF CUT-UP EFFECT IS A BIG DEAL THESE DAYS.
I WANTED TO SATIRIZE THE WHOLE ART-HOUSE THING... BUT...
THE RESULT LOOKED MORE LIKE MY LETTER OF RESIGNATION.
IT'S GOING TO BE THE END OF MY LIFE IN MOVIES.
NO, IT'S NOT THE END. YOU WILL TURN A NEW PAGE.
HUH ?
I HAVE EVERY CONFIDENCE IN YOU... YOU DESERVE ANOTHER CHANCE.
WE WOULD LIKE YOU TO DIRECT.
A MOVIE ?
NO... REAL LIFE. I MEAN, WE WOULD LIKE YOU TO DIRECT THIS WORLD.

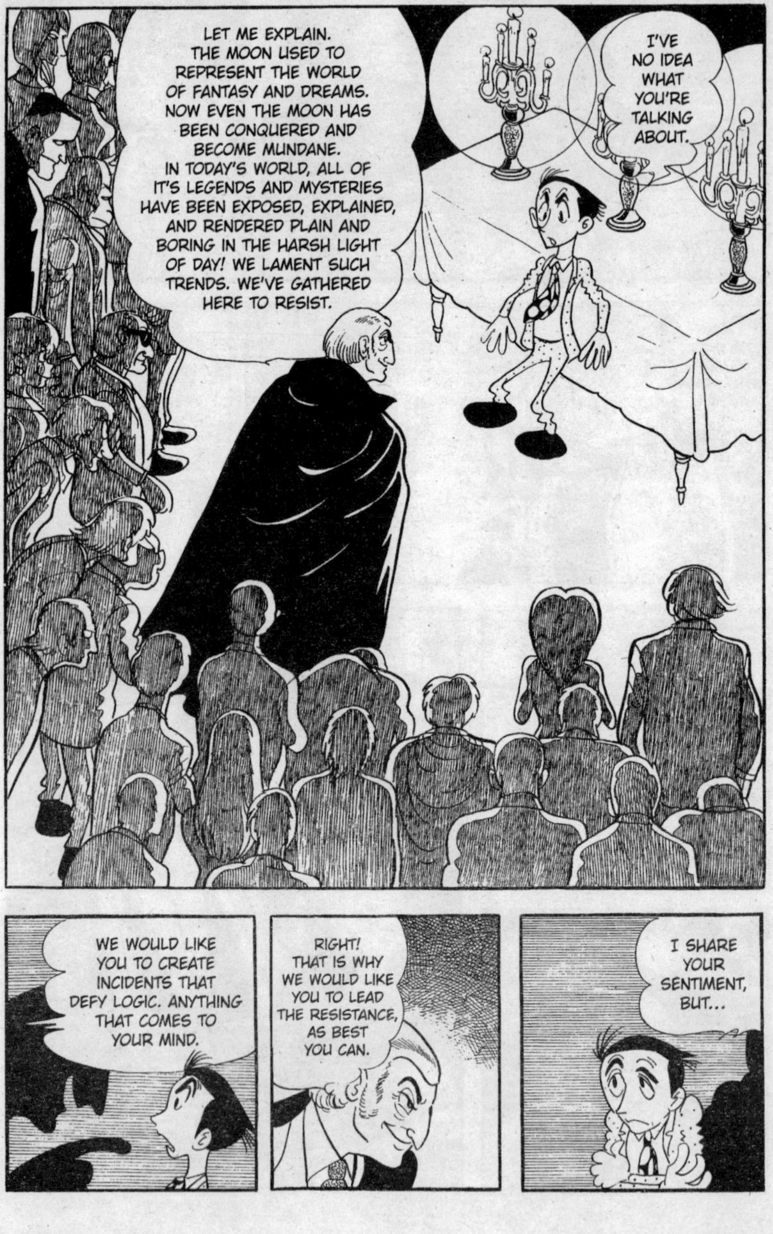
I'VE NO IDEA WHAT YOU'RE TALKING ABOUT.
LET ME EXPLAIN. THE MOON USED TO REPRESENT THE WORLD OF FANTASY AND DREAMS. NOW EVEN THE MOON HAS BEEN CONQUERED AND BECOME MUNDANE. IN TODAY'S WORLD, ALL OF IT'S LEGENDS AND MYSTERIES HAVE BEEN EXPOSED, EXPLAINED, AND RENDERED PLAIN AND BORING IN THE HARSH LIGHT OF DAY! WE LAMENT SUCH TRENDS. WE'VE GATHERED HERE TO RESIST.
I SHARE YOUR SENTIMENT, BUT...
RIGHT! THAT IS WHY WE WOULD LIKE YOU TO LEAD THE RESISTANCE, AS BEST YOU CAN.
WE WOULD LIKE YOU TO CREATE INCIDENTS THAT DEFY LOGIC. ANYTHING THAT COMES TO YOUR MIND.

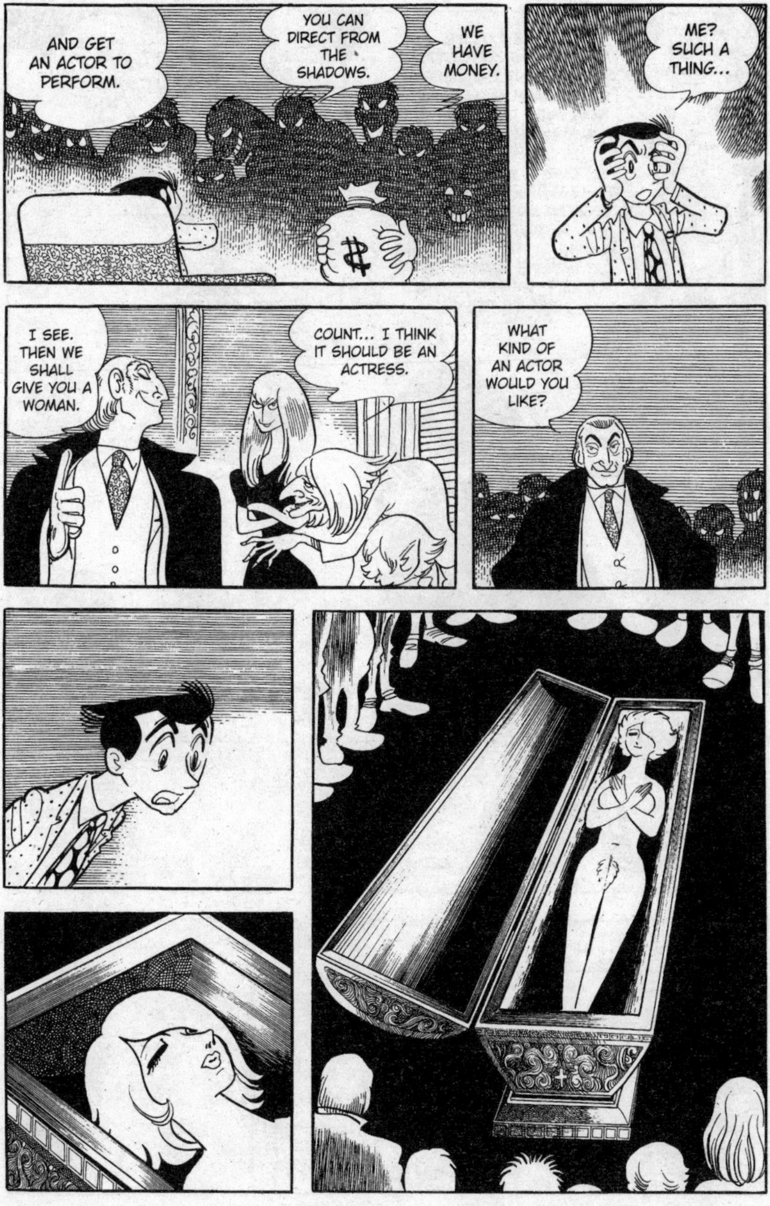
ME? SUCH A THING...
WE HAVE MONEY.
YOU CAN DIRECT FROM THE SHADOWS.
AND GET AN ACTOR TO PERFORM.
WHAT KIND OF AN ACTOR WOULD YOU LIKE?
COUNT... I THINK IT SHOULD BE AN ACTRESS.
I SEE. THEN WE SHALL GIVE YOU A WOMAN.

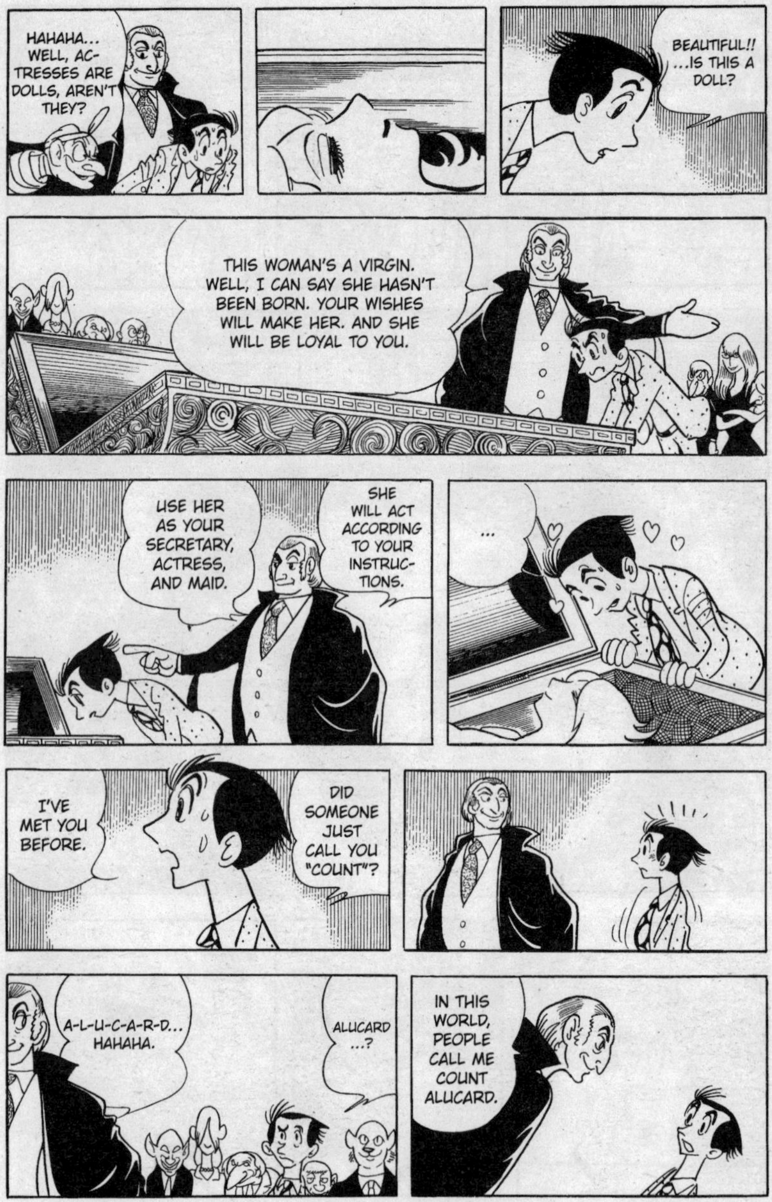
BEAUTIFUL!! ...IS THIS A DOLL?
HAHAHA... WELL, ACTRESSES ARE DOLLS, AREN'T THEY?
THIS WOMAN'S A VIRGIN. WELL, I CAN SAY SHE HASN'T BEEN BORN. YOUR WISHES WILL MAKE HER. AND SHE WILL BE LOYAL TO YOU.
...
SHE WILL ACT ACCORDING TO YOUR INSTRUCTIONS.
USE HER AS YOUR SECRETARY, ACTRESS, AND MAID.
DID SOMEONE JUST CALL YOU "COUNT"?
I'VE MET YOU BEFORE.
IN THIS WORLD, PEOPLE CALL ME COUNT ALUCARD.
ALUCARD ...?
A-L-U-C-A-R-D... HAHAHA.

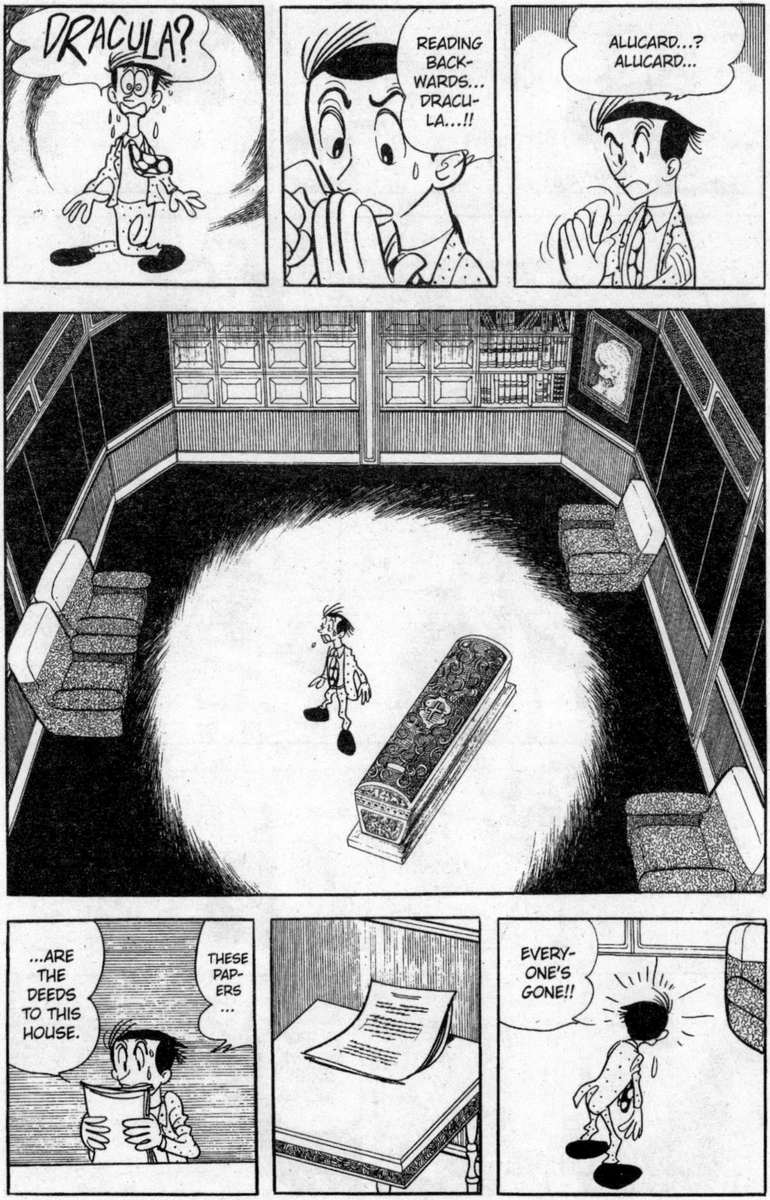
ALUCARD...? ALUCARD...
READING BACKWARDS... DRACULA...!!
DRACULA?
EVERYONE'S GONE!!
THESE PAPERS...
...ARE THE DEEDS TO THIS HOUSE.

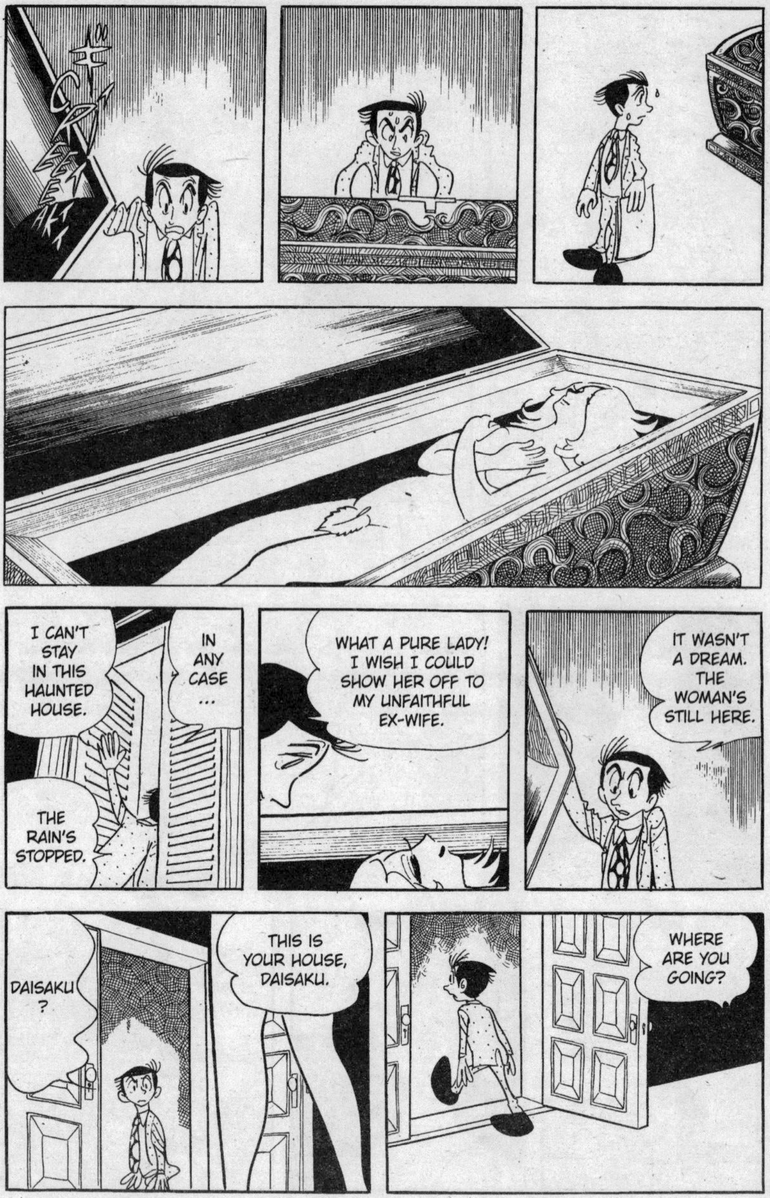
ギー
CREEEAKK
IT WASN'T A DREAM. THE WOMAN'S STILL HERE.
WHAT A PURE LADY! I WISH I COULD SHOW HER OFF TO MY UNFAITHFUL EX-WIFE.
IN ANY CASE ...
I CAN'T STAY IN THIS HAUNTED HOUSE.
THE RAIN'S STOPPED.
WHERE ARE YOU GOING?
THIS IS YOUR HOUSE, DAISAKU.
DAISAKU ?

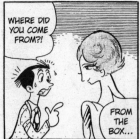

K... KAYOKO ?!
WHERE DID YOU COME FROM?!
FROM THE BOX...
BUT WHY DO YOU HAVE MY EX-WIFE'S FACE?!
BECAUSE THAT'S WHAT YOU WANTED...
I DIDN'T WANT THAT. I NEVER WANT TO SEE HER AGAIN.
CAN'T YOU TAKE OFF THE MAKEUP?! PUT ON A DIFFERENT ONE...
SORRY ...
H-HANG ON. WHAT IS YOUR NAME?
I.L...
I.L? SOUNDS LIKE A CODE. OH WELL, I'LL CALL YOU WHATEVER.
AS FOR ME... ALL THE ACTORS CALL ME DIREC-TOR.

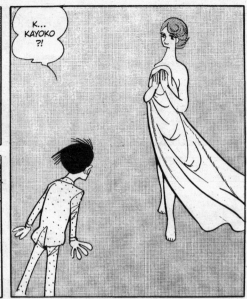

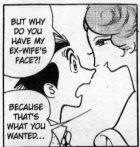

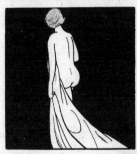

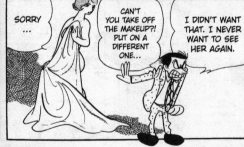

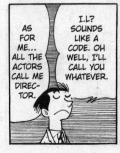

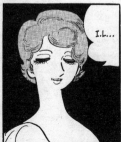

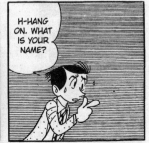

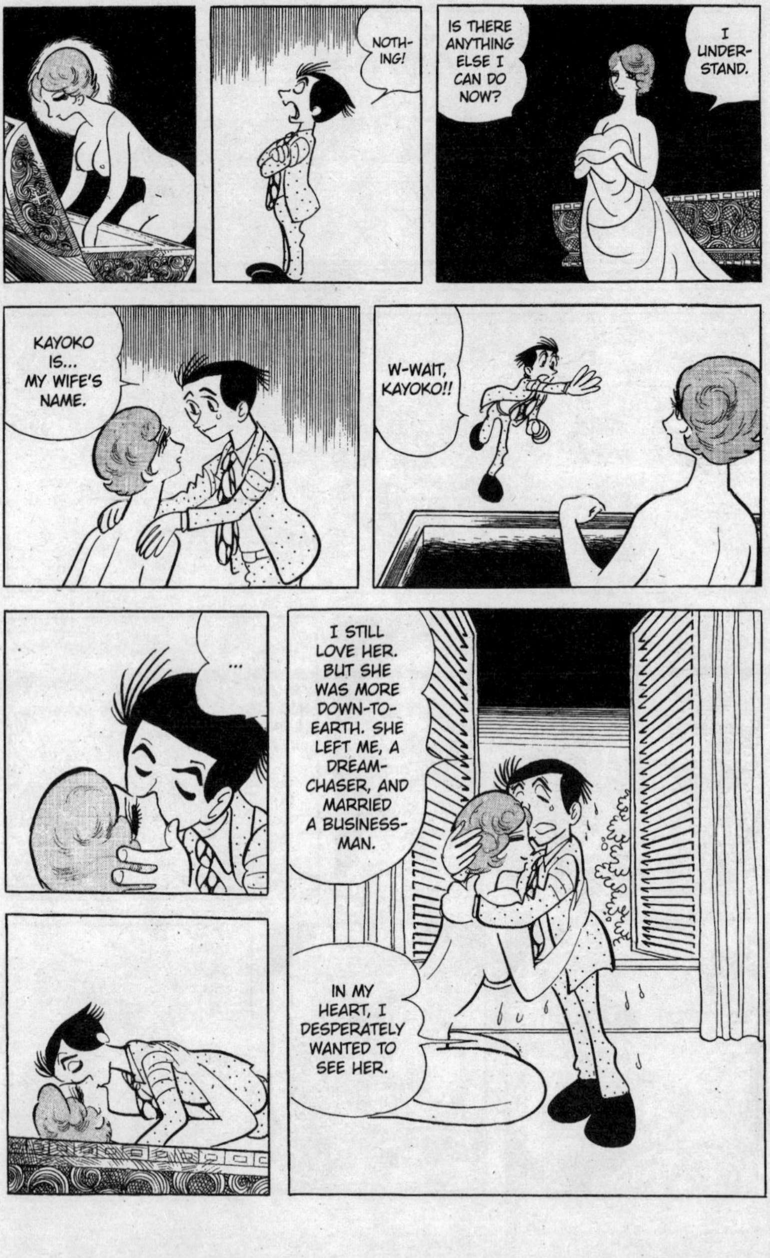
I UNDERSTAND.
IS THERE ANYTHING ELSE I CAN DO NOW?
NOTHING!
W-WAIT, KAYOKO!!
KAYOKO IS... MY WIFE'S NAME.
I STILL LOVE HER. BUT SHE WAS MORE DOWN-TO-EARTH. SHE LEFT ME, A DREAM-CHASER, AND MARRIED A BUSINESSMAN.
IN MY HEART, I DESPERATELY WANTED TO SEE HER.
...

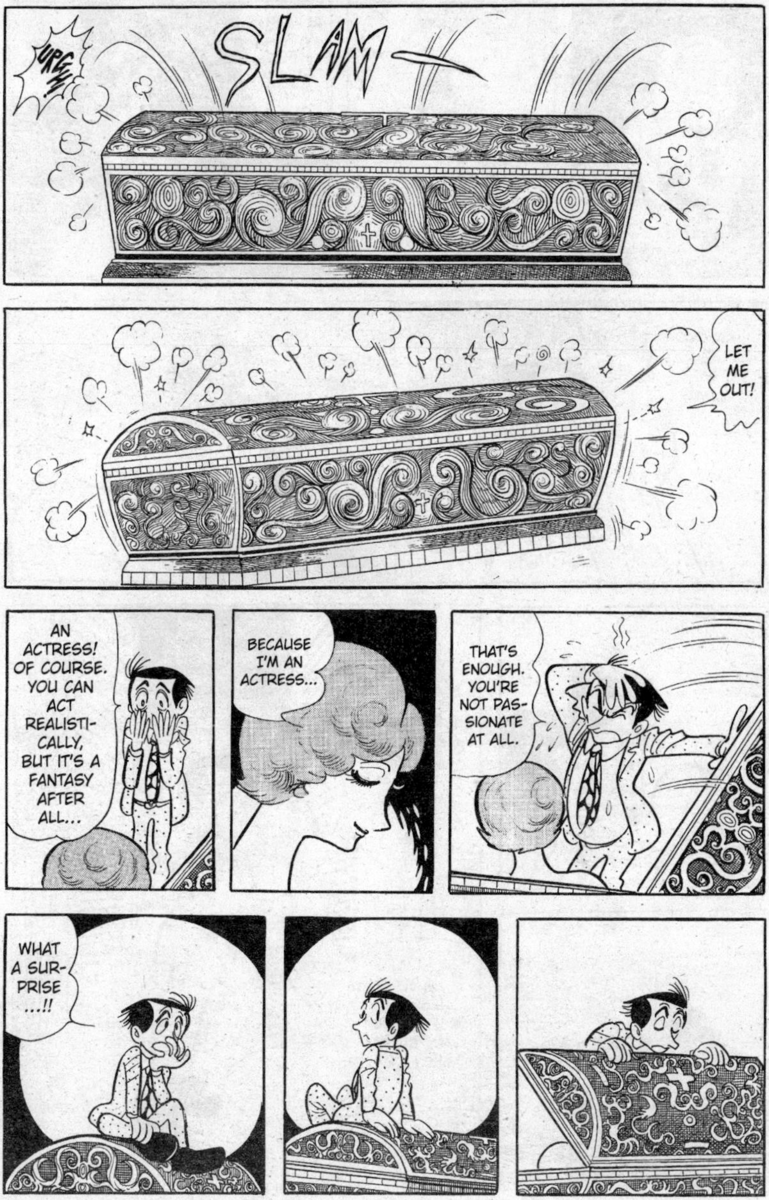
SLAM
URGH!
LET ME OUT!
THAT'S ENOUGH. YOU'RE NOT PASSIONATE AT ALL.
BECAUSE I'M AN ACTRESS...
AN ACTRESS! OF COURSE. YOU CAN ACT REALISTICALLY, BUT IT'S A FANTASY AFTER ALL...
WHAT A SURPRISE ...!!

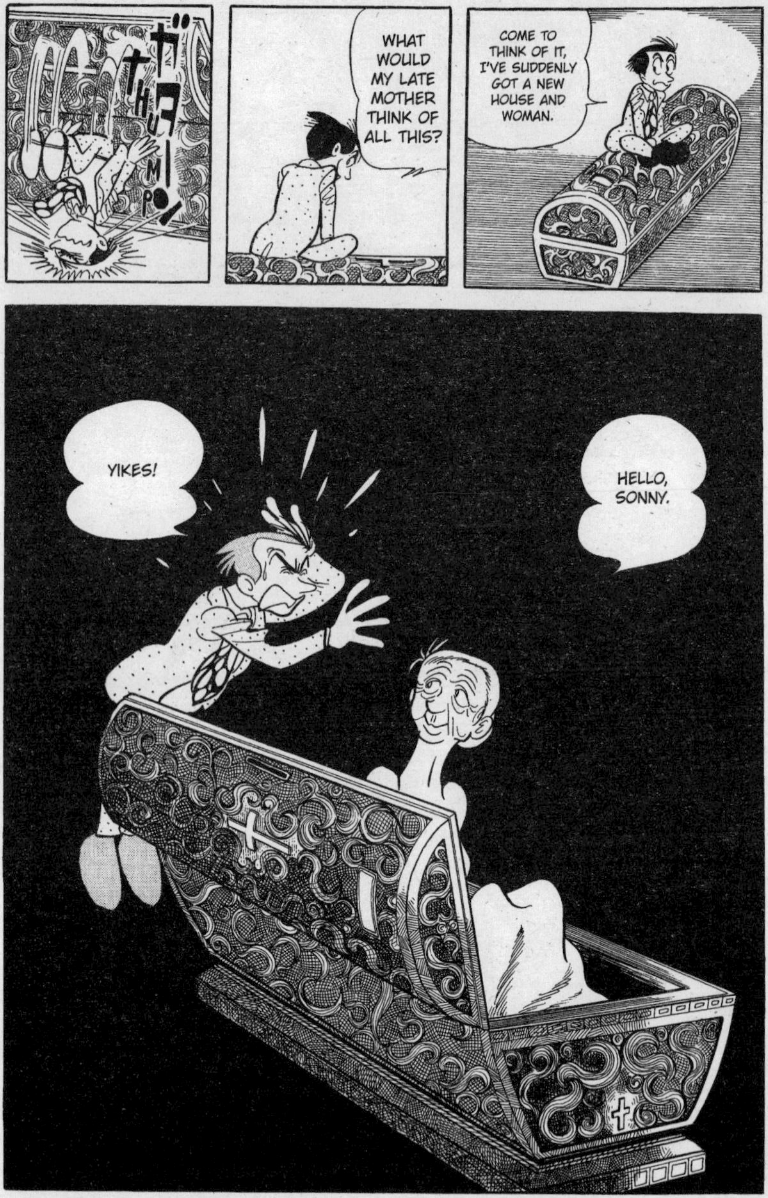
COME TO THINK OF IT, I'VE SUDDENLY GOT A NEW HOUSE AND WOMAN.
WHAT WOULD MY LATE MOTHER THINK OF ALL THIS?
THUMP
HELLO, SONNY.
YIKES!

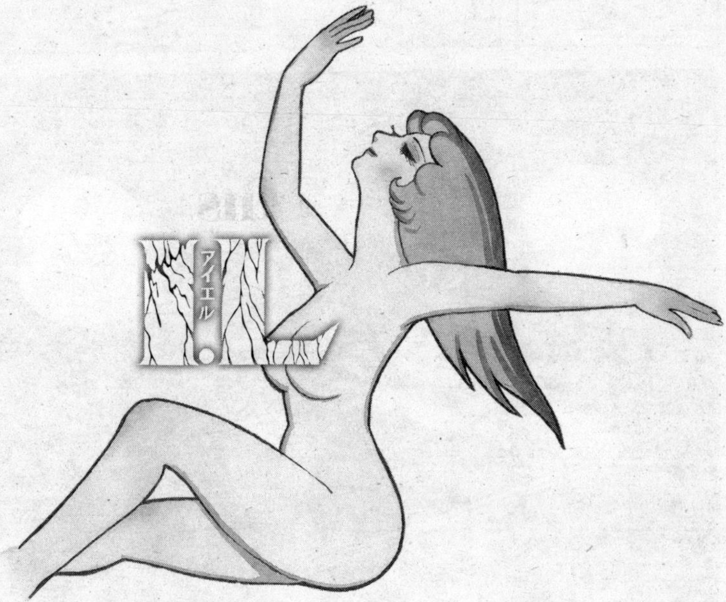
I.L
アイエル

# EPISODE 2
# The Moths

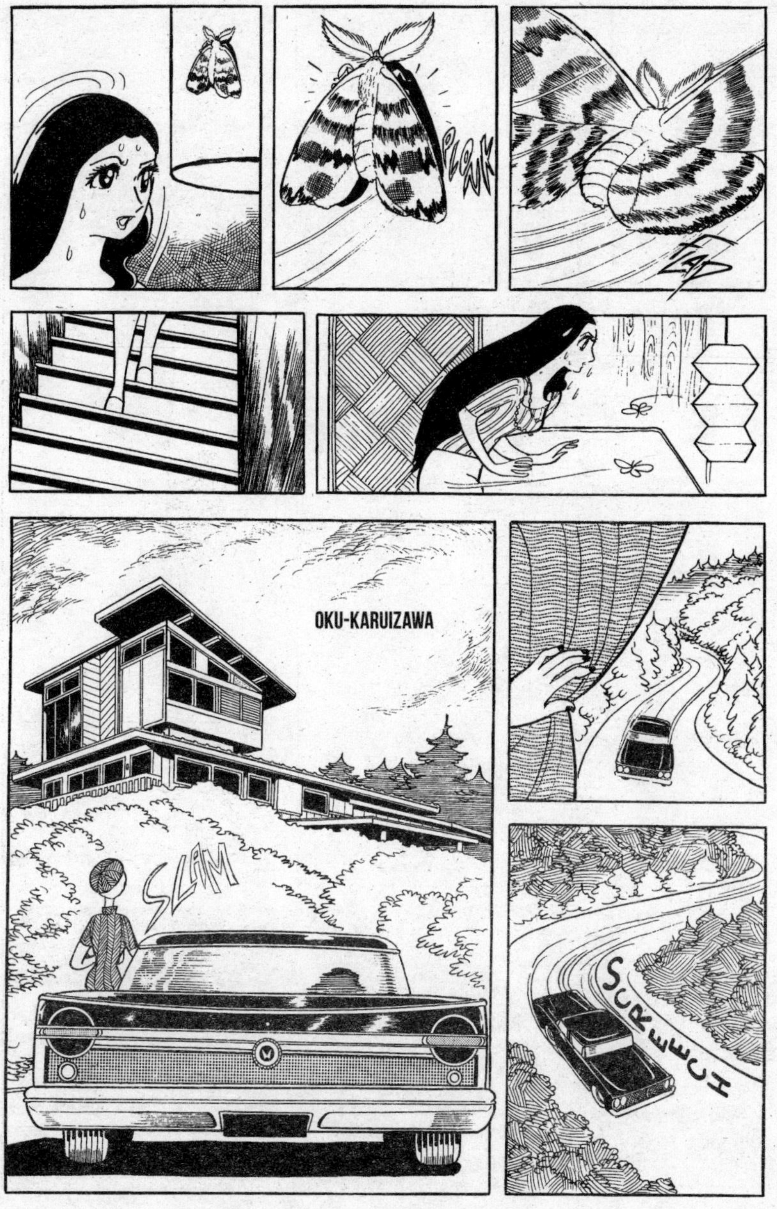
FLAP
PLONK
SCREECH
OKU-KARUIZAWA
SLAM

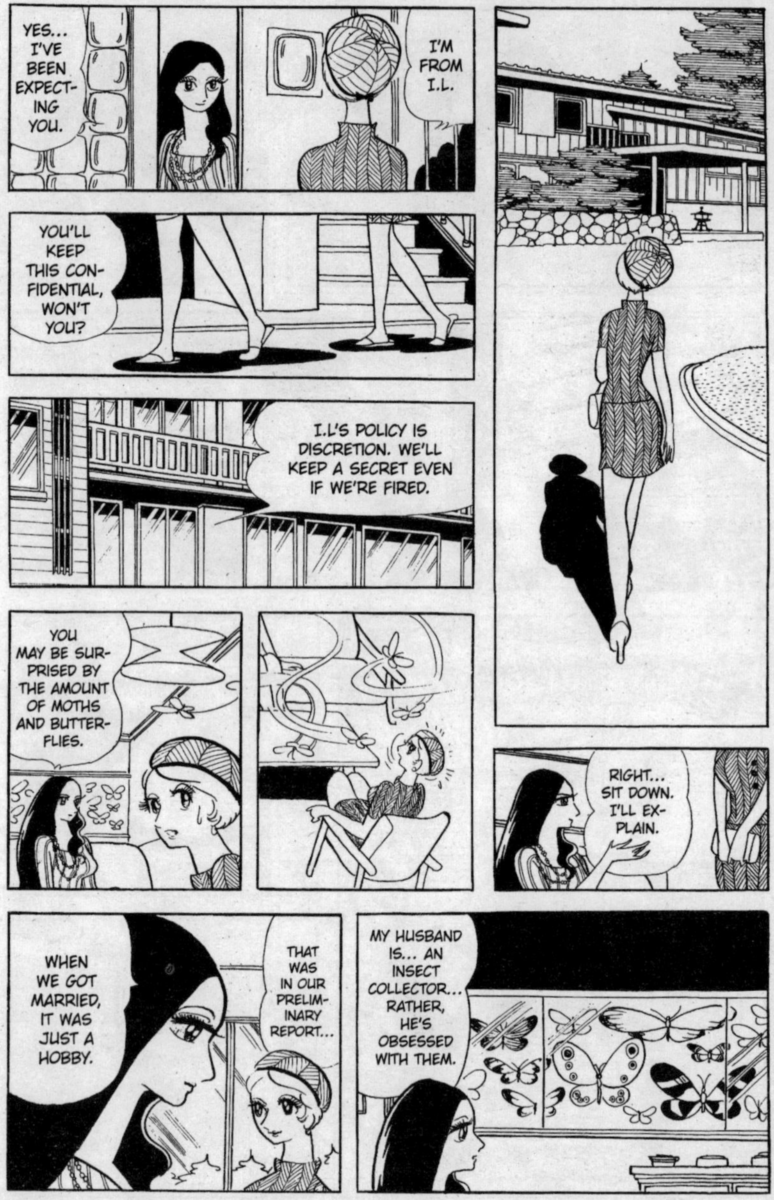
I'M FROM I.L.
YES... I'VE BEEN EXPECTING YOU.
YOU'LL KEEP THIS CONFIDENTIAL, WON'T YOU?
I.L'S POLICY IS DISCRETION. WE'LL KEEP A SECRET EVEN IF WE'RE FIRED.
RIGHT... SIT DOWN. I'LL EXPLAIN.
YOU MAY BE SURPRISED BY THE AMOUNT OF MOTHS AND BUTTERFLIES.
MY HUSBAND IS... AN INSECT COLLECTOR... RATHER, HE'S OBSESSED WITH THEM.
THAT WAS IN OUR PRELIMINARY REPORT...
WHEN WE GOT MARRIED, IT WAS JUST A HOBBY.

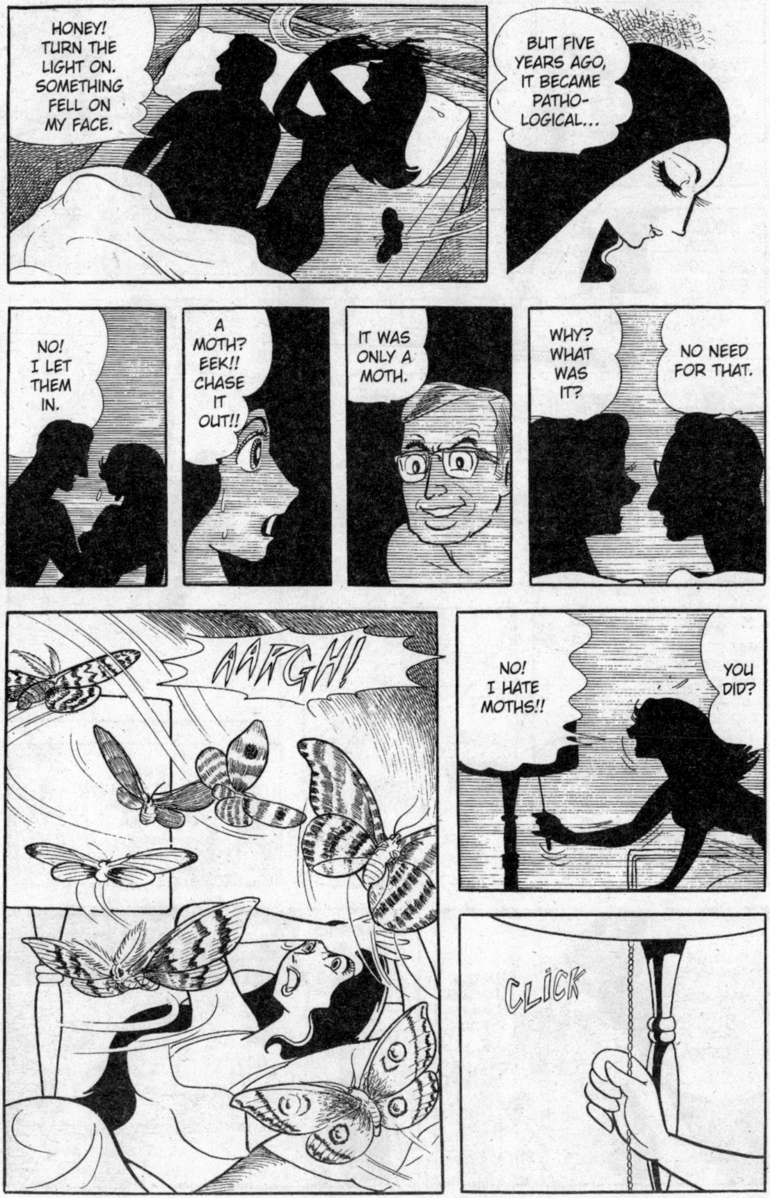
BUT FIVE YEARS AGO, IT BECAME PATHO-LOGICAL...
HONEY! TURN THE LIGHT ON. SOMETHING FELL ON MY FACE.
NO NEED FOR THAT.
WHY? WHAT WAS IT?
IT WAS ONLY A MOTH.
A MOTH? EEK!! CHASE IT OUT!!
NO! I LET THEM IN.
YOU DID?
NO! I HATE MOTHS!!
CLICK
AARGH!

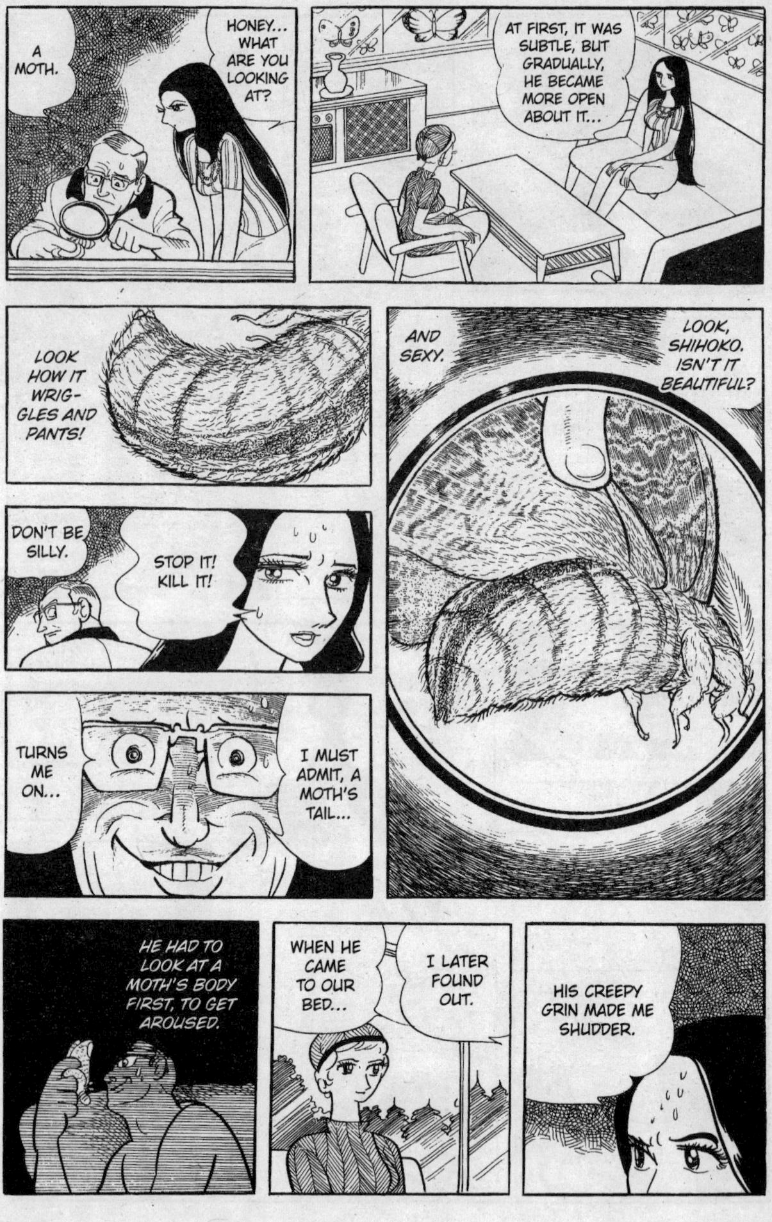
AT FIRST, IT WAS SUBTLE, BUT GRADUALLY, HE BECAME MORE OPEN ABOUT IT...
HONEY... WHAT ARE YOU LOOKING AT?
A MOTH.
LOOK, SHIHOKO. ISN'T IT BEAUTIFUL?
AND SEXY.
LOOK HOW IT WRIG-GLES AND PANTS!
STOP IT! KILL IT!
DON'T BE SILLY.
I MUST ADMIT, A MOTH'S TAIL...
TURNS ME ON...
HIS CREEPY GRIN MADE ME SHUDDER.
I LATER FOUND OUT.
WHEN HE CAME TO OUR BED...
HE HAD TO LOOK AT A MOTH'S BODY FIRST, TO GET AROUSED.

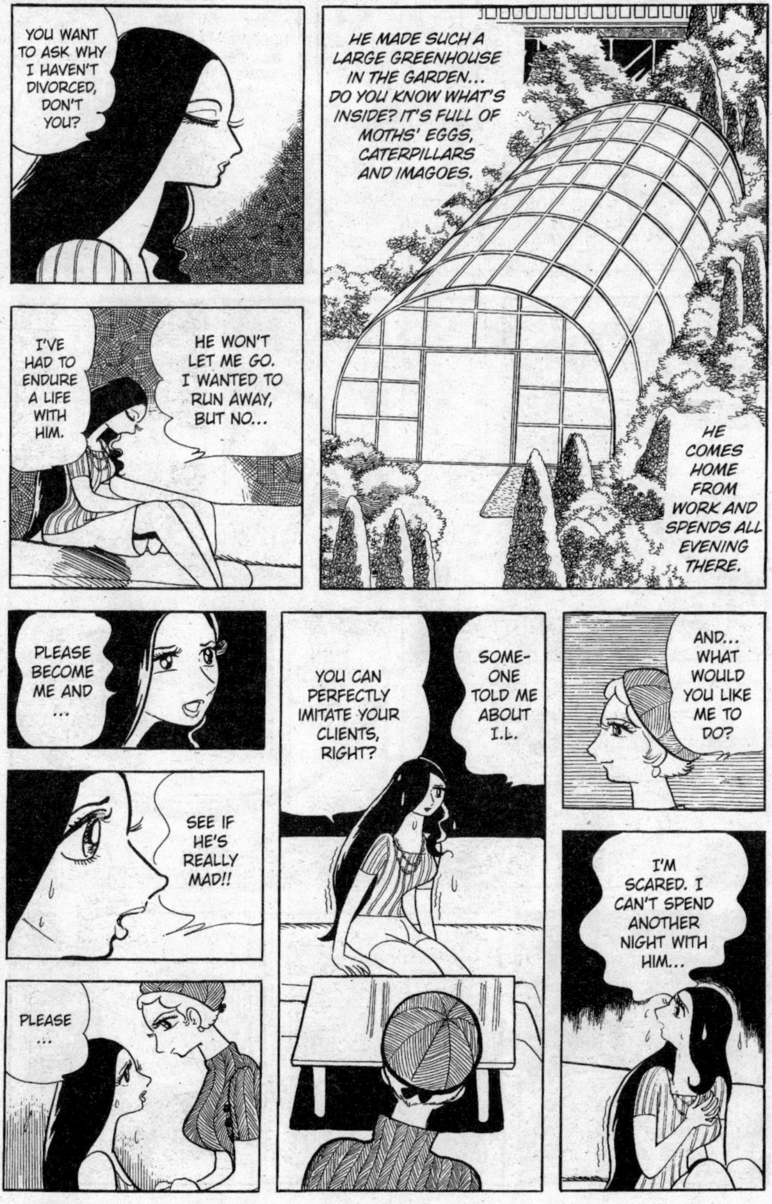
HE MADE SUCH A LARGE GREENHOUSE IN THE GARDEN... DO YOU KNOW WHAT'S INSIDE? IT'S FULL OF MOTHS' EGGS, CATERPILLARS AND IMAGOES.
HE COMES HOME FROM WORK AND SPENDS ALL EVENING THERE.
YOU WANT TO ASK WHY I HAVEN'T DIVORCED, DON'T YOU?
HE WON'T LET ME GO. I WANTED TO RUN AWAY, BUT NO...
I'VE HAD TO ENDURE A LIFE WITH HIM.
AND... WHAT WOULD YOU LIKE ME TO DO?
I'M SCARED. I CAN'T SPEND ANOTHER NIGHT WITH HIM...
SOME-ONE TOLD ME ABOUT I.L.
YOU CAN PERFECTLY IMITATE YOUR CLIENTS, RIGHT?
PLEASE BECOME ME AND ...
SEE IF HE'S REALLY MAD!!
PLEASE ...

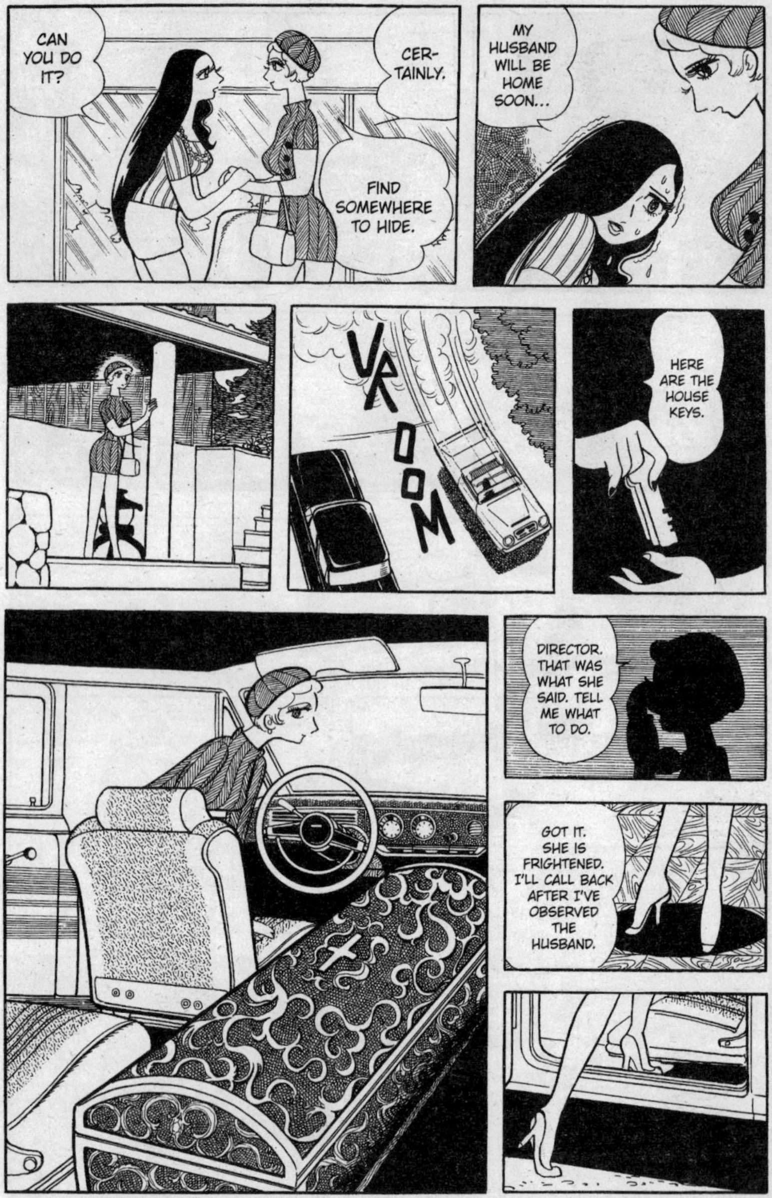
MY HUSBAND WILL BE HOME SOON...
CER-TAINLY.
CAN YOU DO IT?
FIND SOMEWHERE TO HIDE.
HERE ARE THE HOUSE KEYS.
VROOM
DIRECTOR. THAT WAS WHAT SHE SAID. TELL ME WHAT TO DO.
GOT IT. SHE IS FRIGHTENED. I'LL CALL BACK AFTER I'VE OBSERVED THE HUSBAND.

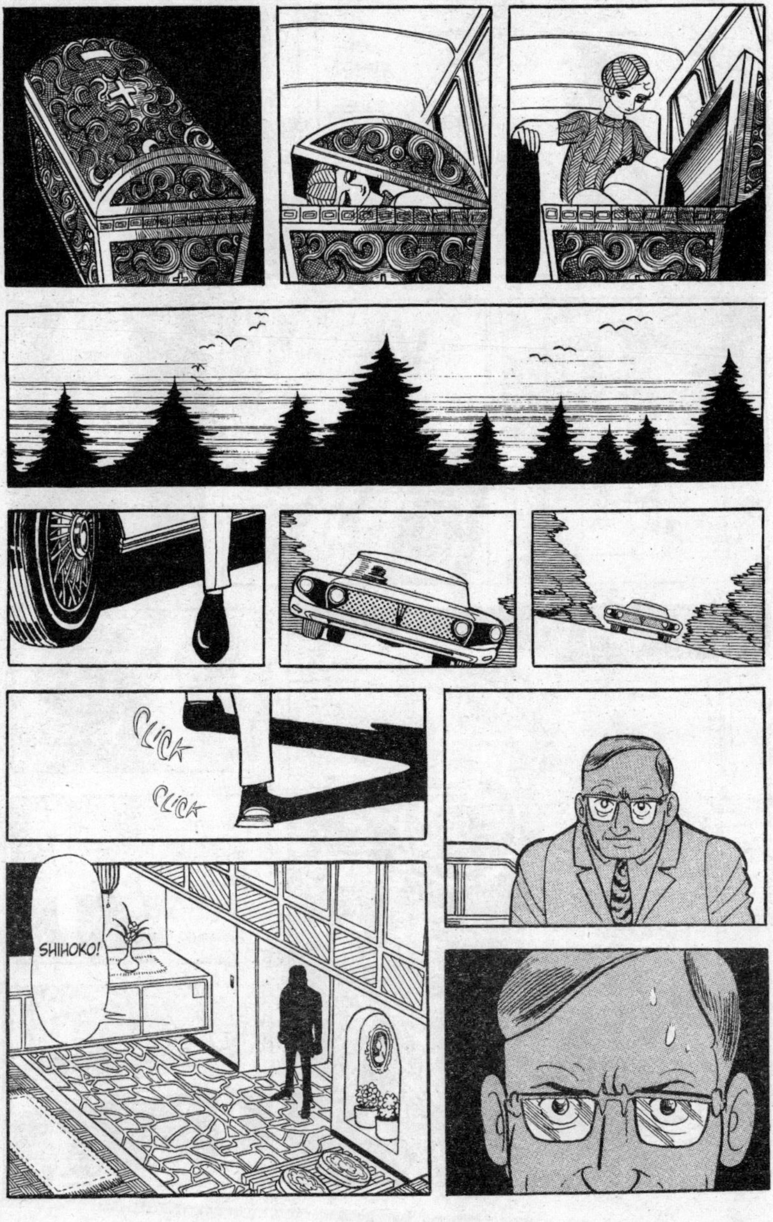
CLICK
CLICK
SHIHOKO!

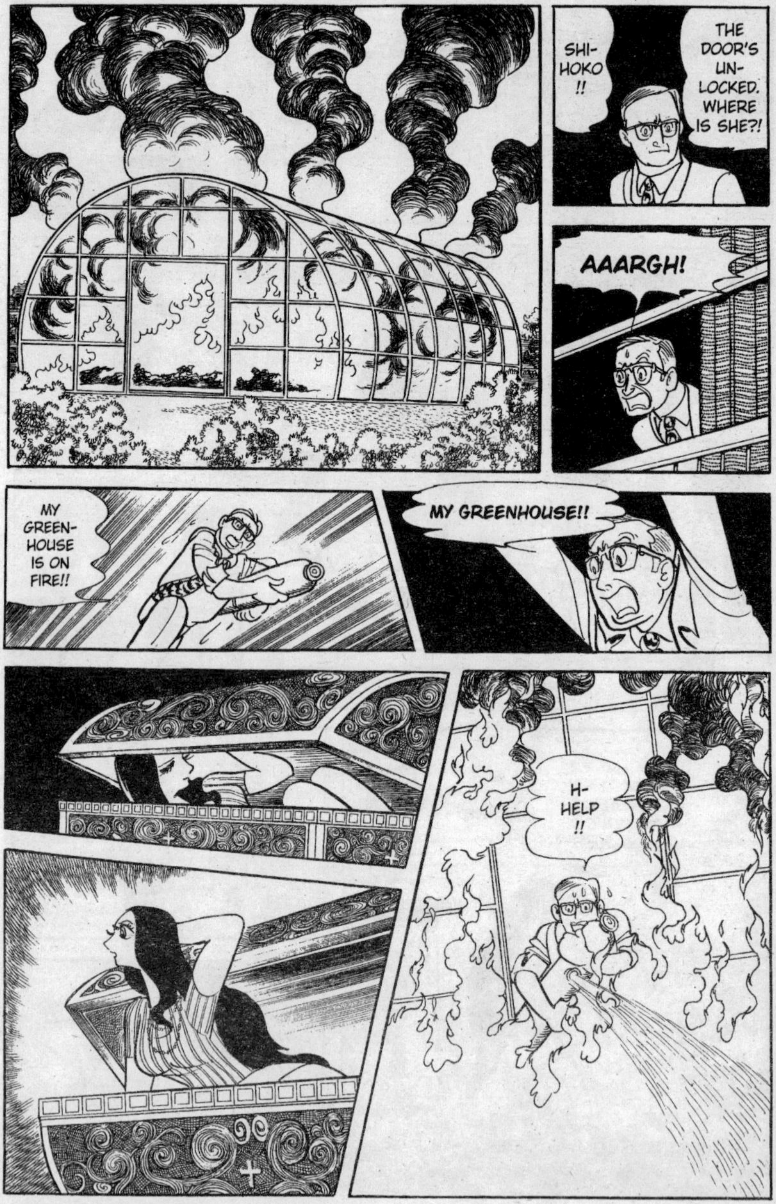
THE DOOR'S UNLOCKED. WHERE IS SHE?!
SHI-HOKO!!
AAARGH!
MY GREENHOUSE!!
MY GREENHOUSE IS ON FIRE!!
H-HELP!!

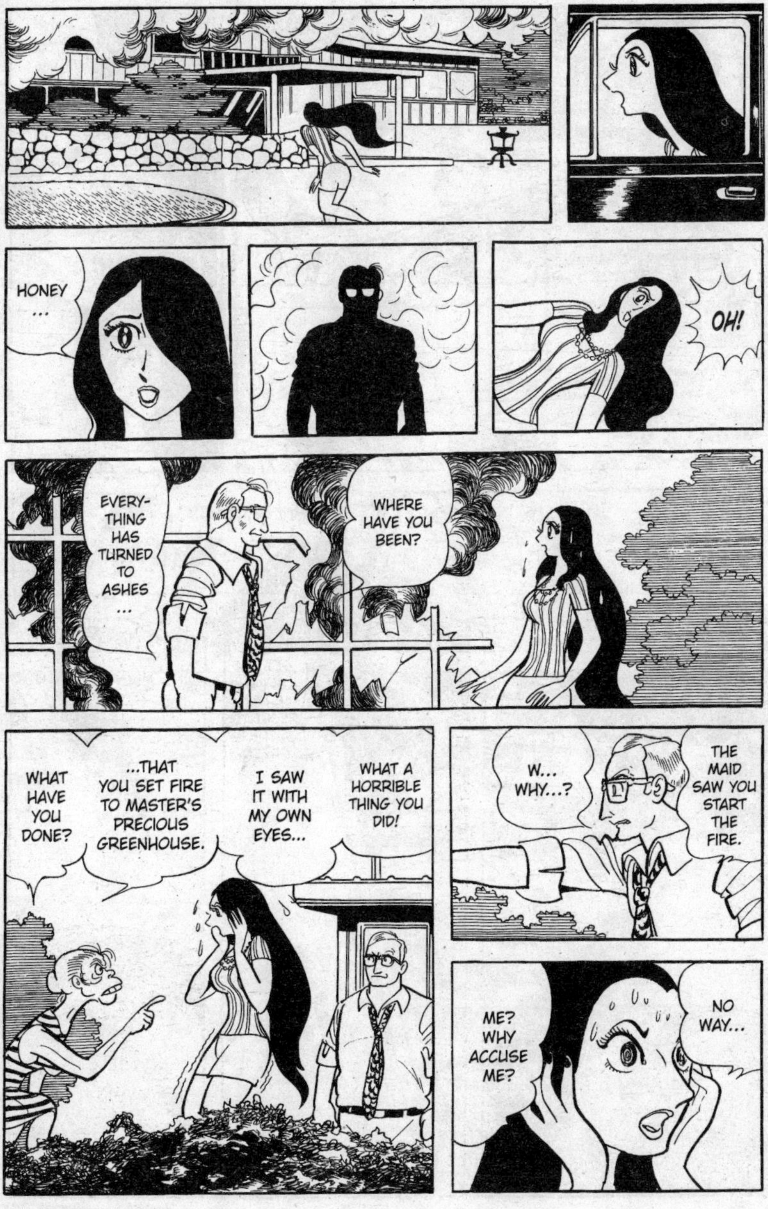
OH!
HONEY ...
WHERE HAVE YOU BEEN?
EVERY-THING HAS TURNED TO ASHES ...
THE MAID SAW YOU START THE FIRE.
W... WHY...?
NO WAY...
ME? WHY ACCUSE ME?
WHAT A HORRIBLE THING YOU DID!
I SAW IT WITH MY OWN EYES...
...THAT YOU SET FIRE TO MASTER'S PRECIOUS GREENHOUSE.
WHAT HAVE YOU DONE?

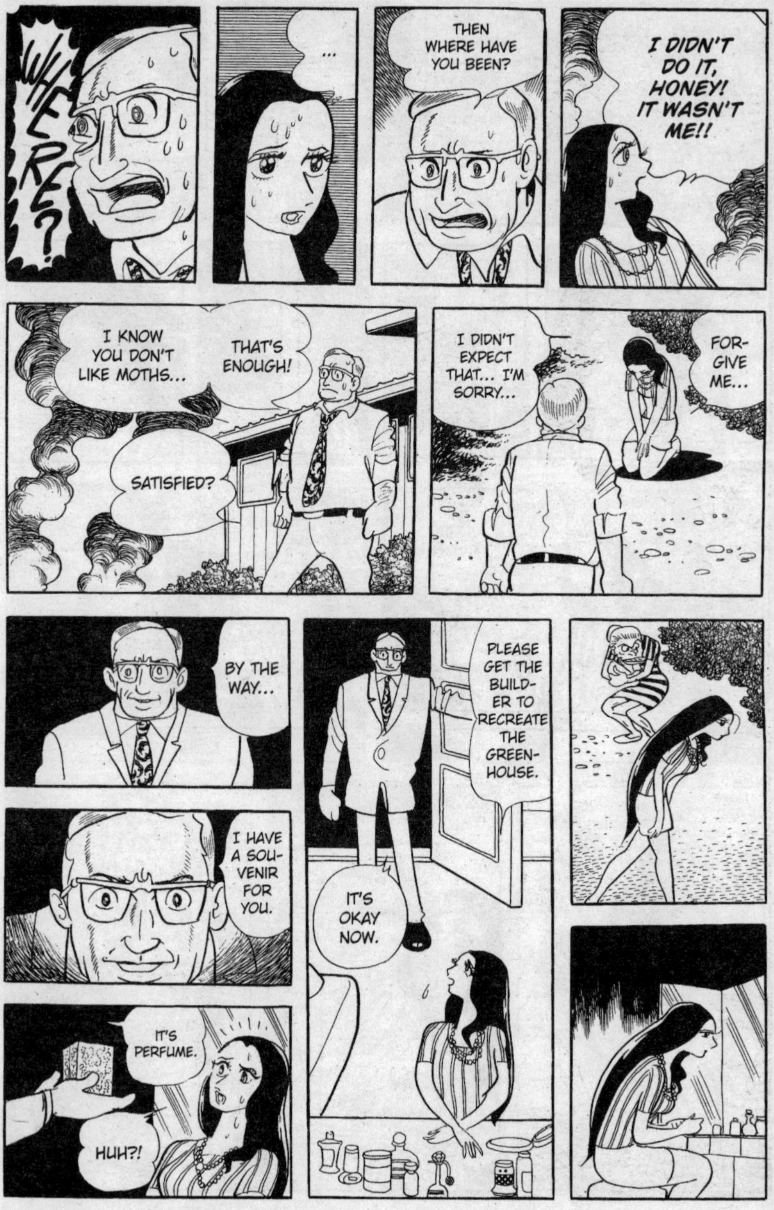
WHERE?
...
THEN WHERE HAVE YOU BEEN?
I DIDN'T DO IT, HONEY! IT WASN'T ME!!
I KNOW YOU DON'T LIKE MOTHS...
THAT'S ENOUGH!
SATISFIED?
I DIDN'T EXPECT THAT... I'M SORRY...
FOR-GIVE ME...
BY THE WAY...
I HAVE A SOU-VENIR FOR YOU.
IT'S PERFUME.
HUH?!
PLEASE GET THE BUILD-ER TO RECREATE THE GREEN-HOUSE.
IT'S OKAY NOW.

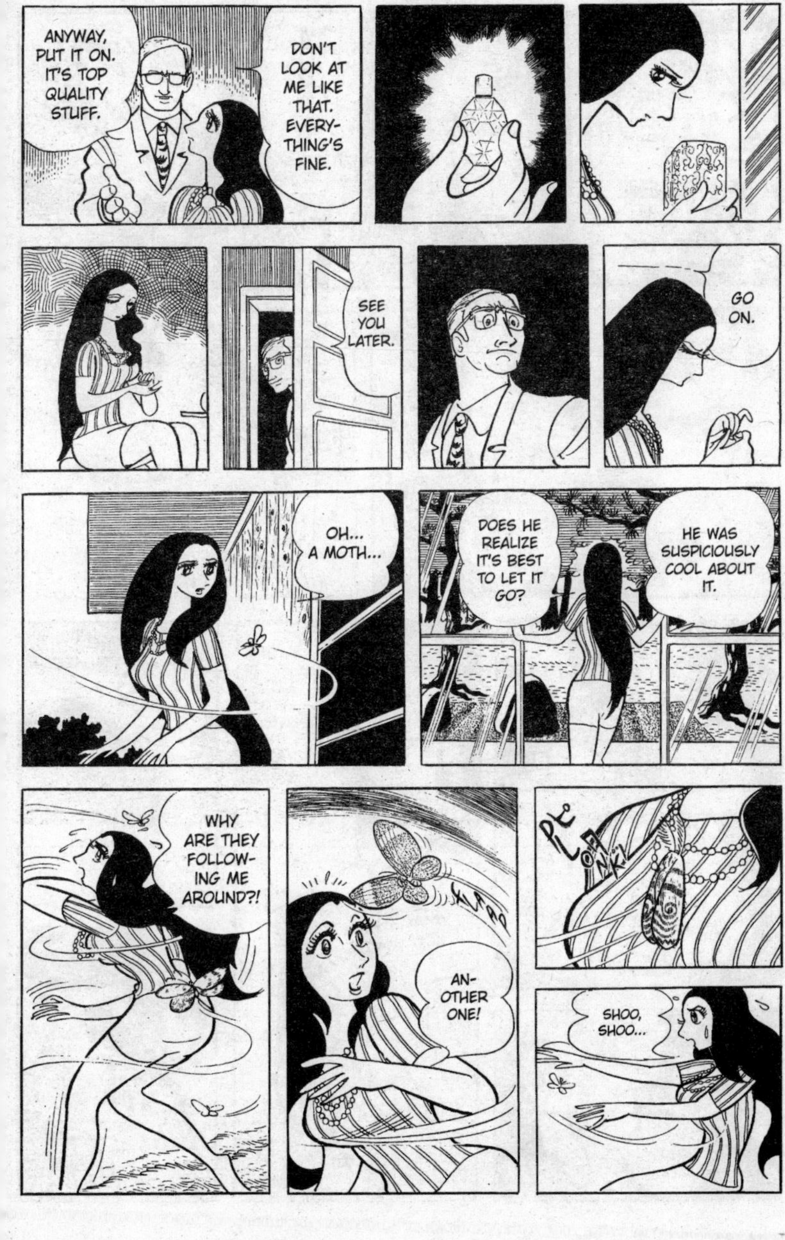
DON'T LOOK AT ME LIKE THAT. EVERYTHING'S FINE.
ANYWAY, PUT IT ON. IT'S TOP QUALITY STUFF.
GO ON.
SEE YOU LATER.
HE WAS SUSPICIOUSLY COOL ABOUT IT.
DOES HE REALIZE IT'S BEST TO LET IT GO?
OH... A MOTH...
PLONK
SHOO, SHOO...
AN-OTHER ONE!
WHY ARE THEY FOLLOWING ME AROUND?!

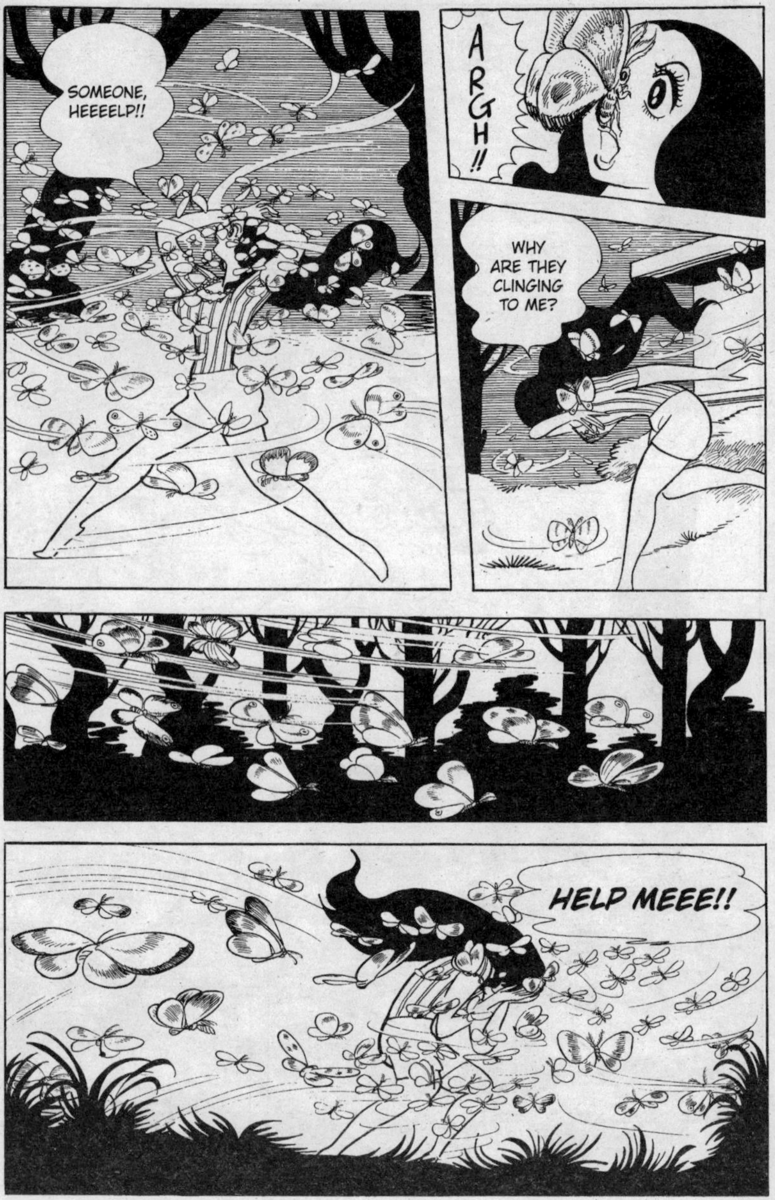
ARGH!!
WHY ARE THEY CLINGING TO ME?
SOMEONE, HEEEELP!!
HELP MEEE!!

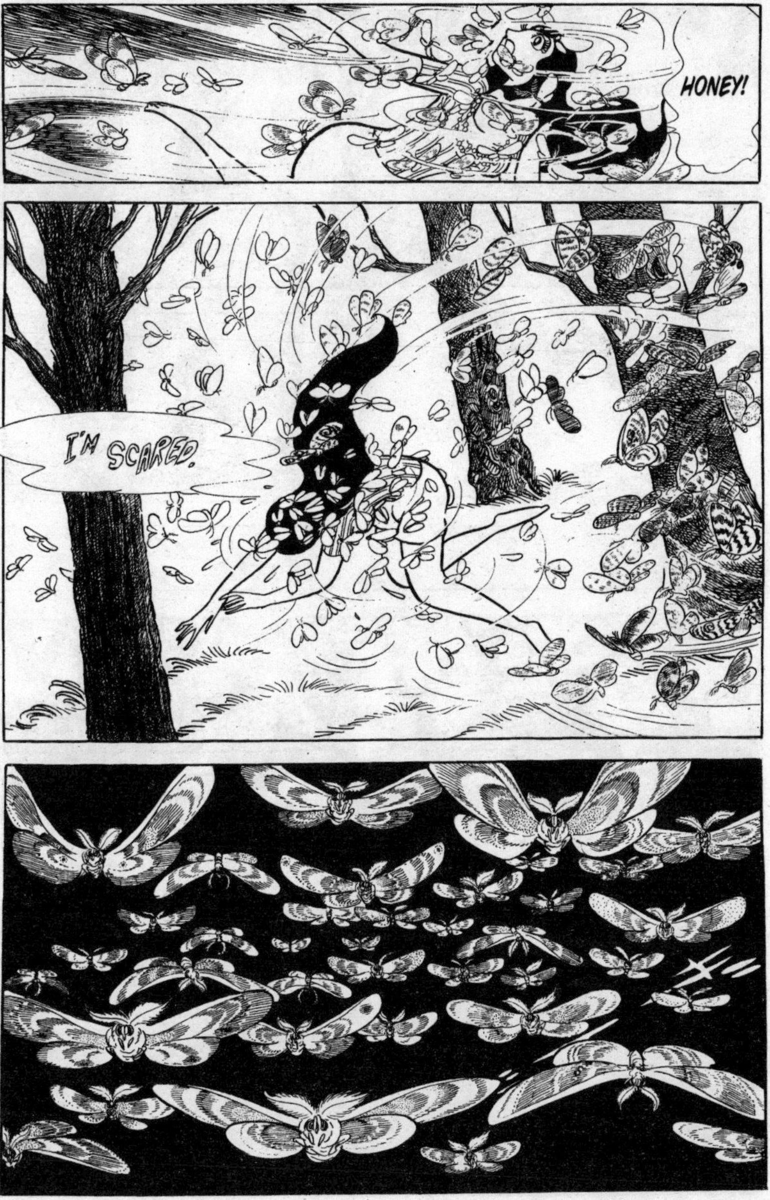
HONEY!
I'M SCARED.

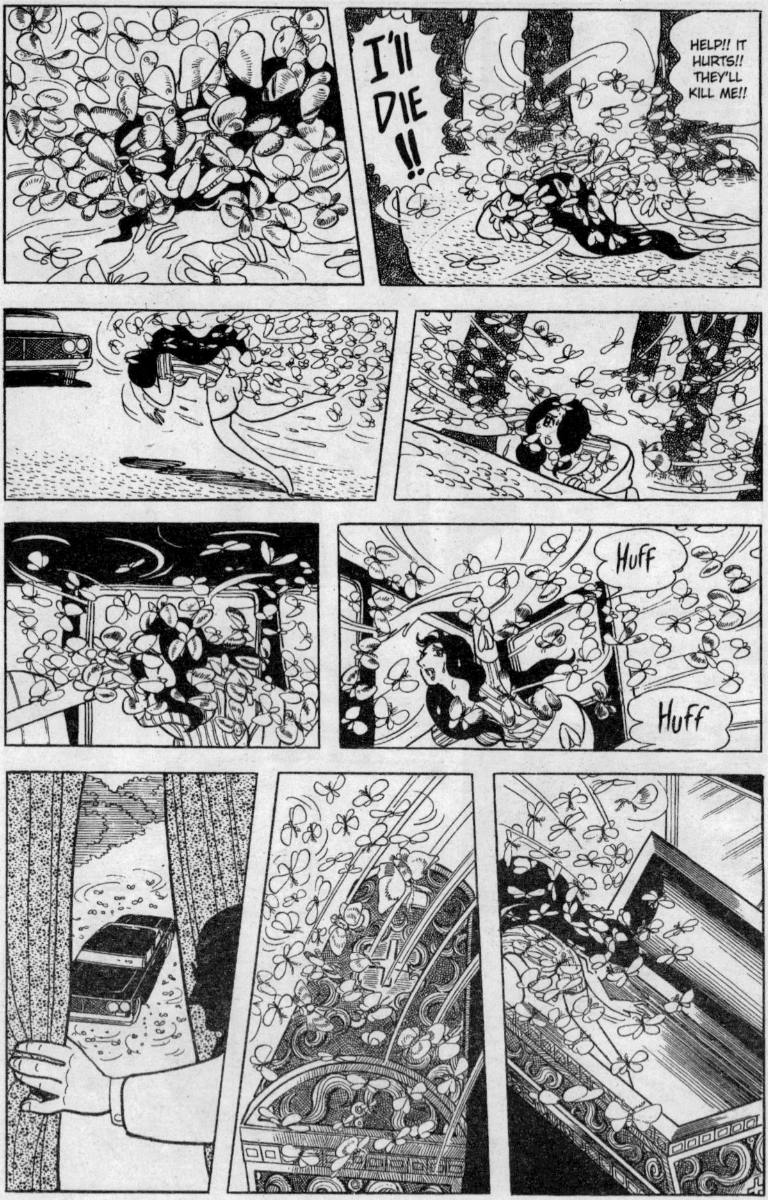
HELP!! IT HURTS!! THEY'LL KILL ME!!
I'll DIE !!
Huff
Huff

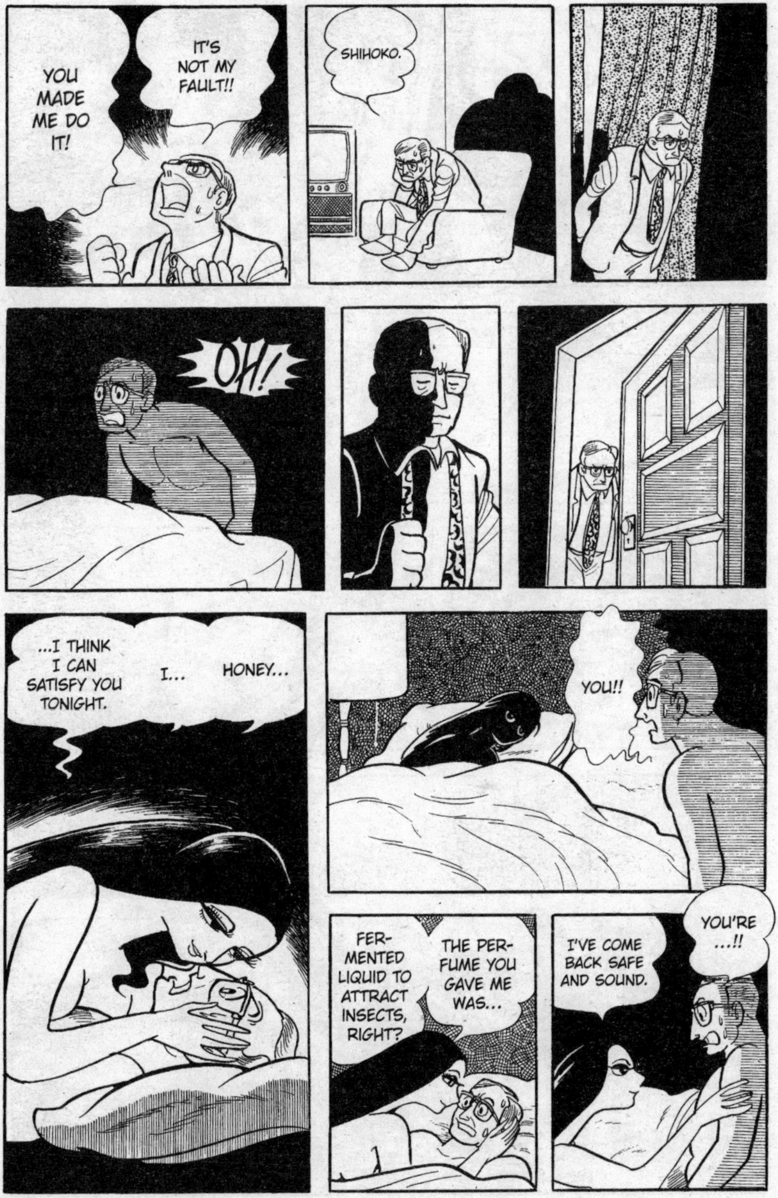
SHIHOKO.
IT'S NOT MY FAULT!!
YOU MADE ME DO IT!
OH!
YOU!!
YOU'RE ...!!
I'VE COME BACK SAFE AND SOUND.
THE PERFUME YOU GAVE ME WAS...
FERMENTED LIQUID TO ATTRACT INSECTS, RIGHT?
HONEY...
I...
...I THINK I CAN SATISFY YOU TONIGHT.

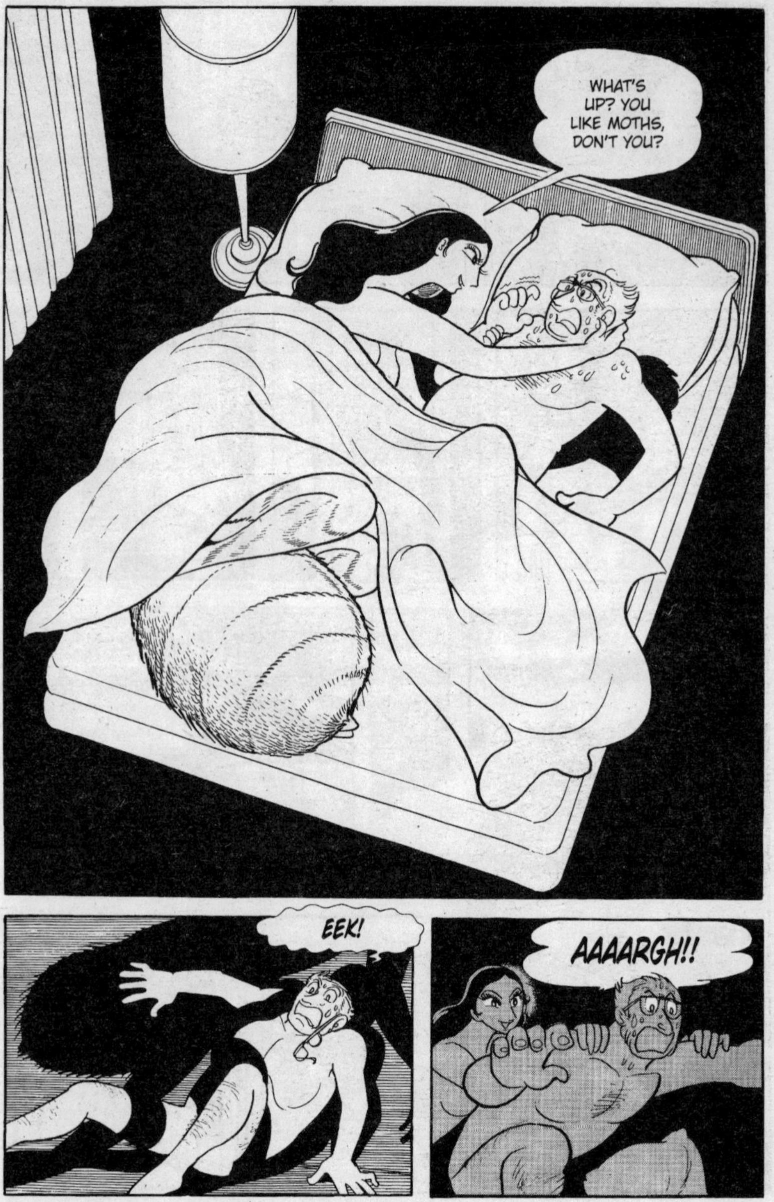
WHAT'S UP? YOU LIKE MOTHS, DON'T YOU?
AAAARGH!!
EEK!

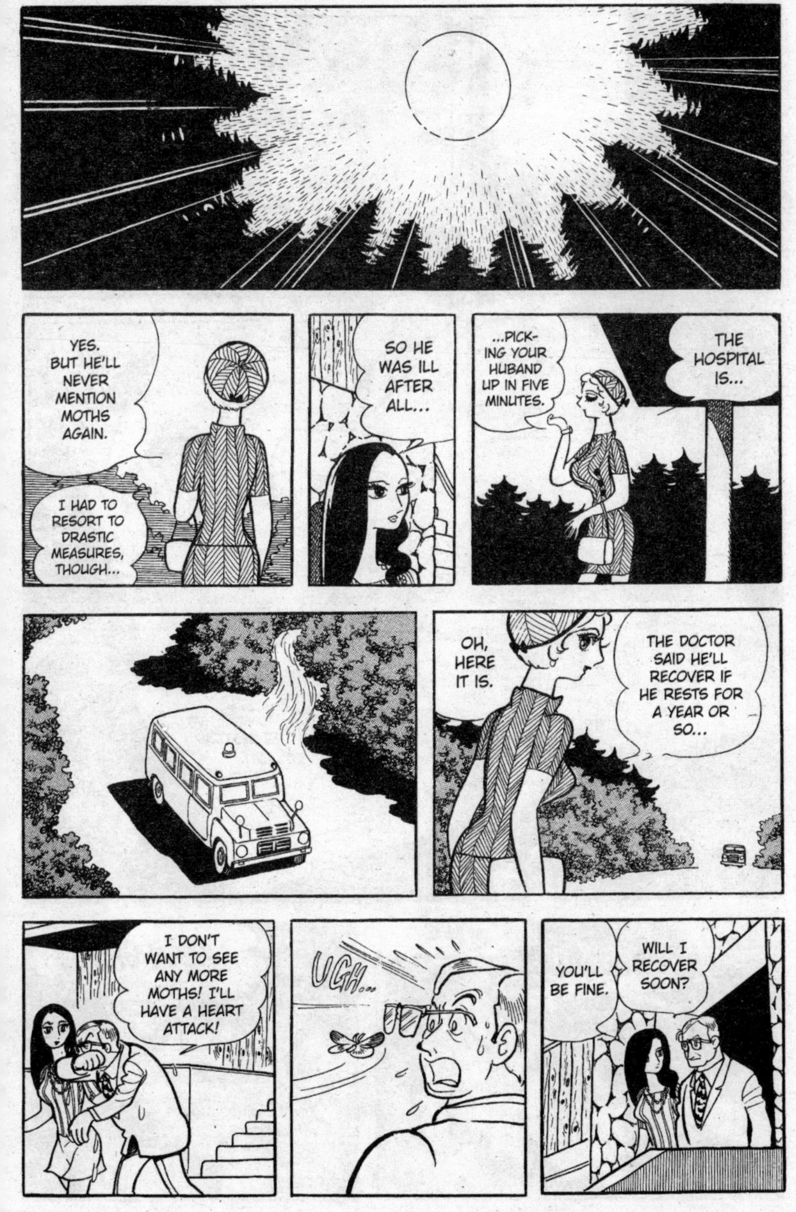
THE HOSPITAL IS...
...PICKING YOUR HUBAND UP IN FIVE MINUTES.
SO HE WAS ILL AFTER ALL...
YES. BUT HE'LL NEVER MENTION MOTHS AGAIN.
I HAD TO RESORT TO DRASTIC MEASURES, THOUGH...
THE DOCTOR SAID HE'LL RECOVER IF HE RESTS FOR A YEAR OR SO...
OH, HERE IT IS.
WILL I RECOVER SOON?
YOU'LL BE FINE.
UGH...
I DON'T WANT TO SEE ANY MORE MOTHS! I'LL HAVE A HEART ATTACK!

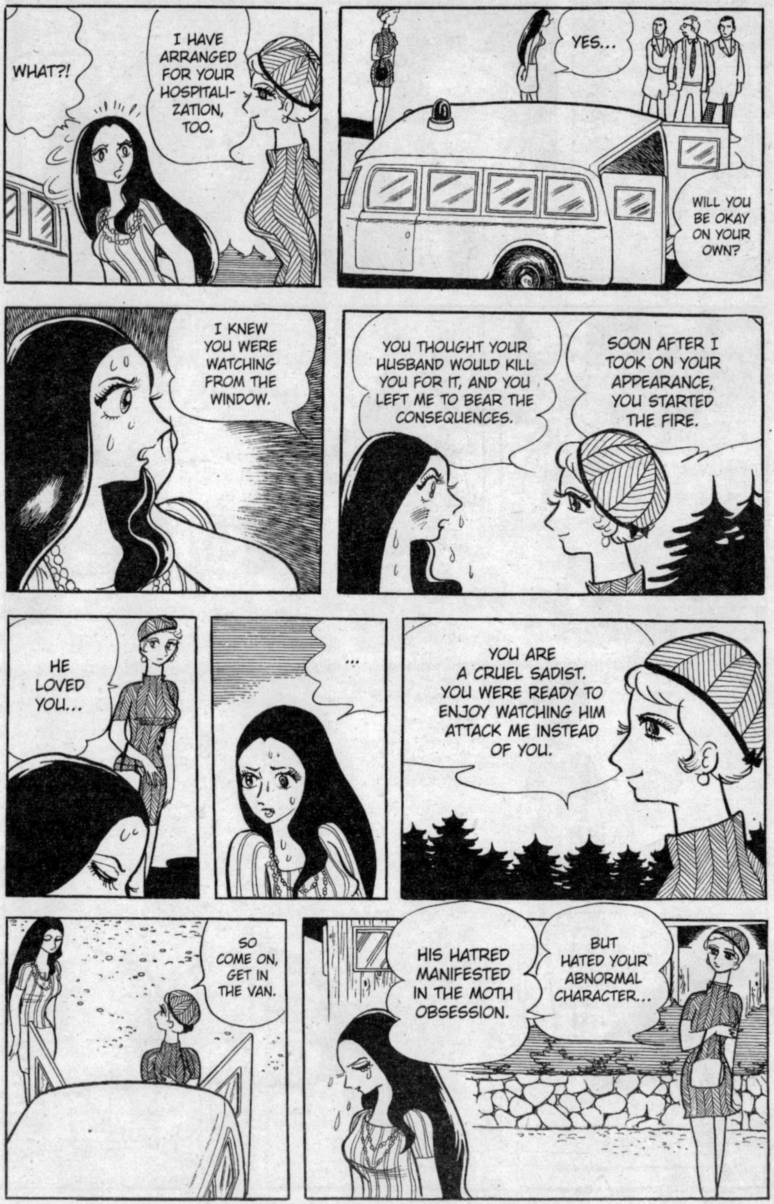
WILL YOU BE OKAY ON YOUR OWN?
YES...
I HAVE ARRANGED FOR YOUR HOSPITALIZATION, TOO.
WHAT?!
SOON AFTER I TOOK ON YOUR APPEARANCE, YOU STARTED THE FIRE.
YOU THOUGHT YOUR HUSBAND WOULD KILL YOU FOR IT, AND YOU LEFT ME TO BEAR THE CONSEQUENCES.
I KNEW YOU WERE WATCHING FROM THE WINDOW.
YOU ARE A CRUEL SADIST. YOU WERE READY TO ENJOY WATCHING HIM ATTACK ME INSTEAD OF YOU.
...
HE LOVED YOU...
BUT HATED YOUR ABNORMAL CHARACTER...
HIS HATRED MANIFESTED IN THE MOTH OBSESSION.
SO COME ON, GET IN THE VAN.

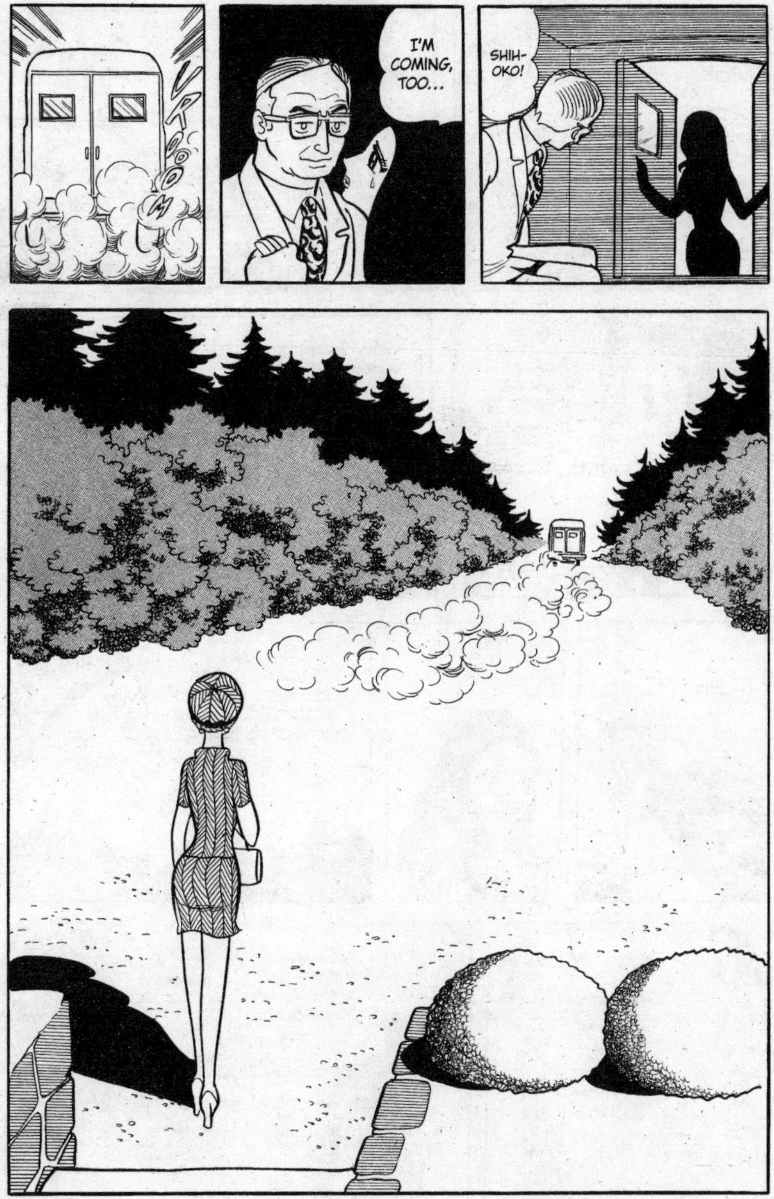
SHIH-OKO!
I'M COMING, TOO...
VROOOM

# EPISODE 3
# The Messenger

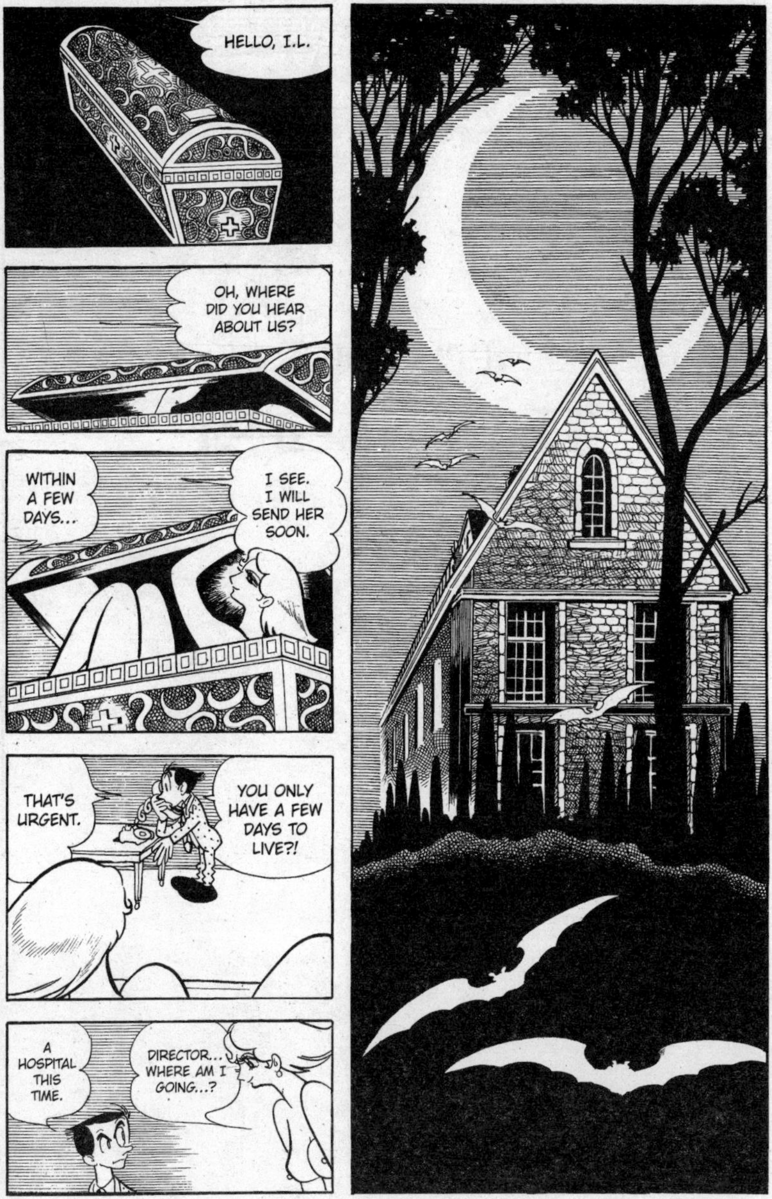
HELLO, I.L.
OH, WHERE DID YOU HEAR ABOUT US?
I SEE. I WILL SEND HER SOON.
WITHIN A FEW DAYS...
YOU ONLY HAVE A FEW DAYS TO LIVE?!
THAT'S URGENT.
DIRECTOR... WHERE AM I GOING...?
A HOSPITAL THIS TIME.

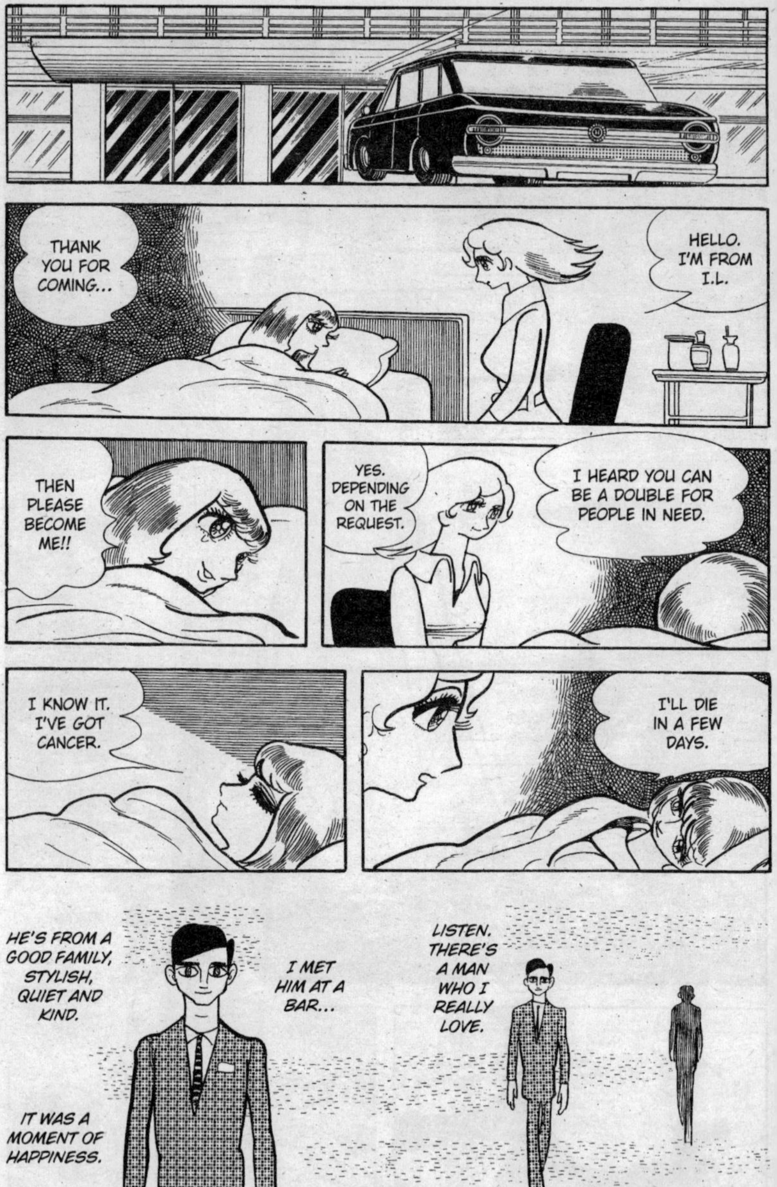
HELLO. I'M FROM I.L.
THANK YOU FOR COMING...
I HEARD YOU CAN BE A DOUBLE FOR PEOPLE IN NEED.
YES. DEPENDING ON THE REQUEST.
THEN PLEASE BECOME ME!!
I'LL DIE IN A FEW DAYS.
I KNOW IT. I'VE GOT CANCER.
LISTEN. THERE'S A MAN WHO I REALLY LOVE.
I MET HIM AT A BAR...
HE'S FROM A GOOD FAMILY, STYLISH, QUIET AND KIND.
IT WAS A MOMENT OF HAPPINESS.

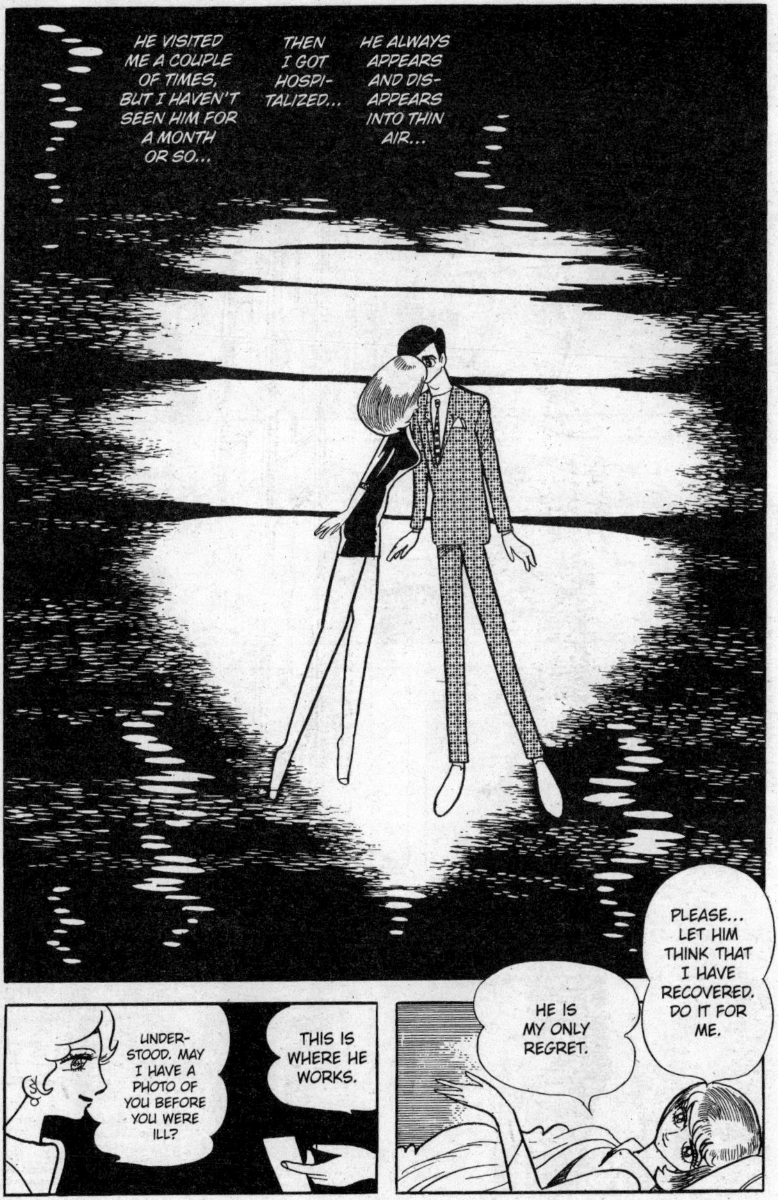
HE ALWAYS APPEARS AND DIS-APPEARS INTO THIN AIR...
THEN I GOT HOSPI-TALIZED...
HE VISITED ME A COUPLE OF TIMES, BUT I HAVEN'T SEEN HIM FOR A MONTH OR SO...
PLEASE... LET HIM THINK THAT I HAVE RECOVERED. DO IT FOR ME.
HE IS MY ONLY REGRET.
THIS IS WHERE HE WORKS.
UNDER-STOOD. MAY I HAVE A PHOTO OF YOU BEFORE YOU WERE ILL?

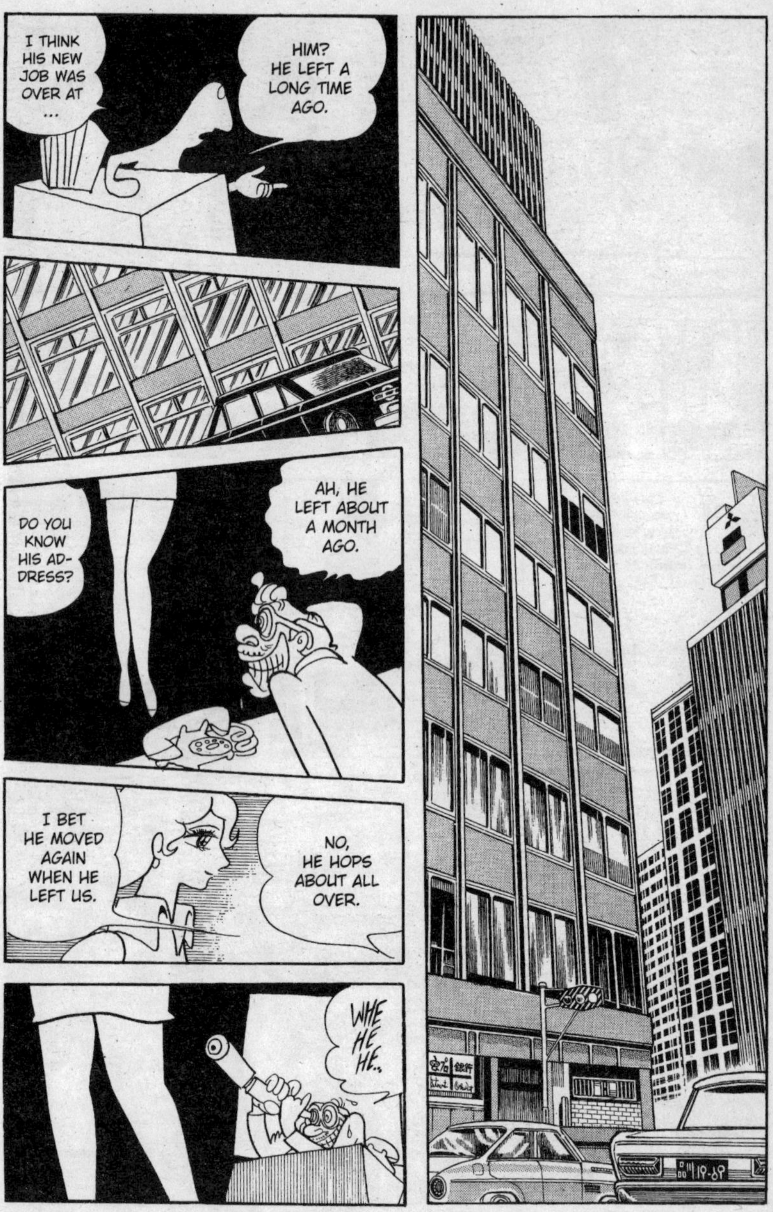
HIM? HE LEFT A LONG TIME AGO.
I THINK HIS NEW JOB WAS OVER AT ...
AH, HE LEFT ABOUT A MONTH AGO.
DO YOU KNOW HIS AD-DRESS?
NO, HE HOPS ABOUT ALL OVER.
I BET HE MOVED AGAIN WHEN HE LEFT US.
WHE HE HE..

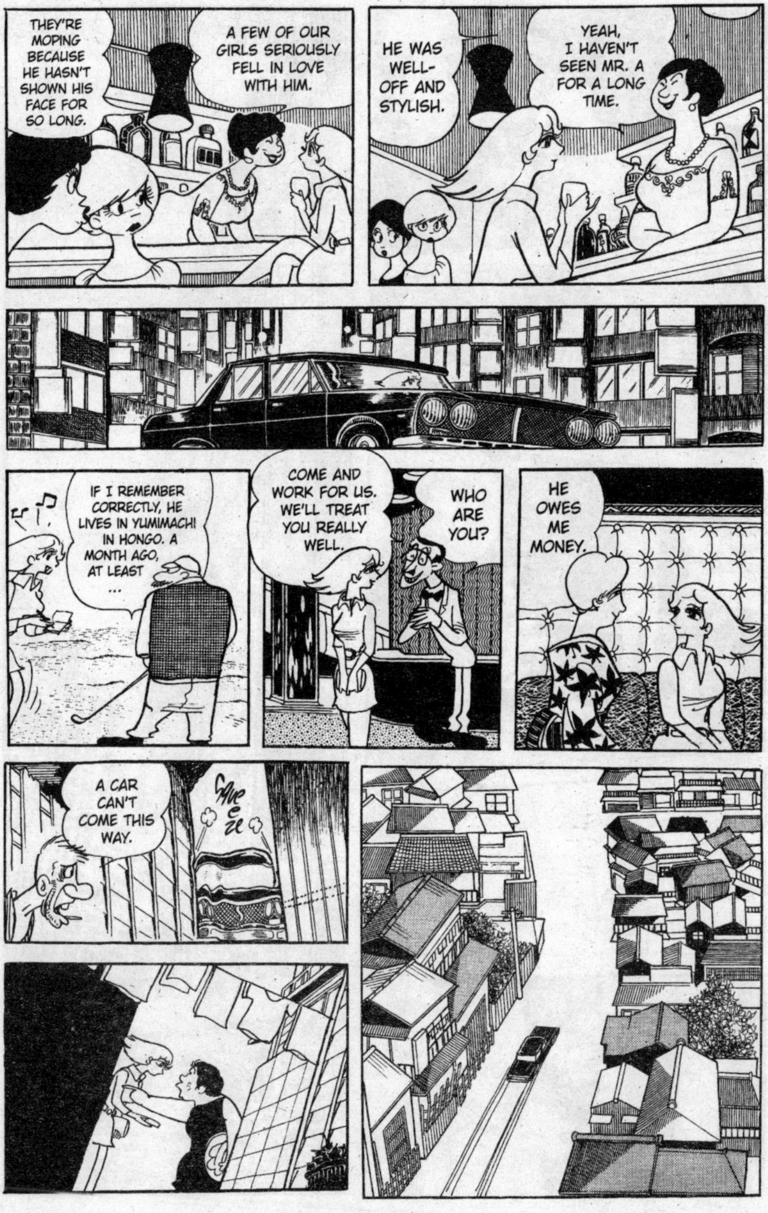
YEAH, I HAVEN'T SEEN MR. A FOR A LONG TIME.
HE WAS WELL-OFF AND STYLISH.
A FEW OF OUR GIRLS SERIOUSLY FELL IN LOVE WITH HIM.
THEY'RE MOPING BECAUSE HE HASN'T SHOWN HIS FACE FOR SO LONG.
HE OWES ME MONEY.
WHO ARE YOU?
COME AND WORK FOR US. WE'LL TREAT YOU REALLY WELL.
IF I REMEMBER CORRECTLY, HE LIVES IN YUMIMACHI IN HONGO. A MONTH AGO, AT LEAST ...
A CAR CAN'T COME THIS WAY.

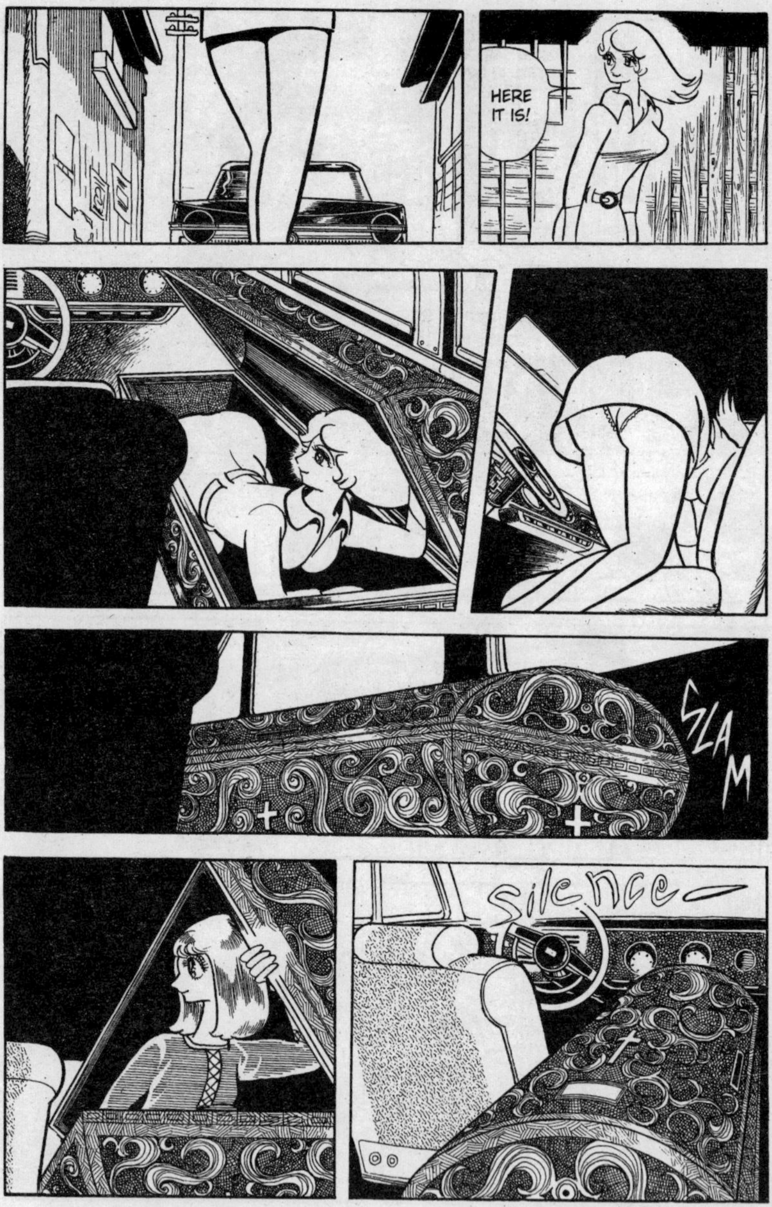
HERE IT IS!
SLAM
silence

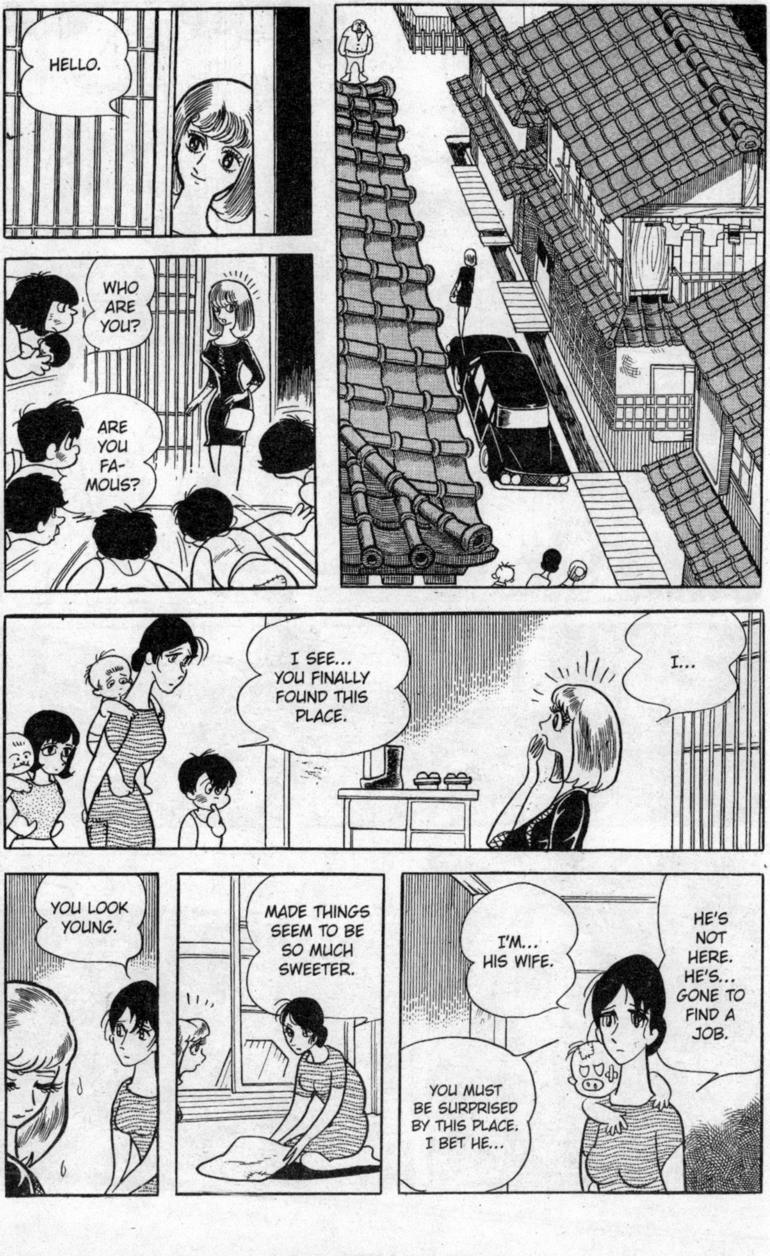
HELLO.
WHO ARE YOU?
ARE YOU FA-MOUS?
I...
I SEE... YOU FINALLY FOUND THIS PLACE.
HE'S NOT HERE. HE'S... GONE TO FIND A JOB.
I'M... HIS WIFE.
YOU MUST BE SURPRISED BY THIS PLACE. I BET HE...
MADE THINGS SEEM TO BE SO MUCH SWEETER.
YOU LOOK YOUNG.

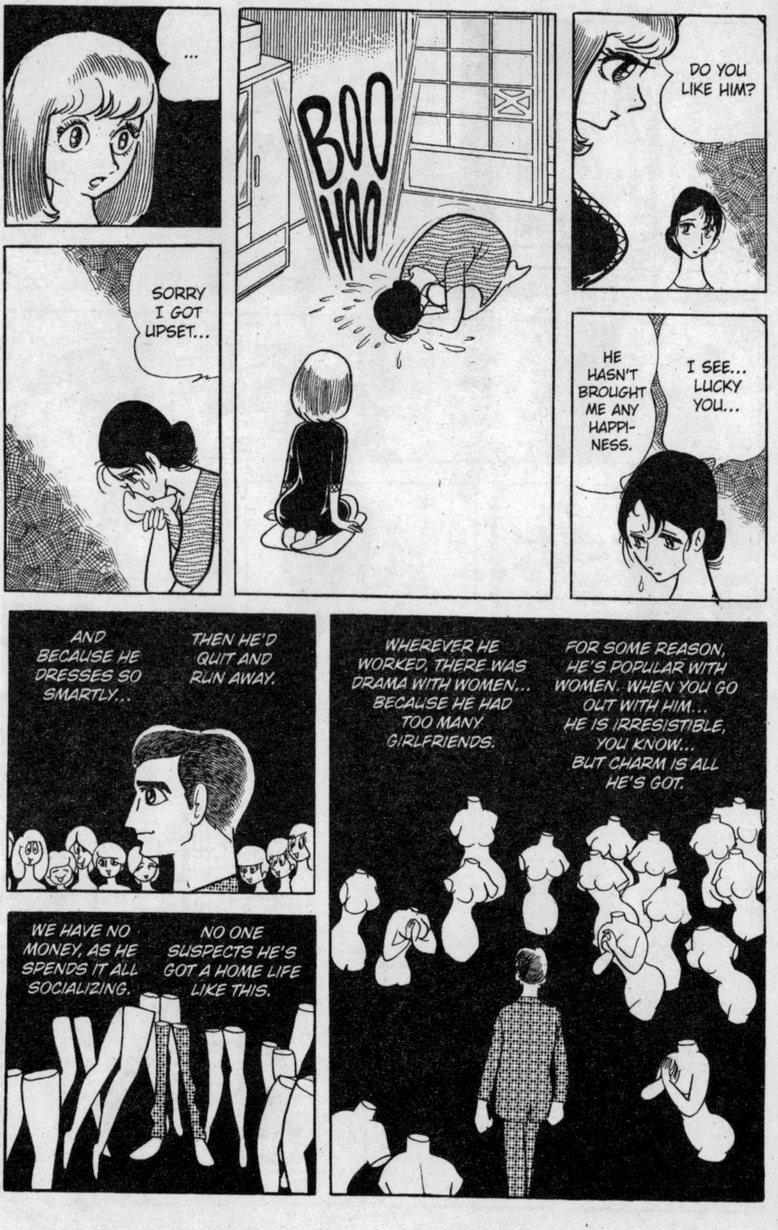
DO YOU LIKE HIM?
I SEE... LUCKY YOU...
HE HASN'T BROUGHT ME ANY HAPPI-NESS.
BOO HOO
...
SORRY I GOT UPSET...
FOR SOME REASON, HE'S POPULAR WITH WOMEN. WHEN YOU GO OUT WITH HIM... HE IS IRRESISTIBLE, YOU KNOW... BUT CHARM IS ALL HE'S GOT.
WHEREVER HE WORKED, THERE WAS DRAMA WITH WOMEN... BECAUSE HE HAD TOO MANY GIRLFRIENDS.
THEN HE'D QUIT AND RUN AWAY.
AND BECAUSE HE DRESSES SO SMARTLY...
NO ONE SUSPECTS HE'S GOT A HOME LIFE LIKE THIS.
WE HAVE NO MONEY, AS HE SPENDS IT ALL SOCIALIZING.

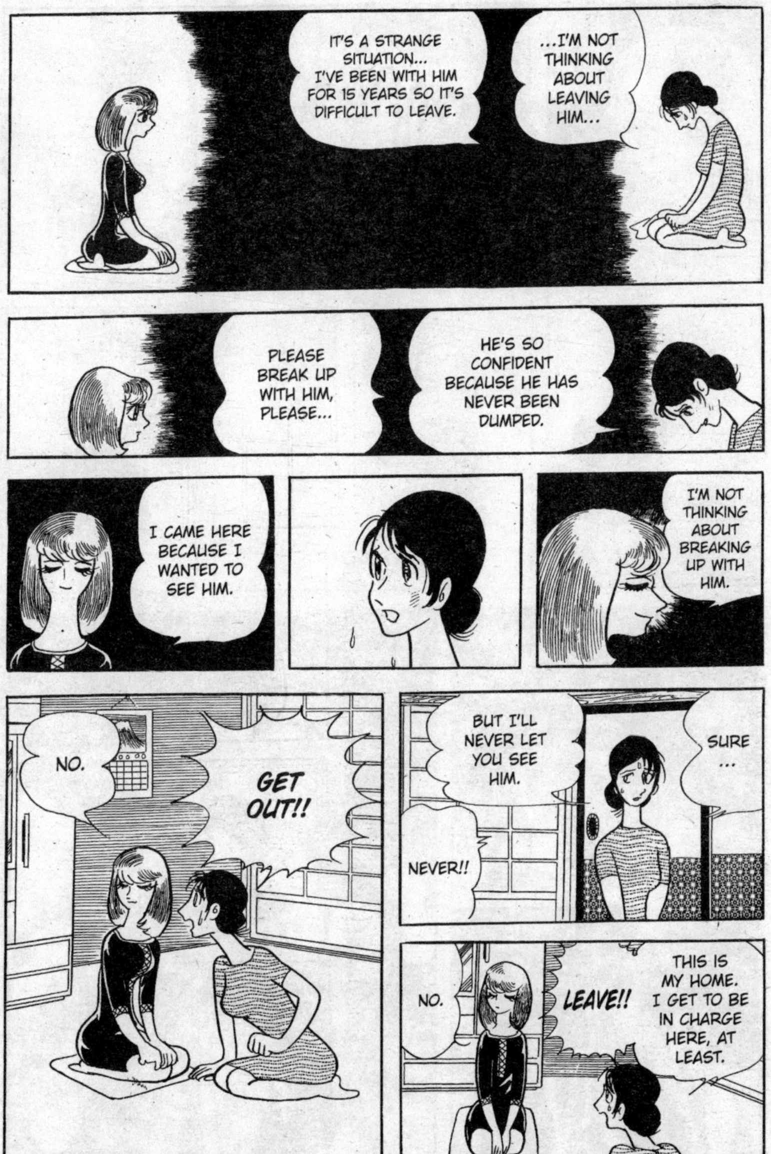
...I'M NOT THINKING ABOUT LEAVING HIM...
IT'S A STRANGE SITUATION... I'VE BEEN WITH HIM FOR 15 YEARS SO IT'S DIFFICULT TO LEAVE.
HE'S SO CONFIDENT BECAUSE HE HAS NEVER BEEN DUMPED.
PLEASE BREAK UP WITH HIM, PLEASE...
I'M NOT THINKING ABOUT BREAKING UP WITH HIM.
I CAME HERE BECAUSE I WANTED TO SEE HIM.
SURE ...
BUT I'LL NEVER LET YOU SEE HIM.
NEVER!!
THIS IS MY HOME. I GET TO BE IN CHARGE HERE, AT LEAST.
LEAVE!!
NO.
GET OUT!!
NO.

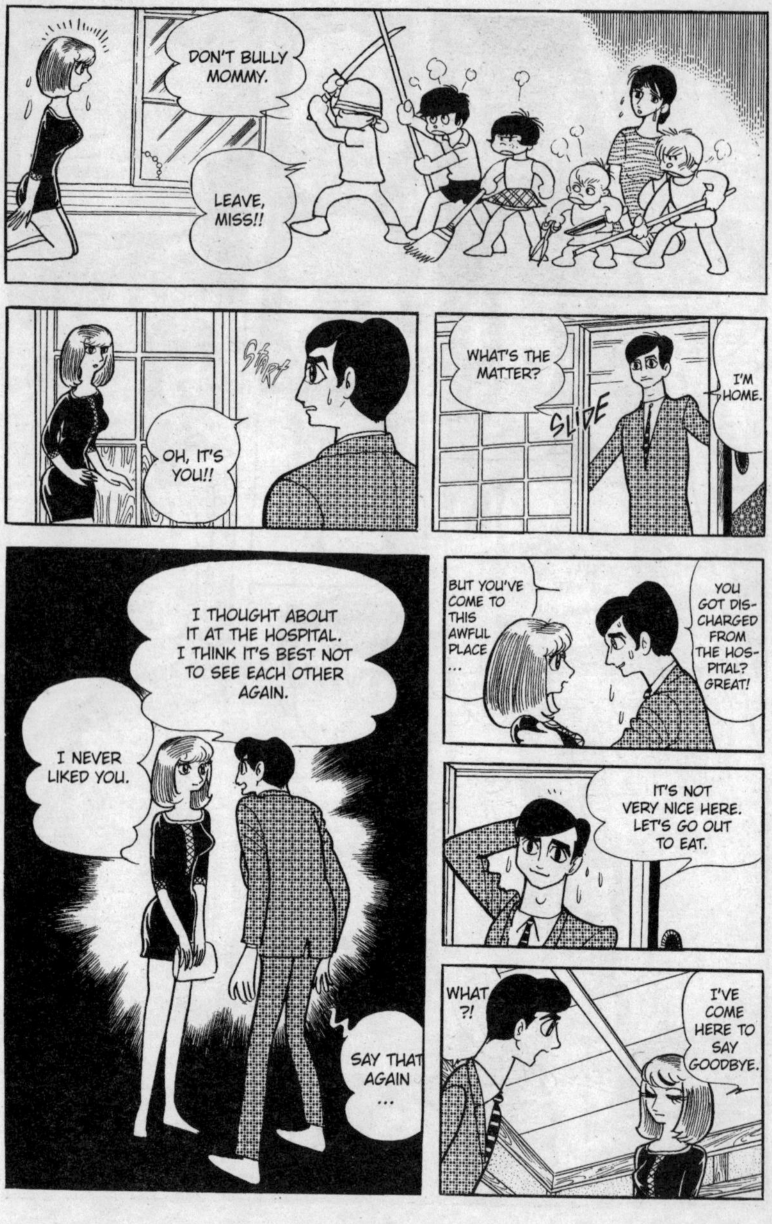
DON'T BULLY MOMMY.
LEAVE, MISS!!
I'M HOME.
SLIDE
WHAT'S THE MATTER?
START
OH, IT'S YOU!!
YOU GOT DISCHARGED FROM THE HOSPITAL? GREAT!
BUT YOU'VE COME TO THIS AWFUL PLACE ...
IT'S NOT VERY NICE HERE. LET'S GO OUT TO EAT.
I'VE COME HERE TO SAY GOODBYE.
WHAT ?!
I THOUGHT ABOUT IT AT THE HOSPITAL. I THINK IT'S BEST NOT TO SEE EACH OTHER AGAIN.
I NEVER LIKED YOU.
SAY THAT AGAIN ...

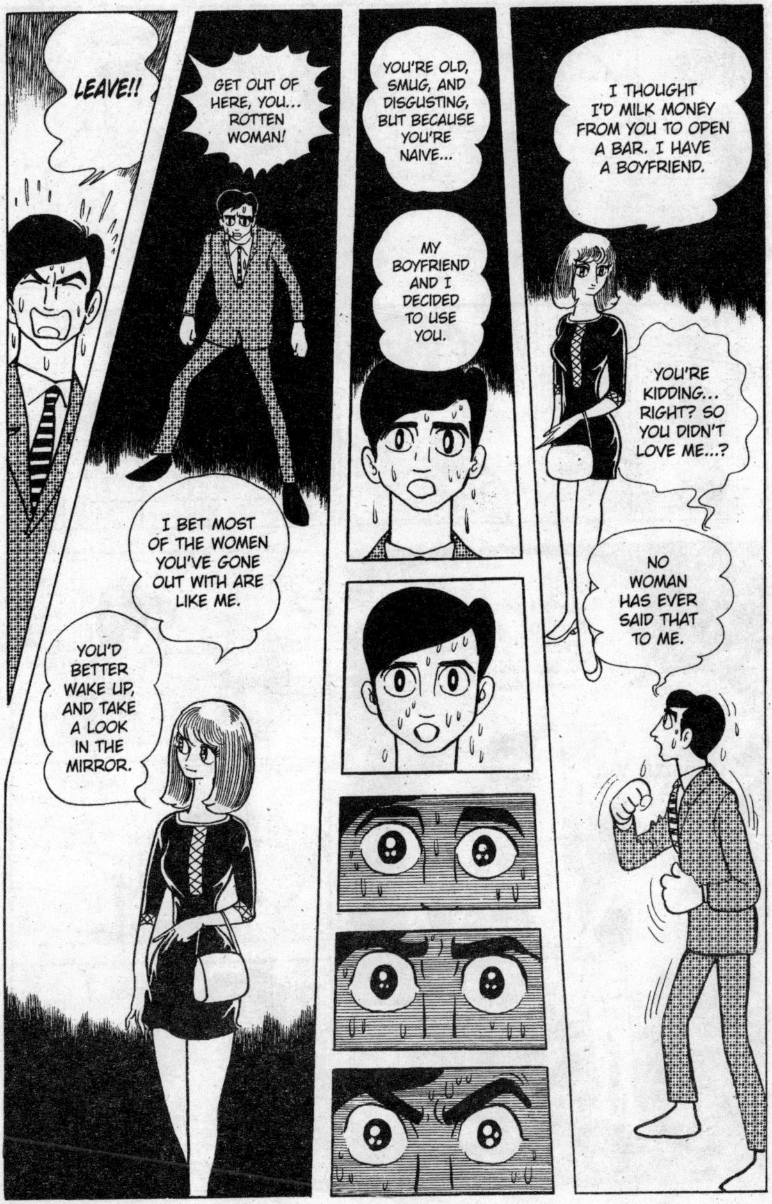
I THOUGHT I'D MILK MONEY FROM YOU TO OPEN A BAR. I HAVE A BOYFRIEND.
YOU'RE KIDDING... RIGHT? SO YOU DIDN'T LOVE ME...?
NO WOMAN HAS EVER SAID THAT TO ME.
YOU'RE OLD, SMUG, AND DISGUSTING, BUT BECAUSE YOU'RE NAIVE...
MY BOYFRIEND AND I DECIDED TO USE YOU.
GET OUT OF HERE, YOU... ROTTEN WOMAN!
I BET MOST OF THE WOMEN YOU'VE GONE OUT WITH ARE LIKE ME.
YOU'D BETTER WAKE UP, AND TAKE A LOOK IN THE MIRROR.
LEAVE!!

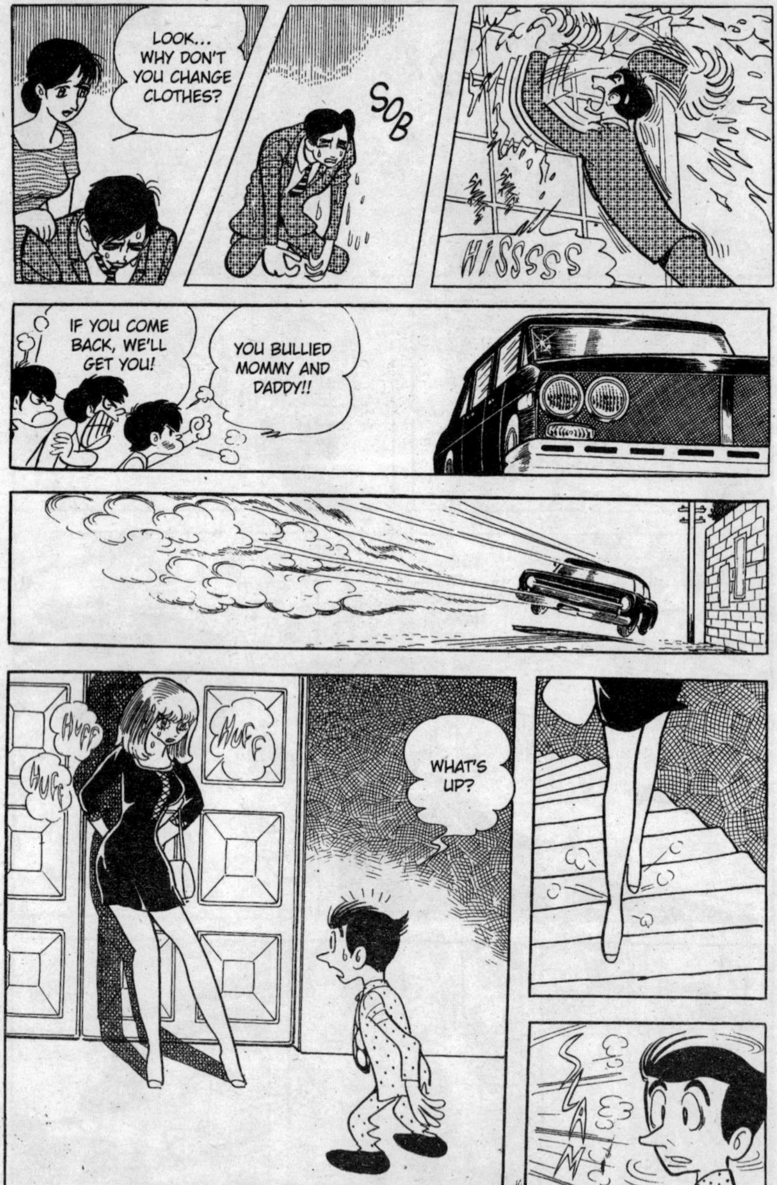
HISSSSS
SOB
LOOK... WHY DON'T YOU CHANGE CLOTHES?
YOU BULLIED MOMMY AND DADDY!!
IF YOU COME BACK, WE'LL GET YOU!
SLAM
WHAT'S UP?
HUFF
HUFF
HUFF

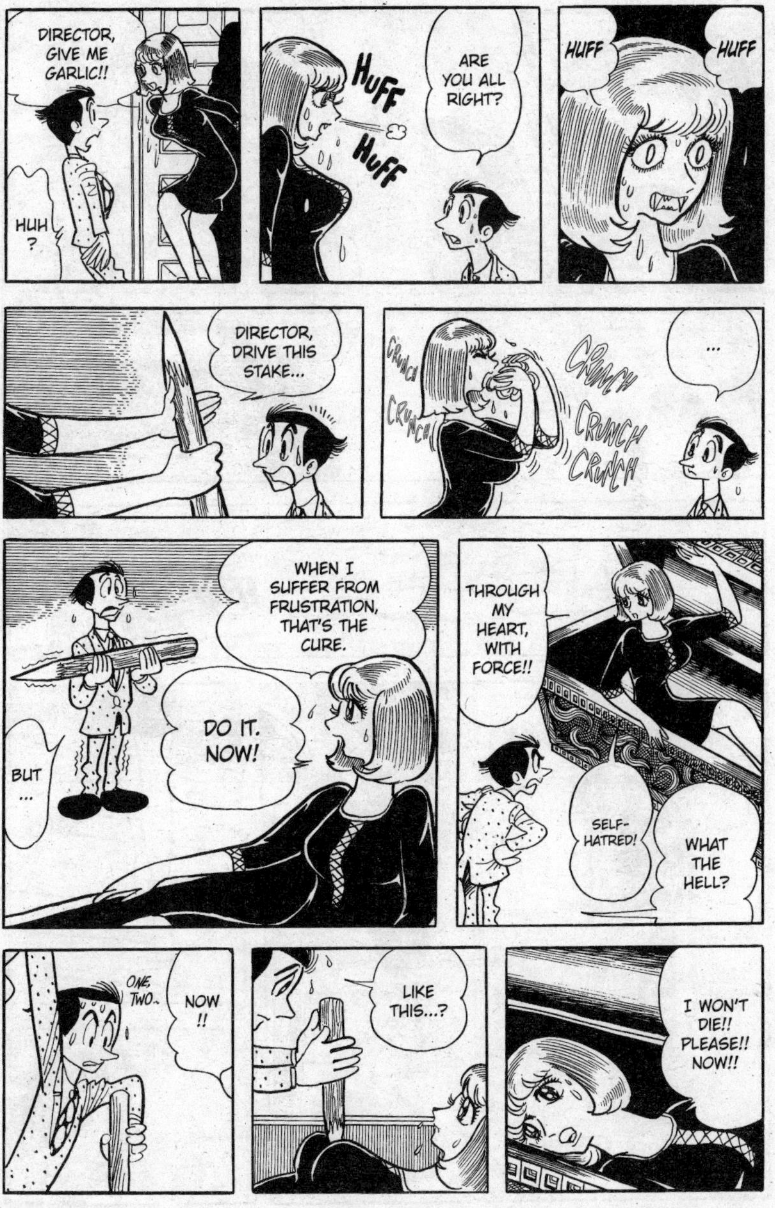
HUFF
HUFF
ARE YOU ALL RIGHT?
HUFF
HUFF
DIRECTOR, GIVE ME GARLIC!!
HUH?
...
CRUNCH
CRUNCH
CRUNCH
CRUNCH
CRUNCH
DIRECTOR, DRIVE THIS STAKE...
THROUGH MY HEART, WITH FORCE!!
WHAT THE HELL?
SELF-HATRED!
WHEN I SUFFER FROM FRUSTRATION, THAT'S THE CURE.
DO IT. NOW!
BUT ...
I WON'T DIE!! PLEASE!! NOW!!
LIKE THIS...?
NOW!!
ONE, TWO..

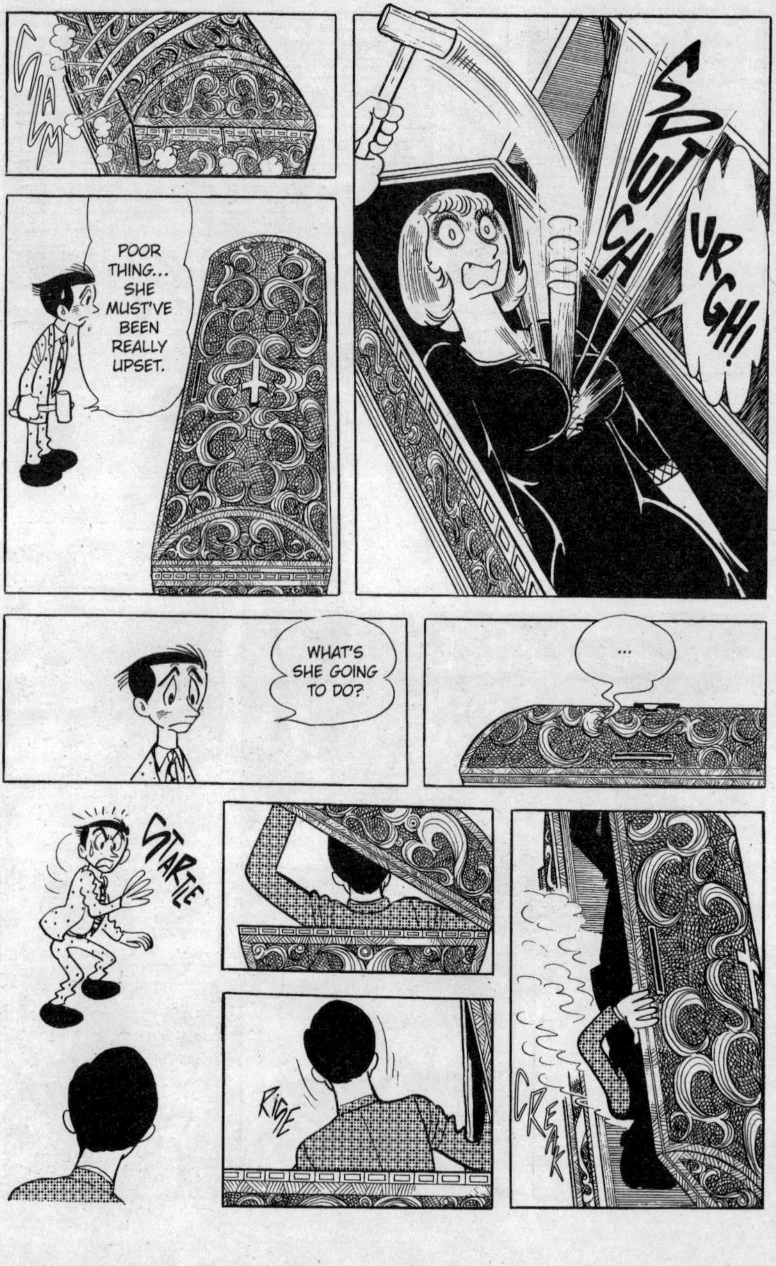
SPUTUCH
URGH!
SLAM
POOR THING... SHE MUST'VE BEEN REALLY UPSET.
...
WHAT'S SHE GOING TO DO?
CREAK
RISE
STARTLE

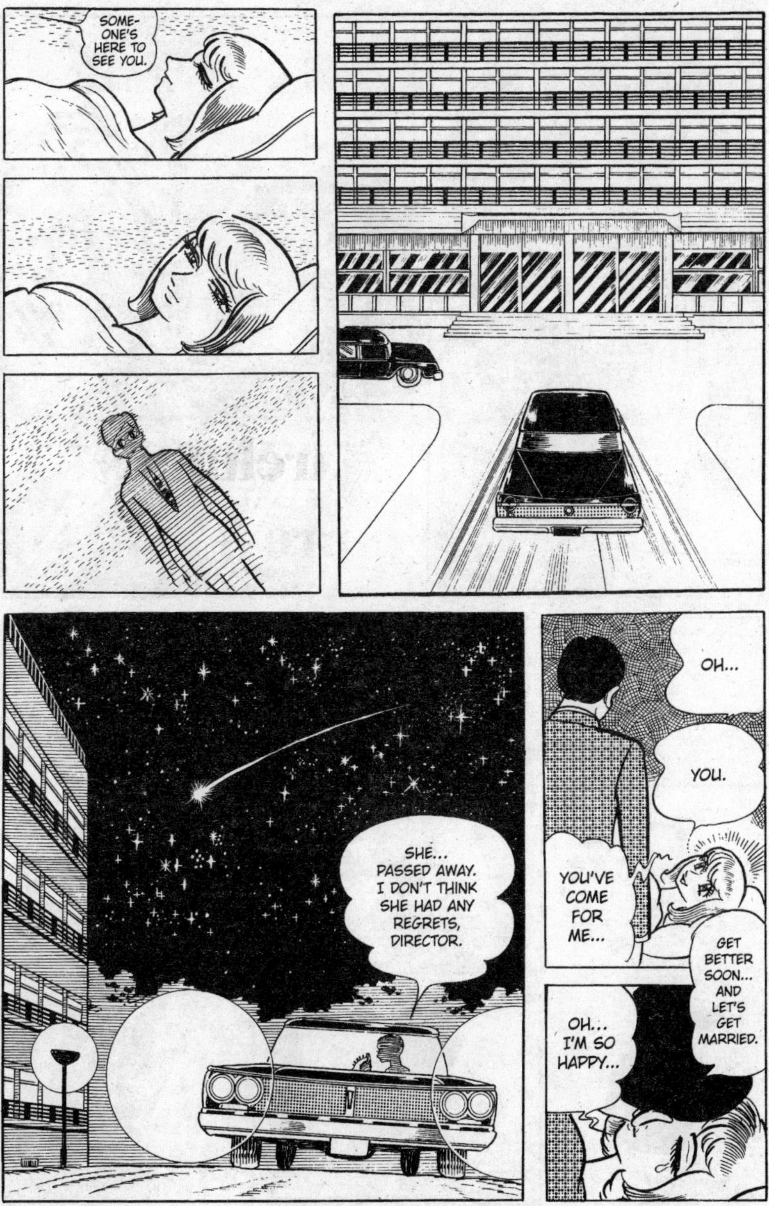
SOME-ONE'S HERE TO SEE YOU.
OH...
YOU.
YOU'VE COME FOR ME...
GET BETTER SOON... AND LET'S GET MARRIED.
OH... I'M SO HAPPY...
SHE... PASSED AWAY. I DON'T THINK SHE HAD ANY REGRETS, DIRECTOR.

# EPISODE 4

# President Flareluno's Treasure

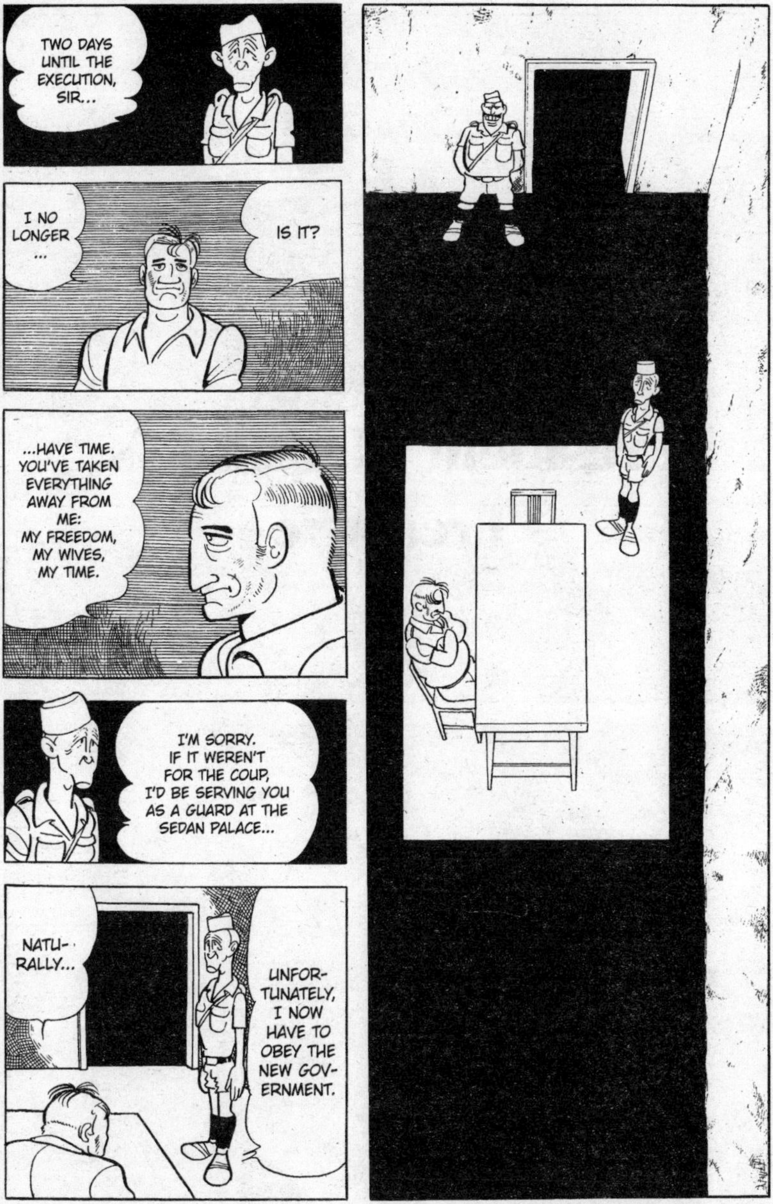
TWO DAYS UNTIL THE EXECUTION, SIR...
IS IT?
I NO LONGER ...
...HAVE TIME. YOU'VE TAKEN EVERYTHING AWAY FROM ME: MY FREEDOM, MY WIVES, MY TIME.
I'M SORRY. IF IT WEREN'T FOR THE COUP, I'D BE SERVING YOU AS A GUARD AT THE SEDAN PALACE...
UNFORTUNATELY, I NOW HAVE TO OBEY THE NEW GOVERNMENT.
NATURALLY...

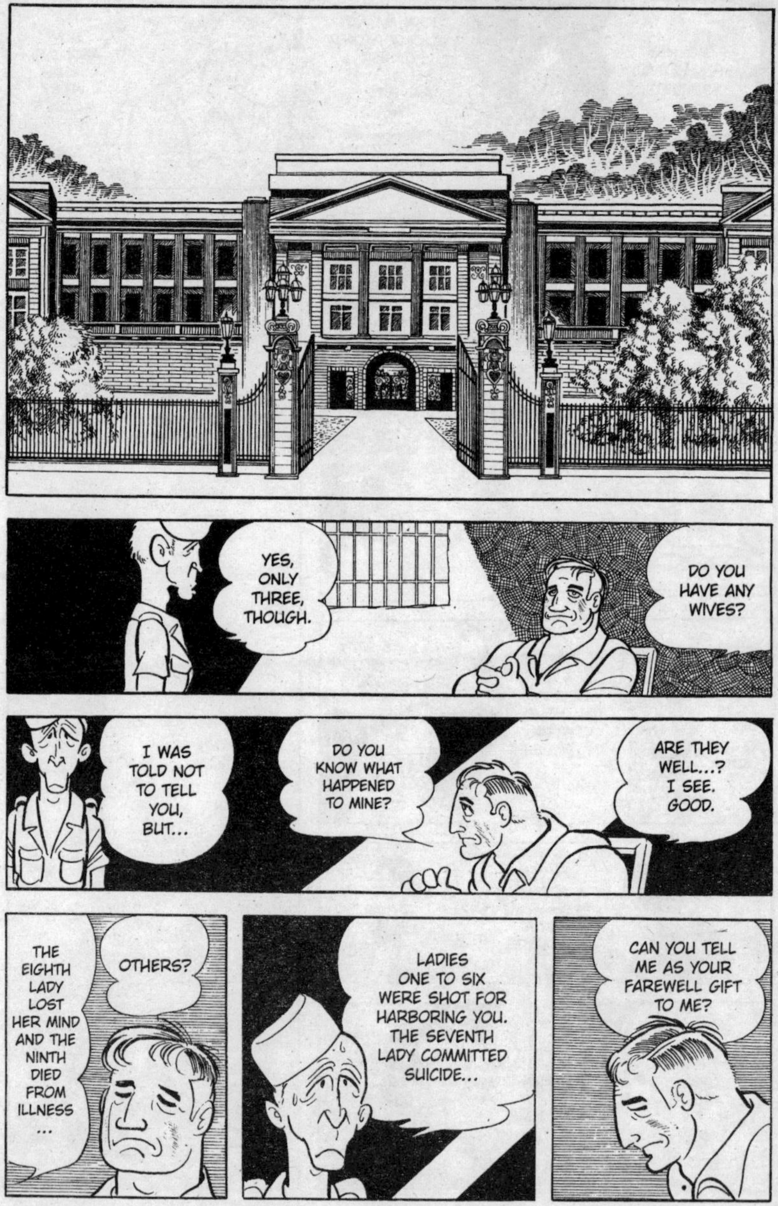
DO YOU HAVE ANY WIVES?
YES, ONLY THREE, THOUGH.
ARE THEY WELL...? I SEE. GOOD.
DO YOU KNOW WHAT HAPPENED TO MINE?
I WAS TOLD NOT TO TELL YOU, BUT...
CAN YOU TELL ME AS YOUR FAREWELL GIFT TO ME?
LADIES ONE TO SIX WERE SHOT FOR HARBORING YOU. THE SEVENTH LADY COMMITTED SUICIDE...
OTHERS?
THE EIGHTH LADY LOST HER MIND AND THE NINTH DIED FROM ILLNESS...

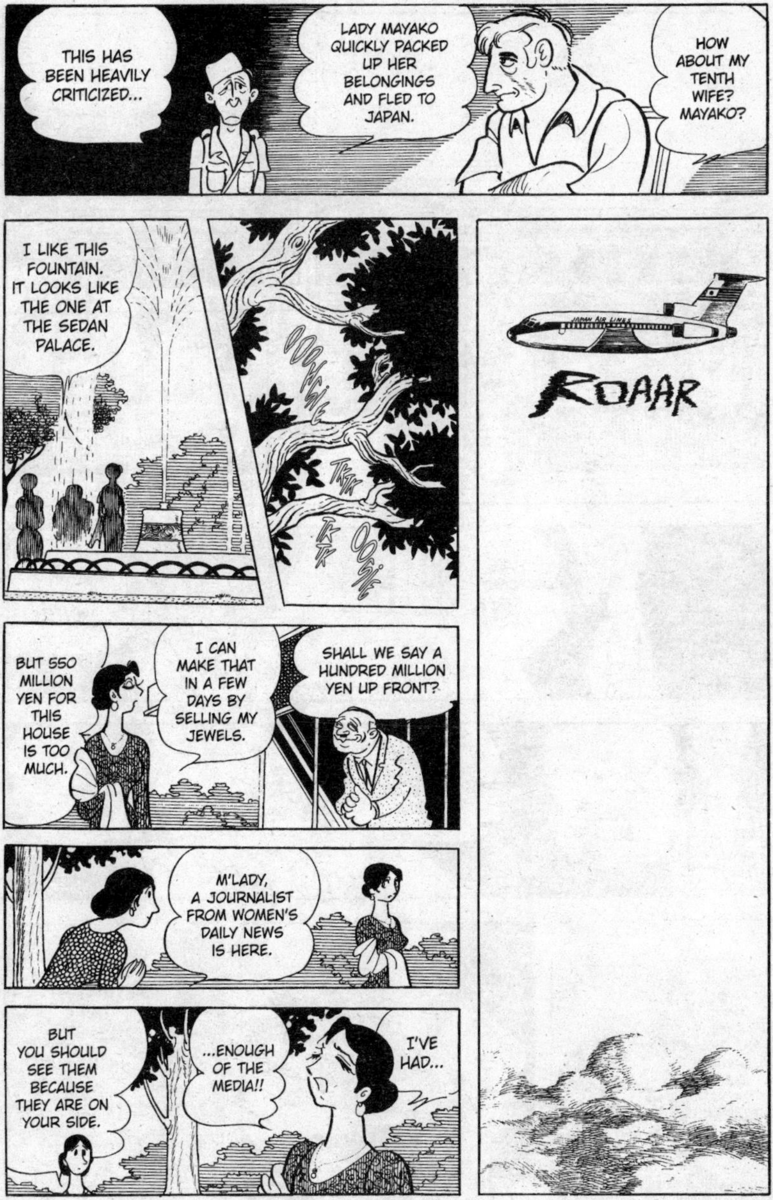
HOW ABOUT MY TENTH WIFE? MAYAKO?
LADY MAYAKO QUICKLY PACKED UP HER BELONGINGS AND FLED TO JAPAN.
THIS HAS BEEN HEAVILY CRITICIZED...
ROAAR
OOOHGIE
TKTK
TKTK
OOGIE
I LIKE THIS FOUNTAIN. IT LOOKS LIKE THE ONE AT THE SEDAN PALACE.
SHALL WE SAY A HUNDRED MILLION YEN UP FRONT?
I CAN MAKE THAT IN A FEW DAYS BY SELLING MY JEWELS.
BUT 550 MILLION YEN FOR THIS HOUSE IS TOO MUCH.
M'LADY, A JOURNALIST FROM WOMEN'S DAILY NEWS IS HERE.
I'VE HAD...
...ENOUGH OF THE MEDIA!!
BUT YOU SHOULD SEE THEM BECAUSE THEY ARE ON YOUR SIDE.

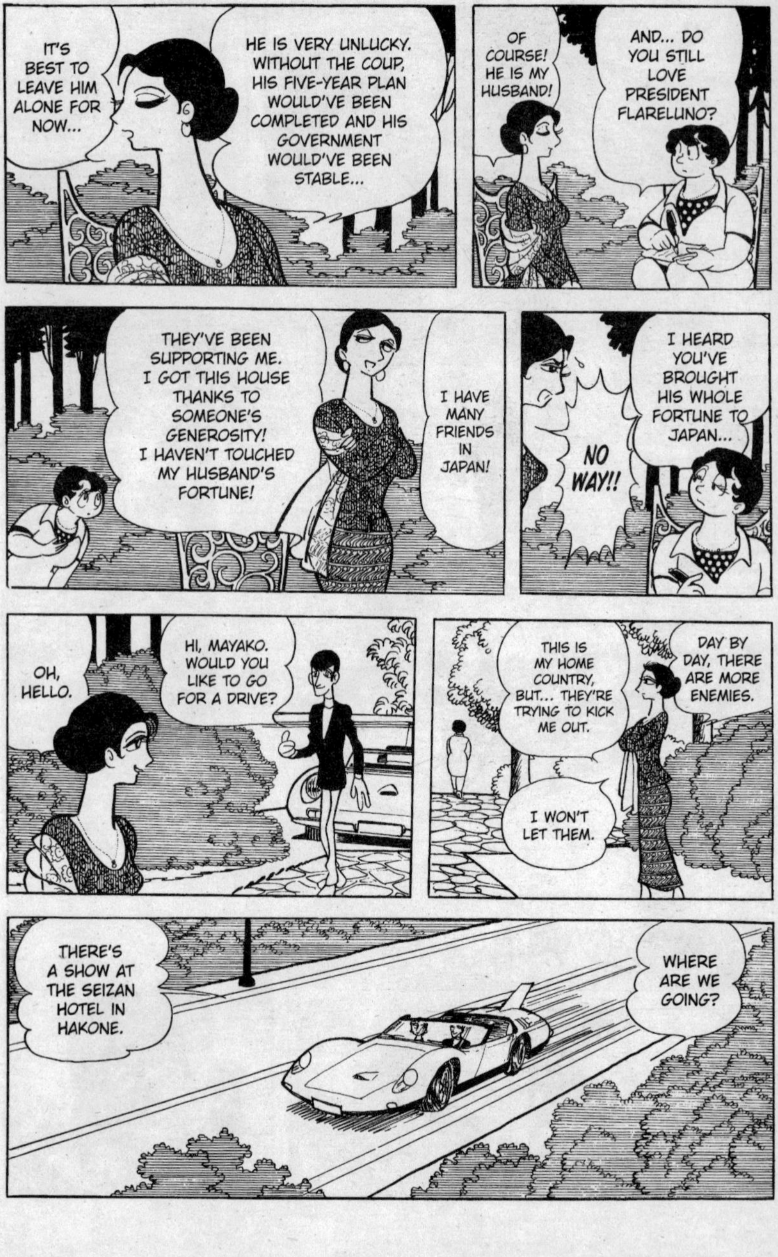

AND... DO YOU STILL LOVE PRESIDENT FLARELUNO?
OF COURSE! HE IS MY HUSBAND!
HE IS VERY UNLUCKY. WITHOUT THE COUP, HIS FIVE-YEAR PLAN WOULD'VE BEEN COMPLETED AND HIS GOVERNMENT WOULD'VE BEEN STABLE...
IT'S BEST TO LEAVE HIM ALONE FOR NOW...
I HEARD YOU'VE BROUGHT HIS WHOLE FORTUNE TO JAPAN...
NO WAY!!
I HAVE MANY FRIENDS IN JAPAN!
THEY'VE BEEN SUPPORTING ME. I GOT THIS HOUSE THANKS TO SOMEONE'S GENEROSITY! I HAVEN'T TOUCHED MY HUSBAND'S FORTUNE!
DAY BY DAY, THERE ARE MORE ENEMIES.
THIS IS MY HOME COUNTRY, BUT... THEY'RE TRYING TO KICK ME OUT.
I WON'T LET THEM.
HI, MAYAKO. WOULD YOU LIKE TO GO FOR A DRIVE?
OH, HELLO.
WHERE ARE WE GOING?
THERE'S A SHOW AT THE SEIZAN HOTEL IN HAKONE.

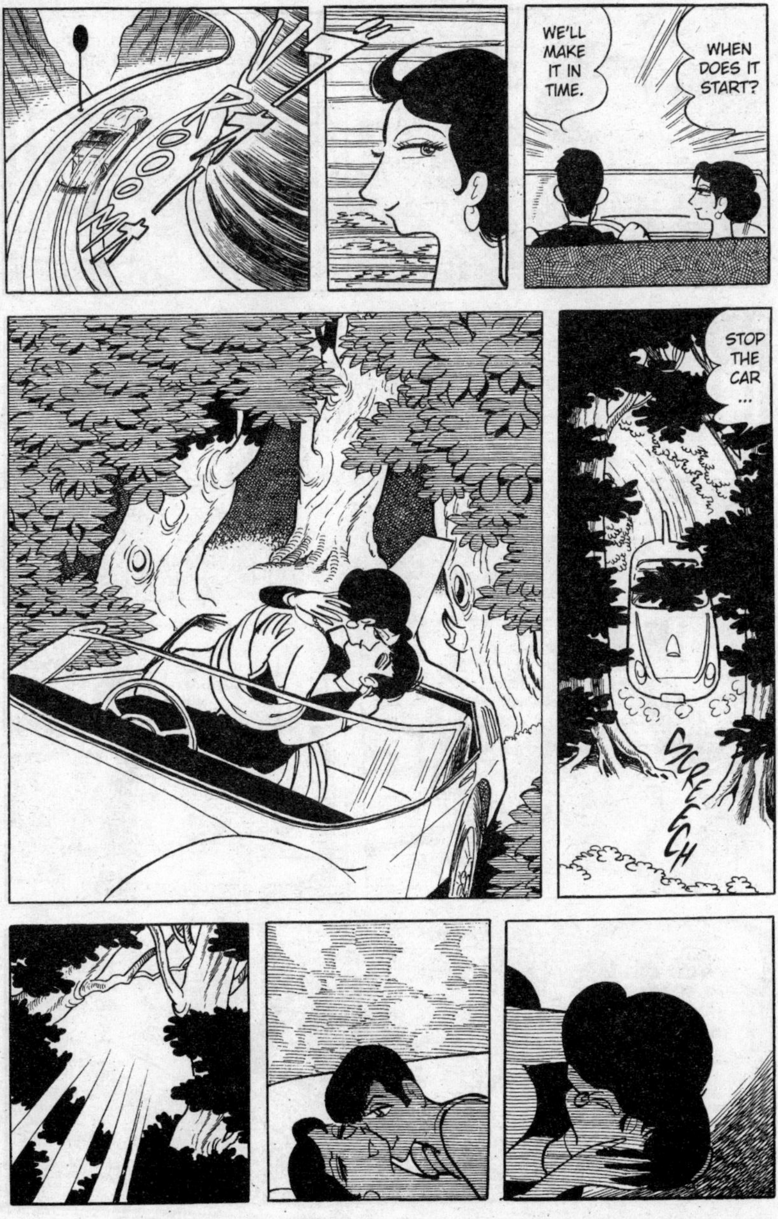
WHEN DOES IT START?
WE'LL MAKE IT IN TIME.
VROOOM
STOP THE CAR ...
SCREECH

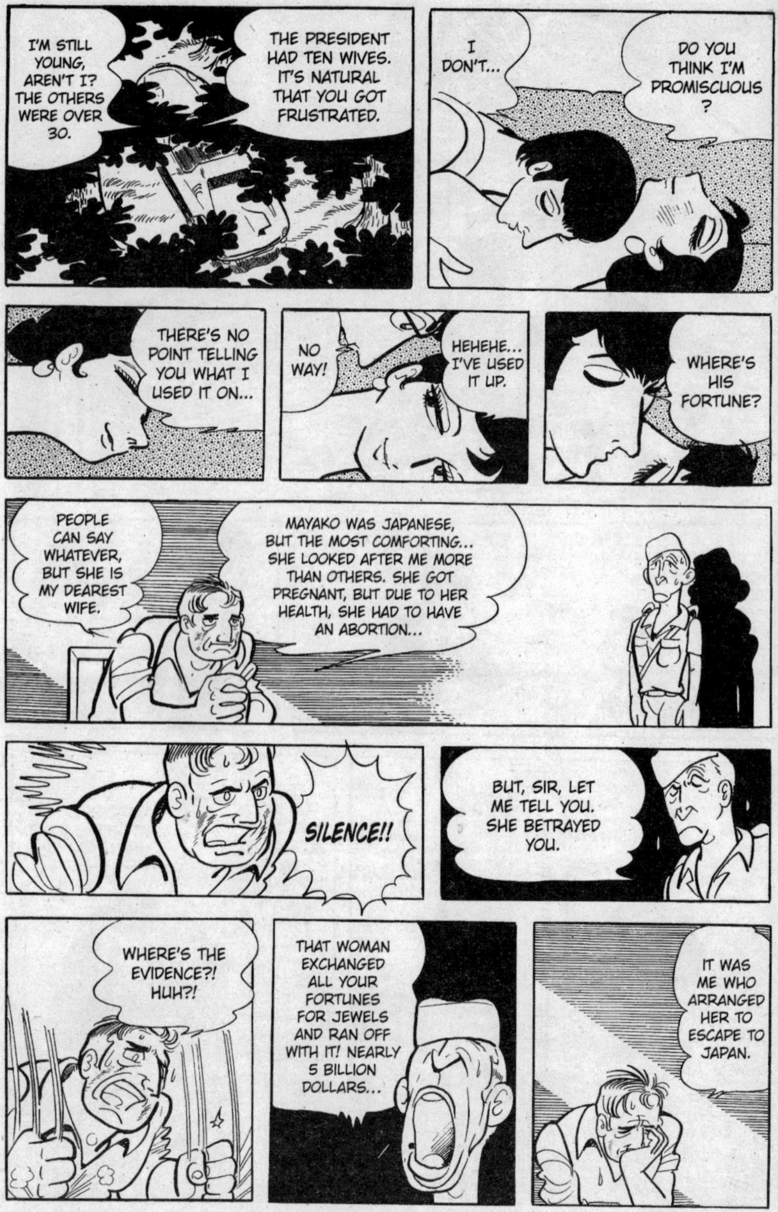
DO YOU THINK I'M PROMISCUOUS ?
I DON'T...
THE PRESIDENT HAD TEN WIVES. IT'S NATURAL THAT YOU GOT FRUSTRATED.
I'M STILL YOUNG, AREN'T I? THE OTHERS WERE OVER 30.
WHERE'S HIS FORTUNE?
HEHEHE... I'VE USED IT UP.
NO WAY!
THERE'S NO POINT TELLING YOU WHAT I USED IT ON...
MAYAKO WAS JAPANESE, BUT THE MOST COMFORTING... SHE LOOKED AFTER ME MORE THAN OTHERS. SHE GOT PREGNANT, BUT DUE TO HER HEALTH, SHE HAD TO HAVE AN ABORTION...
PEOPLE CAN SAY WHATEVER, BUT SHE IS MY DEAREST WIFE.
BUT, SIR, LET ME TELL YOU. SHE BETRAYED YOU.
SILENCE!!
IT WAS ME WHO ARRANGED HER TO ESCAPE TO JAPAN.
THAT WOMAN EXCHANGED ALL YOUR FORTUNES FOR JEWELS AND RAN OFF WITH IT! NEARLY 5 BILLION DOLLARS...
WHERE'S THE EVIDENCE?! HUH?!

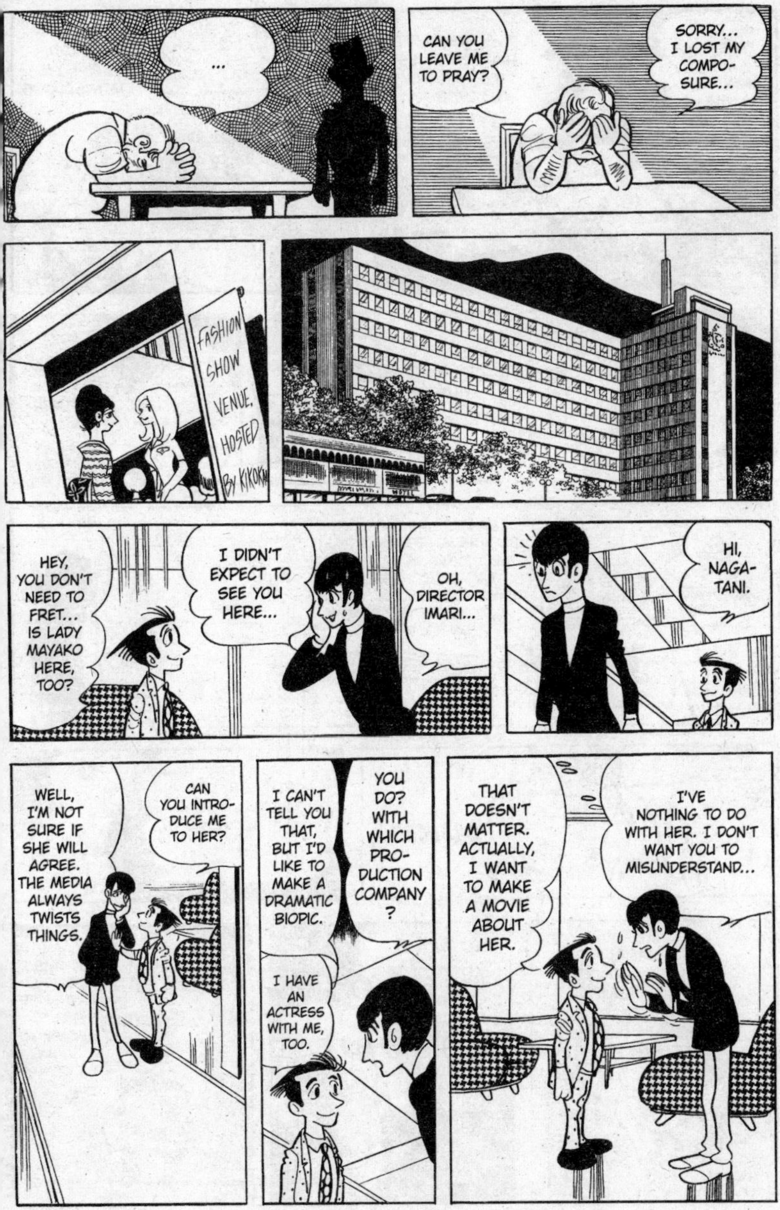
SORRY... I LOST MY COMPOSURE...
CAN YOU LEAVE ME TO PRAY?
...
FASHION SHOW VENUE, HOSTED BY KIKOK
HI, NAGATANI.
OH, DIRECTOR IMARI...
I DIDN'T EXPECT TO SEE YOU HERE...
HEY, YOU DON'T NEED TO FRET... IS LADY MAYAKO HERE, TOO?
I'VE NOTHING TO DO WITH HER. I DON'T WANT YOU TO MISUNDERSTAND...
THAT DOESN'T MATTER. ACTUALLY, I WANT TO MAKE A MOVIE ABOUT HER.
YOU DO? WITH WHICH PRODUCTION COMPANY?
I CAN'T TELL YOU THAT, BUT I'D LIKE TO MAKE A DRAMATIC BIOPIC.
I HAVE AN ACTRESS WITH ME, TOO.
CAN YOU INTRODUCE ME TO HER?
WELL, I'M NOT SURE IF SHE WILL AGREE. THE MEDIA ALWAYS TWISTS THINGS.

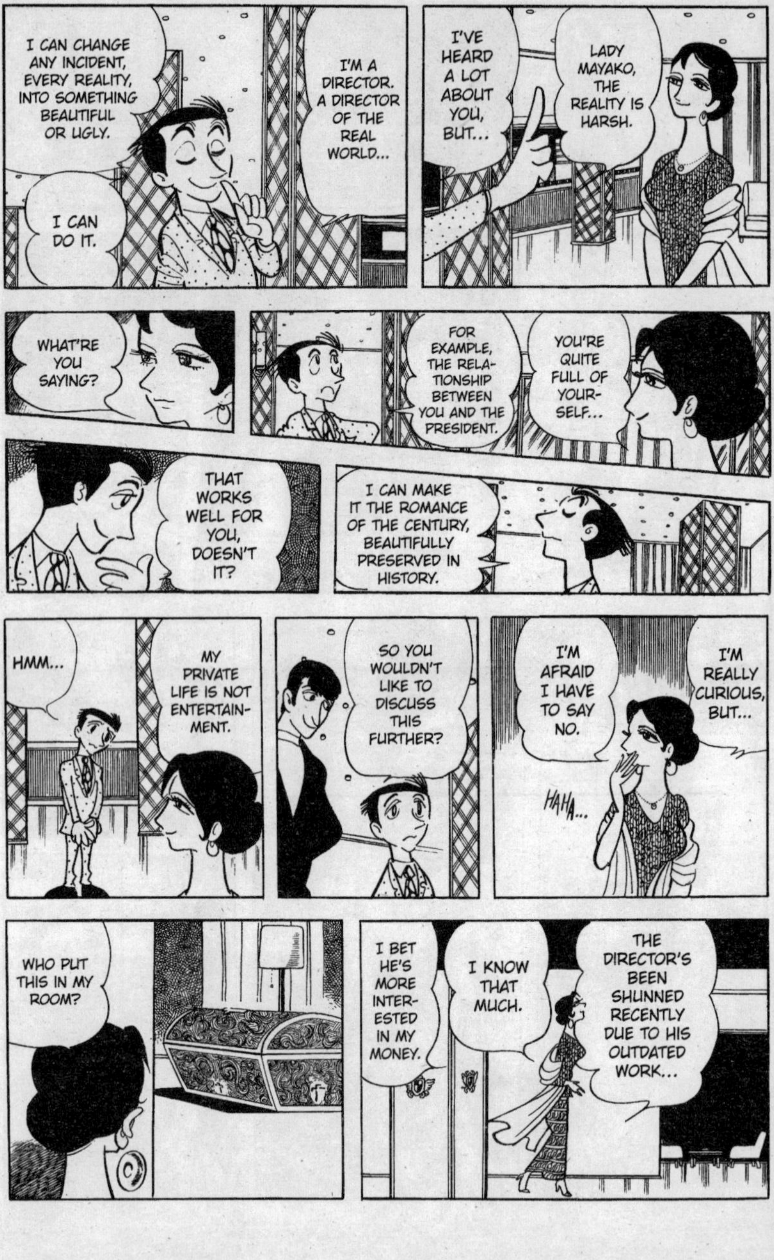
LADY MAYAKO, THE REALITY IS HARSH.
I'VE HEARD A LOT ABOUT YOU, BUT...
I'M A DIRECTOR. A DIRECTOR OF THE REAL WORLD...
I CAN CHANGE ANY INCIDENT, EVERY REALITY, INTO SOMETHING BEAUTIFUL OR UGLY.
I CAN DO IT.
YOU'RE QUITE FULL OF YOURSELF...
FOR EXAMPLE, THE RELATIONSHIP BETWEEN YOU AND THE PRESIDENT.
WHAT'RE YOU SAYING?
I CAN MAKE IT THE ROMANCE OF THE CENTURY, BEAUTIFULLY PRESERVED IN HISTORY.
THAT WORKS WELL FOR YOU, DOESN'T IT?
I'M REALLY CURIOUS, BUT...
I'M AFRAID I HAVE TO SAY NO.
HAHA...
SO YOU WOULDN'T LIKE TO DISCUSS THIS FURTHER?
MY PRIVATE LIFE IS NOT ENTERTAINMENT.
HMM...
THE DIRECTOR'S BEEN SHUNNED RECENTLY DUE TO HIS OUTDATED WORK...
I KNOW THAT MUCH.
I BET HE'S MORE INTERESTED IN MY MONEY.
WHO PUT THIS IN MY ROOM?

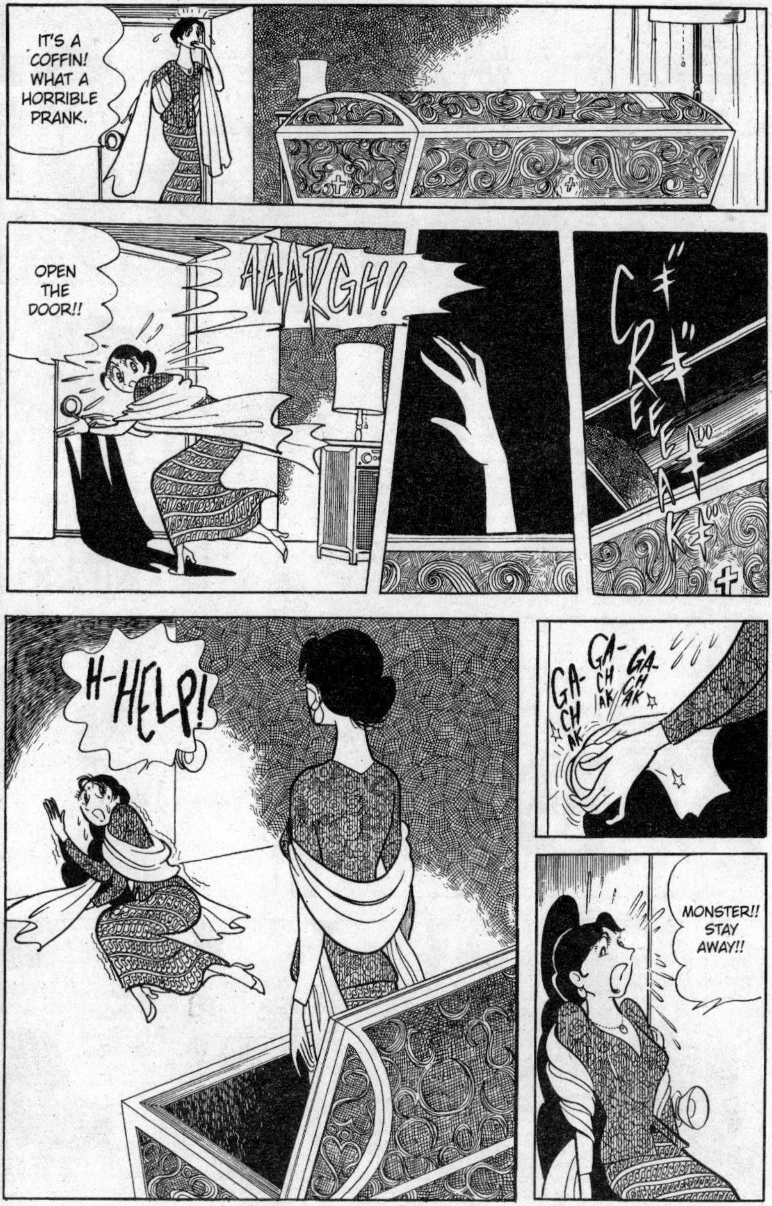
IT'S A COFFIN! WHAT A HORRIBLE PRANK.
CREEEAK
AAAARGH!
OPEN THE DOOR!!
GA-CHAK GA-CHAK GA-CHAK
MONSTER!! STAY AWAY!!
H-HELP!

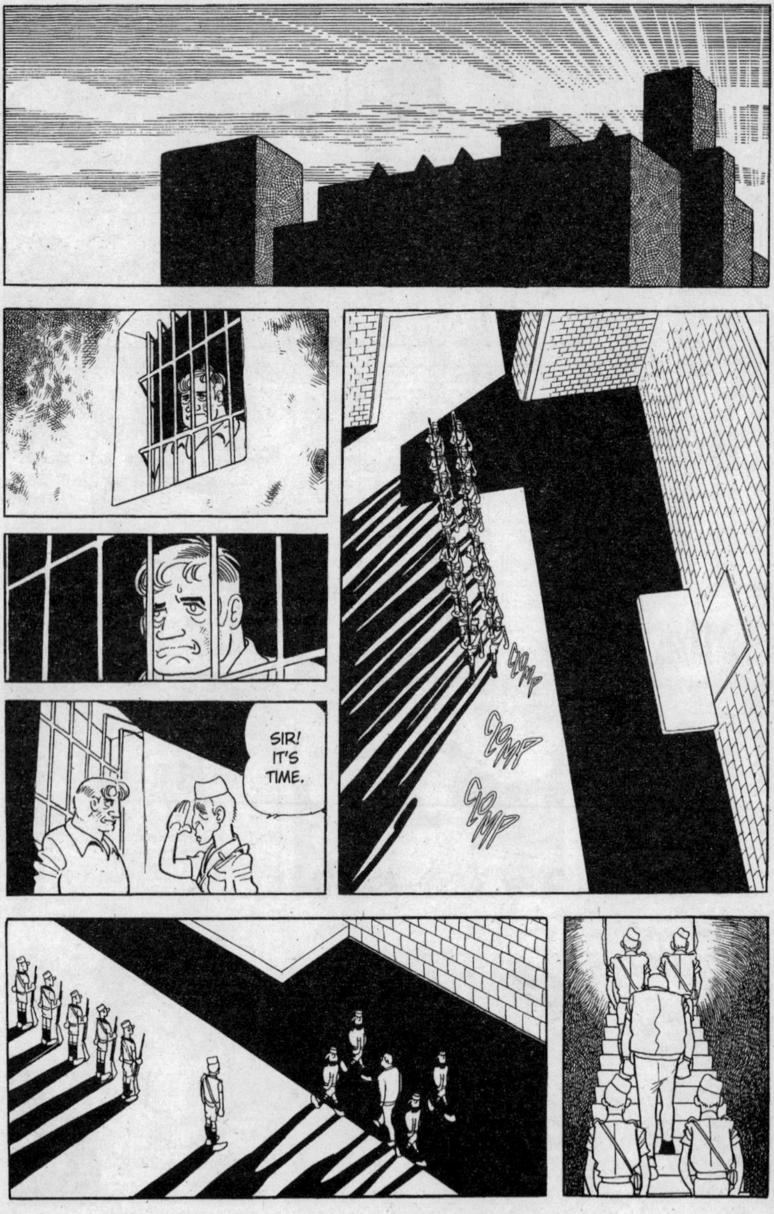
CLOMP
CLOMP
CLOMP
SIR! IT'S TIME.

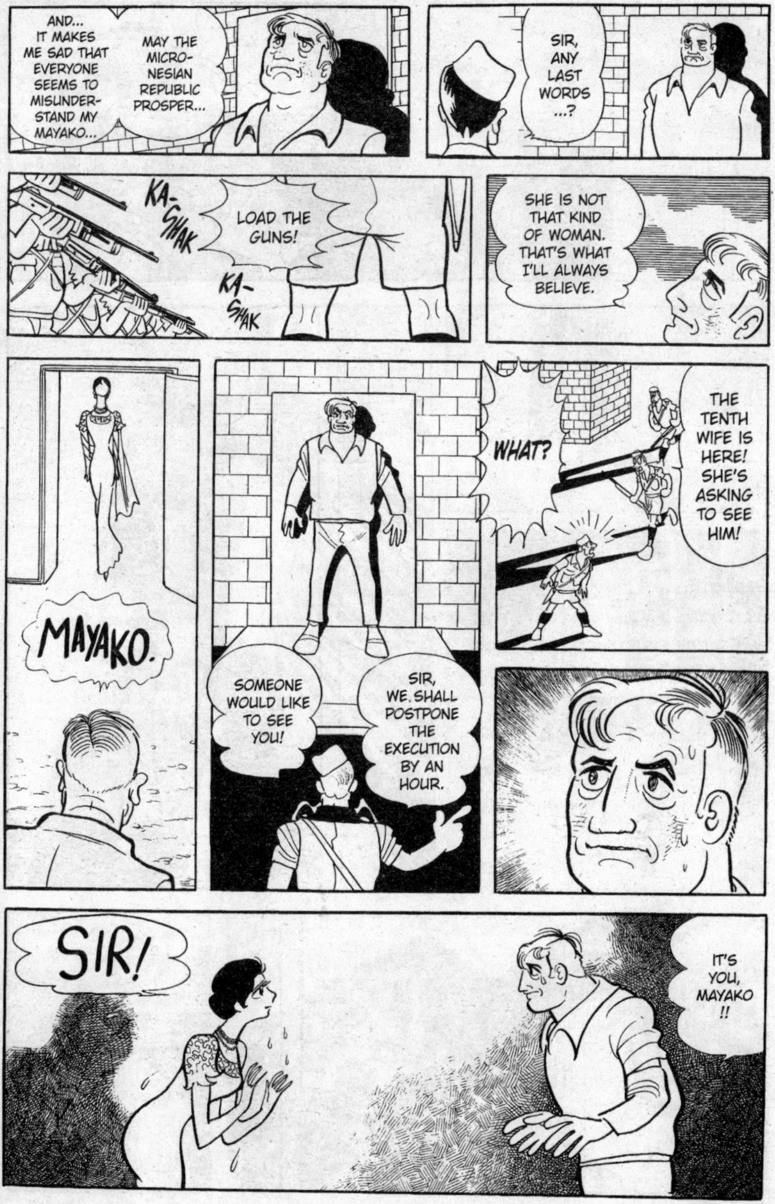
SIR, ANY LAST WORDS ...?
MAY THE MICRO-NESIAN REPUBLIC PROSPER...
AND... IT MAKES ME SAD THAT EVERYONE SEEMS TO MISUNDER-STAND MY MAYAKO...
SHE IS NOT THAT KIND OF WOMAN. THAT'S WHAT I'LL ALWAYS BELIEVE.
LOAD THE GUNS!
KA-SHAK
KA-SHAK
THE TENTH WIFE IS HERE! SHE'S ASKING TO SEE HIM!
WHAT?
SIR, WE SHALL POSTPONE THE EXECUTION BY AN HOUR.
SOMEONE WOULD LIKE TO SEE YOU!
MAYAKO.
IT'S YOU, MAYAKO !!
SIR!

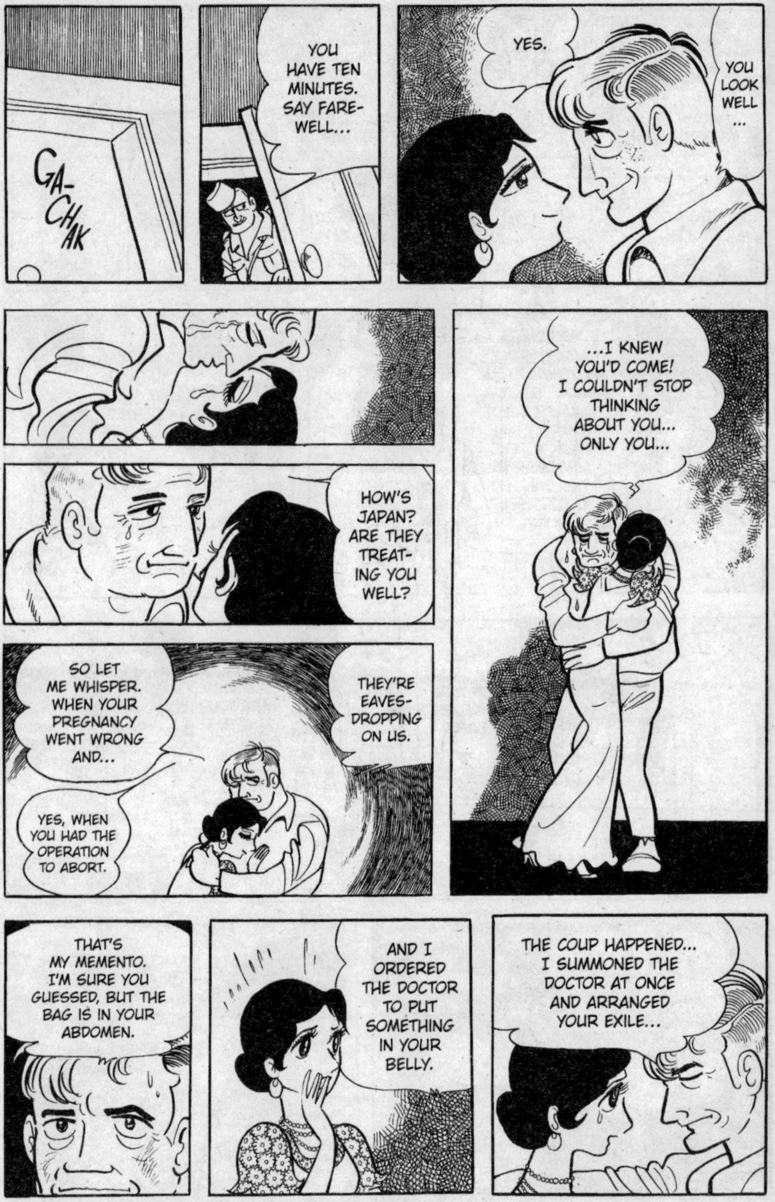
YOU LOOK WELL ...
YES.
YOU HAVE TEN MINUTES. SAY FARE-WELL...
GA-CHAK
...I KNEW YOU'D COME! I COULDN'T STOP THINKING ABOUT YOU... ONLY YOU...
HOW'S JAPAN? ARE THEY TREAT-ING YOU WELL?
THEY'RE EAVES-DROPPING ON US.
SO LET ME WHISPER. WHEN YOUR PREGNANCY WENT WRONG AND...
YES, WHEN YOU HAD THE OPERATION TO ABORT.
THE COUP HAPPENED... I SUMMONED THE DOCTOR AT ONCE AND ARRANGED YOUR EXILE...
AND I ORDERED THE DOCTOR TO PUT SOMETHING IN YOUR BELLY.
THAT'S MY MEMENTO. I'M SURE YOU GUESSED, BUT THE BAG IS IN YOUR ABDOMEN.

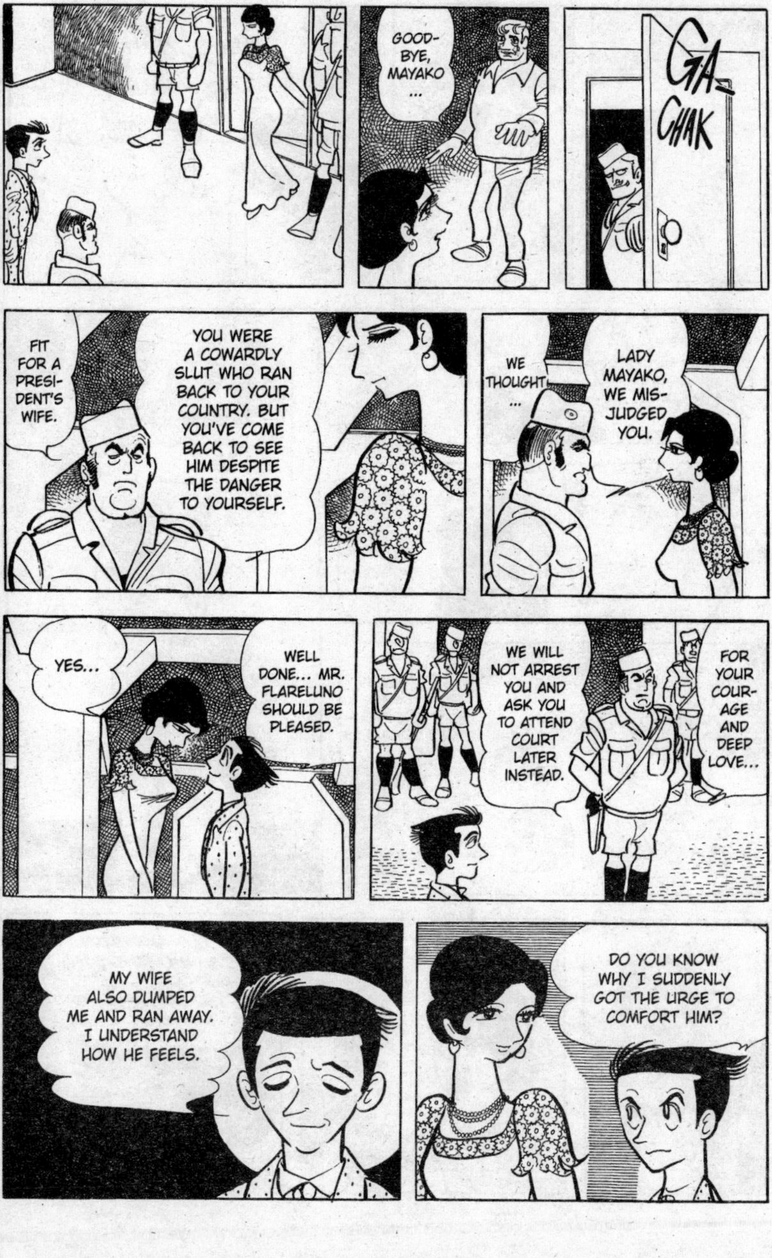
GA-CHAK
GOOD-BYE, MAYAKO ...
LADY MAYAKO, WE MIS-JUDGED YOU.
WE THOUGHT ...
YOU WERE A COWARDLY SLUT WHO RAN BACK TO YOUR COUNTRY. BUT YOU'VE COME BACK TO SEE HIM DESPITE THE DANGER TO YOURSELF.
FIT FOR A PRESI-DENT'S WIFE.
FOR YOUR COUR-AGE AND DEEP LOVE...
WE WILL NOT ARREST YOU AND ASK YOU TO ATTEND COURT LATER INSTEAD.
WELL DONE... MR. FLARELUNO SHOULD BE PLEASED.
YES...
DO YOU KNOW WHY I SUDDENLY GOT THE URGE TO COMFORT HIM?
MY WIFE ALSO DUMPED ME AND RAN AWAY. I UNDERSTAND HOW HE FEELS.

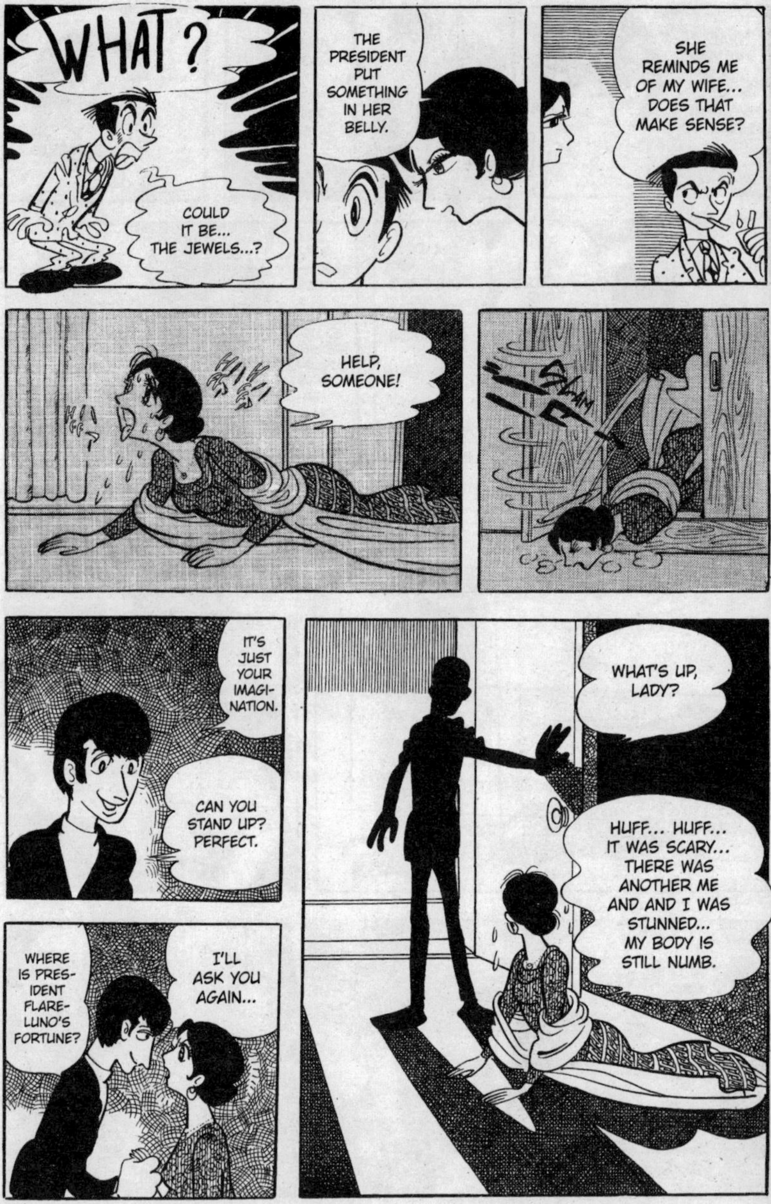
SHE REMINDS ME OF MY WIFE... DOES THAT MAKE SENSE?
THE PRESIDENT PUT SOMETHING IN HER BELLY.
WHAT?
COULD IT BE... THE JEWELS...?
SLAM
HELP, SOMEONE!
WHAT'S UP, LADY?
HUFF... HUFF... IT WAS SCARY... THERE WAS ANOTHER ME AND AND I WAS STUNNED... MY BODY IS STILL NUMB.
IT'S JUST YOUR IMAGINATION.
CAN YOU STAND UP? PERFECT.
I'LL ASK YOU AGAIN...
WHERE IS PRESIDENT FLARELUNO'S FORTUNE?

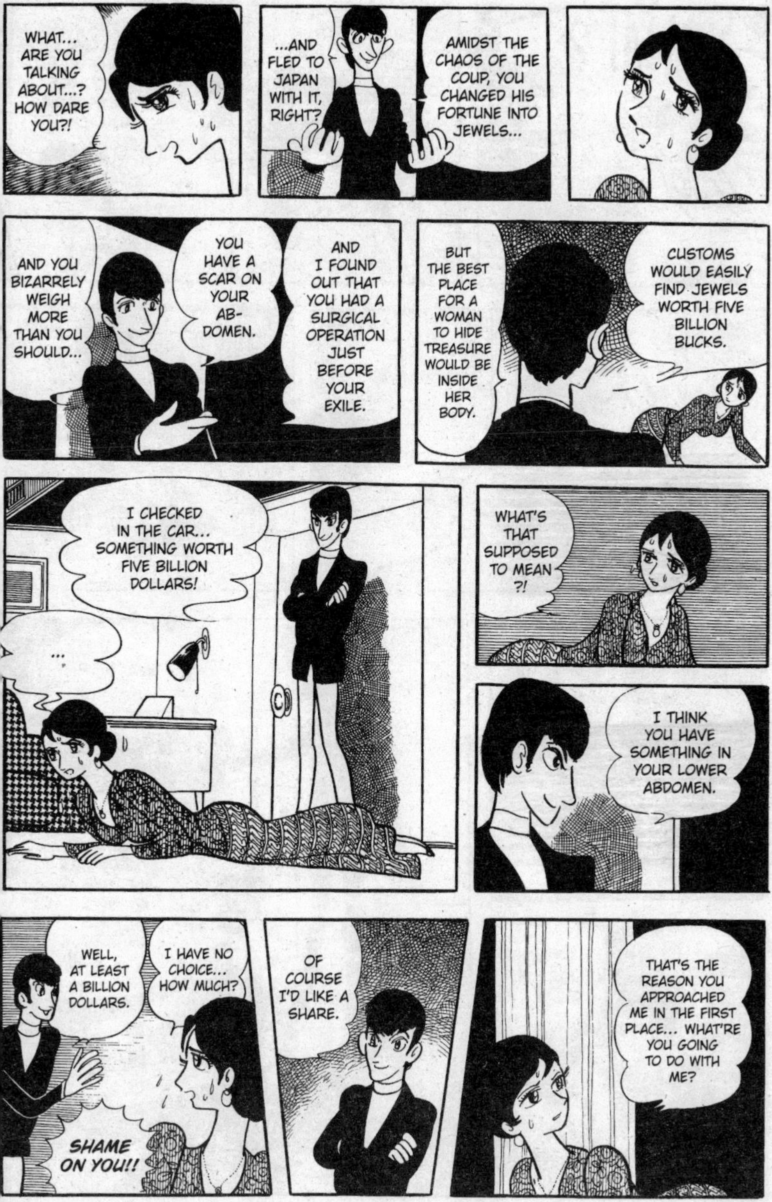
AMIDST THE CHAOS OF THE COUP, YOU CHANGED HIS FORTUNE INTO JEWELS...
...AND FLED TO JAPAN WITH IT, RIGHT?
WHAT... ARE YOU TALKING ABOUT...? HOW DARE YOU?!
CUSTOMS WOULD EASILY FIND JEWELS WORTH FIVE BILLION BUCKS.
BUT THE BEST PLACE FOR A WOMAN TO HIDE TREASURE WOULD BE INSIDE HER BODY.
AND I FOUND OUT THAT YOU HAD A SURGICAL OPERATION JUST BEFORE YOUR EXILE.
YOU HAVE A SCAR ON YOUR AB- DOMEN.
AND YOU BIZARRELY WEIGH MORE THAN YOU SHOULD...
WHAT'S THAT SUPPOSED TO MEAN ?!
I THINK YOU HAVE SOMETHING IN YOUR LOWER ABDOMEN.
I CHECKED IN THE CAR... SOMETHING WORTH FIVE BILLION DOLLARS!
...
THAT'S THE REASON YOU APPROACHED ME IN THE FIRST PLACE... WHAT'RE YOU GOING TO DO WITH ME?
OF COURSE I'D LIKE A SHARE.
I HAVE NO CHOICE... HOW MUCH?
WELL, AT LEAST A BILLION DOLLARS.
SHAME ON YOU!!

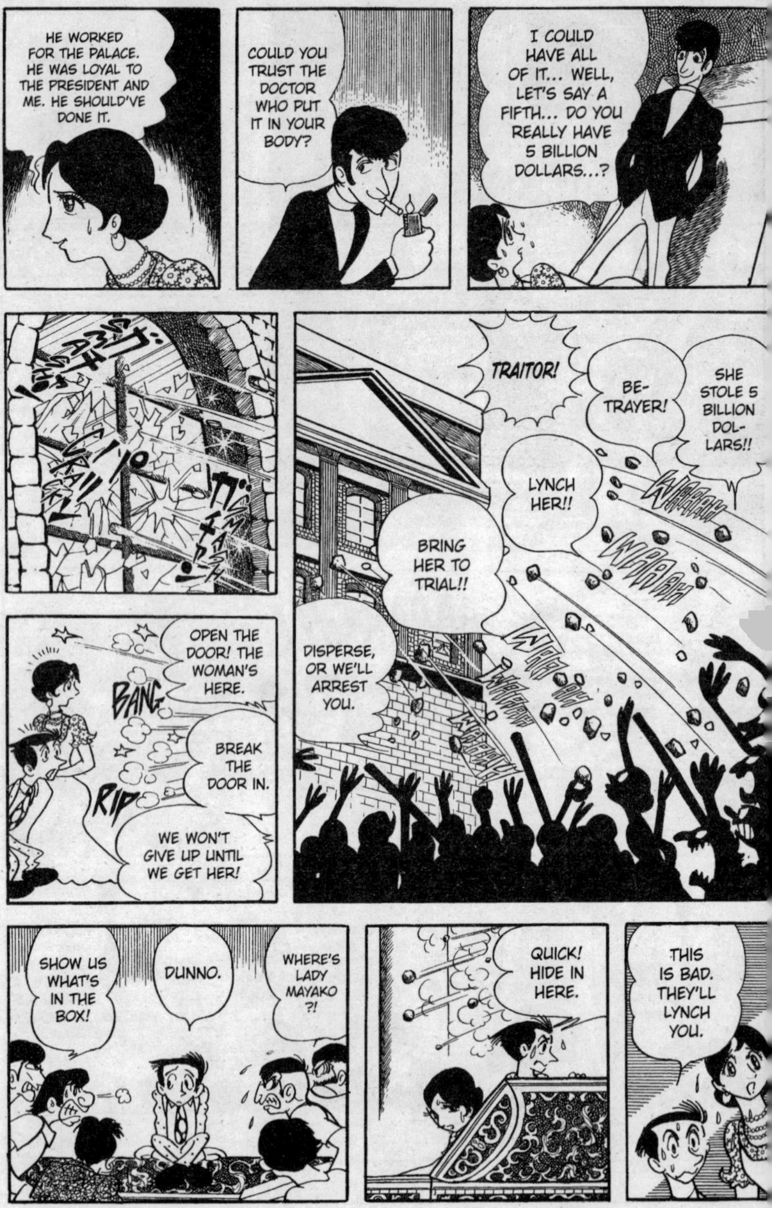
I COULD HAVE ALL OF IT... WELL, LET'S SAY A FIFTH... DO YOU REALLY HAVE 5 BILLION DOLLARS...?
COULD YOU TRUST THE DOCTOR WHO PUT IT IN YOUR BODY?
HE WORKED FOR THE PALACE. HE WAS LOYAL TO THE PRESIDENT AND ME. HE SHOULD'VE DONE IT.
SHE STOLE 5 BILLION DOL-LARS!!
BE-TRAYER!
TRAITOR!
LYNCH HER!!
BRING HER TO TRIAL!!
DISPERSE, OR WE'LL ARREST YOU.
OPEN THE DOOR! THE WOMAN'S HERE.
BANG
BREAK THE DOOR IN.
RIP
WE WON'T GIVE UP UNTIL WE GET HER!
THIS IS BAD. THEY'LL LYNCH YOU.
QUICK! HIDE IN HERE.
WHERE'S LADY MAYAKO?!
DUNNO.
SHOW US WHAT'S IN THE BOX!

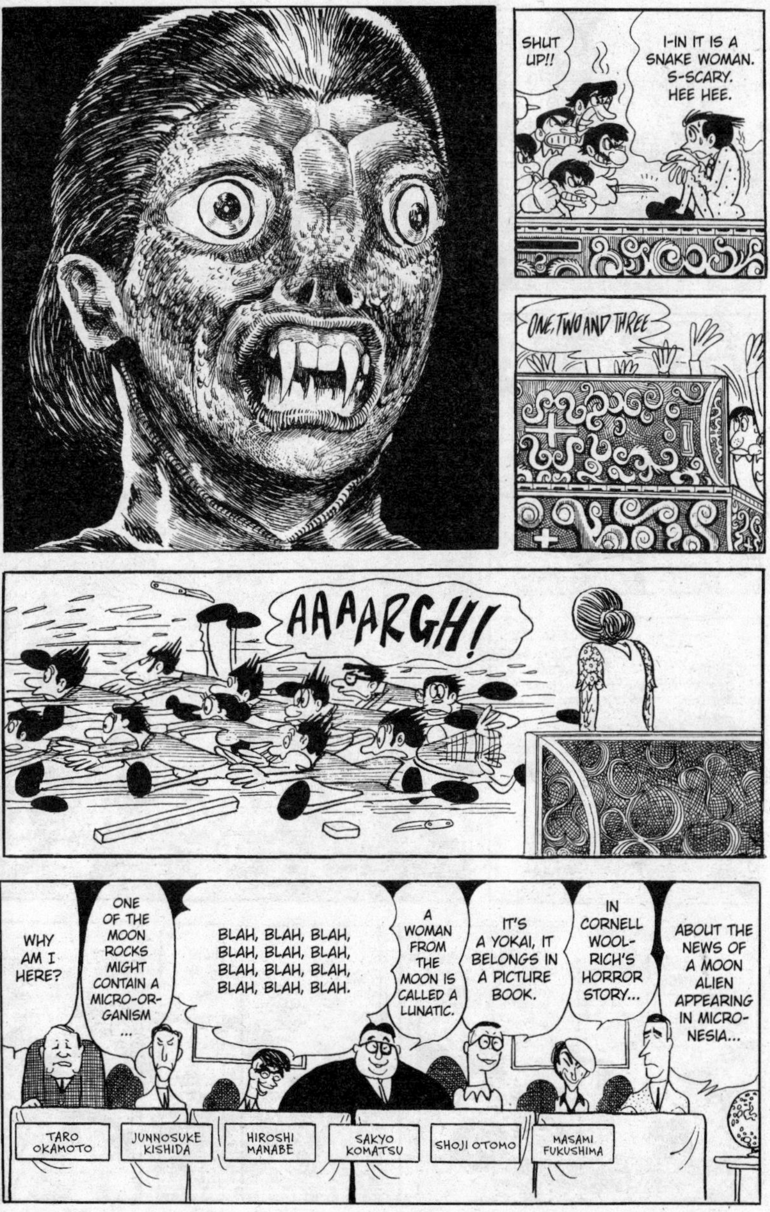
I-IN IT IS A SNAKE WOMAN. S-SCARY. HEE HEE.
SHUT UP!!
ONE, TWO AND THREE
AAAARGH!
ABOUT THE NEWS OF A MOON ALIEN APPEARING IN MICRO-NESIA...
IN CORNELL WOOL-RICH'S HORROR STORY...
IT'S A YOKAI, IT BELONGS IN A PICTURE BOOK.
A WOMAN FROM THE MOON IS CALLED A LUNATIC.
BLAH, BLAH, BLAH, BLAH, BLAH, BLAH, BLAH, BLAH, BLAH, BLAH, BLAH, BLAH.
ONE OF THE MOON ROCKS MIGHT CONTAIN A MICRO-OR-GANISM ...
WHY AM I HERE?
MASAMI FUKUSHIMA
SHOJI OTOMO
SAKYO KOMATSU
HIROSHI MANABE
JUNNOSUKE KISHIDA
TARO OKAMOTO

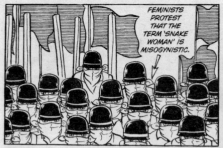

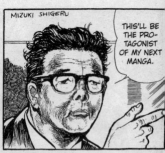

MIZUKI SHIGERU
THIS'LL BE THE PROTAGONIST OF MY NEXT MANGA.
FEMINISTS PROTEST THAT THE TERM 'SNAKE WOMAN' IS MISOGYNISTIC.
HAS THE OPERATION ON LADY MAYAKO FINISHED?
YES.
DID YOU EXTRACT WHAT WAS INSIDE OF HER?
WE'VE TAKEN IT OUT. IT WAS A BAG.
AND... WHAT'S INSIDE?
WE HAVEN'T OPENED IT.
WAIT. WE'LL OPEN IT ONCE SHE'S WOKEN UP.

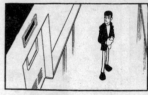

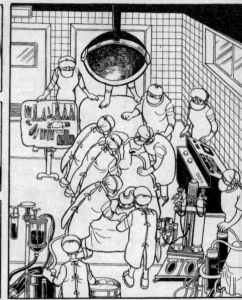

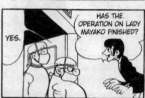

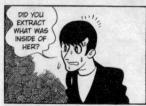

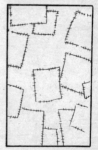

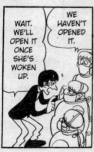

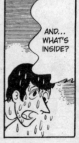

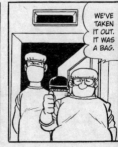

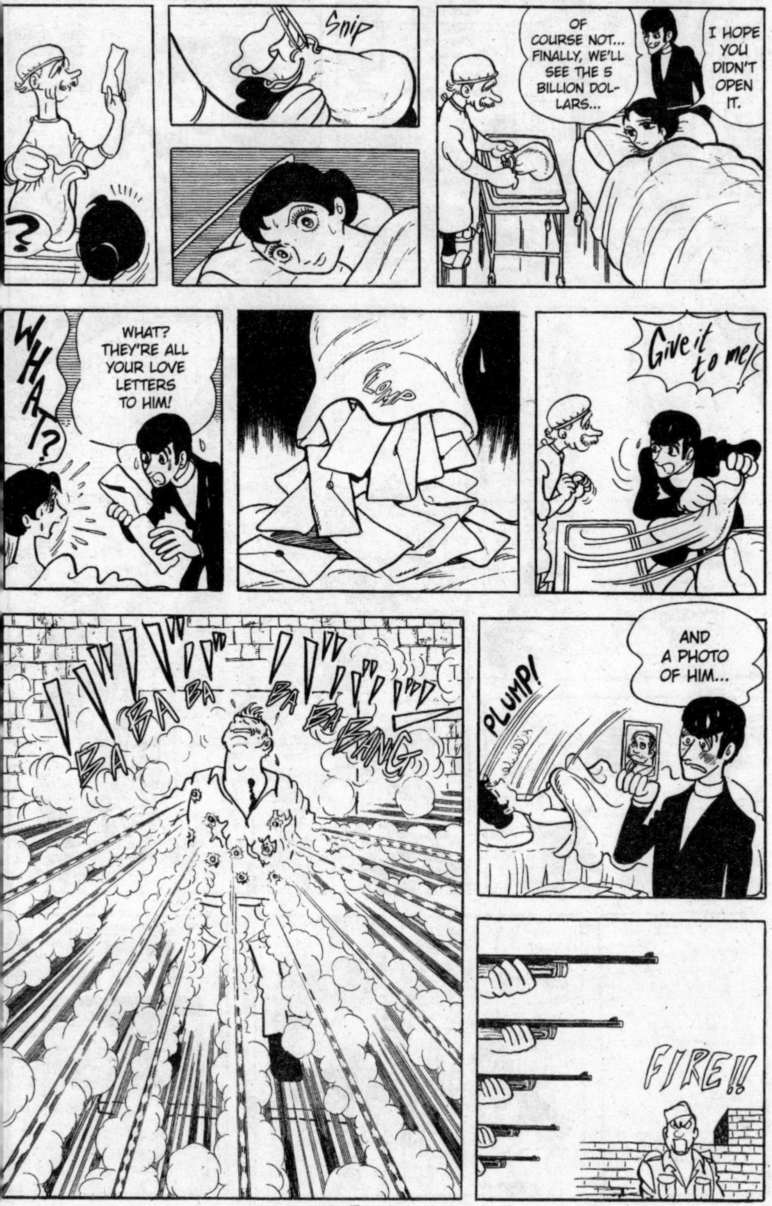
I HOPE YOU DIDN'T OPEN IT.
OF COURSE NOT... FINALLY, WE'LL SEE THE 5 BILLION DOL-LARS...
Snip
Give it to me!
FLOMP
WHAT? THEY'RE ALL YOUR LOVE LETTERS TO HIM!
WHAT?
AND A PHOTO OF HIM...
PLUMP!
FIRE!!
BA BA BA BA BA BANG

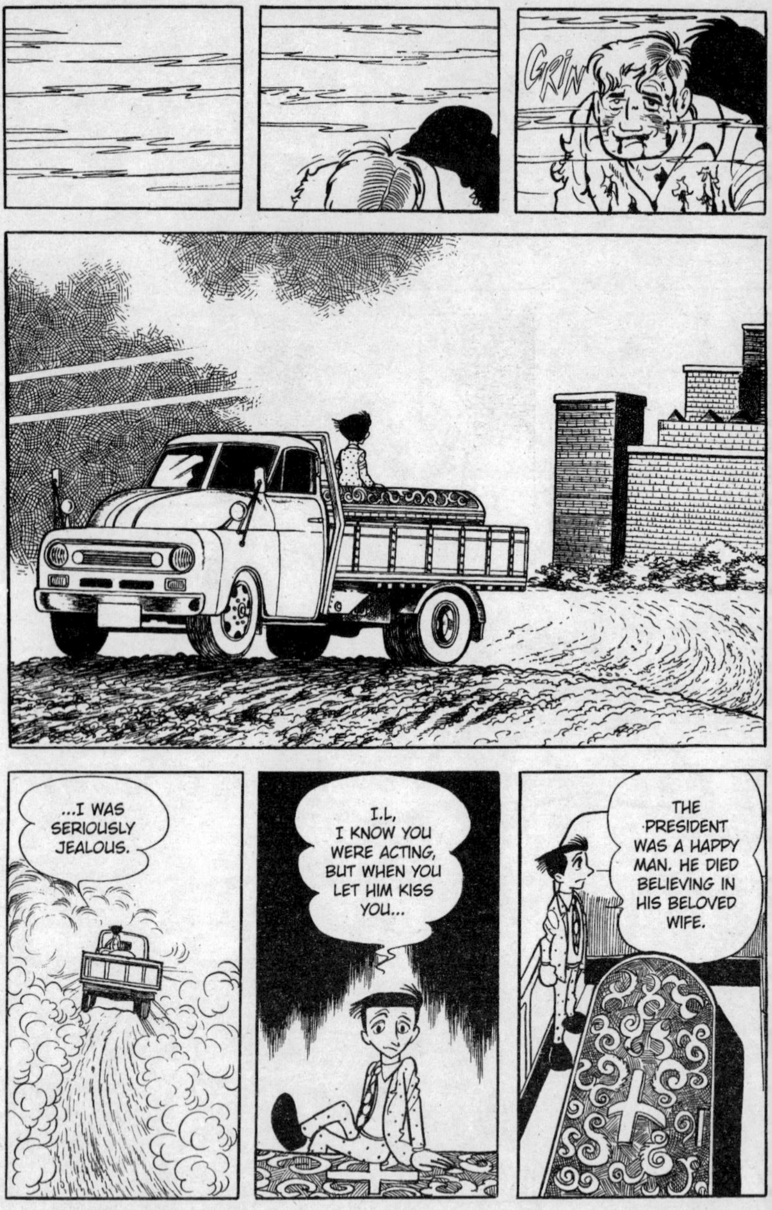
GRIN
THE PRESIDENT WAS A HAPPY MAN. HE DIED BELIEVING IN HIS BELOVED WIFE.
I.L, I KNOW YOU WERE ACTING, BUT WHEN YOU LET HIM KISS YOU...
...I WAS SERIOUSLY JEALOUS.

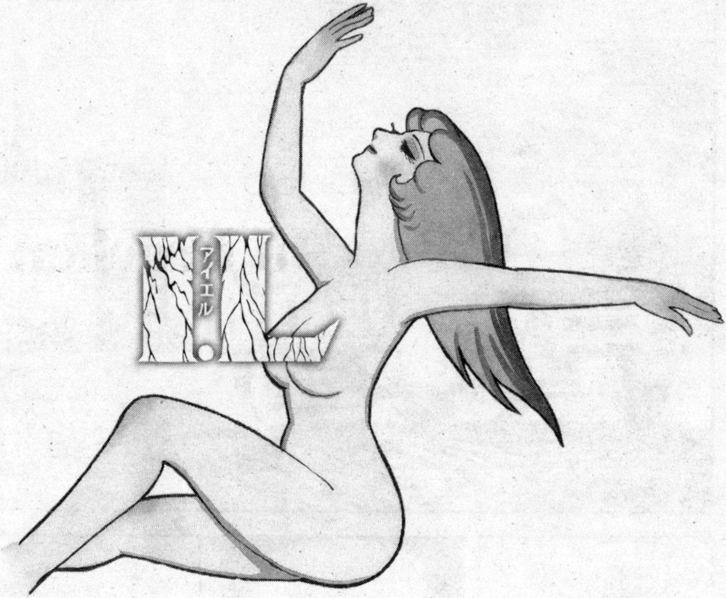
アイエル

# EPISODE 5
# The Monster In Brocken

SRABRIA
PEOPLE'S
REPUBLIC,
BAGRA CITY

Lunka Puppet Institute

Srabria National
Puppet Film
Productions

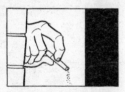

CLICK

CLICK CLICK
CLICK

RATTLE RATTLE

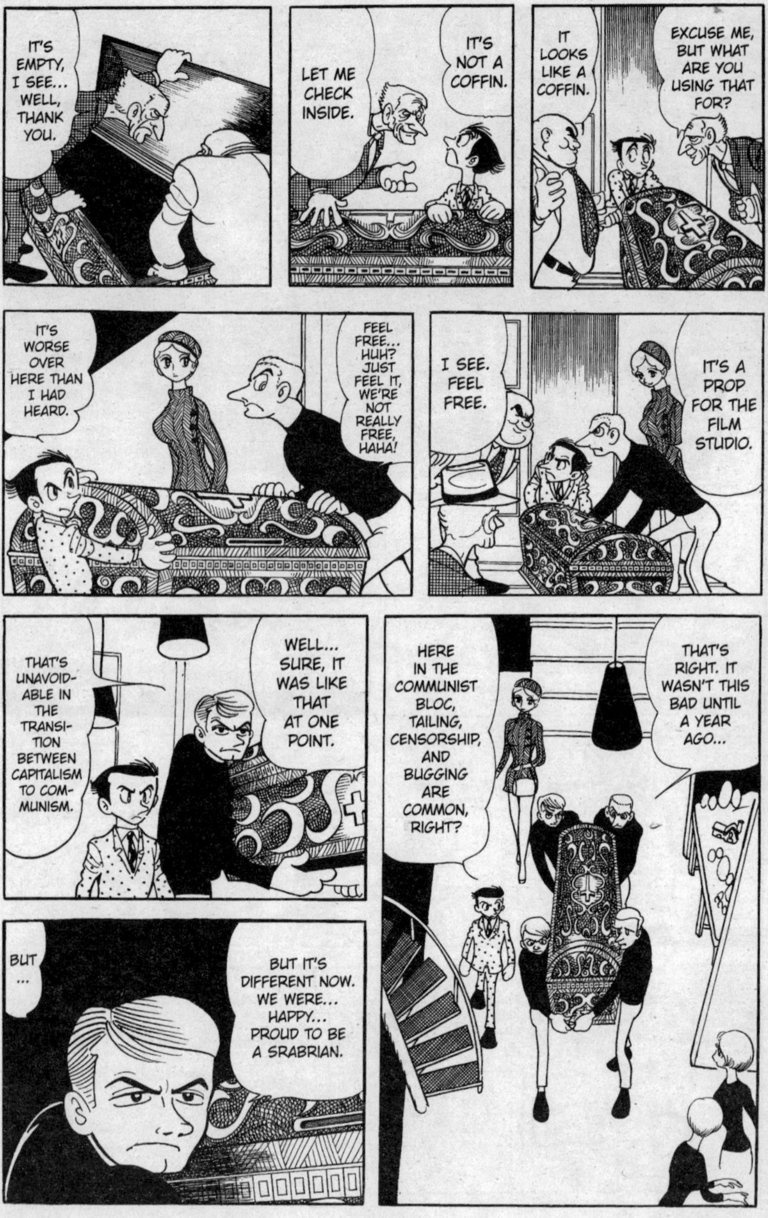
EXCUSE ME, BUT WHAT ARE YOU USING THAT FOR?
IT LOOKS LIKE A COFFIN.
IT'S NOT A COFFIN.
LET ME CHECK INSIDE.
IT'S EMPTY, I SEE... WELL, THANK YOU.
IT'S A PROP FOR THE FILM STUDIO.
I SEE. FEEL FREE.
FEEL FREE... HUH? JUST FEEL IT, WE'RE NOT REALLY FREE, HAHA!
IT'S WORSE OVER HERE THAN I HAD HEARD.
THAT'S RIGHT. IT WASN'T THIS BAD UNTIL A YEAR AGO...
HERE IN THE COMMUNIST BLOC, TAILING, CENSORSHIP, AND BUGGING ARE COMMON, RIGHT?
WELL... SURE, IT WAS LIKE THAT AT ONE POINT.
THAT'S UNAVOIDABLE IN THE TRANSITION BETWEEN CAPITALISM TO COMMUNISM.
BUT IT'S DIFFERENT NOW. WE WERE... HAPPY... PROUD TO BE A SRABRIAN.
BUT ...

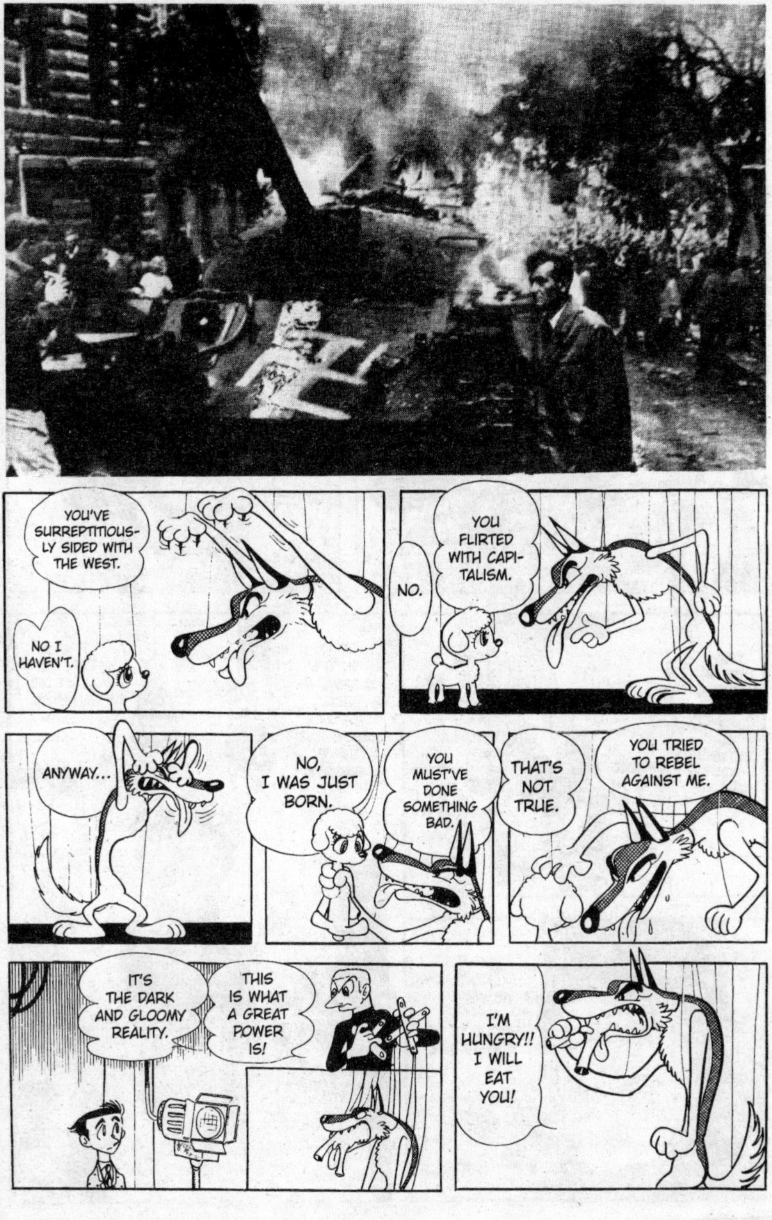
YOU FLIRTED WITH CAPI-TALISM.
NO.
YOU'VE SURREPTITIOUS-LY SIDED WITH THE WEST.
NO I HAVEN'T.
YOU TRIED TO REBEL AGAINST ME.
THAT'S NOT TRUE.
YOU MUST'VE DONE SOMETHING BAD.
NO, I WAS JUST BORN.
ANYWAY...
I'M HUNGRY!! I WILL EAT YOU!
THIS IS WHAT A GREAT POWER IS!
IT'S THE DARK AND GLOOMY REALITY.

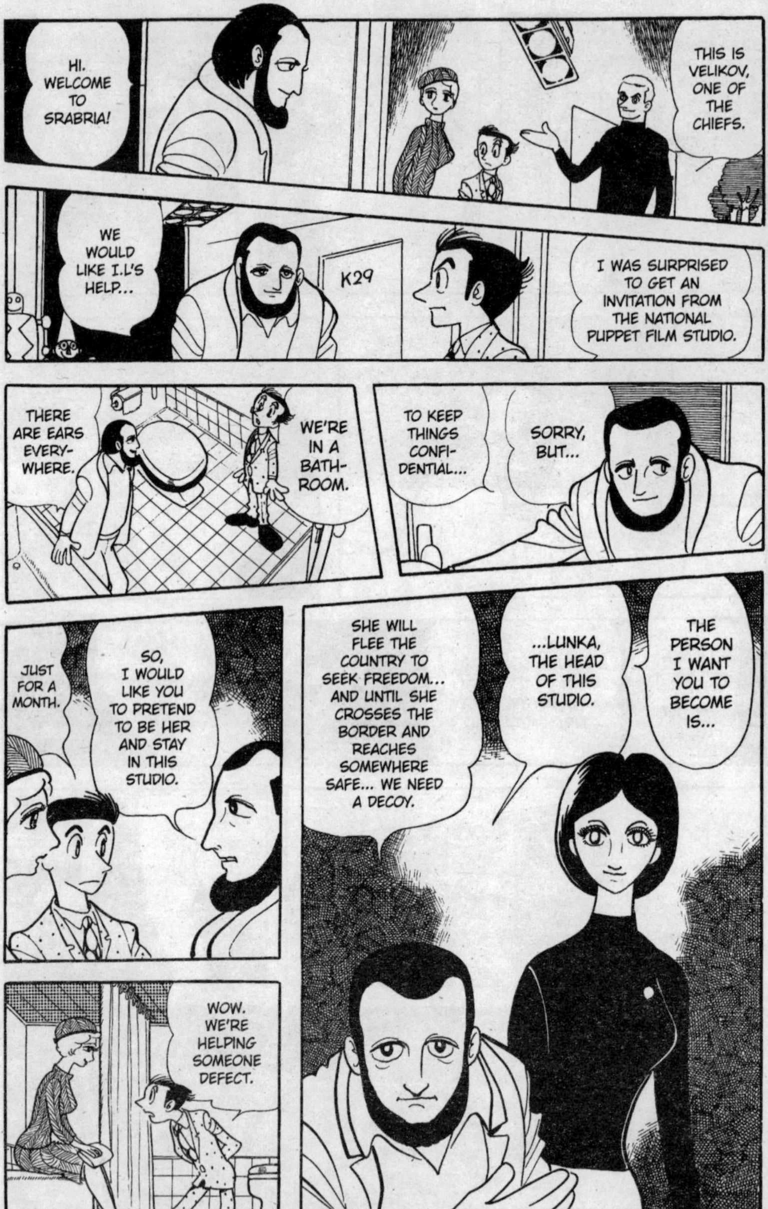
THIS IS VELIKOV, ONE OF THE CHIEFS.
HI. WELCOME TO SRABRIA!
I WAS SURPRISED TO GET AN INVITATION FROM THE NATIONAL PUPPET FILM STUDIO.
K29
WE WOULD LIKE I.L'S HELP...
SORRY, BUT...
TO KEEP THINGS CONFIDENTIAL...
WE'RE IN A BATHROOM.
THERE ARE EARS EVERYWHERE.
THE PERSON I WANT YOU TO BECOME IS...
...LUNKA, THE HEAD OF THIS STUDIO.
SHE WILL FLEE THE COUNTRY TO SEEK FREEDOM... AND UNTIL SHE CROSSES THE BORDER AND REACHES SOMEWHERE SAFE... WE NEED A DECOY.
SO, I WOULD LIKE YOU TO PRETEND TO BE HER AND STAY IN THIS STUDIO.
JUST FOR A MONTH.
WOW. WE'RE HELPING SOMEONE DEFECT.

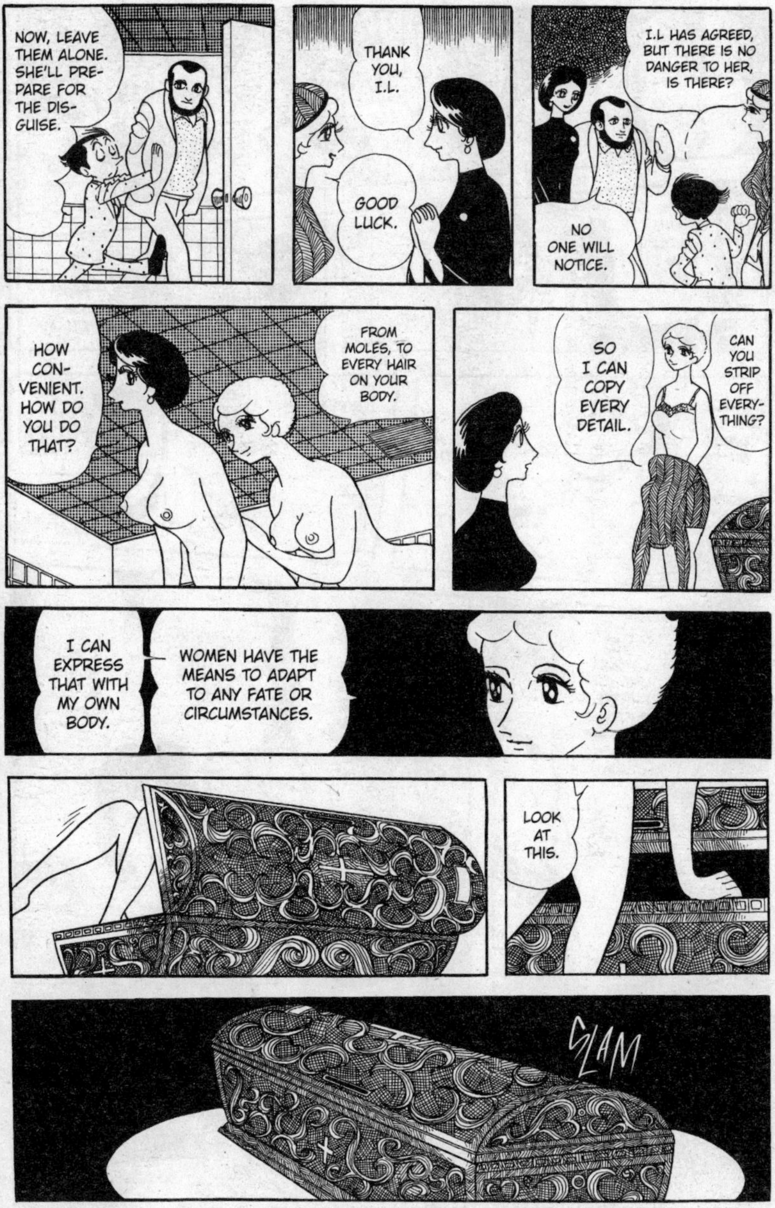
I.L HAS AGREED, BUT THERE IS NO DANGER TO HER, IS THERE?
NO ONE WILL NOTICE.
THANK YOU, I.L.
GOOD LUCK.
NOW, LEAVE THEM ALONE. SHE'LL PREPARE FOR THE DISGUISE.
CAN YOU STRIP OFF EVERYTHING?
SO I CAN COPY EVERY DETAIL.
FROM MOLES, TO EVERY HAIR ON YOUR BODY.
HOW CONVENIENT. HOW DO YOU DO THAT?
WOMEN HAVE THE MEANS TO ADAPT TO ANY FATE OR CIRCUMSTANCES.
I CAN EXPRESS THAT WITH MY OWN BODY.
LOOK AT THIS.
SLAM

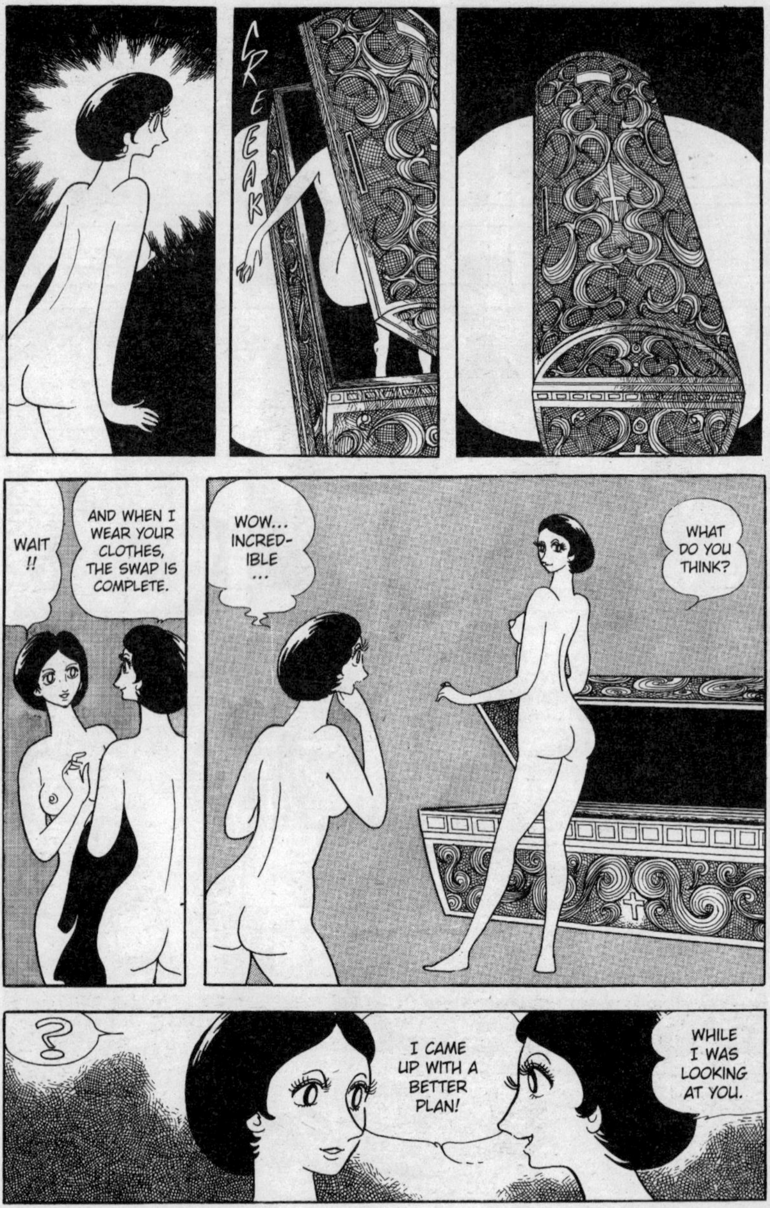
CREEAK
WHAT DO YOU THINK?
WOW... INCRED-IBLE ...
AND WHEN I WEAR YOUR CLOTHES, THE SWAP IS COMPLETE.
WAIT !!
WHILE I WAS LOOKING AT YOU.
I CAME UP WITH A BETTER PLAN!
?

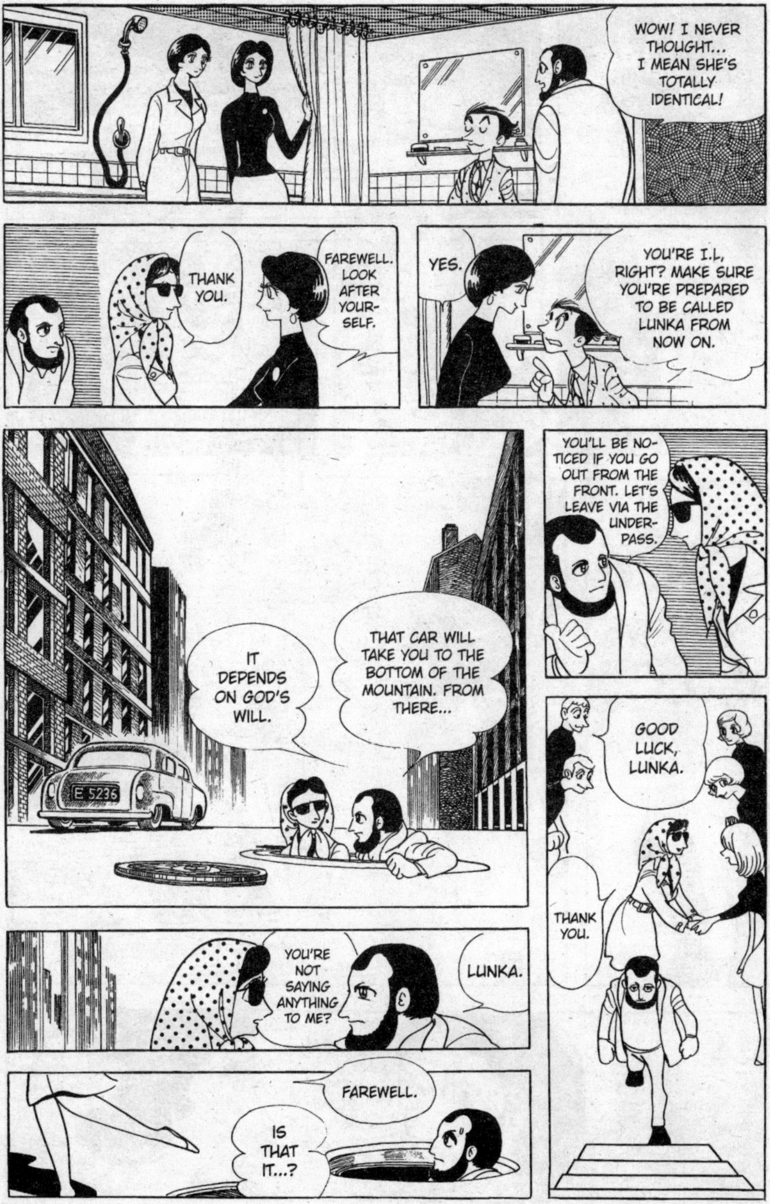
WOW! I NEVER THOUGHT... I MEAN SHE'S TOTALLY IDENTICAL!
YOU'RE I.L, RIGHT? MAKE SURE YOU'RE PREPARED TO BE CALLED LUNKA FROM NOW ON.
YES.
FAREWELL. LOOK AFTER YOURSELF.
THANK YOU.
YOU'LL BE NOTICED IF YOU GO OUT FROM THE FRONT. LET'S LEAVE VIA THE UNDERPASS.
GOOD LUCK, LUNKA.
THANK YOU.
THAT CAR WILL TAKE YOU TO THE BOTTOM OF THE MOUNTAIN. FROM THERE...
IT DEPENDS ON GOD'S WILL.
E 5236
LUNKA.
YOU'RE NOT SAYING ANYTHING TO ME?
FAREWELL.
IS THAT IT...?

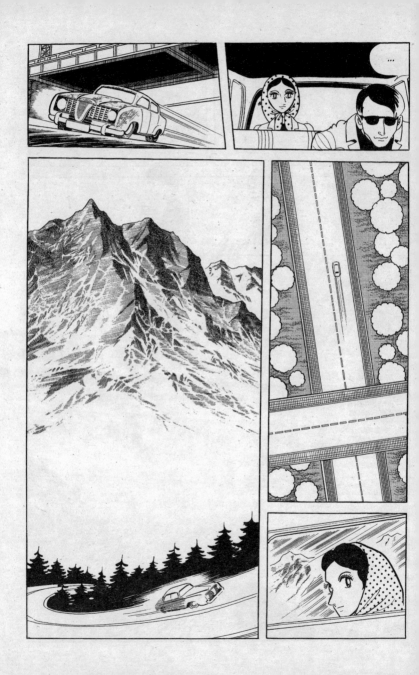

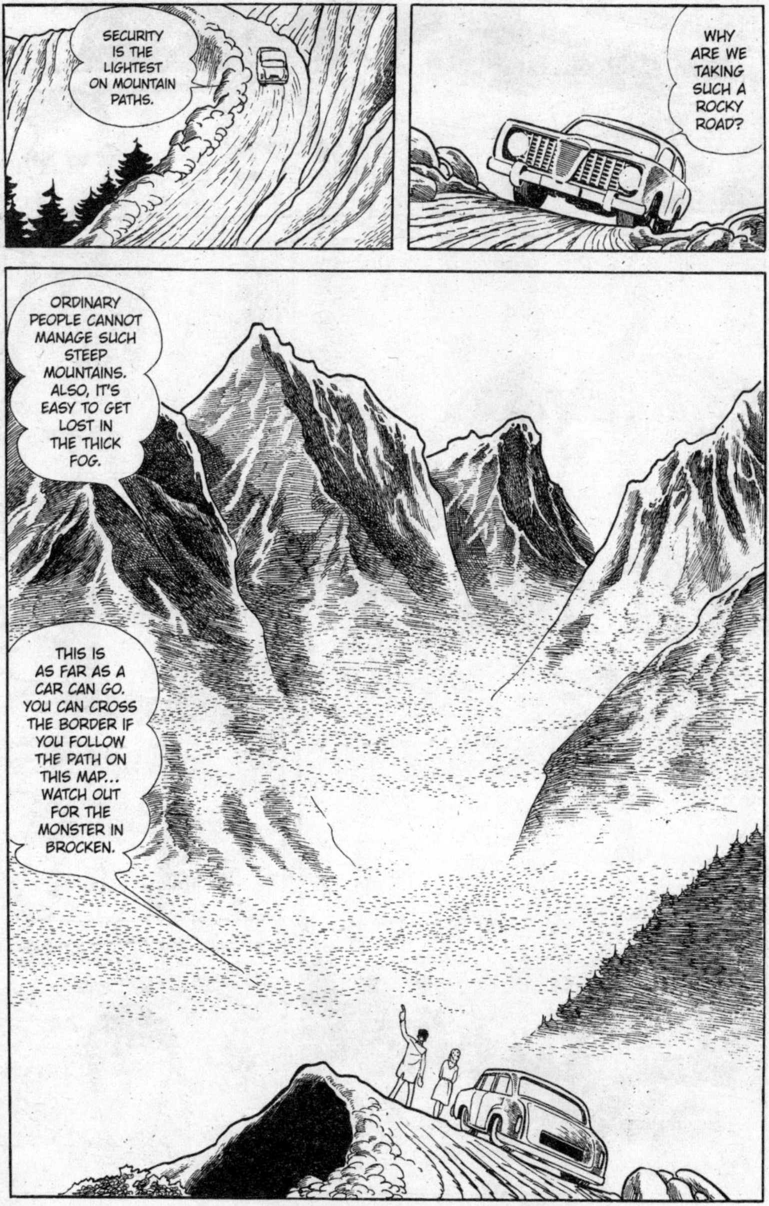
WHY ARE WE TAKING SUCH A ROCKY ROAD?
SECURITY IS THE LIGHTEST ON MOUNTAIN PATHS.
ORDINARY PEOPLE CANNOT MANAGE SUCH STEEP MOUNTAINS. ALSO, IT'S EASY TO GET LOST IN THE THICK FOG.
THIS IS AS FAR AS A CAR CAN GO. YOU CAN CROSS THE BORDER IF YOU FOLLOW THE PATH ON THIS MAP... WATCH OUT FOR THE MONSTER IN BROCKEN.

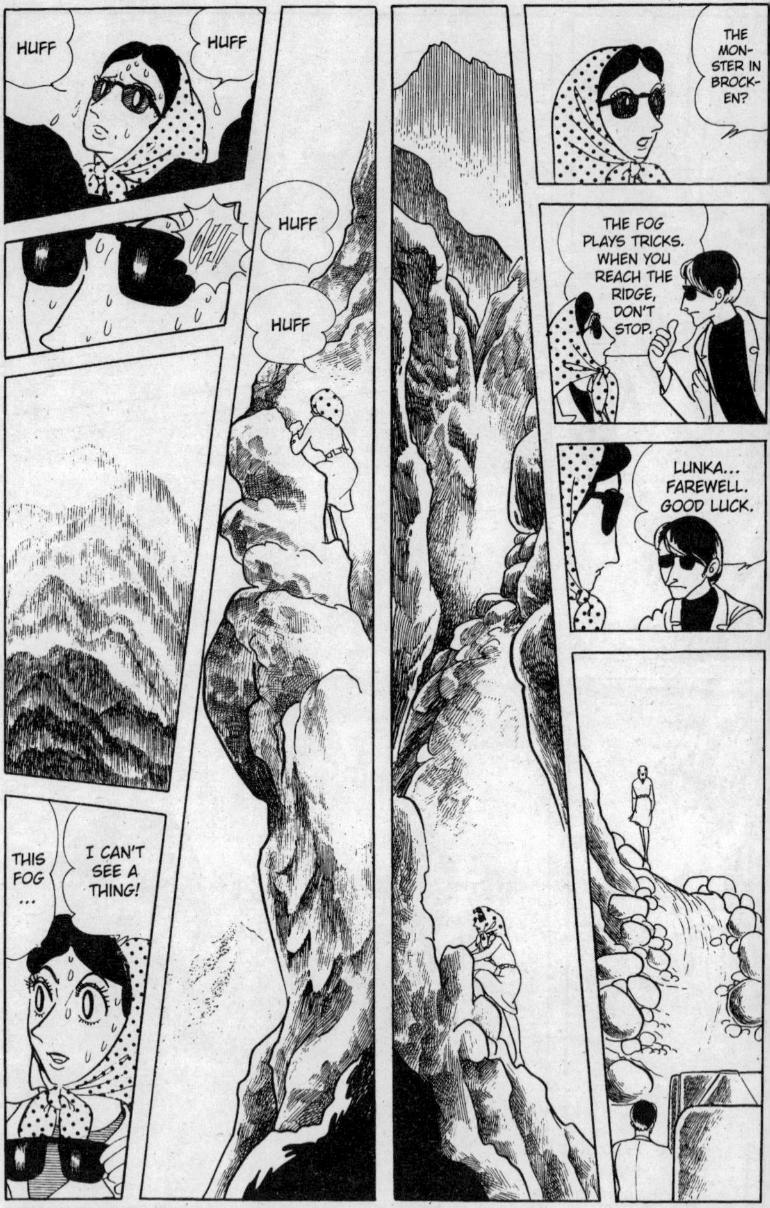
THE MONSTER IN BROCKEN?
THE FOG PLAYS TRICKS. WHEN YOU REACH THE RIDGE, DON'T STOP.
LUNKA... FAREWELL. GOOD LUCK.
HUFF
HUFF
HUFF
HUFF
I CAN'T SEE A THING!
THIS FOG ...

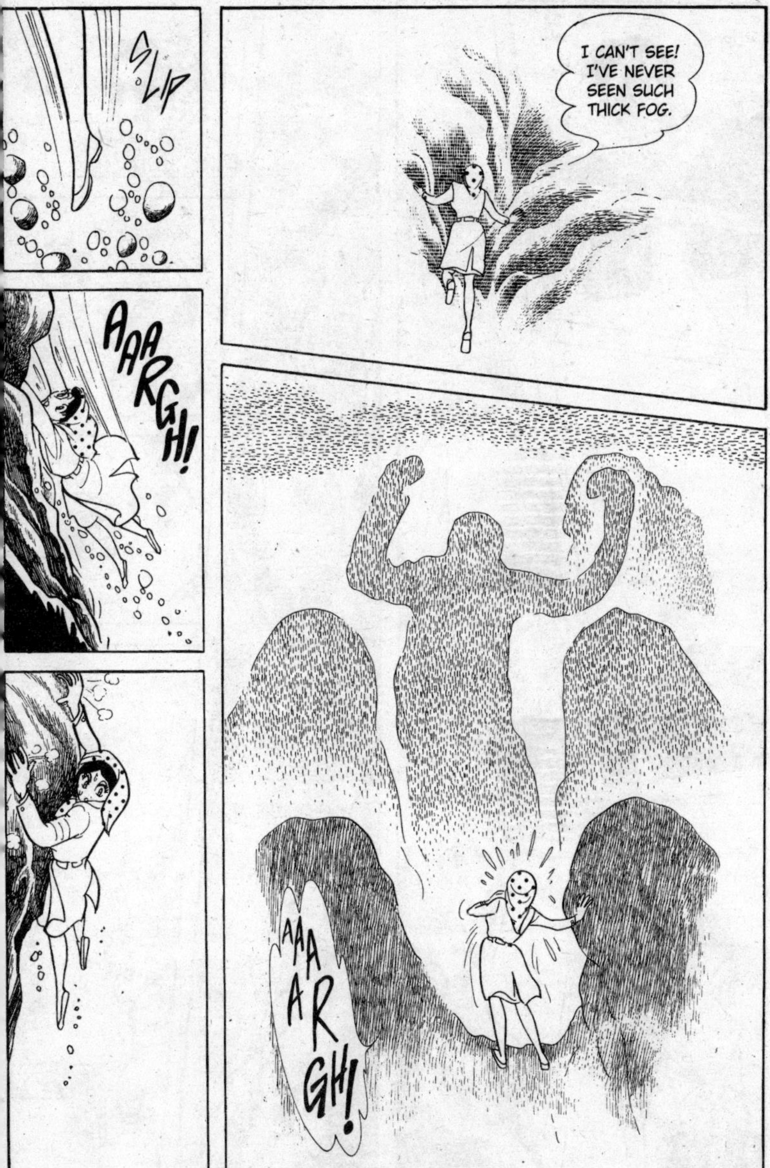
I CAN'T SEE! I'VE NEVER SEEN SUCH THICK FOG.
AAAARGH!
SLIP
AARGH!

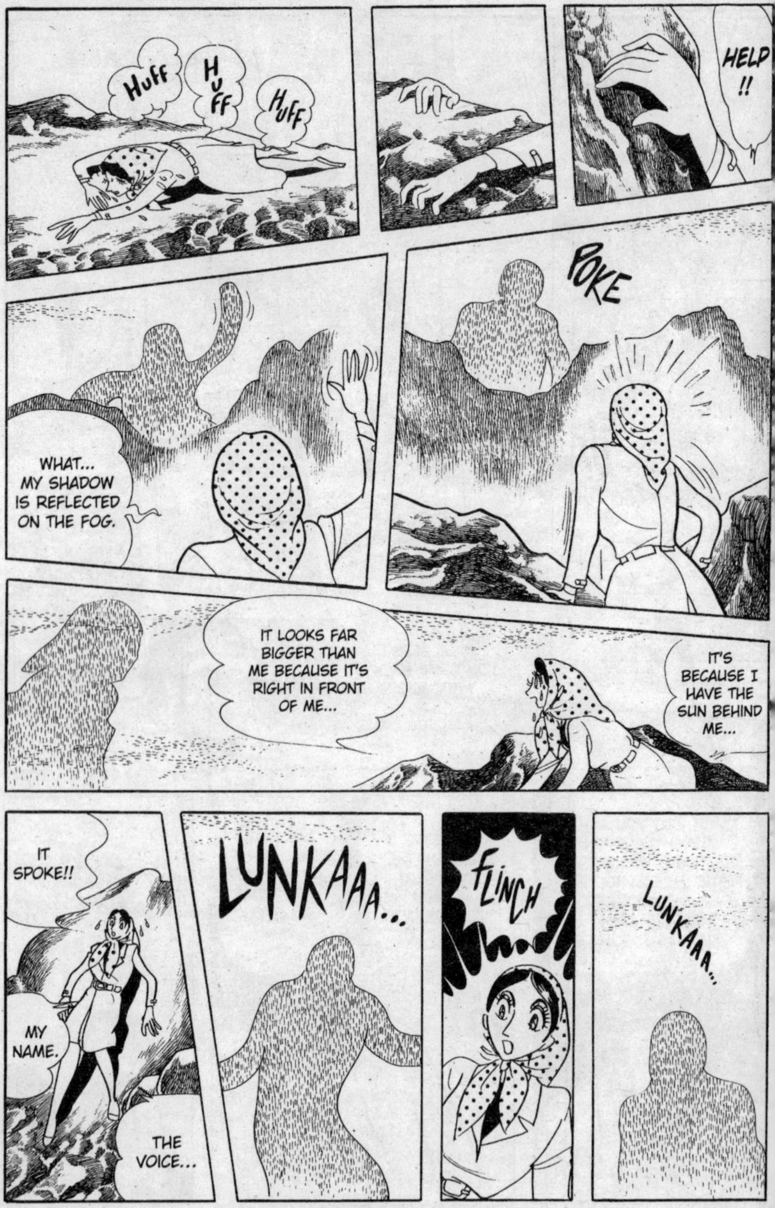
HELP !!
HUFF
HUFF
HUFF
POKE
WHAT... MY SHADOW IS REFLECTED ON THE FOG.
IT'S BECAUSE I HAVE THE SUN BEHIND ME...
IT LOOKS FAR BIGGER THAN ME BECAUSE IT'S RIGHT IN FRONT OF ME...
LUNKAAA...
FLINCH
LUNKAAA...
IT SPOKE!!
MY NAME.
THE VOICE...

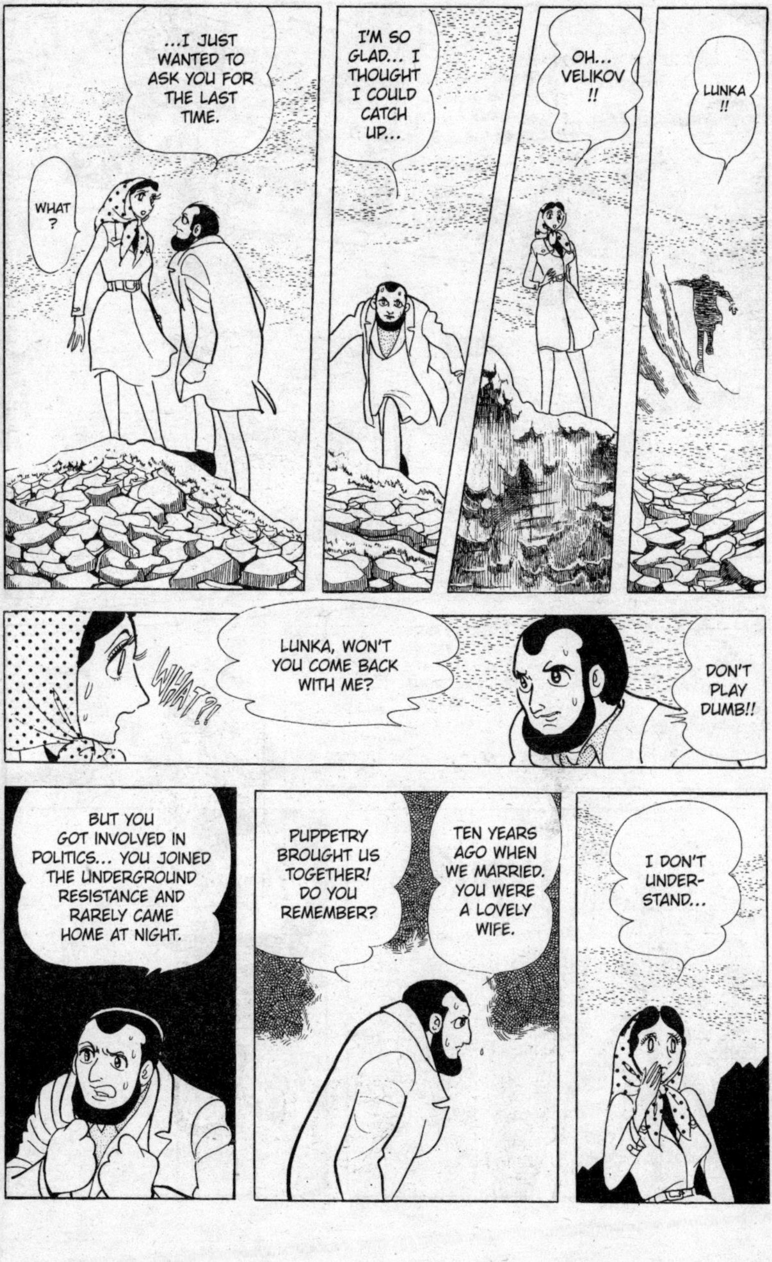
LUNKA !!
OH... VELIKOV !!
I'M SO GLAD... I THOUGHT I COULD CATCH UP...
...I JUST WANTED TO ASK YOU FOR THE LAST TIME.
WHAT ?
DON'T PLAY DUMB!!
LUNKA, WON'T YOU COME BACK WITH ME?
WHAT?!
I DON'T UNDER-STAND...
TEN YEARS AGO WHEN WE MARRIED. YOU WERE A LOVELY WIFE.
PUPPETRY BROUGHT US TOGETHER! DO YOU REMEMBER?
BUT YOU GOT INVOLVED IN POLITICS... YOU JOINED THE UNDERGROUND RESISTANCE AND RARELY CAME HOME AT NIGHT.

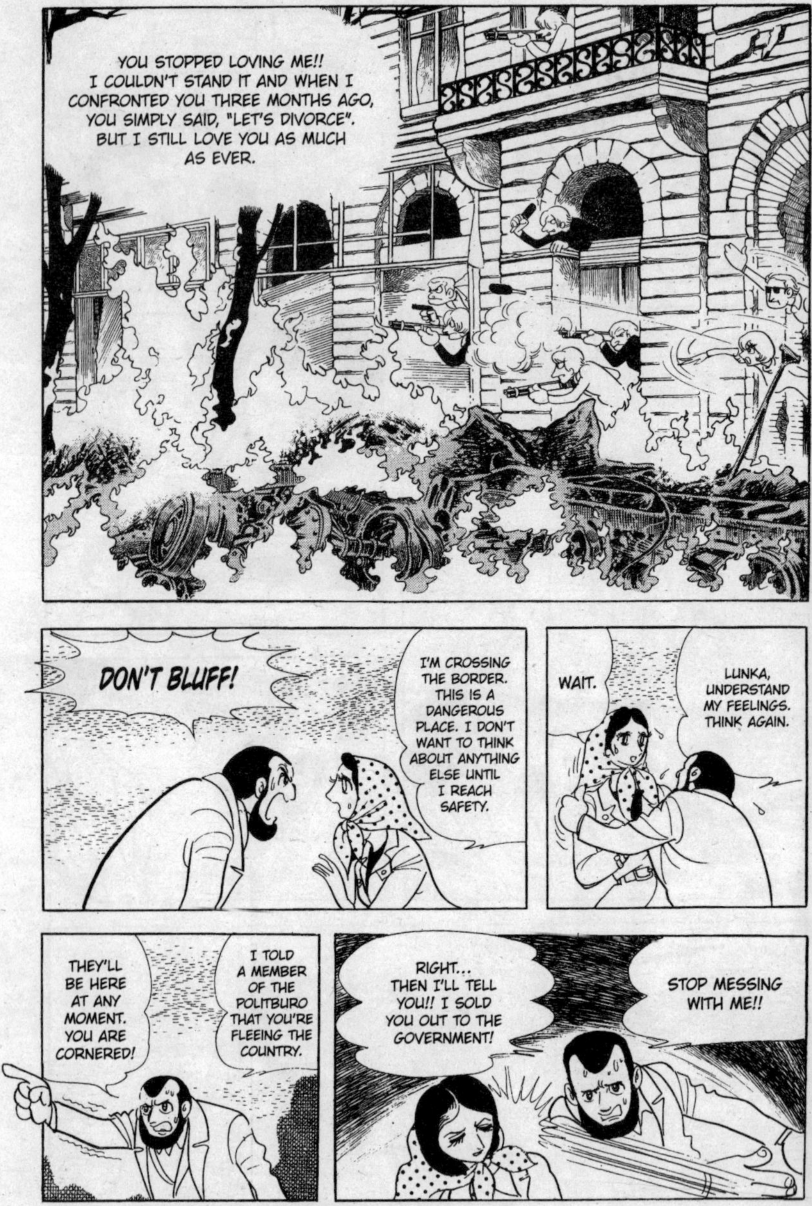
YOU STOPPED LOVING ME!! I COULDN'T STAND IT AND WHEN I CONFRONTED YOU THREE MONTHS AGO, YOU SIMPLY SAID, "LET'S DIVORCE". BUT I STILL LOVE YOU AS MUCH AS EVER.
LUNKA, UNDERSTAND MY FEELINGS. THINK AGAIN.
WAIT.
I'M CROSSING THE BORDER. THIS IS A DANGEROUS PLACE. I DON'T WANT TO THINK ABOUT ANYTHING ELSE UNTIL I REACH SAFETY.
DON'T BLUFF!
STOP MESSING WITH ME!!
RIGHT... THEN I'LL TELL YOU!! I SOLD YOU OUT TO THE GOVERNMENT!
I TOLD A MEMBER OF THE POLITBURO THAT YOU'RE FLEEING THE COUNTRY.
THEY'LL BE HERE AT ANY MOMENT. YOU ARE CORNERED!

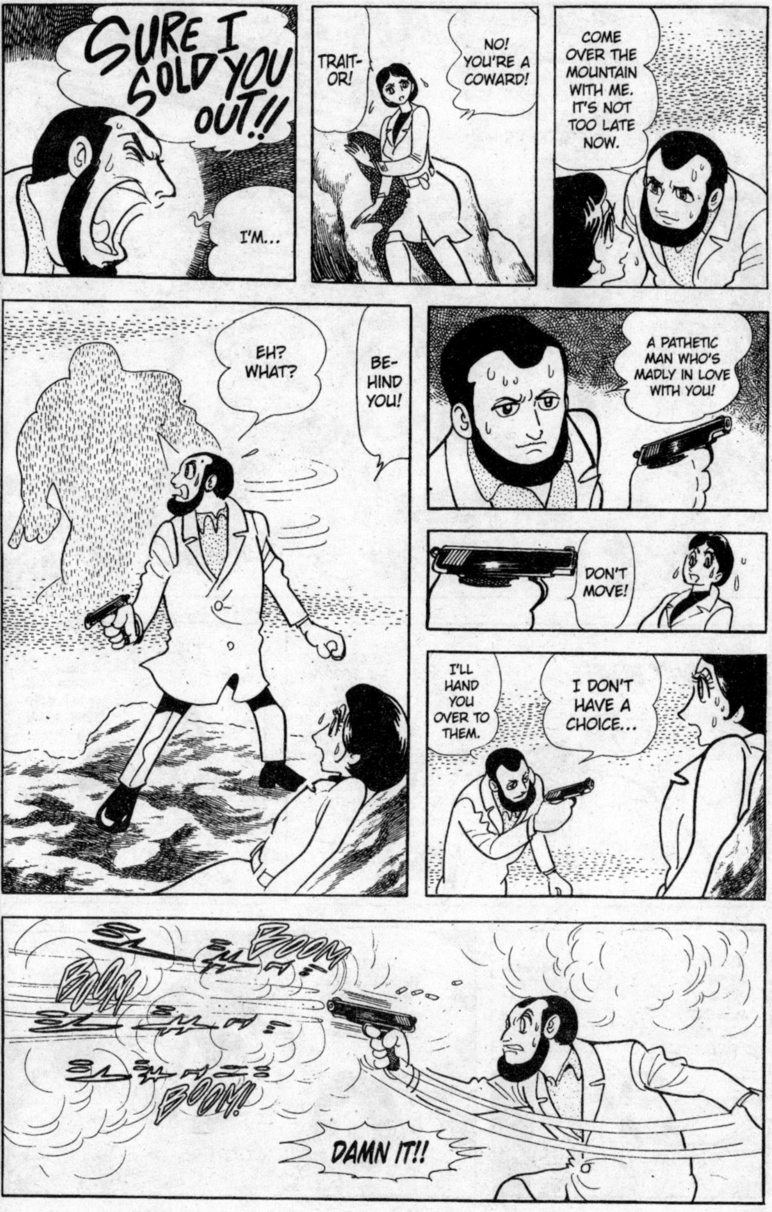
COME OVER THE MOUNTAIN WITH ME. IT'S NOT TOO LATE NOW.
NO! YOU'RE A COWARD!
TRAIT-OR!
SURE I SOLD YOU OUT!!
I'M...
A PATHETIC MAN WHO'S MADLY IN LOVE WITH YOU!
DON'T MOVE!
I DON'T HAVE A CHOICE...
I'LL HAND YOU OVER TO THEM.
BE-HIND YOU!
EH? WHAT?
BOOM
BOOM
BOOM!
DAMN IT!!

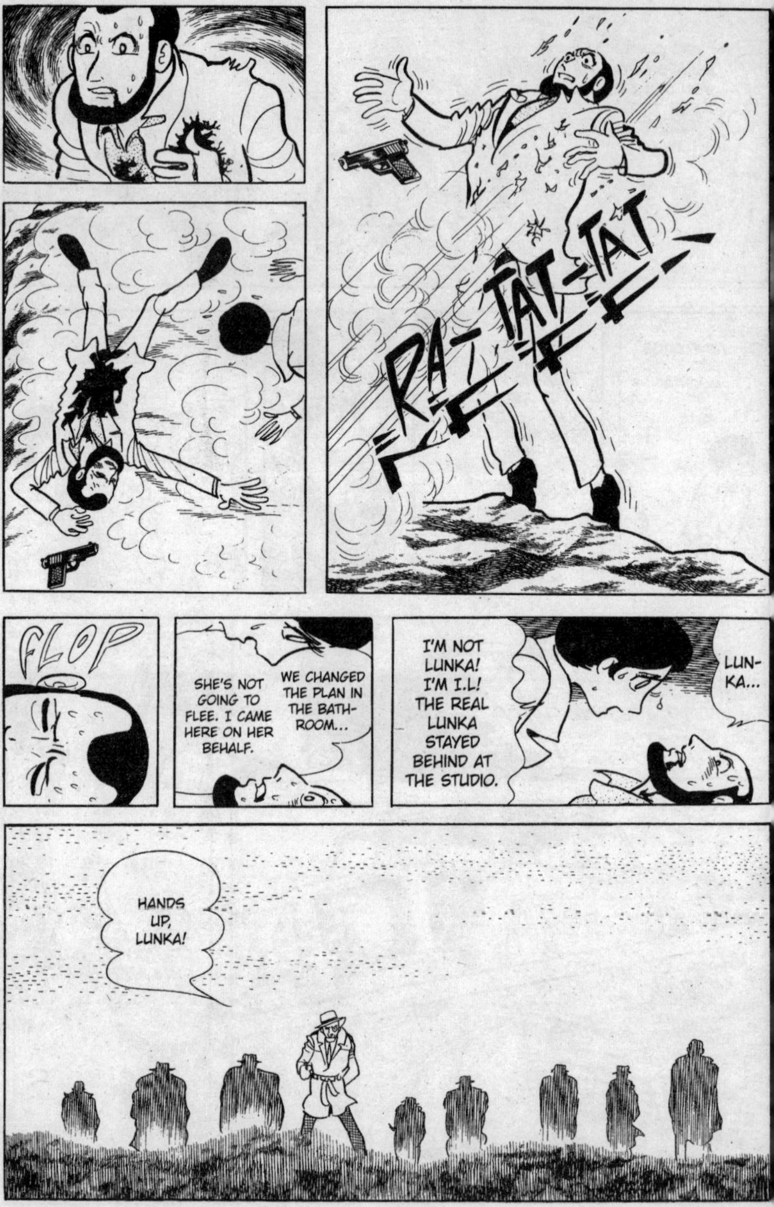
RA-TAT-TAT
LUN-KA...
I'M NOT LUNKA! I'M I.L! THE REAL LUNKA STAYED BEHIND AT THE STUDIO.
WE CHANGED THE PLAN IN THE BATH-ROOM...
SHE'S NOT GOING TO FLEE. I CAME HERE ON HER BEHALF.
FLOP
HANDS UP, LUNKA!

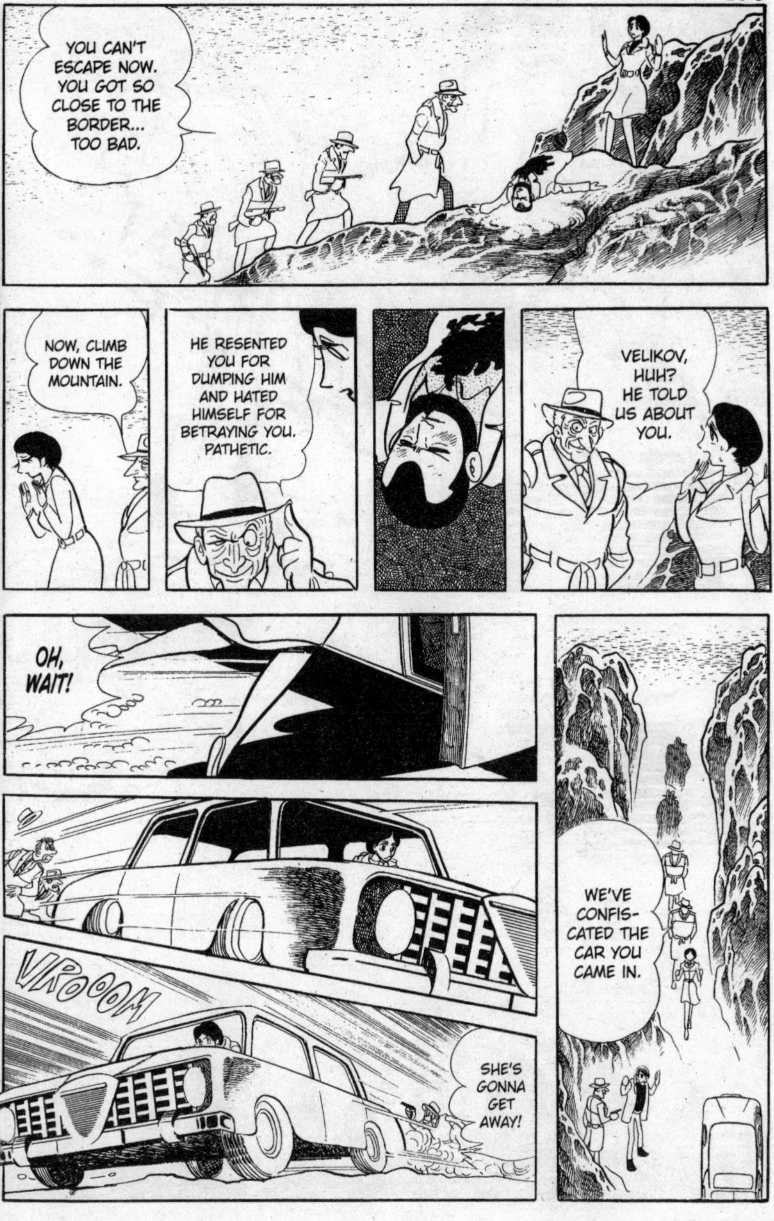
YOU CAN'T ESCAPE NOW. YOU GOT SO CLOSE TO THE BORDER... TOO BAD.
VELIKOV, HUH? HE TOLD US ABOUT YOU.
HE RESENTED YOU FOR DUMPING HIM AND HATED HIMSELF FOR BETRAYING YOU. PATHETIC.
NOW, CLIMB DOWN THE MOUNTAIN.
WE'VE CONFIS-CATED THE CAR YOU CAME IN.
OH, WAIT!
VROOOM
SHE'S GONNA GET AWAY!

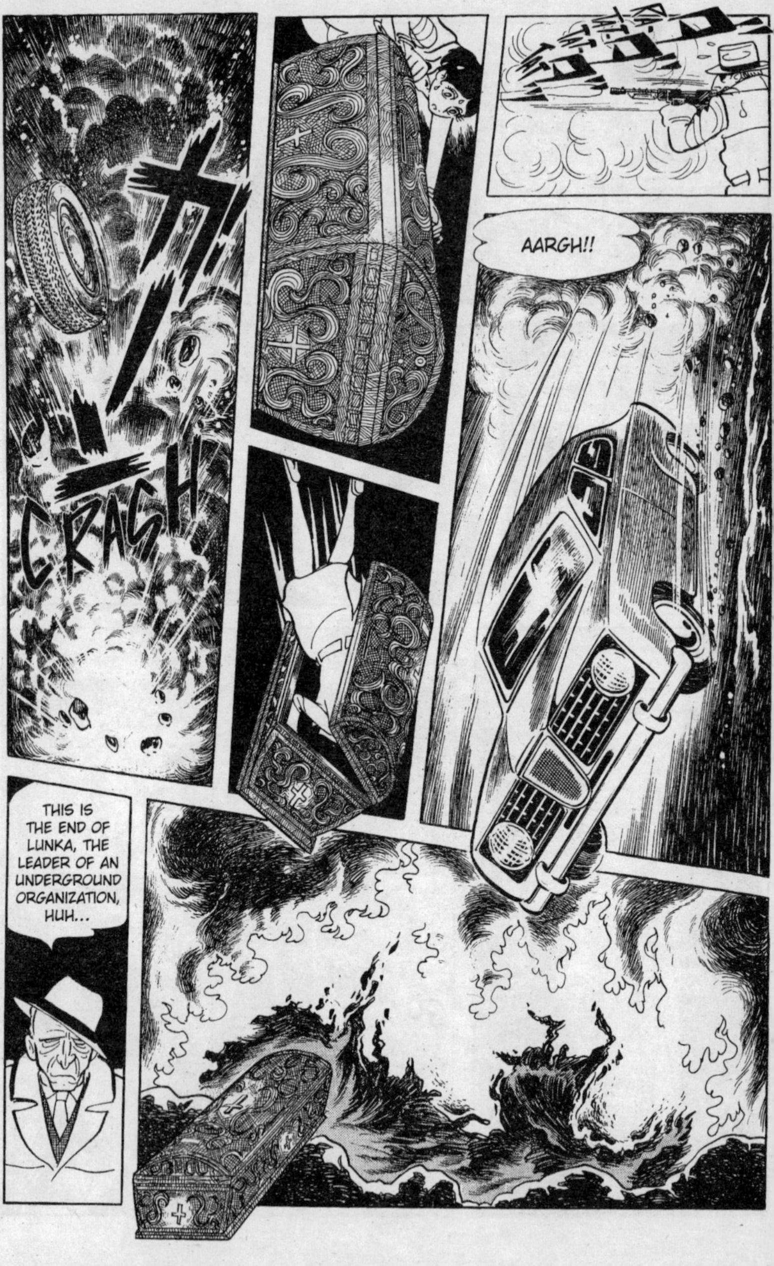
KA-TAT-TAT
AARGH!!
CRASH
THIS IS THE END OF LUNKA, THE LEADER OF AN UNDERGROUND ORGANIZATION, HUH...

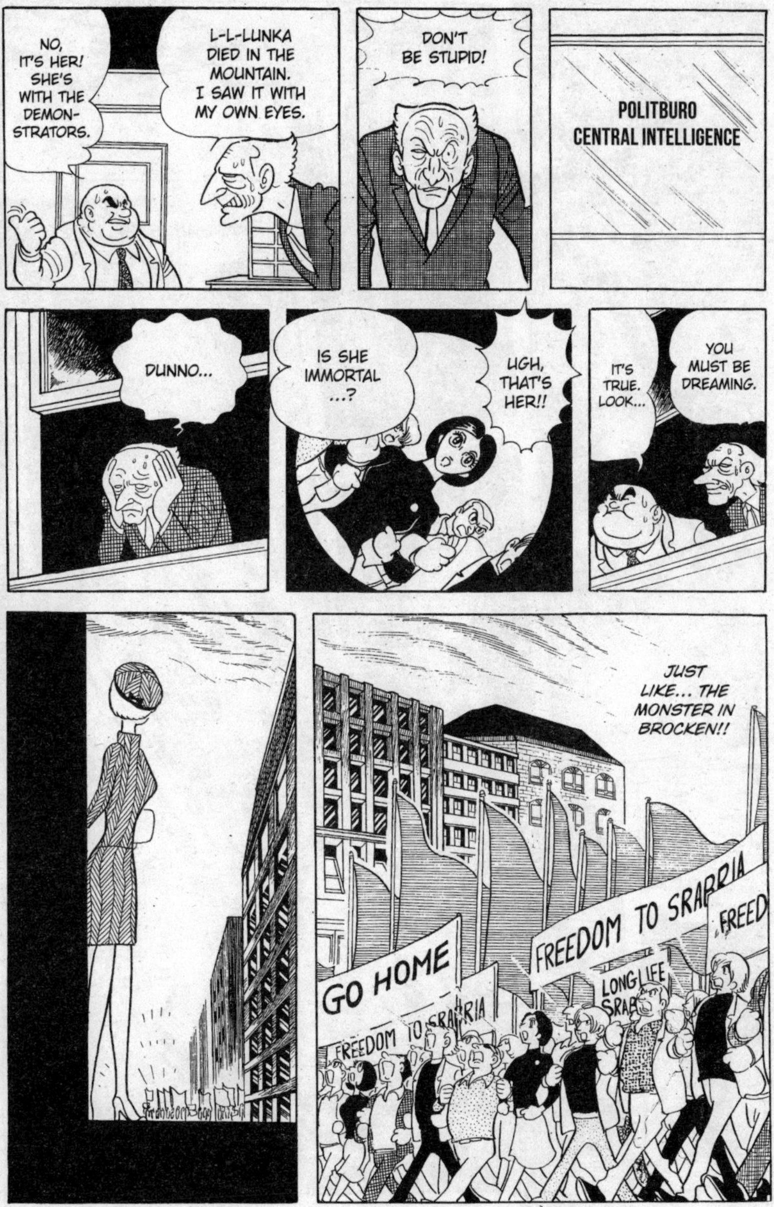
POLITBURO
CENTRAL INTELLIGENCE
DON'T BE STUPID!
L-L-LUNKA DIED IN THE MOUNTAIN. I SAW IT WITH MY OWN EYES.
NO, IT'S HER! SHE'S WITH THE DEMON-STRATORS.
YOU MUST BE DREAMING.
IT'S TRUE. LOOK...
UGH, THAT'S HER!!
IS SHE IMMORTAL ...?
DUNNO...
JUST LIKE... THE MONSTER IN BROCKEN!!
FREEDOM TO SRABRIA
FREED
LONG LIFE SRAB
GO HOME
FREEDOM TO SRABRIA

# EPISODE 6
# Ransom

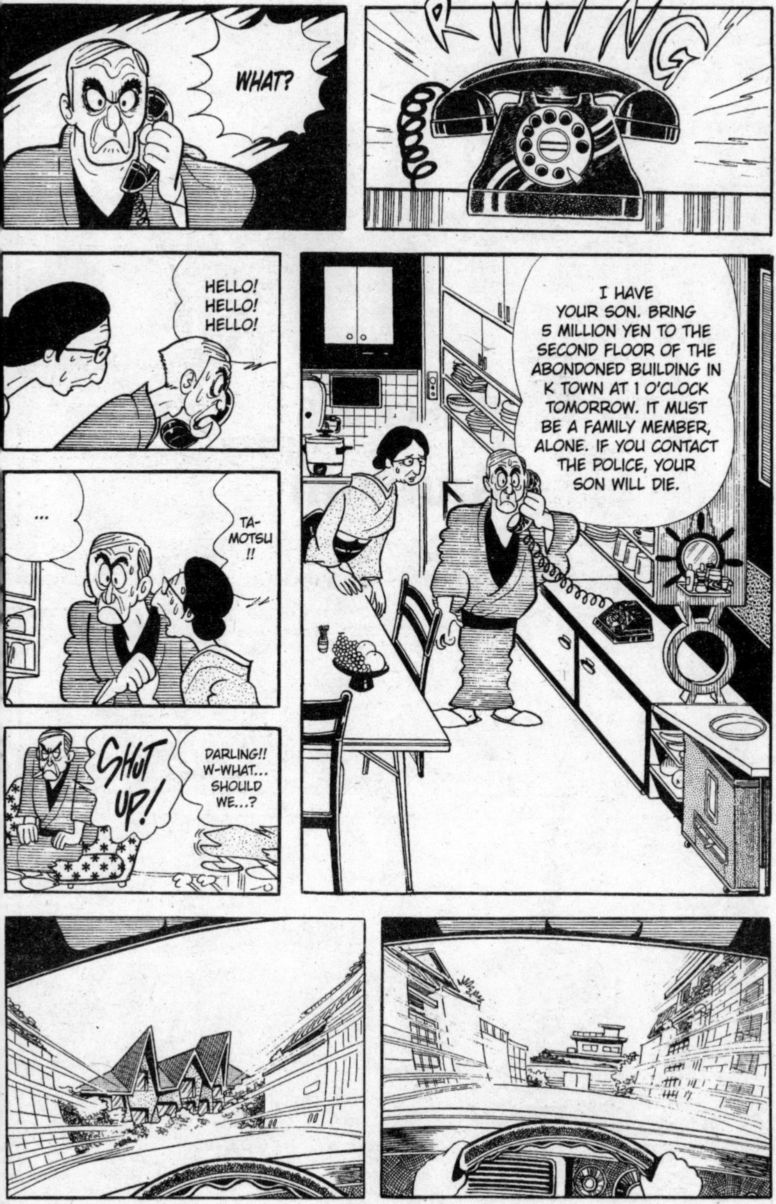
RIIIING
WHAT?
I HAVE YOUR SON. BRING 5 MILLION YEN TO THE SECOND FLOOR OF THE ABONDONED BUILDING IN K TOWN AT 1 O'CLOCK TOMORROW. IT MUST BE A FAMILY MEMBER, ALONE. IF YOU CONTACT THE POLICE, YOUR SON WILL DIE.
HELLO! HELLO! HELLO!
TA-MOTSU !!
...
DARLING!! W-WHAT... SHOULD WE...?
SHUT UP!

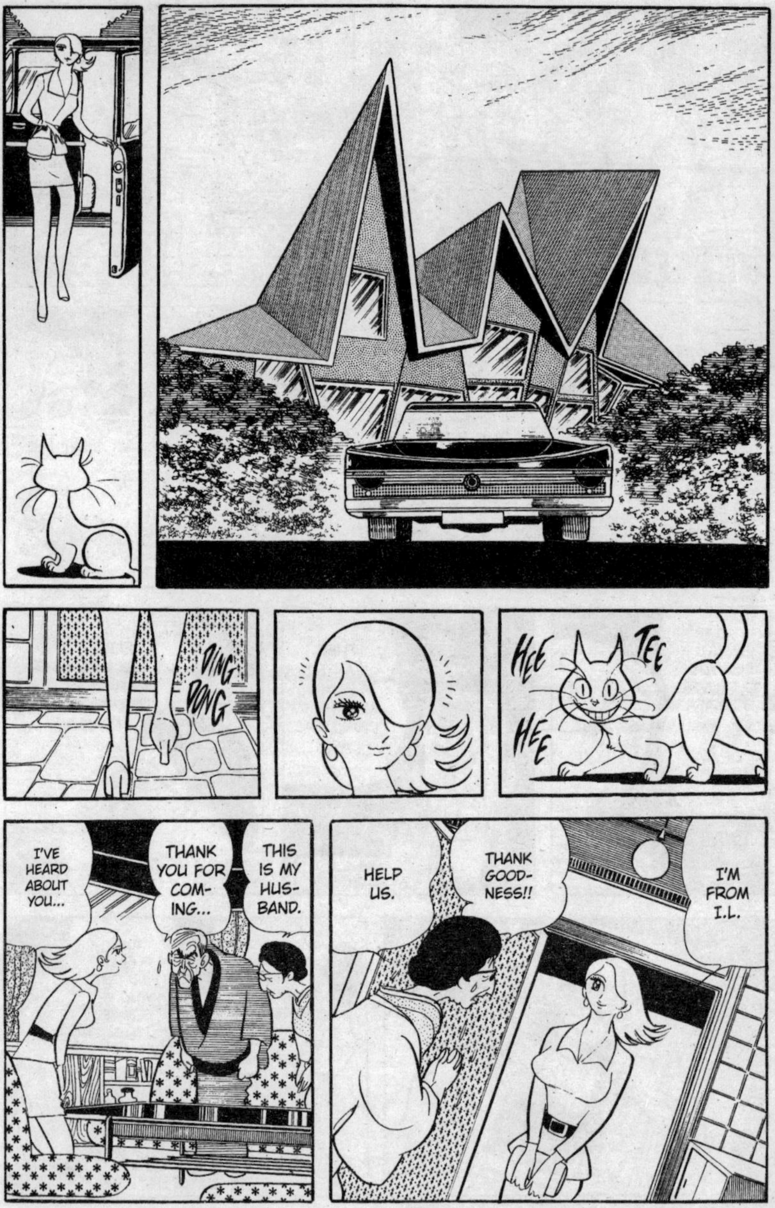
HEE TEE HEE
DING DONG
I'M FROM I.L.
THANK GOODNESS!!
HELP US.
THIS IS MY HUS-BAND.
THANK YOU FOR COM-ING...
I'VE HEARD ABOUT YOU...

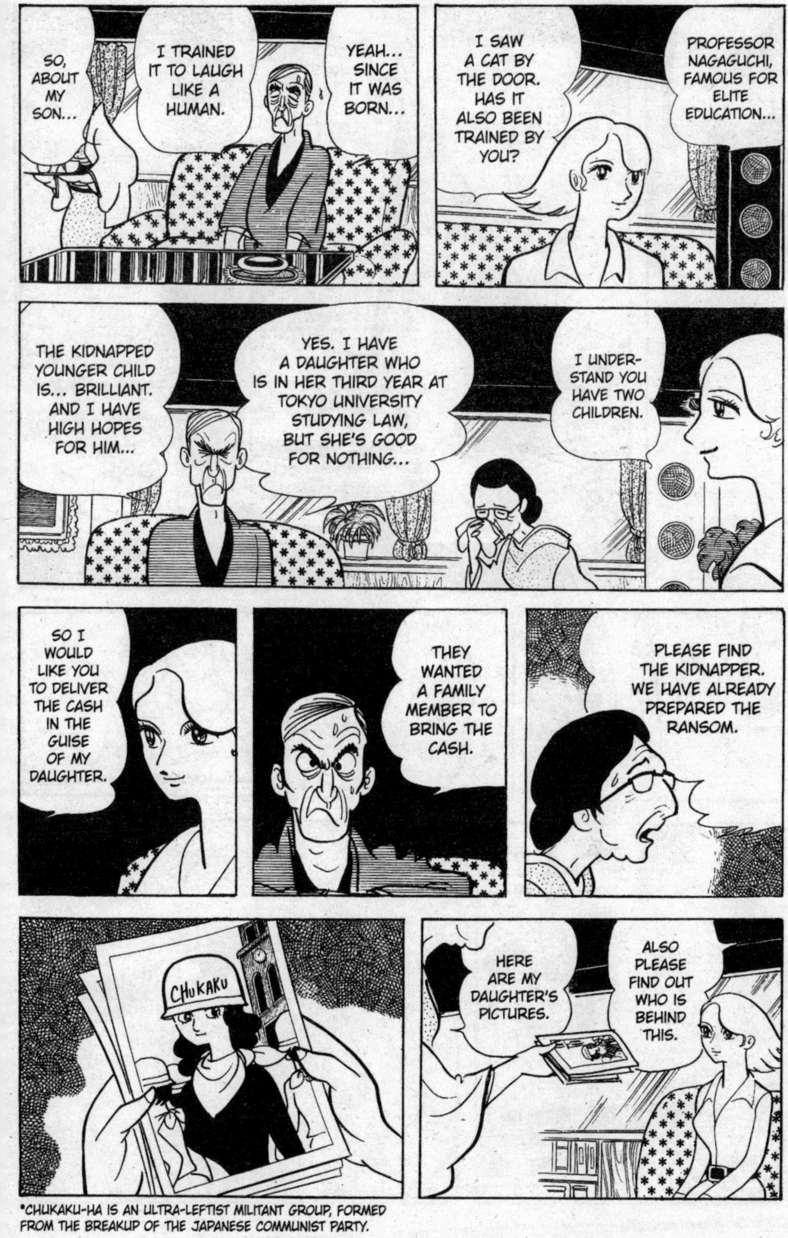
PROFESSOR NAGAGUCHI, FAMOUS FOR ELITE EDUCATION...
I SAW A CAT BY THE DOOR. HAS IT ALSO BEEN TRAINED BY YOU?
YEAH... SINCE IT WAS BORN...
I TRAINED IT TO LAUGH LIKE A HUMAN.
SO, ABOUT MY SON...
I UNDER-STAND YOU HAVE TWO CHILDREN.
YES. I HAVE A DAUGHTER WHO IS IN HER THIRD YEAR AT TOKYO UNIVERSITY STUDYING LAW, BUT SHE'S GOOD FOR NOTHING...
THE KIDNAPPED YOUNGER CHILD IS... BRILLIANT. AND I HAVE HIGH HOPES FOR HIM...
PLEASE FIND THE KIDNAPPER. WE HAVE ALREADY PREPARED THE RANSOM.
THEY WANTED A FAMILY MEMBER TO BRING THE CASH.
SO I WOULD LIKE YOU TO DELIVER THE CASH IN THE GUISE OF MY DAUGHTER.
ALSO PLEASE FIND OUT WHO IS BEHIND THIS.
HERE ARE MY DAUGHTER'S PICTURES.
CHUKAKU

*CHUKAKU-HA IS AN ULTRA-LEFTIST MILITANT GROUP, FORMED FROM THE BREAKUP OF THE JAPANESE COMMUNIST PARTY.

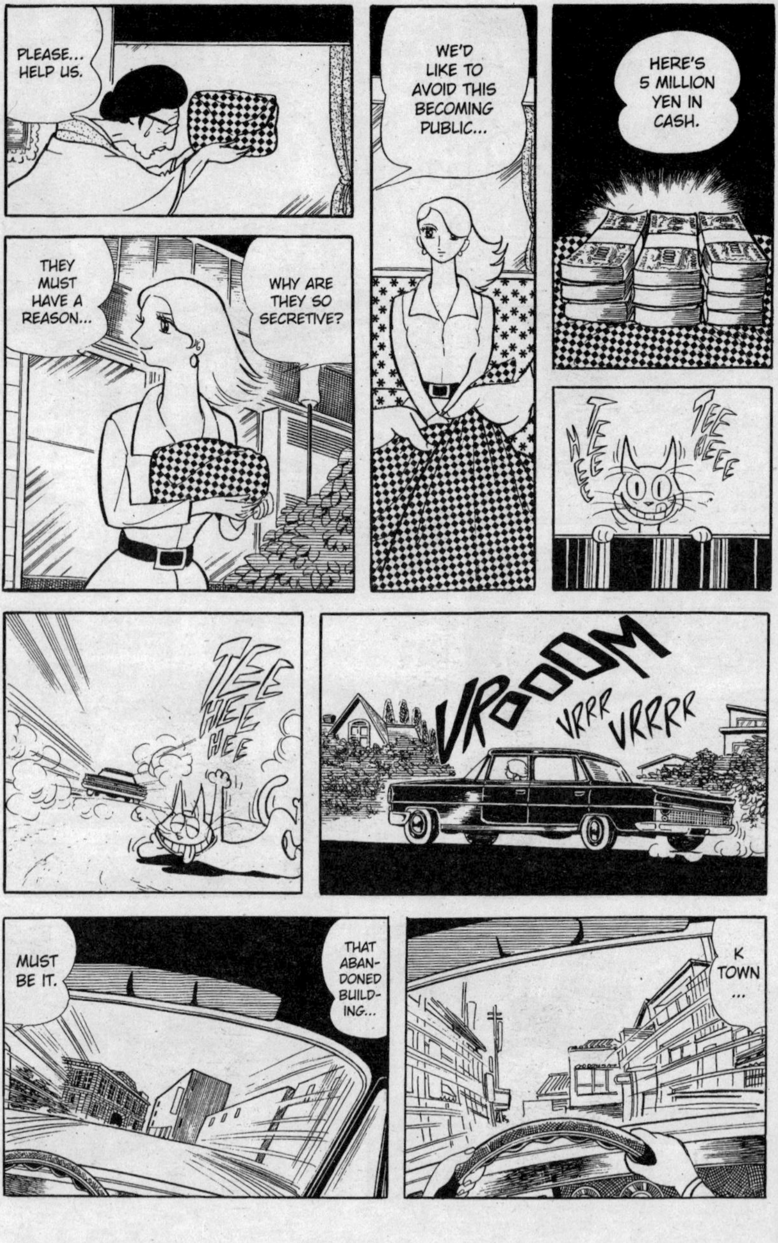
HERE'S 5 MILLION YEN IN CASH.
TEE HEE
TEE HEEE
WE'D LIKE TO AVOID THIS BECOMING PUBLIC...
PLEASE... HELP US.
WHY ARE THEY SO SECRETIVE?
THEY MUST HAVE A REASON...
VROOOM
VRRR VRRRR
TEE HEE HEE HEE
K TOWN ...
THAT ABAN-DONED BUILD-ING...
MUST BE IT.

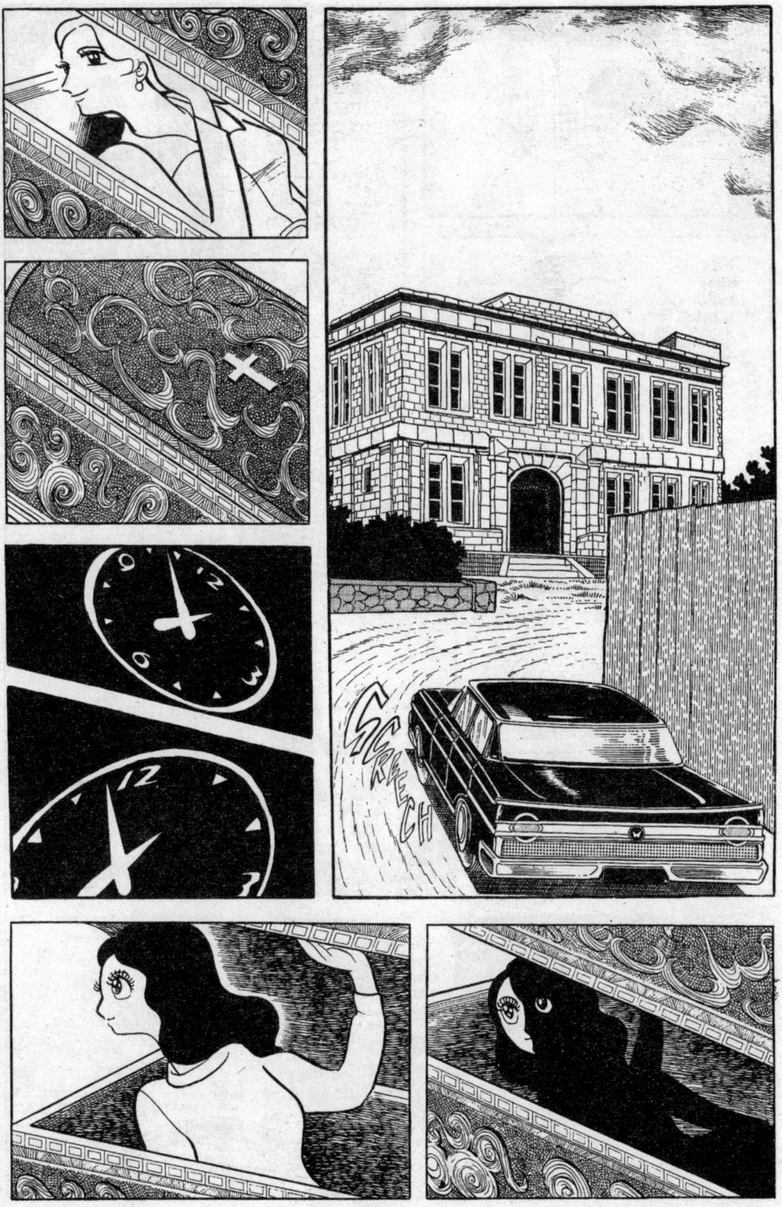
SCREECH

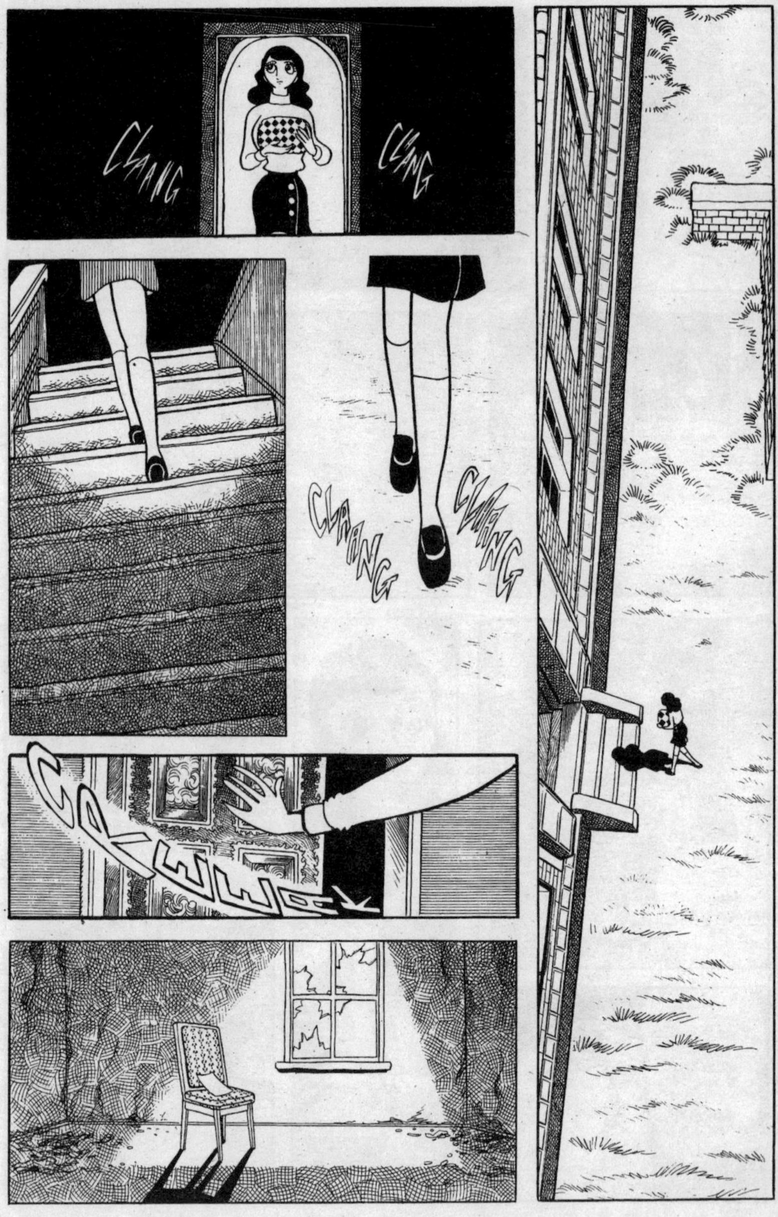
CLANG
CLAANG
CLAANG
CLAANG
CREEEAK

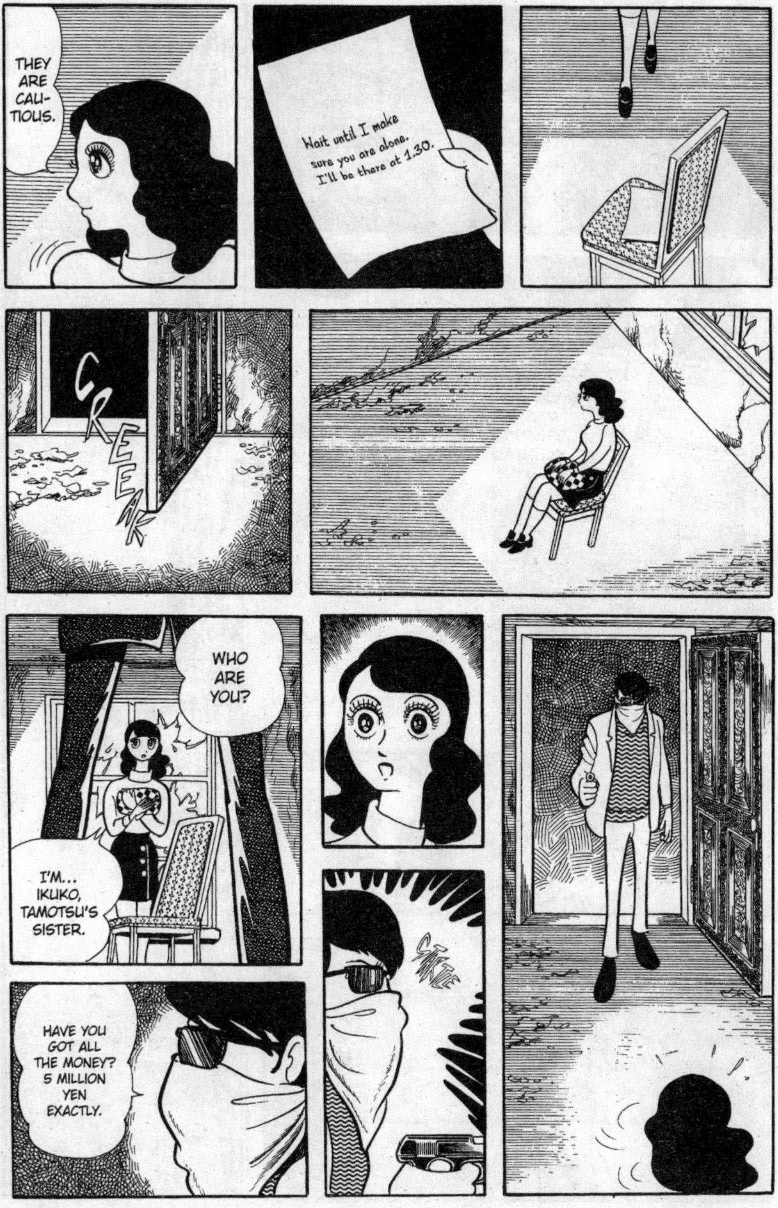
Wait until I make sure you are alone. I'll be there at 1.30.
THEY ARE CAU-TIOUS.
CREEAK
WHO ARE YOU?
I'M... IKUKO, TAMOTSU'S SISTER.
HAVE YOU GOT ALL THE MONEY? 5 MILLION YEN EXACTLY.

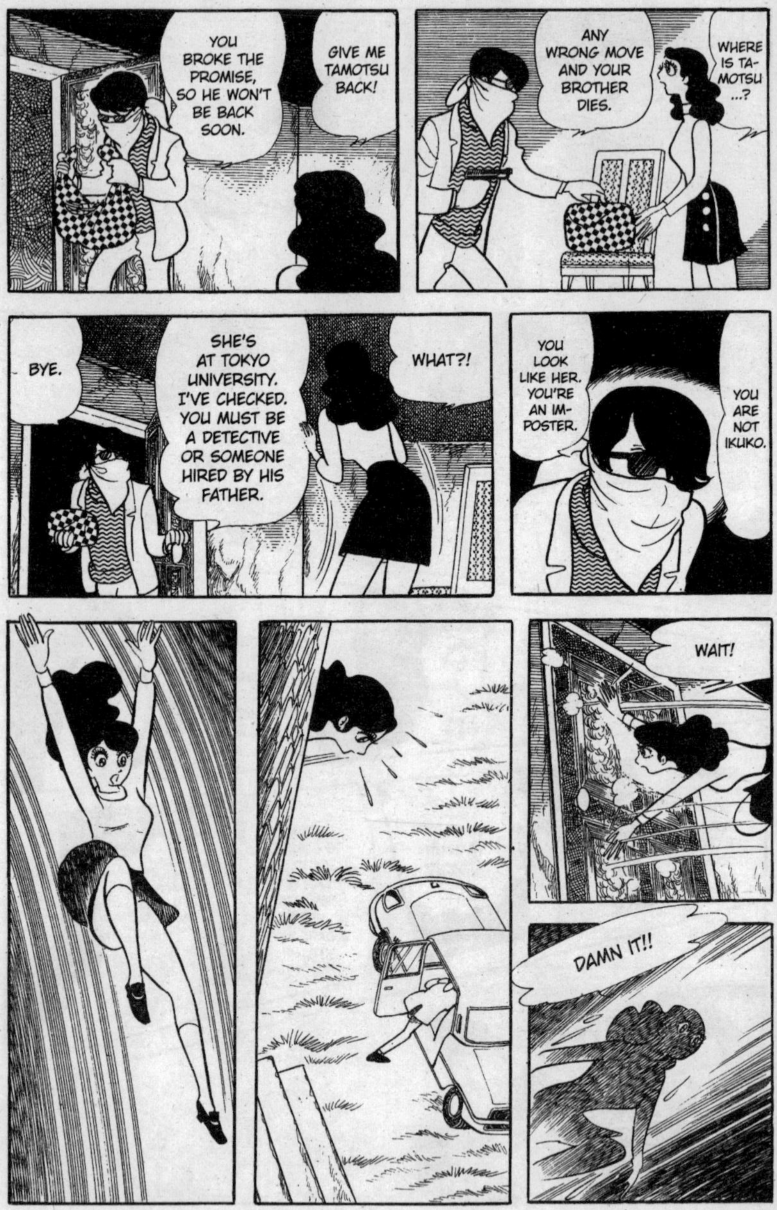
WHERE IS TA-MOTSU ...?
ANY WRONG MOVE AND YOUR BROTHER DIES.
GIVE ME TAMOTSU BACK!
YOU BROKE THE PROMISE, SO HE WON'T BE BACK SOON.
YOU ARE NOT IKUKO.
YOU LOOK LIKE HER. YOU'RE AN IM-POSTER.
WHAT?!
SHE'S AT TOKYO UNIVERSITY. I'VE CHECKED. YOU MUST BE A DETECTIVE OR SOMEONE HIRED BY HIS FATHER.
BYE.
WAIT!
DAMN IT!!

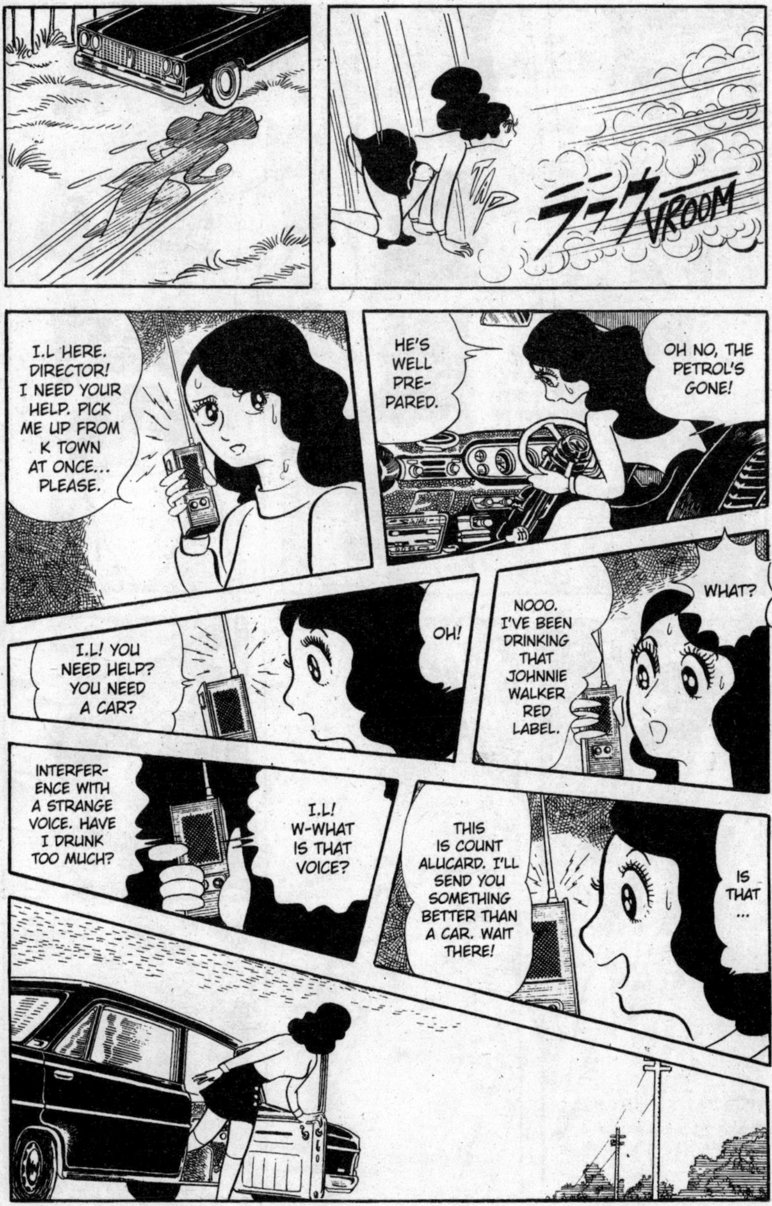
TAP
VROOM
OH NO, THE PETROL'S GONE!
HE'S WELL PRE-PARED.
I.L HERE. DIRECTOR! I NEED YOUR HELP. PICK ME UP FROM K TOWN AT ONCE... PLEASE.
WHAT?
NOOO. I'VE BEEN DRINKING THAT JOHNNIE WALKER RED LABEL.
OH!
I.L! YOU NEED HELP? YOU NEED A CAR?
IS THAT ...
THIS IS COUNT ALUCARD. I'LL SEND YOU SOMETHING BETTER THAN A CAR. WAIT THERE!
I.L! W-WHAT IS THAT VOICE?
INTERFER-ENCE WITH A STRANGE VOICE. HAVE I DRUNK TOO MUCH?

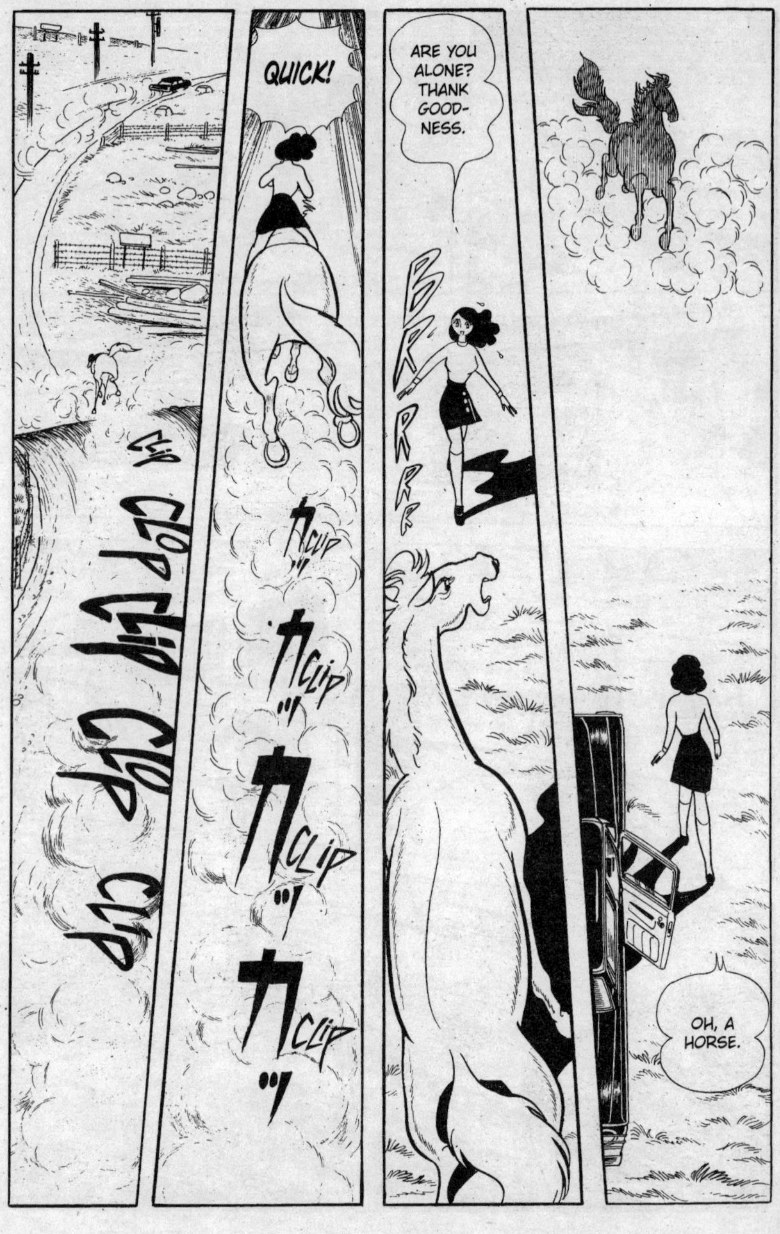
OH, A HORSE.
ARE YOU ALONE? THANK GOODNESS.
BRRRRRF
QUICK!
カCLIP ッ
カCLIP ッ
カCLIP ッ
カCLIP ッ
CLIP CLIP CLIP CLIP CLIP CLIP

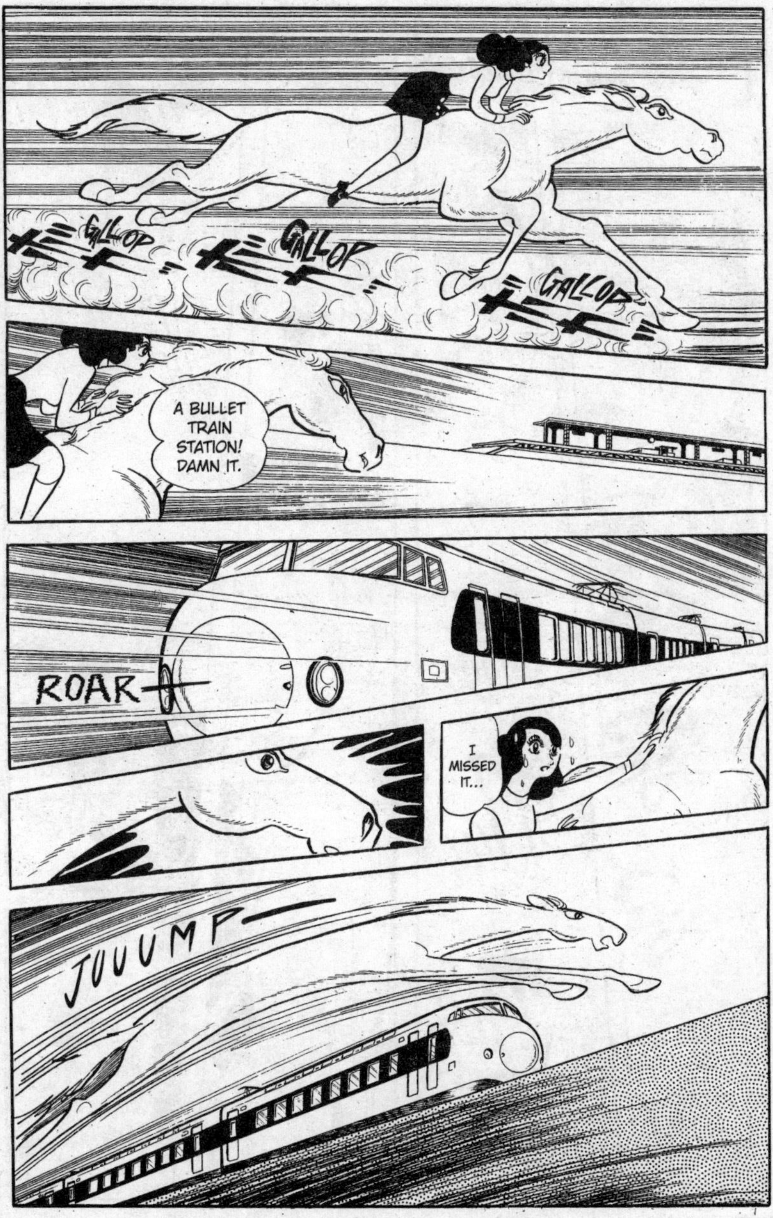
GALLOP
GALLOP
GALLOP
A BULLET TRAIN STATION! DAMN IT.
ROAR
I MISSED IT...
JUUUMP

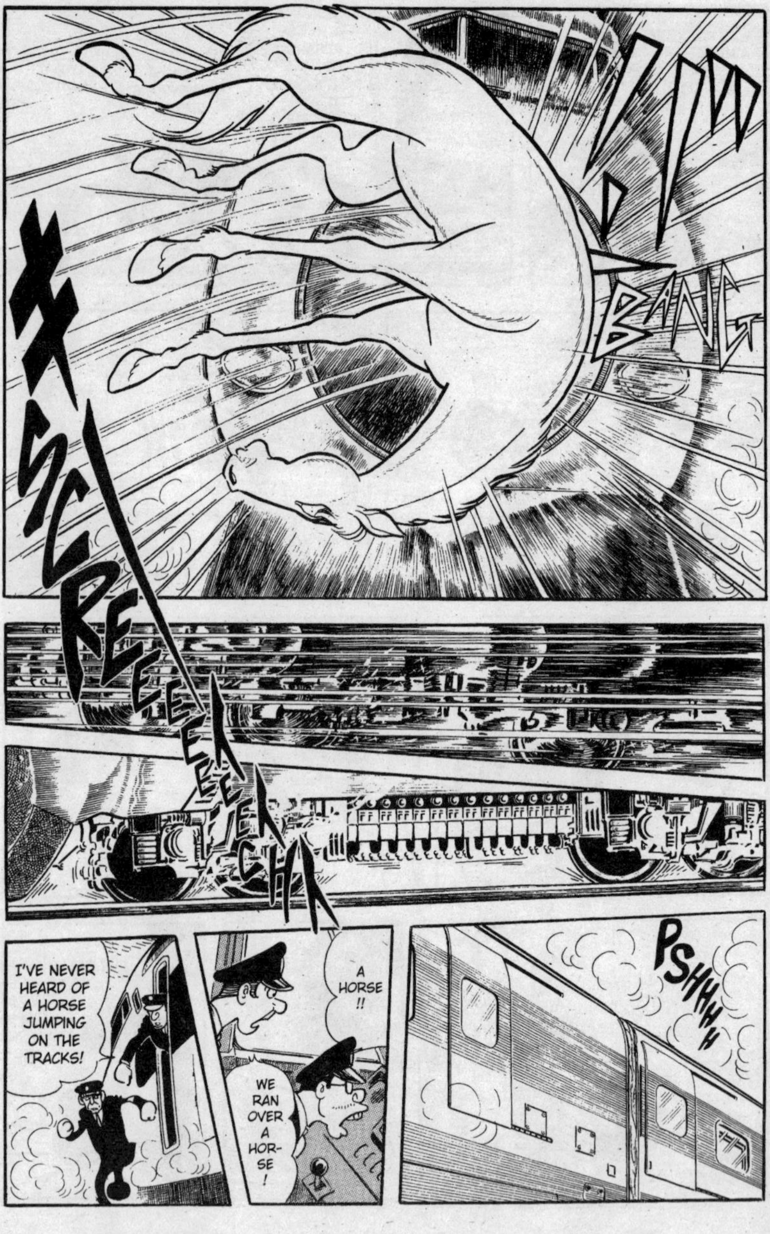
BANG
SCREEEEEECH
PSHHHH
A HORSE !!
WE RAN OVER A HORSE!
I'VE NEVER HEARD OF A HORSE JUMPING ON THE TRACKS!

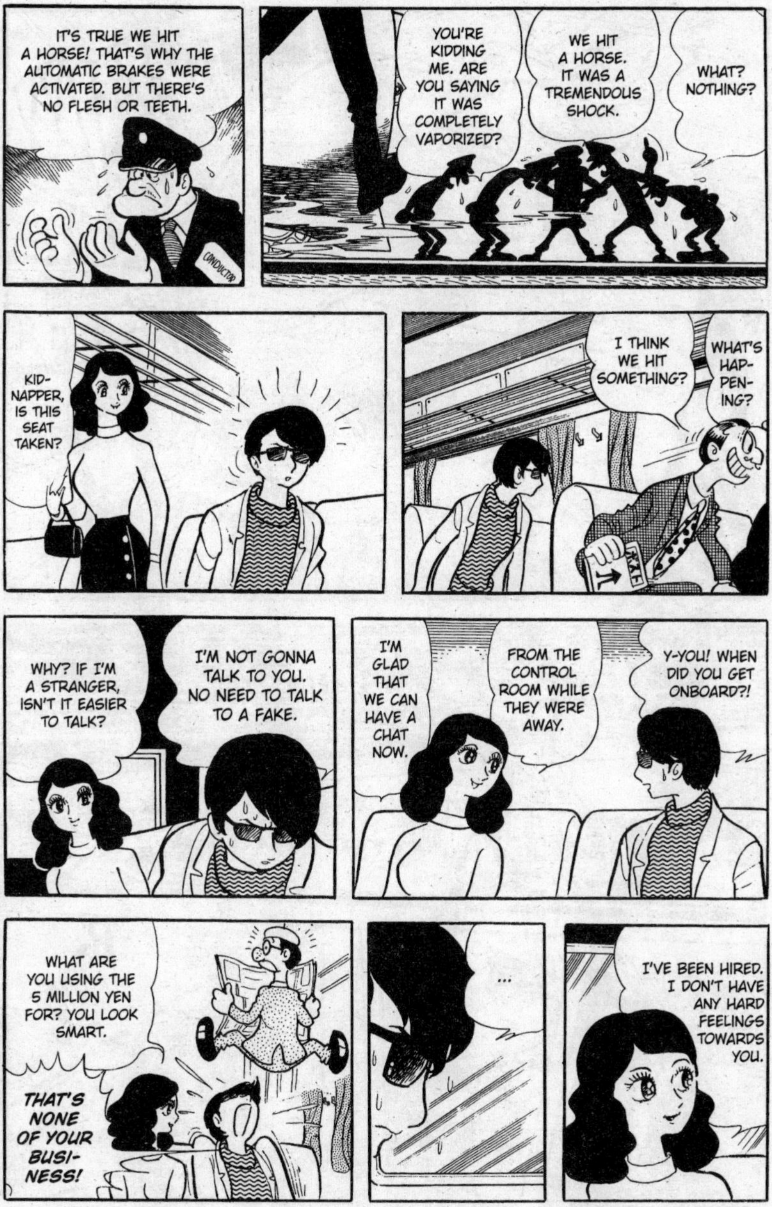
WHAT? NOTHING?
WE HIT A HORSE. IT WAS A TREMENDOUS SHOCK.
YOU'RE KIDDING ME. ARE YOU SAYING IT WAS COMPLETELY VAPORIZED?
IT'S TRUE WE HIT A HORSE! THAT'S WHY THE AUTOMATIC BRAKES WERE ACTIVATED. BUT THERE'S NO FLESH OR TEETH.
CONDUCTOR
WHAT'S HAP-PEN-ING?
I THINK WE HIT SOMETHING?
KID-NAPPER, IS THIS SEAT TAKEN?
Y-YOU! WHEN DID YOU GET ONBOARD?!
FROM THE CONTROL ROOM WHILE THEY WERE AWAY.
I'M GLAD THAT WE CAN HAVE A CHAT NOW.
I'M NOT GONNA TALK TO YOU. NO NEED TO TALK TO A FAKE.
WHY? IF I'M A STRANGER, ISN'T IT EASIER TO TALK?
I'VE BEEN HIRED. I DON'T HAVE ANY HARD FEELINGS TOWARDS YOU.
...
WHAT ARE YOU USING THE 5 MILLION YEN FOR? YOU LOOK SMART.
THAT'S NONE OF YOUR BUSI-NESS!

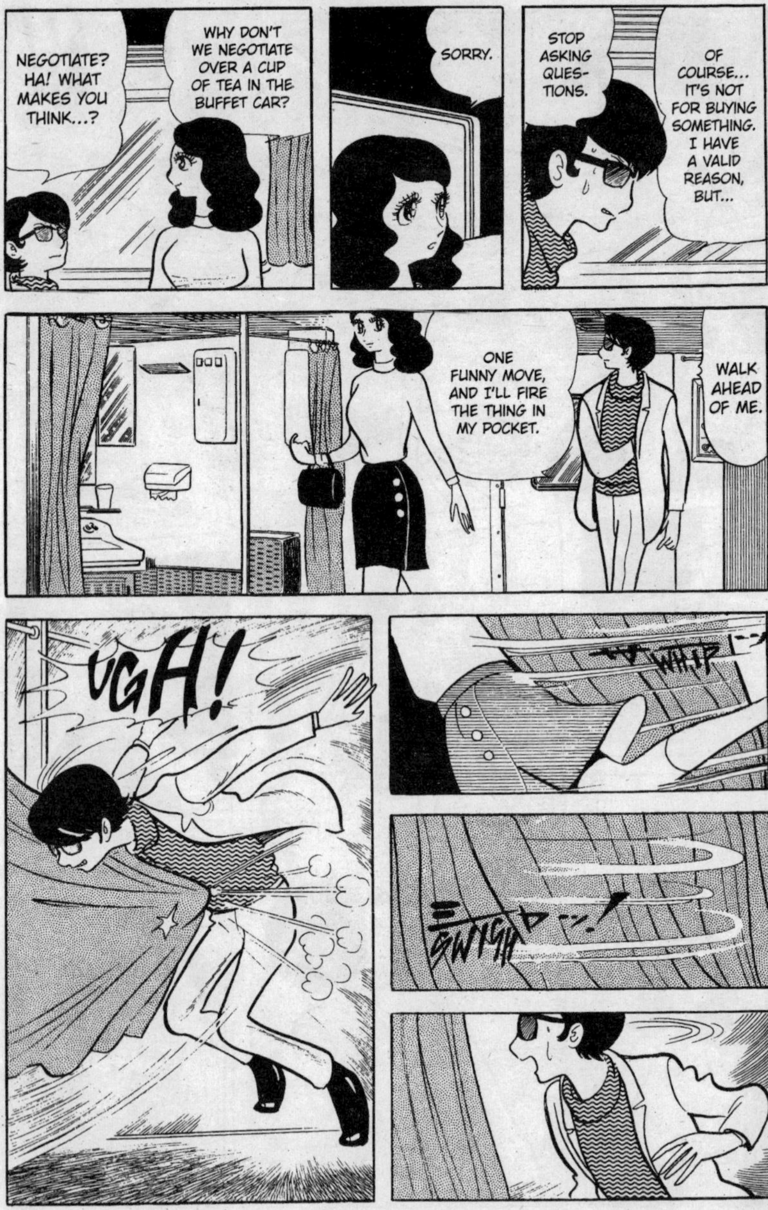
OF COURSE... IT'S NOT FOR BUYING SOMETHING. I HAVE A VALID REASON, BUT...
STOP ASKING QUES-TIONS.
SORRY.
WHY DON'T WE NEGOTIATE OVER A CUP OF TEA IN THE BUFFET CAR?
NEGOTIATE? HA! WHAT MAKES YOU THINK...?
WALK AHEAD OF ME.
ONE FUNNY MOVE, AND I'LL FIRE THE THING IN MY POCKET.
WHIP
SWISH
UGH!

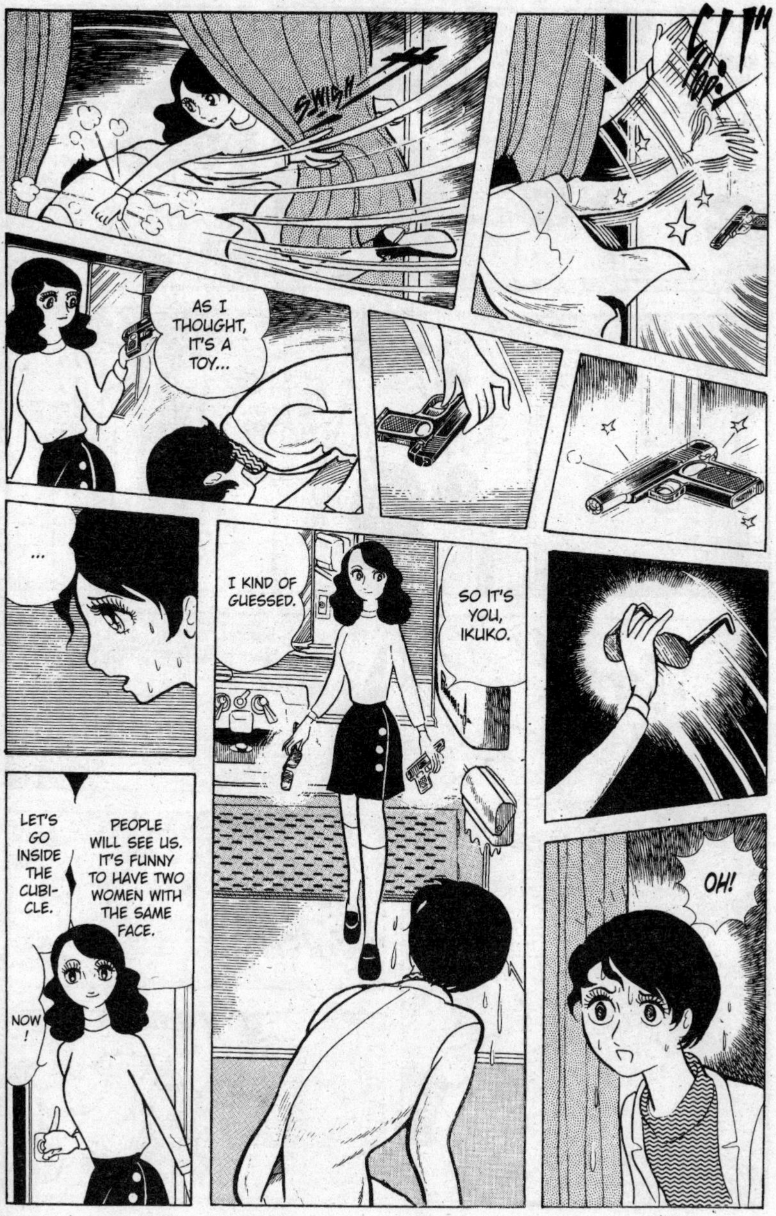
SWISH
AS I THOUGHT, IT'S A TOY...
SO IT'S YOU, IKUKO.
I KIND OF GUESSED.
OH!
...
PEOPLE WILL SEE US. IT'S FUNNY TO HAVE TWO WOMEN WITH THE SAME FACE.
LET'S GO INSIDE THE CUBICLE.
NOW!

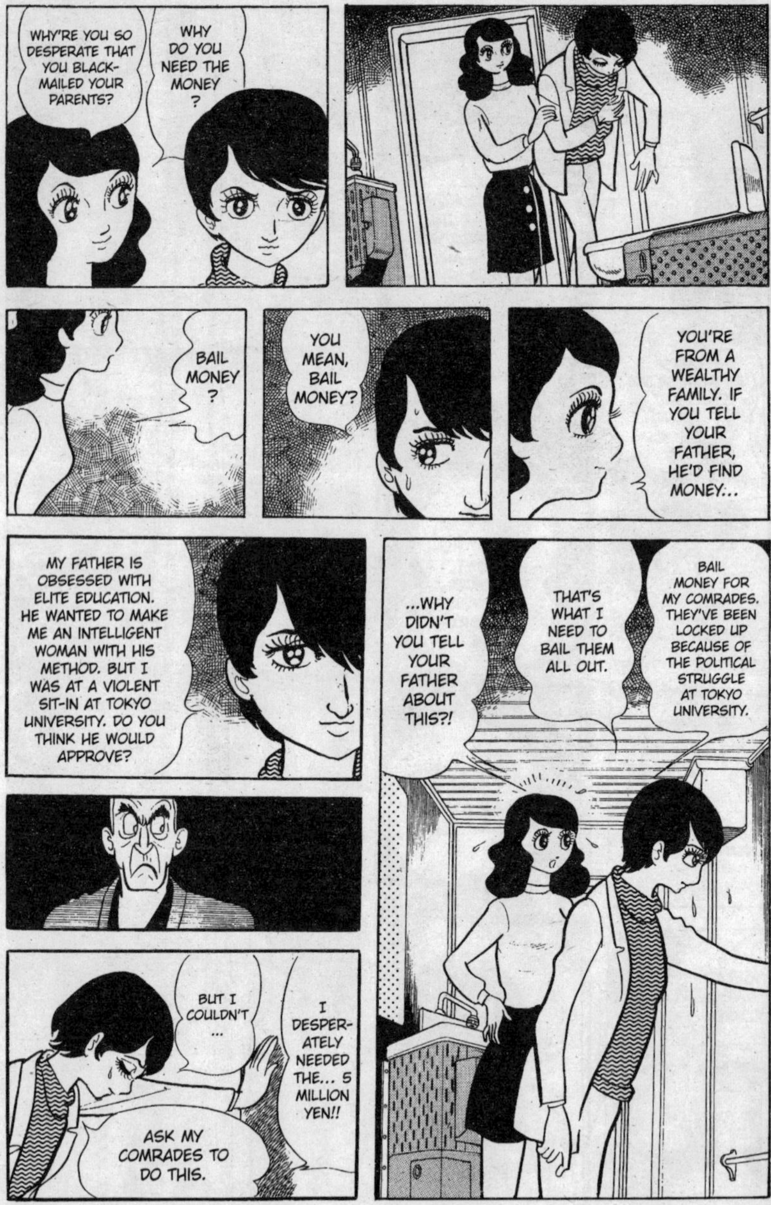
WHY DO YOU NEED THE MONEY ?
WHY'RE YOU SO DESPERATE THAT YOU BLACK-MAILED YOUR PARENTS?
YOU'RE FROM A WEALTHY FAMILY. IF YOU TELL YOUR FATHER, HE'D FIND MONEY...
YOU MEAN, BAIL MONEY?
BAIL MONEY ?
BAIL MONEY FOR MY COMRADES. THEY'VE BEEN LOCKED UP BECAUSE OF THE POLITICAL STRUGGLE AT TOKYO UNIVERSITY.
THAT'S WHAT I NEED TO BAIL THEM ALL OUT.
...WHY DIDN'T YOU TELL YOUR FATHER ABOUT THIS?!
MY FATHER IS OBSESSED WITH ELITE EDUCATION. HE WANTED TO MAKE ME AN INTELLIGENT WOMAN WITH HIS METHOD. BUT I WAS AT A VIOLENT SIT-IN AT TOKYO UNIVERSITY. DO YOU THINK HE WOULD APPROVE?
I DESPER-ATELY NEEDED THE... 5 MILLION YEN!!
BUT I COULDN'T ...
ASK MY COMRADES TO DO THIS.

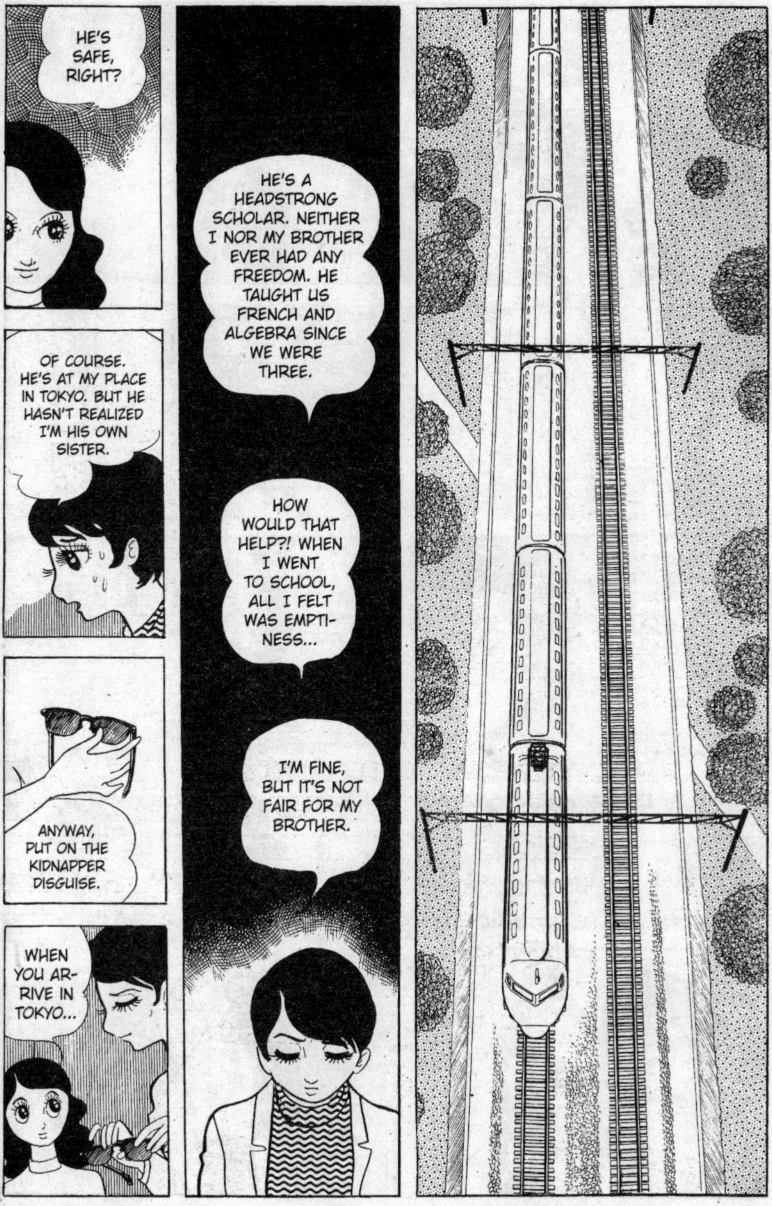
HE'S A HEADSTRONG SCHOLAR. NEITHER I NOR MY BROTHER EVER HAD ANY FREEDOM. HE TAUGHT US FRENCH AND ALGEBRA SINCE WE WERE THREE.
HOW WOULD THAT HELP?! WHEN I WENT TO SCHOOL, ALL I FELT WAS EMPTI-NESS...
I'M FINE, BUT IT'S NOT FAIR FOR MY BROTHER.
HE'S SAFE, RIGHT?
OF COURSE. HE'S AT MY PLACE IN TOKYO. BUT HE HASN'T REALIZED I'M HIS OWN SISTER.
ANYWAY, PUT ON THE KIDNAPPER DISGUISE.
WHEN YOU AR-RIVE IN TOKYO...

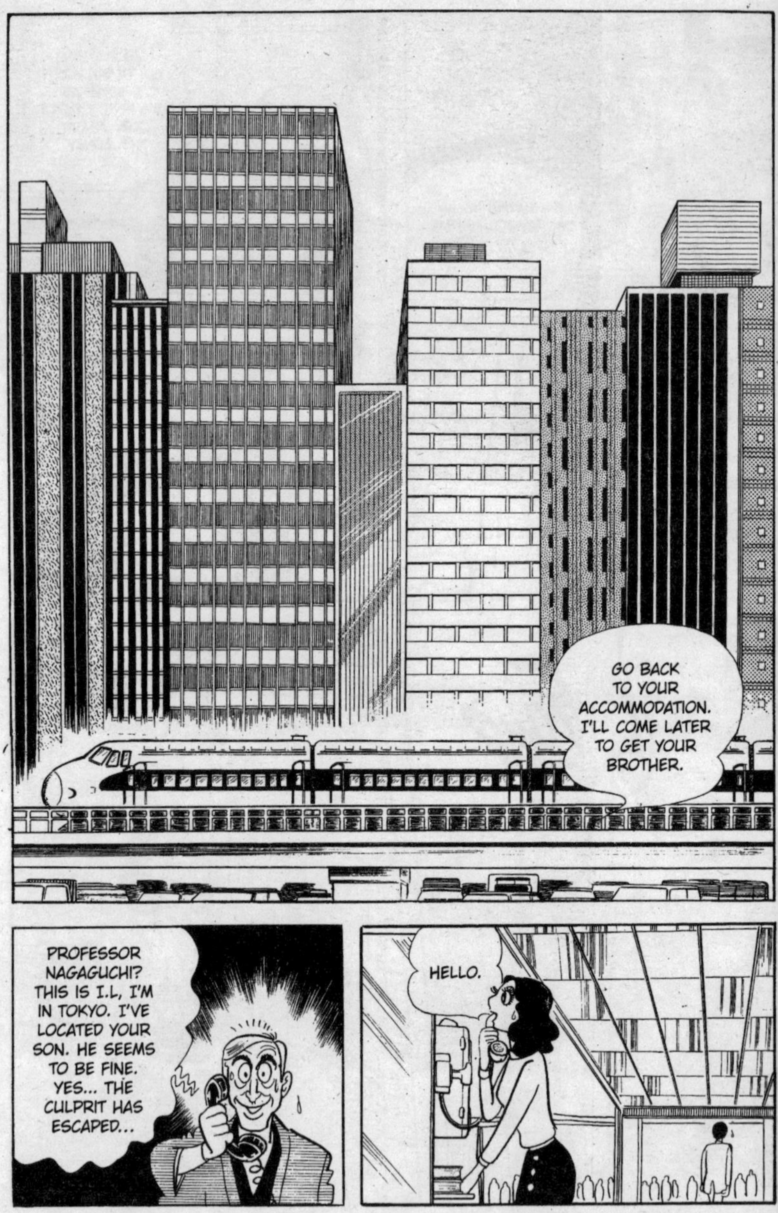
GO BACK TO YOUR ACCOMMODATION. I'LL COME LATER TO GET YOUR BROTHER.
HELLO.
PROFESSOR NAGAGUCHI? THIS IS I.L, I'M IN TOKYO. I'VE LOCATED YOUR SON. HE SEEMS TO BE FINE. YES... THE CULPRIT HAS ESCAPED...

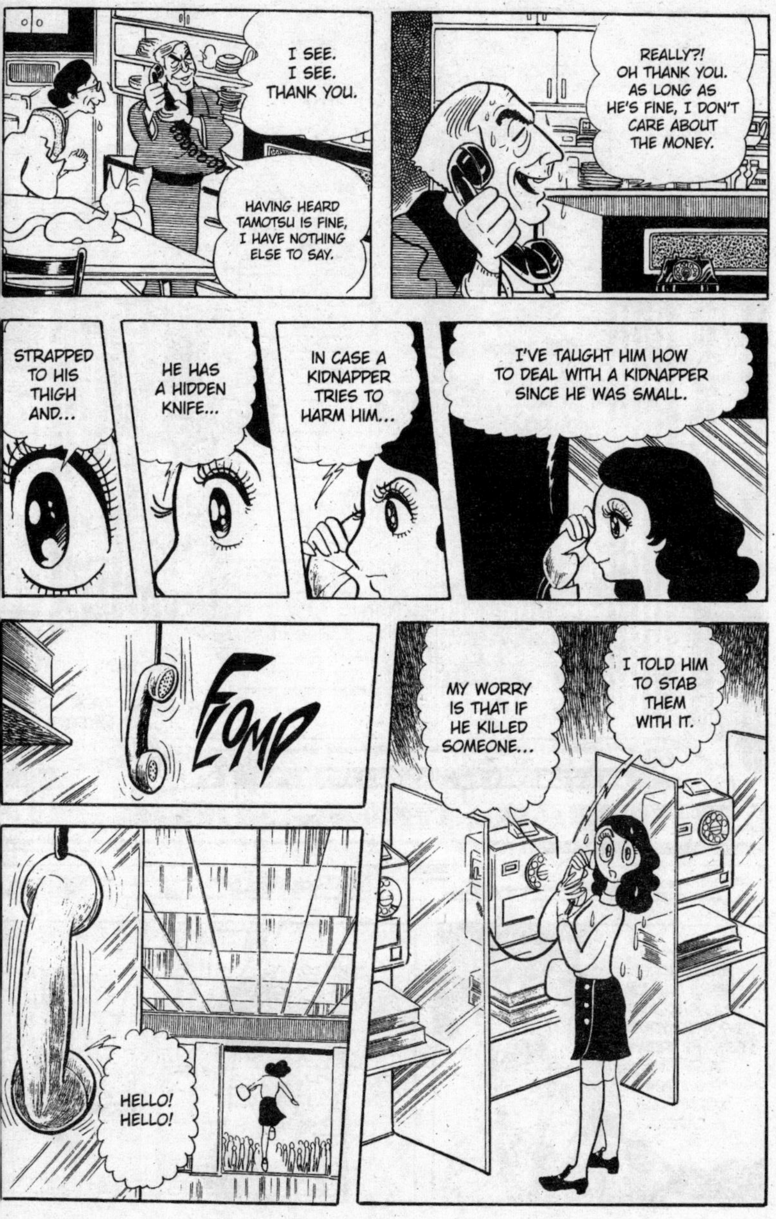
REALLY?! OH THANK YOU. AS LONG AS HE'S FINE, I DON'T CARE ABOUT THE MONEY.
I SEE. I SEE. THANK YOU.
HAVING HEARD TAMOTSU IS FINE, I HAVE NOTHING ELSE TO SAY.
I'VE TAUGHT HIM HOW TO DEAL WITH A KIDNAPPER SINCE HE WAS SMALL.
IN CASE A KIDNAPPER TRIES TO HARM HIM...
HE HAS A HIDDEN KNIFE...
STRAPPED TO HIS THIGH AND...
I TOLD HIM TO STAB THEM WITH IT.
MY WORRY IS THAT IF HE KILLED SOMEONE...
FLOMP
HELLO! HELLO!

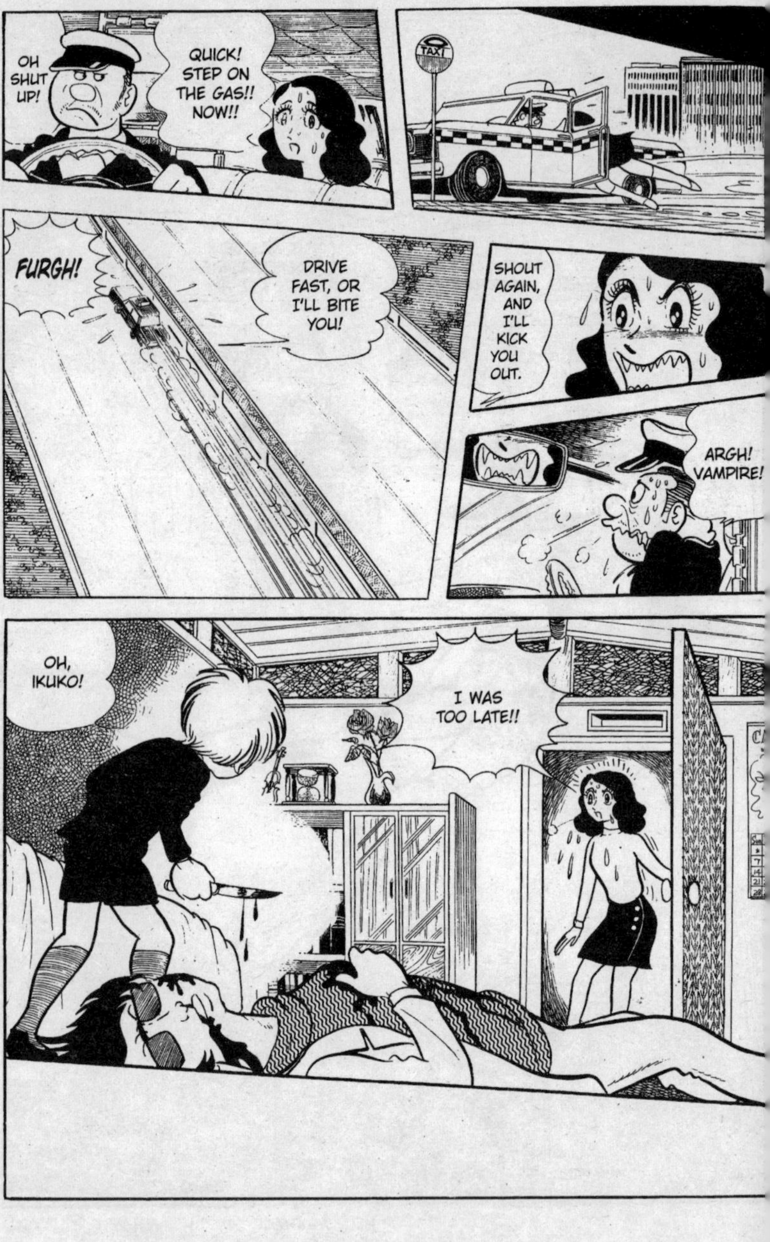
QUICK! STEP ON THE GAS!! NOW!!
OH SHUT UP!
SHOUT AGAIN, AND I'LL KICK YOU OUT.
ARGH! VAMPIRE!
DRIVE FAST, OR I'LL BITE YOU!
FURGH!
I WAS TOO LATE!!
OH, IKUKO!

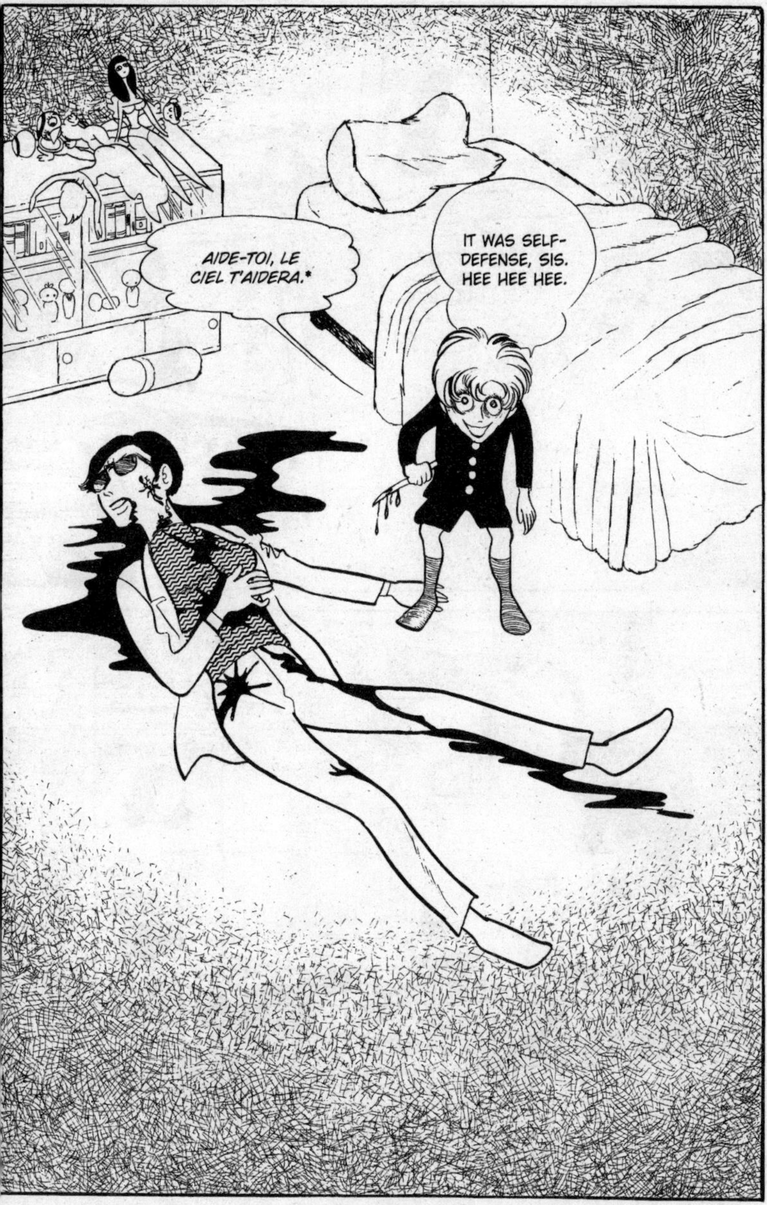
IT WAS SELF-DEFENSE, SIS. HEE HEE HEE.
AIDE-TOI, LE CIEL T'AIDERA.*

* HELP YOURSELF, (AND) HEAVEN WILL HELP YOU.

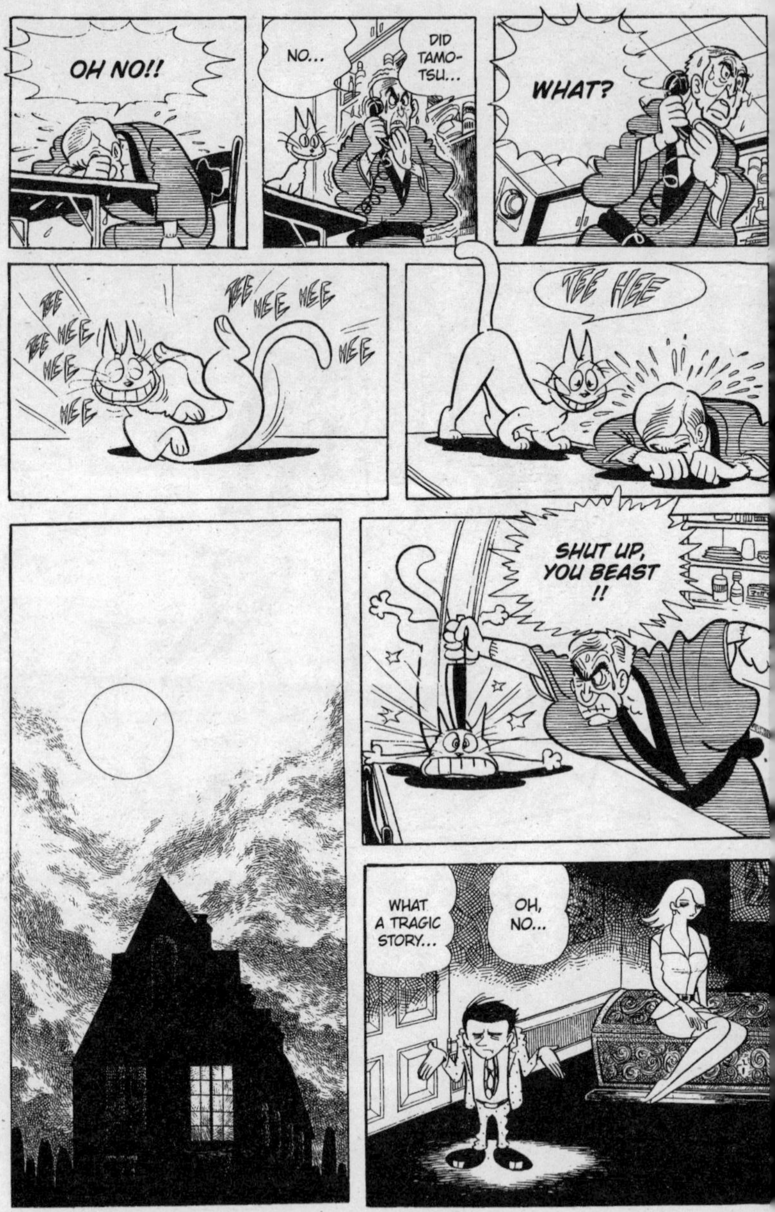
WHAT?
DID TAMO-TSU...
NO...
OH NO!!
TEE HEE
TEE HEE HEE
HEE
TEE HEE
TEE HEE
HEE
HEE
SHUT UP, YOU BEAST !!
OH, NO...
WHAT A TRAGIC STORY...

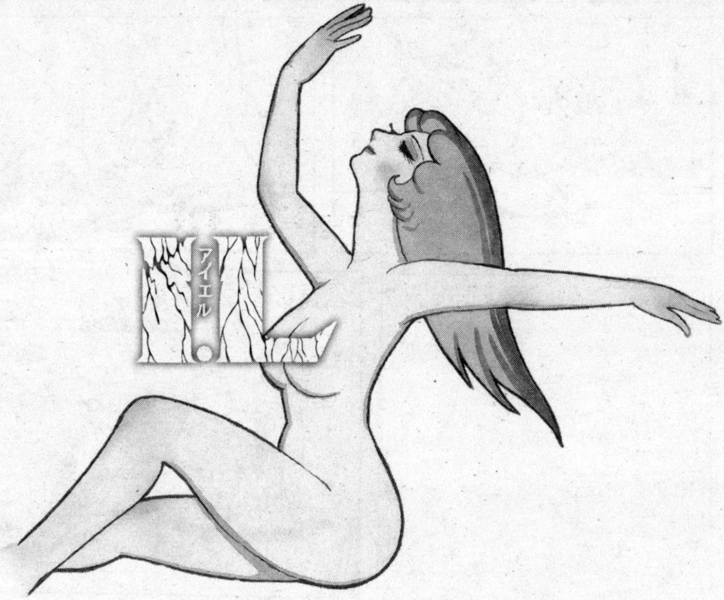
アイエル

# EPISODE 7
# The Story of
# Hippie Yoshiko

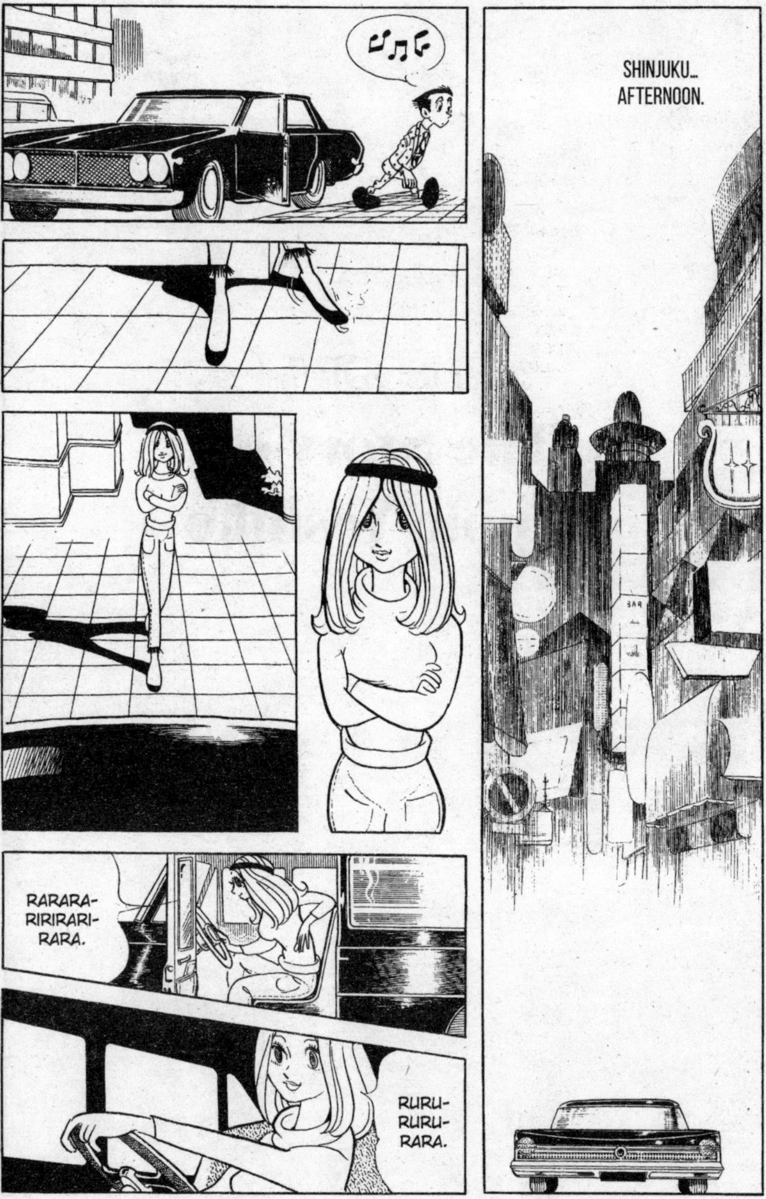
SHINJUKU... AFTERNOON.
RARARA-RIRIRARI-RARA.
RURU-RURU-RARA.

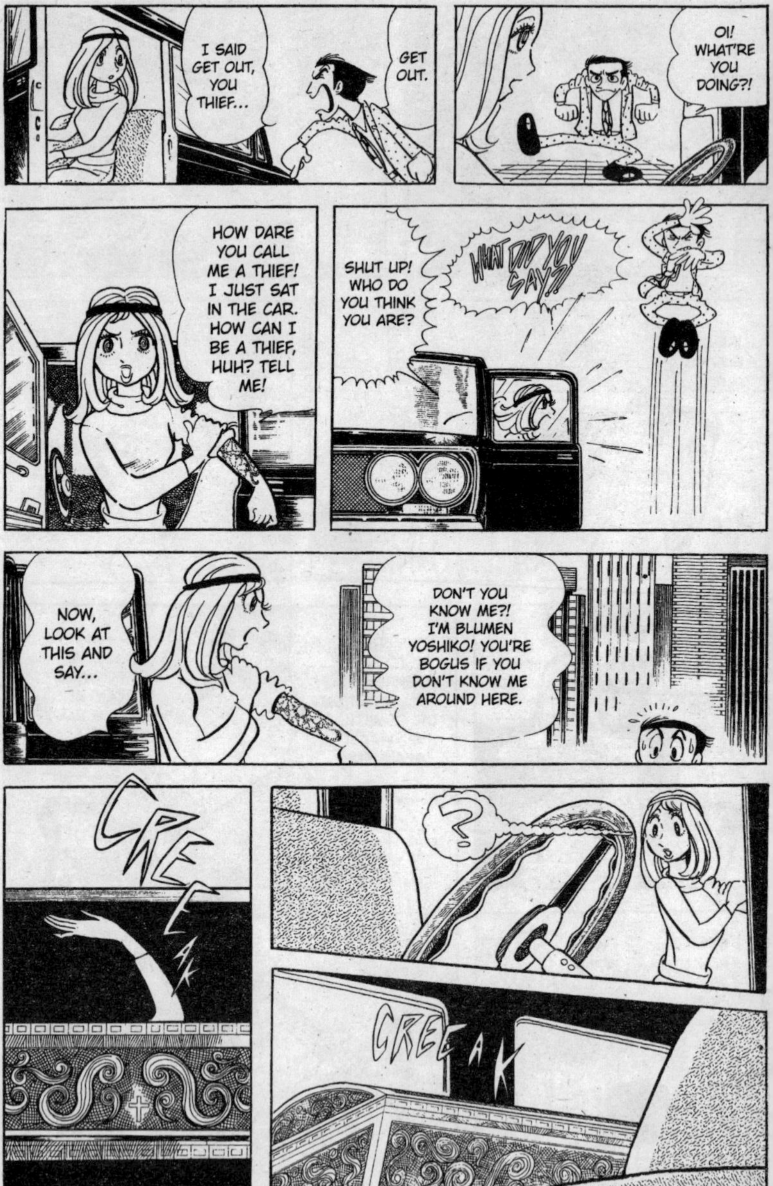
OI! WHAT'RE YOU DOING?!
GET OUT.
I SAID GET OUT, YOU THIEF...
WHAT DID YOU SAY?!
SHUT UP! WHO DO YOU THINK YOU ARE?
HOW DARE YOU CALL ME A THIEF! I JUST SAT IN THE CAR. HOW CAN I BE A THIEF, HUH? TELL ME!
DON'T YOU KNOW ME?! I'M BLUMEN YOSHIKO! YOU'RE BOGUS IF YOU DON'T KNOW ME AROUND HERE.
NOW, LOOK AT THIS AND SAY...
?
CREEAK
CREEAK

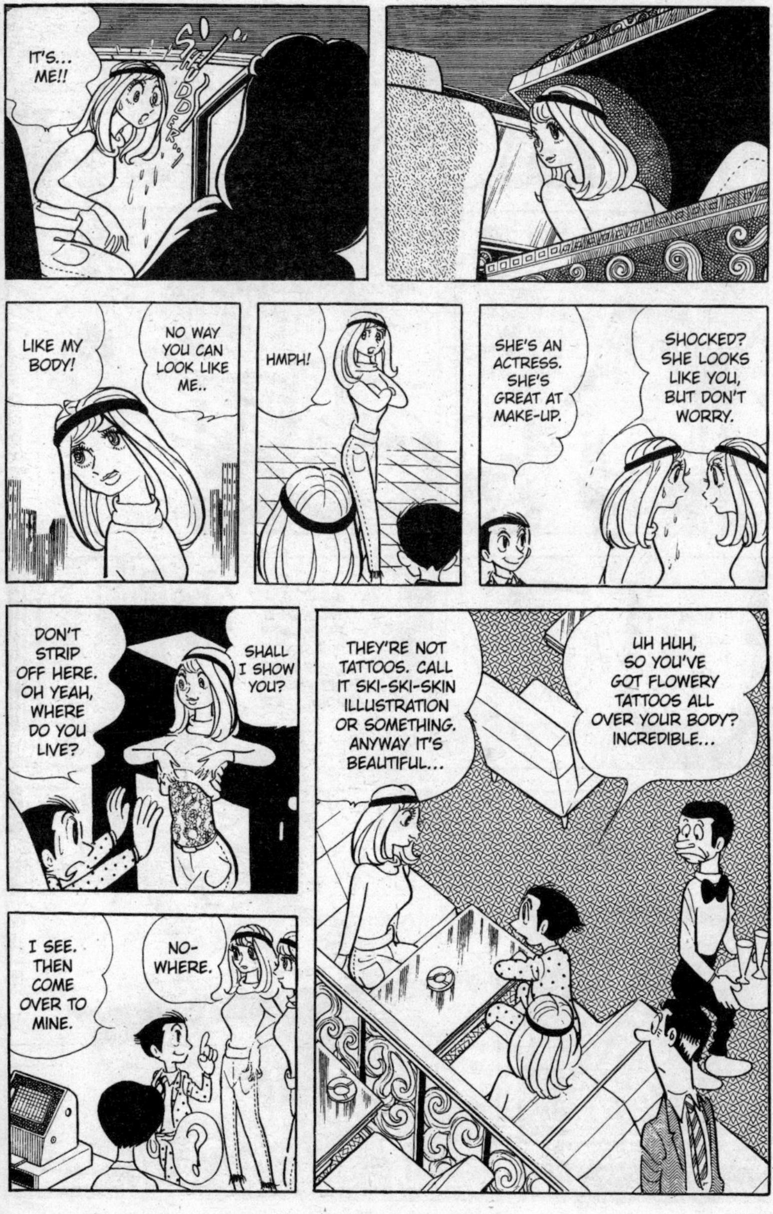
IT'S... ME!!
SHUDDER..!
SHOCKED? SHE LOOKS LIKE YOU, BUT DON'T WORRY.
SHE'S AN ACTRESS. SHE'S GREAT AT MAKE-UP.
HMPH!
NO WAY YOU CAN LOOK LIKE ME..
LIKE MY BODY!
UH HUH, SO YOU'VE GOT FLOWERY TATTOOS ALL OVER YOUR BODY? INCREDIBLE...
THEY'RE NOT TATTOOS. CALL IT SKI-SKI-SKIN ILLUSTRATION OR SOMETHING. ANYWAY IT'S BEAUTIFUL...
SHALL I SHOW YOU?
DON'T STRIP OFF HERE. OH YEAH, WHERE DO YOU LIVE?
NO-WHERE.
I SEE. THEN COME OVER TO MINE.
?

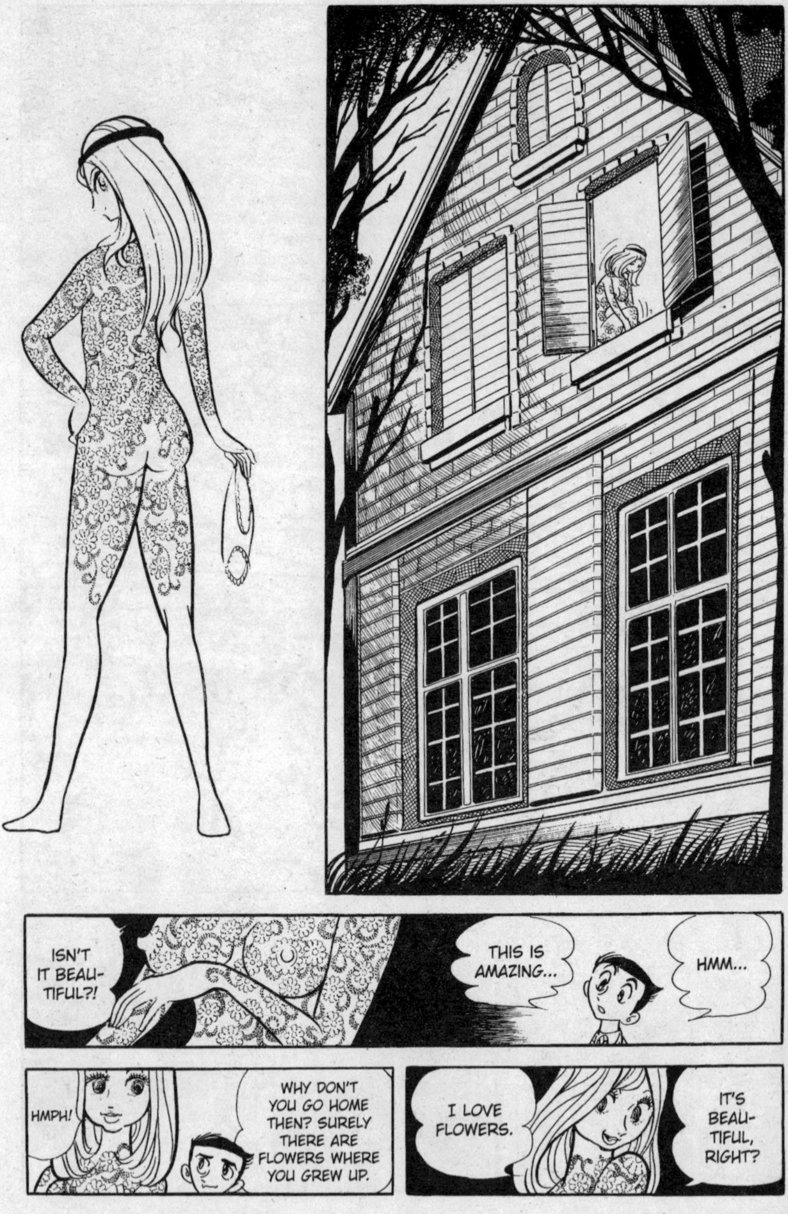
HMM...
THIS IS AMAZING...
ISN'T IT BEAUTIFUL?!
IT'S BEAUTIFUL, RIGHT?
I LOVE FLOWERS.
WHY DON'T YOU GO HOME THEN? SURELY THERE ARE FLOWERS WHERE YOU GREW UP.
HMPH!

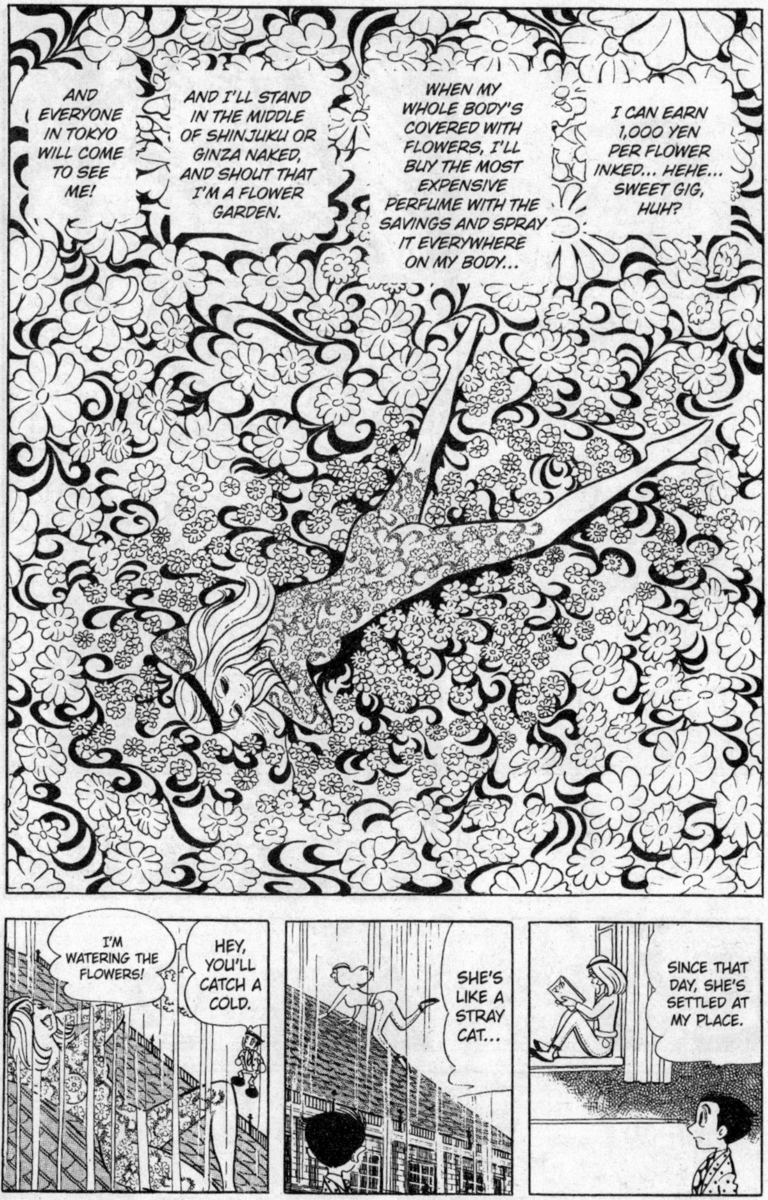
I CAN EARN 1,000 YEN PER FLOWER INKED... HEHE... SWEET GIG, HUH?
WHEN MY WHOLE BODY'S COVERED WITH FLOWERS, I'LL BUY THE MOST EXPENSIVE PERFUME WITH THE SAVINGS AND SPRAY IT EVERYWHERE ON MY BODY...
AND I'LL STAND IN THE MIDDLE OF SHINJUKU OR GINZA NAKED, AND SHOUT THAT I'M A FLOWER GARDEN.
AND EVERYONE IN TOKYO WILL COME TO SEE ME!
SINCE THAT DAY, SHE'S SETTLED AT MY PLACE.
SHE'S LIKE A STRAY CAT...
HEY, YOU'LL CATCH A COLD.
I'M WATERING THE FLOWERS!

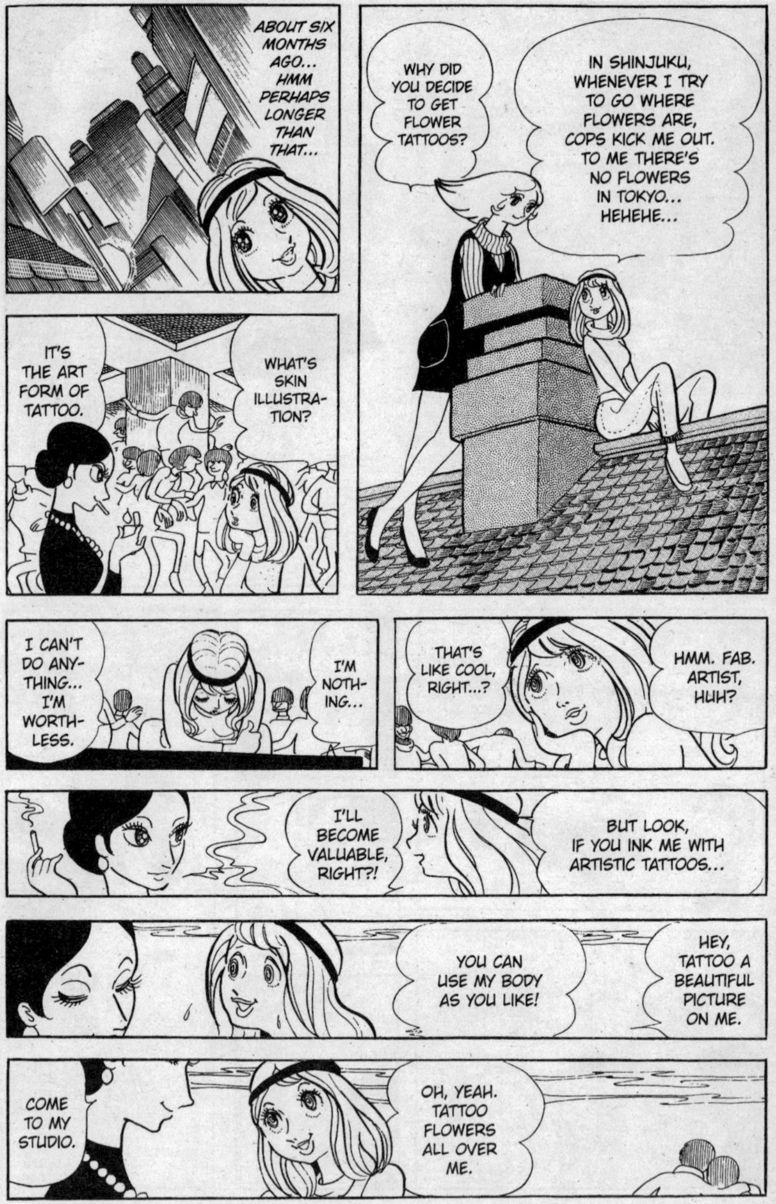
IN SHINJUKU, WHENEVER I TRY TO GO WHERE FLOWERS ARE, COPS KICK ME OUT. TO ME THERE'S NO FLOWERS IN TOKYO... HEHEHE...
WHY DID YOU DECIDE TO GET FLOWER TATTOOS?
ABOUT SIX MONTHS AGO... HMM PERHAPS LONGER THAN THAT...
WHAT'S SKIN ILLUSTRATION?
IT'S THE ART FORM OF TATTOO.
HMM. FAB. ARTIST, HUH?
THAT'S LIKE COOL, RIGHT...?
I'M NOTHING...
I CAN'T DO ANYTHING... I'M WORTHLESS.
BUT LOOK, IF YOU INK ME WITH ARTISTIC TATTOOS...
I'LL BECOME VALUABLE, RIGHT?!
HEY, TATTOO A BEAUTIFUL PICTURE ON ME.
YOU CAN USE MY BODY AS YOU LIKE!
OH, YEAH. TATTOO FLOWERS ALL OVER ME.
COME TO MY STUDIO.

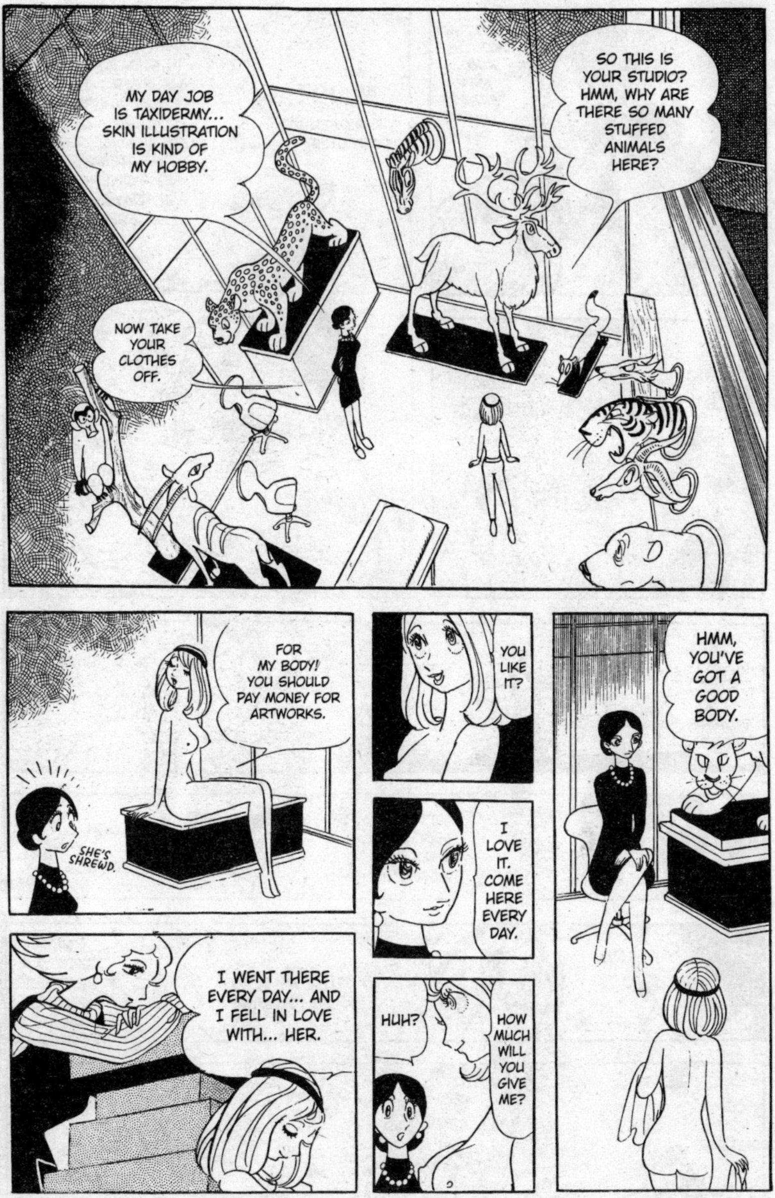
SO THIS IS YOUR STUDIO? HMM, WHY ARE THERE SO MANY STUFFED ANIMALS HERE?
MY DAY JOB IS TAXIDERMY... SKIN ILLUSTRATION IS KIND OF MY HOBBY.
NOW TAKE YOUR CLOTHES OFF.
HMM, YOU'VE GOT A GOOD BODY.
YOU LIKE IT?
I LOVE IT. COME HERE EVERY DAY.
HOW MUCH WILL YOU GIVE ME?
HUH?
FOR MY BODY! YOU SHOULD PAY MONEY FOR ARTWORKS.
SHE'S SHREWD.
I WENT THERE EVERY DAY... AND I FELL IN LOVE WITH... HER.

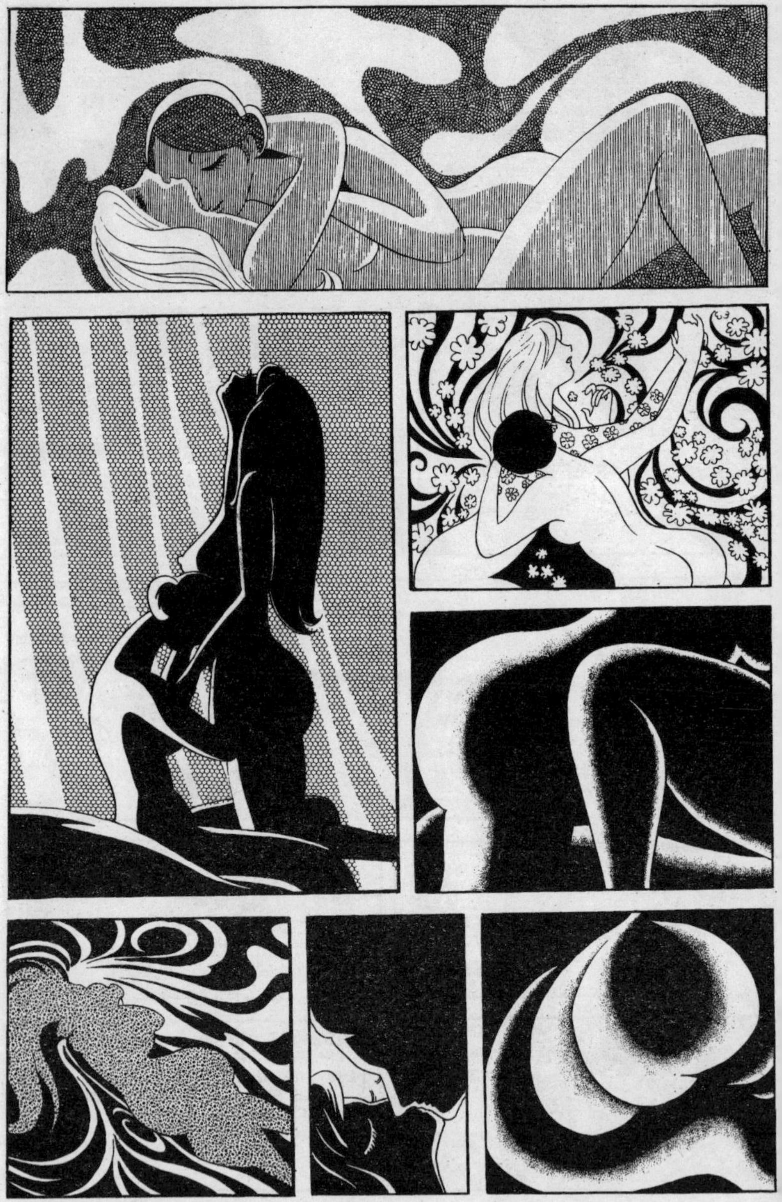

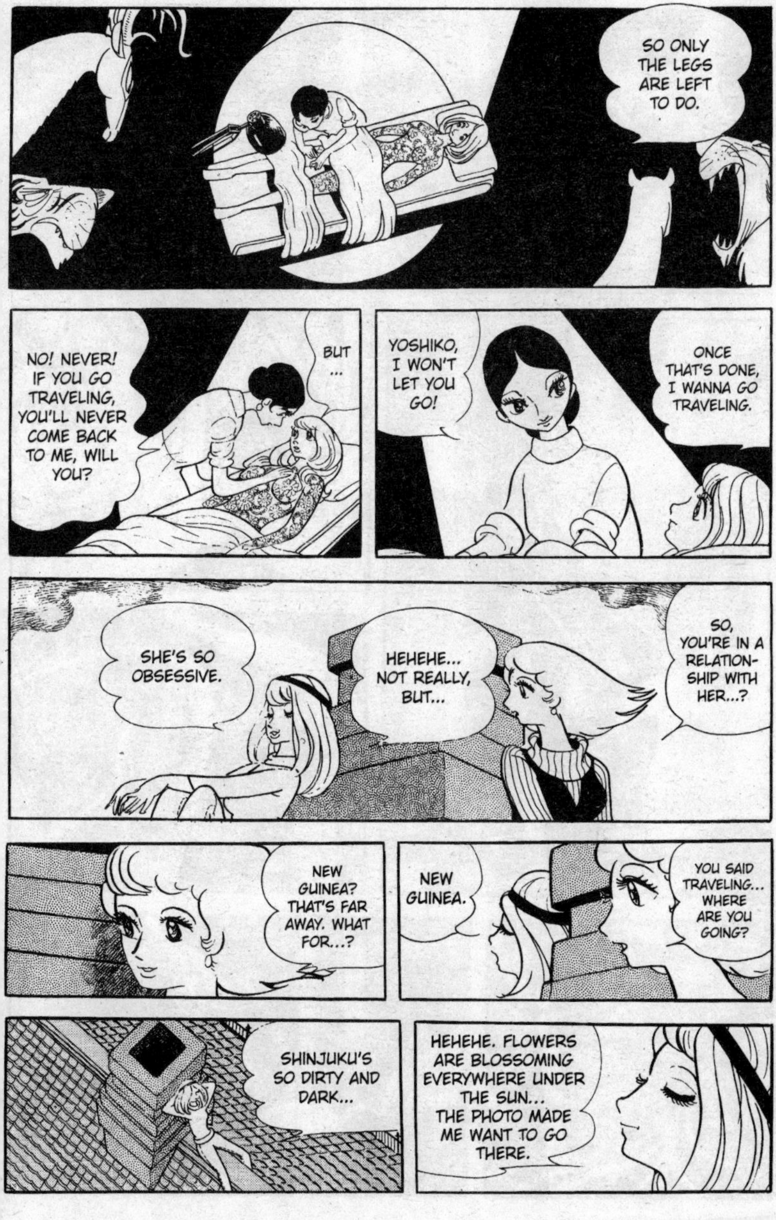
SO ONLY THE LEGS ARE LEFT TO DO.
ONCE THAT'S DONE, I WANNA GO TRAVELING.
YOSHIKO, I WON'T LET YOU GO!
BUT ...
NO! NEVER! IF YOU GO TRAVELING, YOU'LL NEVER COME BACK TO ME, WILL YOU?
SO, YOU'RE IN A RELATIONSHIP WITH HER...?
HEHEHE... NOT REALLY, BUT...
SHE'S SO OBSESSIVE.
YOU SAID TRAVELING... WHERE ARE YOU GOING?
NEW GUINEA.
NEW GUINEA? THAT'S FAR AWAY. WHAT FOR...?
HEHEHE. FLOWERS ARE BLOSSOMING EVERYWHERE UNDER THE SUN... THE PHOTO MADE ME WANT TO GO THERE.
SHINJUKU'S SO DIRTY AND DARK...

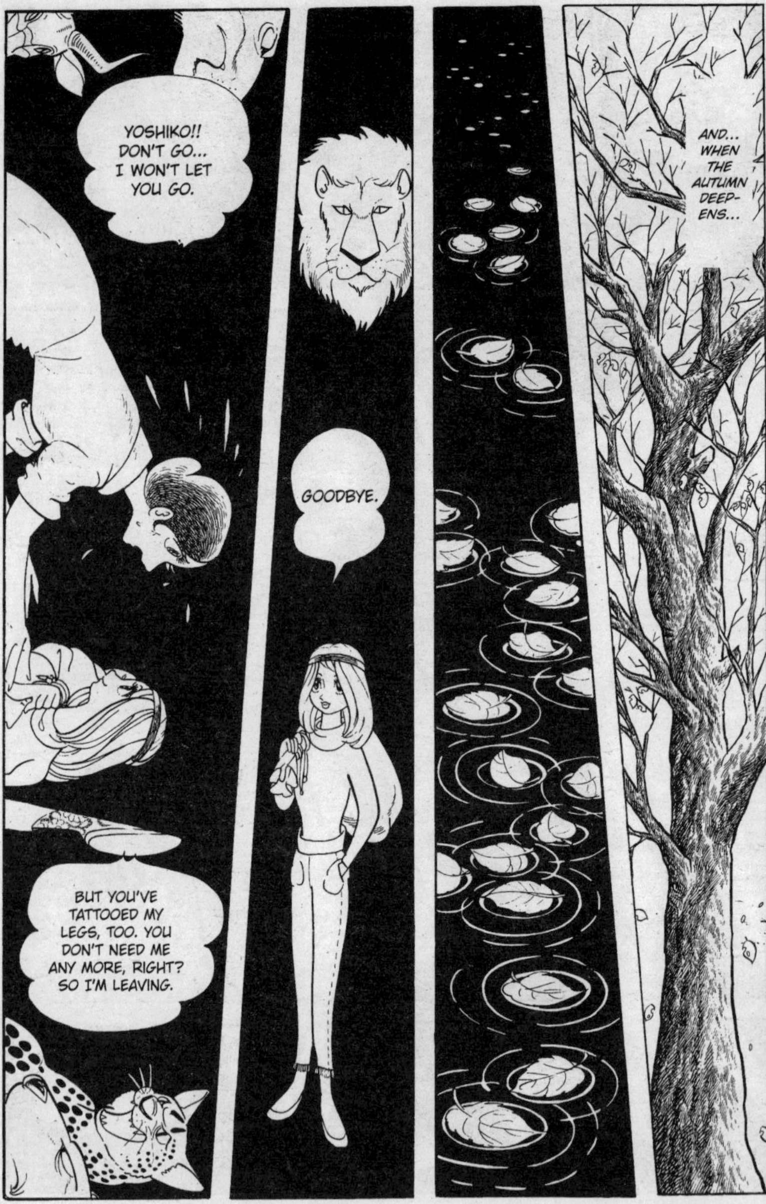
AND... WHEN THE AUTUMN DEEP- ENS...
GOODBYE.
YOSHIKO!! DON'T GO... I WON'T LET YOU GO.
BUT YOU'VE TATTOOED MY LEGS, TOO. YOU DON'T NEED ME ANY MORE, RIGHT? SO I'M LEAVING.

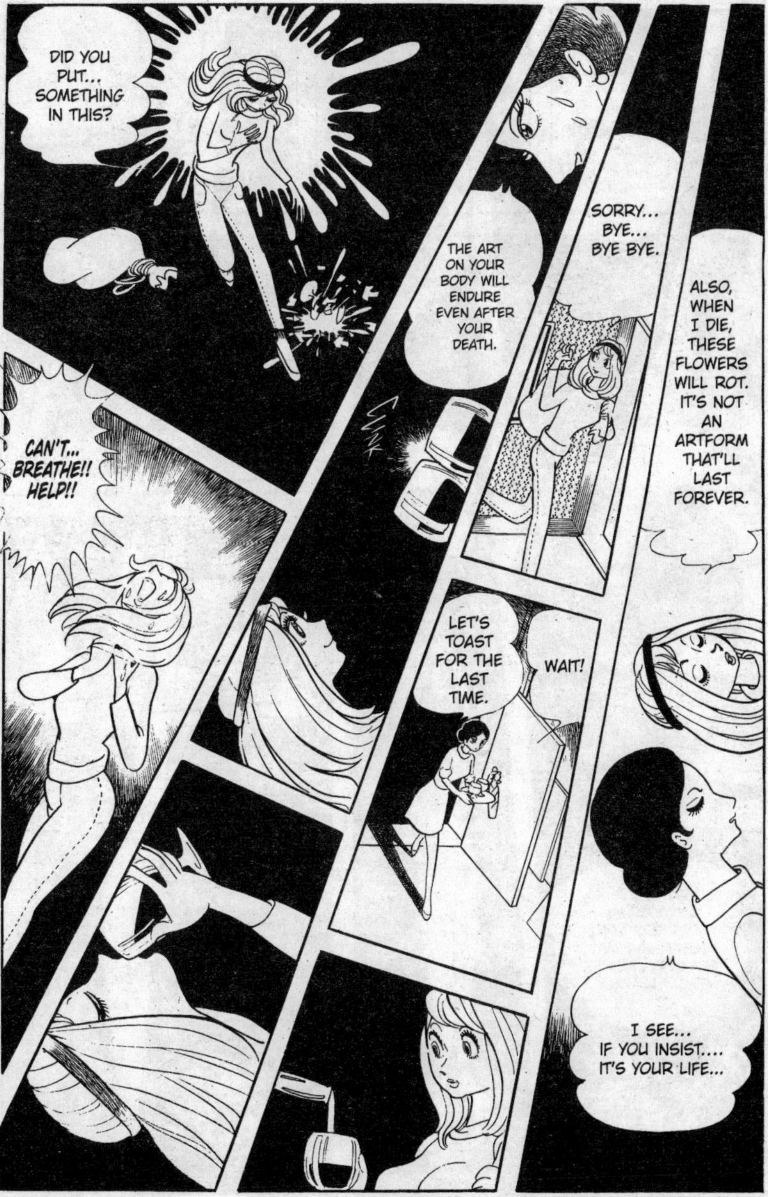

ALSO, WHEN I DIE, THESE FLOWERS WILL ROT. IT'S NOT AN ARTFORM THAT'LL LAST FOREVER.
I SEE... IF YOU INSIST.... IT'S YOUR LIFE...
SORRY... BYE... BYE BYE.
THE ART ON YOUR BODY WILL ENDURE EVEN AFTER YOUR DEATH.
WAIT!
LET'S TOAST FOR THE LAST TIME.
CLINK
DID YOU PUT... SOMETHING IN THIS?
CAN'T... BREATHE!! HELP!!

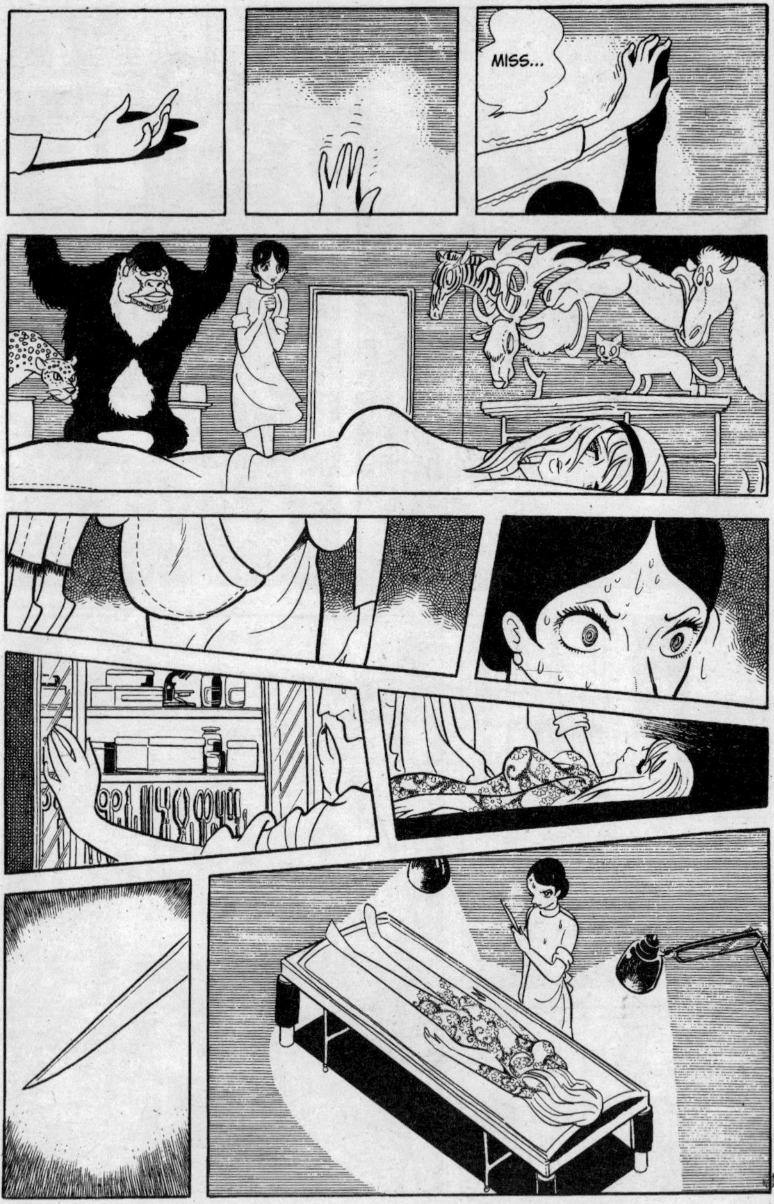
MISS...

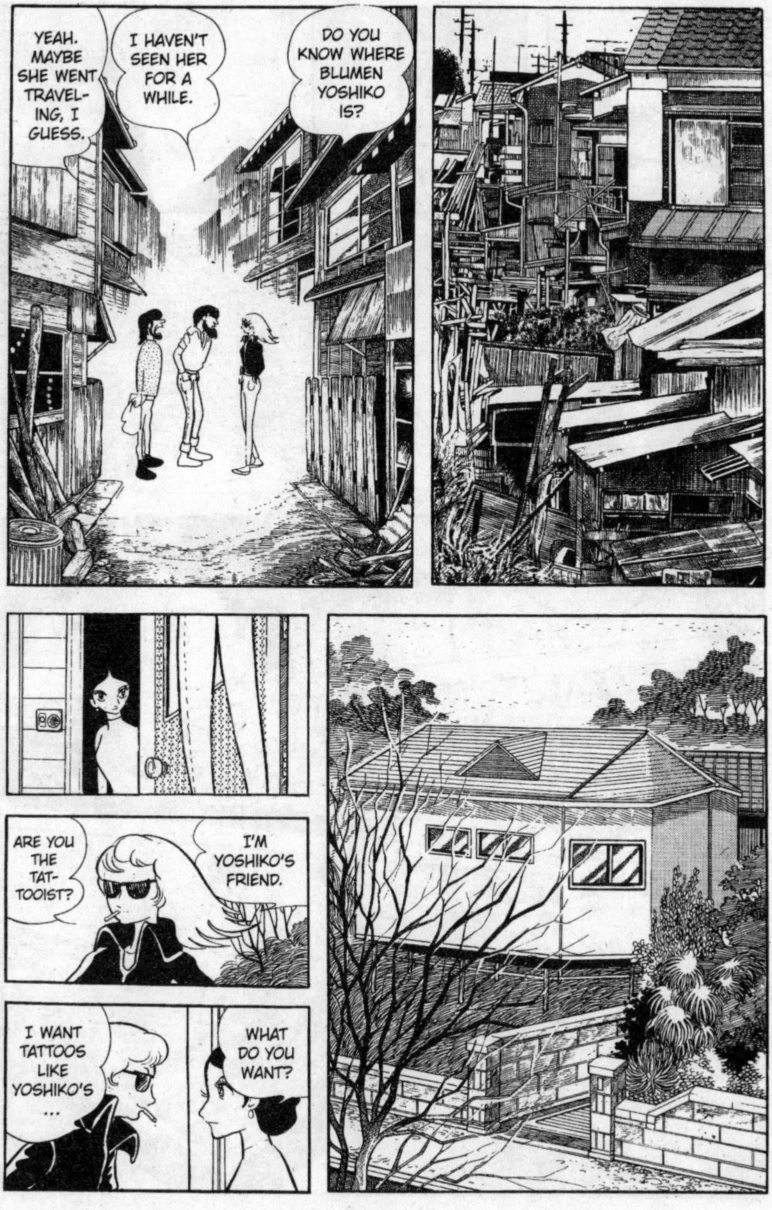
DO YOU KNOW WHERE BLUMEN YOSHIKO IS?
I HAVEN'T SEEN HER FOR A WHILE.
YEAH. MAYBE SHE WENT TRAVEL-ING, I GUESS.
I'M YOSHIKO'S FRIEND.
ARE YOU THE TAT-TOOIST?
WHAT DO YOU WANT?
I WANT TATTOOS LIKE YOSHIKO'S ...

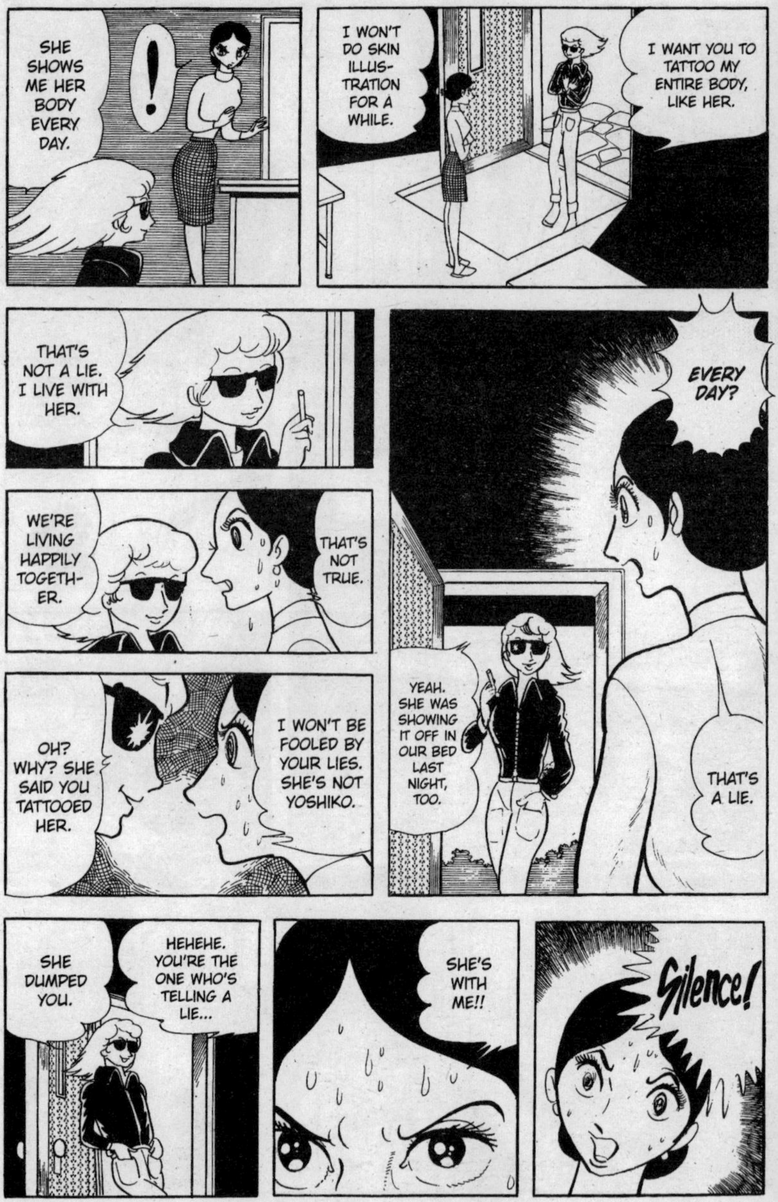
I WANT YOU TO TATTOO MY ENTIRE BODY, LIKE HER.
I WON'T DO SKIN ILLUS-TRATION FOR A WHILE.
!
SHE SHOWS ME HER BODY EVERY DAY.
EVERY DAY?
THAT'S A LIE.
YEAH. SHE WAS SHOWING IT OFF IN OUR BED LAST NIGHT, TOO.
THAT'S NOT A LIE. I LIVE WITH HER.
THAT'S NOT TRUE.
WE'RE LIVING HAPPILY TOGETH-ER.
I WON'T BE FOOLED BY YOUR LIES. SHE'S NOT YOSHIKO.
OH? WHY? SHE SAID YOU TATTOOED HER.
Silence!
SHE'S WITH ME!!
HEHEHE. YOU'RE THE ONE WHO'S TELLING A LIE...
SHE DUMPED YOU.

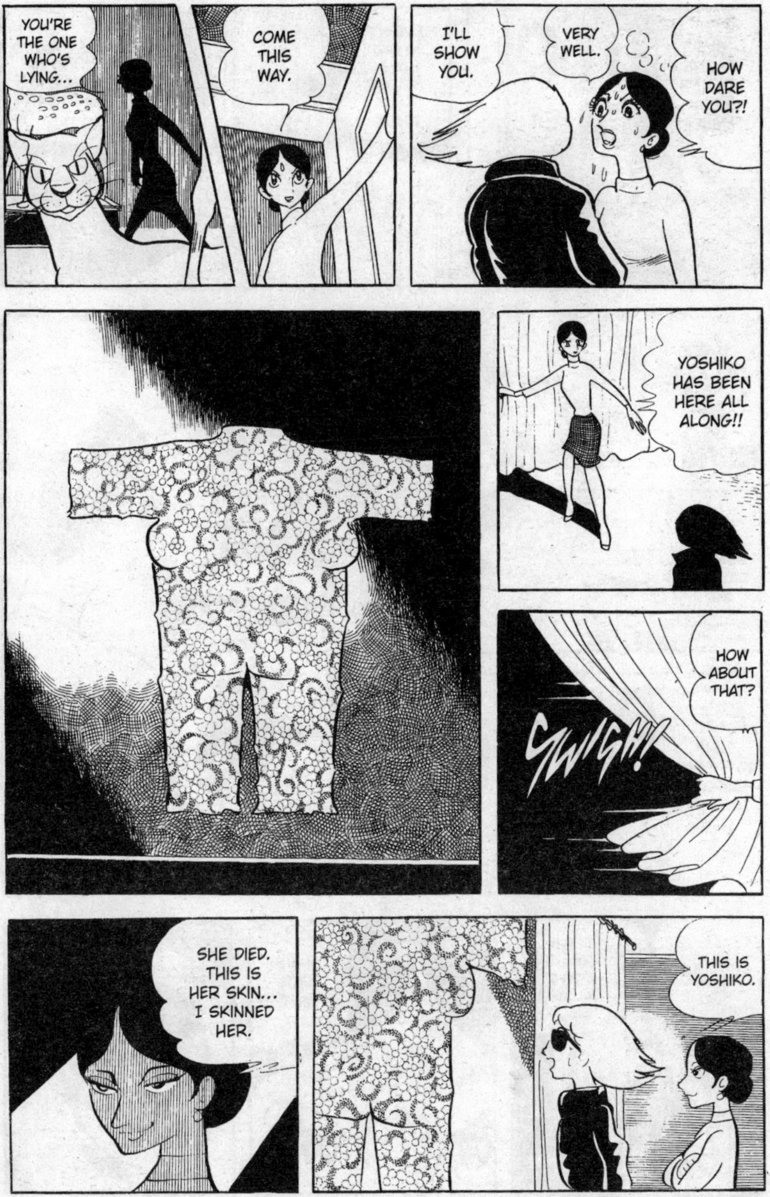
HOW DARE YOU?!
VERY WELL.
I'LL SHOW YOU.
COME THIS WAY.
YOU'RE THE ONE WHO'S LYING...
YOSHIKO HAS BEEN HERE ALL ALONG!!
HOW ABOUT THAT?
SWISH!
THIS IS YOSHIKO.
SHE DIED. THIS IS HER SKIN... I SKINNED HER.

SHE IS FOREVER MINE! NO ONE CAN TAKE HER AWAY FROM ME, UNDERSTOOD?

YOSHIKO!!

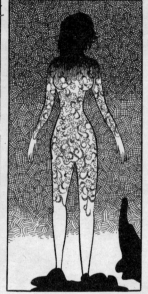

AAARGH!! AARGH!!

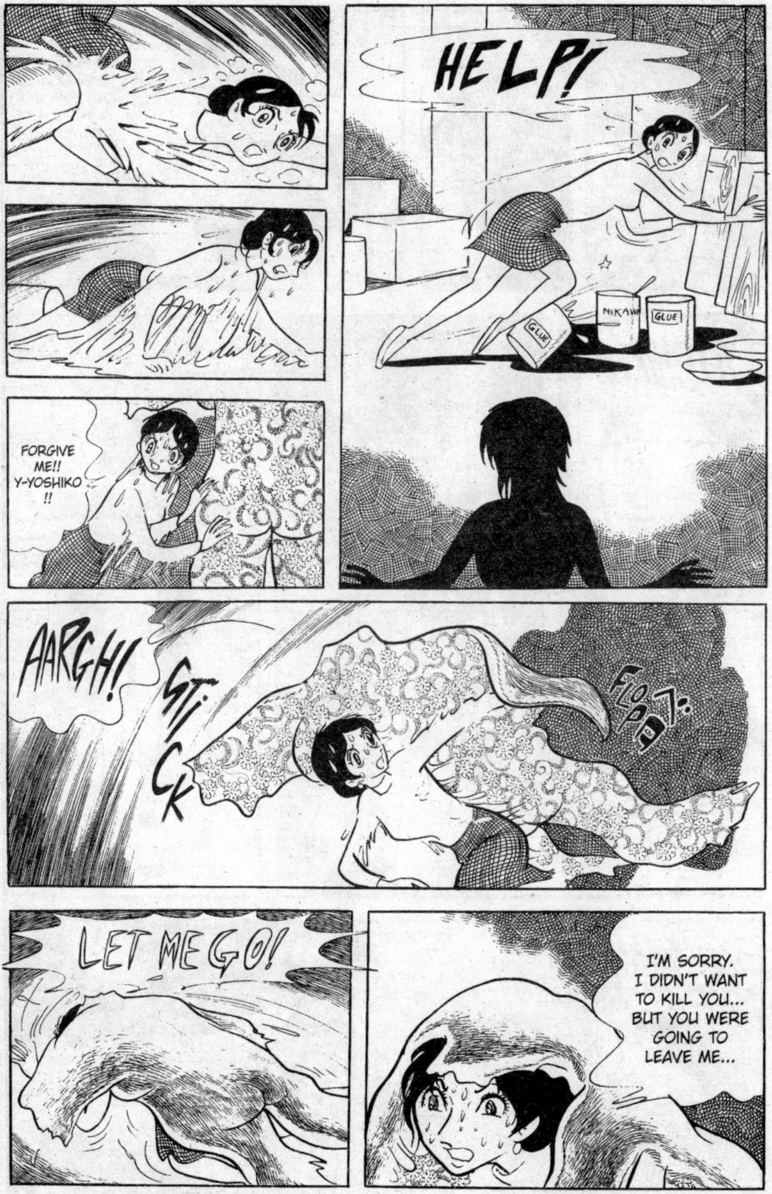
HELP!
NIKAWA
GLUE
GLUE
FORGIVE ME!! Y-YOSHIKO !!
FLOPPA
STICK
AARGH!
I'M SORRY. I DIDN'T WANT TO KILL YOU... BUT YOU WERE GOING TO LEAVE ME...
LET ME GO!

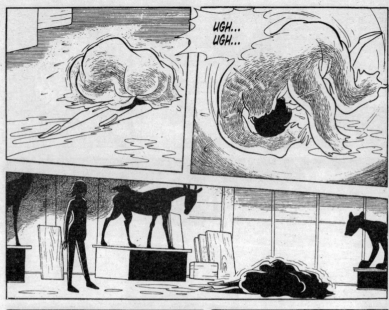

UGH... UGH...
SCREEECH
THERE ARE SO MANY BEAU-TIFUL PLACES.
WHY DO PEOPLE LONG FOR A LIFE IN TOKYO?
THEY'D BE DISAPPOINTED BY THE TWISTED CULTURE AND END UP TORMENTED AND KILLED LIKE YOSHIKO...

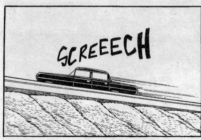

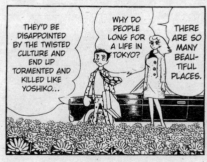

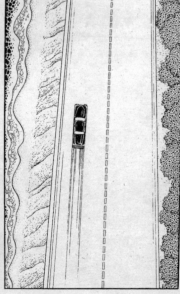

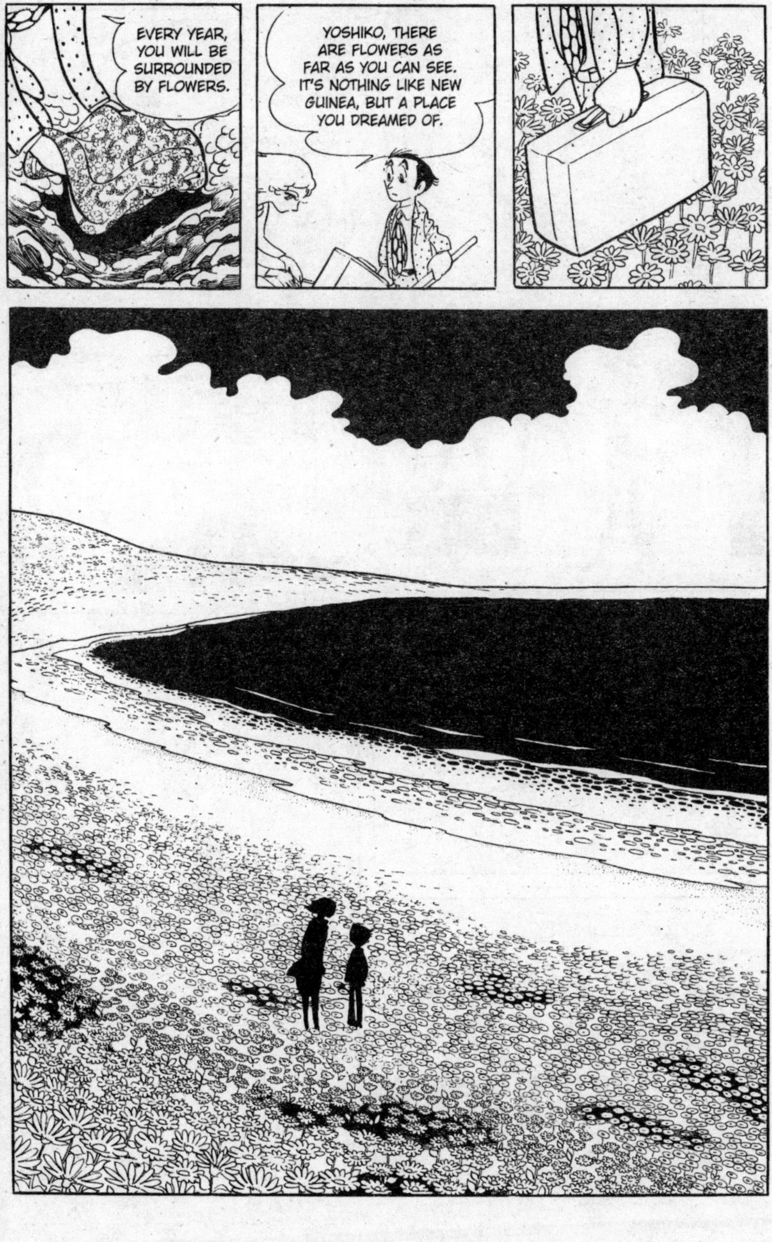
YOSHIKO, THERE ARE FLOWERS AS FAR AS YOU CAN SEE. IT'S NOTHING LIKE NEW GUINEA, BUT A PLACE YOU DREAMED OF.
EVERY YEAR, YOU WILL BE SURROUNDED BY FLOWERS.

# EPISODE 8
# **Mannequin**

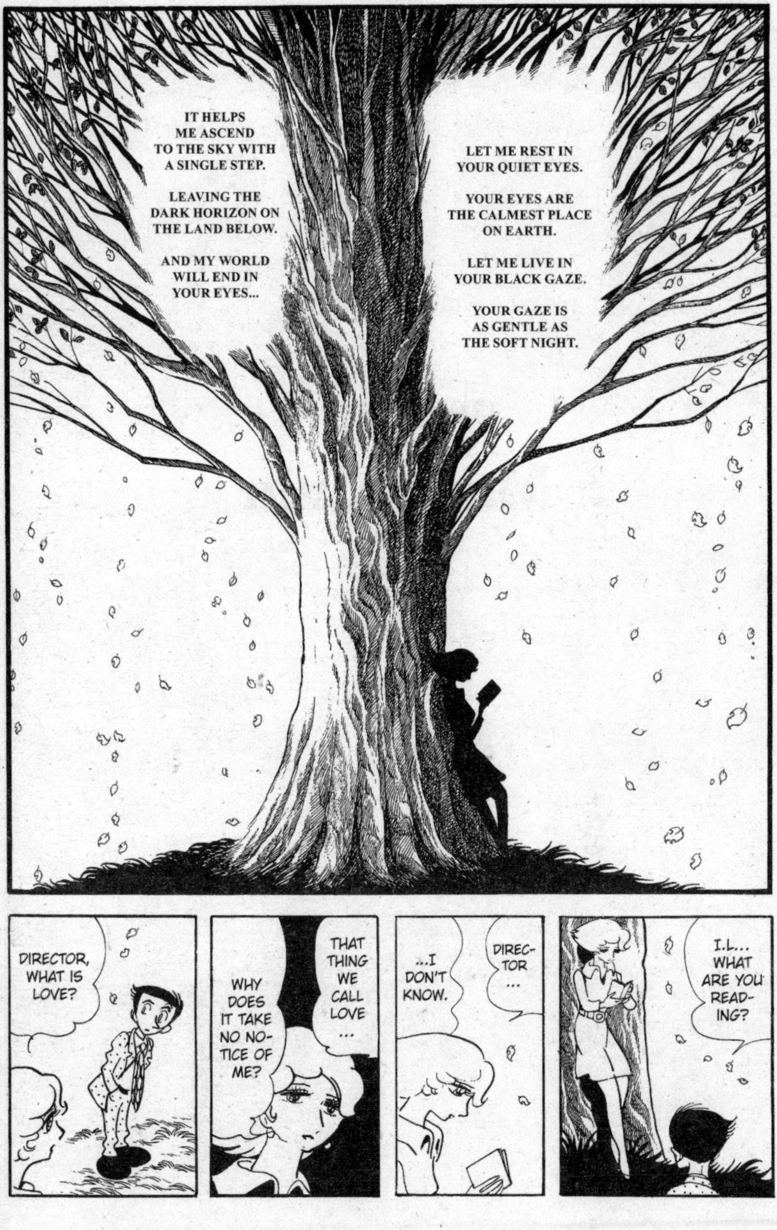
LET ME REST IN YOUR QUIET EYES.
YOUR EYES ARE THE CALMEST PLACE ON EARTH.
LET ME LIVE IN YOUR BLACK GAZE.
YOUR GAZE IS AS GENTLE AS THE SOFT NIGHT.
IT HELPS ME ASCEND TO THE SKY WITH A SINGLE STEP.
LEAVING THE DARK HORIZON ON THE LAND BELOW.
AND MY WORLD WILL END IN YOUR EYES...
I.L... WHAT ARE YOU READING?
DIRECTOR...
...I DON'T KNOW.
THAT THING WE CALL LOVE...
WHY DOES IT TAKE NO NOTICE OF ME?
DIRECTOR, WHAT IS LOVE?

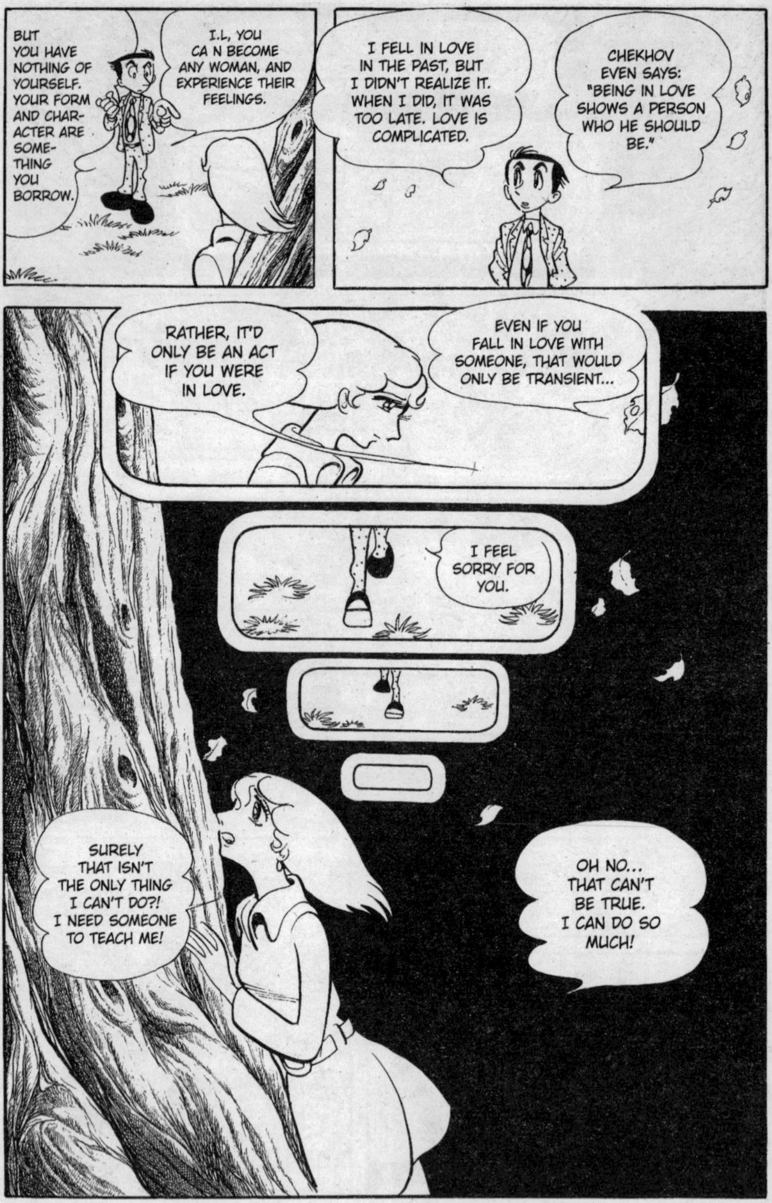
CHEKHOV EVEN SAYS: "BEING IN LOVE SHOWS A PERSON WHO HE SHOULD BE."
I FELL IN LOVE IN THE PAST, BUT I DIDN'T REALIZE IT. WHEN I DID, IT WAS TOO LATE. LOVE IS COMPLICATED.
I.L, YOU CA N BECOME ANY WOMAN, AND EXPERIENCE THEIR FEELINGS.
BUT YOU HAVE NOTHING OF YOURSELF. YOUR FORM AND CHARACTER ARE SOMETHING YOU BORROW.
EVEN IF YOU FALL IN LOVE WITH SOMEONE, THAT WOULD ONLY BE TRANSIENT...
RATHER, IT'D ONLY BE AN ACT IF YOU WERE IN LOVE.
I FEEL SORRY FOR YOU.
OH NO... THAT CAN'T BE TRUE. I CAN DO SO MUCH!
SURELY THAT ISN'T THE ONLY THING I CAN'T DO?! I NEED SOMEONE TO TEACH ME!

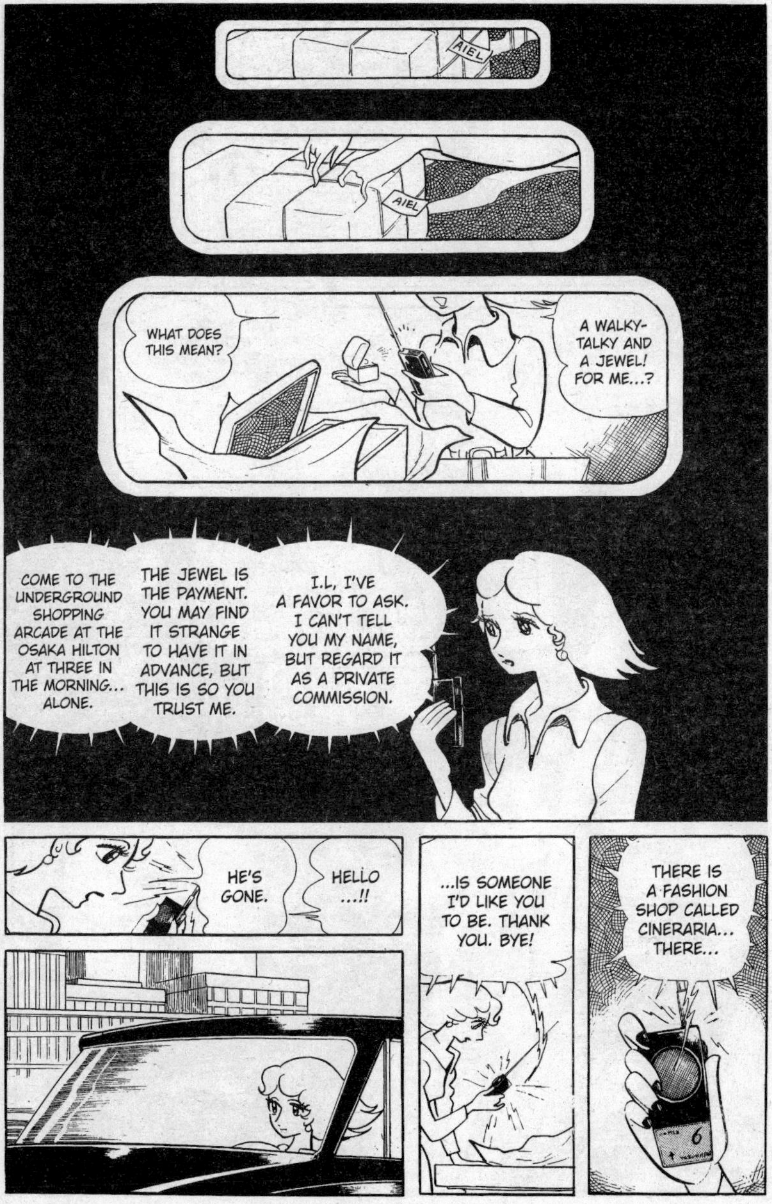
AIEL
AIEL
A WALKY-TALKY AND A JEWEL! FOR ME...?
WHAT DOES THIS MEAN?
I.L, I'VE A FAVOR TO ASK. I CAN'T TELL YOU MY NAME, BUT REGARD IT AS A PRIVATE COMMISSION.
THE JEWEL IS THE PAYMENT. YOU MAY FIND IT STRANGE TO HAVE IT IN ADVANCE, BUT THIS IS SO YOU TRUST ME.
COME TO THE UNDERGROUND SHOPPING ARCADE AT THE OSAKA HILTON AT THREE IN THE MORNING... ALONE.
THERE IS A FASHION SHOP CALLED CINERARIA... THERE...
...IS SOMEONE I'D LIKE YOU TO BE. THANK YOU. BYE!
HELLO ...!!
HE'S GONE.

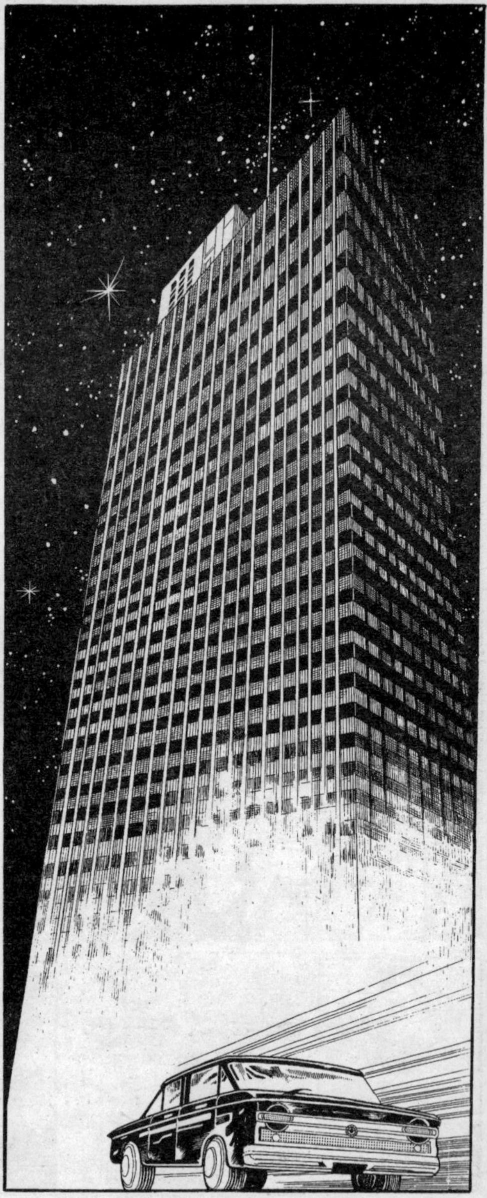

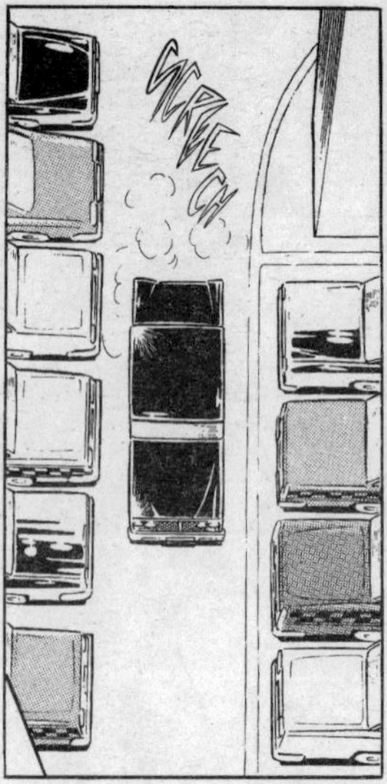
SCREECH

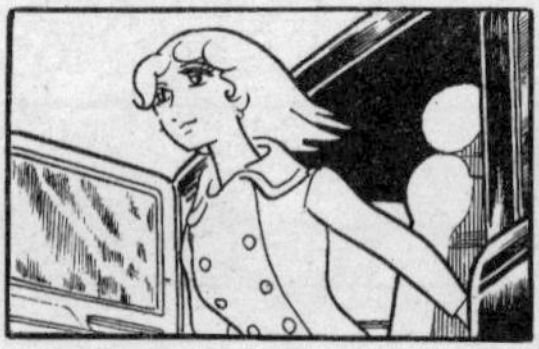

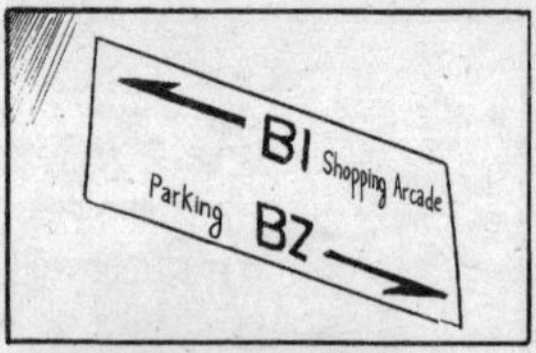
B1 Shopping Arcade
Parking B2

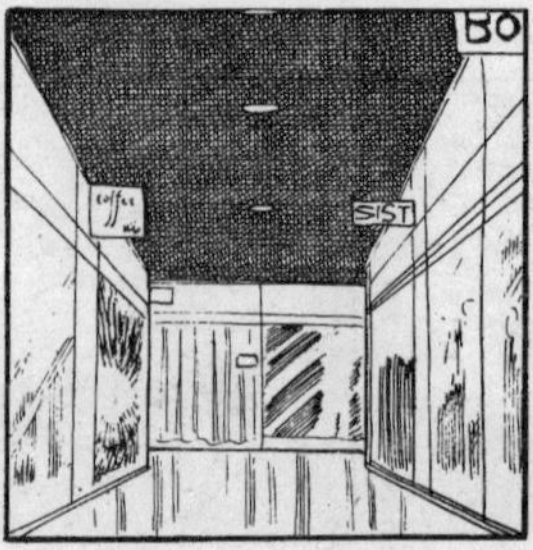
BO
SIST

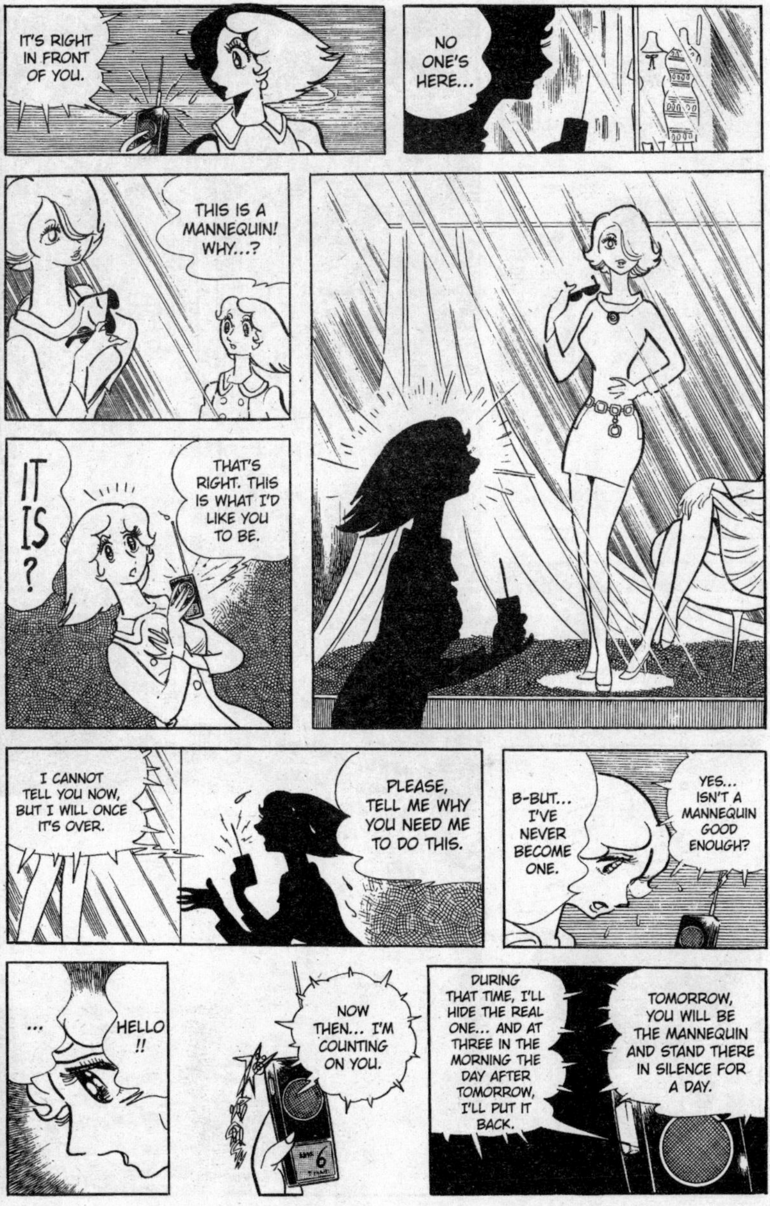
NO ONE'S HERE...
IT'S RIGHT IN FRONT OF YOU.
THIS IS A MANNEQUIN! WHY...?
THAT'S RIGHT. THIS IS WHAT I'D LIKE YOU TO BE.
IT IS?
YES... ISN'T A MANNEQUIN GOOD ENOUGH?
B-BUT... I'VE NEVER BECOME ONE.
PLEASE, TELL ME WHY YOU NEED ME TO DO THIS.
I CANNOT TELL YOU NOW, BUT I WILL ONCE IT'S OVER.
TOMORROW, YOU WILL BE THE MANNEQUIN AND STAND THERE IN SILENCE FOR A DAY.
DURING THAT TIME, I'LL HIDE THE REAL ONE... AND AT THREE IN THE MORNING THE DAY AFTER TOMORROW, I'LL PUT IT BACK.
NOW THEN... I'M COUNTING ON YOU.
HELLO !!
...

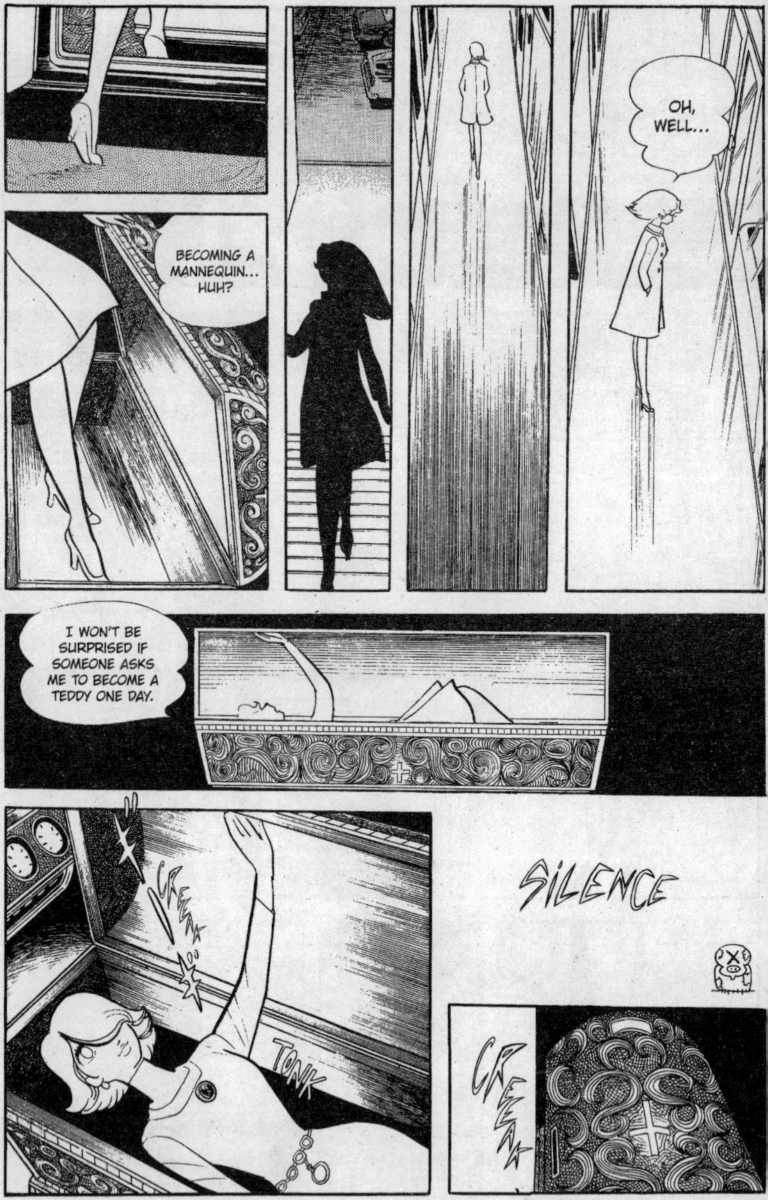
OH, WELL...
BECOMING A MANNEQUIN... HUH?
I WON'T BE SURPRISED IF SOMEONE ASKS ME TO BECOME A TEDDY ONE DAY.
SILENCE
CREEAK
CREEAK
TONK

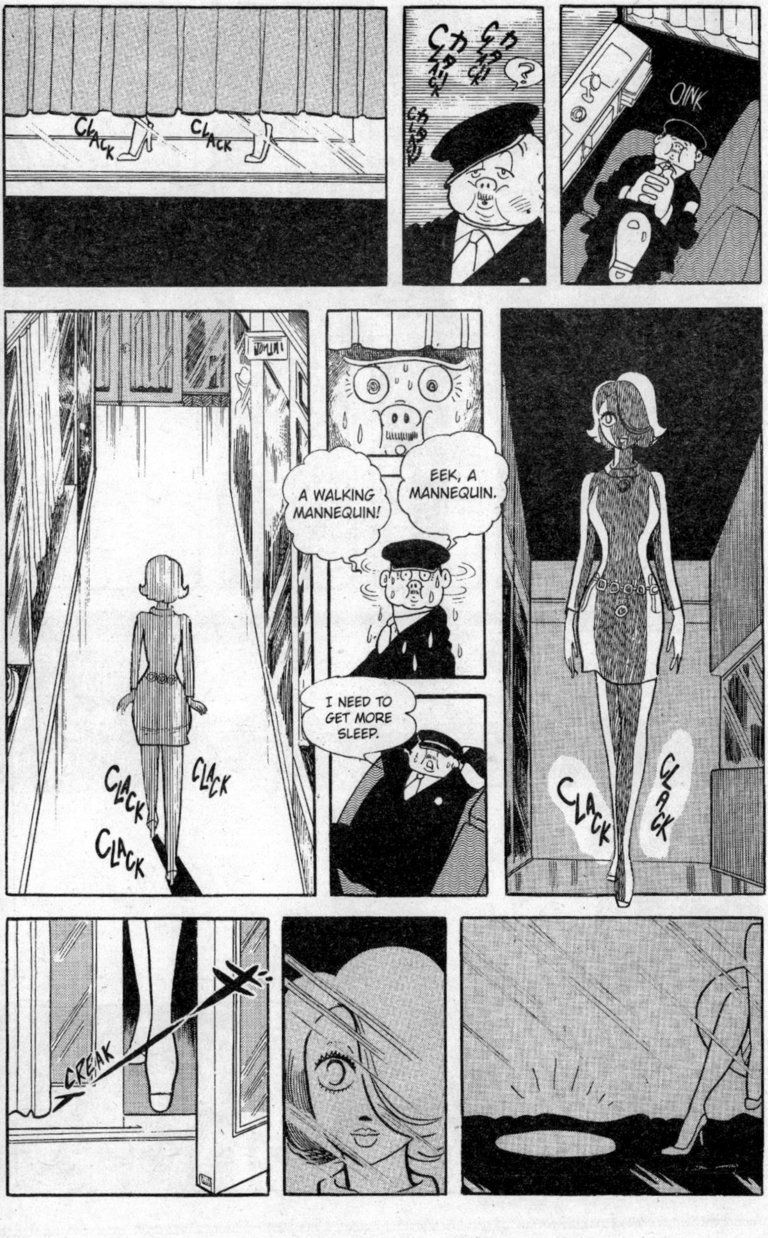
OINK
CLACK
CLACK
CLACK
?
CLACK
CLACK
CLACK
CLACK
EEK, A MANNEQUIN.
A WALKING MANNEQUIN!
I NEED TO GET MORE SLEEP.
CLACK
CLACK
CLACK
CREAK

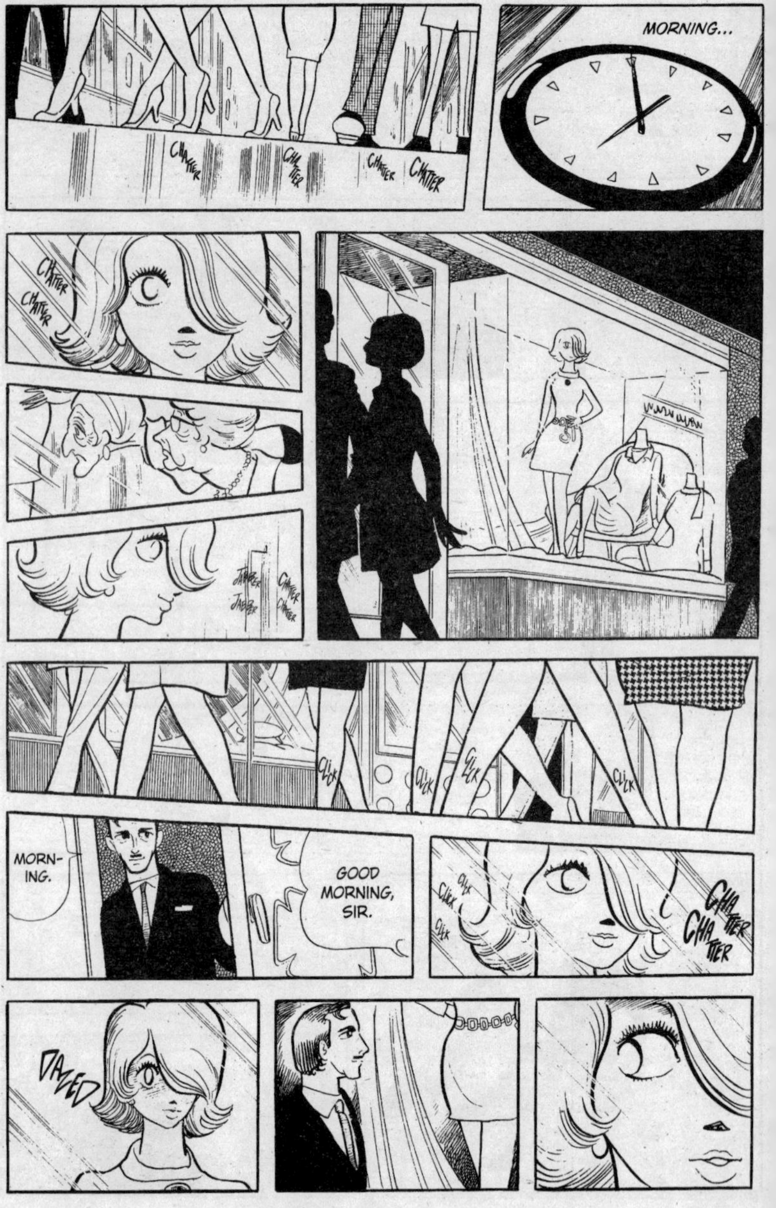
MORNING...
CHATTER
CHATTER
CHATTER
CHATTER
CHATTER
CHATTER
CHATTER
CHATTER
JABBER
JABBER
CLICK
CLICK
CLICK
CLICK
CHATTER
CHATTER
CLICK
CLICK
CLICK
GOOD MORNING, SIR.
MORN-ING.
DAZED

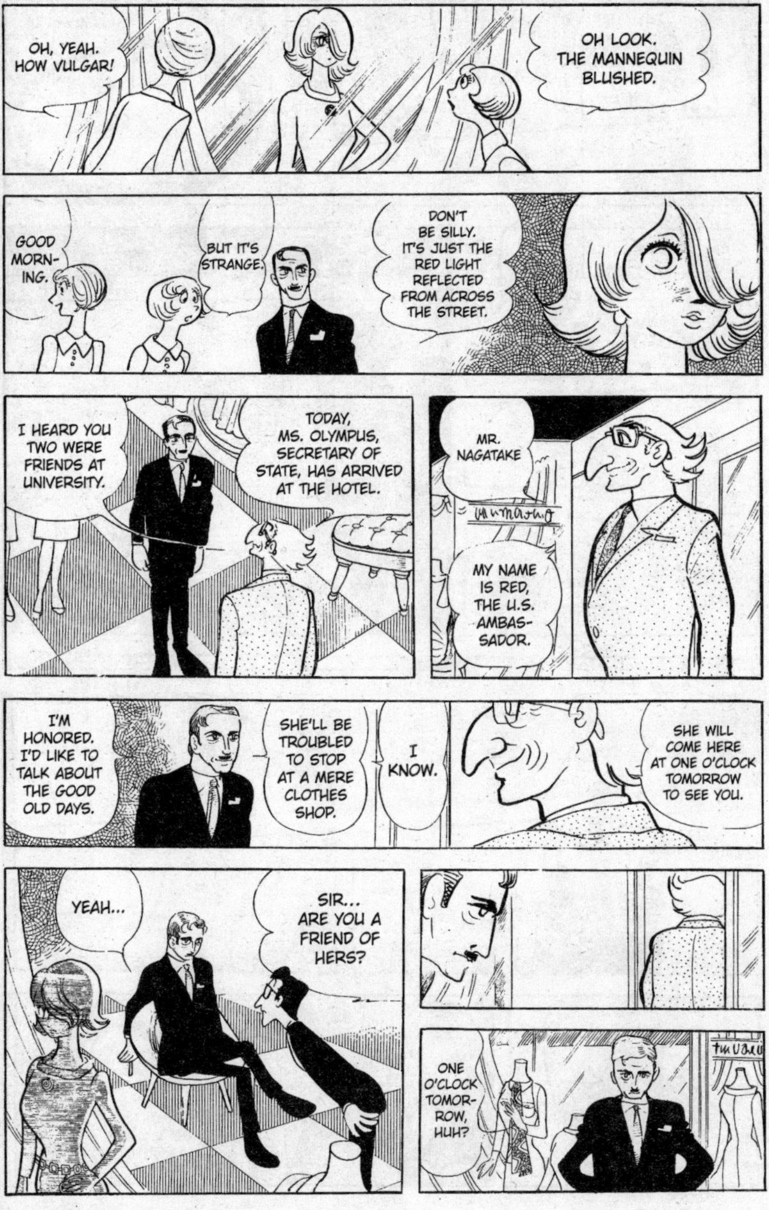
OH LOOK. THE MANNEQUIN BLUSHED.
OH, YEAH. HOW VULGAR!
DON'T BE SILLY. IT'S JUST THE RED LIGHT REFLECTED FROM ACROSS THE STREET.
BUT IT'S STRANGE.
GOOD MORN-ING.
MR. NAGATAKE
MY NAME IS RED, THE U.S. AMBAS-SADOR.
TODAY, MS. OLYMPUS, SECRETARY OF STATE, HAS ARRIVED AT THE HOTEL.
I HEARD YOU TWO WERE FRIENDS AT UNIVERSITY.
SHE WILL COME HERE AT ONE O'CLOCK TOMORROW TO SEE YOU.
I KNOW.
SHE'LL BE TROUBLED TO STOP AT A MERE CLOTHES SHOP.
I'M HONORED. I'D LIKE TO TALK ABOUT THE GOOD OLD DAYS.
ONE O'CLOCK TOMOR-ROW, HUH?
SIR... ARE YOU A FRIEND OF HERS?
YEAH...

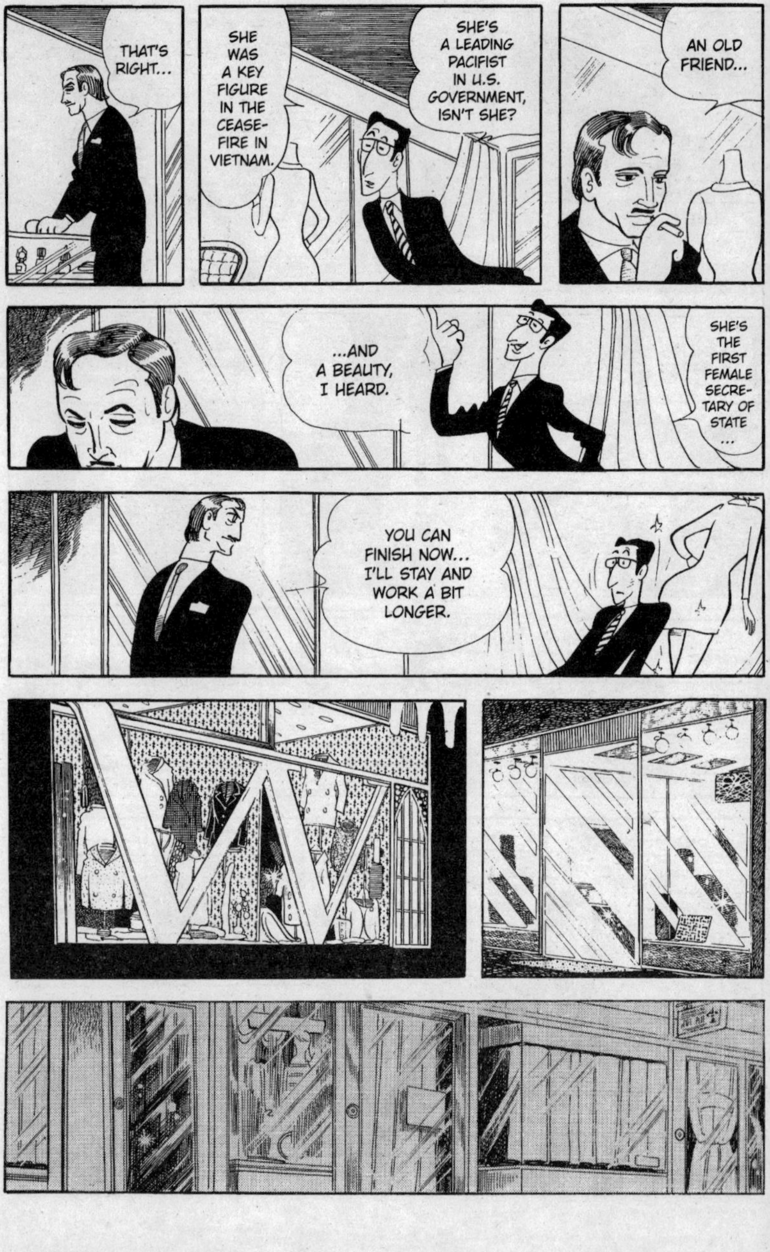
AN OLD FRIEND...
SHE'S A LEADING PACIFIST IN U.S. GOVERNMENT, ISN'T SHE?
SHE WAS A KEY FIGURE IN THE CEASE-FIRE IN VIETNAM.
THAT'S RIGHT...
SHE'S THE FIRST FEMALE SECRETARY OF STATE ...
...AND A BEAUTY, I HEARD.
YOU CAN FINISH NOW... I'LL STAY AND WORK A BIT LONGER.

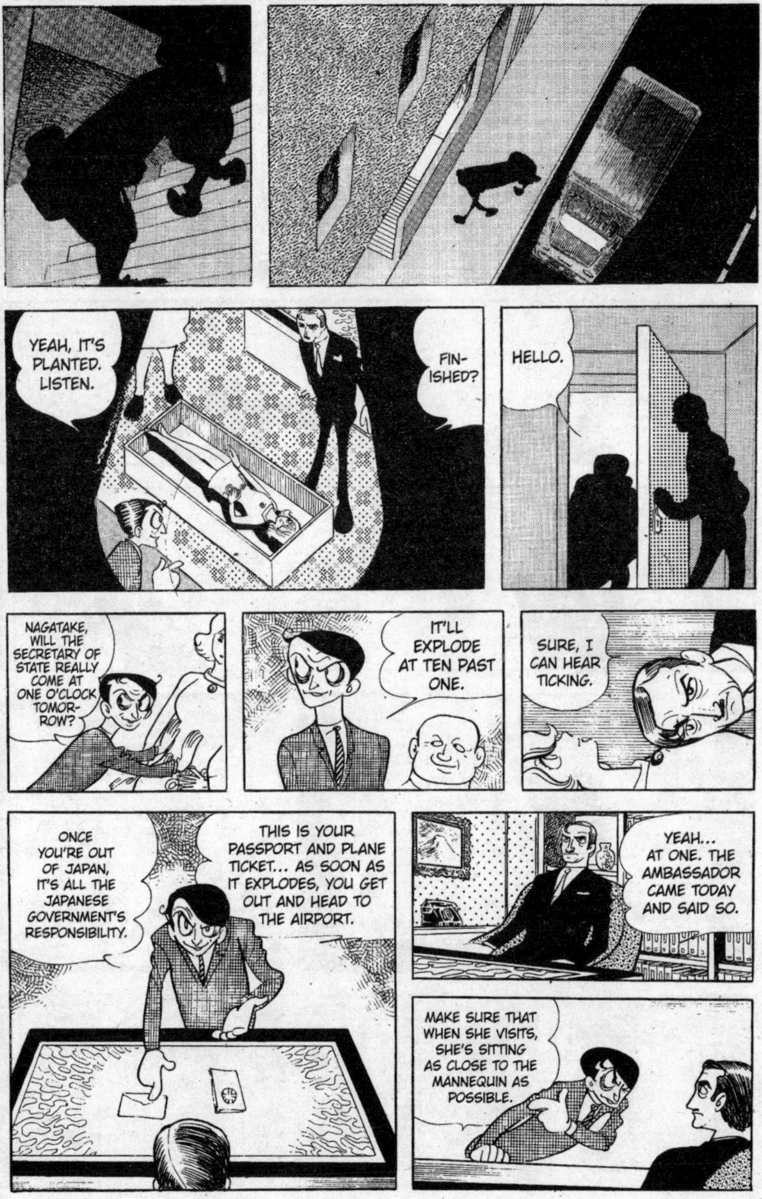
HELLO.
FIN-ISHED?
YEAH, IT'S PLANTED. LISTEN.
SURE, I CAN HEAR TICKING.
IT'LL EXPLODE AT TEN PAST ONE.
NAGATAKE, WILL THE SECRETARY OF STATE REALLY COME AT ONE O'CLOCK TOMOR-ROW?
YEAH... AT ONE. THE AMBASSADOR CAME TODAY AND SAID SO.
MAKE SURE THAT WHEN SHE VISITS, SHE'S SITTING AS CLOSE TO THE MANNEQUIN AS POSSIBLE.
THIS IS YOUR PASSPORT AND PLANE TICKET... AS SOON AS IT EXPLODES, YOU GET OUT AND HEAD TO THE AIRPORT.
ONCE YOU'RE OUT OF JAPAN, IT'S ALL THE JAPANESE GOVERNMENT'S RESPONSIBILITY.

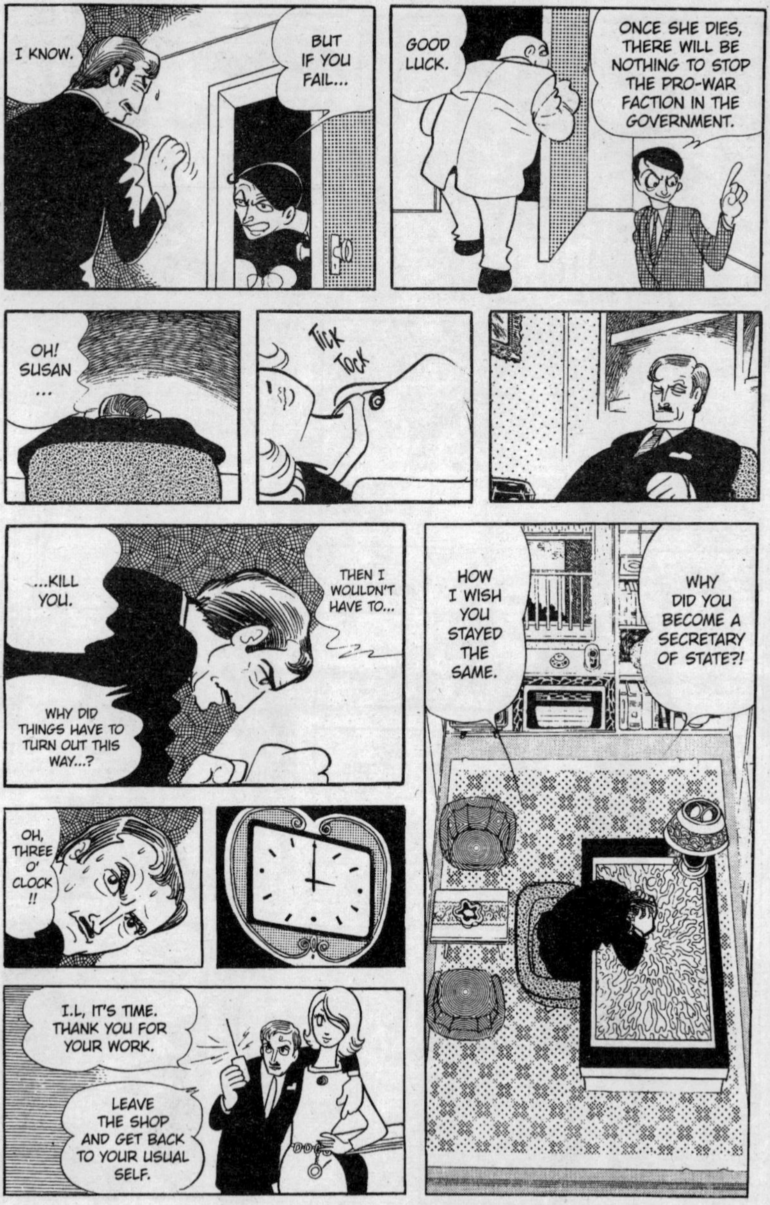
ONCE SHE DIES, THERE WILL BE NOTHING TO STOP THE PRO-WAR FACTION IN THE GOVERNMENT.
GOOD LUCK.
BUT IF YOU FAIL...
I KNOW.
TICK TOCK
OH! SUSAN ...
WHY DID YOU BECOME A SECRETARY OF STATE?!
HOW I WISH YOU STAYED THE SAME.
THEN I WOULDN'T HAVE TO...
...KILL YOU.
WHY DID THINGS HAVE TO TURN OUT THIS WAY...?
OH, THREE O' CLOCK !!
I.L, IT'S TIME. THANK YOU FOR YOUR WORK.
LEAVE THE SHOP AND GET BACK TO YOUR USUAL SELF.

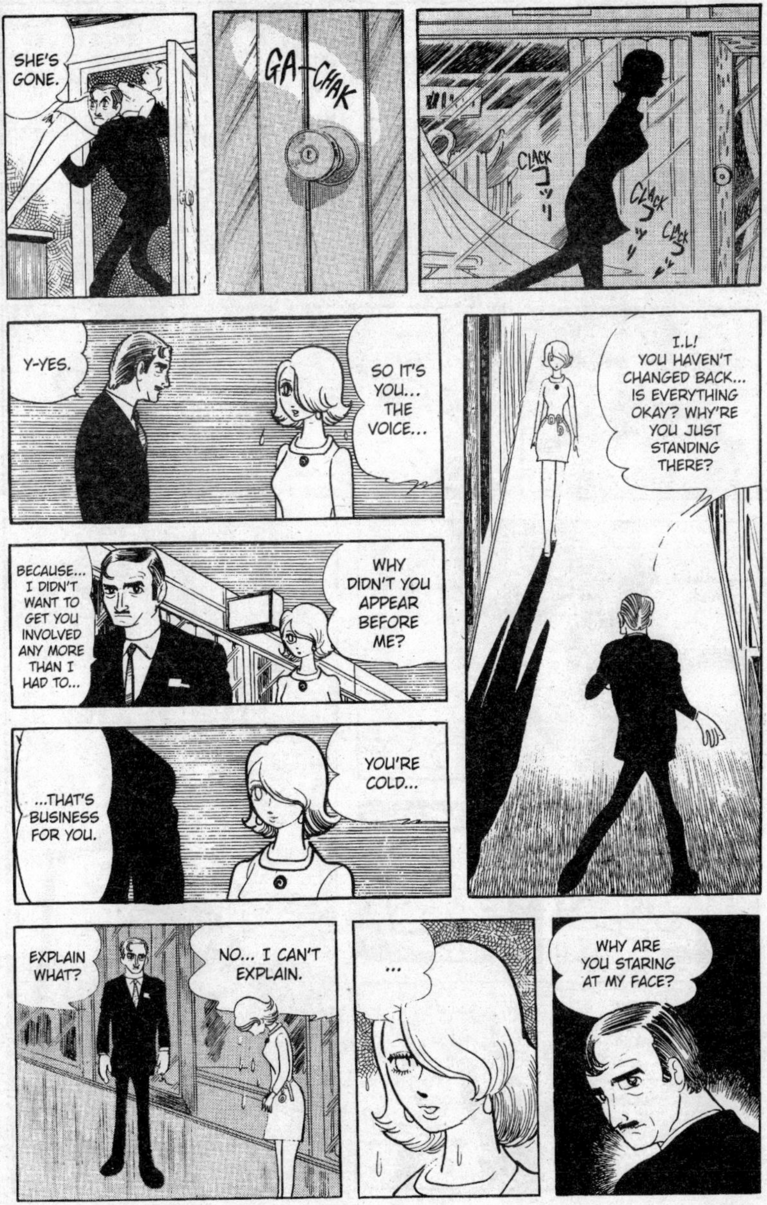
CLACK
CLACK
CLACK
GA-CHAK
SHE'S GONE.
I.L! YOU HAVEN'T CHANGED BACK... IS EVERYTHING OKAY? WHY'RE YOU JUST STANDING THERE?
SO IT'S YOU... THE VOICE...
Y-YES.
WHY DIDN'T YOU APPEAR BEFORE ME?
BECAUSE... I DIDN'T WANT TO GET YOU INVOLVED ANY MORE THAN I HAD TO...
YOU'RE COLD...
...THAT'S BUSINESS FOR YOU.
WHY ARE YOU STARING AT MY FACE?
...
NO... I CAN'T EXPLAIN.
EXPLAIN WHAT?

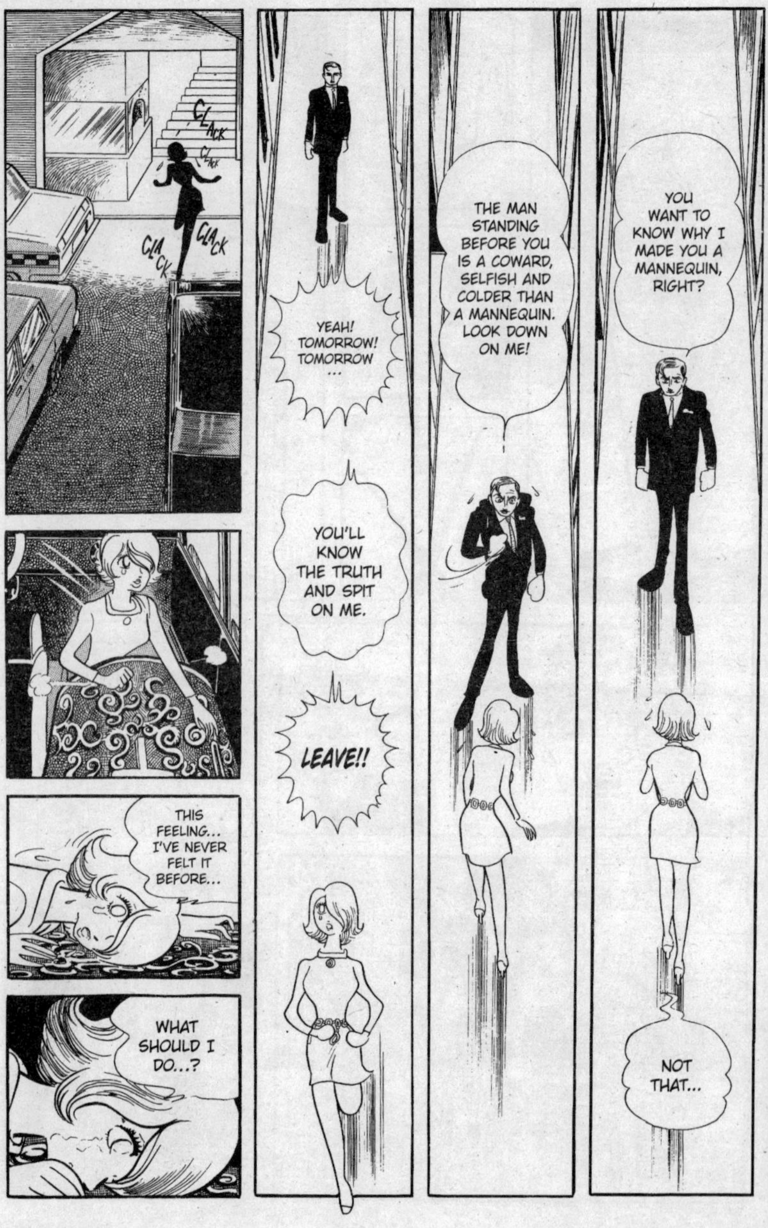
YOU WANT TO KNOW WHY I MADE YOU A MANNEQUIN, RIGHT?
NOT THAT...
THE MAN STANDING BEFORE YOU IS A COWARD, SELFISH AND COLDER THAN A MANNEQUIN. LOOK DOWN ON ME!
YEAH! TOMORROW! TOMORROW ...
YOU'LL KNOW THE TRUTH AND SPIT ON ME.
LEAVE!!
CLACK
CLACK
CLACK
CLACK
THIS FEELING... I'VE NEVER FELT IT BEFORE...
WHAT SHOULD I DO...?

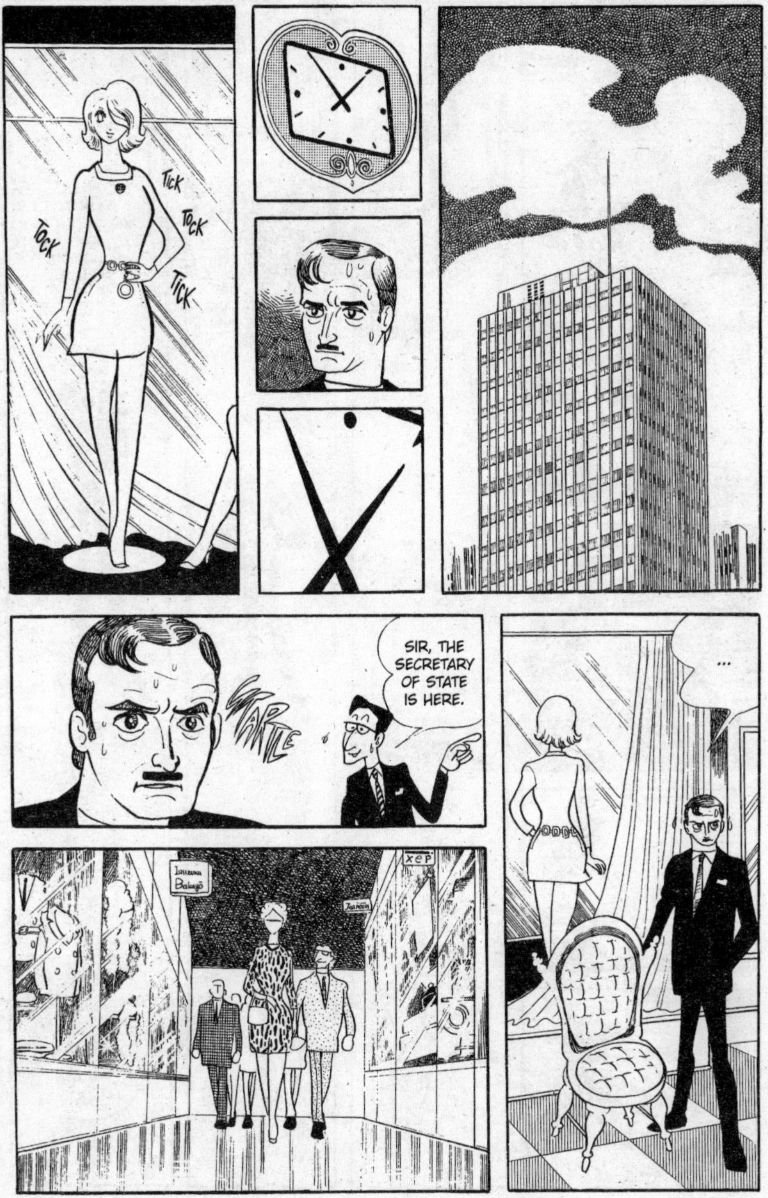
TICK
TOCK
TOCK
TICK
...
SIR, THE SECRETARY OF STATE IS HERE.
STARTLE

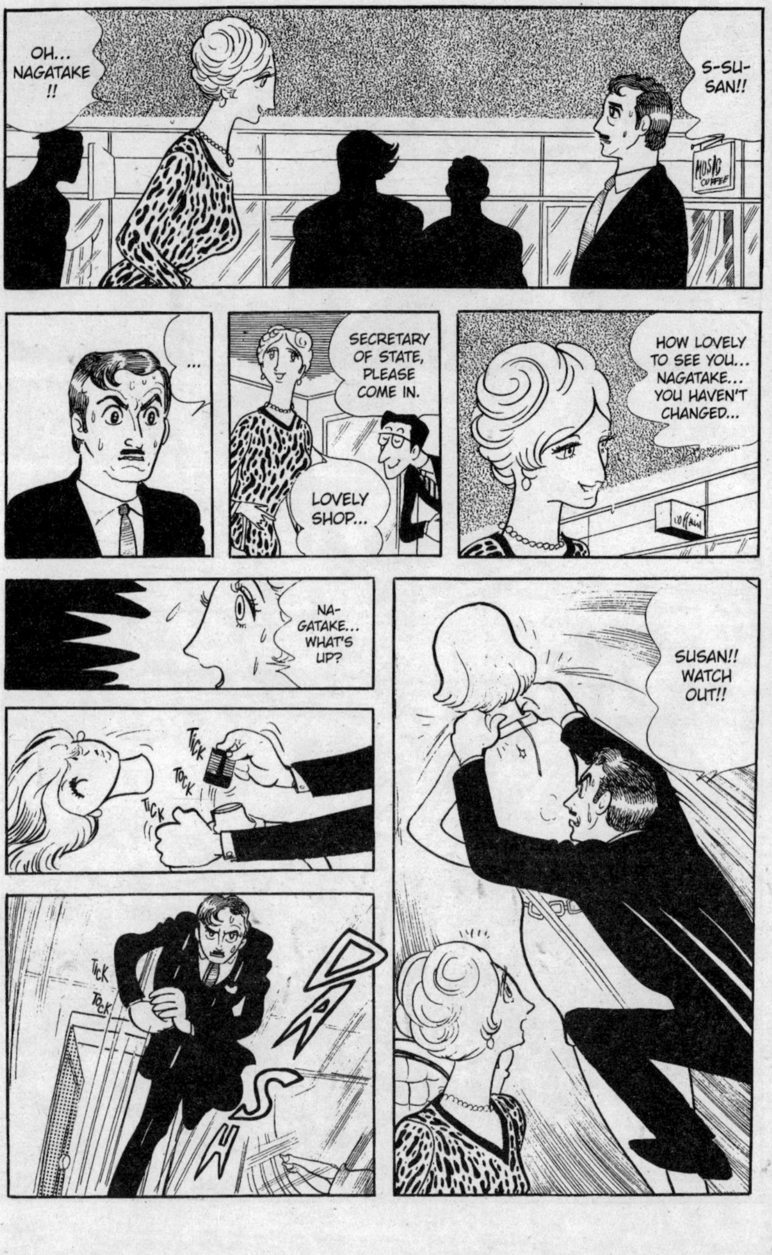
S-SU-SAN!!
OH... NAGATAKE !!
HOW LOVELY TO SEE YOU... NAGATAKE... YOU HAVEN'T CHANGED...
SECRETARY OF STATE, PLEASE COME IN.
LOVELY SHOP...
...
SUSAN!! WATCH OUT!!
NA-GATAKE... WHAT'S UP?
TICK
TOCK
TICK
TICK
TOCK
DASH

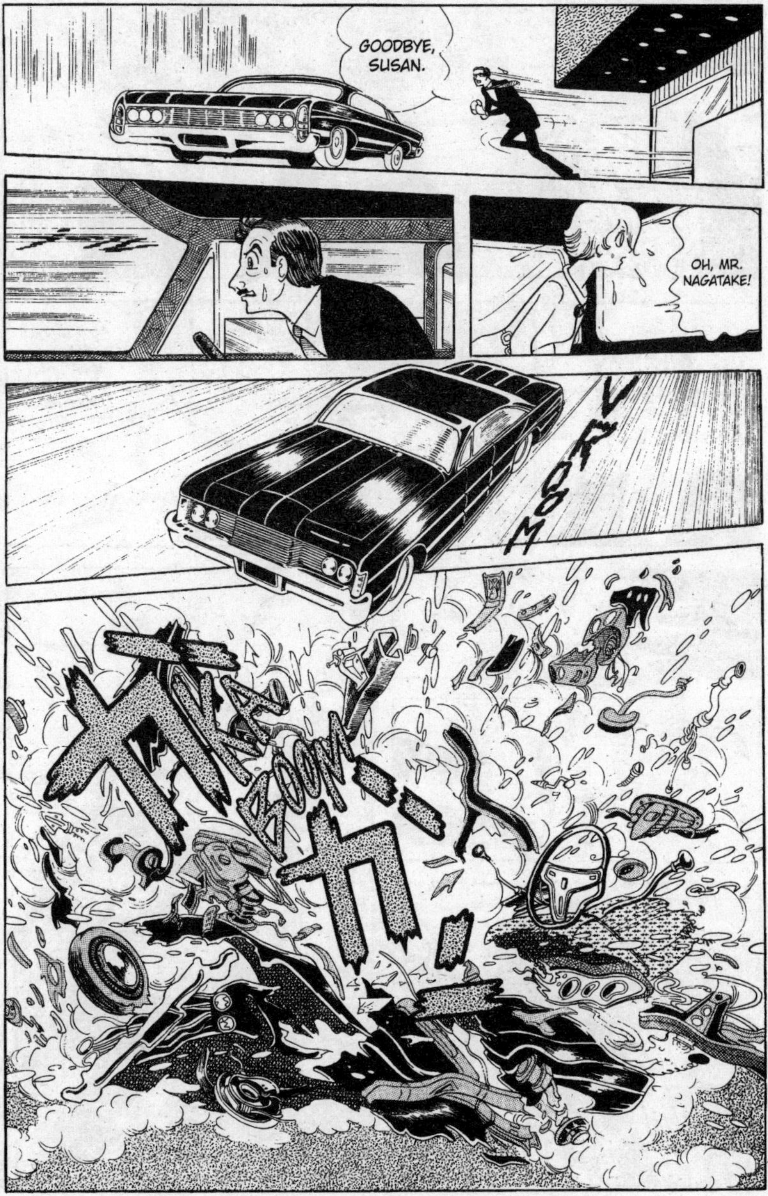
GOODBYE, SUSAN.
OH, MR. NAGATAKE!
VROOM
KA BOOM

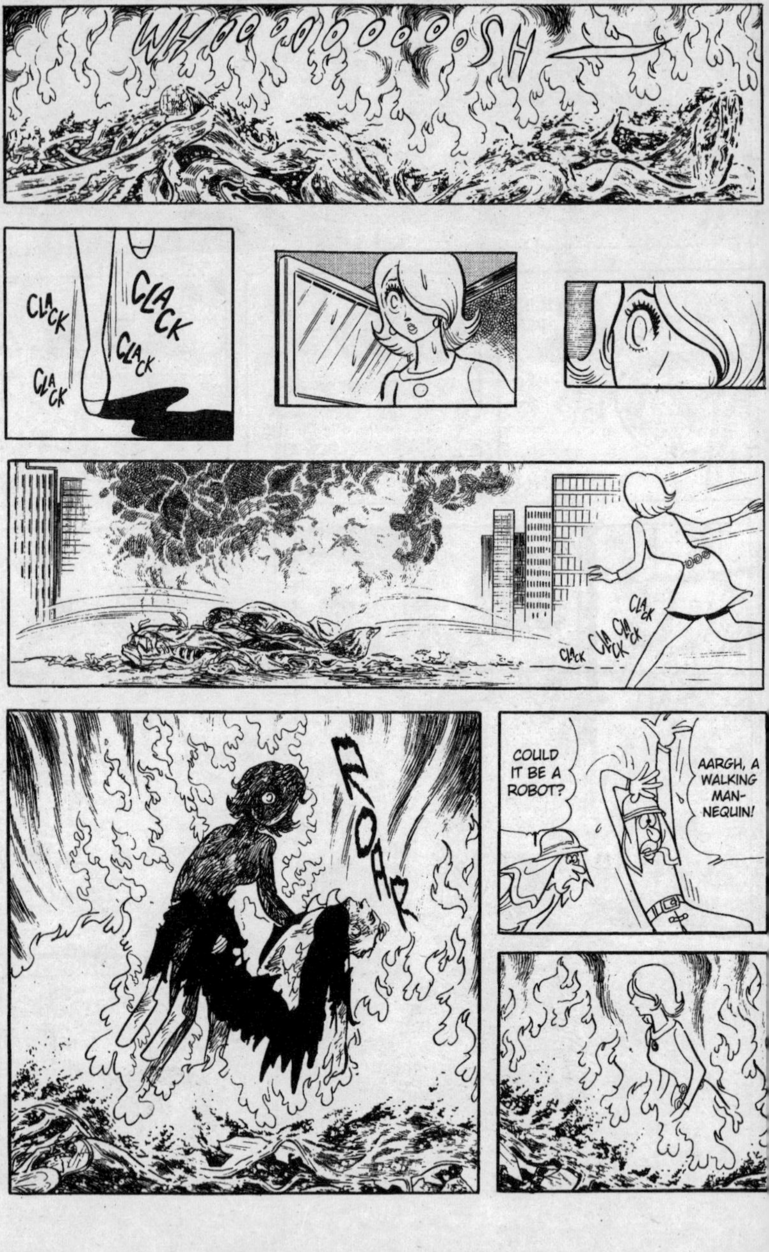
WHOOOOOOOOSH
CLACK
CLACK
CLACK
CLACK
CLACK
CLACK
CLACK
CLACK
AARGH, A WALKING MAN-NEQUIN!
COULD IT BE A ROBOT?
ROAR

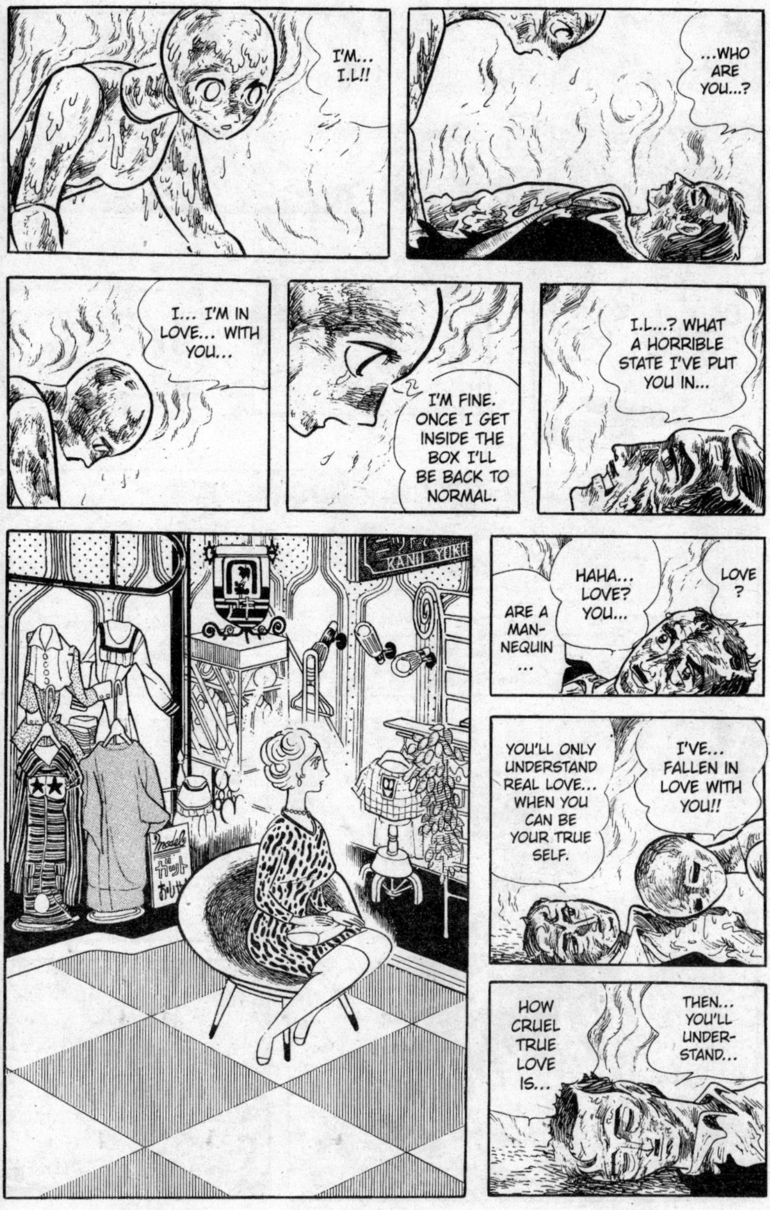
...WHO ARE YOU...?
I'M... I.L!!
I.L...? WHAT A HORRIBLE STATE I'VE PUT YOU IN...
I'M FINE. ONCE I GET INSIDE THE BOX I'LL BE BACK TO NORMAL.
I... I'M IN LOVE... WITH YOU...
LOVE?
HAHA... LOVE? YOU...
ARE A MANNEQUIN...
I'VE... FALLEN IN LOVE WITH YOU!!
YOU'LL ONLY UNDERSTAND REAL LOVE... WHEN YOU CAN BE YOUR TRUE SELF.
THEN... YOU'LL UNDERSTAND...
HOW CRUEL TRUE LOVE IS...

# EPISODE 9
# The Law of Glory

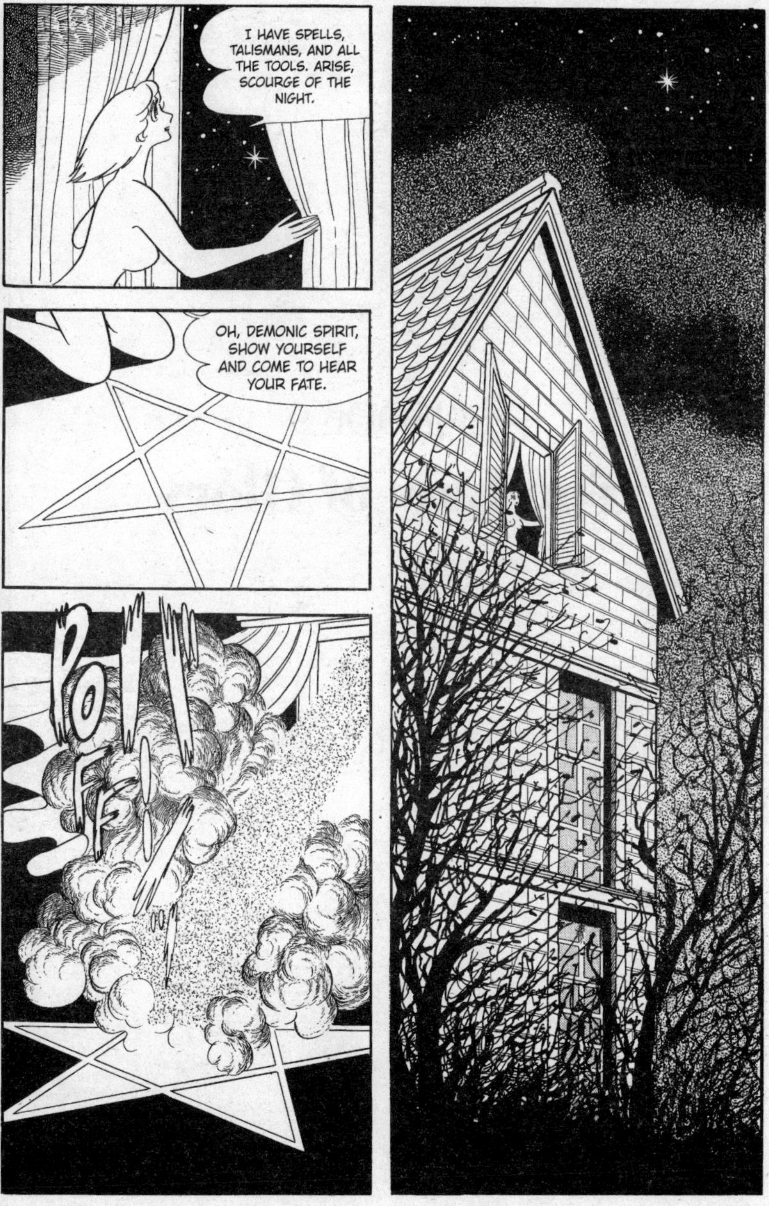
I HAVE SPELLS, TALISMANS, AND ALL THE TOOLS. ARISE, SCOURGE OF THE NIGHT.
OH, DEMONIC SPIRIT, SHOW YOURSELF AND COME TO HEAR YOUR FATE.
POFF

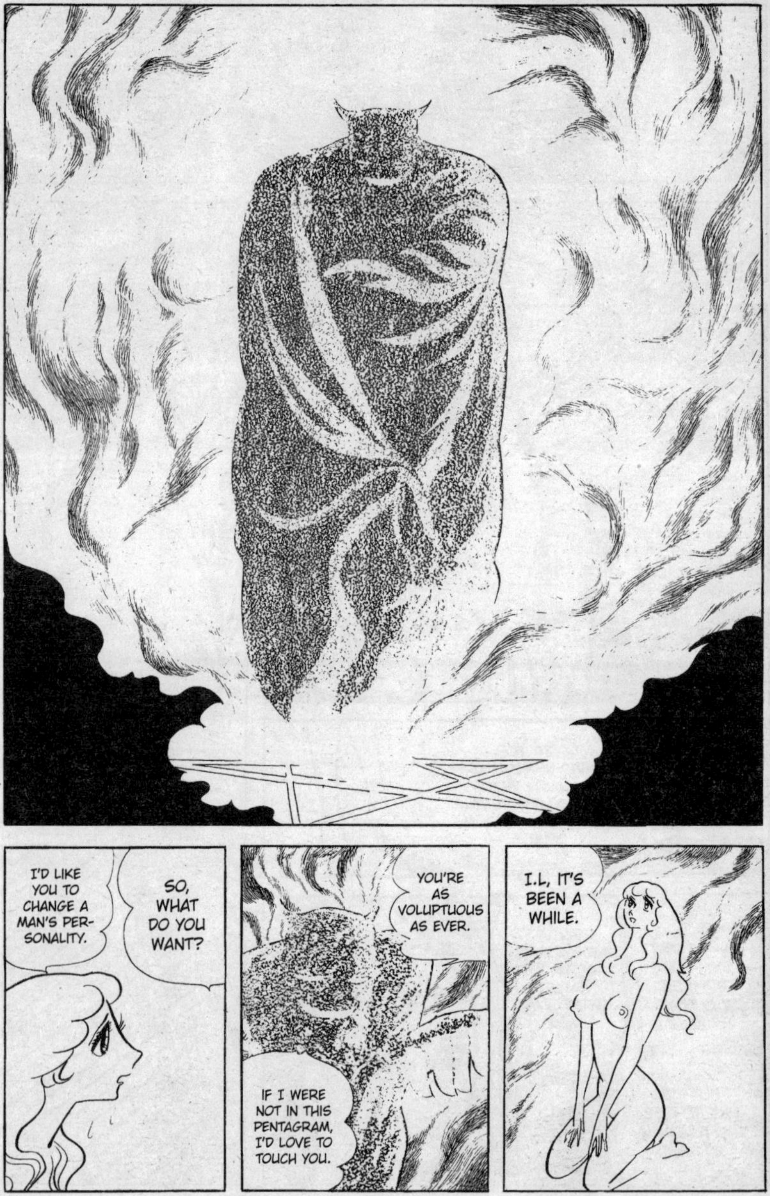
I.L, IT'S BEEN A WHILE.
YOU'RE AS VOLUPTUOUS AS EVER.
IF I WERE NOT IN THIS PENTAGRAM, I'D LOVE TO TOUCH YOU.
SO, WHAT DO YOU WANT?
I'D LIKE YOU TO CHANGE A MAN'S PER-SONALITY.

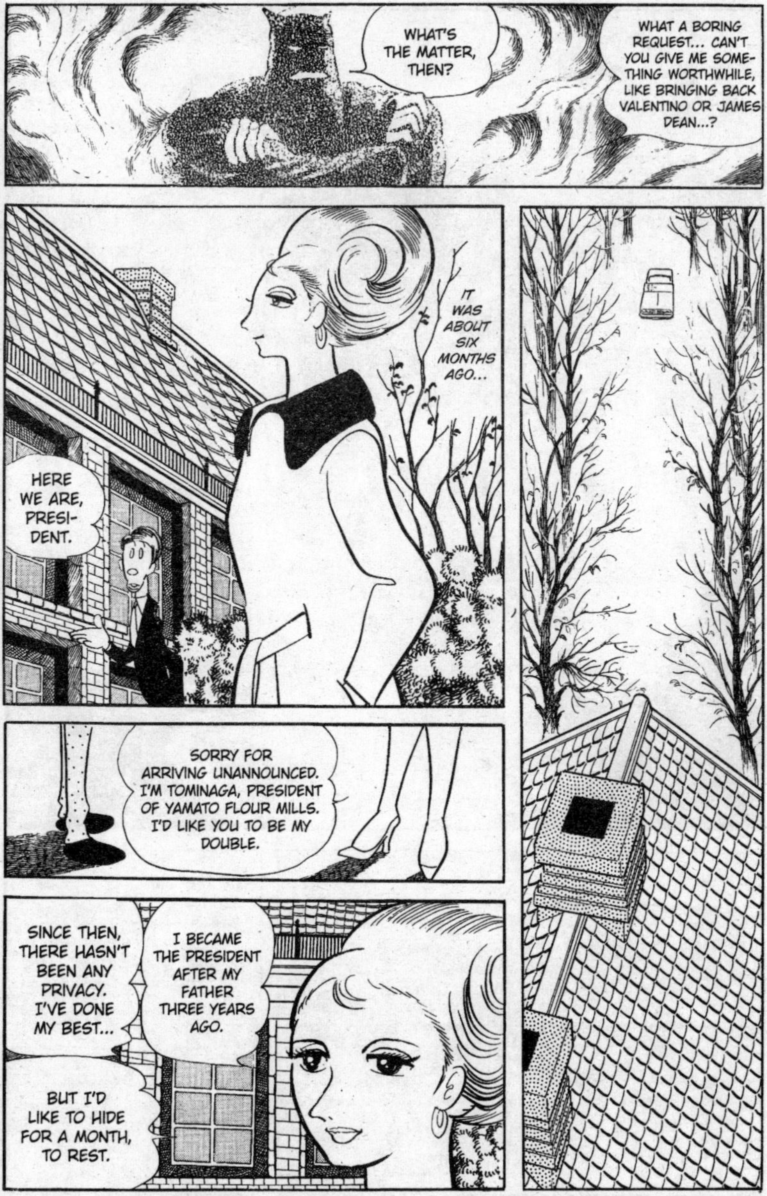
WHAT A BORING REQUEST... CAN'T YOU GIVE ME SOME-THING WORTHWHILE, LIKE BRINGING BACK VALENTINO OR JAMES DEAN...?
WHAT'S THE MATTER, THEN?
IT WAS ABOUT SIX MONTHS AGO...
HERE WE ARE, PRESI-DENT.
SORRY FOR ARRIVING UNANNOUNCED. I'M TOMINAGA, PRESIDENT OF YAMATO FLOUR MILLS. I'D LIKE YOU TO BE MY DOUBLE.
I BECAME THE PRESIDENT AFTER MY FATHER THREE YEARS AGO.
SINCE THEN, THERE HASN'T BEEN ANY PRIVACY. I'VE DONE MY BEST...
BUT I'D LIKE TO HIDE FOR A MONTH, TO REST.

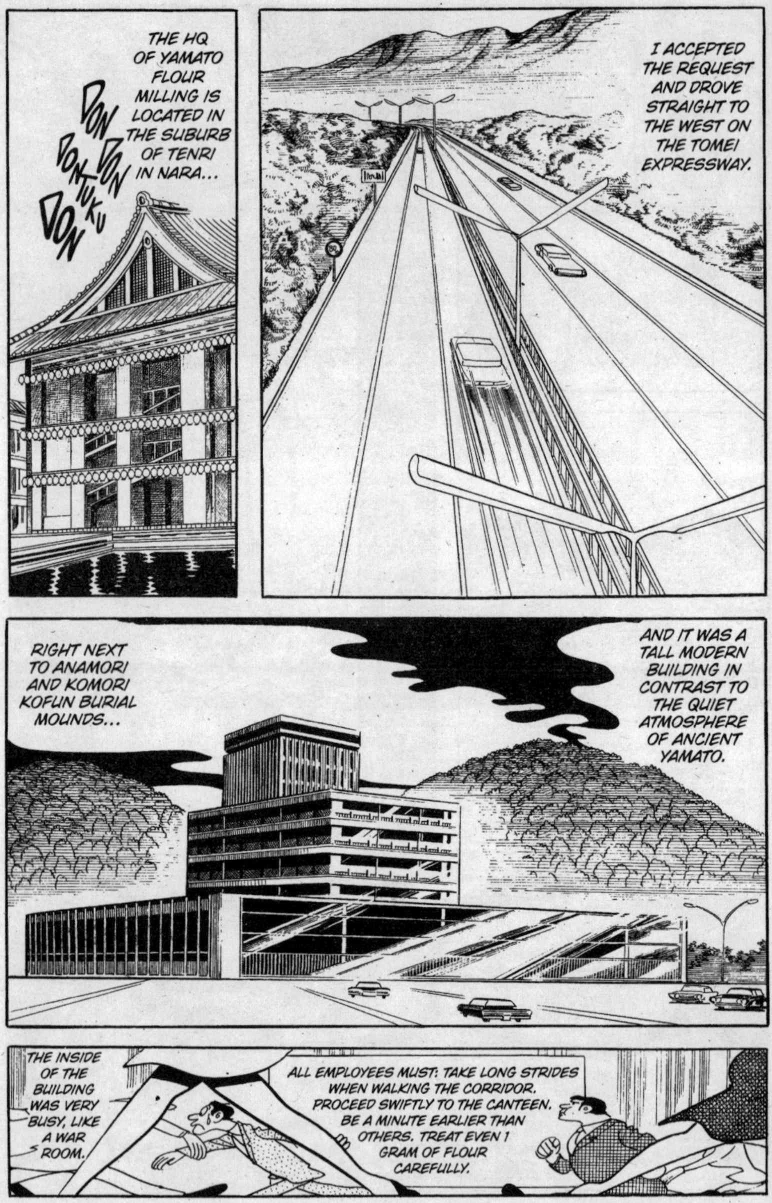
I ACCEPTED THE REQUEST AND DROVE STRAIGHT TO THE WEST ON THE TOMEI EXPRESSWAY.
THE HQ OF YAMATO FLOUR MILLING IS LOCATED IN THE SUBURB OF TENRI IN NARA...
DON DON DONTUKU DON
RIGHT NEXT TO ANAMORI AND KOMORI KOFUN BURIAL MOUNDS...
AND IT WAS A TALL MODERN BUILDING IN CONTRAST TO THE QUIET ATMOSPHERE OF ANCIENT YAMATO.
ALL EMPLOYEES MUST: TAKE LONG STRIDES WHEN WALKING THE CORRIDOR. PROCEED SWIFTLY TO THE CANTEEN. BE A MINUTE EARLIER THAN OTHERS. TREAT EVEN 1 GRAM OF FLOUR CAREFULLY.
THE INSIDE OF THE BUILDING WAS VERY BUSY, LIKE A WAR ROOM.

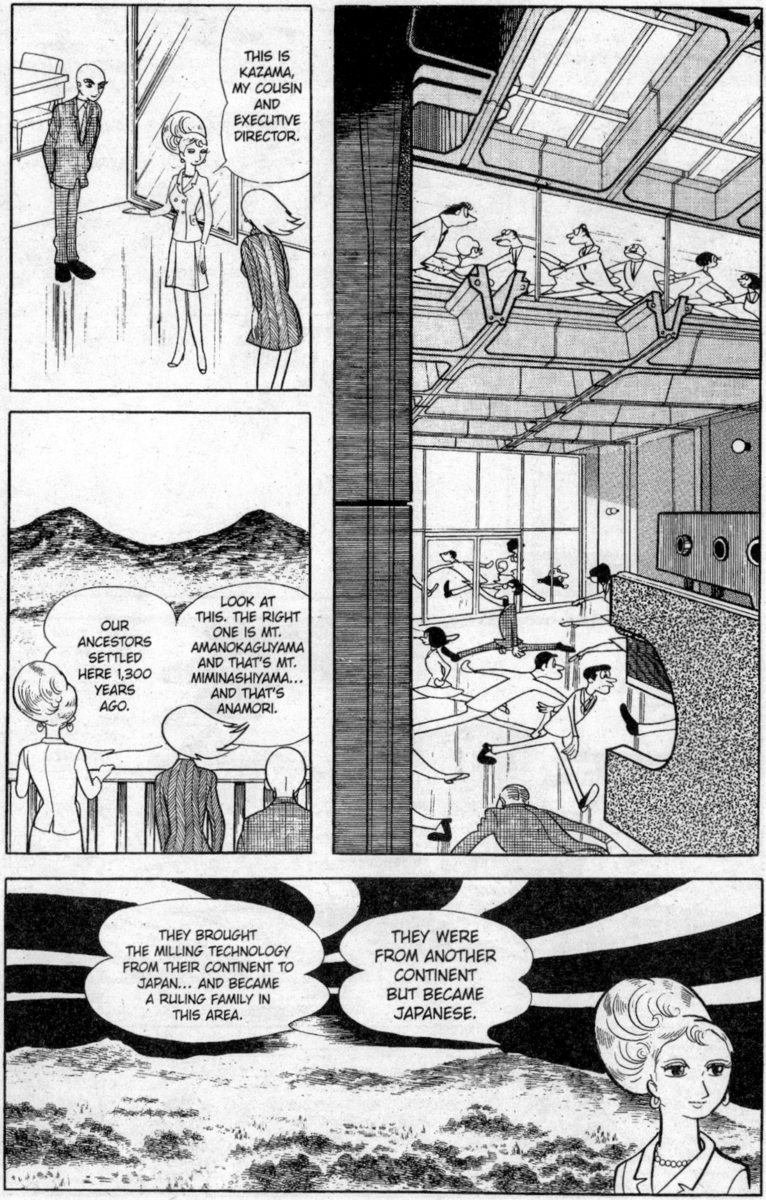
THIS IS KAZAMA, MY COUSIN AND EXECUTIVE DIRECTOR.
LOOK AT THIS. THE RIGHT ONE IS MT. AMANOKAGUYAMA AND THAT'S MT. MIMINASHIYAMA... AND THAT'S ANAMORI.
OUR ANCESTORS SETTLED HERE 1,300 YEARS AGO.
THEY WERE FROM ANOTHER CONTINENT BUT BECAME JAPANESE.
THEY BROUGHT THE MILLING TECHNOLOGY FROM THEIR CONTINENT TO JAPAN... AND BECAME A RULING FAMILY IN THIS AREA.

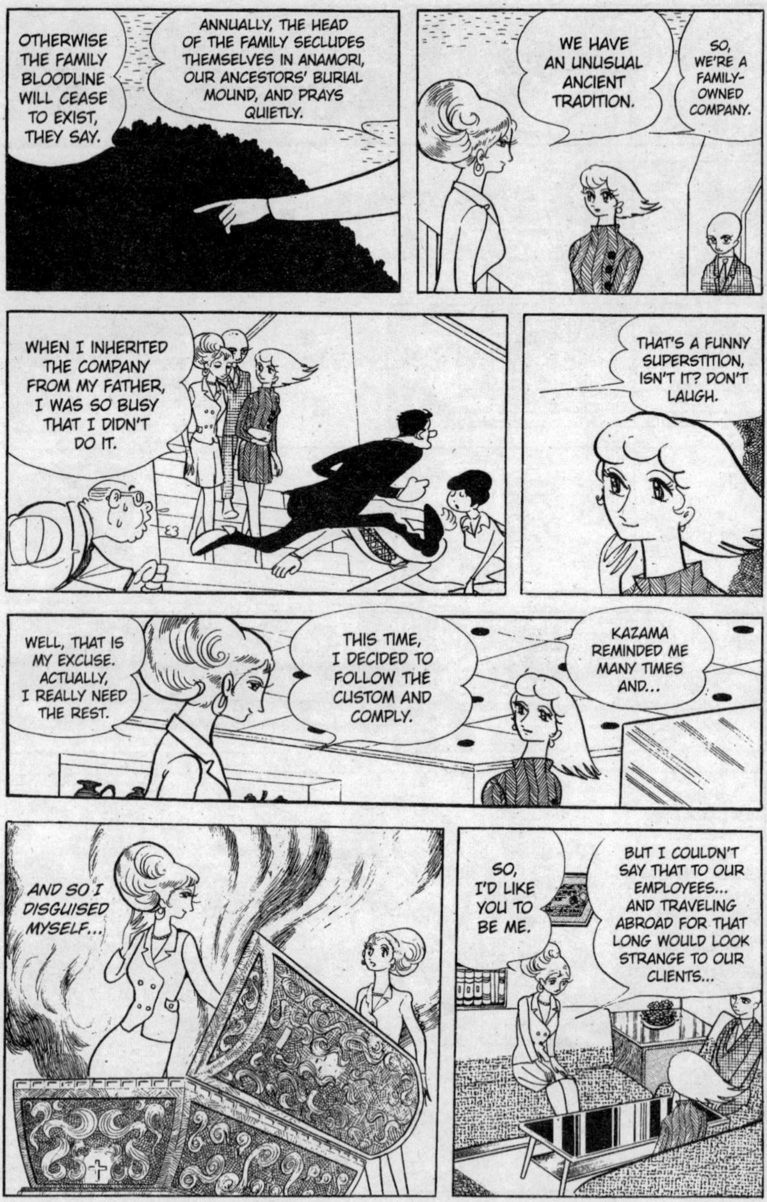
SO, WE'RE A FAMILY-OWNED COMPANY.
WE HAVE AN UNUSUAL ANCIENT TRADITION.
ANNUALLY, THE HEAD OF THE FAMILY SECLUDES THEMSELVES IN ANAMORI, OUR ANCESTORS' BURIAL MOUND, AND PRAYS QUIETLY.
OTHERWISE THE FAMILY BLOODLINE WILL CEASE TO EXIST, THEY SAY.
THAT'S A FUNNY SUPERSTITION, ISN'T IT? DON'T LAUGH.
WHEN I INHERITED THE COMPANY FROM MY FATHER, I WAS SO BUSY THAT I DIDN'T DO IT.
KAZAMA REMINDED ME MANY TIMES AND...
THIS TIME, I DECIDED TO FOLLOW THE CUSTOM AND COMPLY.
WELL, THAT IS MY EXCUSE. ACTUALLY, I REALLY NEED THE REST.
BUT I COULDN'T SAY THAT TO OUR EMPLOYEES... AND TRAVELING ABROAD FOR THAT LONG WOULD LOOK STRANGE TO OUR CLIENTS...
SO, I'D LIKE YOU TO BE ME.
AND SO I DISGUISED MYSELF...

...AS PRESIDENT TOMINAGA. THE REAL PRESIDENT QUIETLY LEFT, BUT FOR SOME REASON SHE LOOKED SAD.

AFTER A FEW DAYS... I WAS SHOCKED.

BY HOW BUSY I WAS.

IT WAS KAZAMA WHO DEALT WITH MATTERS DECISIVELY AND EFFECTIVELY. HE WAS AN EFFICIENT BUSINESS PERSON.

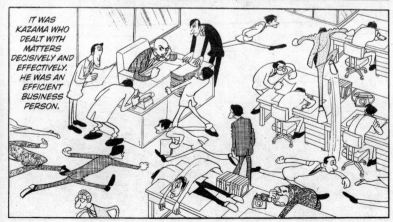

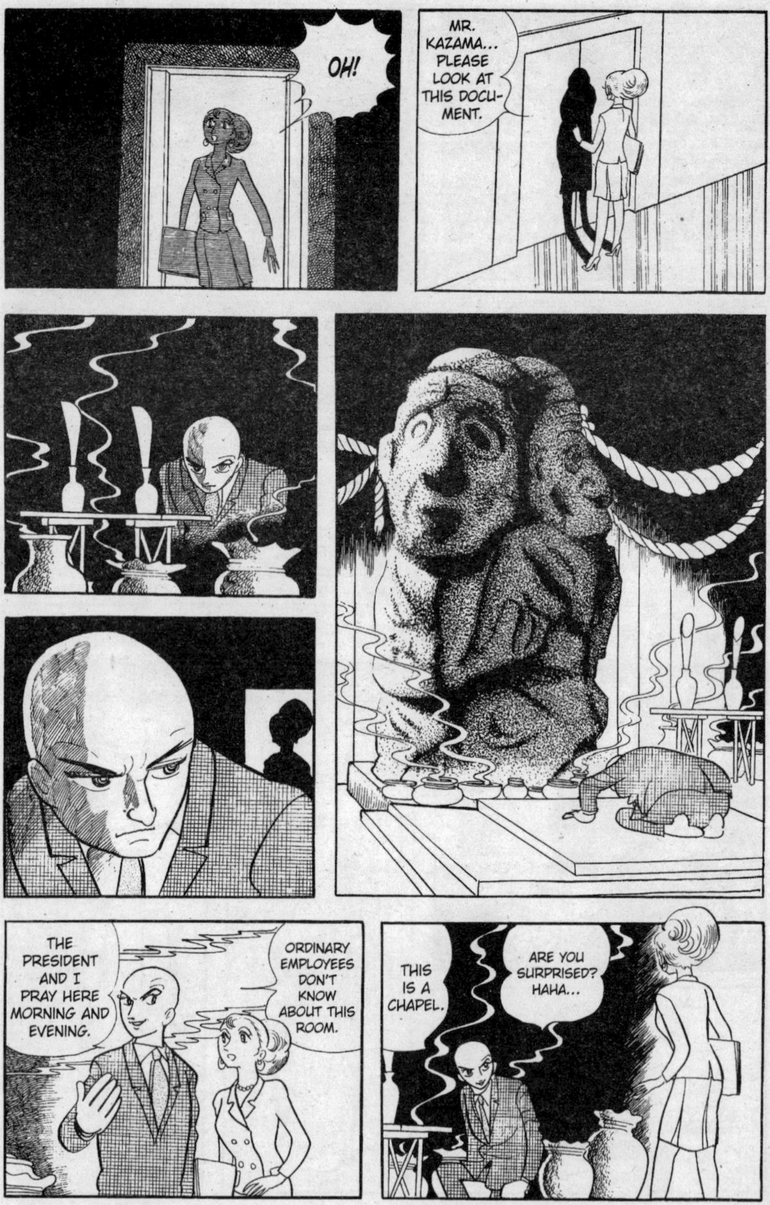
MR. KAZAMA... PLEASE LOOK AT THIS DOCUMENT.
OH!
ARE YOU SURPRISED? HAHA...
THIS IS A CHAPEL.
ORDINARY EMPLOYEES DON'T KNOW ABOUT THIS ROOM.
THE PRESIDENT AND I PRAY HERE MORNING AND EVENING.

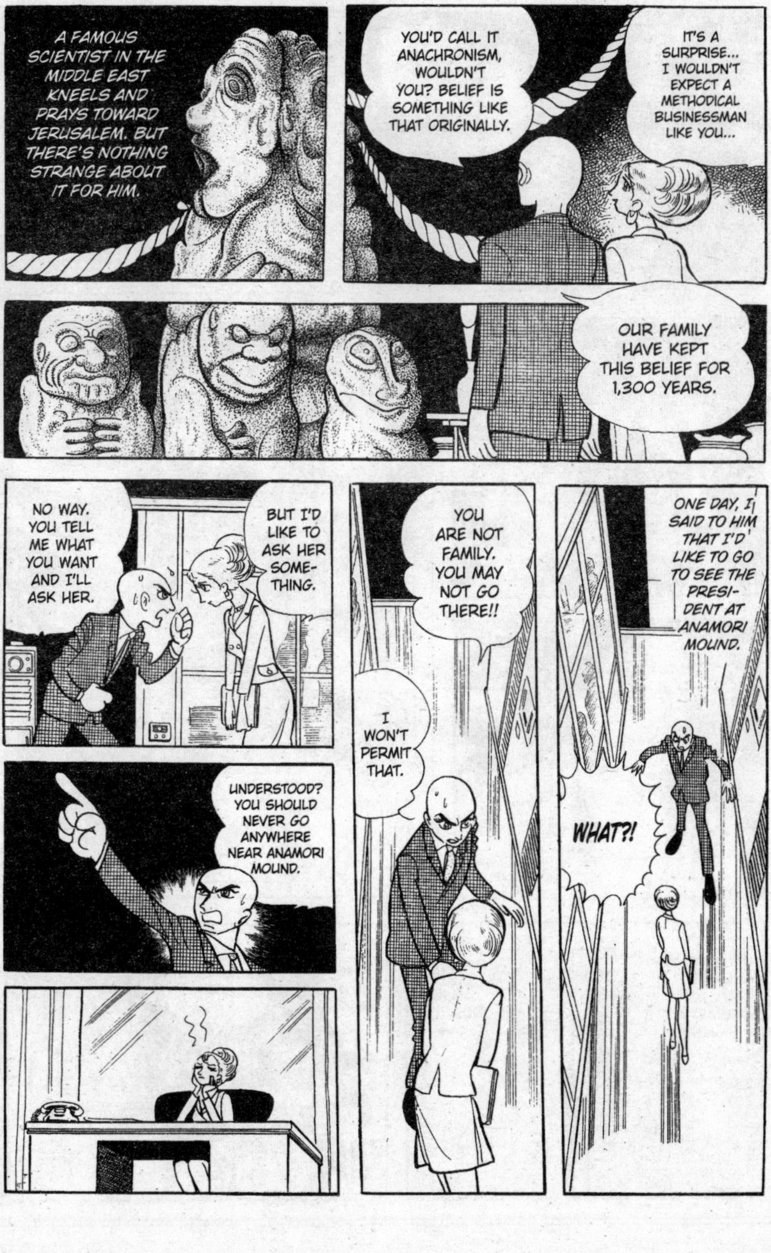
IT'S A SURPRISE... I WOULDN'T EXPECT A METHODICAL BUSINESSMAN LIKE YOU...
YOU'D CALL IT ANACHRONISM, WOULDN'T YOU? BELIEF IS SOMETHING LIKE THAT ORIGINALLY.
A FAMOUS SCIENTIST IN THE MIDDLE EAST KNEELS AND PRAYS TOWARD JERUSALEM. BUT THERE'S NOTHING STRANGE ABOUT IT FOR HIM.
OUR FAMILY HAVE KEPT THIS BELIEF FOR 1,300 YEARS.
ONE DAY, I SAID TO HIM THAT I'D LIKE TO GO TO SEE THE PRESI- DENT AT ANAMORI MOUND.
WHAT?!
YOU ARE NOT FAMILY. YOU MAY NOT GO THERE!!
I WON'T PERMIT THAT.
BUT I'D LIKE TO ASK HER SOME- THING.
NO WAY. YOU TELL ME WHAT YOU WANT AND I'LL ASK HER.
UNDERSTOOD? YOU SHOULD NEVER GO ANYWHERE NEAR ANAMORI MOUND.

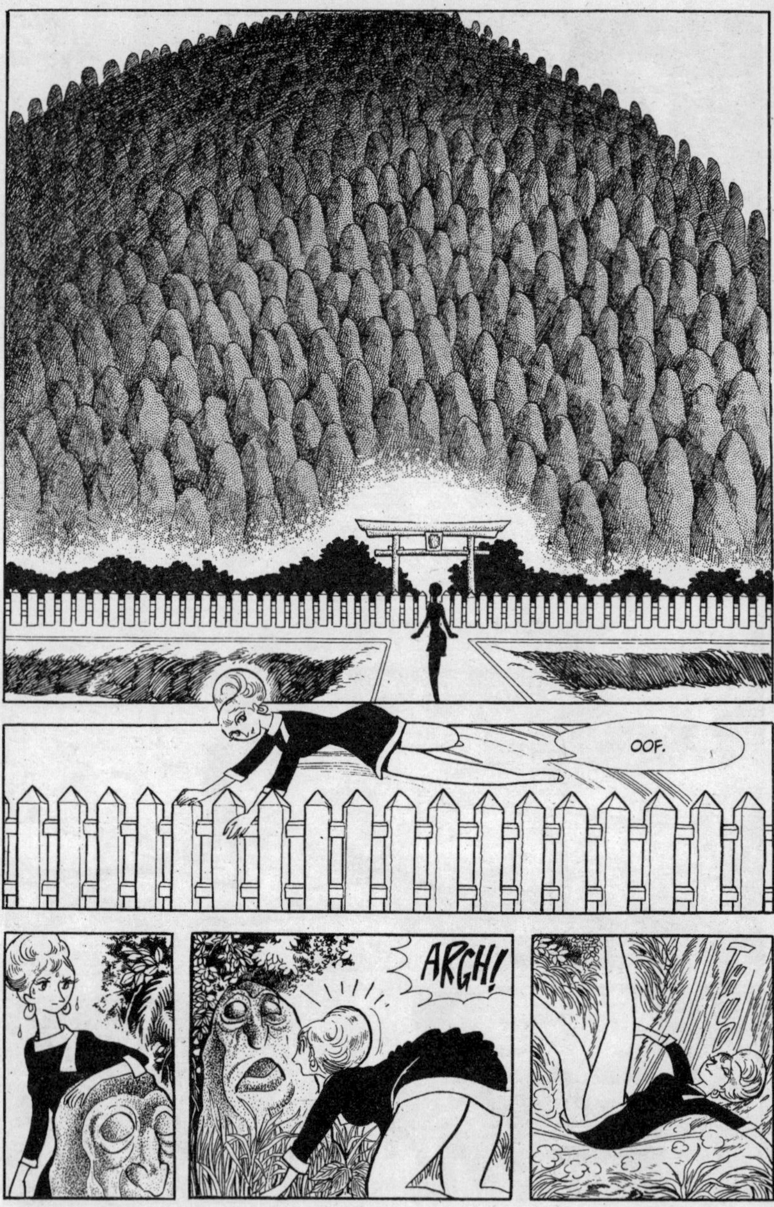
OOF.
THUD
ARGH!

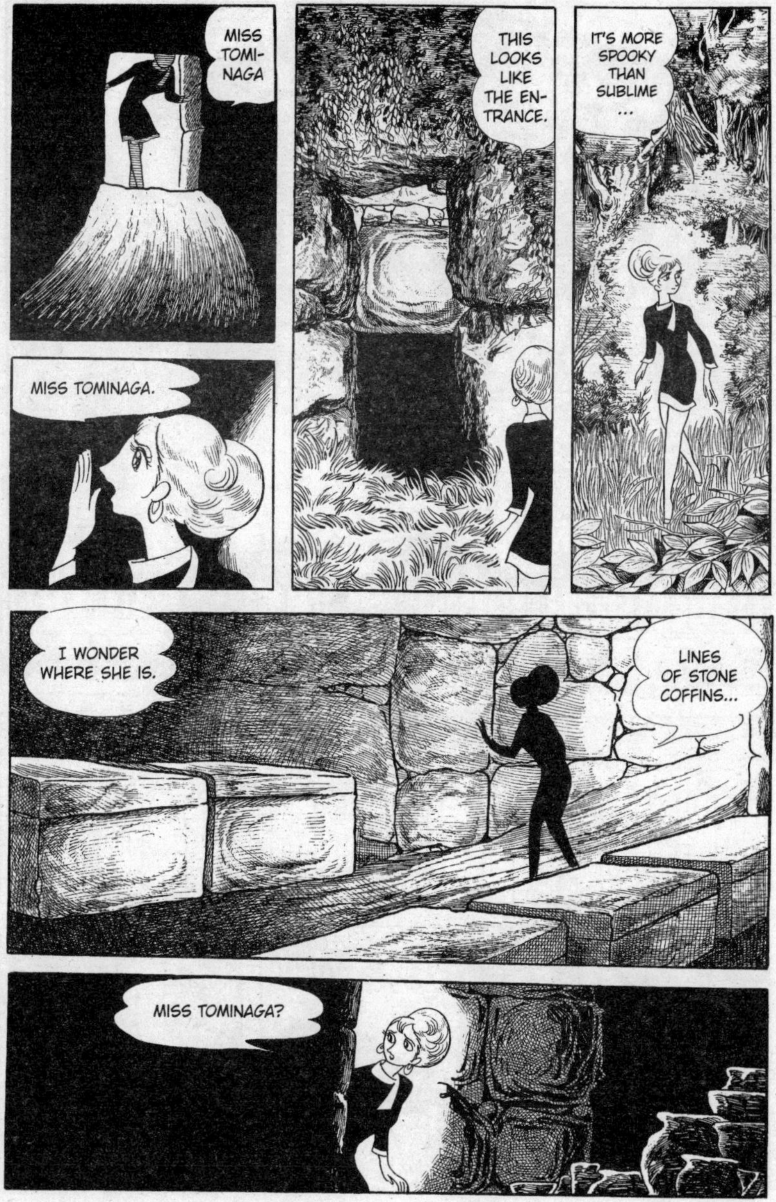
IT'S MORE SPOOKY THAN SUBLIME ...
THIS LOOKS LIKE THE EN- TRANCE.
MISS TOMI- NAGA
MISS TOMINAGA.
LINES OF STONE COFFINS...
I WONDER WHERE SHE IS.
MISS TOMINAGA?

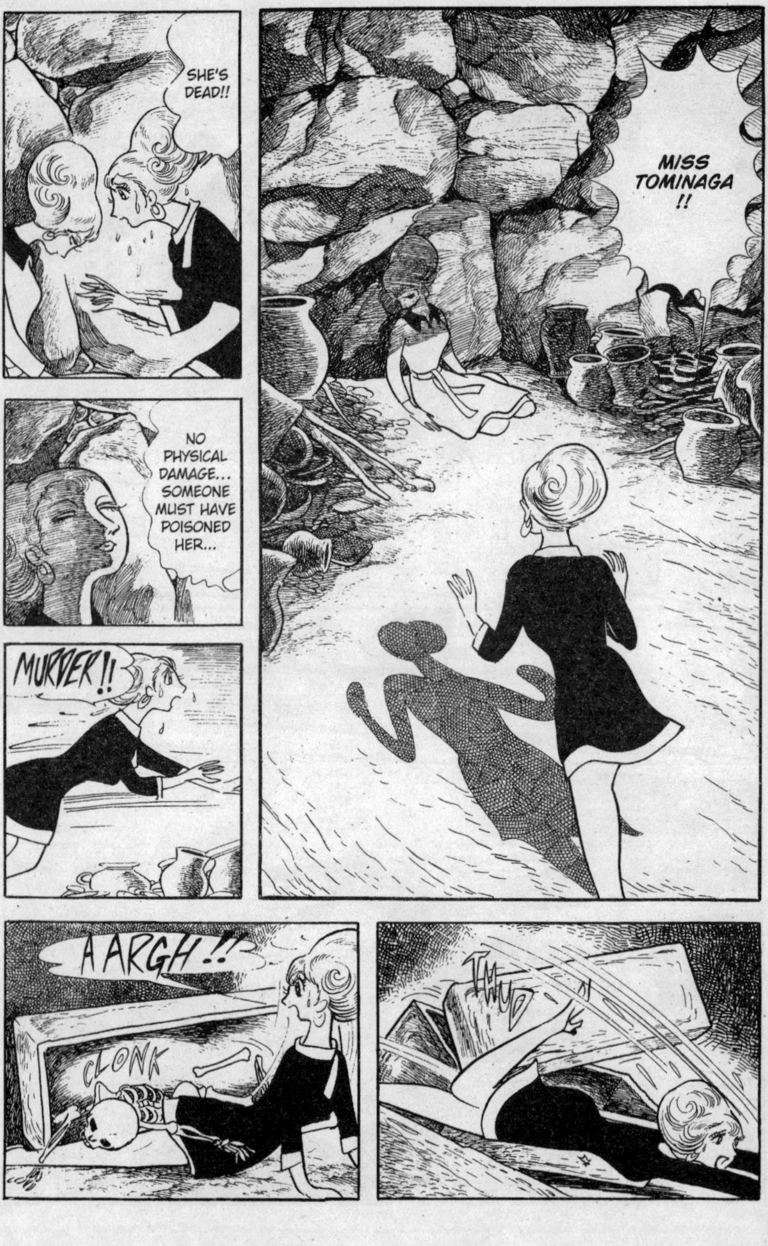
MISS TOMINAGA !!
SHE'S DEAD!!
NO PHYSICAL DAMAGE... SOMEONE MUST HAVE POISONED HER...
MURDER!!
THUD
AARGH!!
CLONK

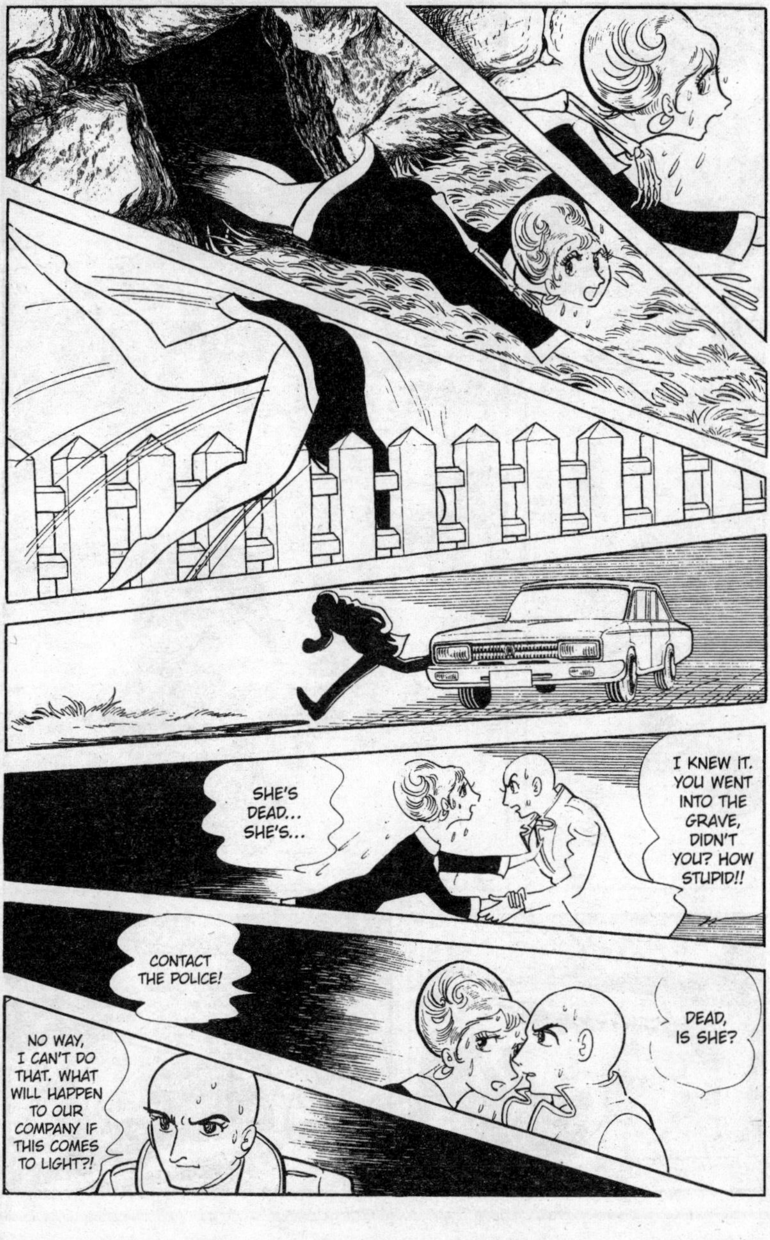
I KNEW IT. YOU WENT INTO THE GRAVE, DIDN'T YOU? HOW STUPID!!
SHE'S DEAD... SHE'S...
DEAD, IS SHE?
CONTACT THE POLICE!
NO WAY, I CAN'T DO THAT. WHAT WILL HAPPEN TO OUR COMPANY IF THIS COMES TO LIGHT?!

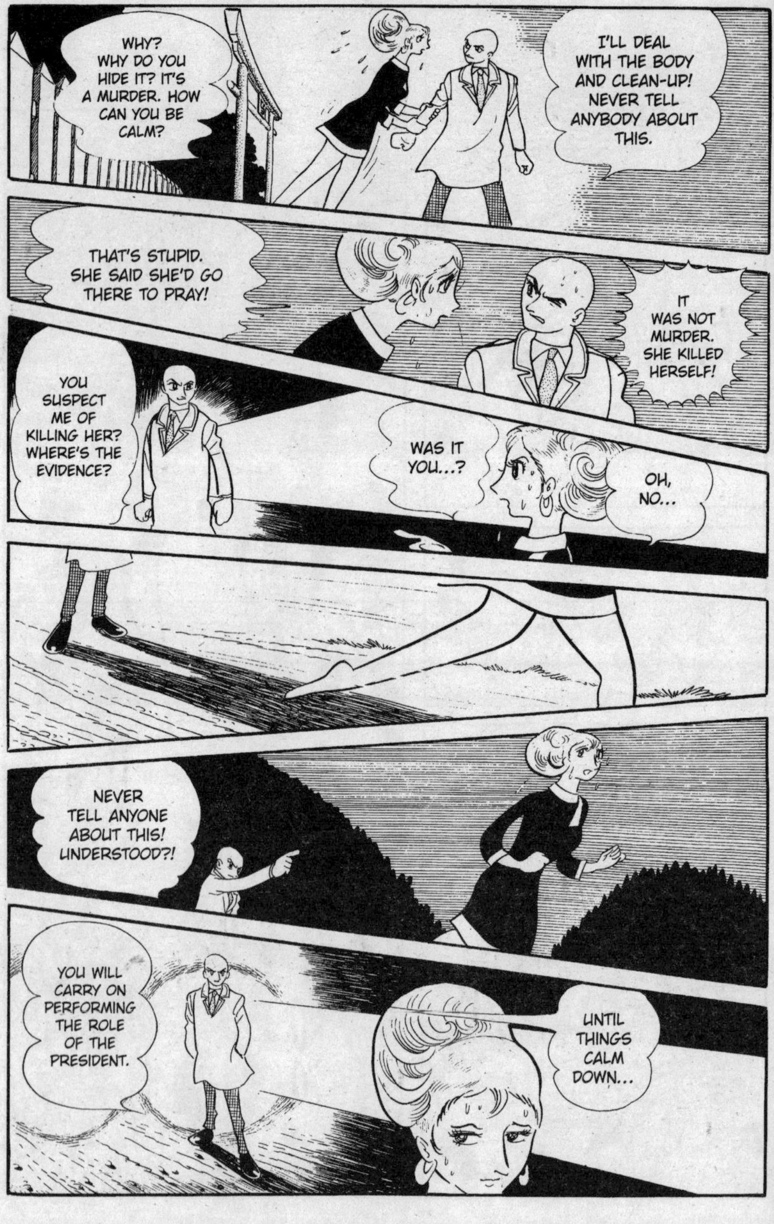

I'LL DEAL WITH THE BODY AND CLEAN-UP! NEVER TELL ANYBODY ABOUT THIS.
WHY? WHY DO YOU HIDE IT? IT'S A MURDER. HOW CAN YOU BE CALM?
IT WAS NOT MURDER. SHE KILLED HERSELF!
THAT'S STUPID. SHE SAID SHE'D GO THERE TO PRAY!
OH, NO...
WAS IT YOU...?
YOU SUSPECT ME OF KILLING HER? WHERE'S THE EVIDENCE?
NEVER TELL ANYONE ABOUT THIS! UNDERSTOOD?!
UNTIL THINGS CALM DOWN...
YOU WILL CARRY ON PERFORMING THE ROLE OF THE PRESIDENT.

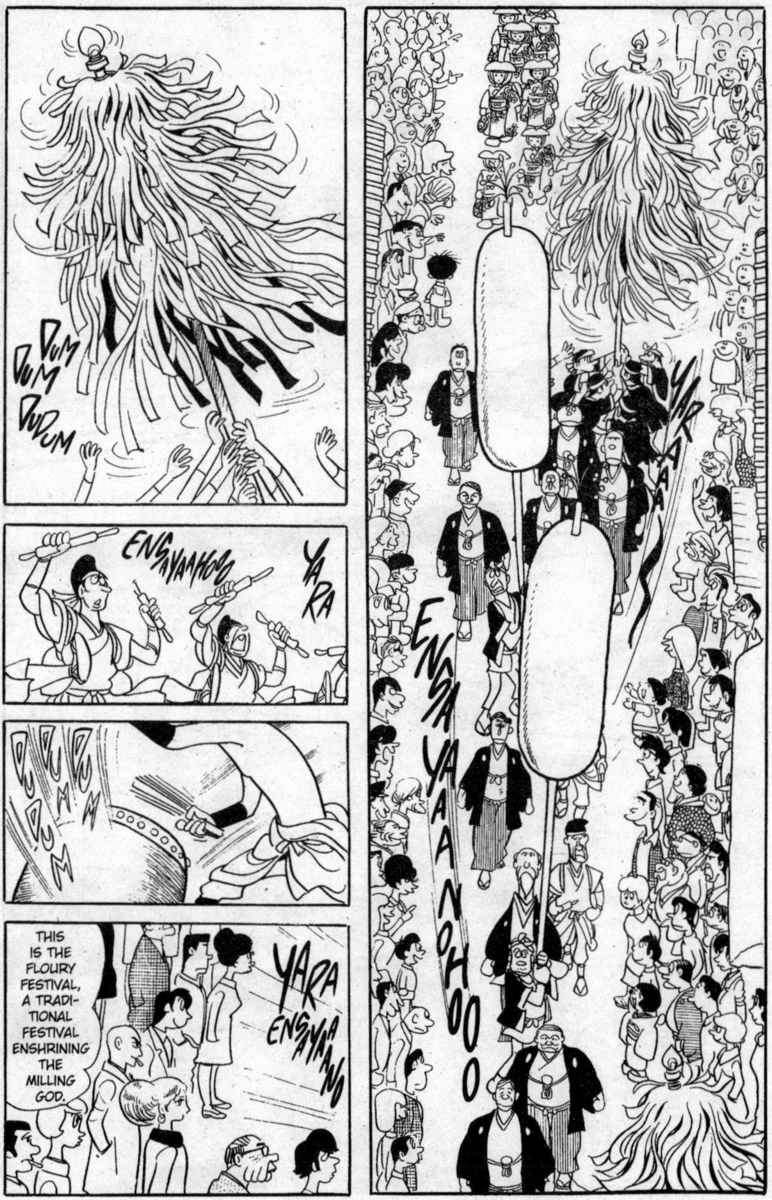
YARAAAA
ENSAYAAANOHOOOO
DUM DUM DUDUM
YARA
ENSAYAAHOO
DUM DUM DUDUM
YARA ENSAYAAANO
THIS IS THE FLOURY FESTIVAL, A TRADITIONAL FESTIVAL ENSHRINING THE MILLING GOD.

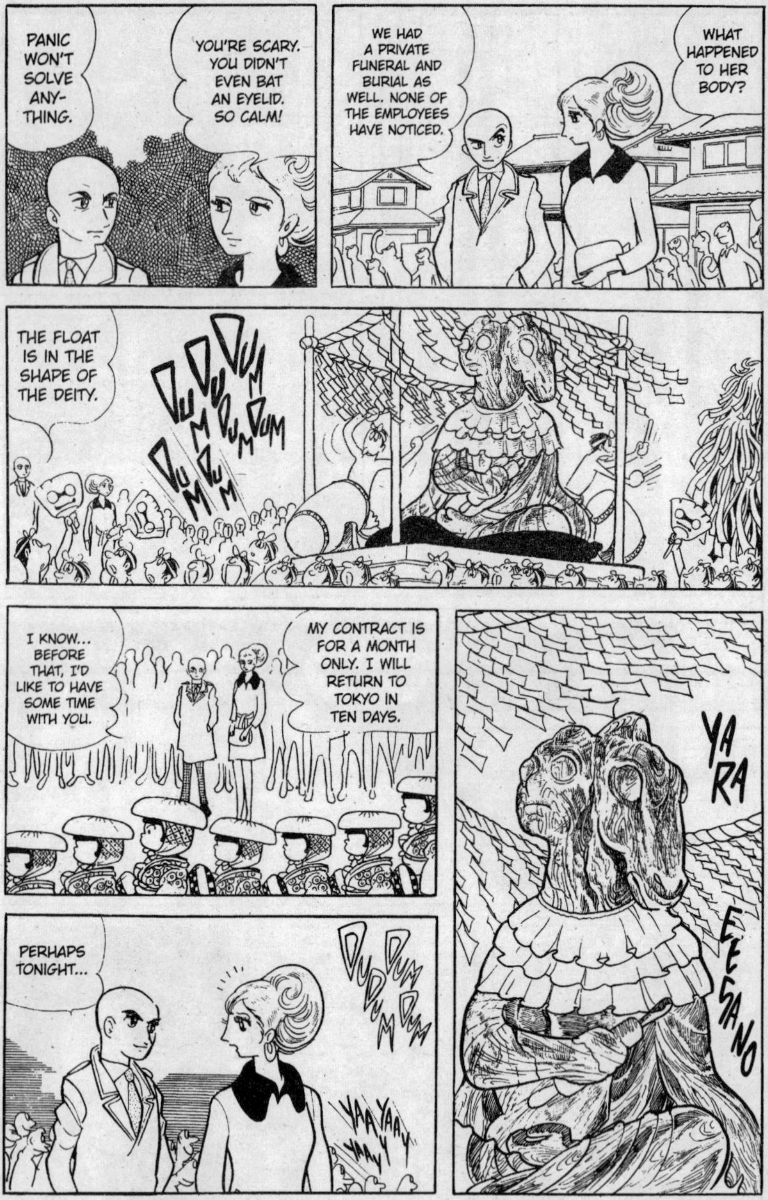
WHAT HAPPENED TO HER BODY?
WE HAD A PRIVATE FUNERAL AND BURIAL AS WELL. NONE OF THE EMPLOYEES HAVE NOTICED.
YOU'RE SCARY. YOU DIDN'T EVEN BAT AN EYELID. SO CALM!
PANIC WON'T SOLVE ANY-THING.
DUM DUM DUM DUM DUM DUM
THE FLOAT IS IN THE SHAPE OF THE DEITY.
YARA
EESANO
MY CONTRACT IS FOR A MONTH ONLY. I WILL RETURN TO TOKYO IN TEN DAYS.
I KNOW... BEFORE THAT, I'D LIKE TO HAVE SOME TIME WITH YOU.
DUM DUM DUM DUM
YAAY YAAY YAAY
PERHAPS TONIGHT...

...
STARTLE
WHAT ARE YOU DOING?!

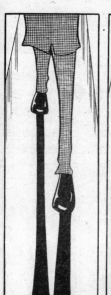

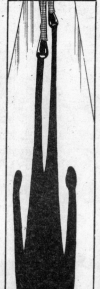

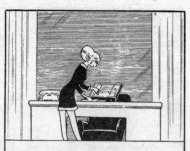

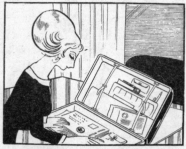

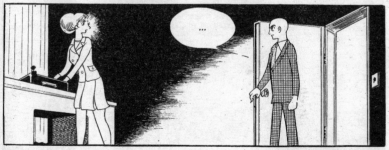

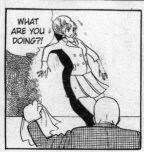

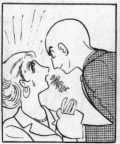

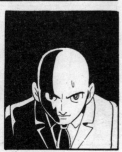

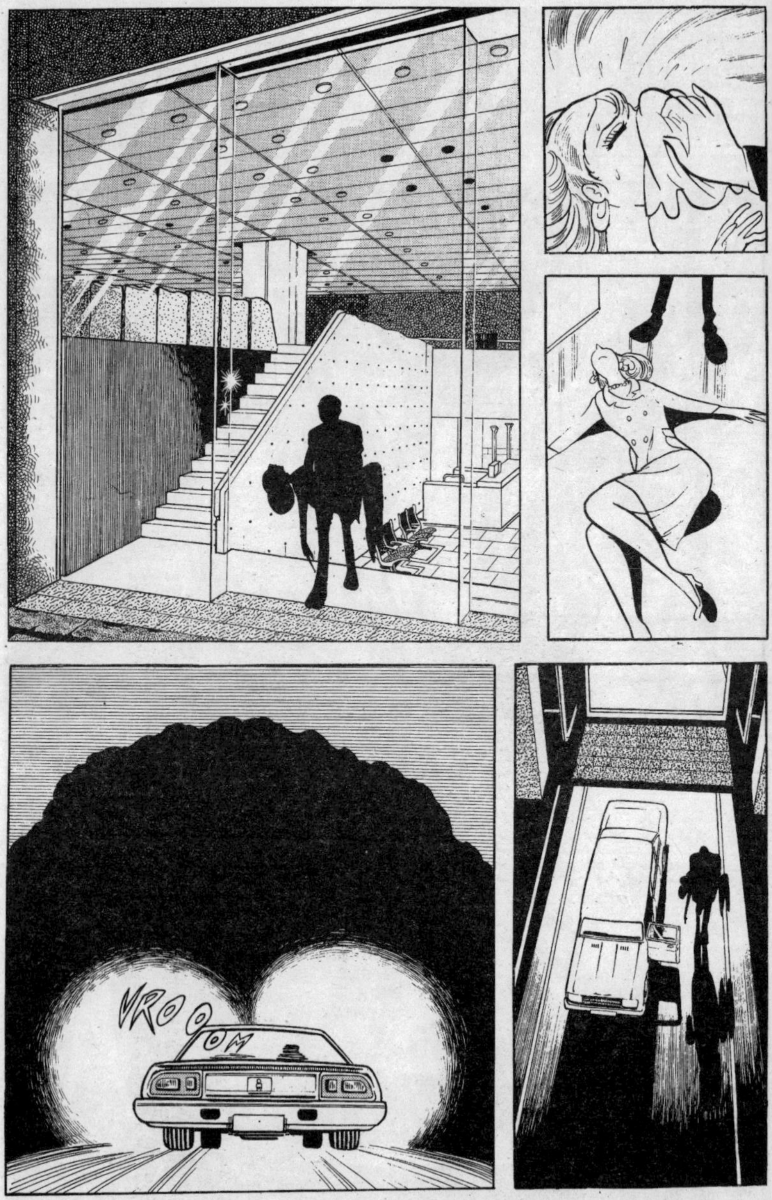
VROOOM

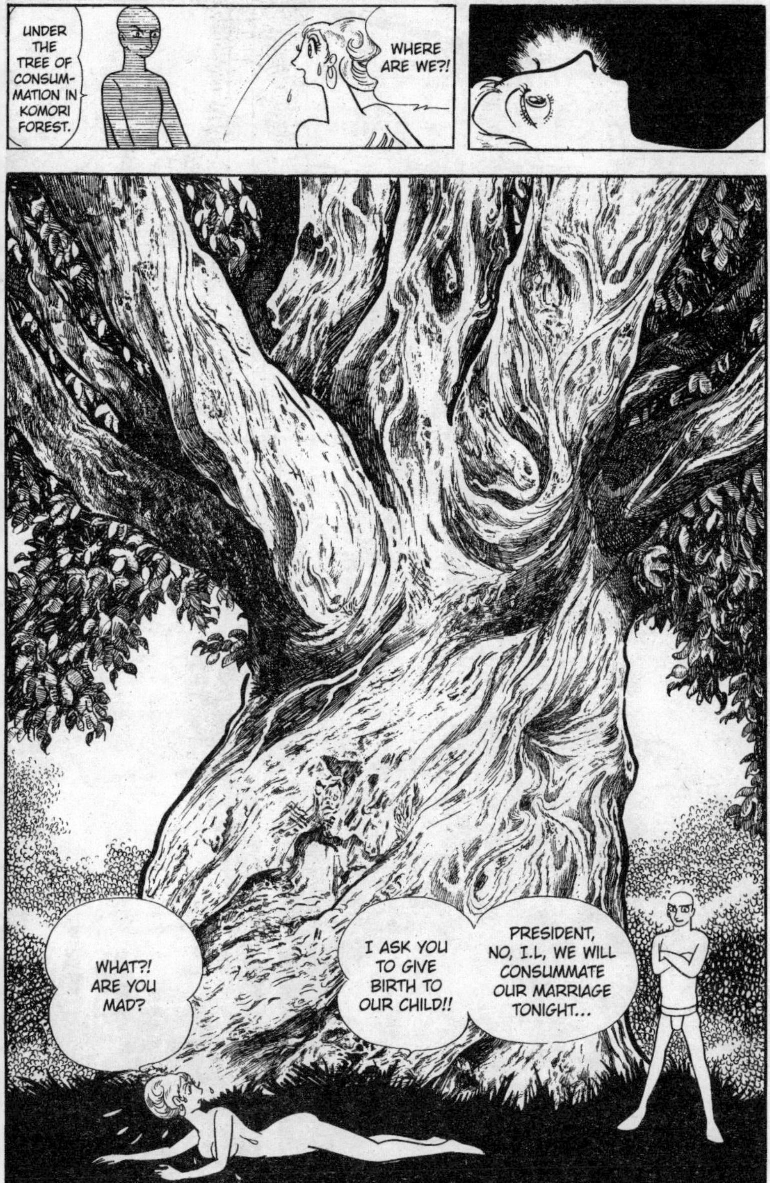
WHERE ARE WE?!
UNDER THE TREE OF CONSUMMATION IN KOMORI FOREST.
PRESIDENT, NO, I.L, WE WILL CONSUMMATE OUR MARRIAGE TONIGHT...
I ASK YOU TO GIVE BIRTH TO OUR CHILD!!
WHAT?! ARE YOU MAD?

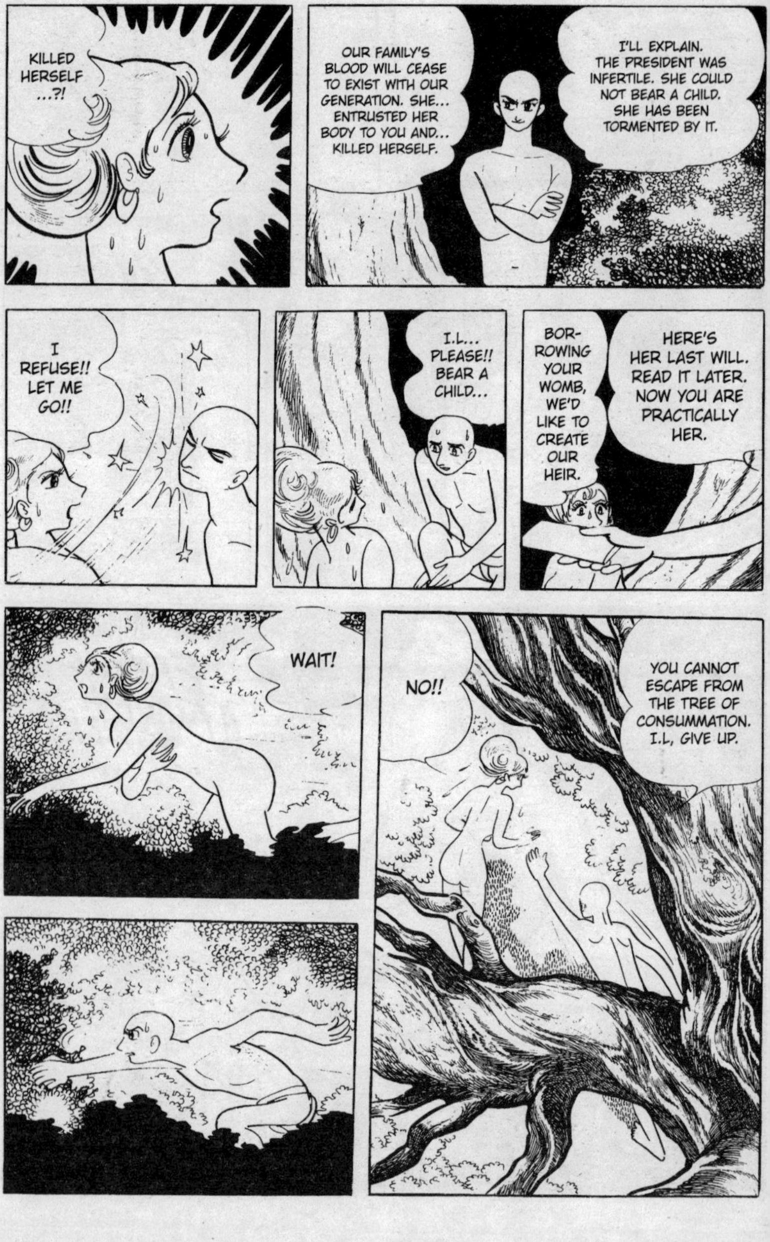
I'LL EXPLAIN. THE PRESIDENT WAS INFERTILE. SHE COULD NOT BEAR A CHILD. SHE HAS BEEN TORMENTED BY IT.
OUR FAMILY'S BLOOD WILL CEASE TO EXIST WITH OUR GENERATION. SHE... ENTRUSTED HER BODY TO YOU AND... KILLED HERSELF.
KILLED HERSELF ...?!
HERE'S HER LAST WILL. READ IT LATER. NOW YOU ARE PRACTICALLY HER.
BOR-ROWING YOUR WOMB, WE'D LIKE TO CREATE OUR HEIR.
I.L... PLEASE!! BEAR A CHILD...
I REFUSE!! LET ME GO!!
YOU CANNOT ESCAPE FROM THE TREE OF CONSUMMATION. I.L, GIVE UP.
NO!!
WAIT!

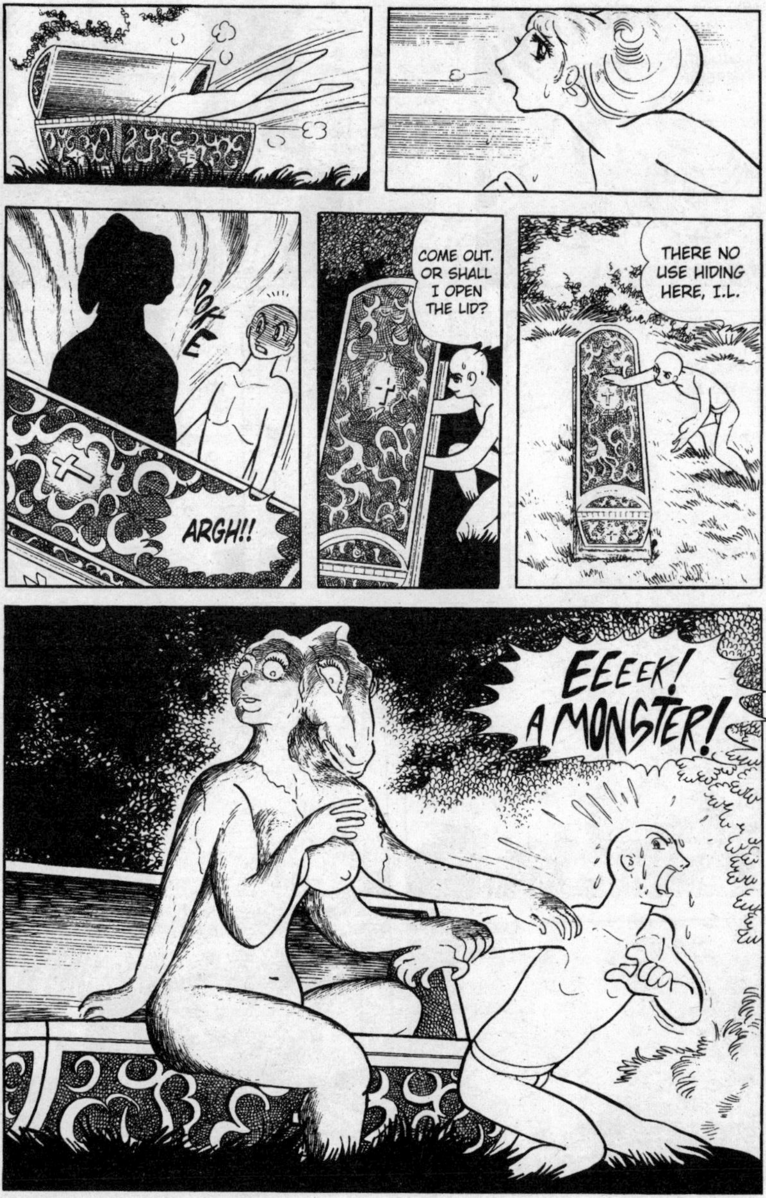
THERE NO USE HIDING HERE, I.L.
COME OUT. OR SHALL I OPEN THE LID?
POKE
ARGH!!
EEEEK! A MONSTER!

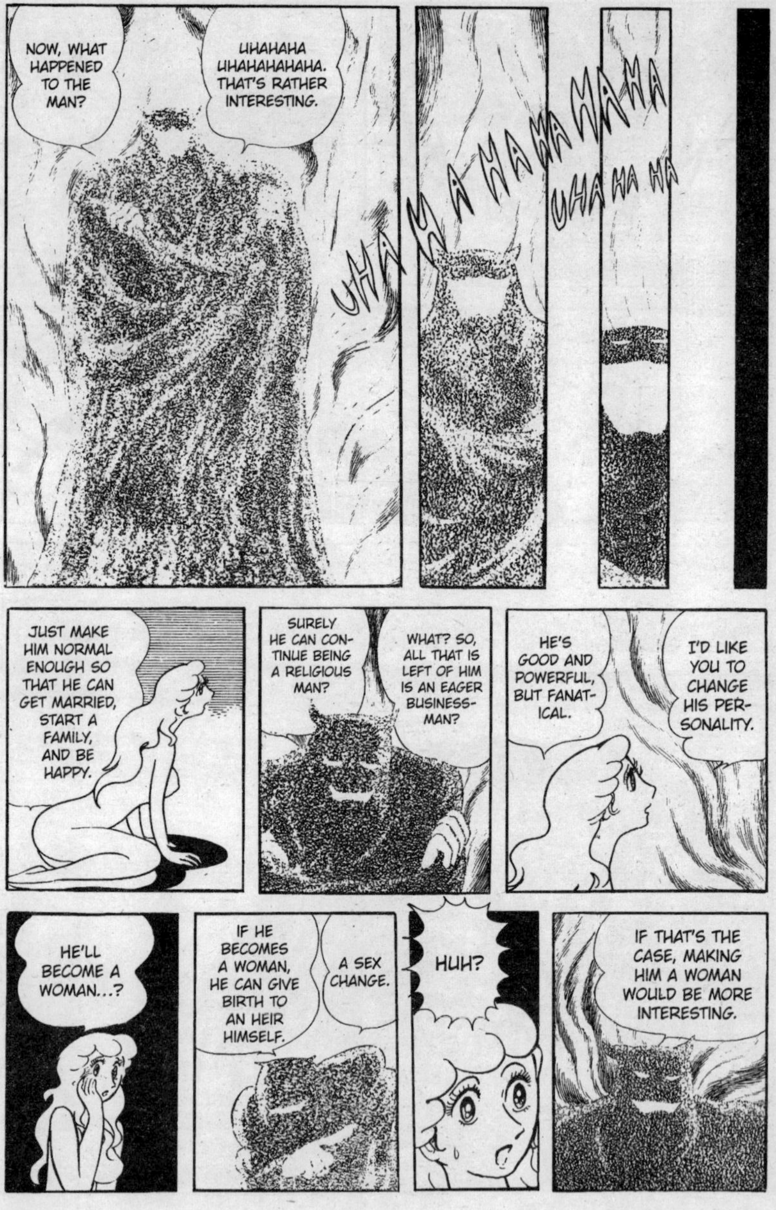
UHAHA HA HA
UHAHAHAHAHAHAHA
UHAHAHA UHAHAHAHAHA. THAT'S RATHER INTERESTING.
NOW, WHAT HAPPENED TO THE MAN?
I'D LIKE YOU TO CHANGE HIS PERSONALITY.
HE'S GOOD AND POWERFUL, BUT FANATICAL.
WHAT? SO, ALL THAT IS LEFT OF HIM IS AN EAGER BUSINESSMAN?
SURELY HE CAN CONTINUE BEING A RELIGIOUS MAN?
JUST MAKE HIM NORMAL ENOUGH SO THAT HE CAN GET MARRIED, START A FAMILY, AND BE HAPPY.
IF THAT'S THE CASE, MAKING HIM A WOMAN WOULD BE MORE INTERESTING.
HUH?
A SEX CHANGE.
IF HE BECOMES A WOMAN, HE CAN GIVE BIRTH TO AN HEIR HIMSELF.
HE'LL BECOME A WOMAN...?

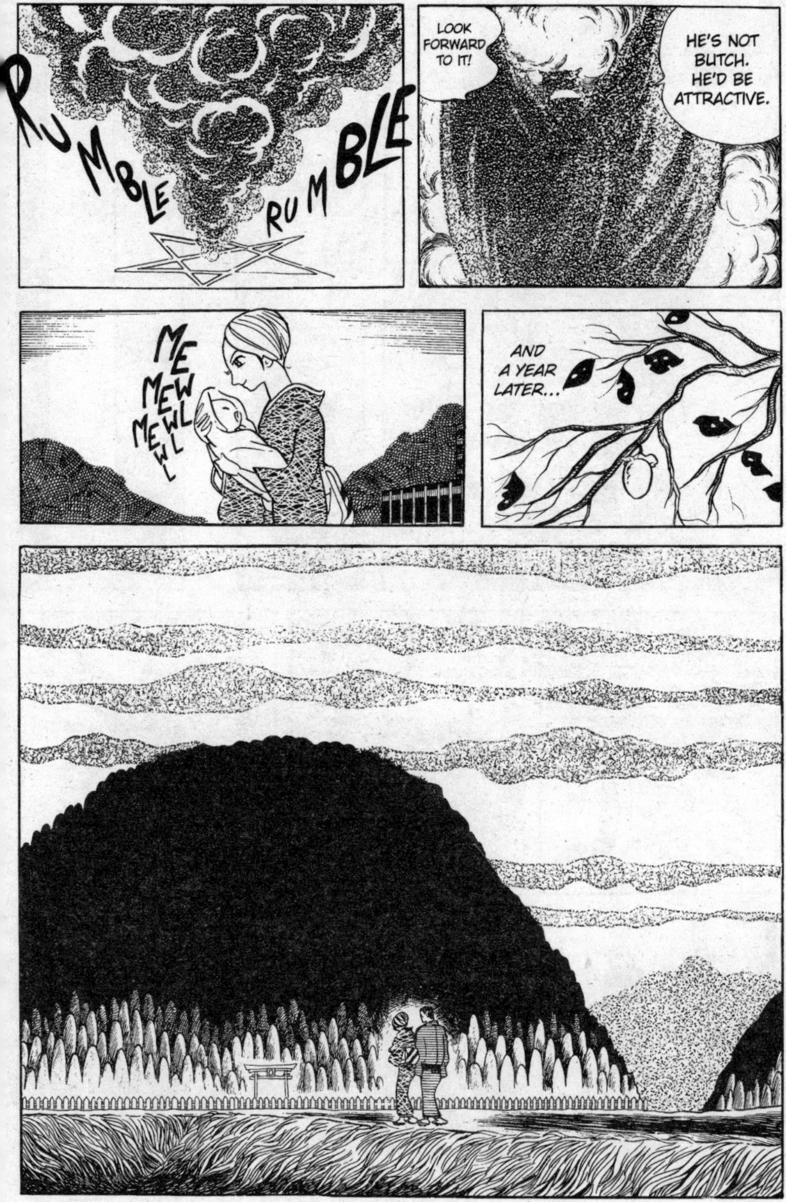
HE'S NOT BUTCH. HE'D BE ATTRACTIVE.
LOOK FORWARD TO IT!
RUMBLE
RUMBLE
AND A YEAR LATER...
MEWL MEWL MEWL

# I.L

アイエル

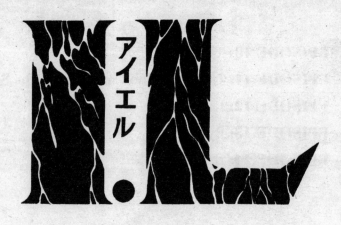

# CONTENTS
## PART 2

# EPISODE 10
## The Seal

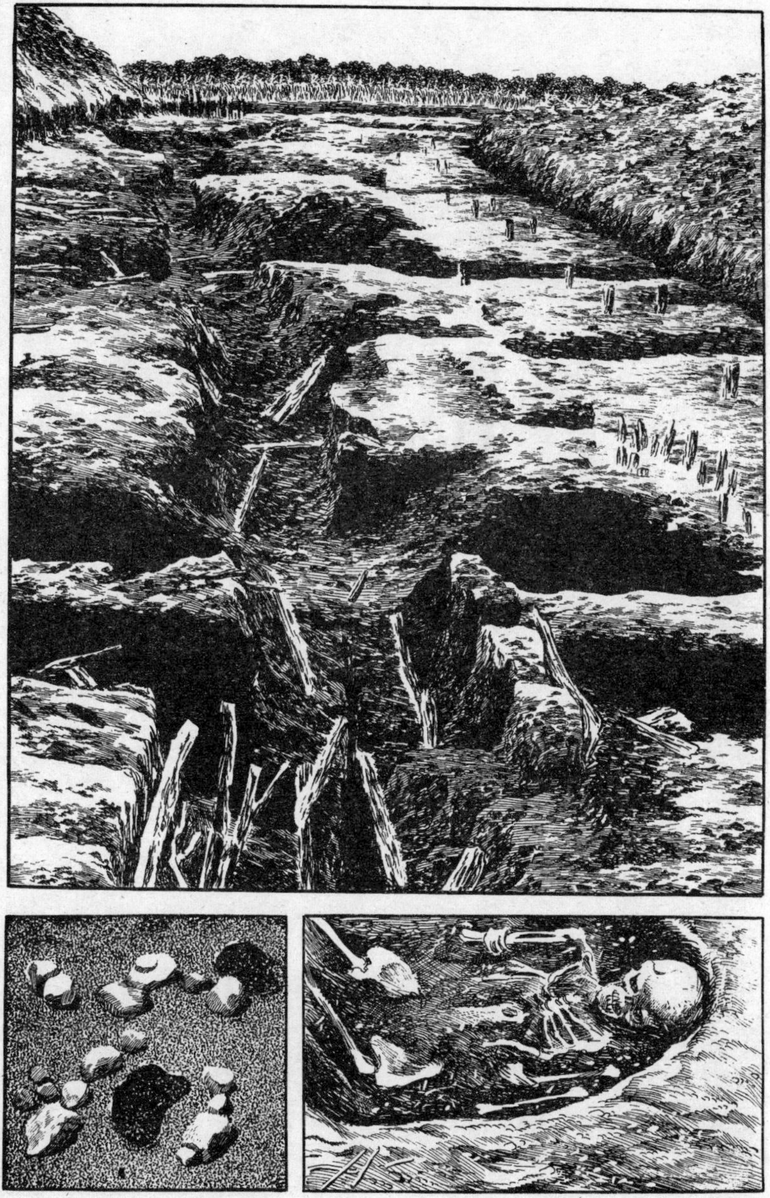

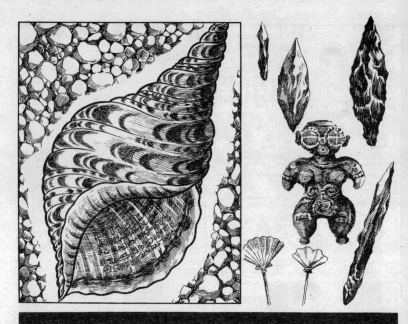

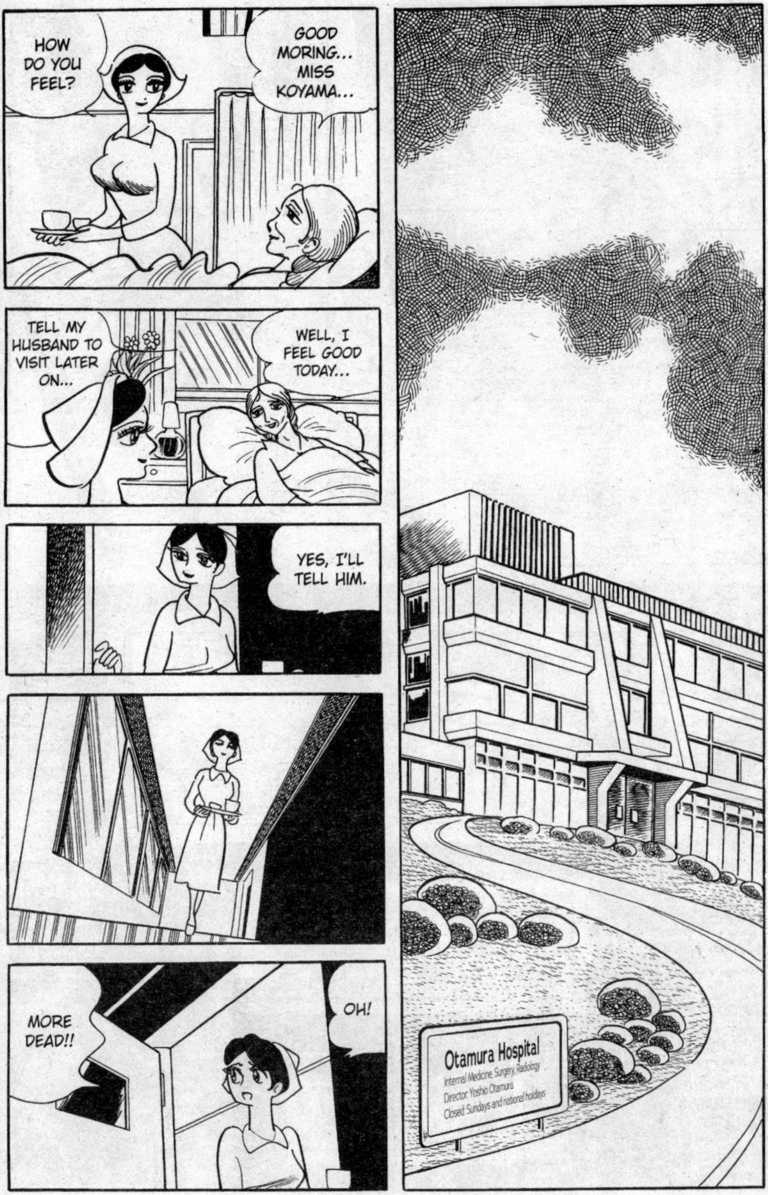
Otamura Hospital
Internal Medicine, Surgery, Radiology
Director: Yoshio Otamura
Closed Sundays and national holidays
GOOD MORING... MISS KOYAMA...
HOW DO YOU FEEL?
WELL, I FEEL GOOD TODAY...
TELL MY HUSBAND TO VISIT LATER ON...
YES, I'LL TELL HIM.
OH!
MORE DEAD!!

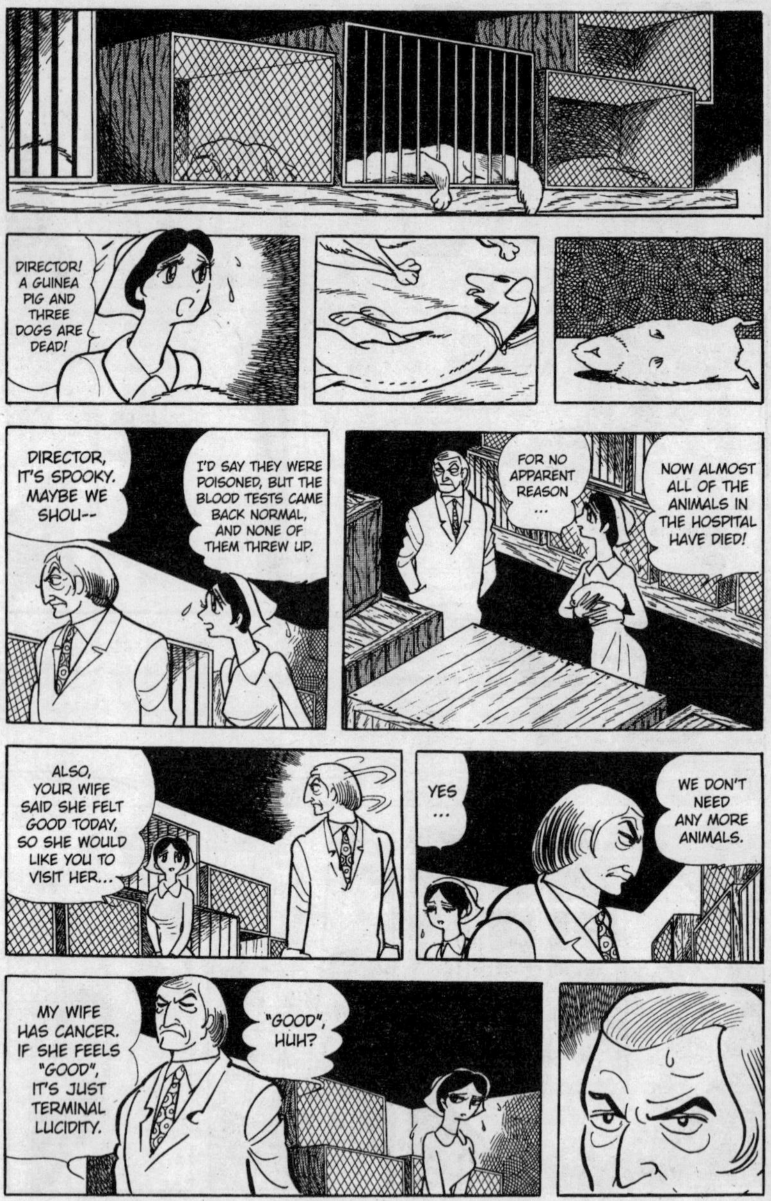
DIRECTOR! A GUINEA PIG AND THREE DOGS ARE DEAD!
NOW ALMOST ALL OF THE ANIMALS IN THE HOSPITAL HAVE DIED!
FOR NO APPARENT REASON ...
I'D SAY THEY WERE POISONED, BUT THE BLOOD TESTS CAME BACK NORMAL, AND NONE OF THEM THREW UP.
DIRECTOR, IT'S SPOOKY. MAYBE WE SHOU--
WE DON'T NEED ANY MORE ANIMALS.
YES ...
ALSO, YOUR WIFE SAID SHE FELT GOOD TODAY, SO SHE WOULD LIKE YOU TO VISIT HER...
"GOOD", HUH?
MY WIFE HAS CANCER. IF SHE FEELS "GOOD", IT'S JUST TERMINAL LUCIDITY.

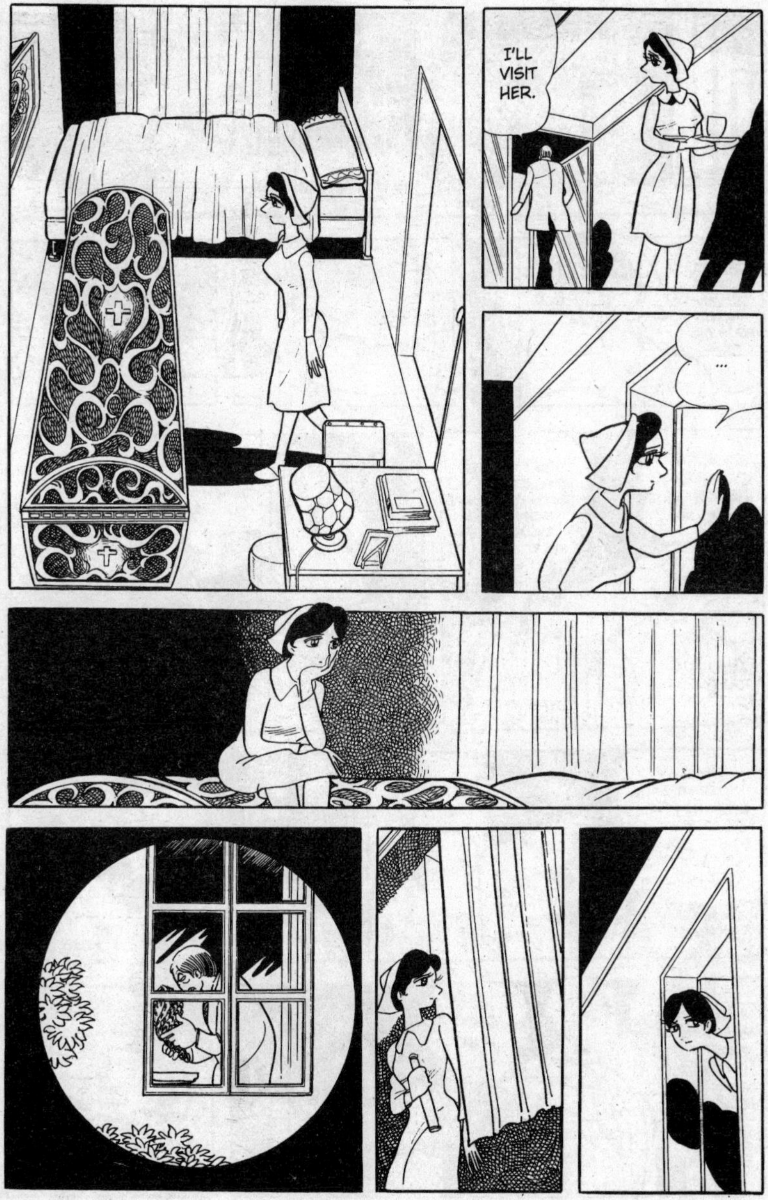
I'LL VISIT HER.
...

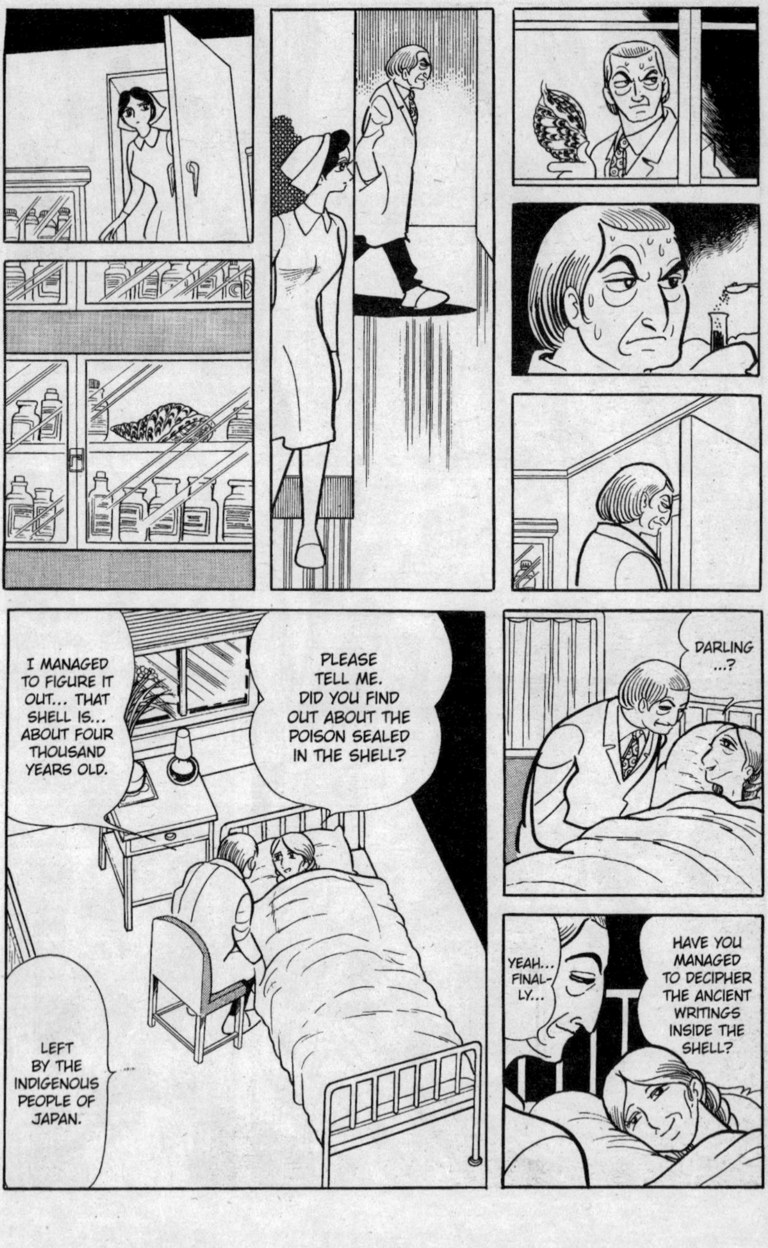
DARLING ...?
HAVE YOU MANAGED TO DECIPHER THE ANCIENT WRITINGS INSIDE THE SHELL?
YEAH... FINAL-LY...
PLEASE TELL ME. DID YOU FIND OUT ABOUT THE POISON SEALED IN THE SHELL?
I MANAGED TO FIGURE IT OUT... THAT SHELL IS... ABOUT FOUR THOUSAND YEARS OLD.
LEFT BY THE INDIGENOUS PEOPLE OF JAPAN.

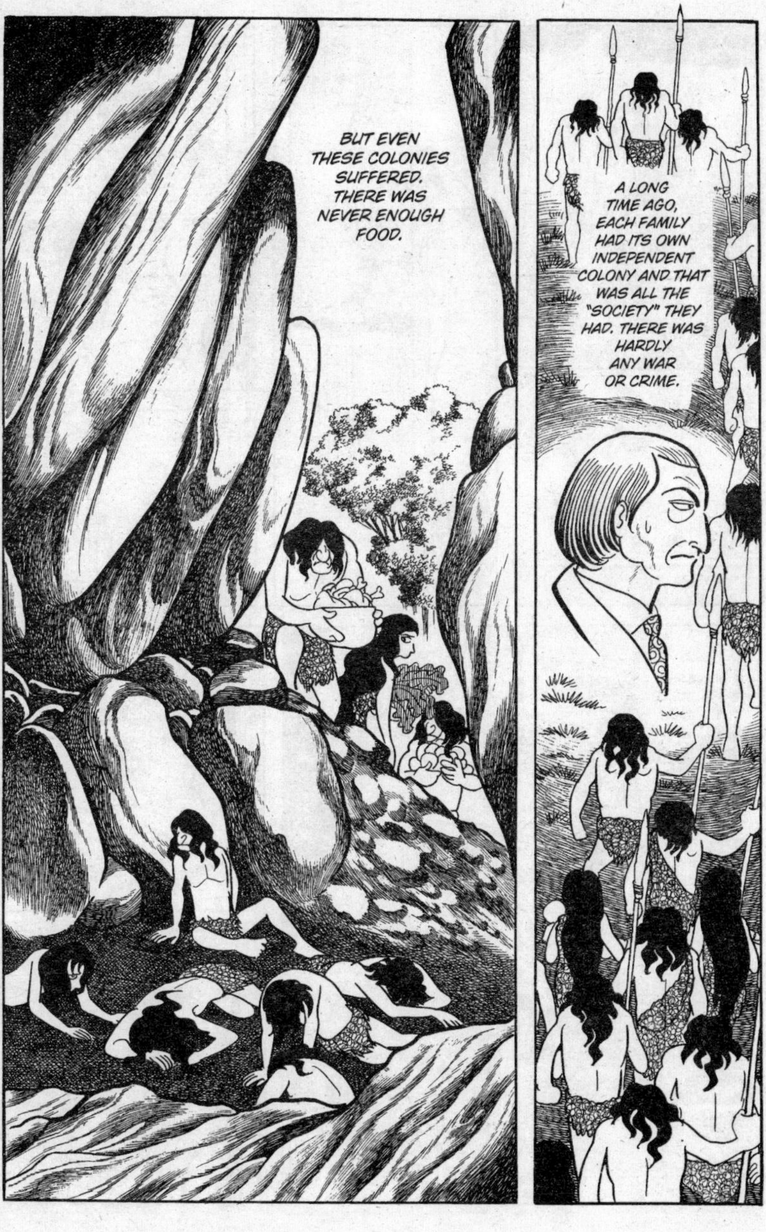
A LONG TIME AGO, EACH FAMILY HAD ITS OWN INDEPENDENT COLONY AND THAT WAS ALL THE "SOCIETY" THEY HAD. THERE WAS HARDLY ANY WAR OR CRIME.
BUT EVEN THESE COLONIES SUFFERED. THERE WAS NEVER ENOUGH FOOD.

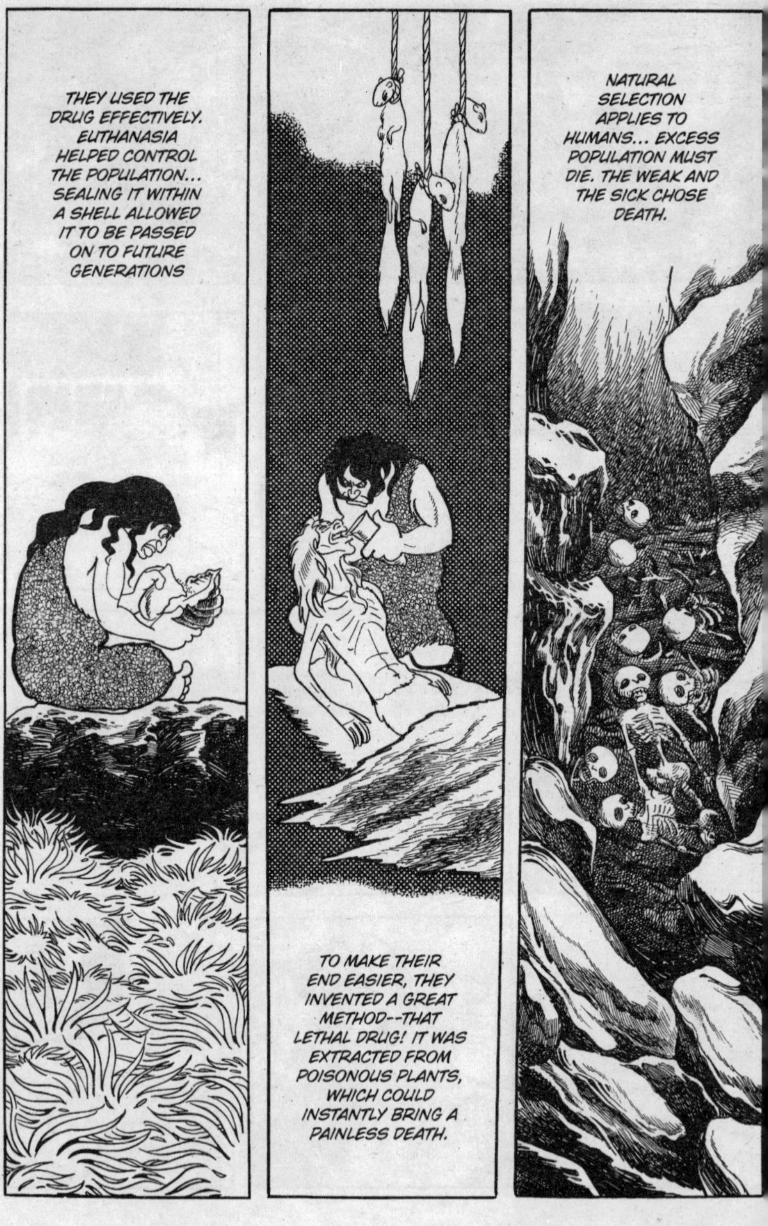
NATURAL SELECTION APPLIES TO HUMANS... EXCESS POPULATION MUST DIE. THE WEAK AND THE SICK CHOSE DEATH.
TO MAKE THEIR END EASIER, THEY INVENTED A GREAT METHOD--THAT LETHAL DRUG! IT WAS EXTRACTED FROM POISONOUS PLANTS, WHICH COULD INSTANTLY BRING A PAINLESS DEATH.
THEY USED THE DRUG EFFECTIVELY. EUTHANASIA HELPED CONTROL THE POPULATION... SEALING IT WITHIN A SHELL ALLOWED IT TO BE PASSED ON TO FUTURE GENERATIONS

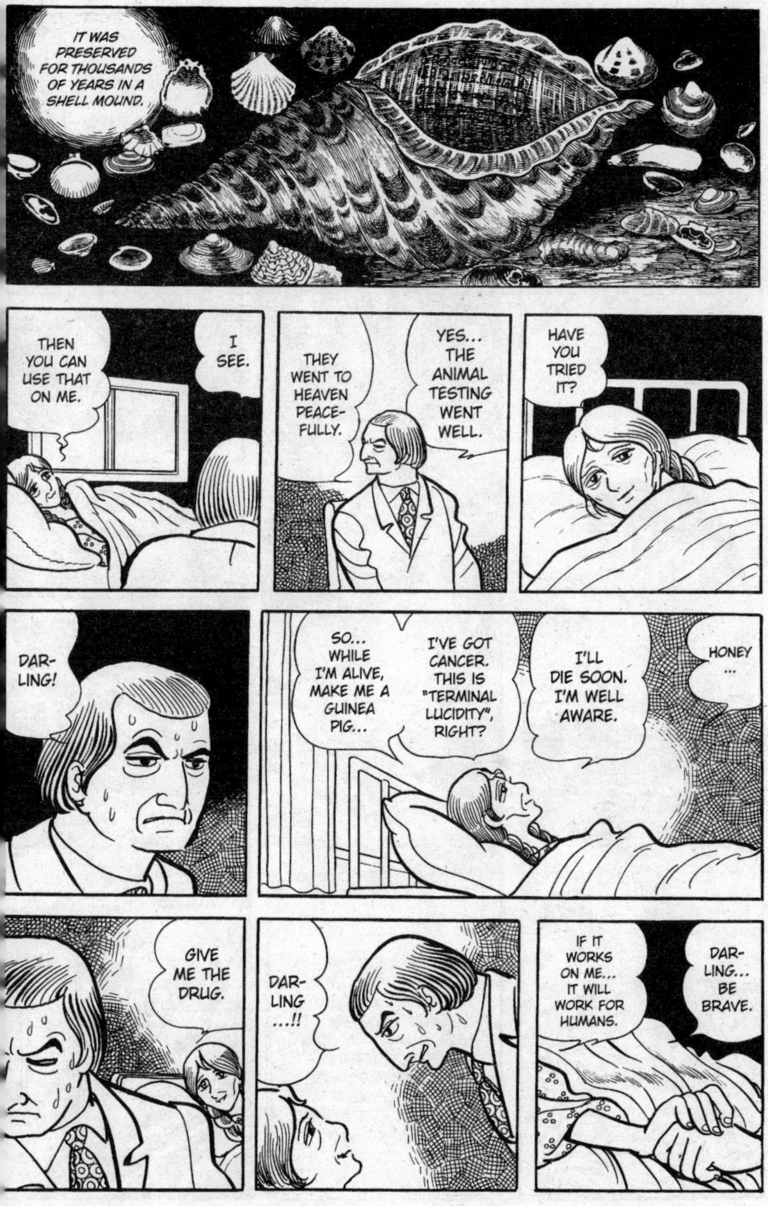
IT WAS PRESERVED FOR THOUSANDS OF YEARS IN A SHELL MOUND.
HAVE YOU TRIED IT?
YES... THE ANIMAL TESTING WENT WELL.
THEY WENT TO HEAVEN PEACE-FULLY.
I SEE.
THEN YOU CAN USE THAT ON ME.
HONEY ...
I'LL DIE SOON. I'M WELL AWARE.
I'VE GOT CANCER. THIS IS "TERMINAL LUCIDITY", RIGHT?
SO... WHILE I'M ALIVE, MAKE ME A GUINEA PIG...
DAR-LING!
DAR-LING... BE BRAVE.
IF IT WORKS ON ME... IT WILL WORK FOR HUMANS.
DAR-LING ...!!
GIVE ME THE DRUG.

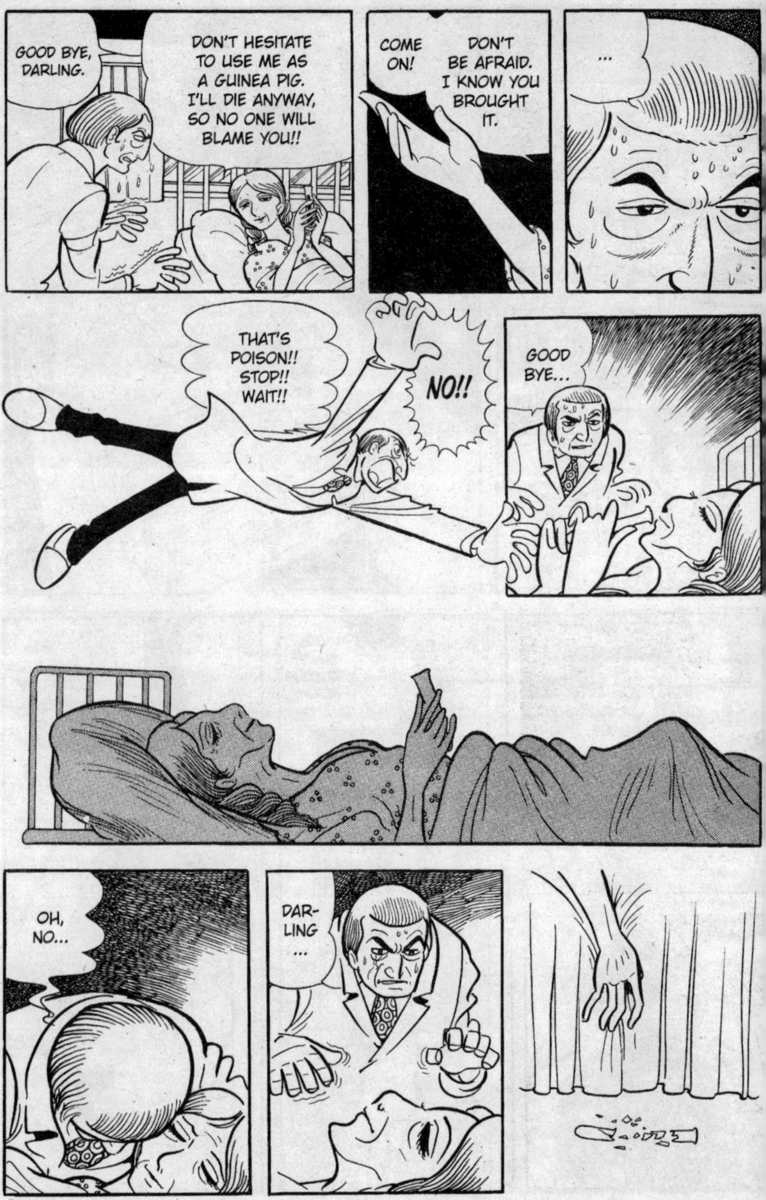
...
DON'T BE AFRAID. I KNOW YOU BROUGHT IT.
COME ON!
DON'T HESITATE TO USE ME AS A GUINEA PIG. I'LL DIE ANYWAY, SO NO ONE WILL BLAME YOU!!
GOOD BYE, DARLING.
GOOD BYE...
NO!!
THAT'S POISON!! STOP!! WAIT!!
DAR- LING ...
OH, NO...

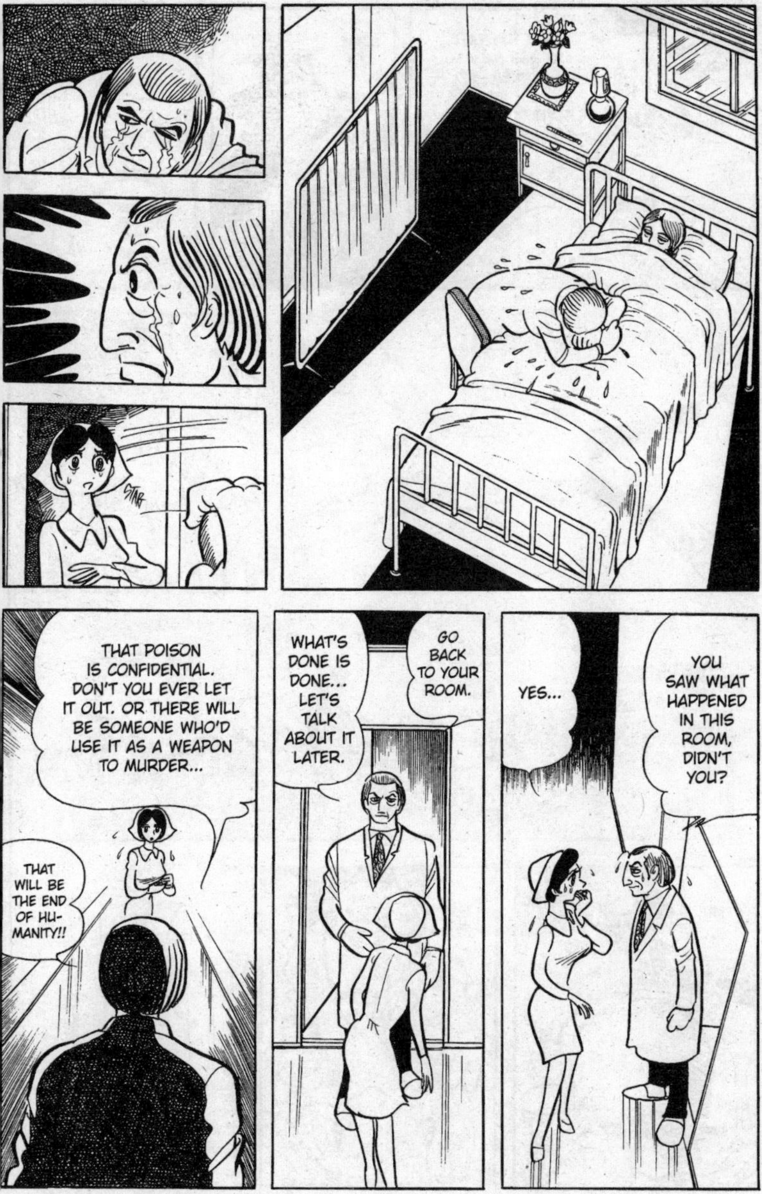
STAR
YOU SAW WHAT HAPPENED IN THIS ROOM, DIDN'T YOU?
YES...
GO BACK TO YOUR ROOM.
WHAT'S DONE IS DONE... LET'S TALK ABOUT IT LATER.
THAT POISON IS CONFIDENTIAL. DON'T YOU EVER LET IT OUT. OR THERE WILL BE SOMEONE WHO'D USE IT AS A WEAPON TO MURDER...
THAT WILL BE THE END OF HU-MANITY!!

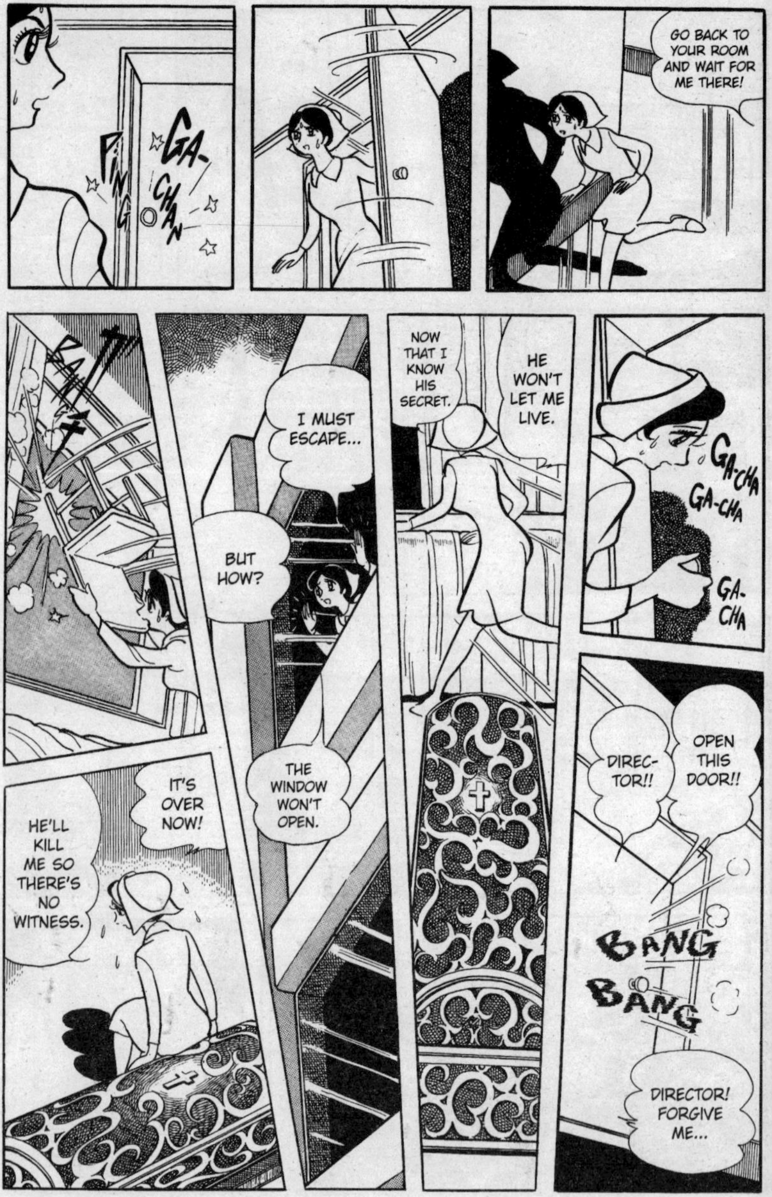
GO BACK TO YOUR ROOM AND WAIT FOR ME THERE!
GA-CHAN
PING
GA-CHA GA-CHA
GA-CHA
OPEN THIS DOOR!!
DIRECTOR!!
BANG BANG
DIRECTOR! FORGIVE ME...
HE WON'T LET ME LIVE.
NOW THAT I KNOW HIS SECRET.
I MUST ESCAPE...
BUT HOW?
THE WINDOW WON'T OPEN.
IT'S OVER NOW!
HE'LL KILL ME SO THERE'S NO WITNESS.

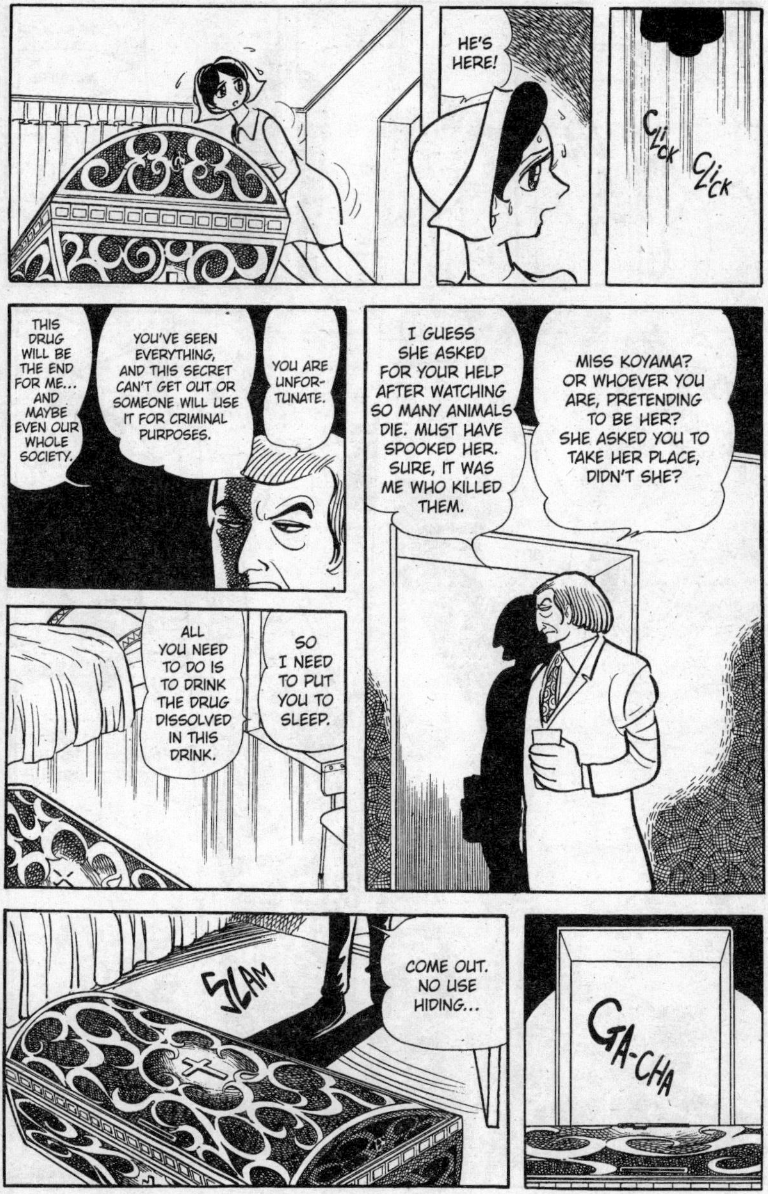
CLICK CLICK
HE'S HERE!
MISS KOYAMA? OR WHOEVER YOU ARE, PRETENDING TO BE HER? SHE ASKED YOU TO TAKE HER PLACE, DIDN'T SHE?
I GUESS SHE ASKED FOR YOUR HELP AFTER WATCHING SO MANY ANIMALS DIE. MUST HAVE SPOOKED HER. SURE, IT WAS ME WHO KILLED THEM.
YOU ARE UNFORTUNATE.
YOU'VE SEEN EVERYTHING, AND THIS SECRET CAN'T GET OUT OR SOMEONE WILL USE IT FOR CRIMINAL PURPOSES.
THIS DRUG WILL BE THE END FOR ME... AND MAYBE EVEN OUR WHOLE SOCIETY.
SO I NEED TO PUT YOU TO SLEEP.
ALL YOU NEED TO DO IS TO DRINK THE DRUG DISSOLVED IN THIS DRINK.
GA-CHA
COME OUT. NO USE HIDING...
SLAM

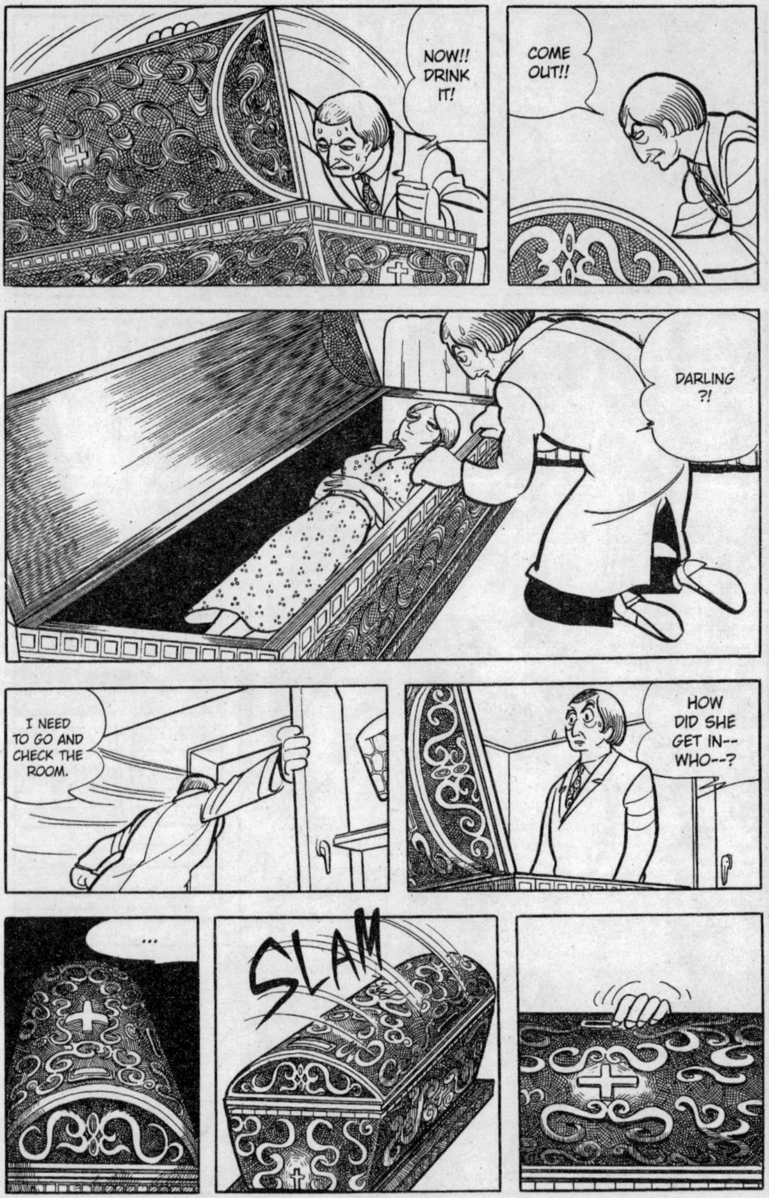
COME OUT!!
NOW!! DRINK IT!
DARLING ?!
HOW DID SHE GET IN-- WHO--?
I NEED TO GO AND CHECK THE ROOM.
SLAM
...

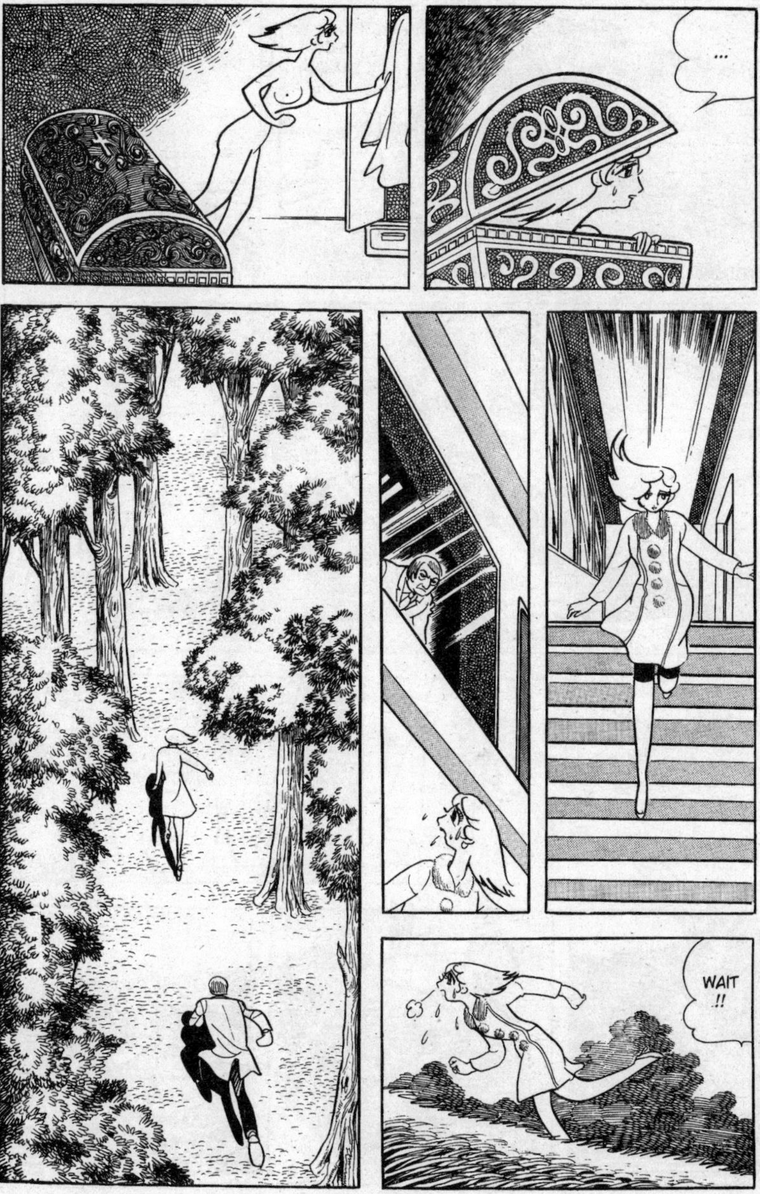
...
WAIT !!

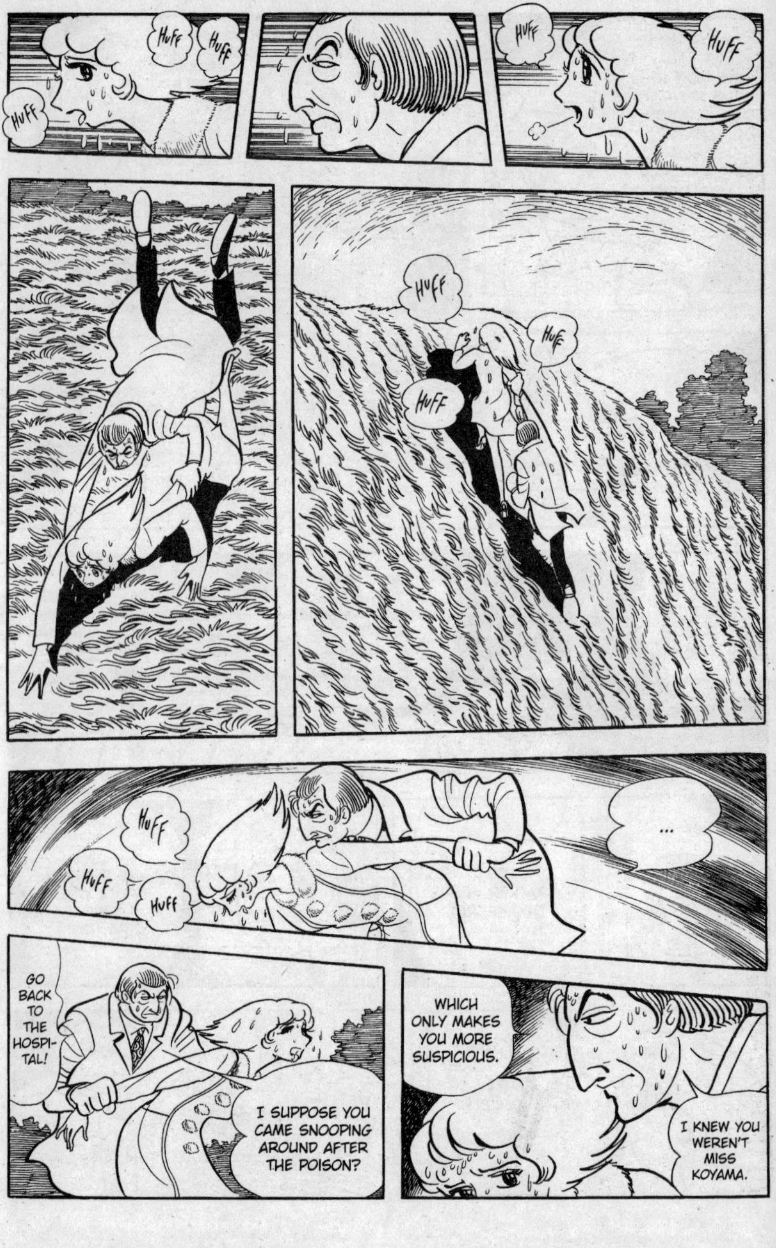
HUFF
HUFF
HUFF
HUFF
HUFF
HUFF
HUFF
HUFF
HUFF
...
HUFF
HUFF
HUFF
I KNEW YOU WEREN'T MISS KOYAMA.
WHICH ONLY MAKES YOU MORE SUSPICIOUS.
I SUPPOSE YOU CAME SNOOPING AROUND AFTER THE POISON?
GO BACK TO THE HOSPI-TAL!

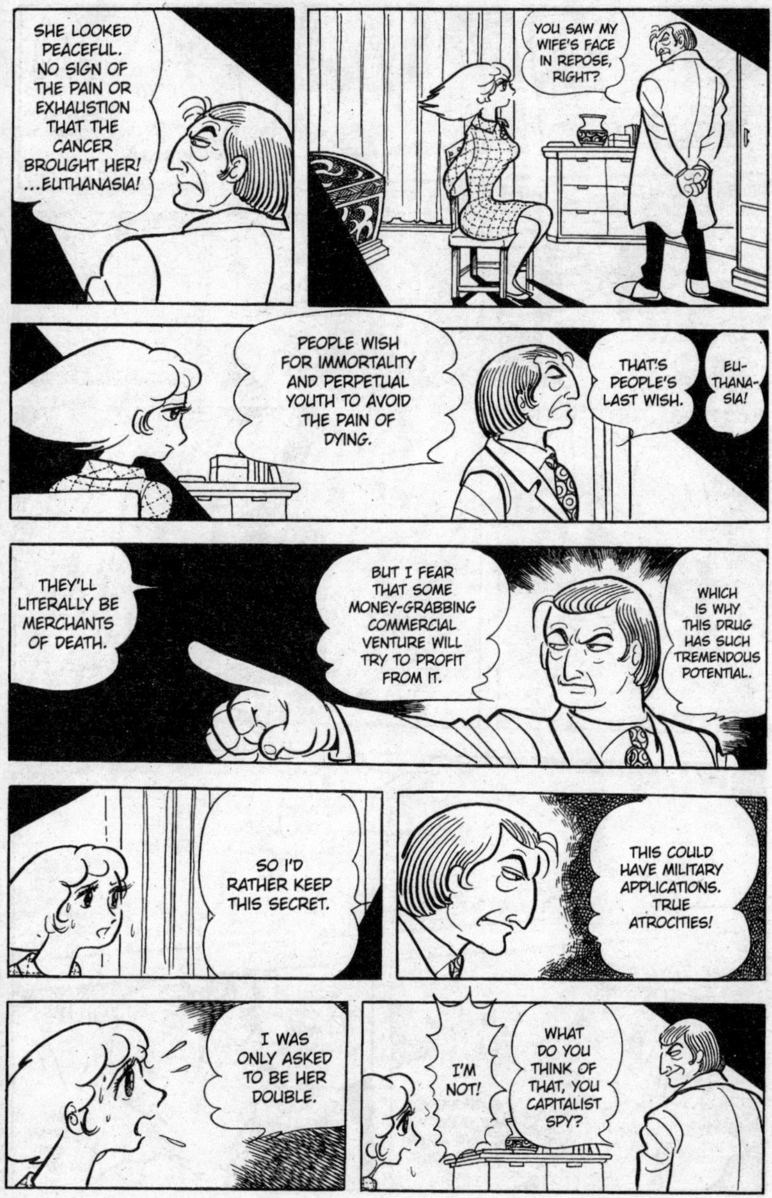
YOU SAW MY WIFE'S FACE IN REPOSE, RIGHT?
SHE LOOKED PEACEFUL. NO SIGN OF THE PAIN OR EXHAUSTION THAT THE CANCER BROUGHT HER! ...EUTHANASIA!
EU-THANA-SIA!
THAT'S PEOPLE'S LAST WISH.
PEOPLE WISH FOR IMMORTALITY AND PERPETUAL YOUTH TO AVOID THE PAIN OF DYING.
WHICH IS WHY THIS DRUG HAS SUCH TREMENDOUS POTENTIAL.
BUT I FEAR THAT SOME MONEY-GRABBING COMMERCIAL VENTURE WILL TRY TO PROFIT FROM IT.
THEY'LL LITERALLY BE MERCHANTS OF DEATH.
THIS COULD HAVE MILITARY APPLICATIONS. TRUE ATROCITIES!
SO I'D RATHER KEEP THIS SECRET.
WHAT DO YOU THINK OF THAT, YOU CAPITALIST SPY?
I'M NOT!
I WAS ONLY ASKED TO BE HER DOUBLE.

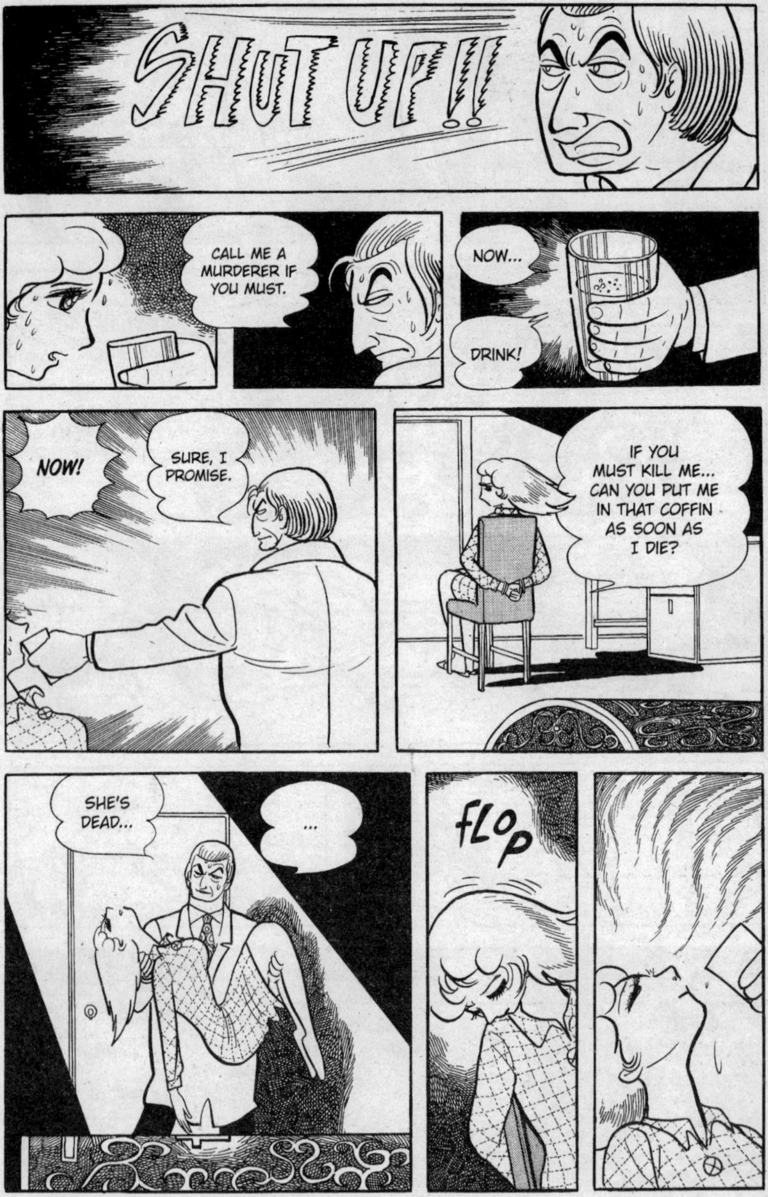
SHUT UP!!
NOW...
DRINK!
CALL ME A MURDERER IF YOU MUST.
IF YOU MUST KILL ME... CAN YOU PUT ME IN THAT COFFIN AS SOON AS I DIE?
SURE, I PROMISE.
NOW!
FLOP
SHE'S DEAD...
...

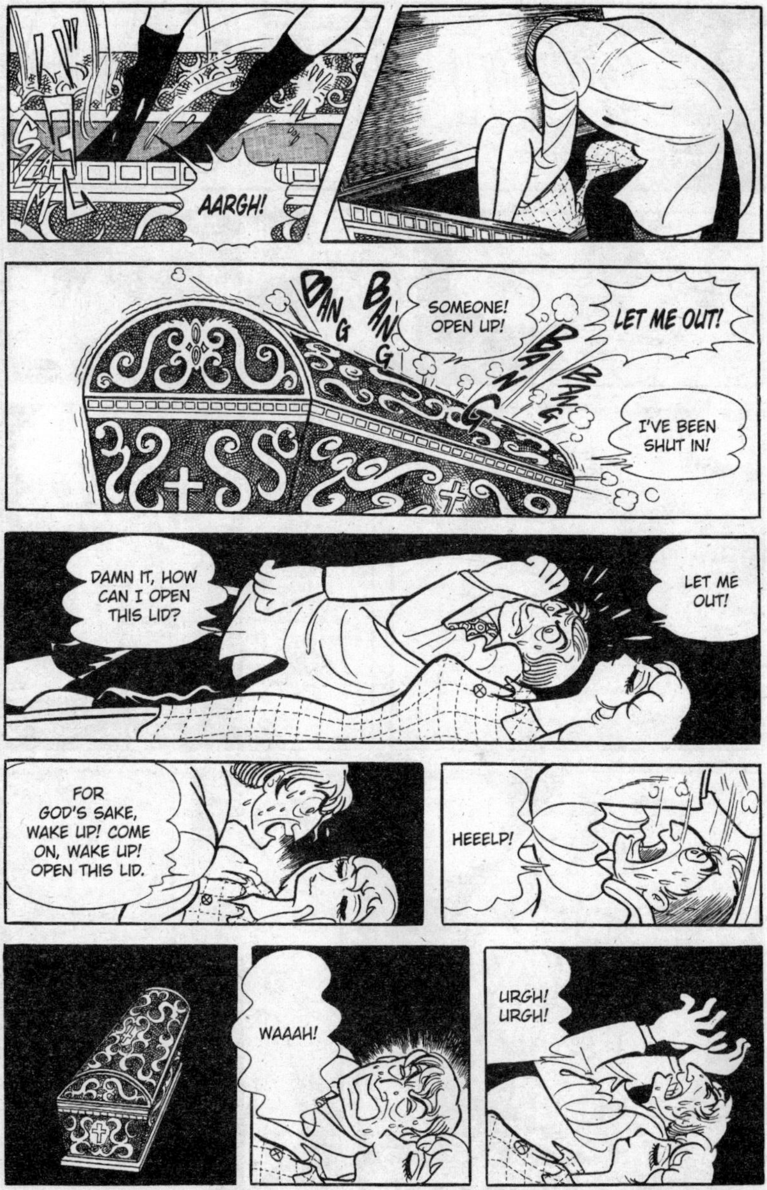
AARGH!
LET ME OUT!
BANG BANG
SOMEONE! OPEN UP!
BANG BANG
I'VE BEEN SHUT IN!
LET ME OUT!
DAMN IT, HOW CAN I OPEN THIS LID?
HEEELP!
FOR GOD'S SAKE, WAKE UP! COME ON, WAKE UP! OPEN THIS LID.
URGH! URGH!
WAAAH!

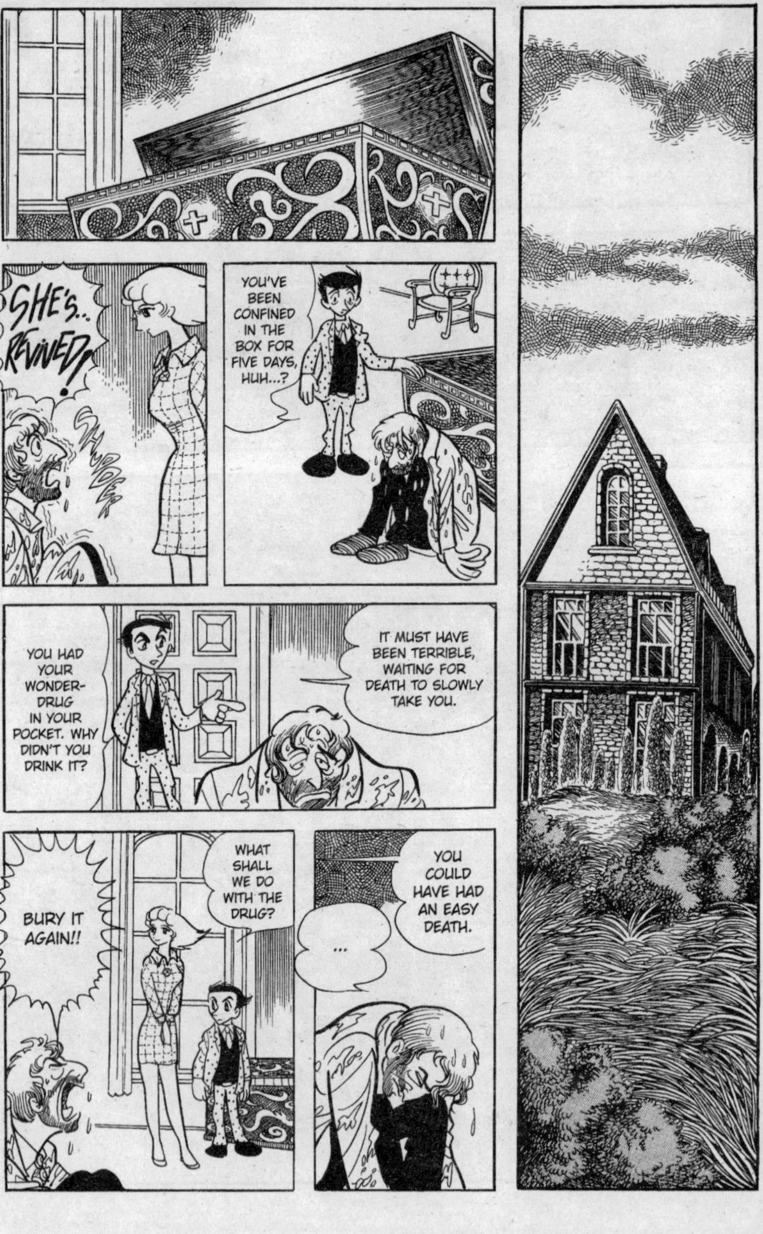
YOU'VE BEEN CONFINED IN THE BOX FOR FIVE DAYS, HUH...?
SHE'S... REVIVED!
SHUDDER
IT MUST HAVE BEEN TERRIBLE, WAITING FOR DEATH TO SLOWLY TAKE YOU.
YOU HAD YOUR WONDER-DRUG IN YOUR POCKET. WHY DIDN'T YOU DRINK IT?
YOU COULD HAVE HAD AN EASY DEATH.
...
WHAT SHALL WE DO WITH THE DRUG?
BURY IT AGAIN!!

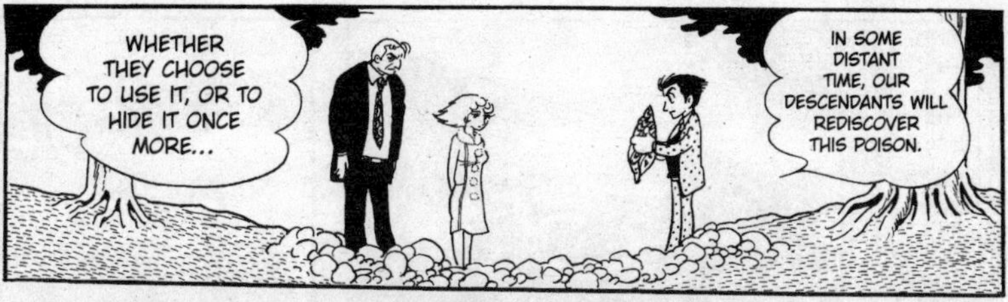
IN SOME DISTANT TIME, OUR DESCENDANTS WILL REDISCOVER THIS POISON.
WHETHER THEY CHOOSE TO USE IT, OR TO HIDE IT ONCE MORE...

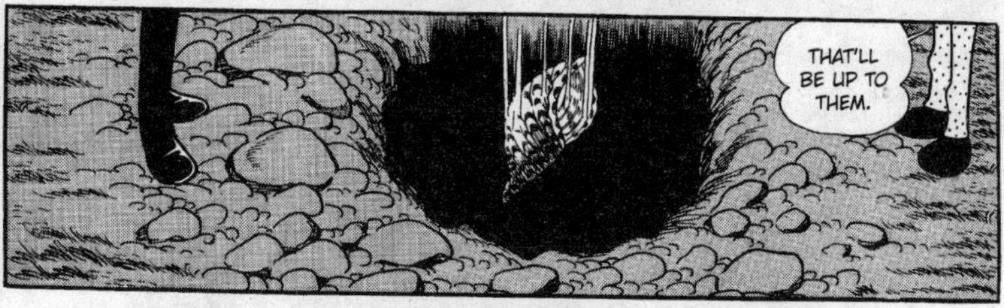
THAT'LL BE UP TO THEM.

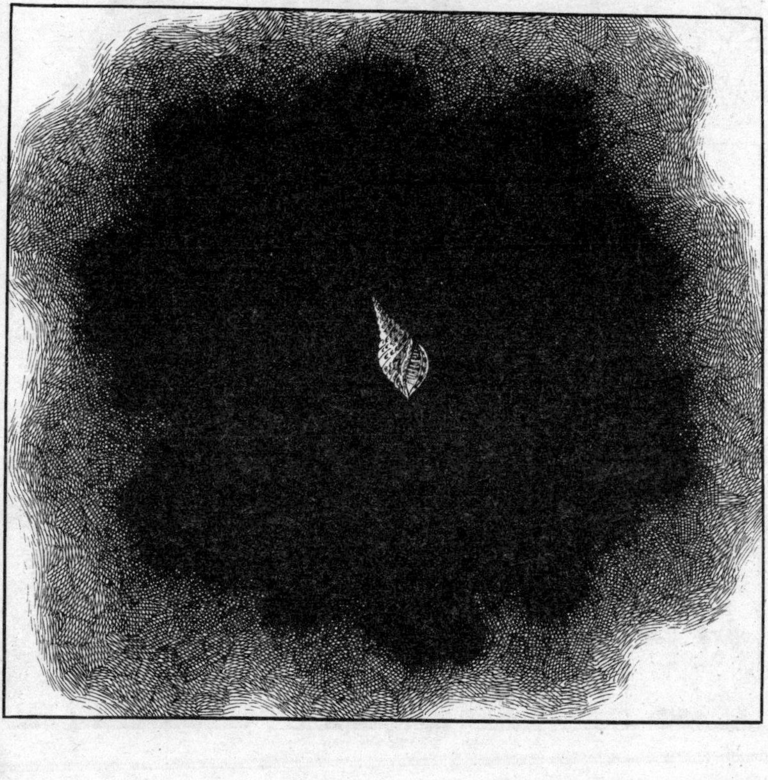

# EPISODE 11
# The Man Who Came From The South

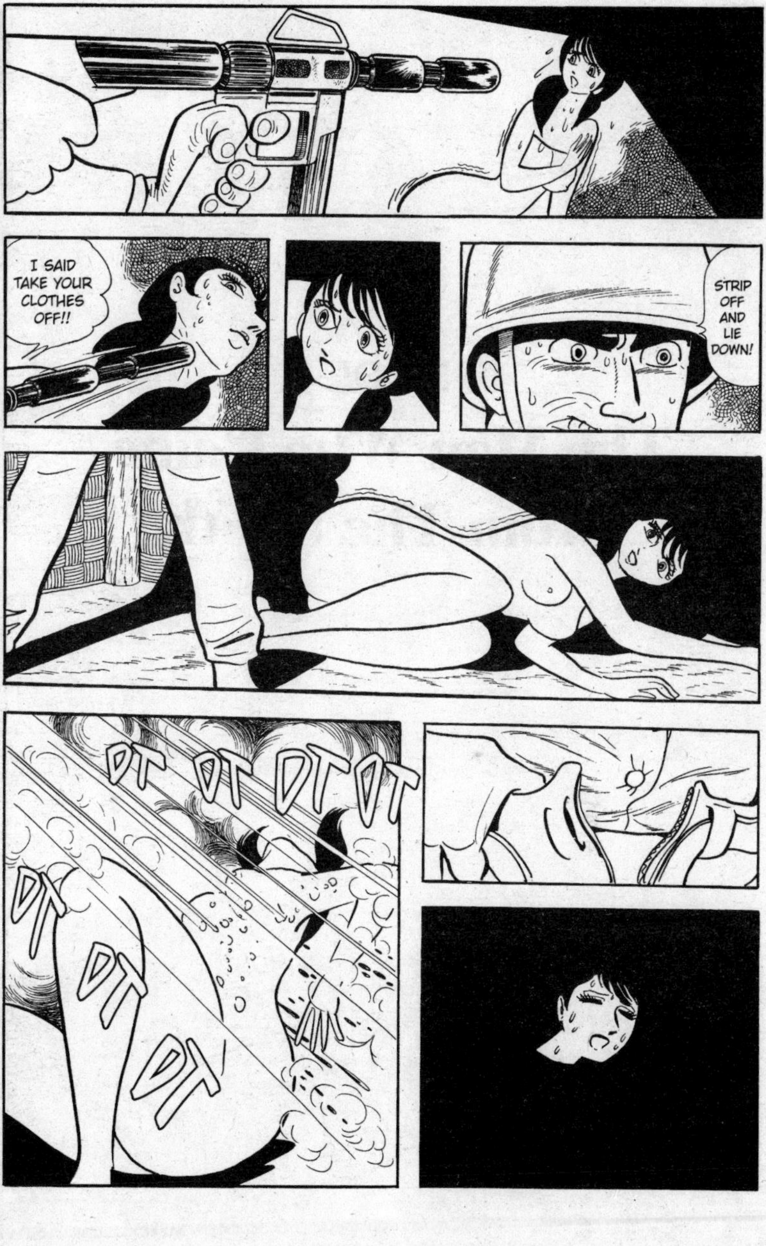
STRIP OFF AND LIE DOWN!
I SAID TAKE YOUR CLOTHES OFF!!
DT DT DT DT
DT DT DT

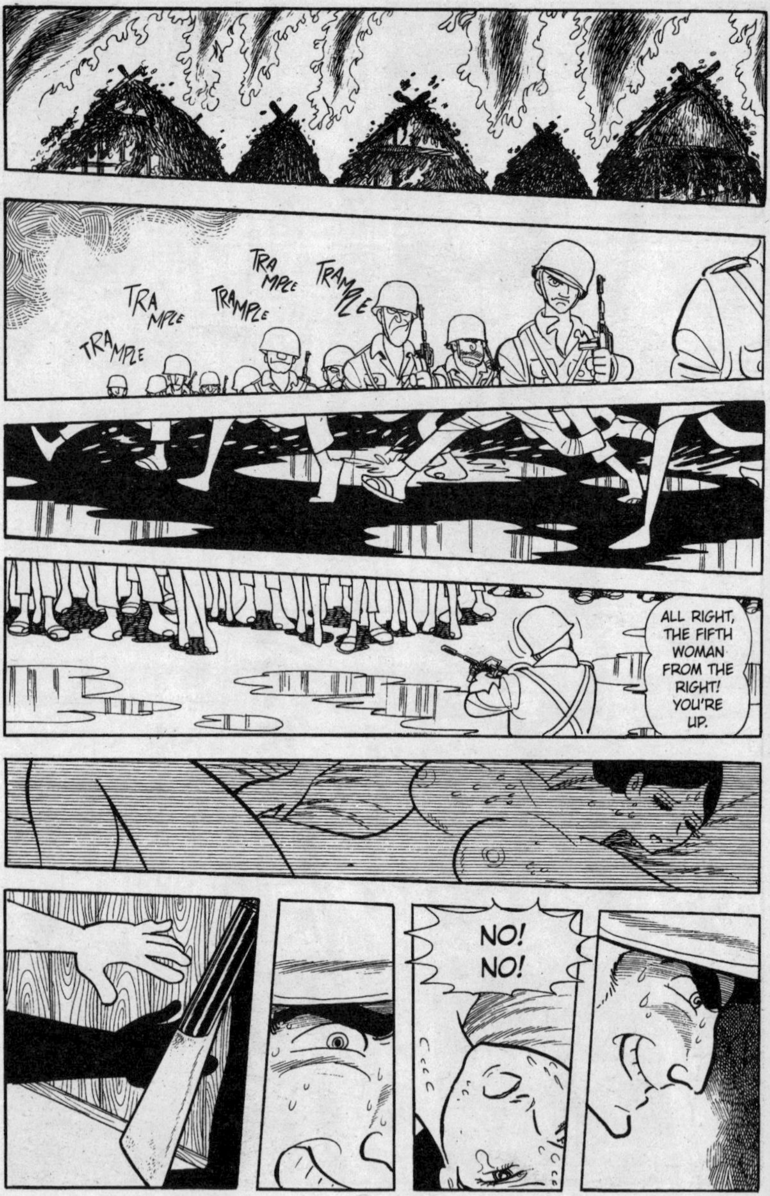
TRAMPLE
TRAMPLE
TRAMPLE
TRAMPLE
TRAMPLE
ALL RIGHT, THE FIFTH WOMAN FROM THE RIGHT! YOU'RE UP.
NO! NO!

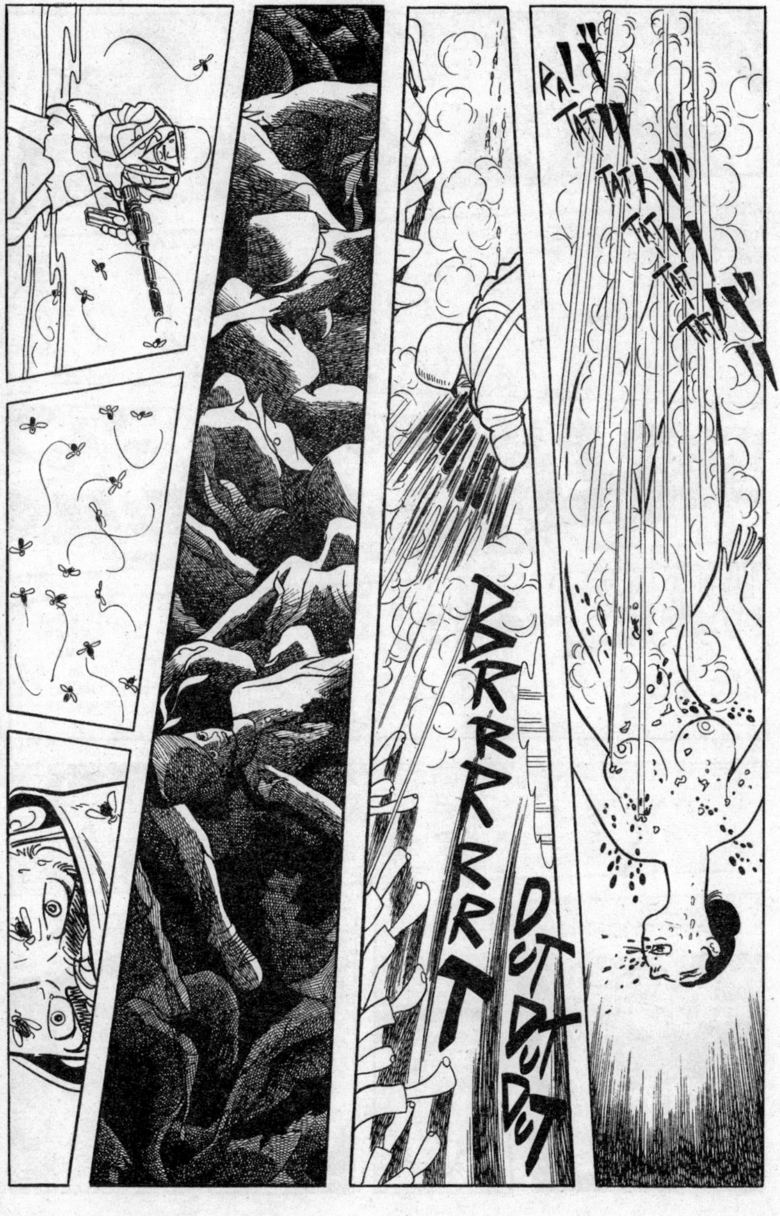
RA! TAT! TAT! TAT! TAT! TAT!
BRRRRRRT
DUT DUT DUT DUT

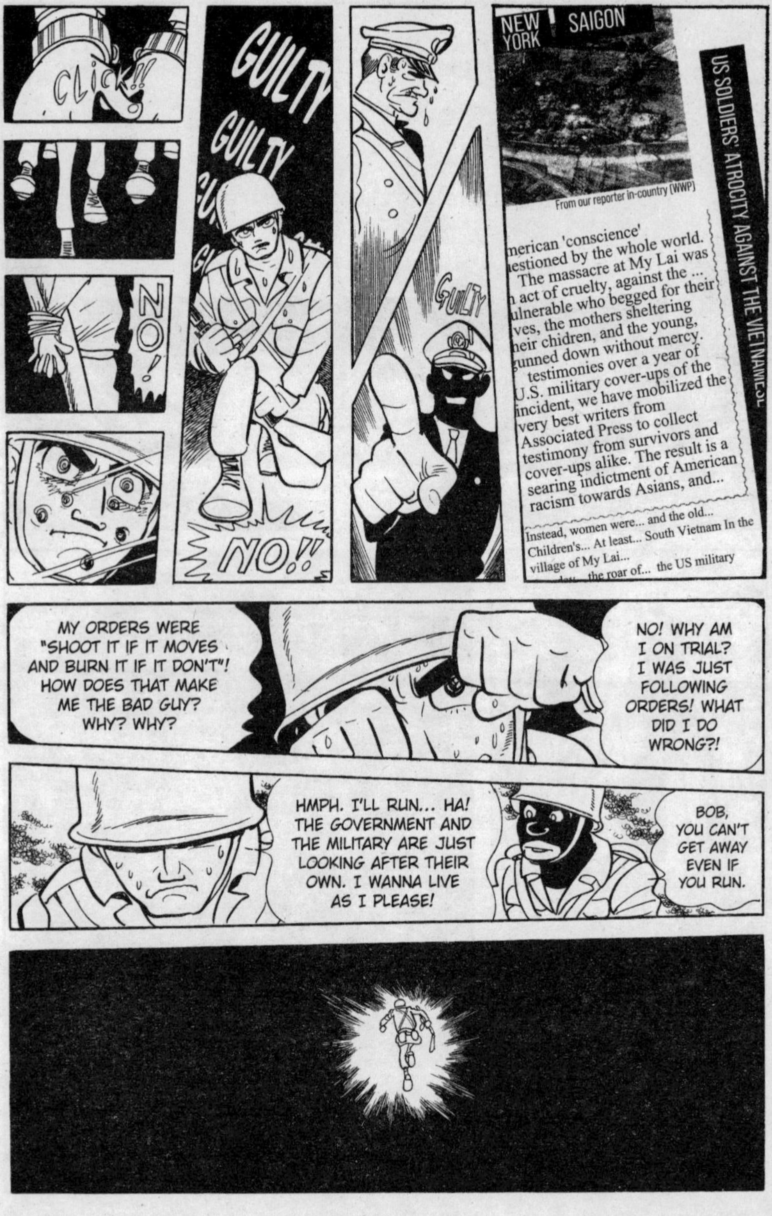
NEW YORK
SAIGON
US SOLDIERS' ATROCITY AGAINST THE VIETNAMESE
From our reporter in-country (WWP)
merican 'conscience'
estioned by the whole world.
The massacre at My Lai was
act of cruelty, against the ...
ulnerable who begged for their
ves, the mothers sheltering
heir chidren, and the young,
gunned down without mercy.
testimonies over a year of
U.S. military cover-ups of the
incident, we have mobilized the
very best writers from
Associated Press to collect
testimony from survivors and
cover-ups alike. The result is a
searing indictment of American
racism towards Asians, and...
Instead, women were... and the old...
Children's... At least... South Vietnam In the
village of My Lai...
the roar of... the US military
GUILTY
GUILTY
GUILTY
GU
NO!!
CLICK!!
NO!
NO! WHY AM I ON TRIAL? I WAS JUST FOLLOWING ORDERS! WHAT DID I DO WRONG?!
MY ORDERS WERE "SHOOT IT IF IT MOVES AND BURN IT IF IT DON'T"! HOW DOES THAT MAKE ME THE BAD GUY? WHY? WHY?
BOB, YOU CAN'T GET AWAY EVEN IF YOU RUN.
HMPH. I'LL RUN... HA! THE GOVERNMENT AND THE MILITARY ARE JUST LOOKING AFTER THEIR OWN. I WANNA LIVE AS I PLEASE!

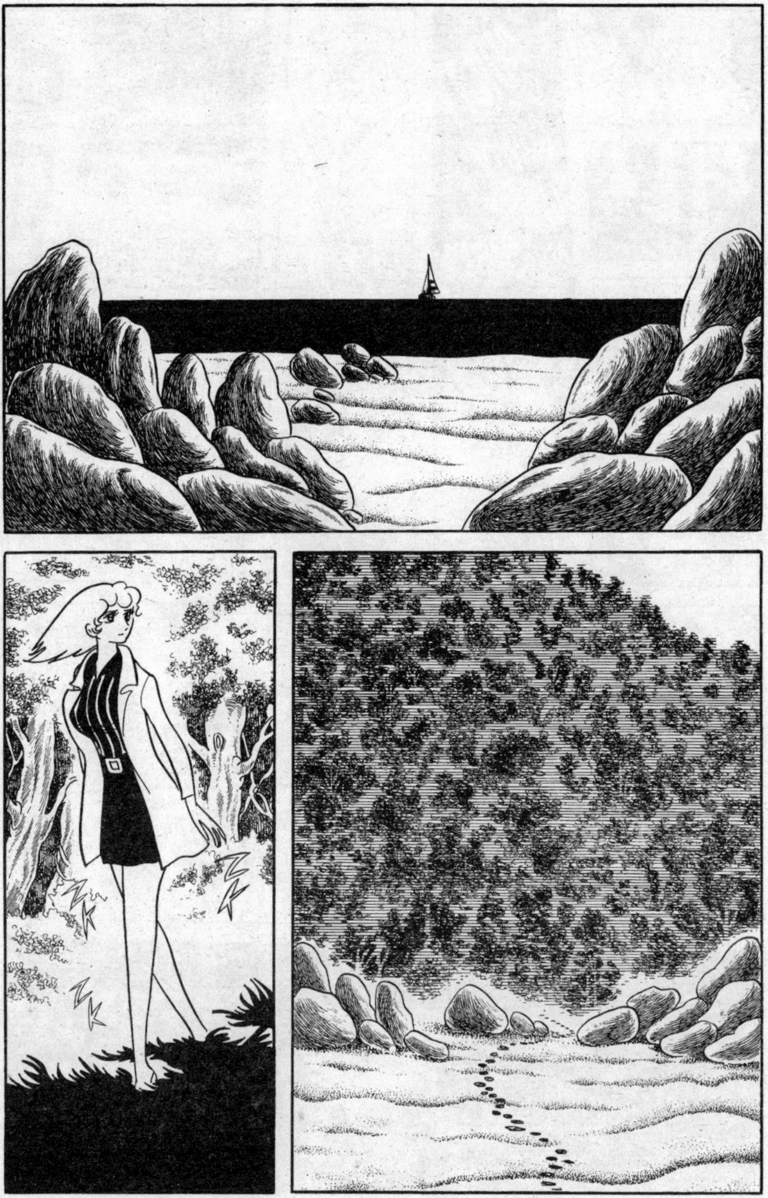

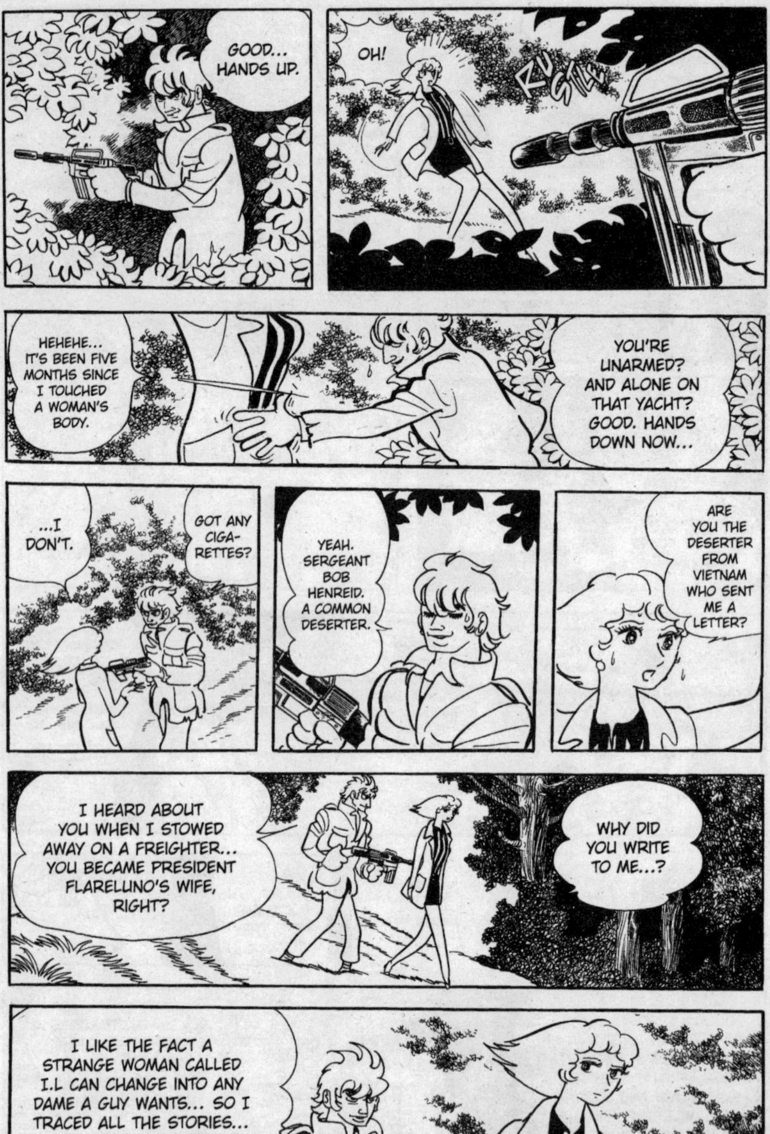
OH!
RUSTLE
GOOD... HANDS UP.
YOU'RE UNARMED? AND ALONE ON THAT YACHT? GOOD. HANDS DOWN NOW...
HEHEHE... IT'S BEEN FIVE MONTHS SINCE I TOUCHED A WOMAN'S BODY.
ARE YOU THE DESERTER FROM VIETNAM WHO SENT ME A LETTER?
YEAH. SERGEANT BOB HENREID. A COMMON DESERTER.
GOT ANY CIGARETTES?
...I DON'T.
WHY DID YOU WRITE TO ME...?
I HEARD ABOUT YOU WHEN I STOWED AWAY ON A FREIGHTER... YOU BECAME PRESIDENT FLARELUNO'S WIFE, RIGHT?
I LIKE THE FACT A STRANGE WOMAN CALLED I.L CAN CHANGE INTO ANY DAME A GUY WANTS... SO I TRACED ALL THE STORIES... I WAS AN INFORMER BACK HOME.

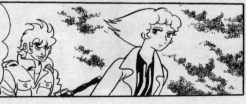

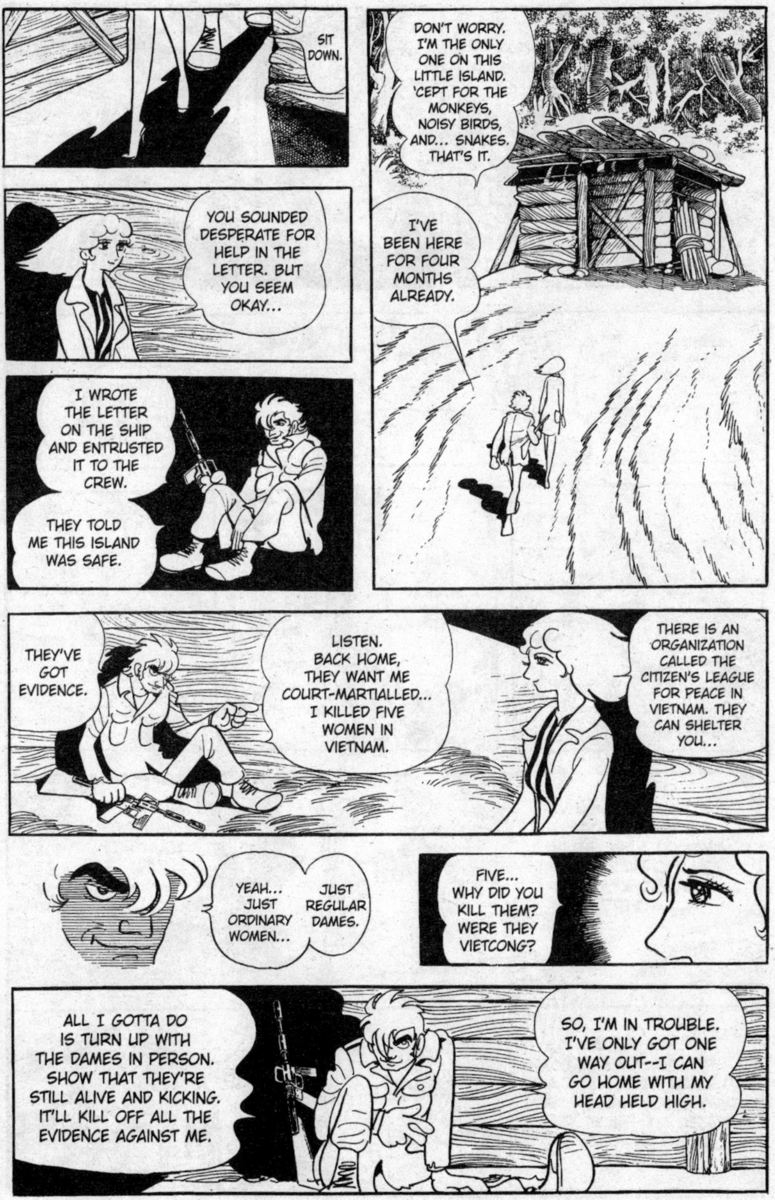
DON'T WORRY. I'M THE ONLY ONE ON THIS LITTLE ISLAND. 'CEPT FOR THE MONKEYS, NOISY BIRDS, AND... SNAKES. THAT'S IT.
I'VE BEEN HERE FOR FOUR MONTHS ALREADY.
SIT DOWN.
YOU SOUNDED DESPERATE FOR HELP IN THE LETTER. BUT YOU SEEM OKAY...
I WROTE THE LETTER ON THE SHIP AND ENTRUSTED IT TO THE CREW.
THEY TOLD ME THIS ISLAND WAS SAFE.
THERE IS AN ORGANIZATION CALLED THE CITIZEN'S LEAGUE FOR PEACE IN VIETNAM. THEY CAN SHELTER YOU...
LISTEN. BACK HOME, THEY WANT ME COURT-MARTIALLED... I KILLED FIVE WOMEN IN VIETNAM.
THEY'VE GOT EVIDENCE.
FIVE... WHY DID YOU KILL THEM? WERE THEY VIETCONG?
JUST REGULAR DAMES.
YEAH... JUST ORDINARY WOMEN...
SO, I'M IN TROUBLE. I'VE ONLY GOT ONE WAY OUT--I CAN GO HOME WITH MY HEAD HELD HIGH.
ALL I GOTTA DO IS TURN UP WITH THE DAMES IN PERSON. SHOW THAT THEY'RE STILL ALIVE AND KICKING. IT'LL KILL OFF ALL THE EVIDENCE AGAINST ME.

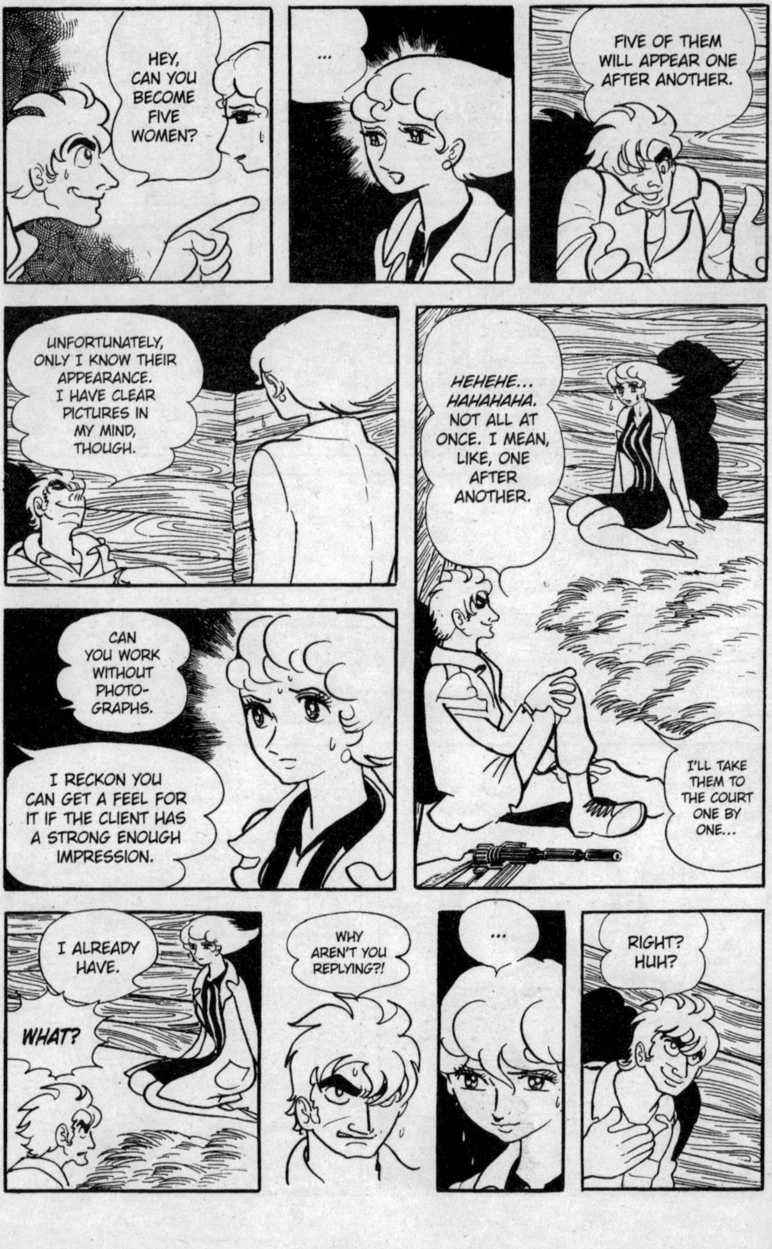
FIVE OF THEM WILL APPEAR ONE AFTER ANOTHER.
...
HEY, CAN YOU BECOME FIVE WOMEN?
HEHEHE... HAHAHAHA. NOT ALL AT ONCE. I MEAN, LIKE, ONE AFTER ANOTHER.
I'LL TAKE THEM TO THE COURT ONE BY ONE...
UNFORTUNATELY, ONLY I KNOW THEIR APPEARANCE. I HAVE CLEAR PICTURES IN MY MIND, THOUGH.
CAN YOU WORK WITHOUT PHOTO-GRAPHS.
I RECKON YOU CAN GET A FEEL FOR IT IF THE CLIENT HAS A STRONG ENOUGH IMPRESSION.
RIGHT? HUH?
...
WHY AREN'T YOU REPLYING?!
I ALREADY HAVE.
WHAT?

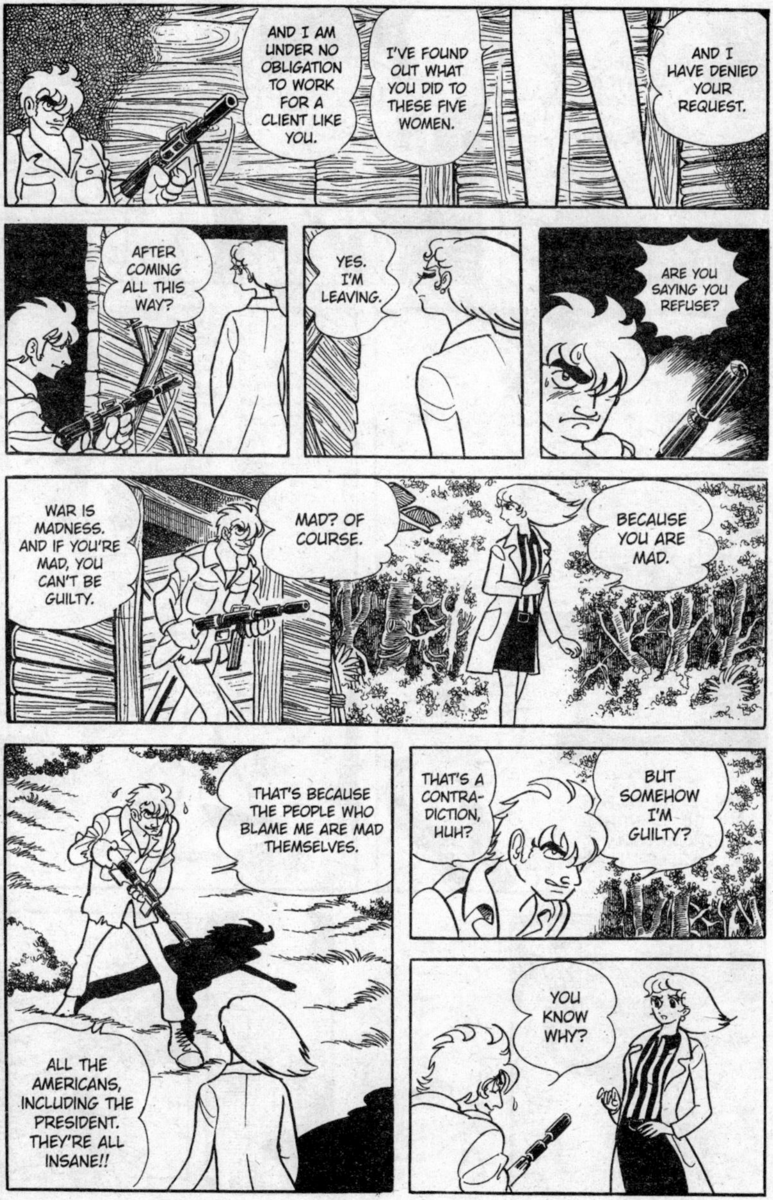
AND I HAVE DENIED YOUR REQUEST.
I'VE FOUND OUT WHAT YOU DID TO THESE FIVE WOMEN.
AND I AM UNDER NO OBLIGATION TO WORK FOR A CLIENT LIKE YOU.
ARE YOU SAYING YOU REFUSE?
YES. I'M LEAVING.
AFTER COMING ALL THIS WAY?
BECAUSE YOU ARE MAD.
MAD? OF COURSE.
WAR IS MADNESS. AND IF YOU'RE MAD, YOU CAN'T BE GUILTY.
BUT SOMEHOW I'M GUILTY?
THAT'S A CONTRADICTION, HUH?
YOU KNOW WHY?
THAT'S BECAUSE THE PEOPLE WHO BLAME ME ARE MAD THEMSELVES.
ALL THE AMERICANS, INCLUDING THE PRESIDENT. THEY'RE ALL INSANE!!

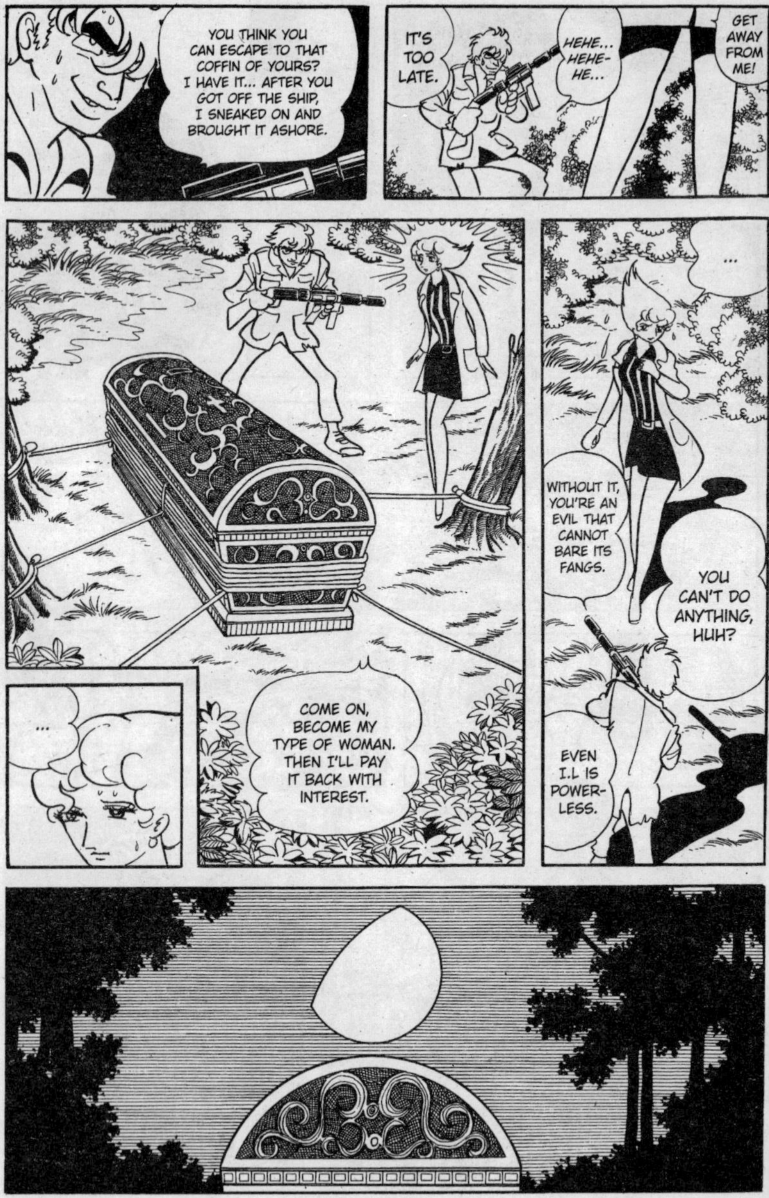
GET AWAY FROM ME!
HEHE... HEHE-HE...
IT'S TOO LATE.
YOU THINK YOU CAN ESCAPE TO THAT COFFIN OF YOURS? I HAVE IT... AFTER YOU GOT OFF THE SHIP, I SNEAKED ON AND BROUGHT IT ASHORE.
...
YOU CAN'T DO ANYTHING, HUH?
WITHOUT IT, YOU'RE AN EVIL THAT CANNOT BARE ITS FANGS.
EVEN I.L IS POWER-LESS.
COME ON, BECOME MY TYPE OF WOMAN. THEN I'LL PAY IT BACK WITH INTEREST.
...

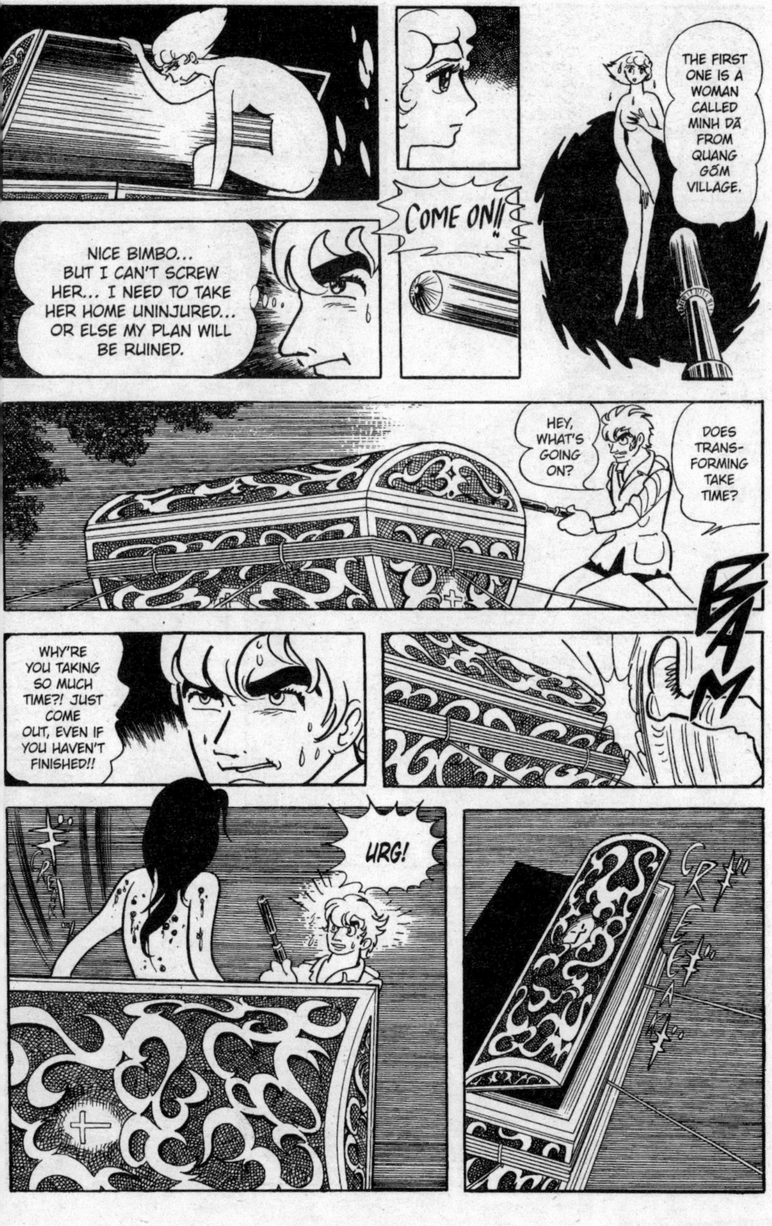
THE FIRST ONE IS A WOMAN CALLED MINH DÃ FROM QUANG GỐM VILLAGE.
COME ON!!
NICE BIMBO... BUT I CAN'T SCREW HER... I NEED TO TAKE HER HOME UNINJURED... OR ELSE MY PLAN WILL BE RUINED.
DOES TRANSFORMING TAKE TIME?
HEY, WHAT'S GOING ON?
BAM
WHY'RE YOU TAKING SO MUCH TIME?! JUST COME OUT, EVEN IF YOU HAVEN'T FINISHED!!
URG!

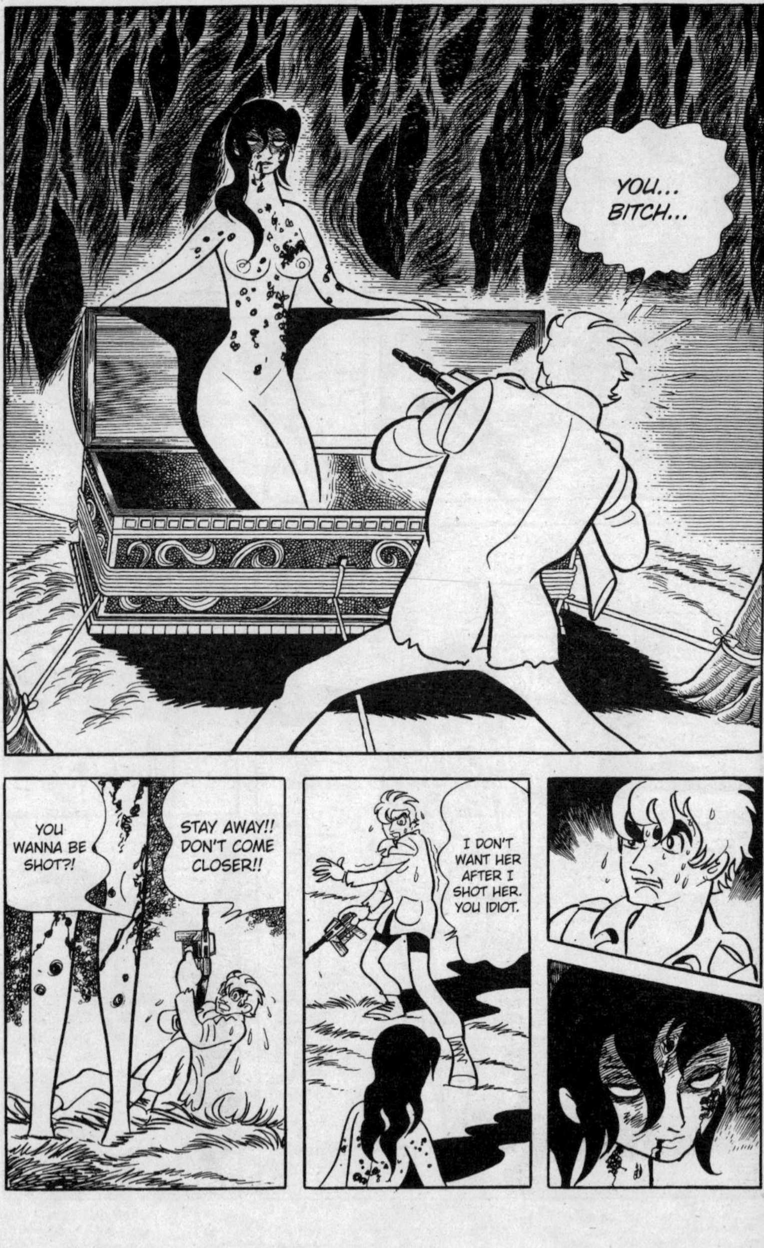
YOU... BITCH...
I DON'T WANT HER AFTER I SHOT HER. YOU IDIOT.
STAY AWAY!! DON'T COME CLOSER!!
YOU WANNA BE SHOT?!

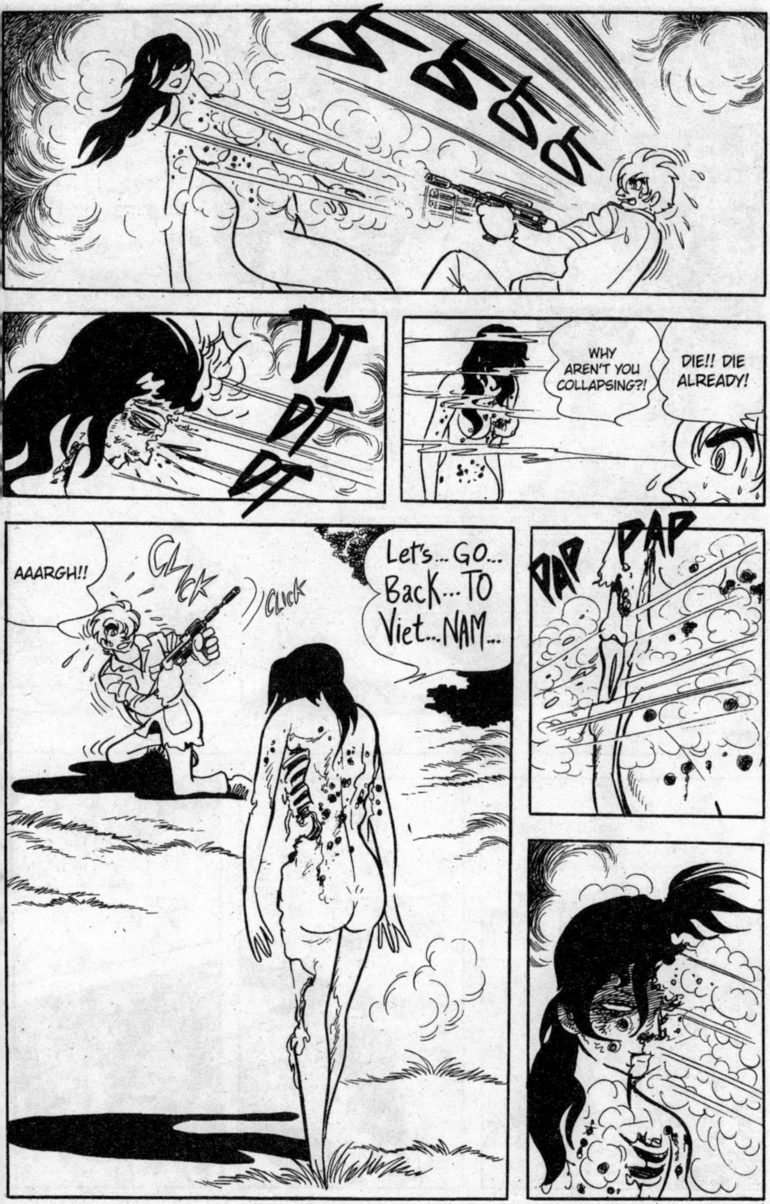
DIE!! DIE ALREADY!
WHY AREN'T YOU COLLAPSING?!
DT DT DT
PAP PAP
Let's... GO... Back... TO Viet... NAM...
CLICK
CLICK
AAARGH!!

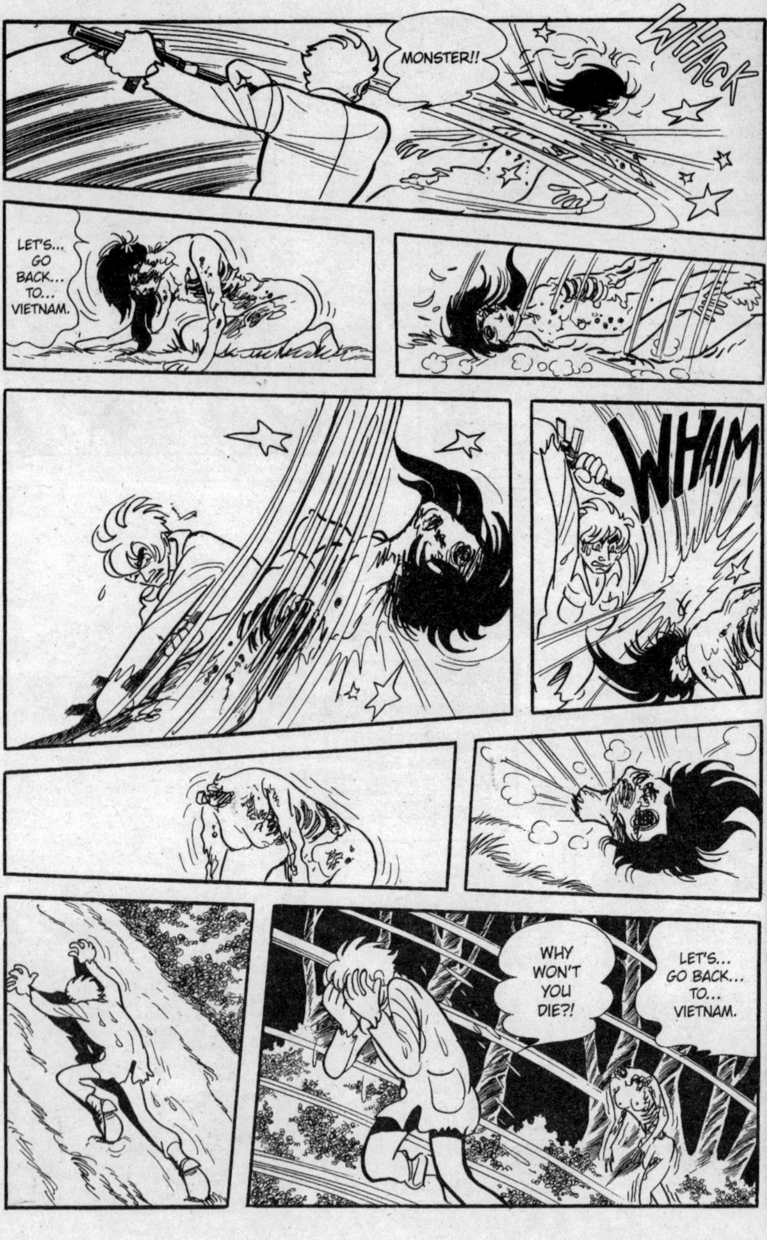
WHACK
MONSTER!!
LET'S... GO BACK... TO... VIETNAM.
WHAM
LET'S... GO BACK... TO... VIETNAM.
WHY WON'T YOU DIE?!

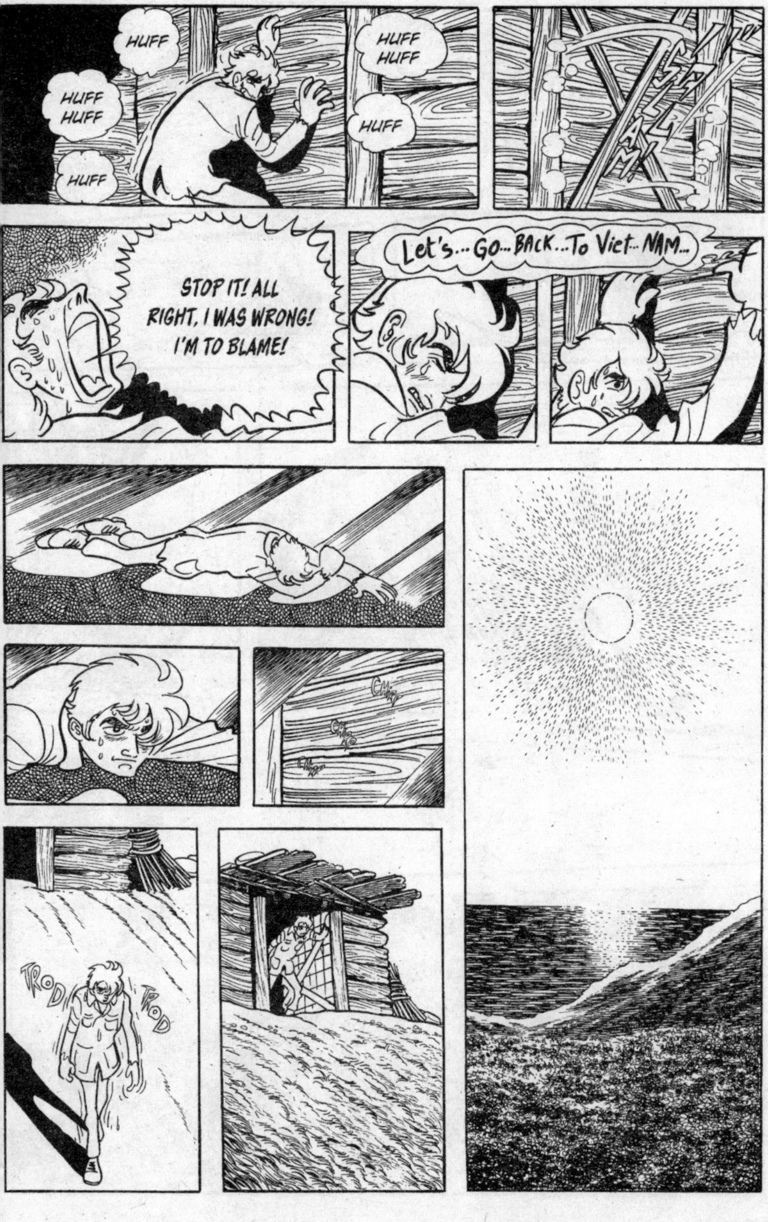
SLAM!
HUFF HUFF
HUFF
HUFF
HUFF HUFF
HUFF
Let's... GO... BACK... To Viet... NAM...
STOP IT! ALL RIGHT, I WAS WRONG! I'M TO BLAME!
TROD TROD

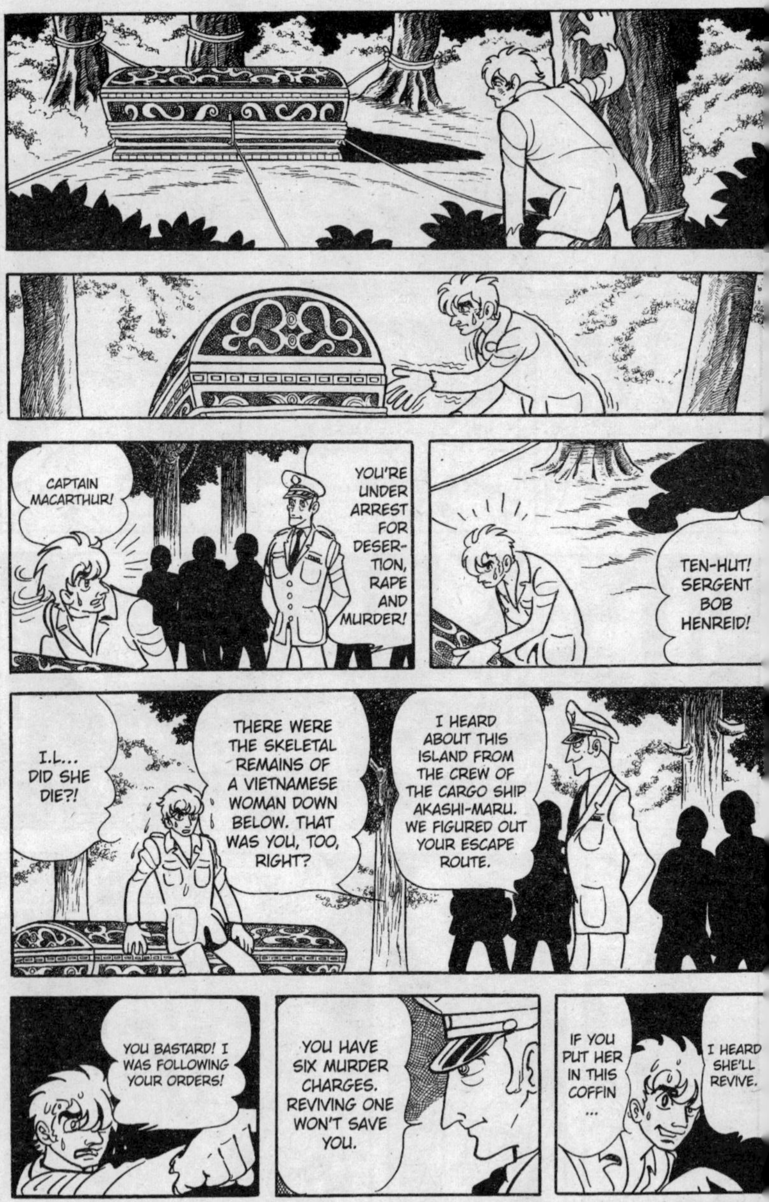
TEN-HUT! SERGENT BOB HENREID!
YOU'RE UNDER ARREST FOR DESER-TION, RAPE AND MURDER!
CAPTAIN MACARTHUR!
I HEARD ABOUT THIS ISLAND FROM THE CREW OF THE CARGO SHIP AKASHI-MARU. WE FIGURED OUT YOUR ESCAPE ROUTE.
THERE WERE THE SKELETAL REMAINS OF A VIETNAMESE WOMAN DOWN BELOW. THAT WAS YOU, TOO, RIGHT?
I.L... DID SHE DIE?!
I HEARD SHE'LL REVIVE.
IF YOU PUT HER IN THIS COFFIN ...
YOU HAVE SIX MURDER CHARGES. REVIVING ONE WON'T SAVE YOU.
YOU BASTARD! I WAS FOLLOWING YOUR ORDERS!

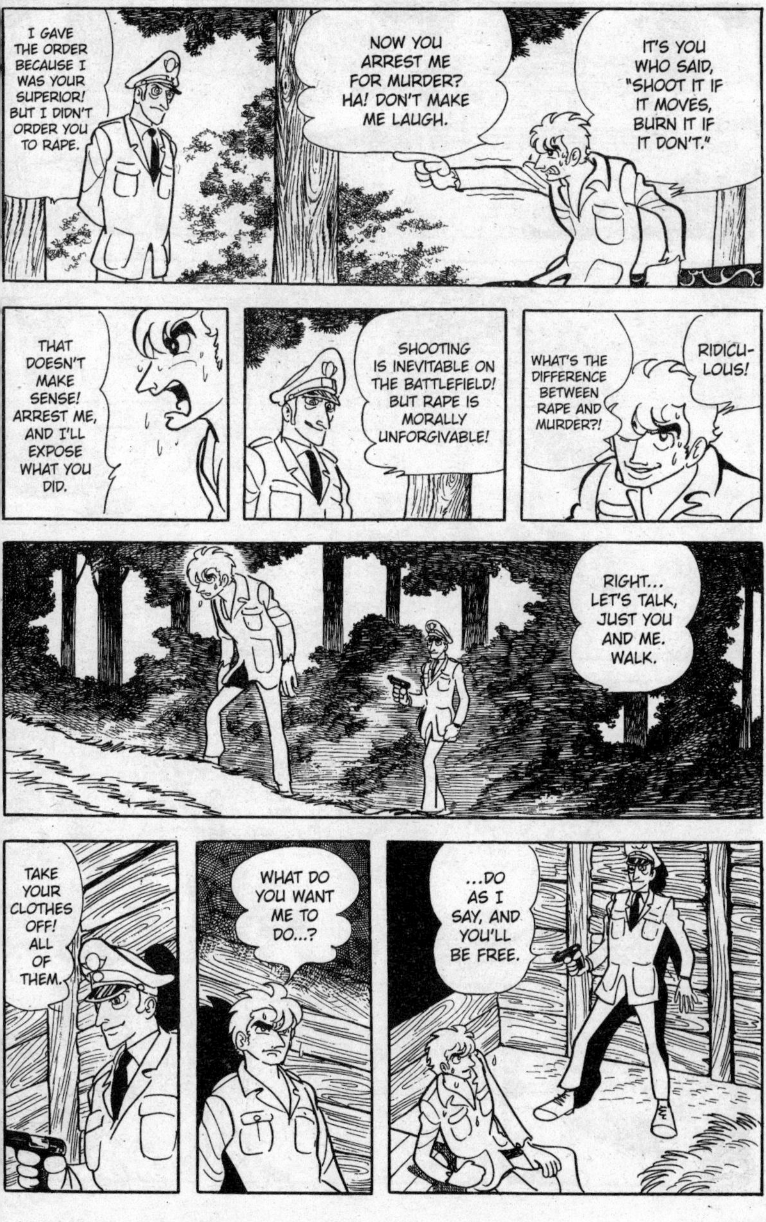
IT'S YOU WHO SAID, "SHOOT IT IF IT MOVES, BURN IT IF IT DON'T."
NOW YOU ARREST ME FOR MURDER? HA! DON'T MAKE ME LAUGH.
I GAVE THE ORDER BECAUSE I WAS YOUR SUPERIOR! BUT I DIDN'T ORDER YOU TO RAPE.
RIDICU-LOUS!
WHAT'S THE DIFFERENCE BETWEEN RAPE AND MURDER?!
SHOOTING IS INEVITABLE ON THE BATTLEFIELD! BUT RAPE IS MORALLY UNFORGIVABLE!
THAT DOESN'T MAKE SENSE! ARREST ME, AND I'LL EXPOSE WHAT YOU DID.
RIGHT... LET'S TALK, JUST YOU AND ME. WALK.
...DO AS I SAY, AND YOU'LL BE FREE.
WHAT DO YOU WANT ME TO DO...?
TAKE YOUR CLOTHES OFF! ALL OF THEM.

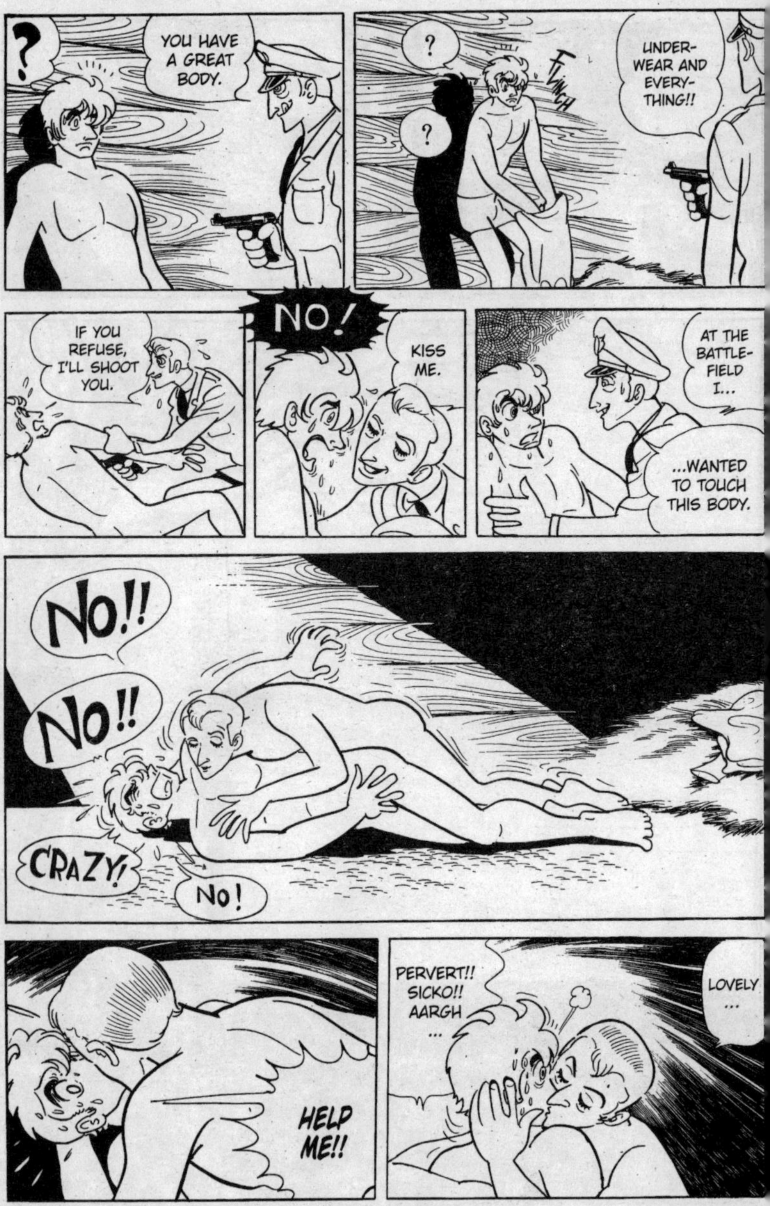
?
YOU HAVE A GREAT BODY.
?
?
FLINCH
UNDER-WEAR AND EVERY-THING!!
IF YOU REFUSE, I'LL SHOOT YOU.
NO!
KISS ME.
AT THE BATTLE-FIELD I...
...WANTED TO TOUCH THIS BODY.
No!!
No!!
CRAZY!
No!
HELP ME!!
PERVERT!! SICKO!! AARGH ...
LOVELY ...

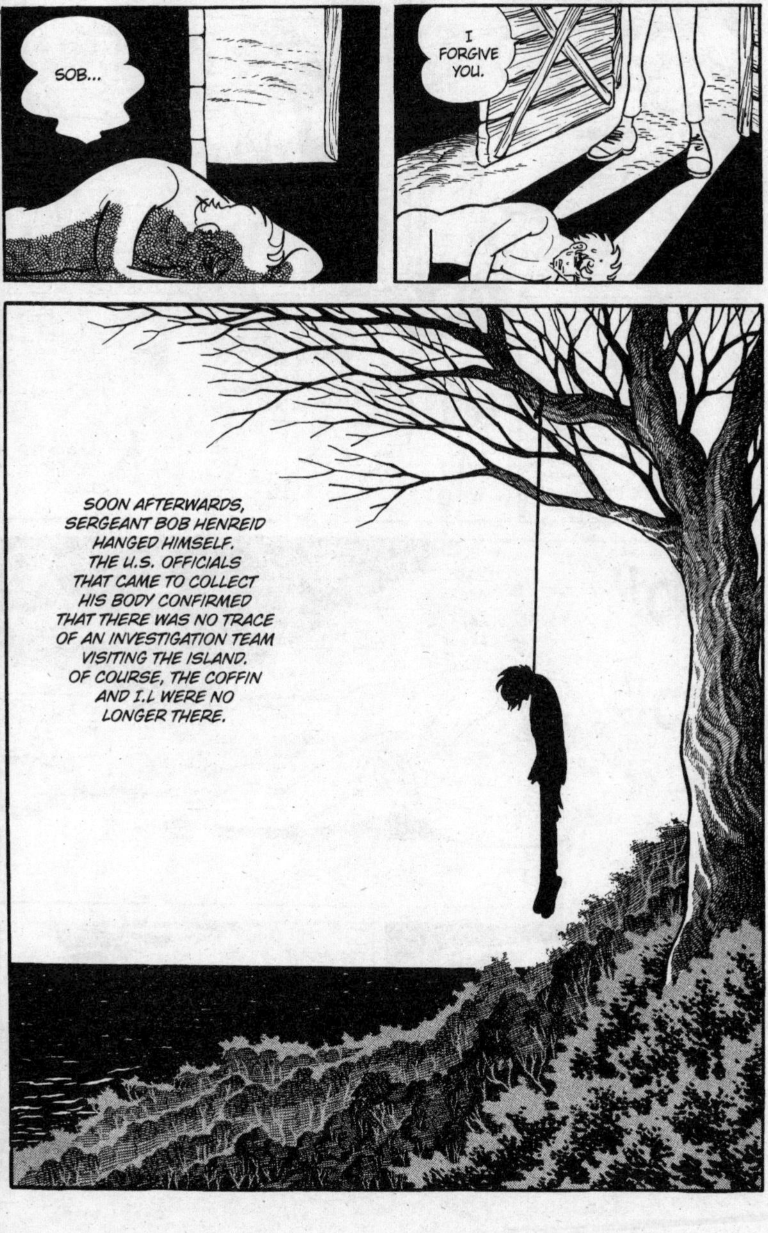
I FORGIVE YOU.
SOB...
SOON AFTERWARDS, SERGEANT BOB HENREID HANGED HIMSELF. THE U.S. OFFICIALS THAT CAME TO COLLECT HIS BODY CONFIRMED THAT THERE WAS NO TRACE OF AN INVESTIGATION TEAM VISITING THE ISLAND. OF COURSE, THE COFFIN AND I.L WERE NO LONGER THERE.

# EPISODE 12
## Rasputin

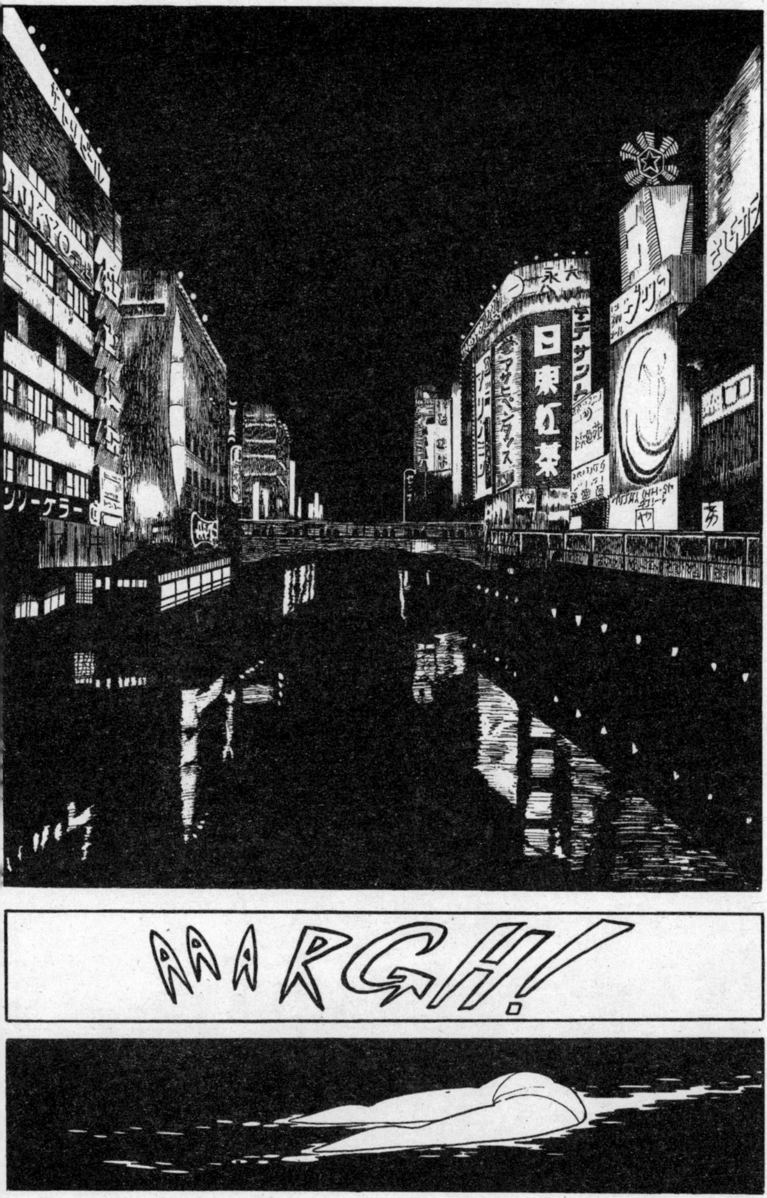
日東紅茶
AAARGH!

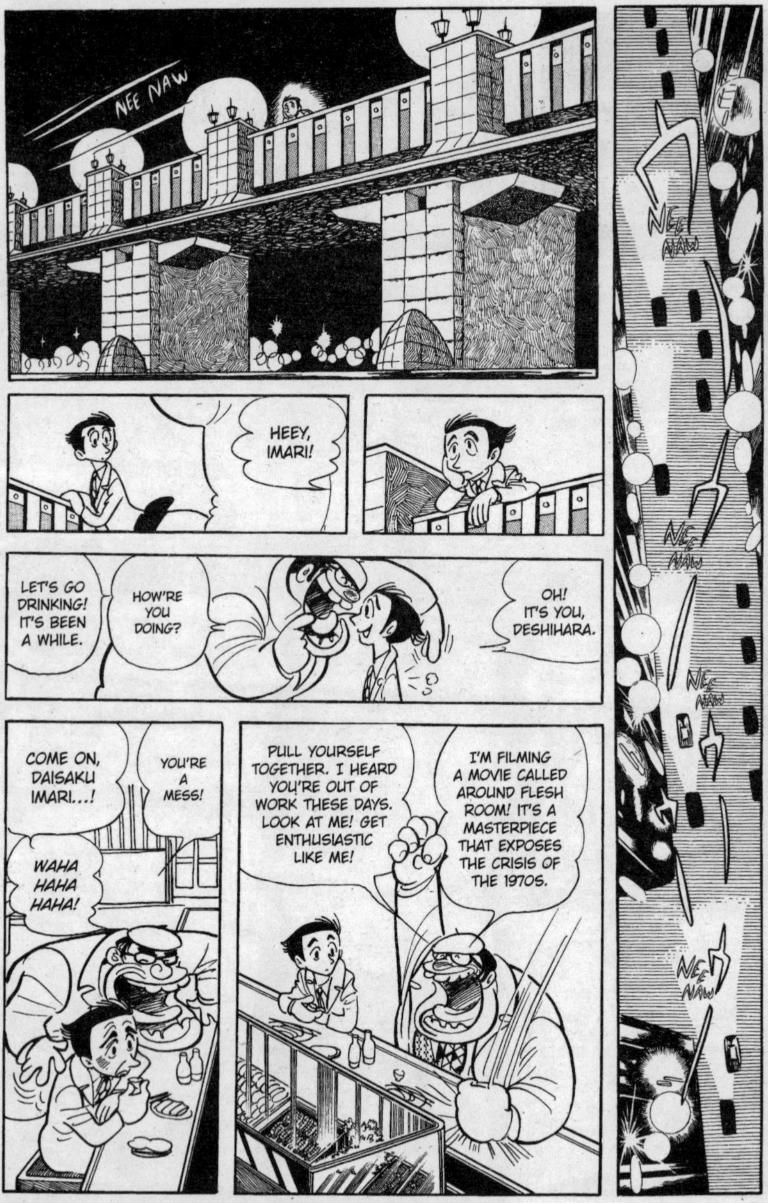
NEE NAW
NEE NAW
NEE NAW
NEE NAW
NEE NAW
HEEY, IMARI!
OH! IT'S YOU, DESHIHARA.
HOW'RE YOU DOING?
LET'S GO DRINKING! IT'S BEEN A WHILE.
I'M FILMING A MOVIE CALLED AROUND FLESH ROOM! IT'S A MASTERPIECE THAT EXPOSES THE CRISIS OF THE 1970S.
PULL YOURSELF TOGETHER. I HEARD YOU'RE OUT OF WORK THESE DAYS. LOOK AT ME! GET ENTHUSIASTIC LIKE ME!
YOU'RE A MESS!
COME ON, DAISAKU IMARI...!
WAHA HAHA HAHA!

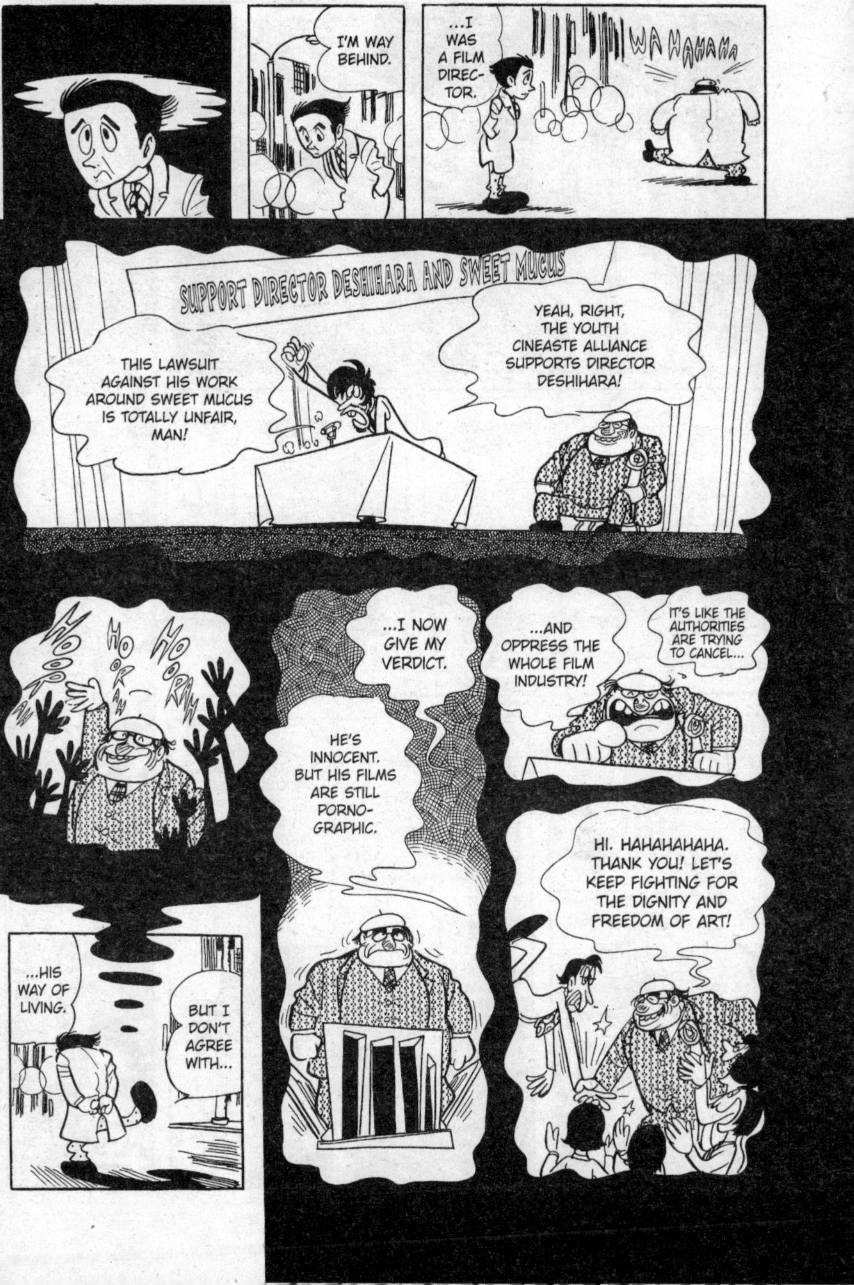
...I WAS A FILM DIRECTOR.
WA HAHAHA
I'M WAY BEHIND.
SUPPORT DIRECTOR DESHIHARA AND SWEET MUCUS
YEAH, RIGHT, THE YOUTH CINEASTE ALLIANCE SUPPORTS DIRECTOR DESHIHARA!
THIS LAWSUIT AGAINST HIS WORK AROUND SWEET MUCUS IS TOTALLY UNFAIR, MAN!
IT'S LIKE THE AUTHORITIES ARE TRYING TO CANCEL...
...AND OPPRESS THE WHOLE FILM INDUSTRY!
HI. HAHAHAHAHA. THANK YOU! LET'S KEEP FIGHTING FOR THE DIGNITY AND FREEDOM OF ART!
...I NOW GIVE MY VERDICT.
HE'S INNOCENT. BUT HIS FILMS ARE STILL PORNO-GRAPHIC.
HOORAH HOORAH HOORAH
BUT I DON'T AGREE WITH...
...HIS WAY OF LIVING.

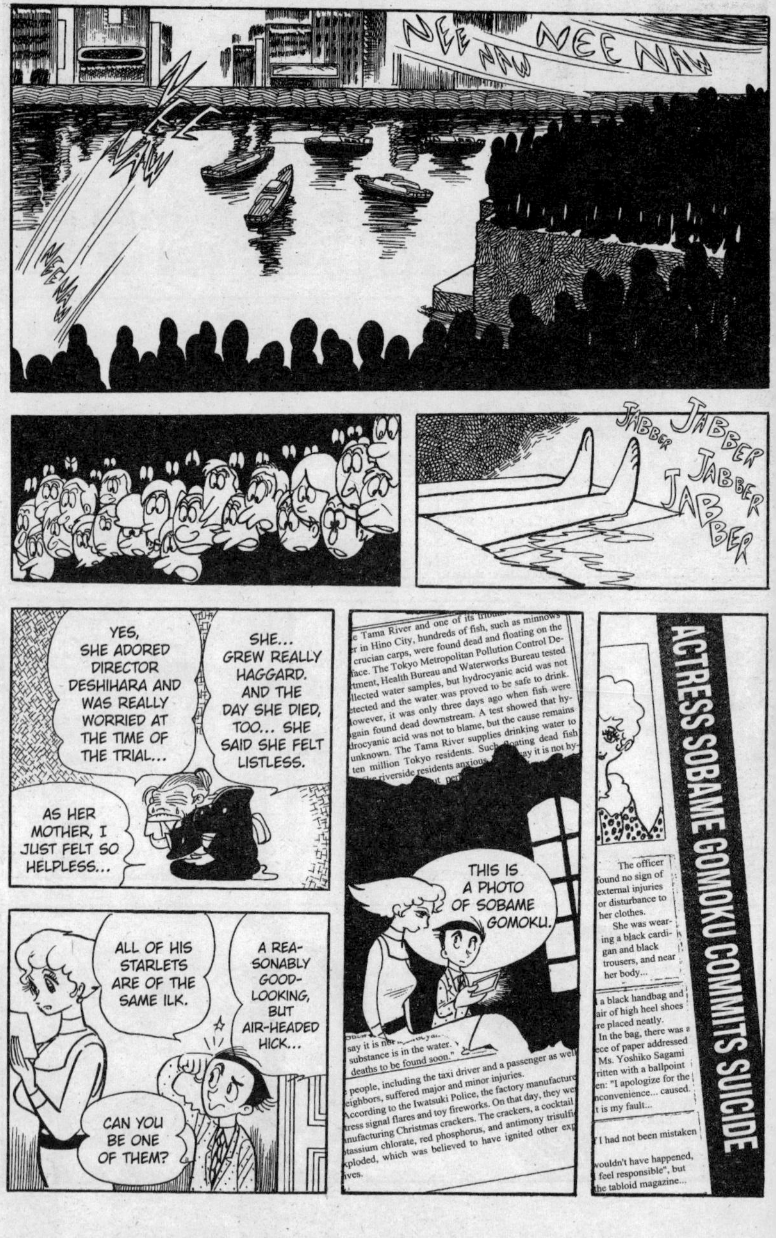
NEE NAW NEE NAW
NEE NAW
NEE NAW
JABBER JABBER JABBER JABBER
ACTRESS SOBAME GOMOKU COMMITS SUICIDE
The officer found no sign of external injuries or disturbance to her clothes.
She was wearing a black cardigan and black trousers, and near her body...
a black handbag and air of high heel shoes re placed neatly.
In the bag, there was a ece of paper addressed Ms. Yoshiko Sagami ritten with a ballpoint en: "I apologize for the nconvenience... caused. t is my fault...
I had not been mistaken
vouldn't have happened, feel responsible", but he tabloid magazine...
e Tama River and one of its r in Hino City, hundreds of fish, such as minnows crucian carps, were found dead and floating on the face. The Tokyo Metropolitan Pollution Control Detment, Health Bureau and Waterworks Bureau tested llected water samples, but hydrocyanic acid was not etected and the water was proved to be safe to drink. owever, it was only three days ago when fish were gain found dead downstream. A test showed that hydrocyanic acid was not to blame, but the cause remains unknown. The Tama River supplies drinking water to ten million Tokyo residents. Such floating dead fish ay it is not hyriverside residents anxious
THIS IS A PHOTO OF SOBAME GOMOKU.
say it is not substance is in the water. deaths to be found soon."
people, including the taxi driver and a passenger as well eighbors, suffered major and minor injuries. According to the Iwatsuki Police, the factory manufacture tress signal flares and toy fireworks. On that day, they we nufacturing Christmas crackers. The crackers, a cocktail tassium chlorate, red phosphorus, and antimony trisulfi ploded, which was believed to have ignited other exp ives.
SHE... GREW REALLY HAGGARD. AND THE DAY SHE DIED, TOO... SHE SAID SHE FELT LISTLESS.
YES, SHE ADORED DIRECTOR DESHIHARA AND WAS REALLY WORRIED AT THE TIME OF THE TRIAL...
AS HER MOTHER, I JUST FELT SO HELPLESS...
A REASONABLY GOOD-LOOKING, BUT AIR-HEADED HICK...
ALL OF HIS STARLETS ARE OF THE SAME ILK.
CAN YOU BE ONE OF THEM?

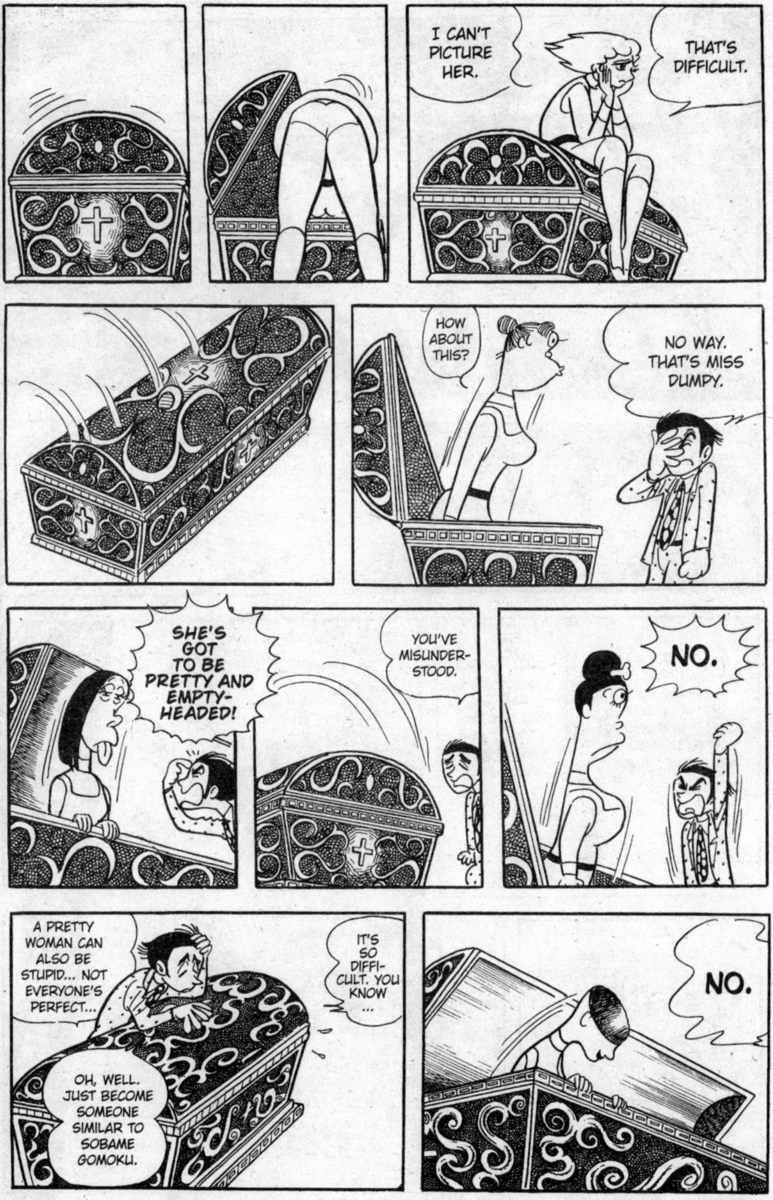
I CAN'T PICTURE HER.
THAT'S DIFFICULT.
HOW ABOUT THIS?
NO WAY. THAT'S MISS DUMPY.
NO.
YOU'VE MISUNDER-STOOD.
SHE'S GOT TO BE PRETTY AND EMPTY-HEADED!
NO.
A PRETTY WOMAN CAN ALSO BE STUPID... NOT EVERYONE'S PERFECT...
IT'S SO DIFFI-CULT. YOU KNOW ...
OH, WELL. JUST BECOME SOMEONE SIMILAR TO SOBAME GOMOKU.

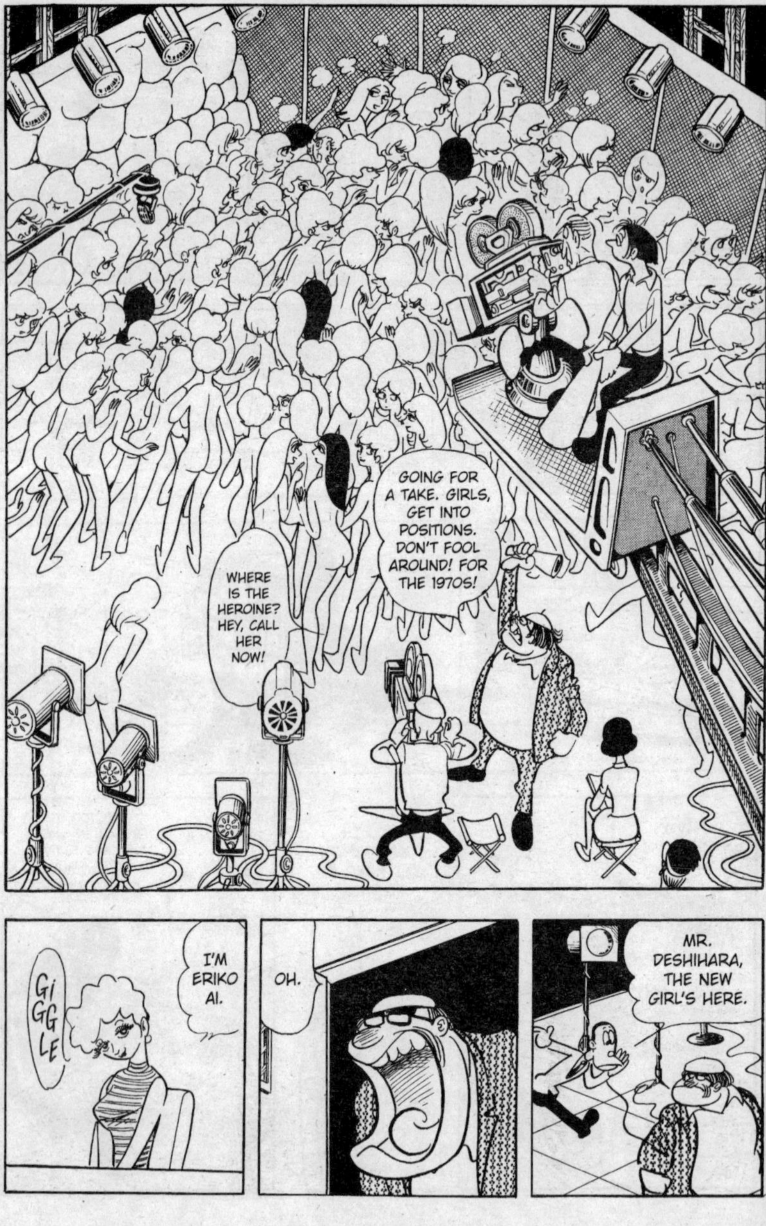
GOING FOR A TAKE. GIRLS, GET INTO POSITIONS. DON'T FOOL AROUND! FOR THE 1970S!
WHERE IS THE HEROINE? HEY, CALL HER NOW!
MR. DESHIHARA, THE NEW GIRL'S HERE.
OH.
I'M ERIKO AI.
GIGGLE

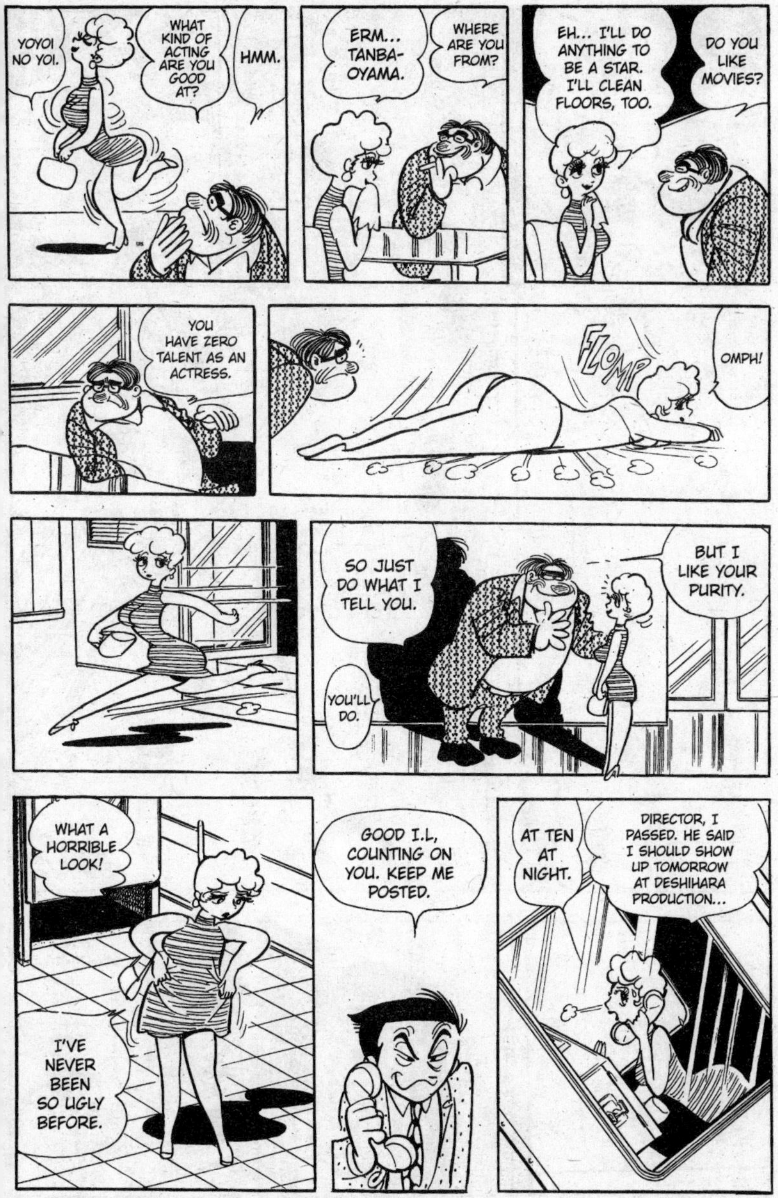
DO YOU LIKE MOVIES?
EH... I'LL DO ANYTHING TO BE A STAR. I'LL CLEAN FLOORS, TOO.
WHERE ARE YOU FROM?
ERM... TANBA-OYAMA.
HMM.
WHAT KIND OF ACTING ARE YOU GOOD AT?
YOYOI NO YOI.
OMPH!
FLOMP
YOU HAVE ZERO TALENT AS AN ACTRESS.
BUT I LIKE YOUR PURITY.
SO JUST DO WHAT I TELL YOU.
YOU'LL DO.
DIRECTOR, I PASSED. HE SAID I SHOULD SHOW UP TOMORROW AT DESHIHARA PRODUCTION...
AT TEN AT NIGHT.
GOOD I.L, COUNTING ON YOU. KEEP ME POSTED.
WHAT A HORRIBLE LOOK!
I'VE NEVER BEEN SO UGLY BEFORE.

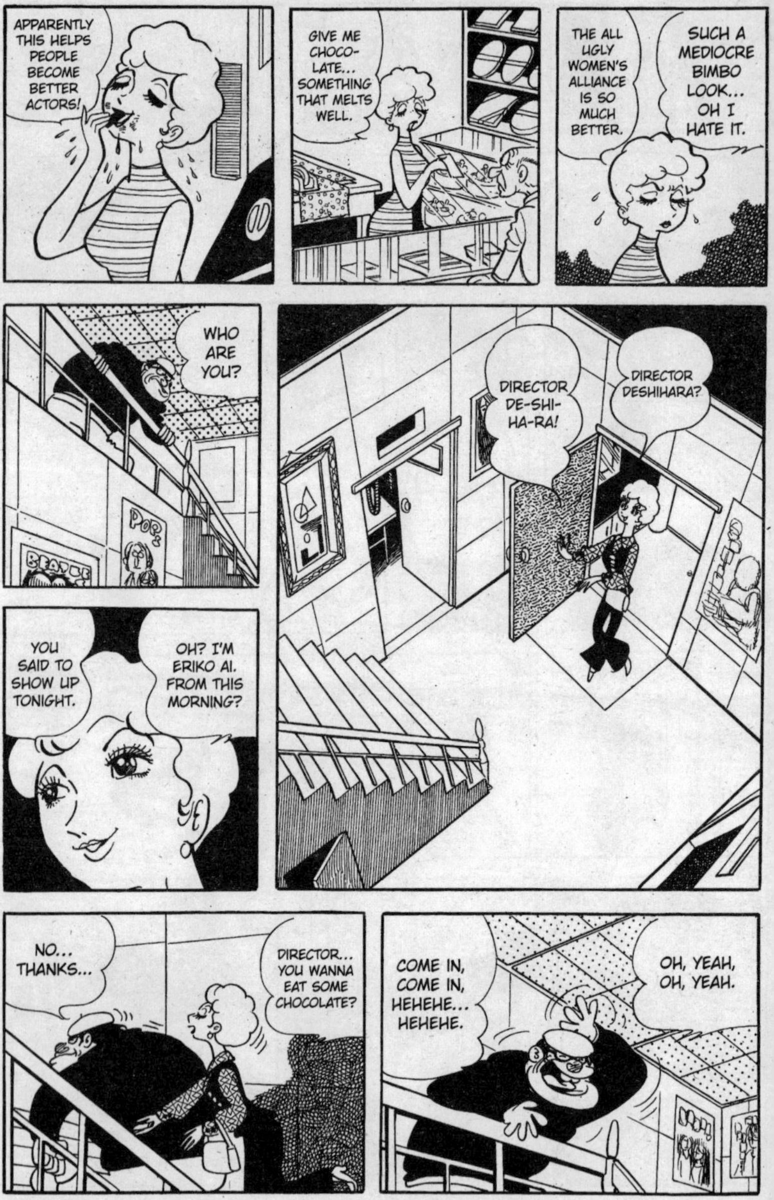

SUCH A MEDIOCRE BIMBO LOOK... OH I HATE IT.
THE ALL UGLY WOMEN'S ALLIANCE IS SO MUCH BETTER.
GIVE ME CHOCO-LATE... SOMETHING THAT MELTS WELL.
APPARENTLY THIS HELPS PEOPLE BECOME BETTER ACTORS!
DIRECTOR DESHIHARA?
DIRECTOR DE-SHI-HA-RA!
WHO ARE YOU?
OH? I'M ERIKO AI. FROM THIS MORNING?
YOU SAID TO SHOW UP TONIGHT.
OH, YEAH, OH, YEAH.
COME IN, COME IN, HEHEHE... HEHEHE.
DIRECTOR... YOU WANNA EAT SOME CHOCOLATE?
NO... THANKS...

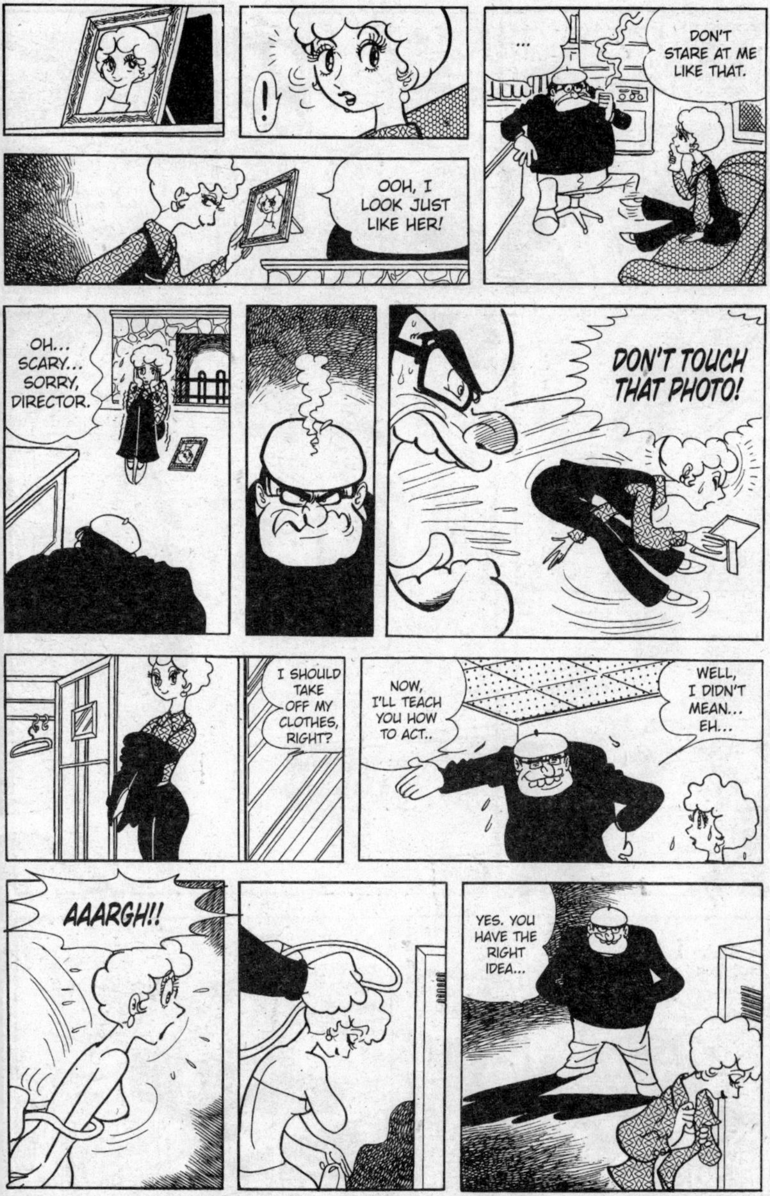
DON'T STARE AT ME LIKE THAT.
...
!
OOH, I LOOK JUST LIKE HER!
DON'T TOUCH THAT PHOTO!
OH... SCARY... SORRY, DIRECTOR.
WELL, I DIDN'T MEAN... EH...
NOW, I'LL TEACH YOU HOW TO ACT..
I SHOULD TAKE OFF MY CLOTHES, RIGHT?
YES. YOU HAVE THE RIGHT IDEA...
AAARGH!!

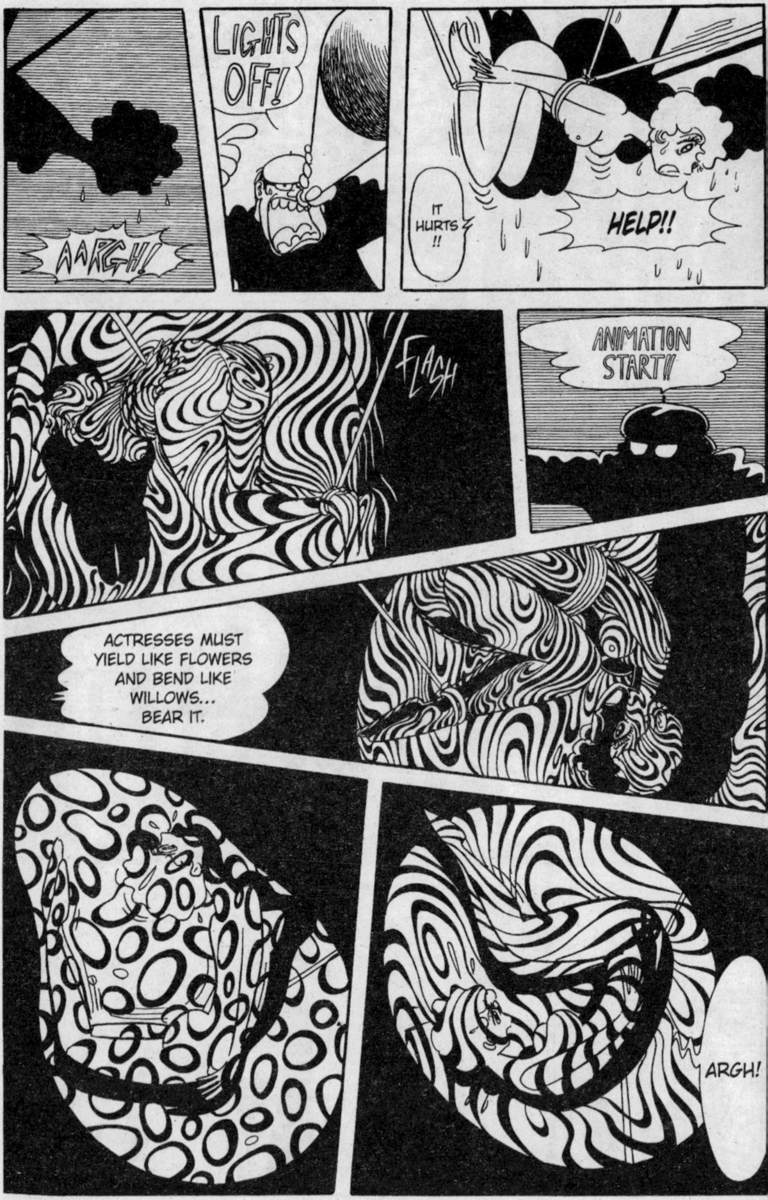
HELP!!
IT HURTS!!
LIGHTS OFF!
AARGH!
ANIMATION START!!
FLASH
ACTRESSES MUST YIELD LIKE FLOWERS AND BEND LIKE WILLOWS... BEAR IT.
ARGH!

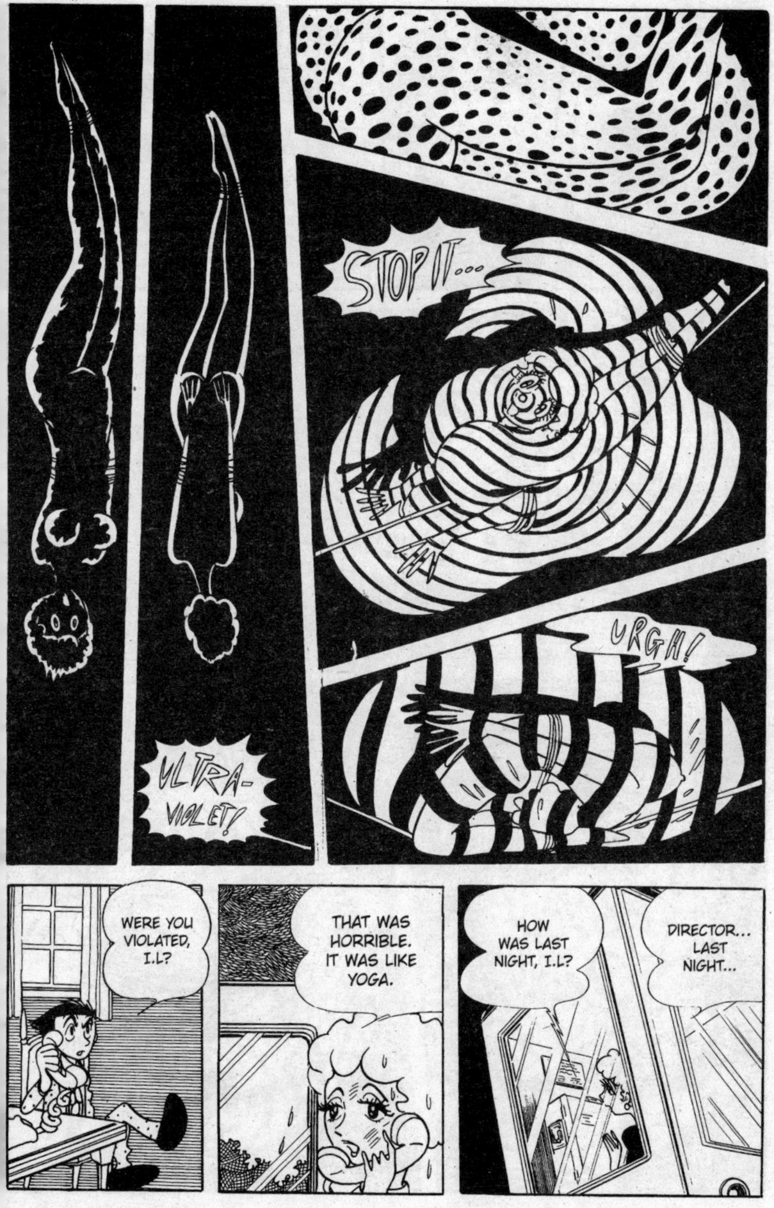
STOP IT...
URGH!
ULTRA-VIOLET!
DIRECTOR... LAST NIGHT...
HOW WAS LAST NIGHT, I.L?
THAT WAS HORRIBLE. IT WAS LIKE YOGA.
WERE YOU VIOLATED, I.L?

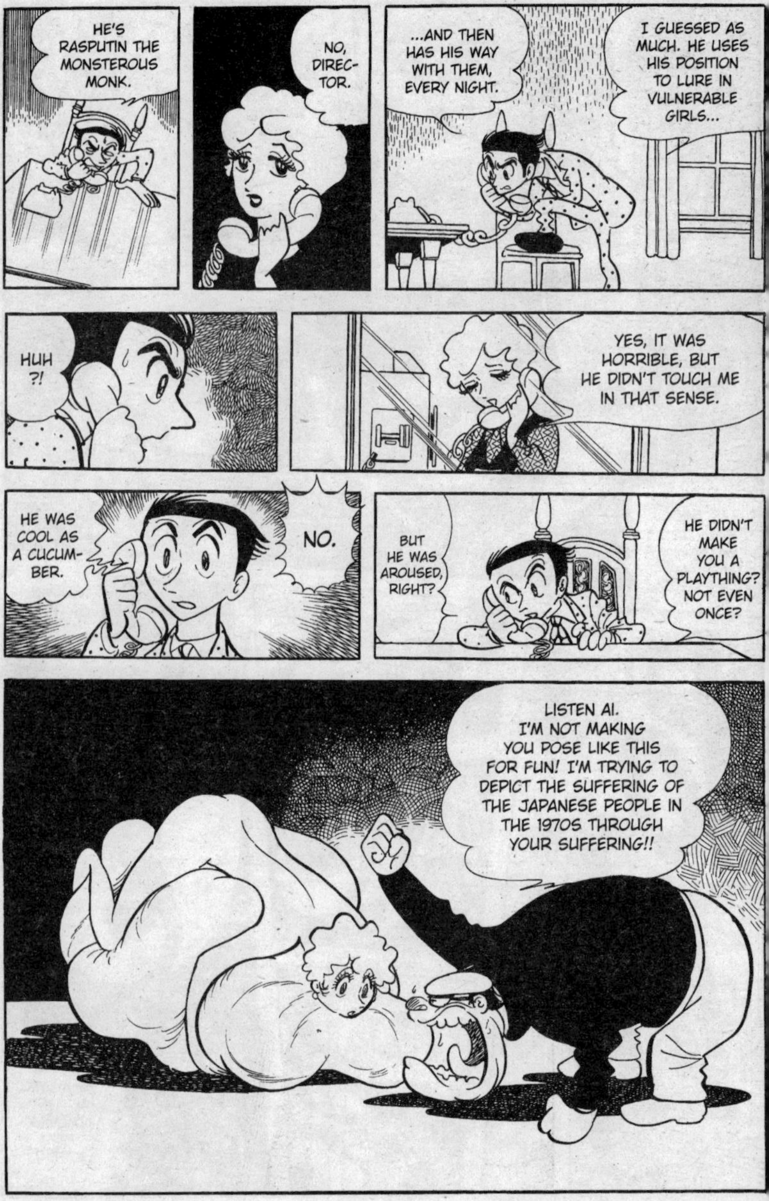
I GUESSED AS MUCH. HE USES HIS POSITION TO LURE IN VULNERABLE GIRLS...
...AND THEN HAS HIS WAY WITH THEM, EVERY NIGHT.
NO, DIRECTOR.
HE'S RASPUTIN THE MONSTEROUS MONK.
YES, IT WAS HORRIBLE, BUT HE DIDN'T TOUCH ME IN THAT SENSE.
HUH ?!
HE DIDN'T MAKE YOU A PLAYTHING? NOT EVEN ONCE?
BUT HE WAS AROUSED, RIGHT?
NO.
HE WAS COOL AS A CUCUMBER.
LISTEN AI. I'M NOT MAKING YOU POSE LIKE THIS FOR FUN! I'M TRYING TO DEPICT THE SUFFERING OF THE JAPANESE PEOPLE IN THE 1970S THROUGH YOUR SUFFERING!!

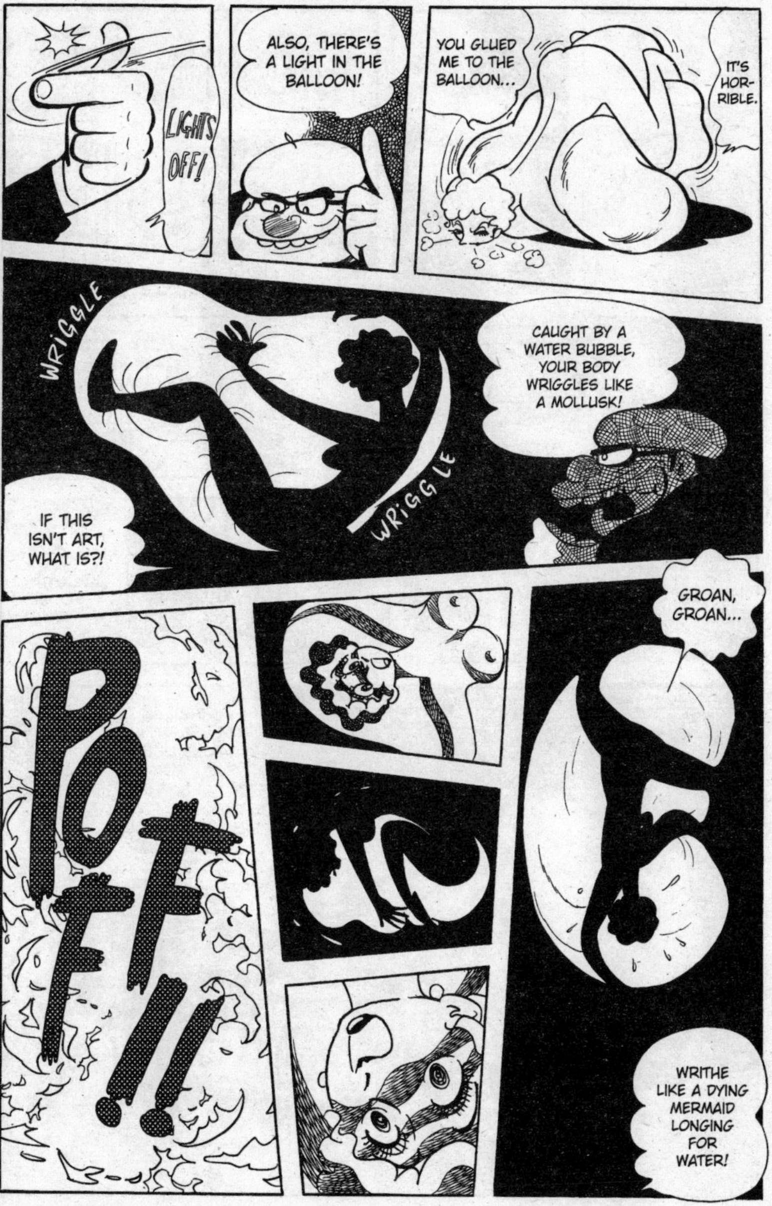
IT'S HOR-RIBLE.
YOU GLUED ME TO THE BALLOON...
ALSO, THERE'S A LIGHT IN THE BALLOON!
LIGHTS OFF!
CAUGHT BY A WATER BUBBLE, YOUR BODY WRIGGLES LIKE A MOLLUSK!
WRIGGLE
WRIGGLE
IF THIS ISN'T ART, WHAT IS?!
GROAN, GROAN...
WRITHE LIKE A DYING MERMAID LONGING FOR WATER!
POFF!!

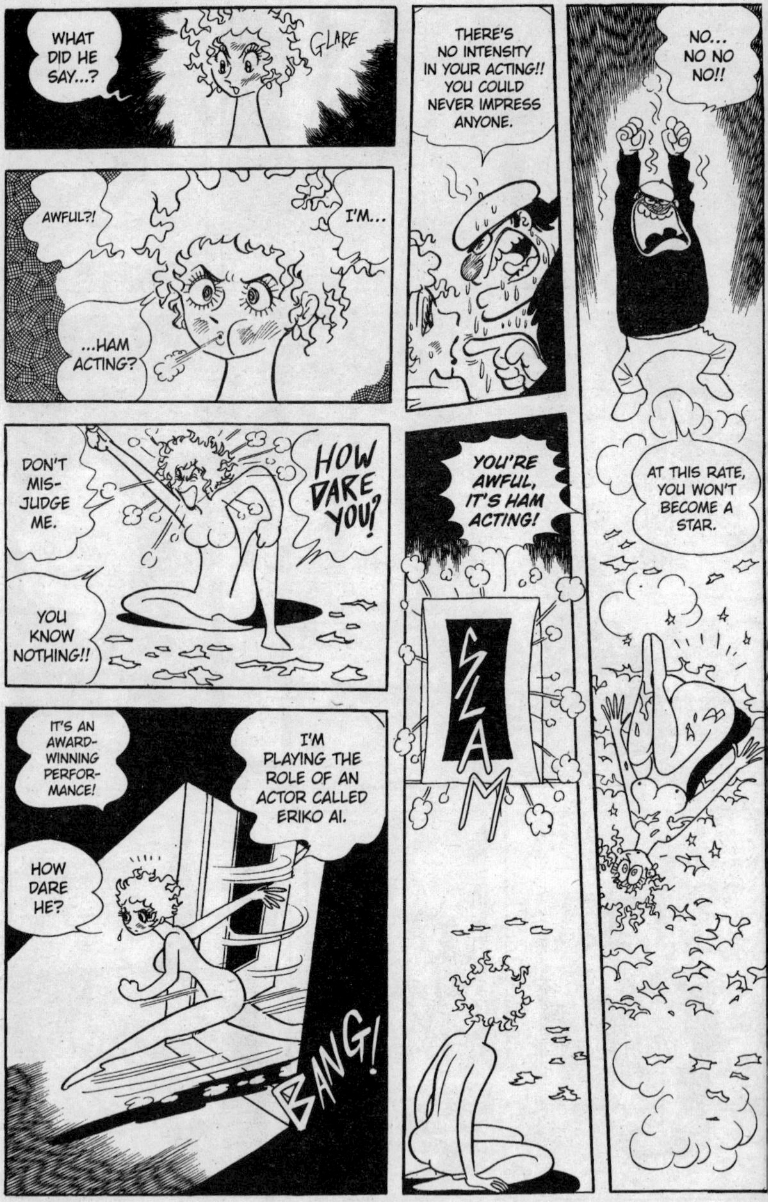
NO... NO NO NO!!
AT THIS RATE, YOU WON'T BECOME A STAR.
THERE'S NO INTENSITY IN YOUR ACTING!! YOU COULD NEVER IMPRESS ANYONE.
YOU'RE AWFUL, IT'S HAM ACTING!
SLAM
WHAT DID HE SAY...?
GLARE
I'M...
AWFUL?!
...HAM ACTING?
HOW DARE YOU?
DON'T MIS-JUDGE ME.
YOU KNOW NOTHING!!
I'M PLAYING THE ROLE OF AN ACTOR CALLED ERIKO AI.
IT'S AN AWARD-WINNING PERFOR-MANCE!
HOW DARE HE?
BANG!

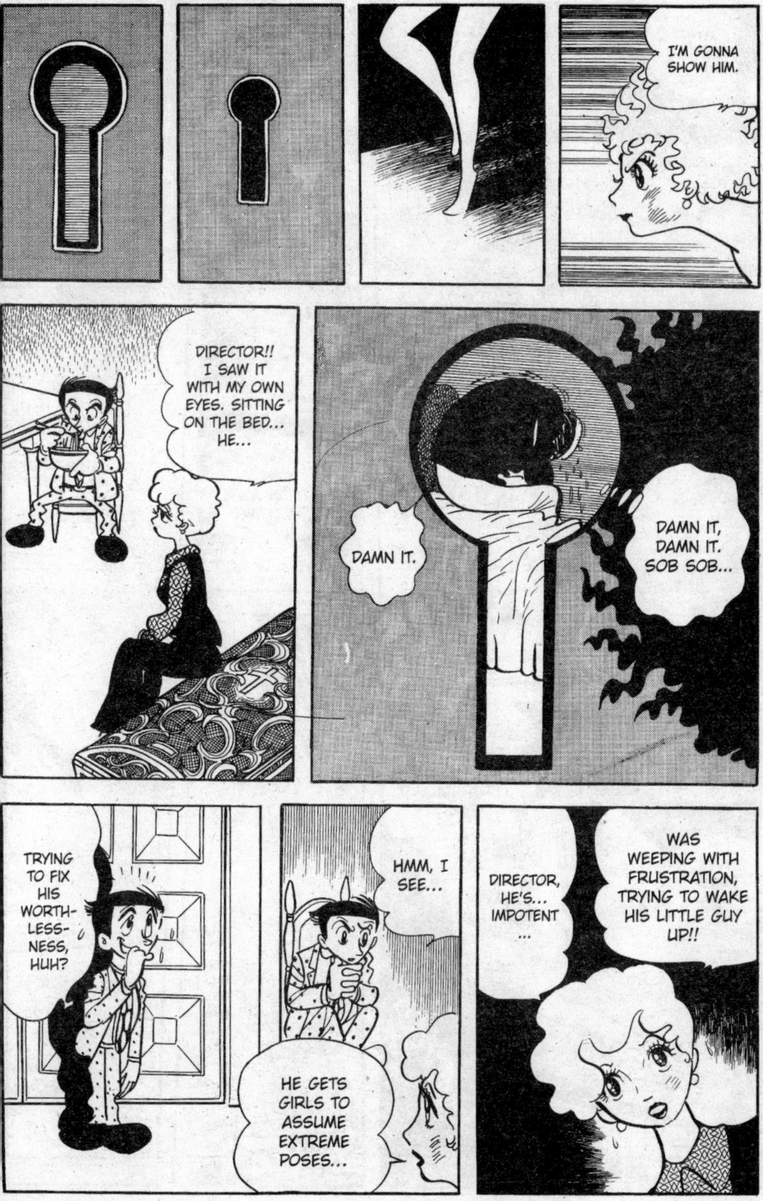
I'M GONNA SHOW HIM.
DAMN IT, DAMN IT. SOB SOB...
DAMN IT.
DIRECTOR!! I SAW IT WITH MY OWN EYES. SITTING ON THE BED... HE...
WAS WEEPING WITH FRUSTRATION, TRYING TO WAKE HIS LITTLE GUY UP!!
DIRECTOR, HE'S... IMPOTENT ...
HMM, I SEE...
HE GETS GIRLS TO ASSUME EXTREME POSES...
TRYING TO FIX HIS WORTH-LESS-NESS, HUH?

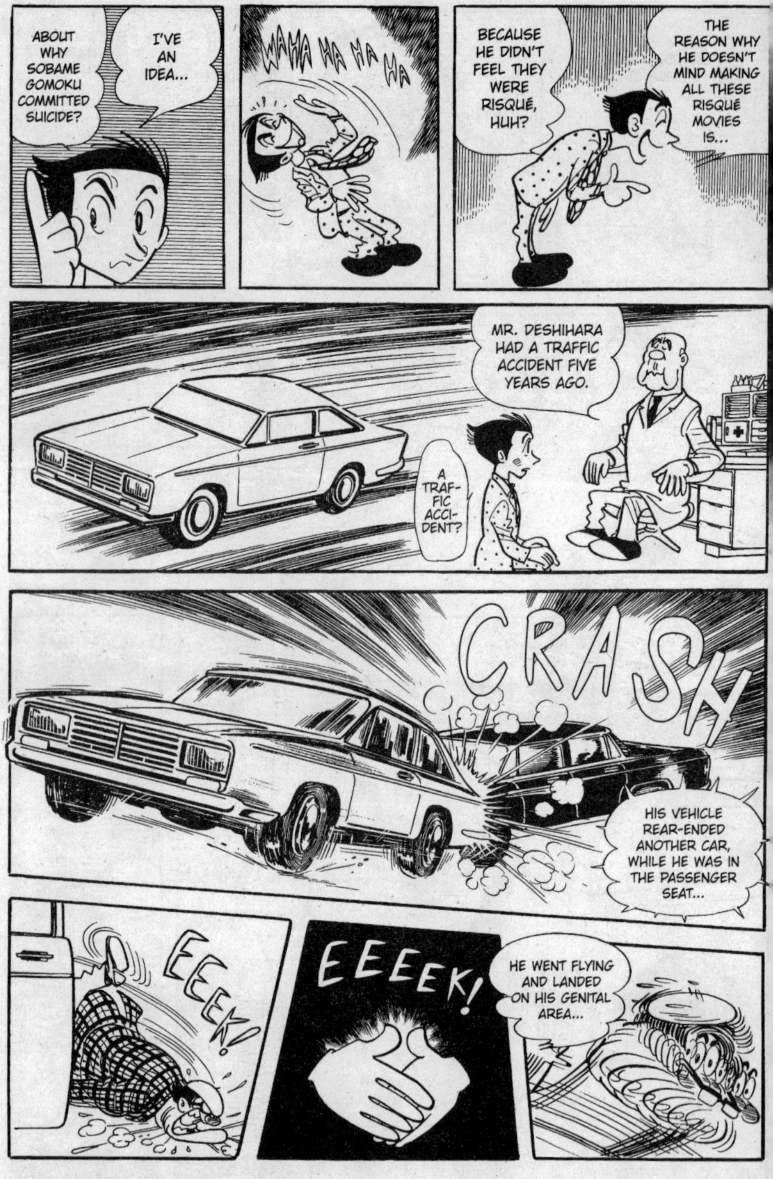
THE REASON WHY HE DOESN'T MIND MAKING ALL THESE RISQUÉ MOVIES IS...
BECAUSE HE DIDN'T FEEL THEY WERE RISQUÉ, HUH?
WAHAHA HA HA HA HA
I'VE AN IDEA...
ABOUT WHY SOBAME GOMOKU COMMITTED SUICIDE?
MR. DESHIHARA HAD A TRAFFIC ACCIDENT FIVE YEARS AGO.
A TRAF-FIC ACCI-DENT?
CRASH
HIS VEHICLE REAR-ENDED ANOTHER CAR, WHILE HE WAS IN THE PASSENGER SEAT...
HE WENT FLYING AND LANDED ON HIS GENITAL AREA...
EEEEK!
EEEK!

THIS IS A PRIVATE MATTER, SO I'M NOT COMFORTABLE TELLING YOU THIS, THOUGH...

HE CANNOT GET AN ERECTION...

HUH?

SINCE THEN, HE HASN'T BEEN THE SAME.

SHE WAS THE CAUSE OF HIS PROBLEM, THEN.

I SEE!

WHO WAS DRIVING?

SOBAME GOMOKU, HIS MISTRESS.

BLANK GAZE

BLANK GAZE

BLANK GAZE

IF I CAN FIX HIM ...

OH... IS THAT THE CAUSE OF HIS PROBLEM? IF SO, THAT'S TRAGIC.

IF WE COULD HEAL THE TRAUMA CAUSED BY THE CRASH...

SOME- HOW...

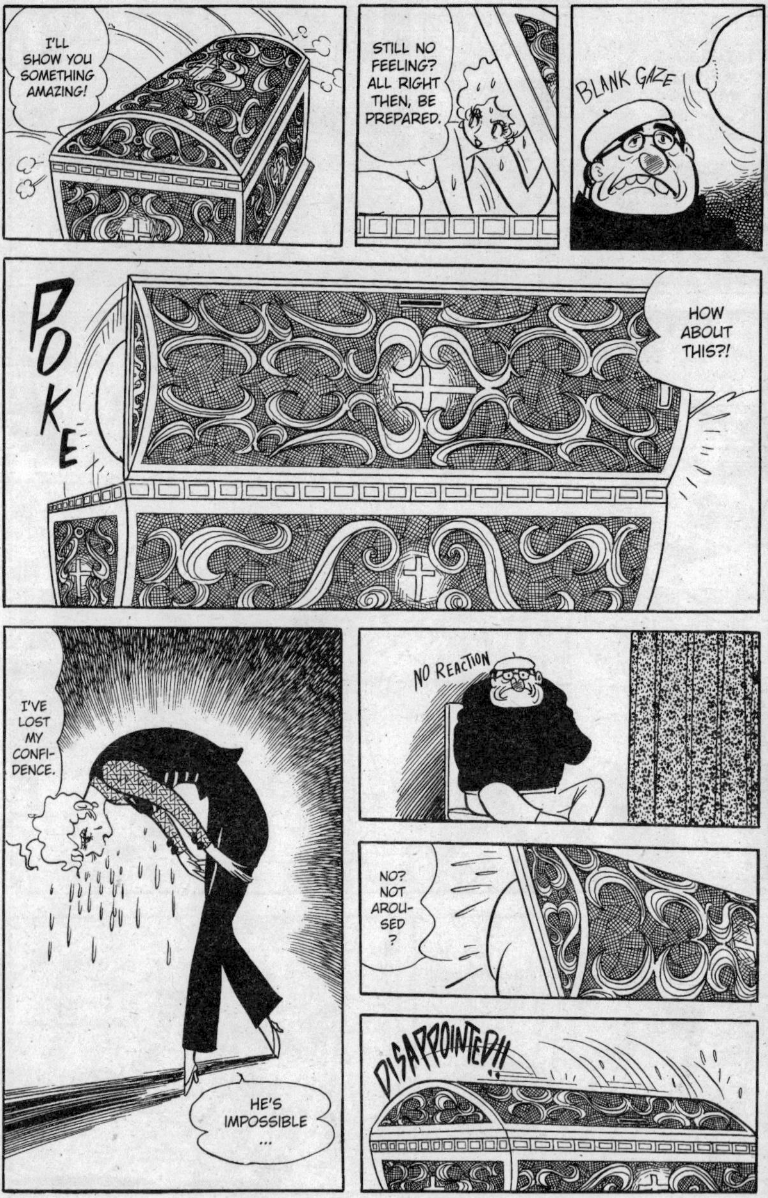
BLANK GAZE
STILL NO FEELING? ALL RIGHT THEN, BE PREPARED.
I'LL SHOW YOU SOMETHING AMAZING!
HOW ABOUT THIS?!
POKE
NO REACTION
NO? NOT AROU-SED ?
DISAPPOINTED!!
I'VE LOST MY CONFI-DENCE.
HE'S IMPOSSIBLE ...

I THINK I UNDERSTAND THE REASON WHY SHE COMMITTED SUICIDE...

DIRECTOR...

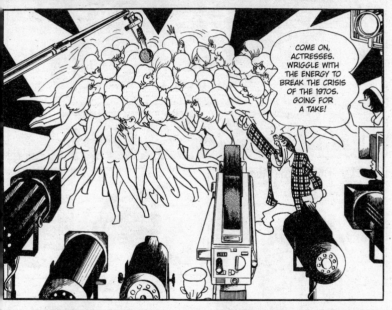

COME ON, ACTRESSES. WRIGGLE WITH THE ENERGY TO BREAK THE CRISIS OF THE 1970S. GOING FOR A TAKE!

...

WA HA HA HA

OH, IMARI, WE MEET AGAIN. BE ENERGETIC. WAHAHAHAHA!

# EPISODE 13
## Eye

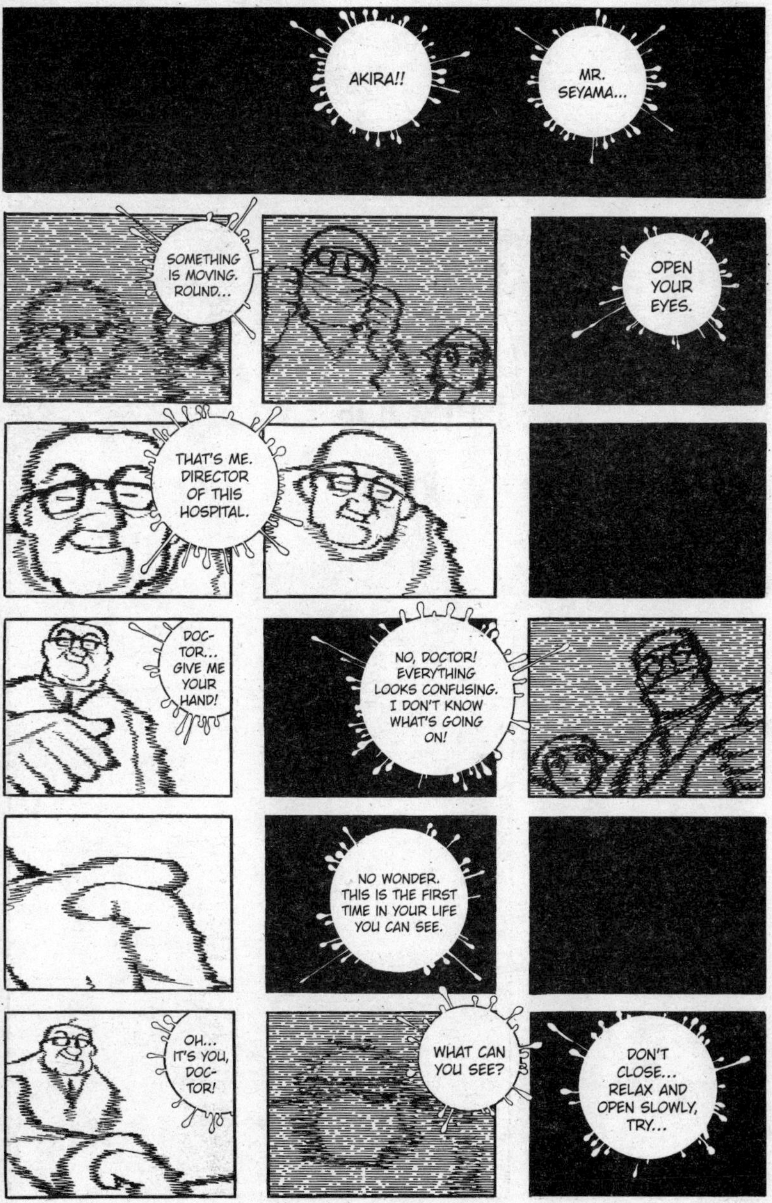
MR. SEYAMA...
AKIRA!!
OPEN YOUR EYES.
SOMETHING IS MOVING. ROUND...
THAT'S ME. DIRECTOR OF THIS HOSPITAL.
NO, DOCTOR! EVERYTHING LOOKS CONFUSING. I DON'T KNOW WHAT'S GOING ON!
DOC-TOR... GIVE ME YOUR HAND!
NO WONDER. THIS IS THE FIRST TIME IN YOUR LIFE YOU CAN SEE.
DON'T CLOSE... RELAX AND OPEN SLOWLY, TRY...
WHAT CAN YOU SEE?
OH... IT'S YOU, DOC-TOR!

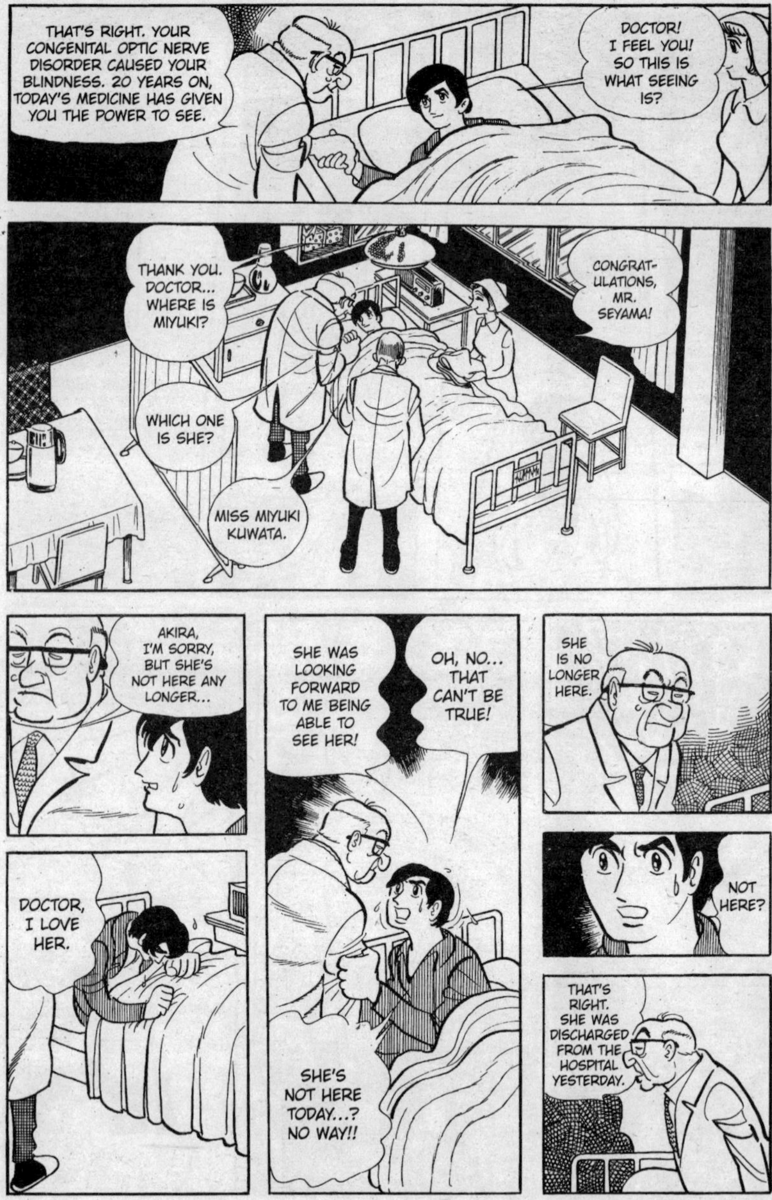
DOCTOR! I FEEL YOU! SO THIS IS WHAT SEEING IS?
THAT'S RIGHT. YOUR CONGENITAL OPTIC NERVE DISORDER CAUSED YOUR BLINDNESS. 20 YEARS ON, TODAY'S MEDICINE HAS GIVEN YOU THE POWER TO SEE.
CONGRAT-ULATIONS, MR. SEYAMA!
THANK YOU. DOCTOR... WHERE IS MIYUKI?
WHICH ONE IS SHE?
MISS MIYUKI KUWATA.
SHE IS NO LONGER HERE.
NOT HERE?
THAT'S RIGHT. SHE WAS DISCHARGED FROM THE HOSPITAL YESTERDAY.
OH, NO... THAT CAN'T BE TRUE!
SHE WAS LOOKING FORWARD TO ME BEING ABLE TO SEE HER!
SHE'S NOT HERE TODAY...? NO WAY!!
AKIRA, I'M SORRY, BUT SHE'S NOT HERE ANY LONGER...
DOCTOR, I LOVE HER.

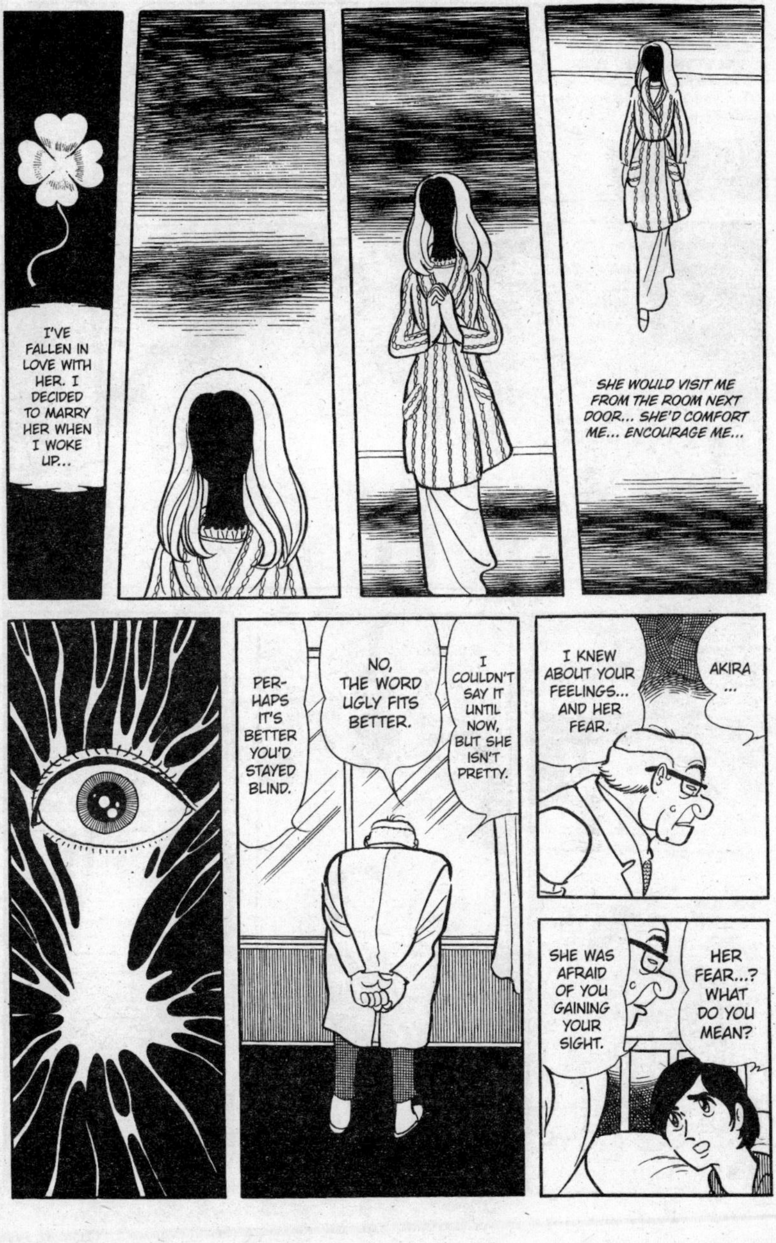
SHE WOULD VISIT ME FROM THE ROOM NEXT DOOR... SHE'D COMFORT ME... ENCOURAGE ME...
I'VE FALLEN IN LOVE WITH HER. I DECIDED TO MARRY HER WHEN I WOKE UP...
AKIRA ...
I KNEW ABOUT YOUR FEELINGS... AND HER FEAR.
HER FEAR...? WHAT DO YOU MEAN?
SHE WAS AFRAID OF YOU GAINING YOUR SIGHT.
I COULDN'T SAY IT UNTIL NOW, BUT SHE ISN'T PRETTY.
NO, THE WORD UGLY FITS BETTER.
PER-HAPS IT'S BETTER YOU'D STAYED BLIND.

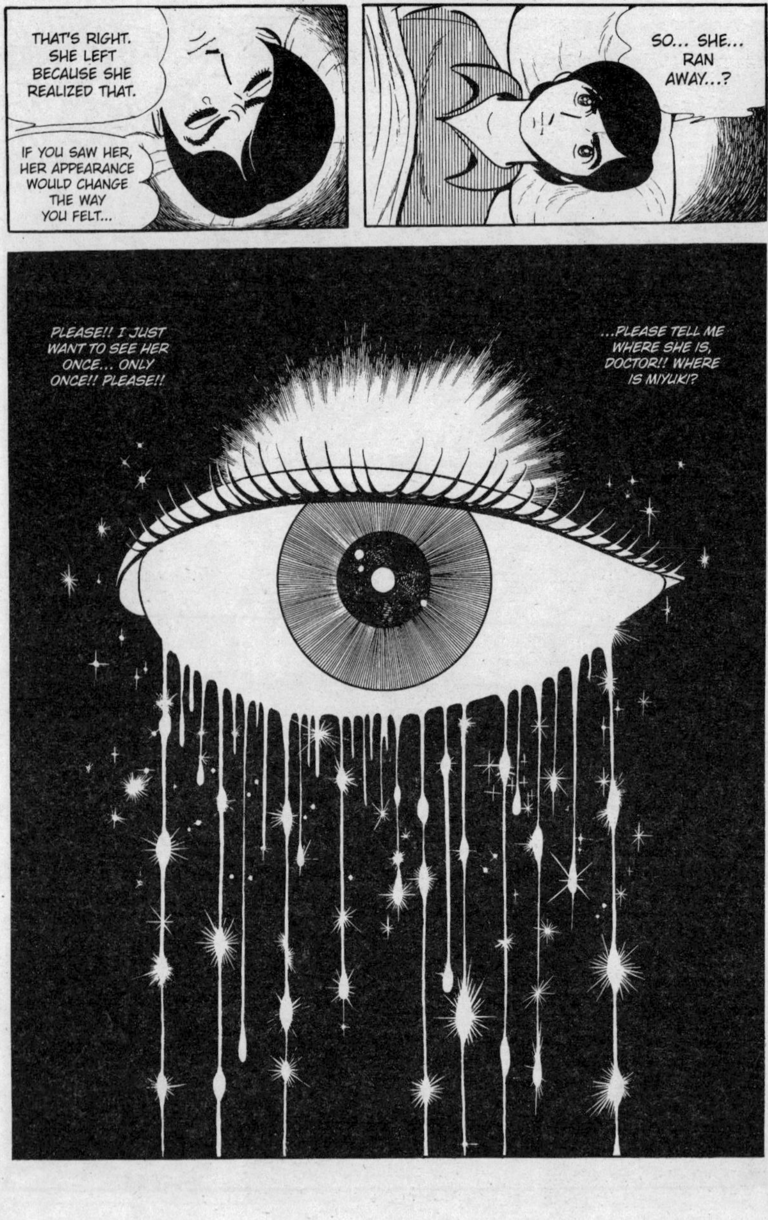
SO... SHE... RAN AWAY...?
THAT'S RIGHT. SHE LEFT BECAUSE SHE REALIZED THAT.
IF YOU SAW HER, HER APPEARANCE WOULD CHANGE THE WAY YOU FELT...
...PLEASE TELL ME WHERE SHE IS, DOCTOR!! WHERE IS MIYUKI?
PLEASE!! I JUST WANT TO SEE HER ONCE... ONLY ONCE!! PLEASE!!

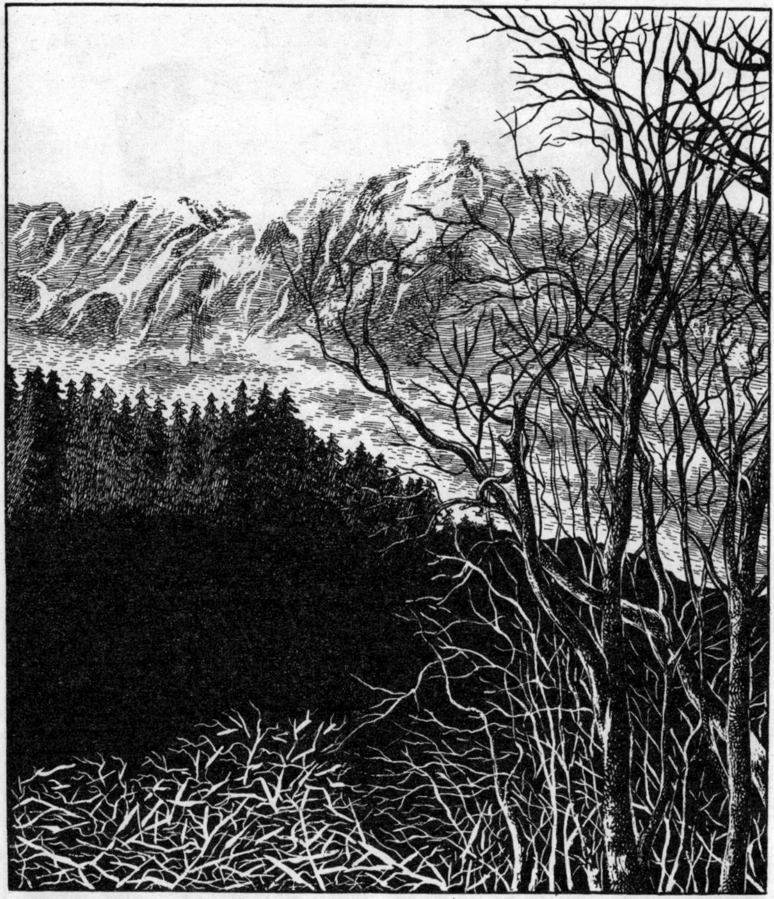
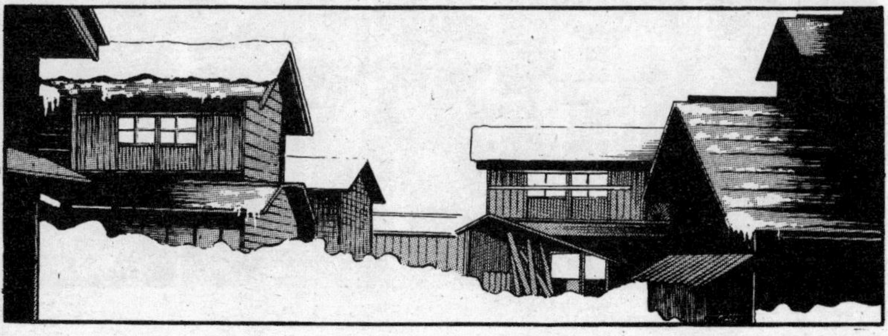

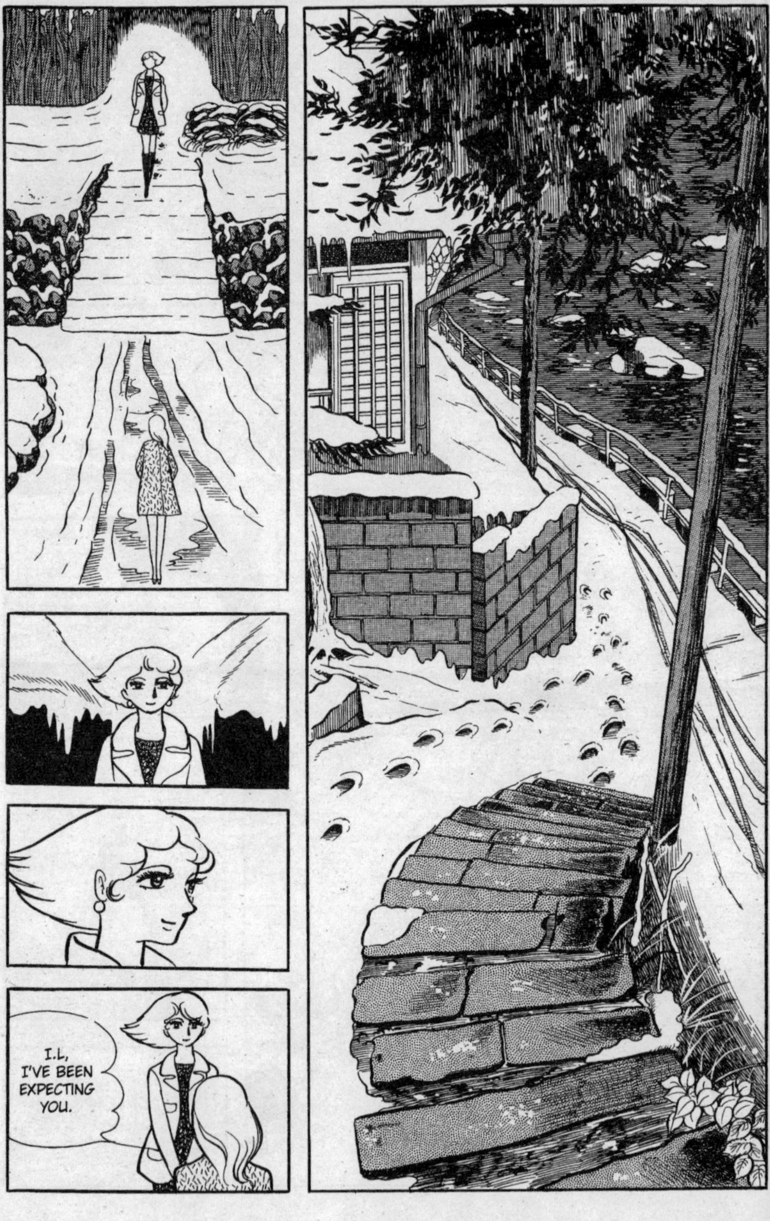
I.L, I'VE BEEN EXPECTING YOU.

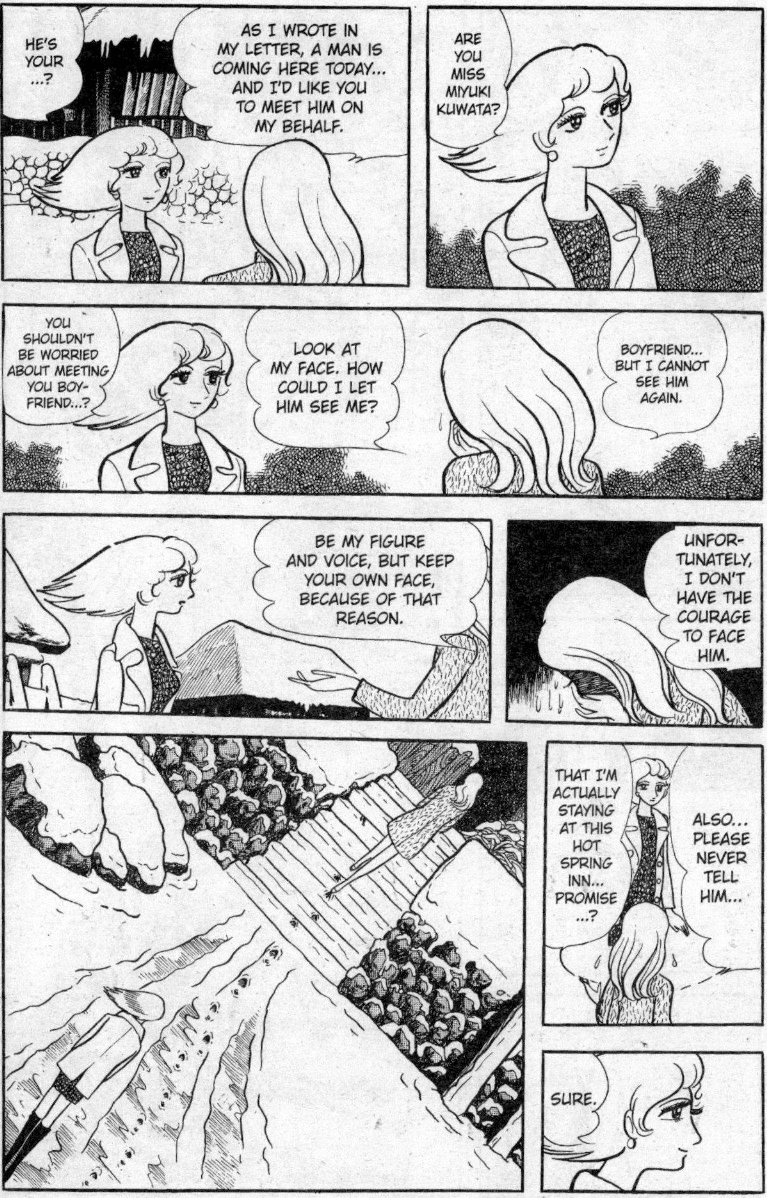
ARE YOU MISS MIYUKI KUWATA?
AS I WROTE IN MY LETTER, A MAN IS COMING HERE TODAY... AND I'D LIKE YOU TO MEET HIM ON MY BEHALF.
HE'S YOUR ...?
BOYFRIEND... BUT I CANNOT SEE HIM AGAIN.
LOOK AT MY FACE. HOW COULD I LET HIM SEE ME?
YOU SHOULDN'T BE WORRIED ABOUT MEETING YOU BOY-FRIEND...?
UNFOR-TUNATELY, I DON'T HAVE THE COURAGE TO FACE HIM.
BE MY FIGURE AND VOICE, BUT KEEP YOUR OWN FACE, BECAUSE OF THAT REASON.
ALSO... PLEASE NEVER TELL HIM...
THAT I'M ACTUALLY STAYING AT THIS HOT SPRING INN... PROMISE ...?
SURE.

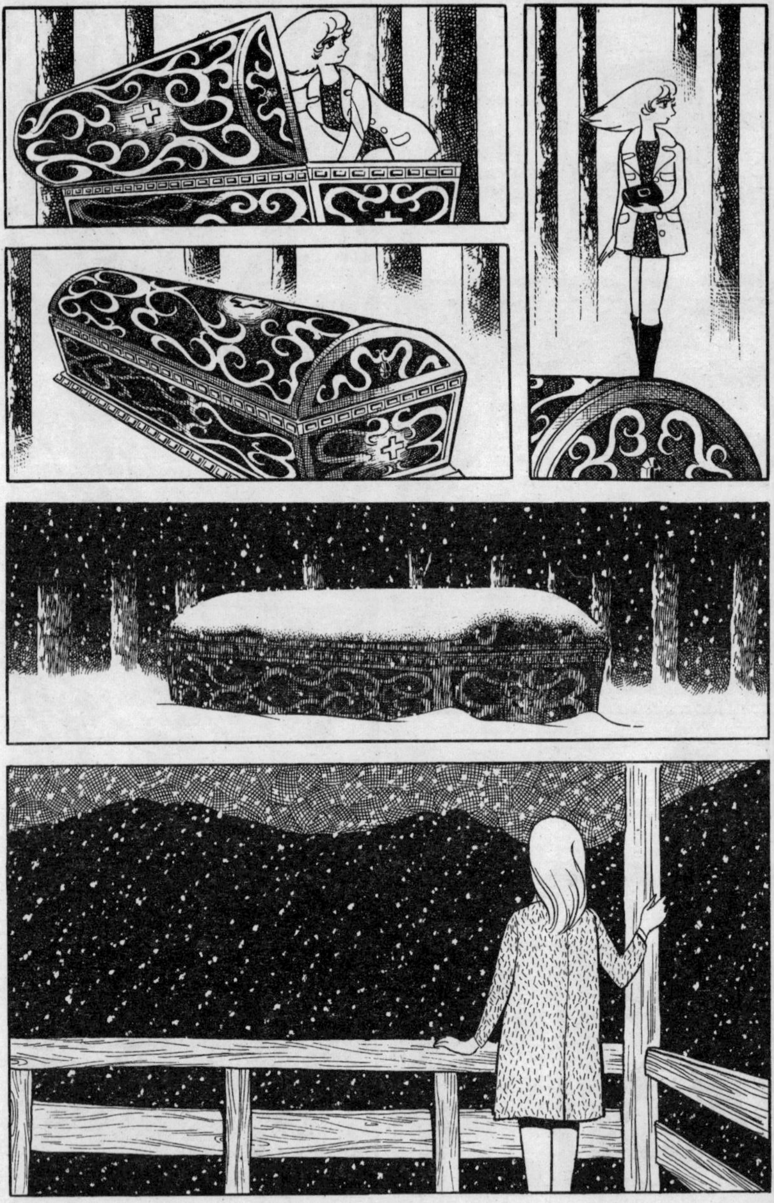

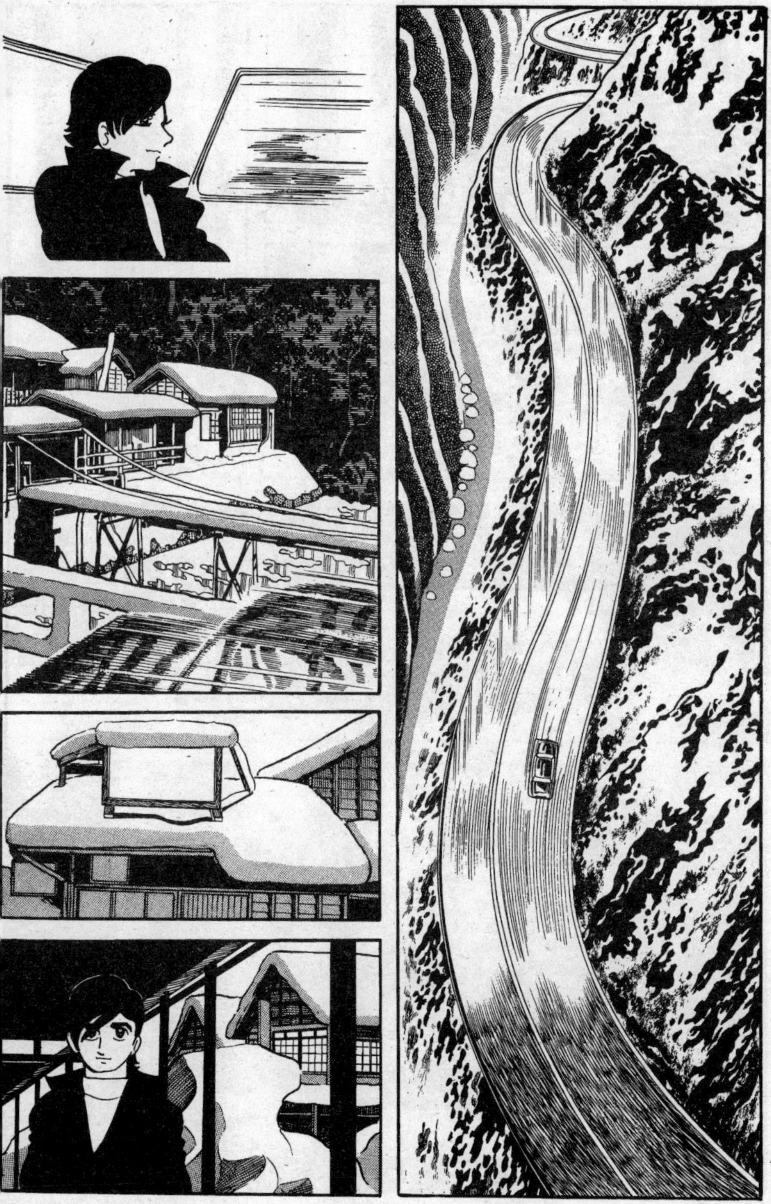

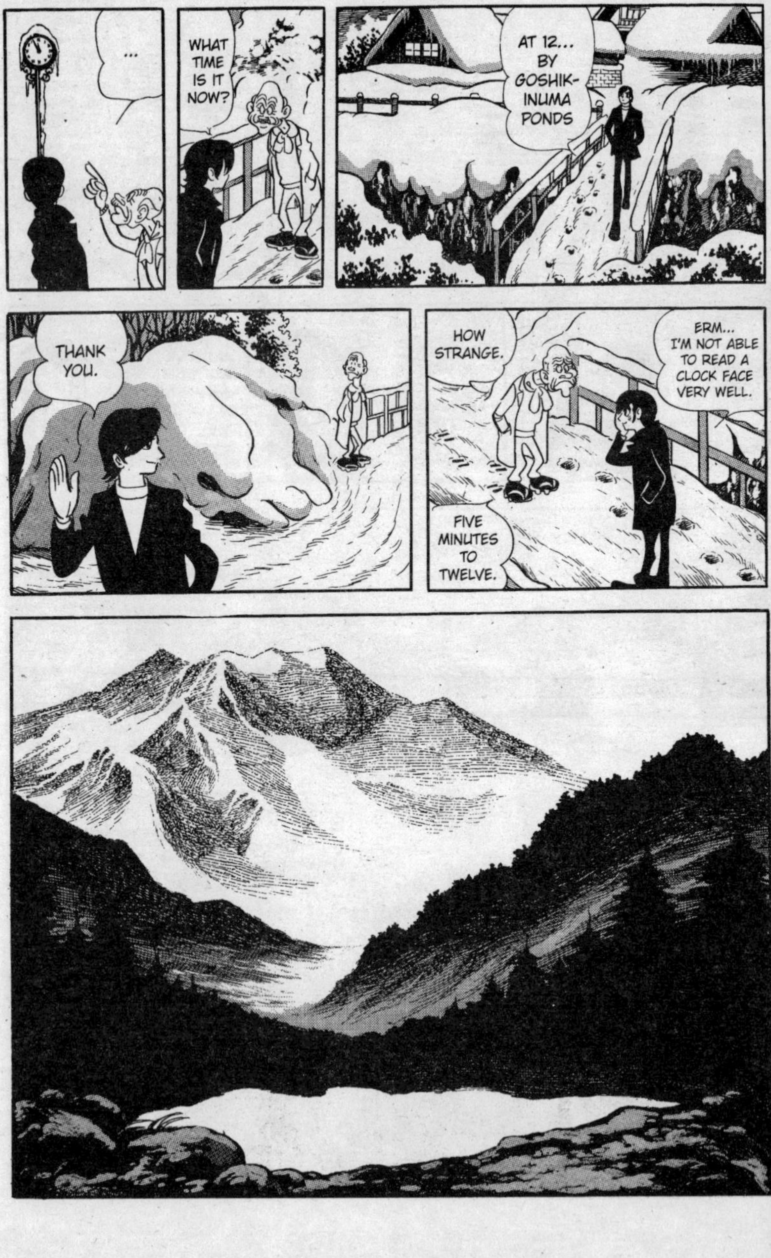
AT 12... BY GOSHIK-INUMA PONDS
WHAT TIME IS IT NOW?
...
ERM... I'M NOT ABLE TO READ A CLOCK FACE VERY WELL.
HOW STRANGE.
FIVE MINUTES TO TWELVE.
THANK YOU.

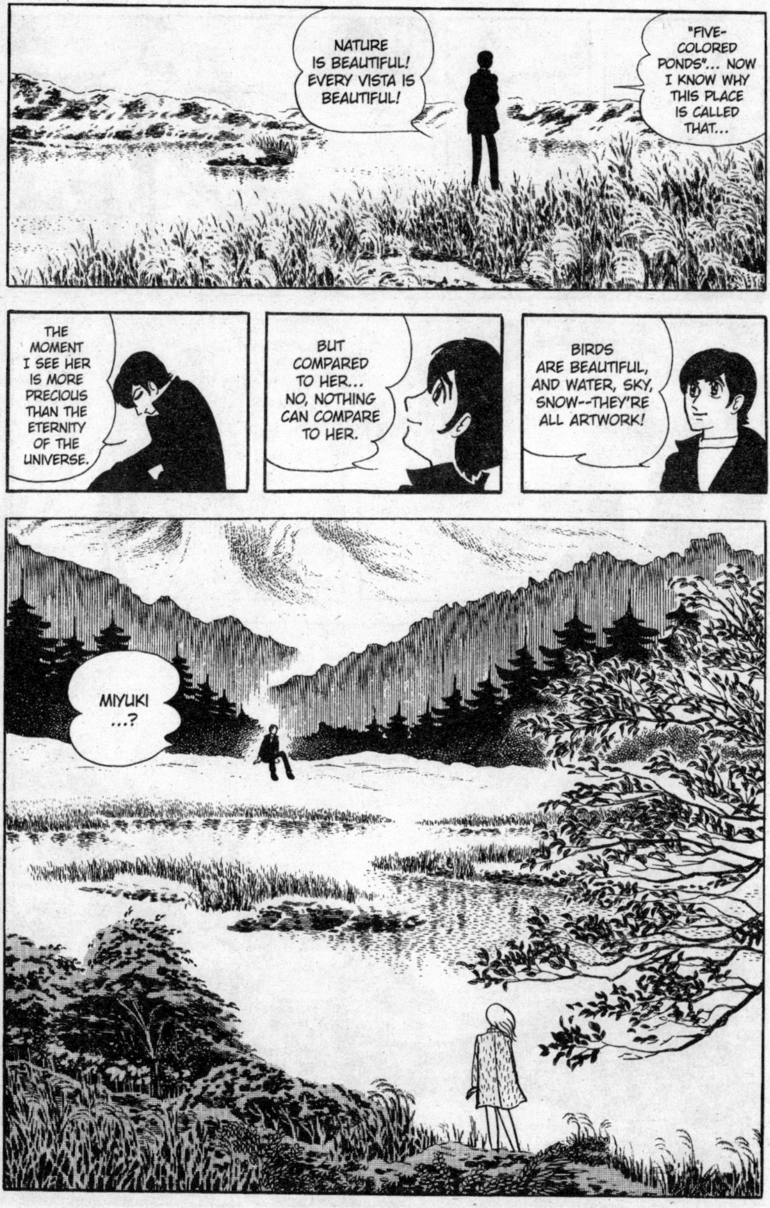
"FIVE-COLORED PONDS"... NOW I KNOW WHY THIS PLACE IS CALLED THAT...
NATURE IS BEAUTIFUL! EVERY VISTA IS BEAUTIFUL!
BIRDS ARE BEAUTIFUL, AND WATER, SKY, SNOW--THEY'RE ALL ARTWORK!
BUT COMPARED TO HER... NO, NOTHING CAN COMPARE TO HER.
THE MOMENT I SEE HER IS MORE PRECIOUS THAN THE ETERNITY OF THE UNIVERSE.
MIYUKI ...?

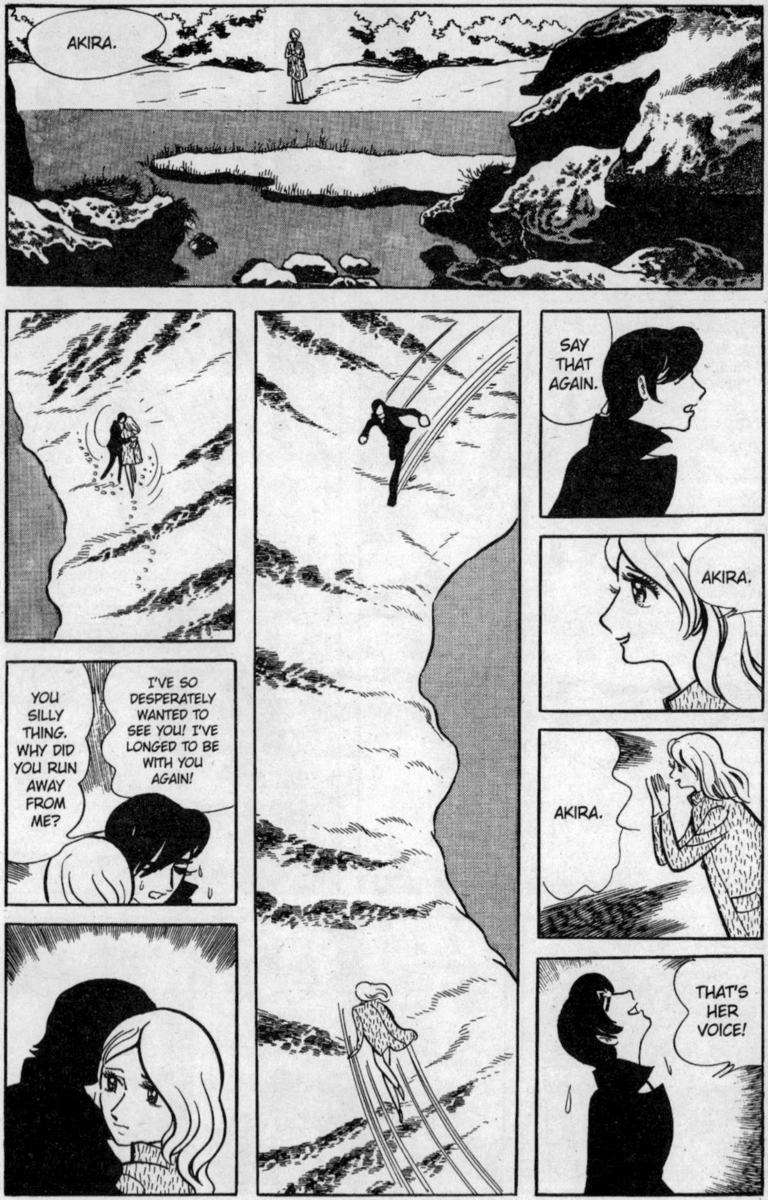
AKIRA.
SAY THAT AGAIN.
AKIRA.
AKIRA.
THAT'S HER VOICE!
I'VE SO DESPERATELY WANTED TO SEE YOU! I'VE LONGED TO BE WITH YOU AGAIN!
YOU SILLY THING. WHY DID YOU RUN AWAY FROM ME?

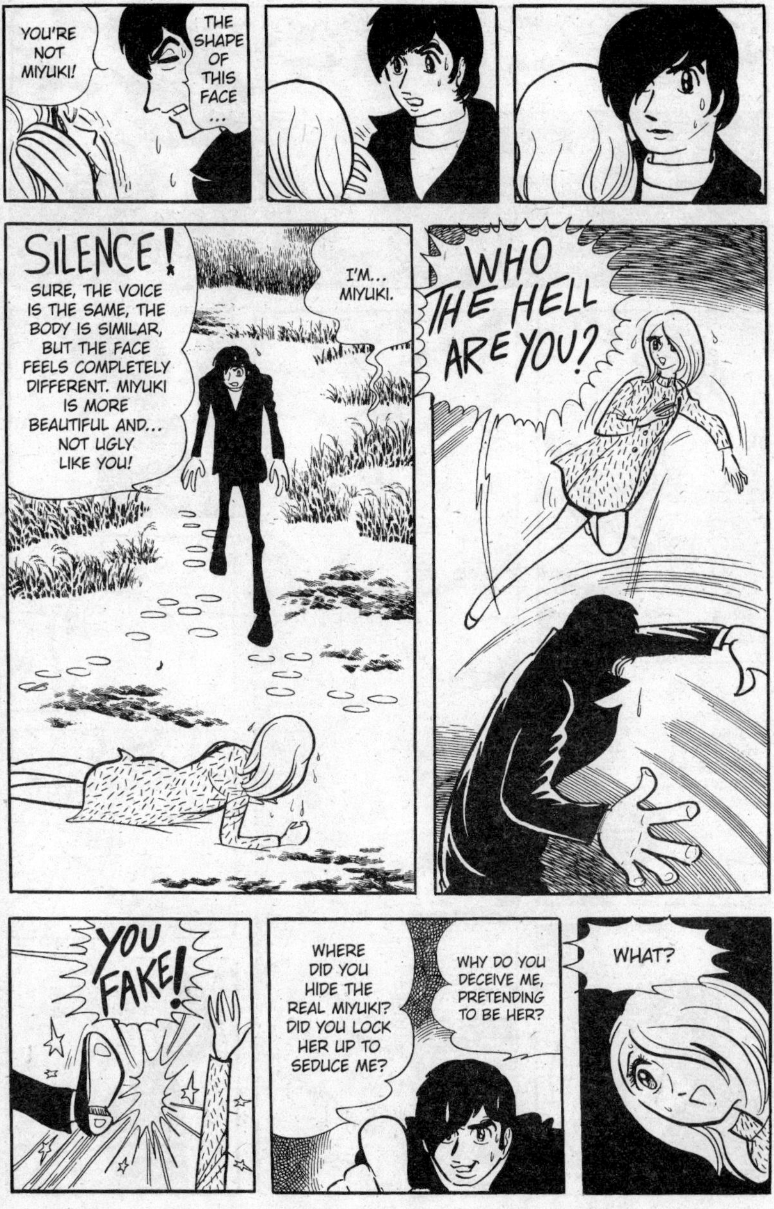
THE SHAPE OF THIS FACE ...
YOU'RE NOT MIYUKI!
WHO THE HELL ARE YOU?
I'M... MIYUKI.
SILENCE! SURE, THE VOICE IS THE SAME, THE BODY IS SIMILAR, BUT THE FACE FEELS COMPLETELY DIFFERENT. MIYUKI IS MORE BEAUTIFUL AND... NOT UGLY LIKE YOU!
WHAT?
WHY DO YOU DECEIVE ME, PRETENDING TO BE HER?
WHERE DID YOU HIDE THE REAL MIYUKI? DID YOU LOCK HER UP TO SEDUCE ME?
YOU FAKE!

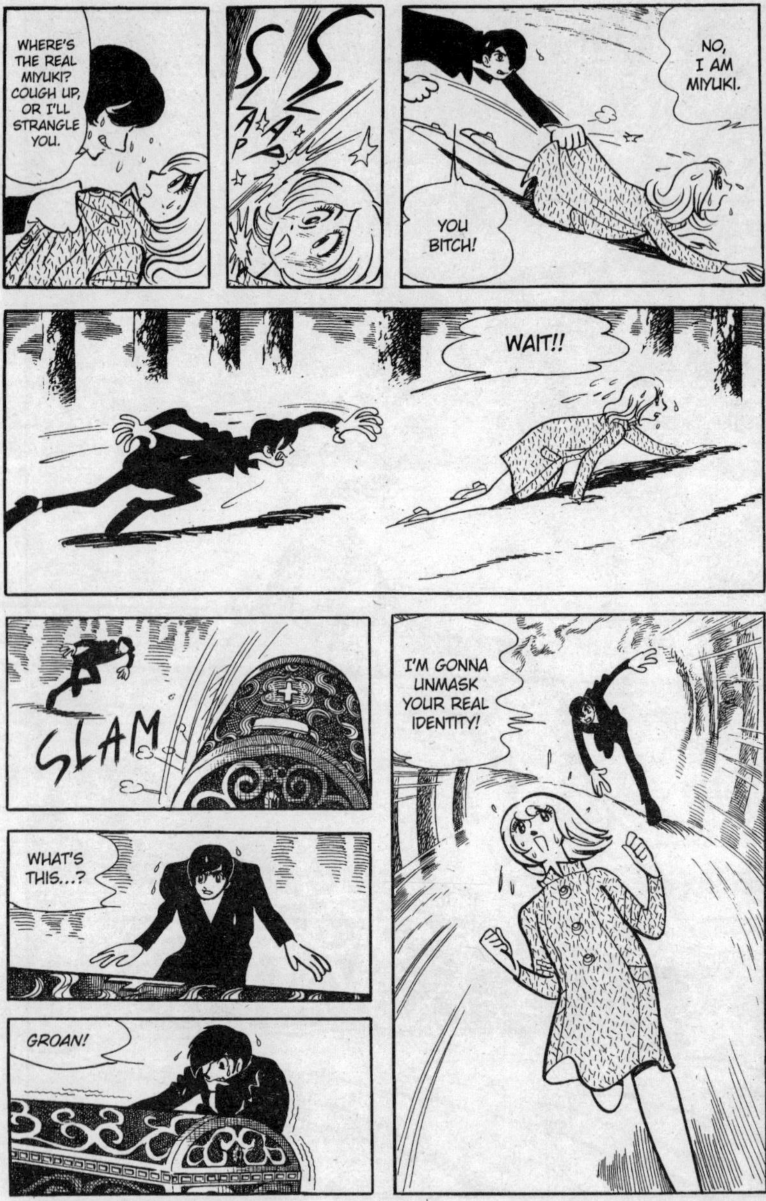
NO, I AM MIYUKI.
YOU BITCH!
SLAP
WHERE'S THE REAL MIYUKI? COUGH UP, OR I'LL STRANGLE YOU.
WAIT!!
I'M GONNA UNMASK YOUR REAL IDENTITY!
SLAM
WHAT'S THIS...?
GROAN!

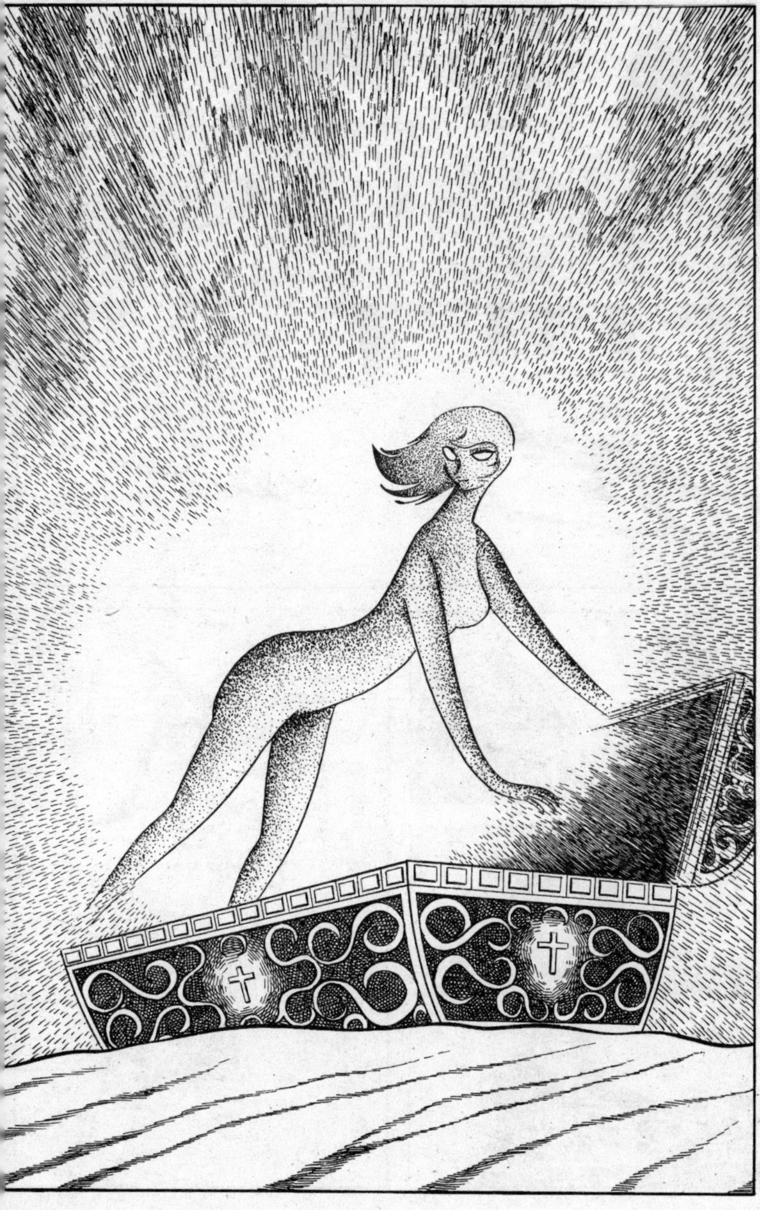

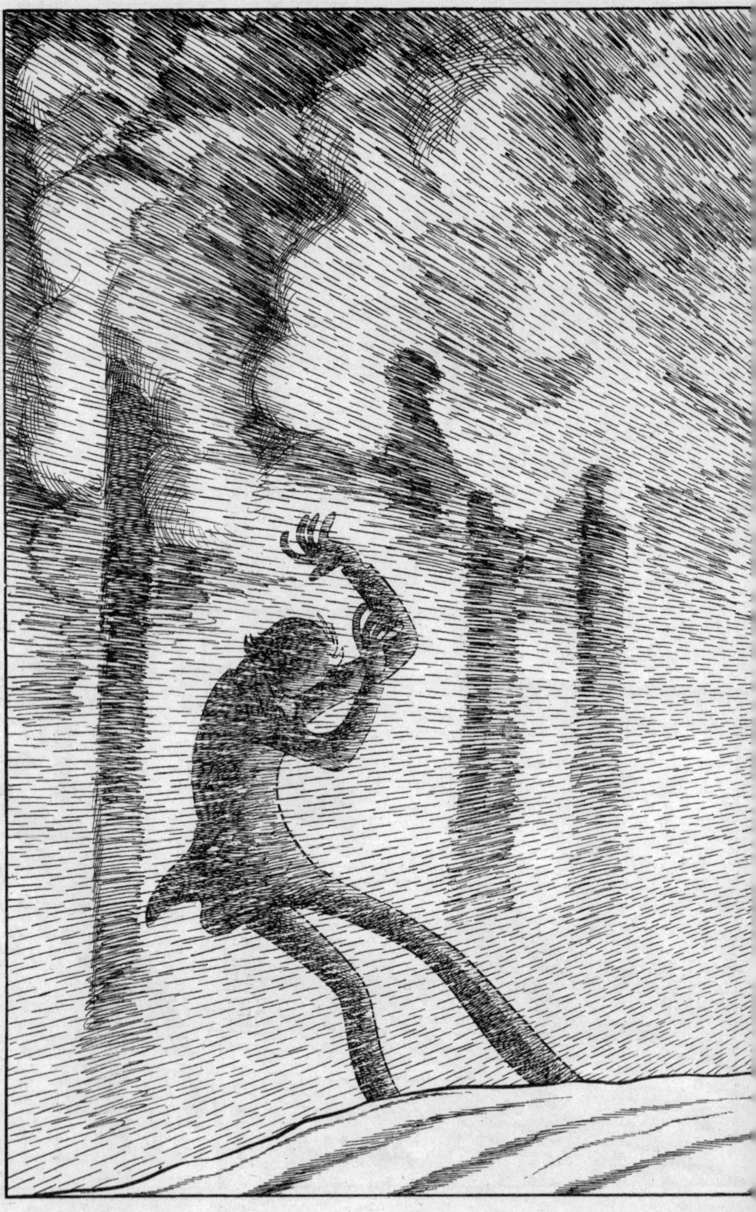

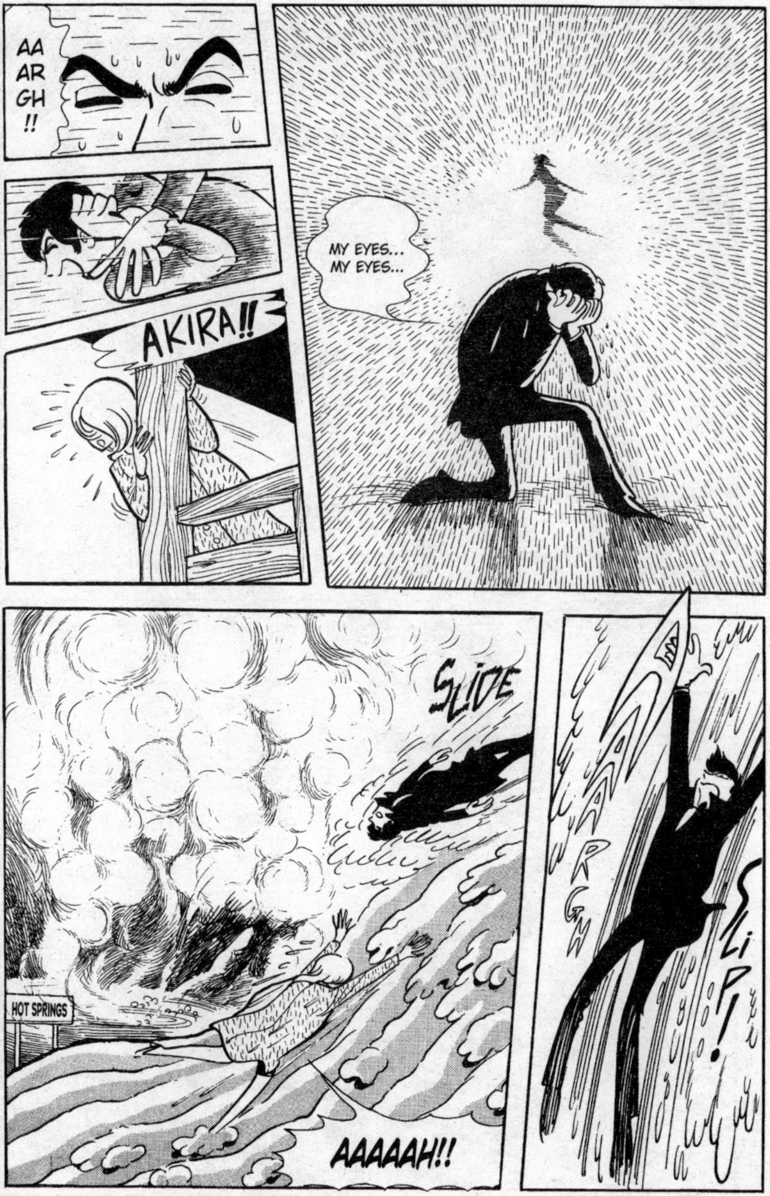
MY EYES... MY EYES...
AA AR GH !!
AKIRA!!
AAARGH
SLIP!
SLIDE
HOT SPRINGS
AAAAAH!!

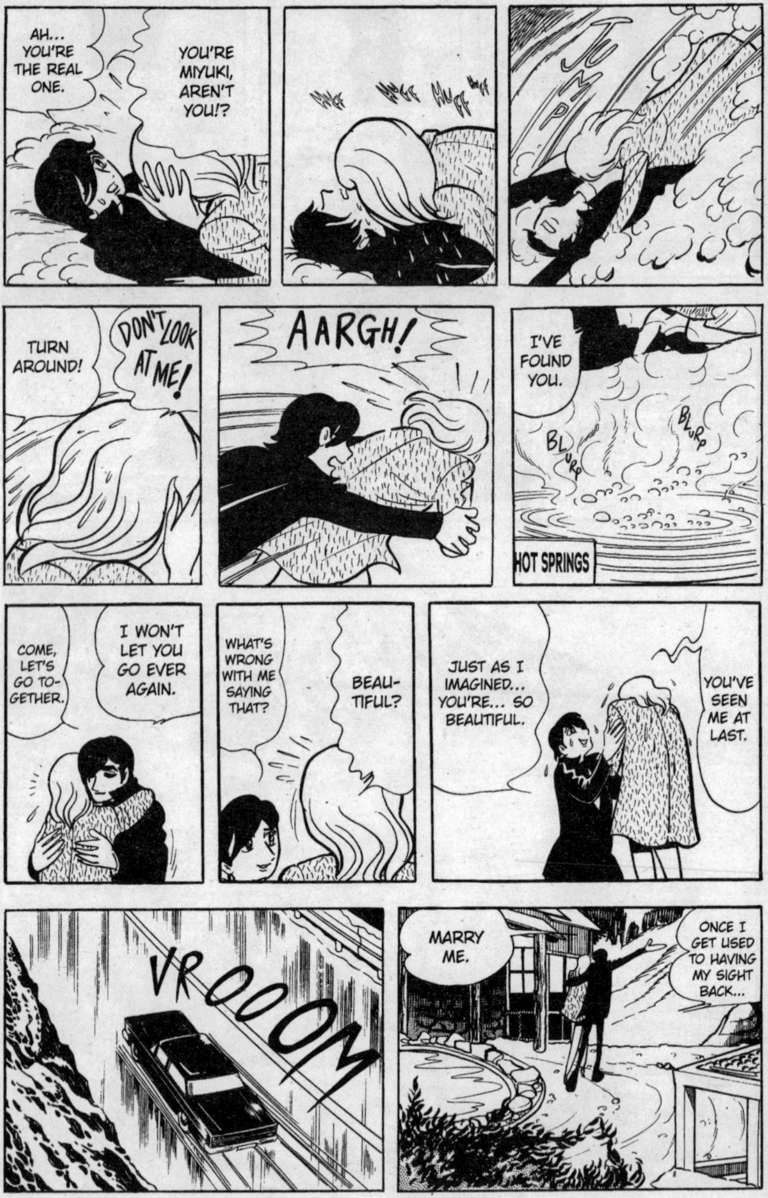
JUMP
HUFF HUFF HUFF HUFF
YOU'RE MIYUKI, AREN'T YOU!?
AH... YOU'RE THE REAL ONE.
I'VE FOUND YOU.
BLURP
BLURP
HOT SPRINGS
AARGH!
DON'T LOOK AT ME!
TURN AROUND!
YOU'VE SEEN ME AT LAST.
JUST AS I IMAGINED... YOU'RE... SO BEAUTIFUL.
BEAU-TIFUL?
WHAT'S WRONG WITH ME SAYING THAT?
I WON'T LET YOU GO EVER AGAIN.
COME, LET'S GO TO-GETHER.
ONCE I GET USED TO HAVING MY SIGHT BACK...
MARRY ME.
VROOOM

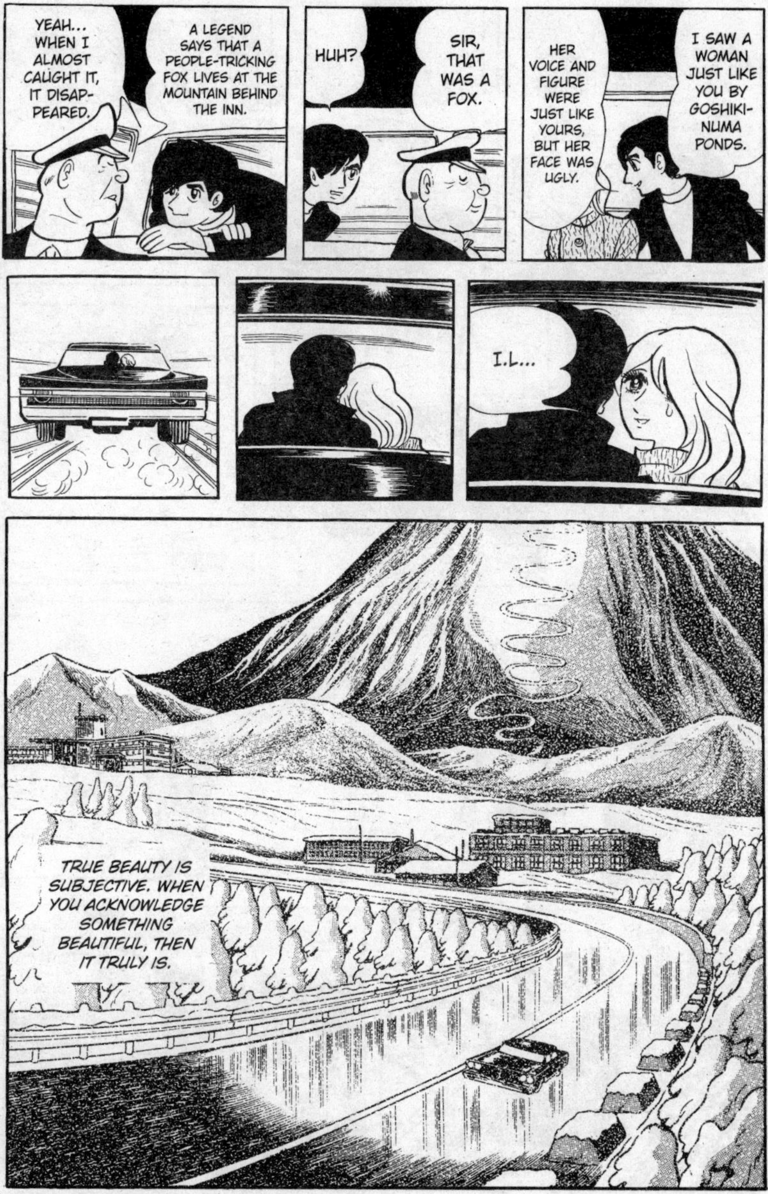
I SAW A WOMAN JUST LIKE YOU BY GOSHIKI-NUMA PONDS.
HER VOICE AND FIGURE WERE JUST LIKE YOURS, BUT HER FACE WAS UGLY.
SIR, THAT WAS A FOX.
HUH?
A LEGEND SAYS THAT A PEOPLE-TRICKING FOX LIVES AT THE MOUNTAIN BEHIND THE INN.
YEAH... WHEN I ALMOST CAUGHT IT, IT DISAPPEARED.
I.L...
TRUE BEAUTY IS SUBJECTIVE. WHEN YOU ACKNOWLEDGE SOMETHING BEAUTIFUL, THEN IT TRULY IS.

# EPISODE 14
# Hyenas

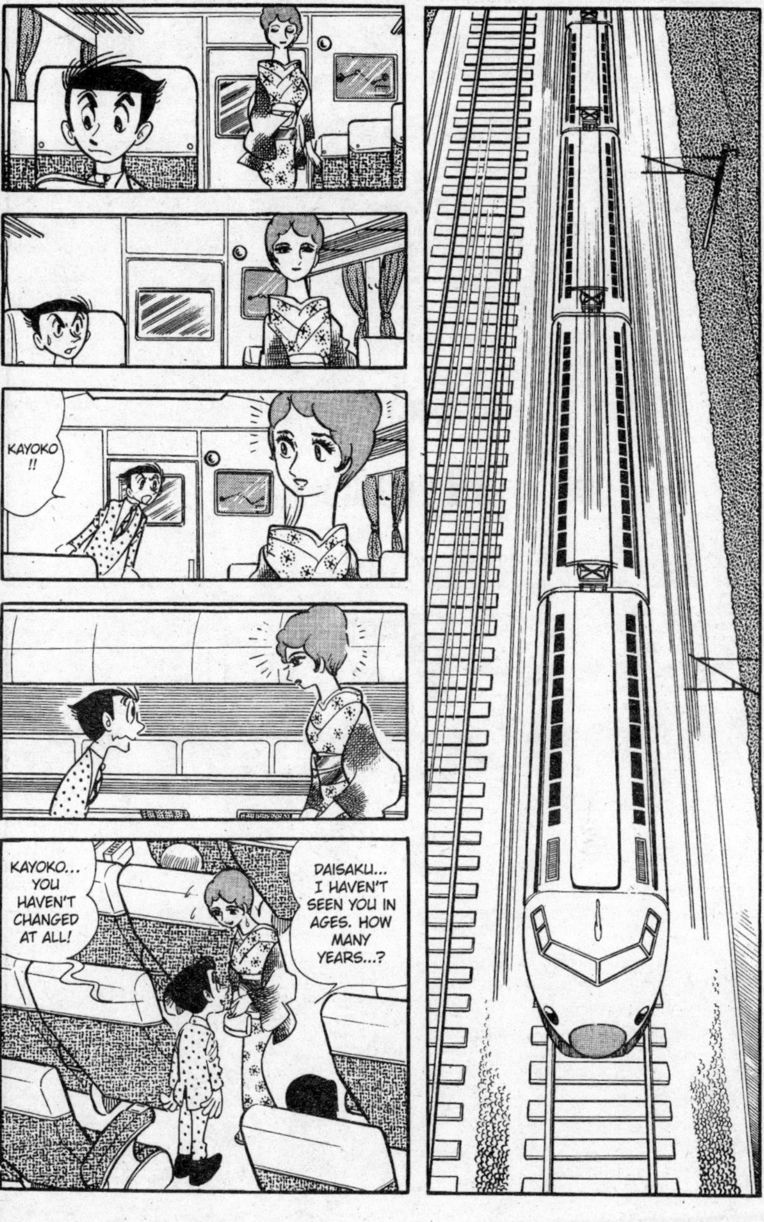
KAYOKO !!
DAISAKU... I HAVEN'T SEEN YOU IN AGES. HOW MANY YEARS...?
KAYOKO... YOU HAVEN'T CHANGED AT ALL!

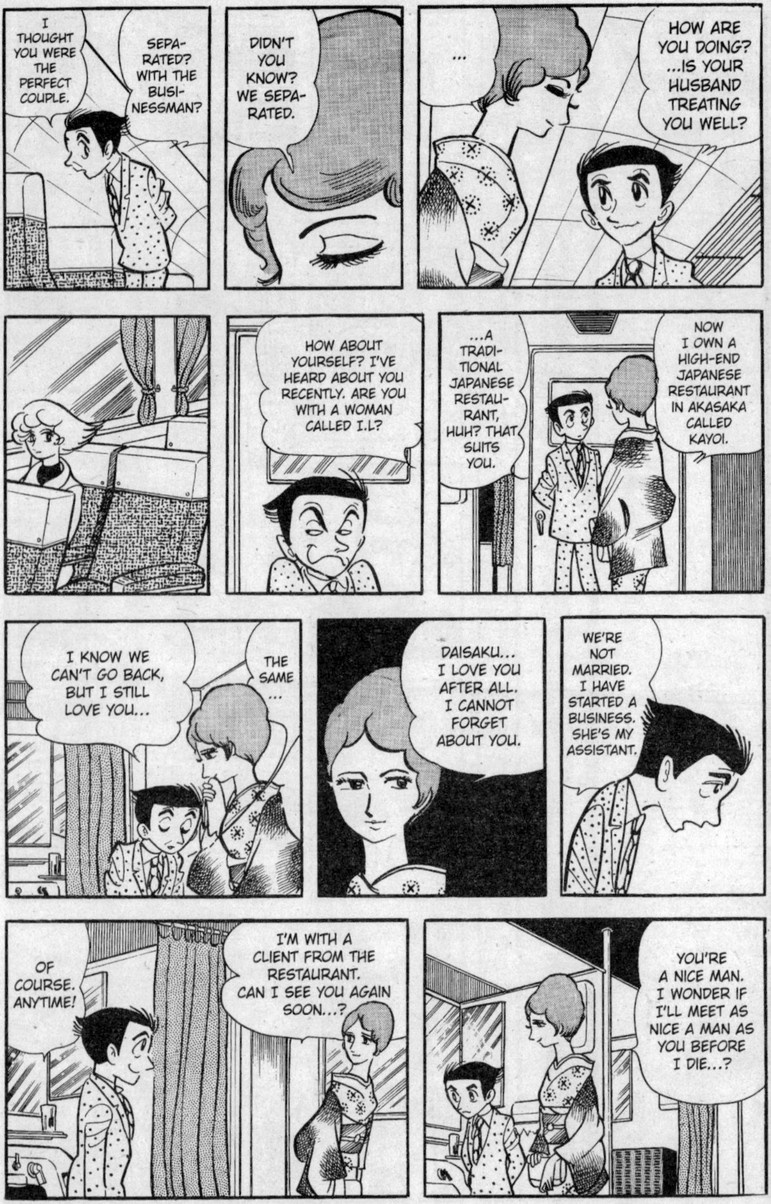
HOW ARE YOU DOING? ...IS YOUR HUSBAND TREATING YOU WELL?
...
DIDN'T YOU KNOW? WE SEPARATED.
SEPARATED? WITH THE BUSINESSMAN?
I THOUGHT YOU WERE THE PERFECT COUPLE.
NOW I OWN A HIGH-END JAPANESE RESTAURANT IN AKASAKA CALLED KAYOI.
...A TRADITIONAL JAPANESE RESTAURANT, HUH? THAT SUITS YOU.
HOW ABOUT YOURSELF? I'VE HEARD ABOUT YOU RECENTLY. ARE YOU WITH A WOMAN CALLED I.L?
WE'RE NOT MARRIED. I HAVE STARTED A BUSINESS. SHE'S MY ASSISTANT.
DAISAKU... I LOVE YOU AFTER ALL. I CANNOT FORGET ABOUT YOU.
THE SAME...
I KNOW WE CAN'T GO BACK, BUT I STILL LOVE YOU...
YOU'RE A NICE MAN. I WONDER IF I'LL MEET AS NICE A MAN AS YOU BEFORE I DIE...?
I'M WITH A CLIENT FROM THE RESTAURANT. CAN I SEE YOU AGAIN SOON...?
OF COURSE. ANYTIME!

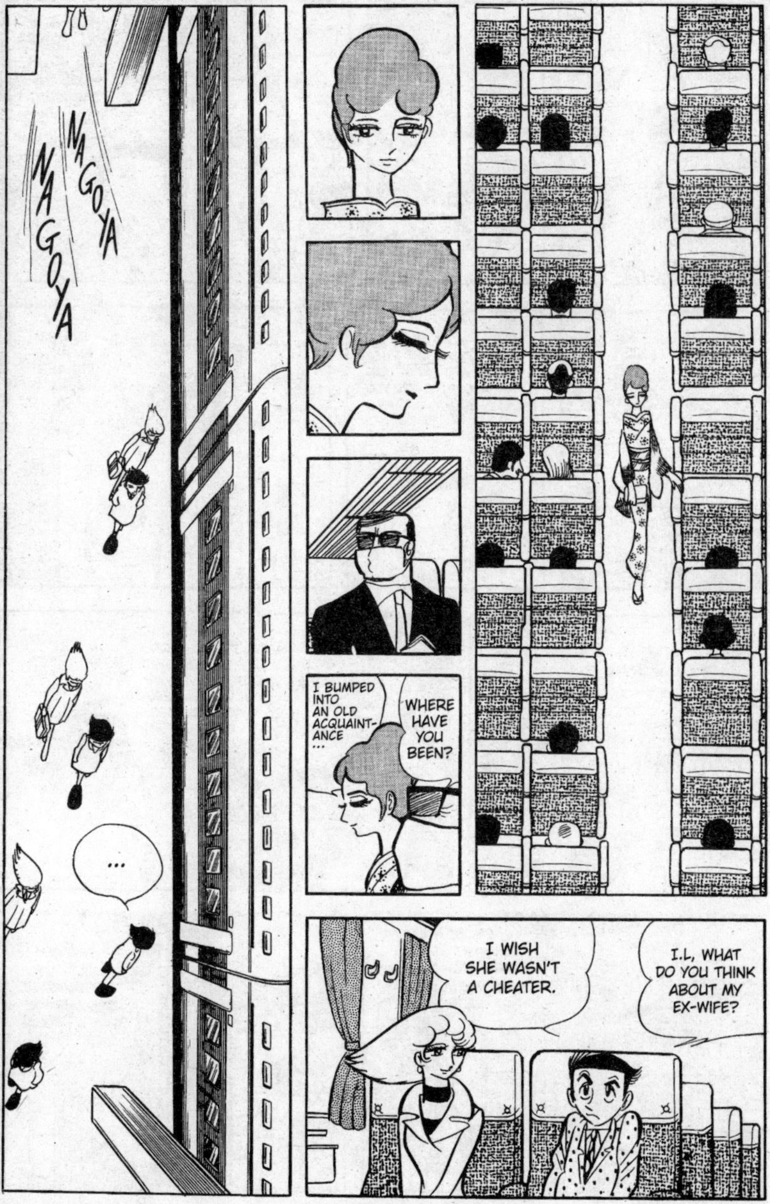
WHERE HAVE YOU BEEN?
I BUMPED INTO AN OLD ACQUAINTANCE...
I.L, WHAT DO YOU THINK ABOUT MY EX-WIFE?
I WISH SHE WASN'T A CHEATER.
NAGOYA
NAGOYA
...

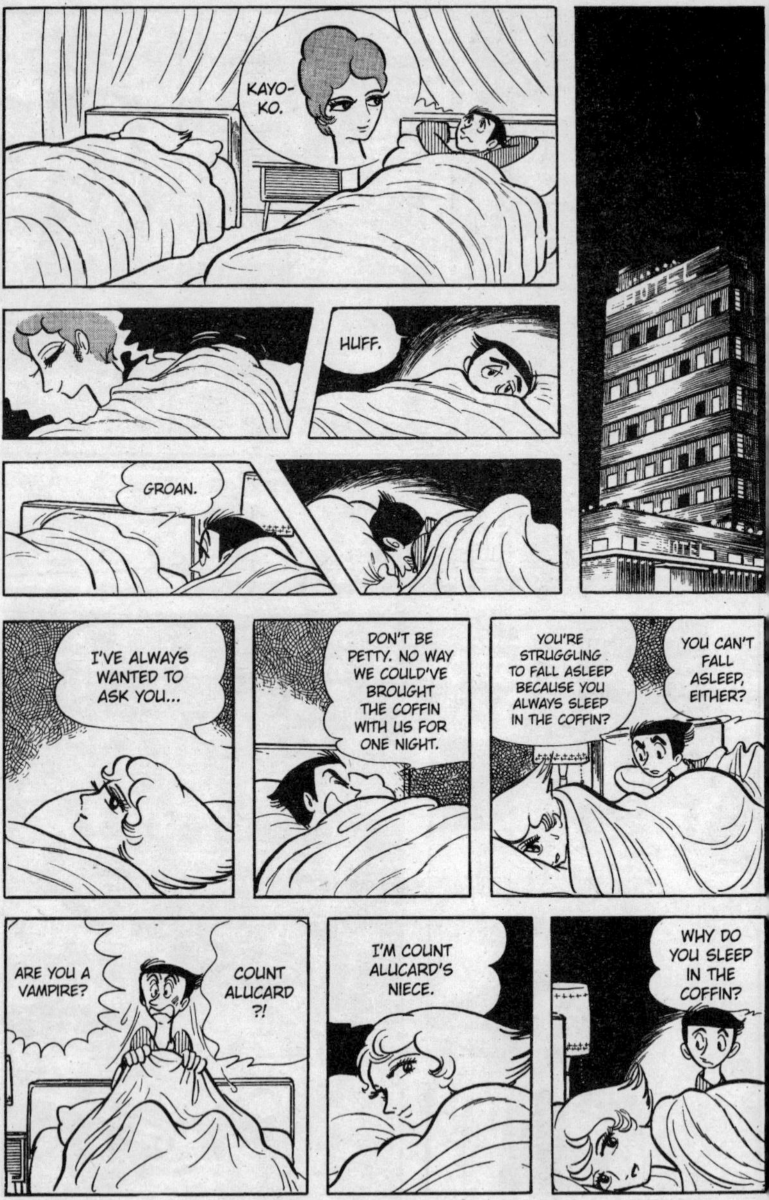
KAYO-KO.
HUFF.
GROAN.
YOU CAN'T FALL ASLEEP, EITHER?
YOU'RE STRUGGLING TO FALL ASLEEP BECAUSE YOU ALWAYS SLEEP IN THE COFFIN?
DON'T BE PETTY. NO WAY WE COULD'VE BROUGHT THE COFFIN WITH US FOR ONE NIGHT.
I'VE ALWAYS WANTED TO ASK YOU...
WHY DO YOU SLEEP IN THE COFFIN?
I'M COUNT ALUCARD'S NIECE.
COUNT ALUCARD ?!
ARE YOU A VAMPIRE?

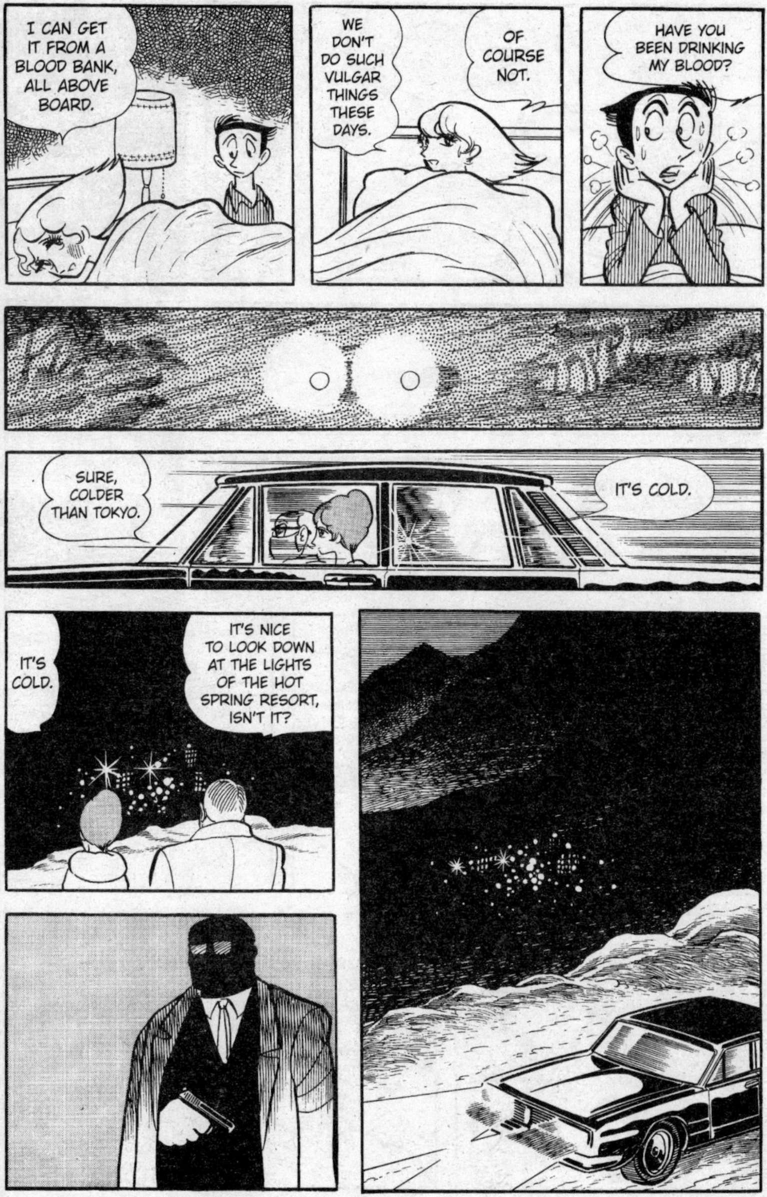
HAVE YOU BEEN DRINKING MY BLOOD?
OF COURSE NOT.
WE DON'T DO SUCH VULGAR THINGS THESE DAYS.
I CAN GET IT FROM A BLOOD BANK, ALL ABOVE BOARD.
IT'S COLD.
SURE, COLDER THAN TOKYO.
IT'S NICE TO LOOK DOWN AT THE LIGHTS OF THE HOT SPRING RESORT, ISN'T IT?
IT'S COLD.

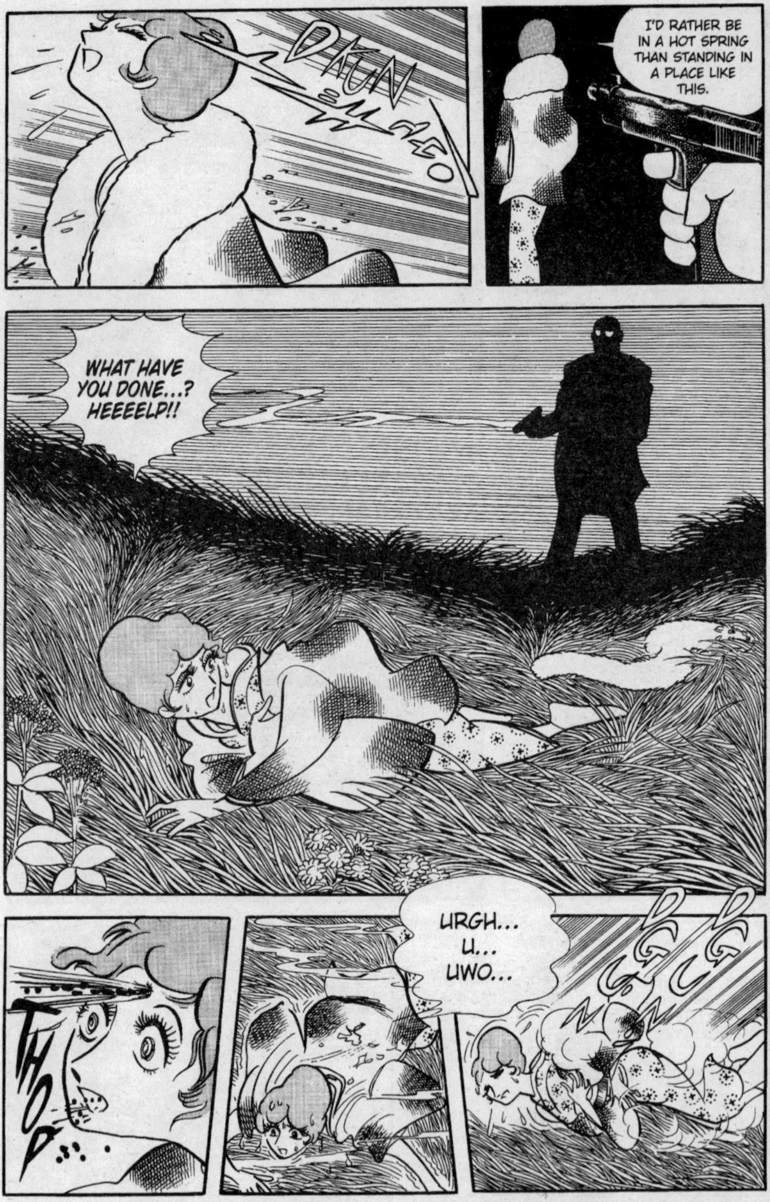
I'D RATHER BE IN A HOT SPRING THAN STANDING IN A PLACE LIKE THIS.
DKUN
WHAT HAVE YOU DONE...? HEEEELP!!
DGUN
DGUN
URGH... U... UWO...
THOD

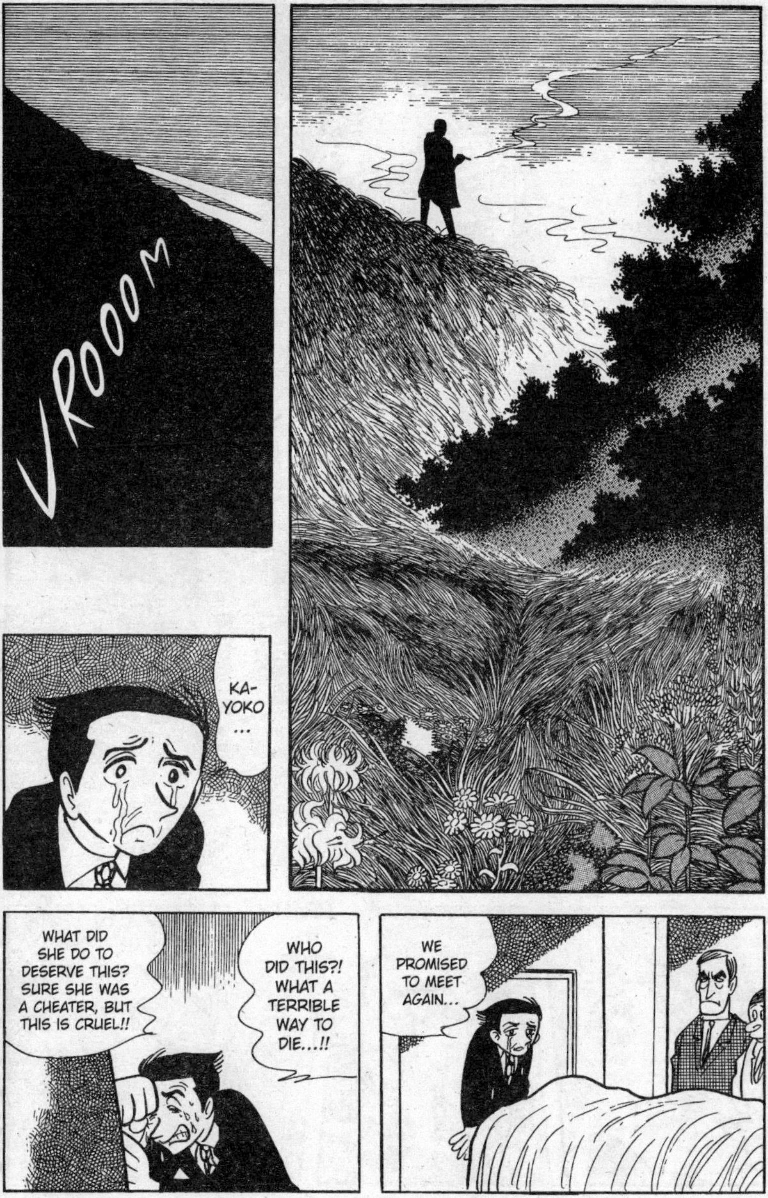
VROOOM
KA-YOKO ...
WE PROMISED TO MEET AGAIN...
WHO DID THIS?! WHAT A TERRIBLE WAY TO DIE...!!
WHAT DID SHE DO TO DESERVE THIS? SURE SHE WAS A CHEATER, BUT THIS IS CRUEL!!

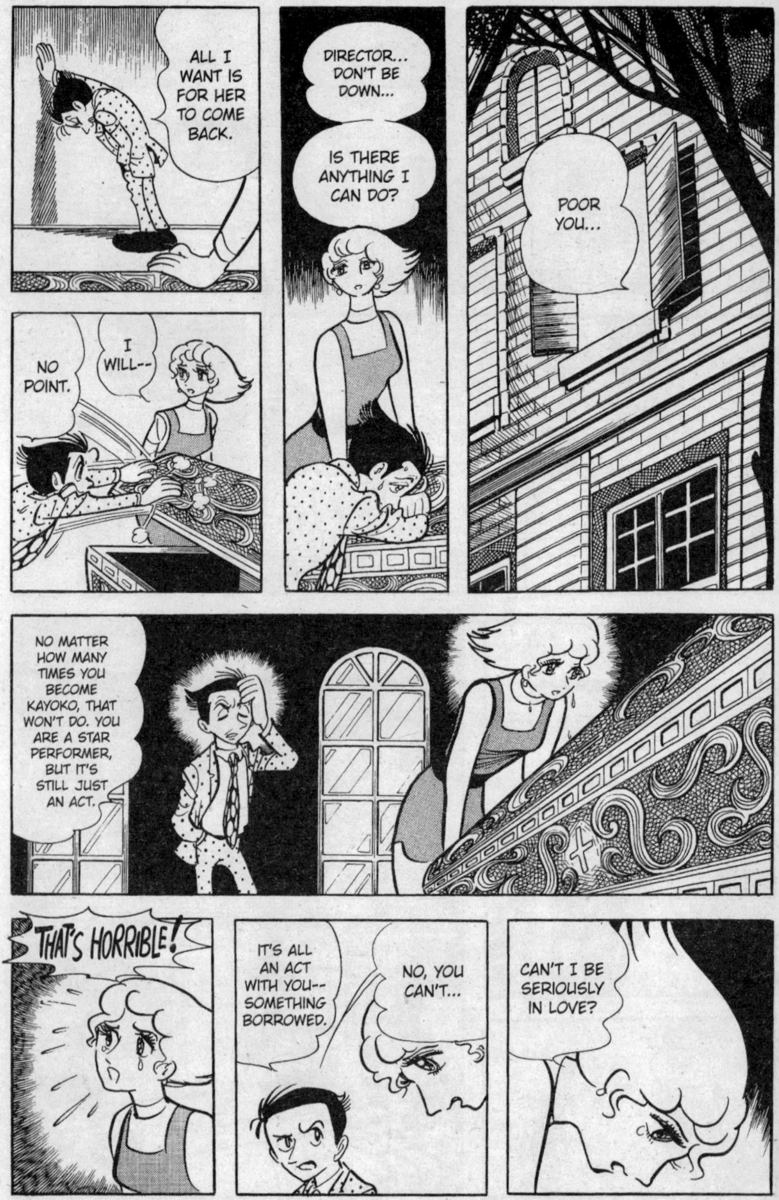
POOR YOU...
DIRECTOR... DON'T BE DOWN...
IS THERE ANYTHING I CAN DO?
ALL I WANT IS FOR HER TO COME BACK.
I WILL--
NO POINT.
NO MATTER HOW MANY TIMES YOU BECOME KAYOKO, THAT WON'T DO. YOU ARE A STAR PERFORMER, BUT IT'S STILL JUST AN ACT.
CAN'T I BE SERIOUSLY IN LOVE?
NO, YOU CAN'T...
IT'S ALL AN ACT WITH YOU-- SOMETHING BORROWED.
THAT'S HORRIBLE!

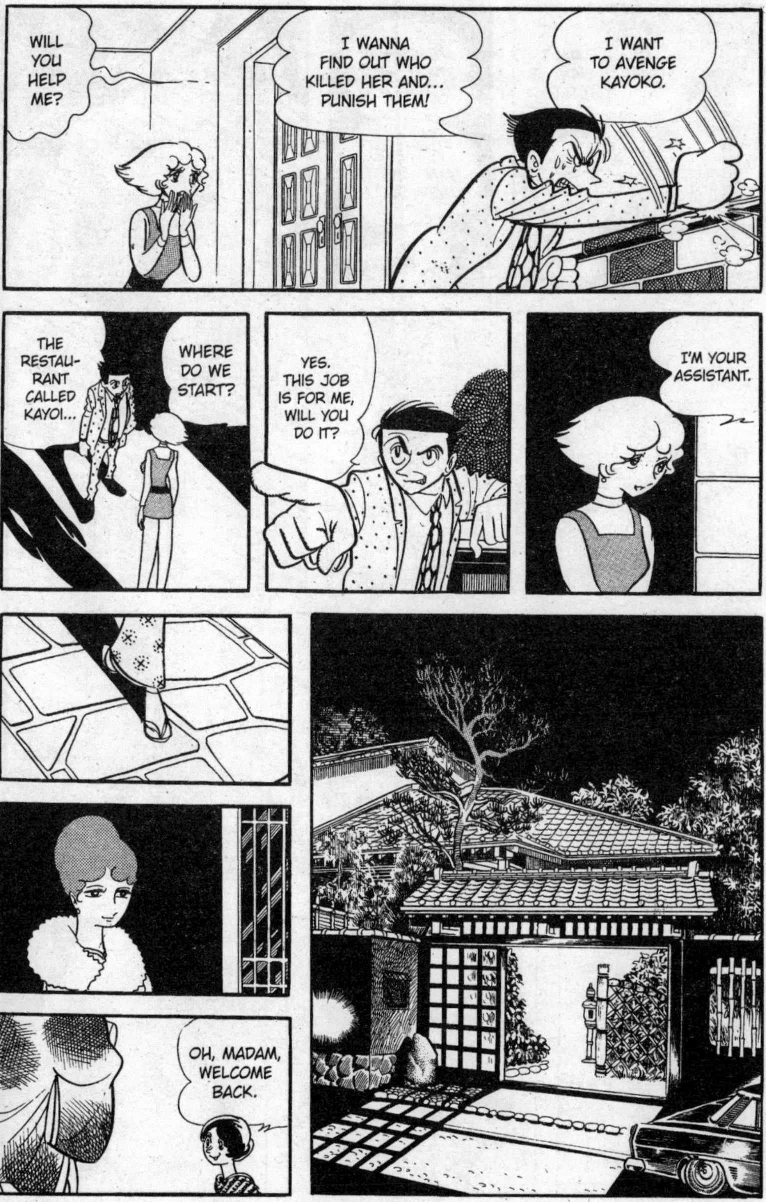
I WANT TO AVENGE KAYOKO.
I WANNA FIND OUT WHO KILLED HER AND... PUNISH THEM!
WILL YOU HELP ME?
I'M YOUR ASSISTANT.
YES. THIS JOB IS FOR ME, WILL YOU DO IT?
WHERE DO WE START?
THE RESTAU-RANT CALLED KAYOI...
OH, MADAM, WELCOME BACK.

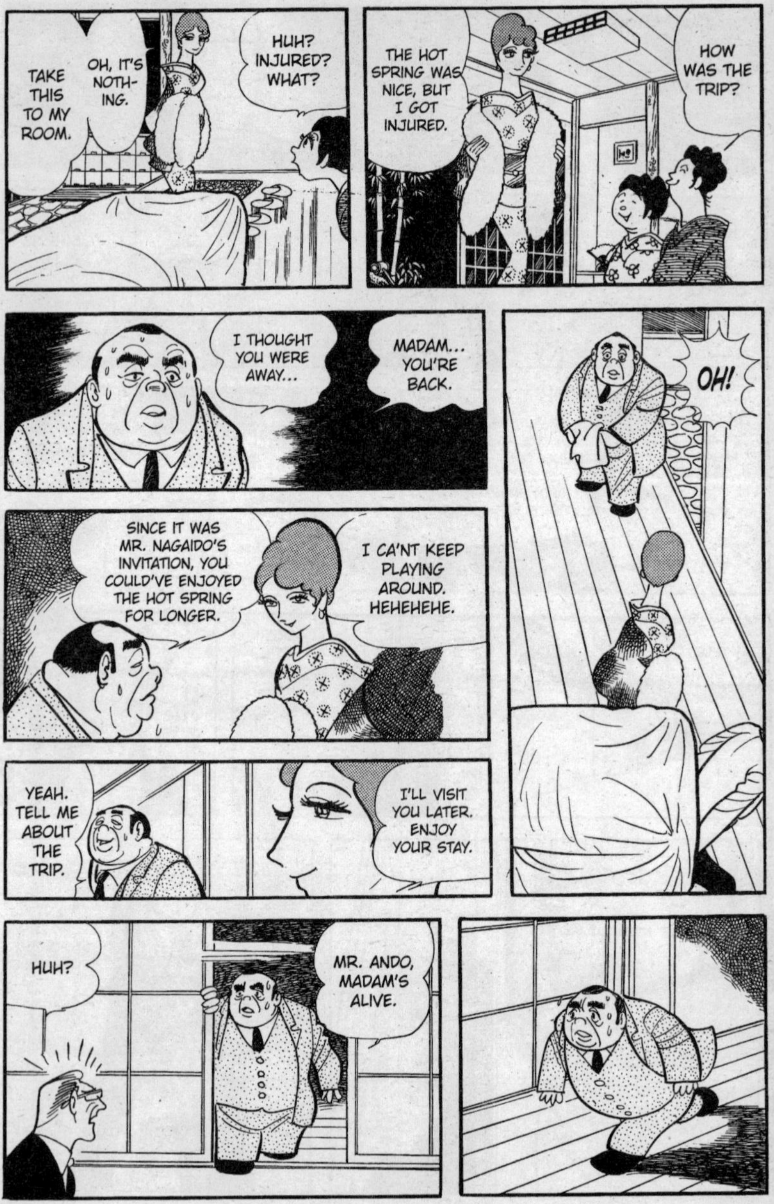
HOW WAS THE TRIP?
THE HOT SPRING WAS NICE, BUT I GOT INJURED.
HUH? INJURED? WHAT?
OH, IT'S NOTHING.
TAKE THIS TO MY ROOM.
OH!
MADAM... YOU'RE BACK.
I THOUGHT YOU WERE AWAY...
I CA'NT KEEP PLAYING AROUND. HEHEHEHE.
SINCE IT WAS MR. NAGAIDO'S INVITATION, YOU COULD'VE ENJOYED THE HOT SPRING FOR LONGER.
I'LL VISIT YOU LATER. ENJOY YOUR STAY.
YEAH. TELL ME ABOUT THE TRIP.
MR. ANDO, MADAM'S ALIVE.
HUH?

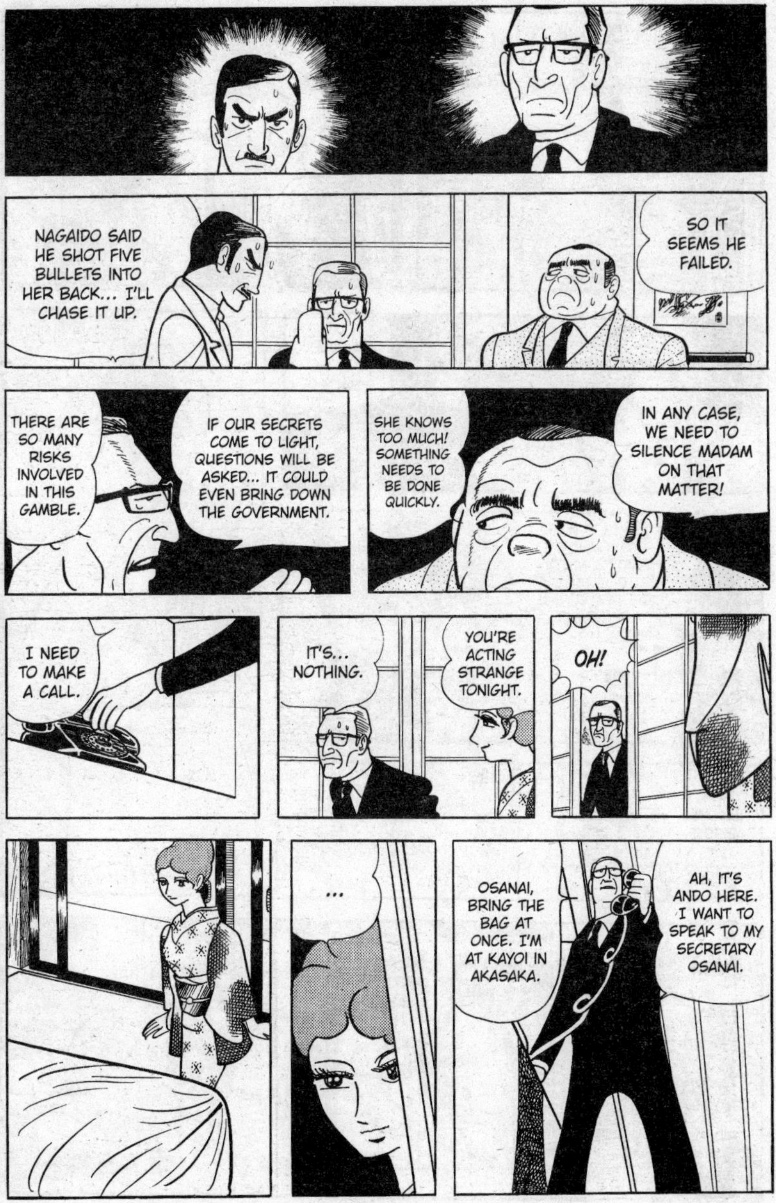
SO IT SEEMS HE FAILED.
NAGAIDO SAID HE SHOT FIVE BULLETS INTO HER BACK... I'LL CHASE IT UP.
IN ANY CASE, WE NEED TO SILENCE MADAM ON THAT MATTER!
SHE KNOWS TOO MUCH! SOMETHING NEEDS TO BE DONE QUICKLY.
IF OUR SECRETS COME TO LIGHT, QUESTIONS WILL BE ASKED... IT COULD EVEN BRING DOWN THE GOVERNMENT.
THERE ARE SO MANY RISKS INVOLVED IN THIS GAMBLE.
OH!
YOU'RE ACTING STRANGE TONIGHT.
IT'S... NOTHING.
I NEED TO MAKE A CALL.
AH, IT'S ANDO HERE. I WANT TO SPEAK TO MY SECRETARY OSANAI.
OSANAI, BRING THE BAG AT ONCE. I'M AT KAYOI IN AKASAKA.
...

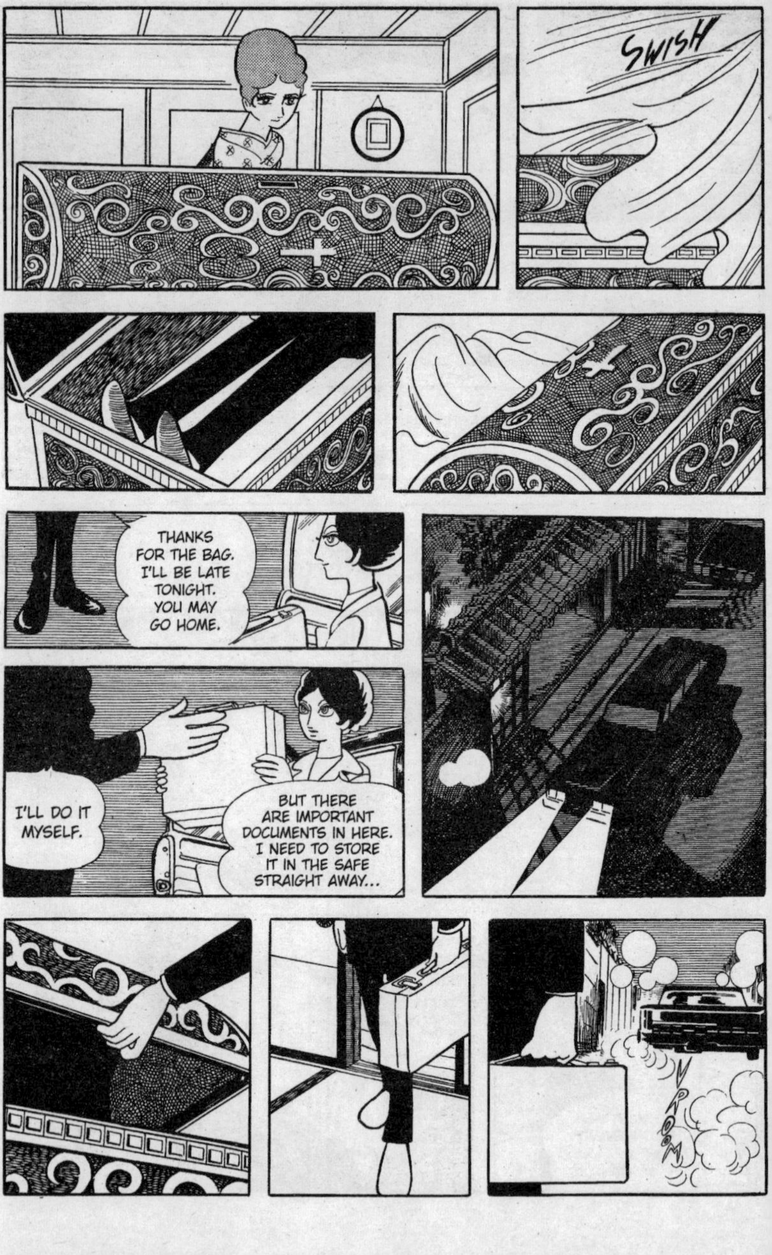
SWISH
THANKS FOR THE BAG. I'LL BE LATE TONIGHT. YOU MAY GO HOME.
BUT THERE ARE IMPORTANT DOCUMENTS IN HERE. I NEED TO STORE IT IN THE SAFE STRAIGHT AWAY...
I'LL DO IT MYSELF.
VROOM

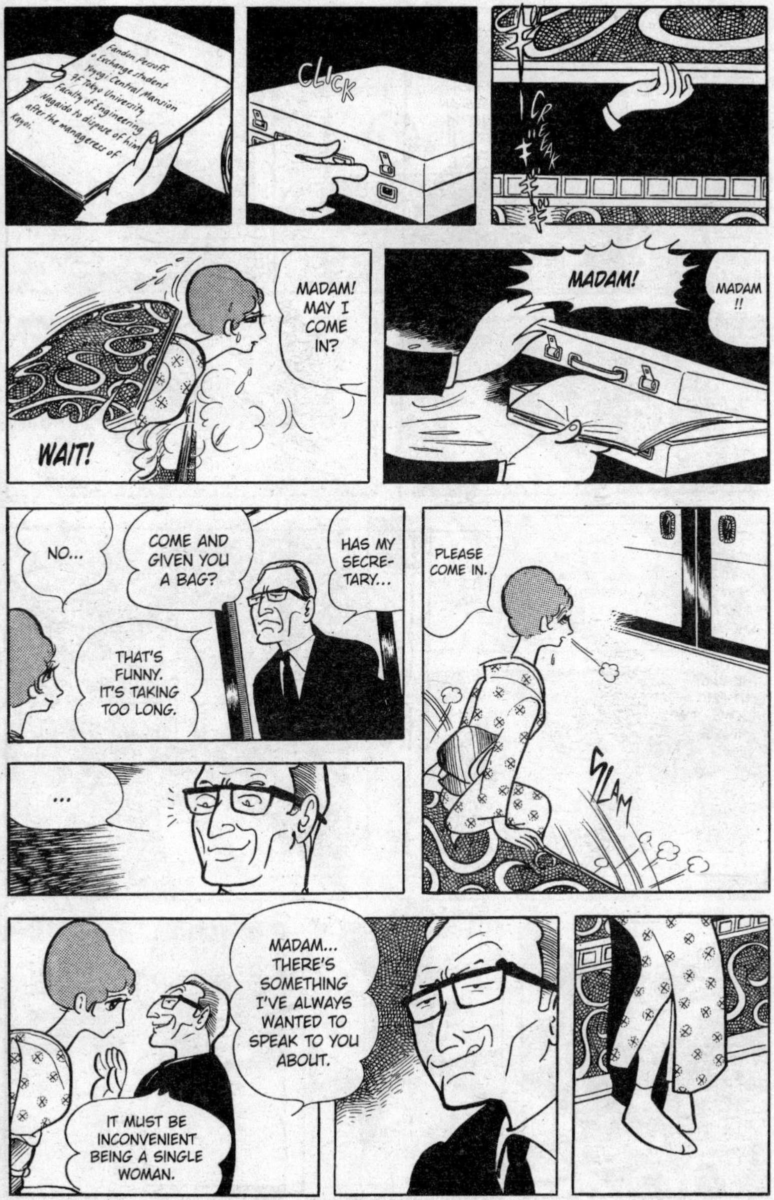
CREEAK
CLICK
Fandon Persoff
o Exchange student
Yoyogi Central Mansion
9F Tokyo University
Faculty of Engineering
Nagaido to dispose of him
after the manageress of
Kayoi.
MADAM !!
MADAM!
MADAM! MAY I COME IN?
WAIT!
PLEASE COME IN.
SLAM
HAS MY SECRE-TARY...
COME AND GIVEN YOU A BAG?
NO...
THAT'S FUNNY. IT'S TAKING TOO LONG.
...
MADAM... THERE'S SOMETHING I'VE ALWAYS WANTED TO SPEAK TO YOU ABOUT.
IT MUST BE INCONVENIENT BEING A SINGLE WOMAN.

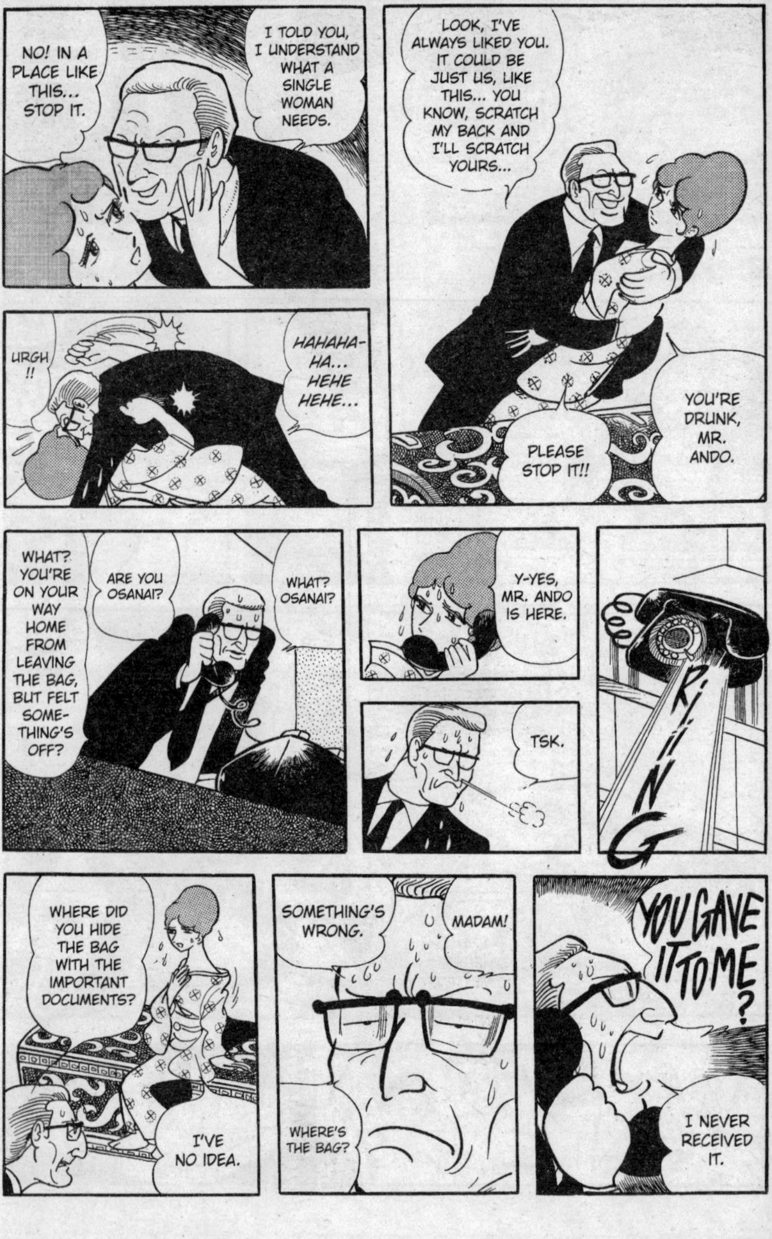
LOOK, I'VE ALWAYS LIKED YOU. IT COULD BE JUST US, LIKE THIS... YOU KNOW, SCRATCH MY BACK AND I'LL SCRATCH YOURS...
YOU'RE DRUNK, MR. ANDO.
PLEASE STOP IT!!
I TOLD YOU, I UNDERSTAND WHAT A SINGLE WOMAN NEEDS.
NO! IN A PLACE LIKE THIS... STOP IT.
HAHAHAHA... HEHE HEHE...
URGH !!
RIIING
Y-YES, MR. ANDO IS HERE.
TSK.
WHAT? OSANAI?
ARE YOU OSANAI?
WHAT? YOU'RE ON YOUR WAY HOME FROM LEAVING THE BAG, BUT FELT SOMETHING'S OFF?
YOU GAVE IT TO ME?
I NEVER RECEIVED IT.
MADAM!
SOMETHING'S WRONG.
WHERE'S THE BAG?
WHERE DID YOU HIDE THE BAG WITH THE IMPORTANT DOCUMENTS?
I'VE NO IDEA.

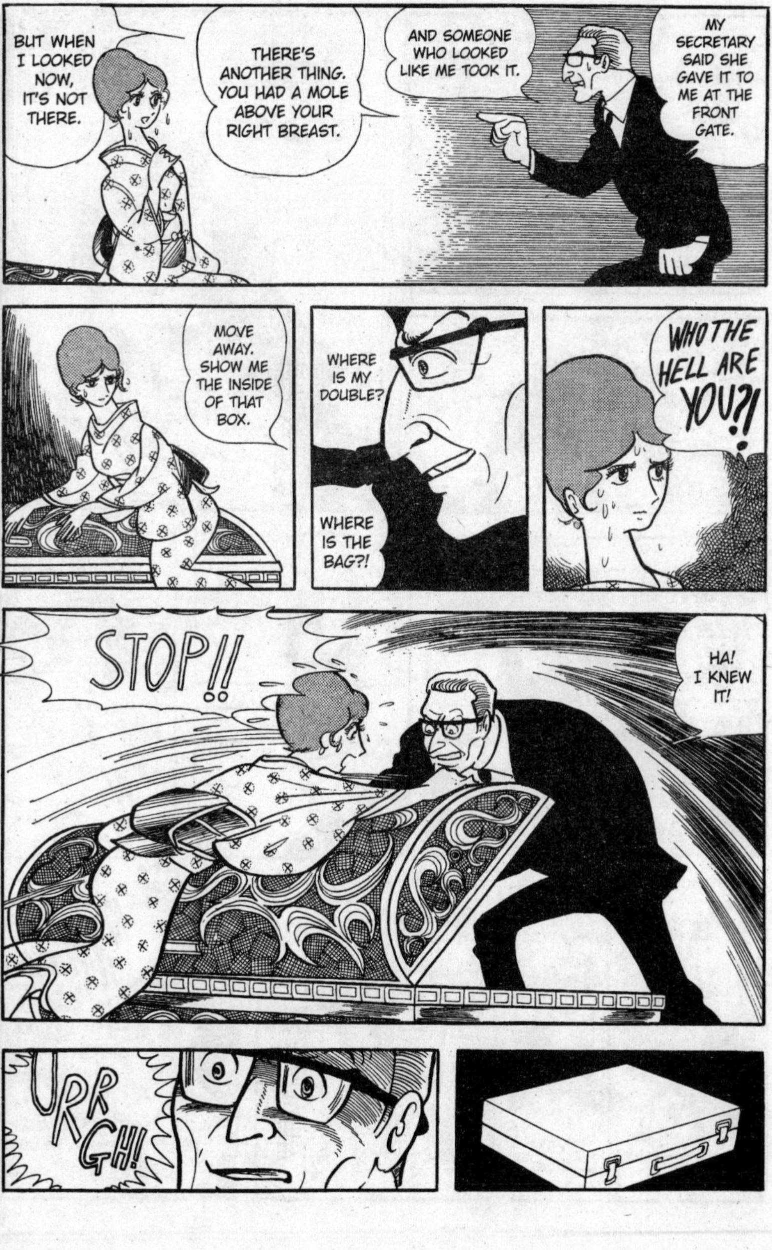
MY SECRETARY SAID SHE GAVE IT TO ME AT THE FRONT GATE.
AND SOMEONE WHO LOOKED LIKE ME TOOK IT.
THERE'S ANOTHER THING. YOU HAD A MOLE ABOVE YOUR RIGHT BREAST.
BUT WHEN I LOOKED NOW, IT'S NOT THERE.
WHO THE HELL ARE YOU?!
WHERE IS MY DOUBLE?
WHERE IS THE BAG?!
MOVE AWAY. SHOW ME THE INSIDE OF THAT BOX.
HA! I KNEW IT!
STOP!!
URRGH!

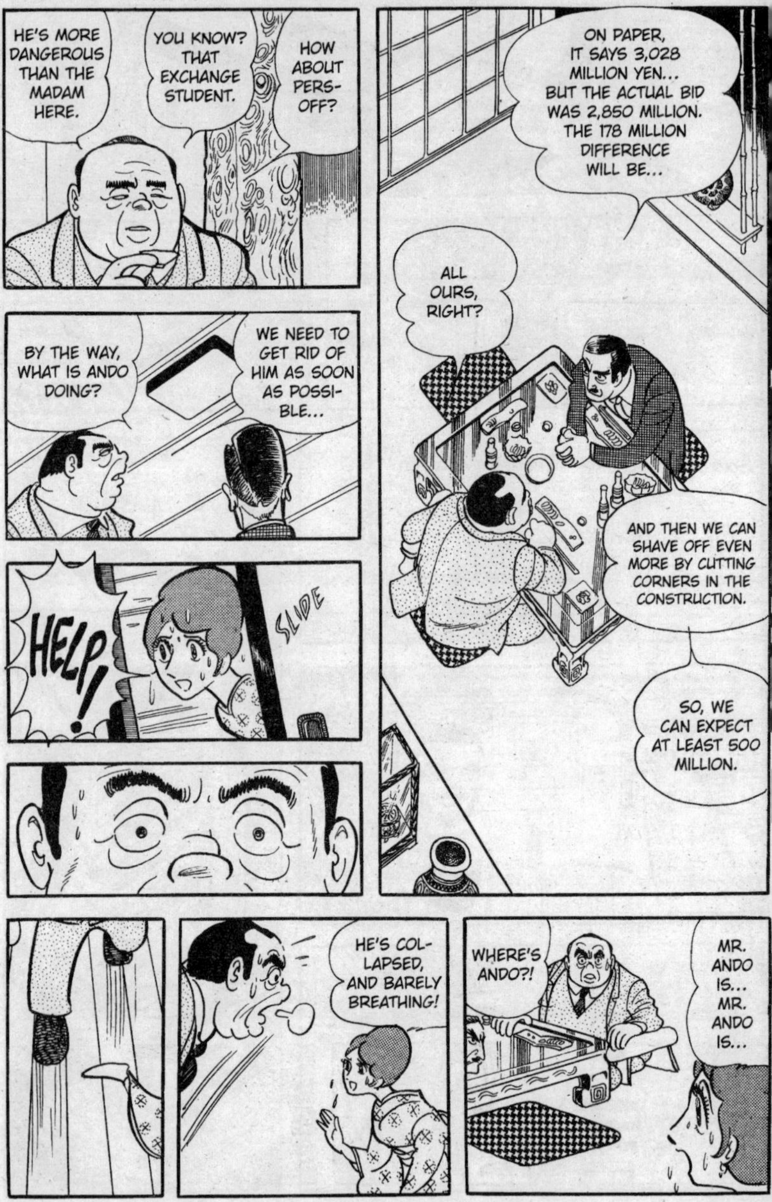
ON PAPER, IT SAYS 3,028 MILLION YEN... BUT THE ACTUAL BID WAS 2,850 MILLION. THE 178 MILLION DIFFERENCE WILL BE...
ALL OURS, RIGHT?
AND THEN WE CAN SHAVE OFF EVEN MORE BY CUTTING CORNERS IN THE CONSTRUCTION.
SO, WE CAN EXPECT AT LEAST 500 MILLION.
HOW ABOUT PERS-OFF?
YOU KNOW? THAT EXCHANGE STUDENT.
HE'S MORE DANGEROUS THAN THE MADAM HERE.
WE NEED TO GET RID OF HIM AS SOON AS POSSI-BLE...
BY THE WAY, WHAT IS ANDO DOING?
SLIDE
HELP!
MR. ANDO IS... MR. ANDO IS...
WHERE'S ANDO?!
HE'S COL-LAPSED, AND BARELY BREATHING!

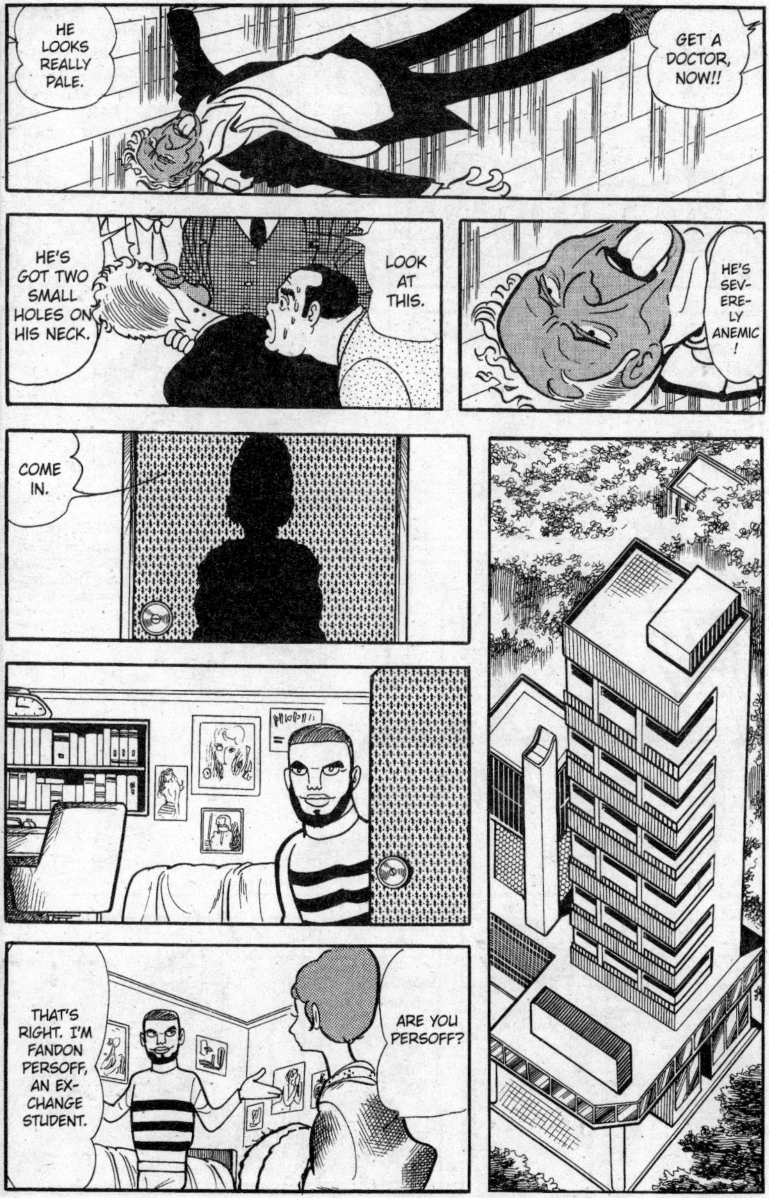
GET A DOCTOR, NOW!!
HE LOOKS REALLY PALE.
HE'S SEV-ERE-LY ANEMIC!
LOOK AT THIS.
HE'S GOT TWO SMALL HOLES ON HIS NECK.
COME IN.
ARE YOU PERSOFF?
THAT'S RIGHT. I'M FANDON PERSOFF, AN EX-CHANGE STUDENT.

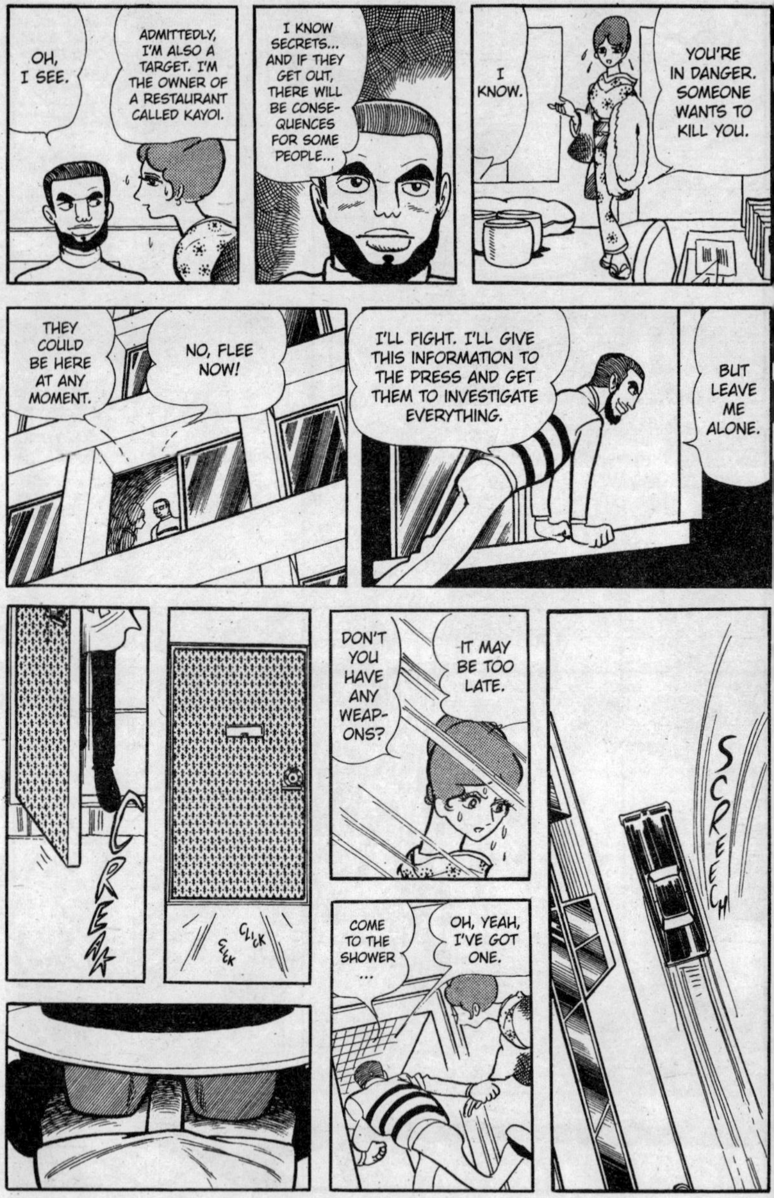
YOU'RE IN DANGER. SOMEONE WANTS TO KILL YOU.
I KNOW.
I KNOW SECRETS... AND IF THEY GET OUT, THERE WILL BE CONSE-QUENCES FOR SOME PEOPLE...
ADMITTEDLY, I'M ALSO A TARGET. I'M THE OWNER OF A RESTAURANT CALLED KAYOI.
OH, I SEE.
BUT LEAVE ME ALONE.
I'LL FIGHT. I'LL GIVE THIS INFORMATION TO THE PRESS AND GET THEM TO INVESTIGATE EVERYTHING.
NO, FLEE NOW!
THEY COULD BE HERE AT ANY MOMENT.
SCREECH
IT MAY BE TOO LATE.
DON'T YOU HAVE ANY WEAP-ONS?
OH, YEAH, I'VE GOT ONE.
COME TO THE SHOWER ...
CLICK
CLICK
CREAK

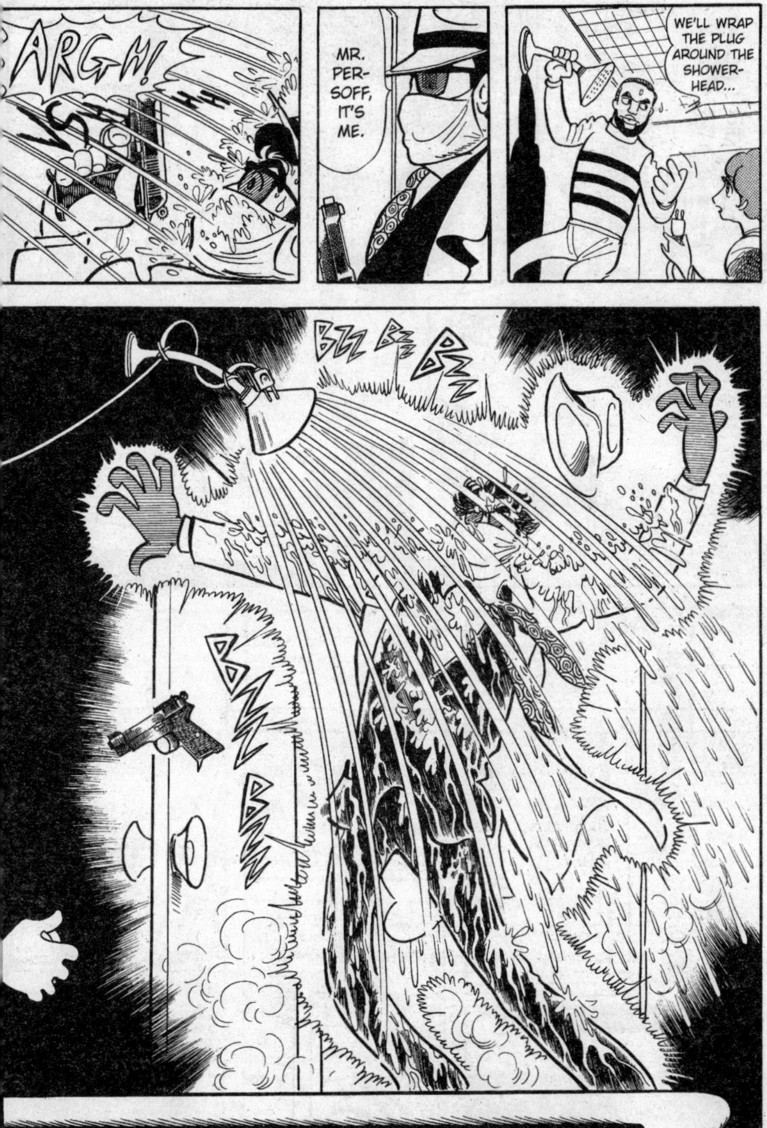
WE'LL WRAP THE PLUG AROUND THE SHOWER-HEAD...
MR. PER-SOFF, IT'S ME.
ARGH!
VSHHH
BZZ
BZZ
BZZ

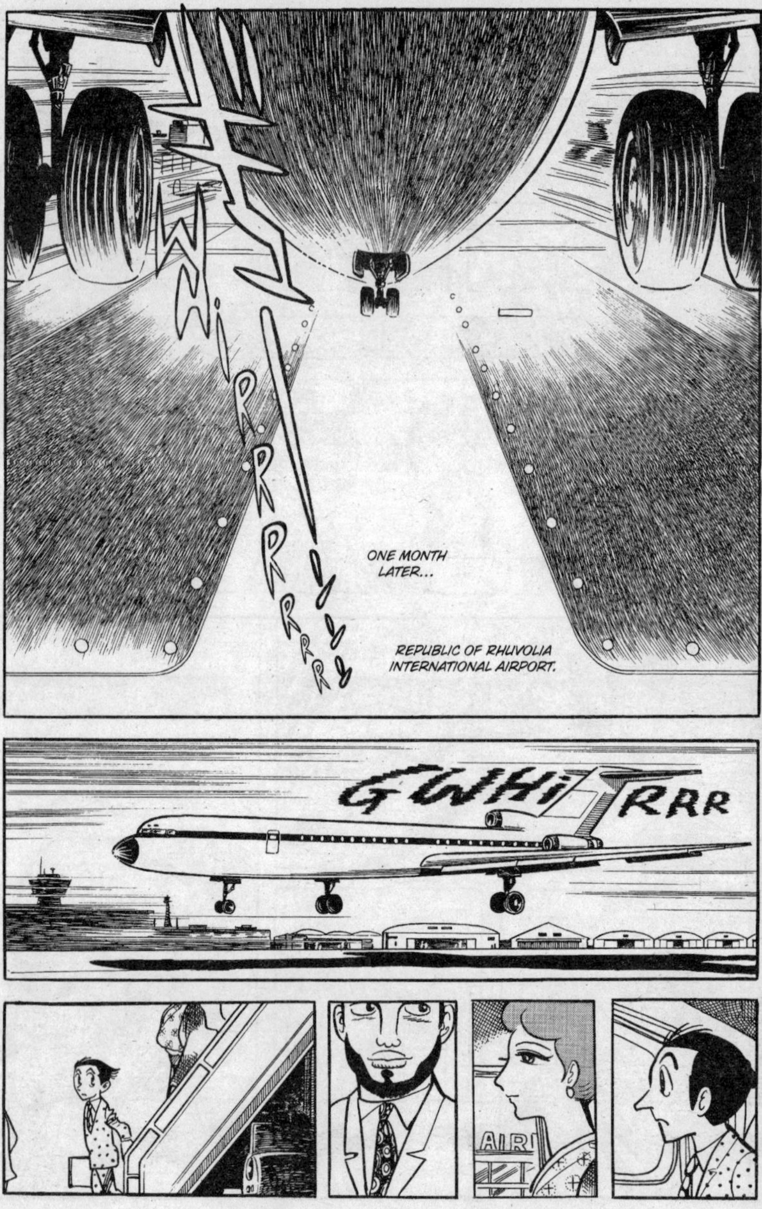
ONE MONTH LATER...
REPUBLIC OF RHUVOLIA INTERNATIONAL AIRPORT.
GWHiRRR

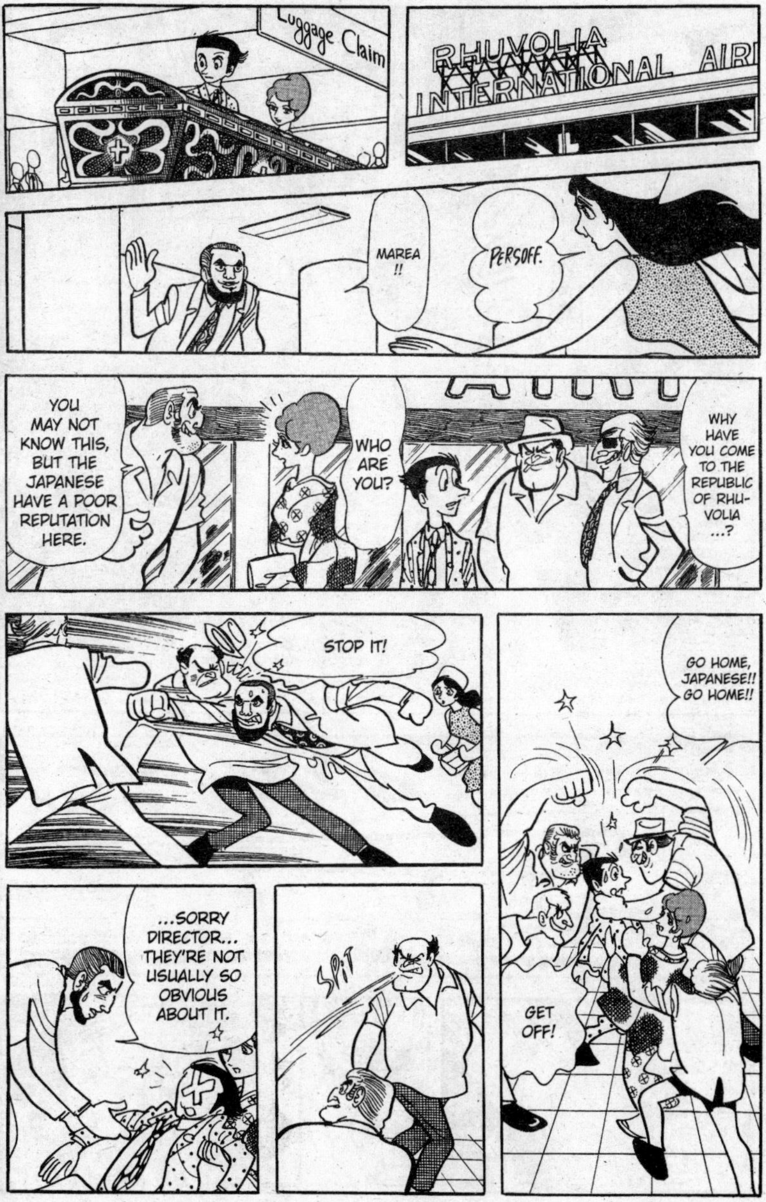
RHUVOLIA
INTERNATIONAL AIR
Luggage Claim
PERSOFF.
MAREA !!
WHY HAVE YOU COME TO THE REPUBLIC OF RHUVOLIA ...?
WHO ARE YOU?
YOU MAY NOT KNOW THIS, BUT THE JAPANESE HAVE A POOR REPUTATION HERE.
GO HOME, JAPANESE!! GO HOME!!
GET OFF!
STOP IT!
SPIT
...SORRY DIRECTOR... THEY'RE NOT USUALLY SO OBVIOUS ABOUT IT.

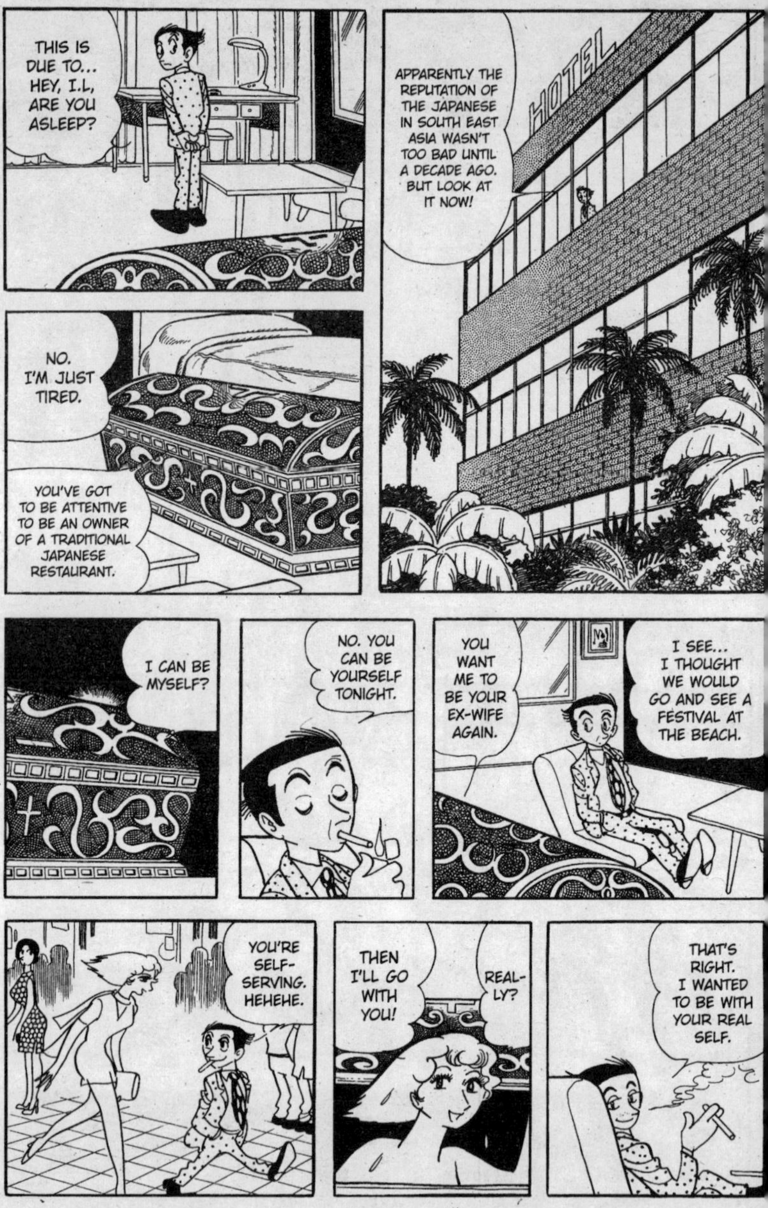
APPARENTLY THE REPUTATION OF THE JAPANESE IN SOUTH EAST ASIA WASN'T TOO BAD UNTIL A DECADE AGO. BUT LOOK AT IT NOW!
HOTEL
THIS IS DUE TO... HEY, I.L, ARE YOU ASLEEP?
NO. I'M JUST TIRED.
YOU'VE GOT TO BE ATTENTIVE TO BE AN OWNER OF A TRADITIONAL JAPANESE RESTAURANT.
I SEE... I THOUGHT WE WOULD GO AND SEE A FESTIVAL AT THE BEACH.
YOU WANT ME TO BE YOUR EX-WIFE AGAIN.
NO. YOU CAN BE YOURSELF TONIGHT.
I CAN BE MYSELF?
THAT'S RIGHT. I WANTED TO BE WITH YOUR REAL SELF.
REAL-LY?
THEN I'LL GO WITH YOU!
YOU'RE SELF-SERVING. HEHEHE.

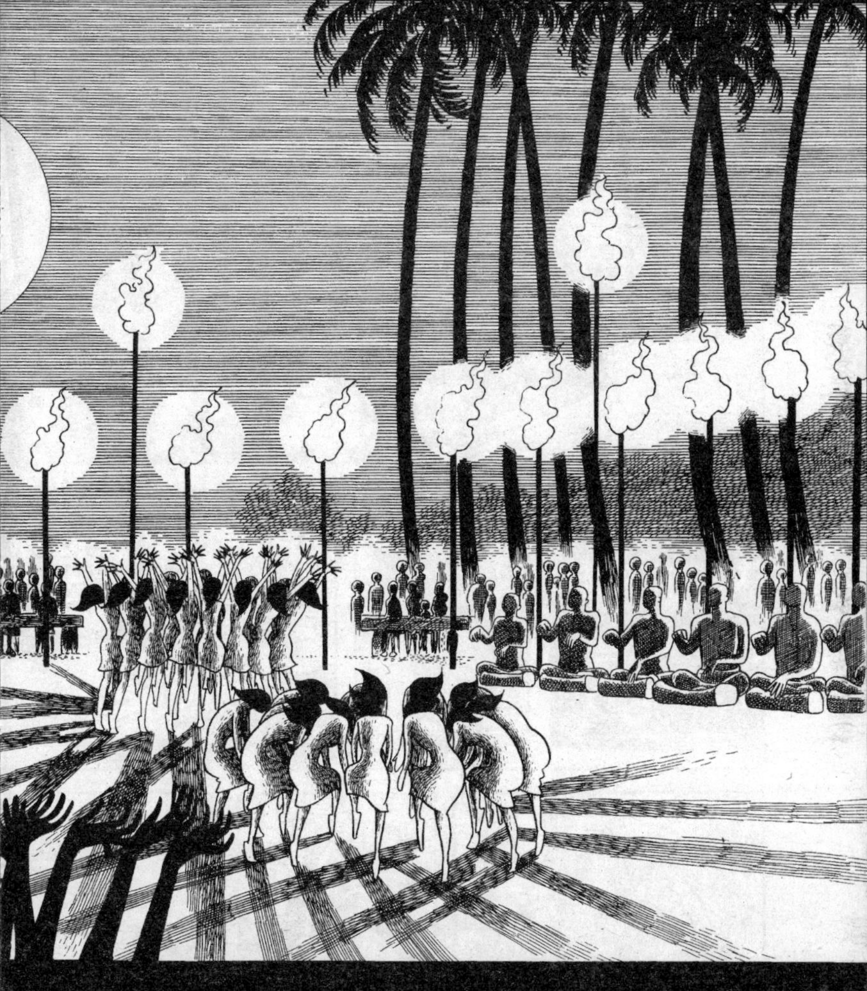

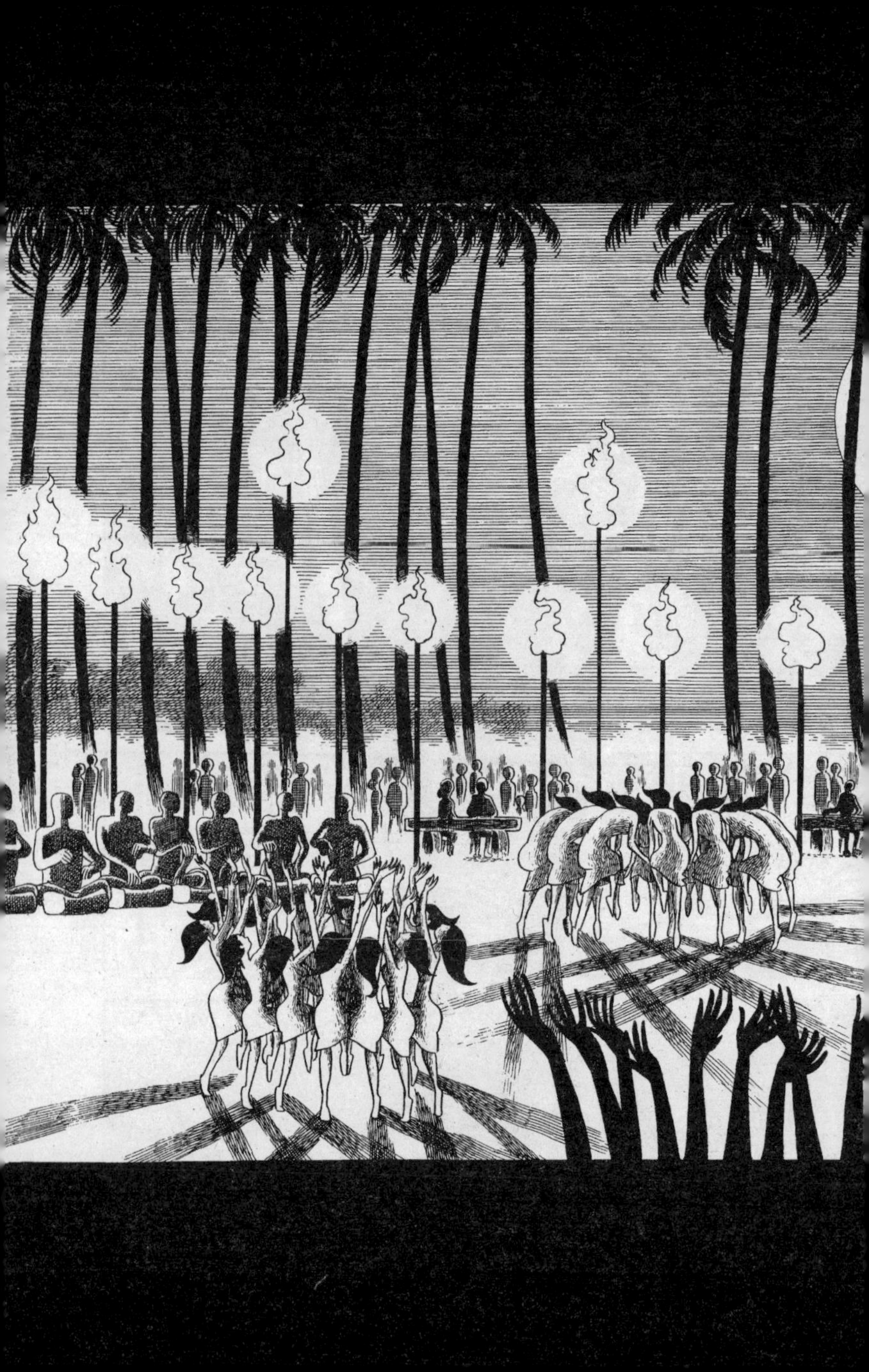

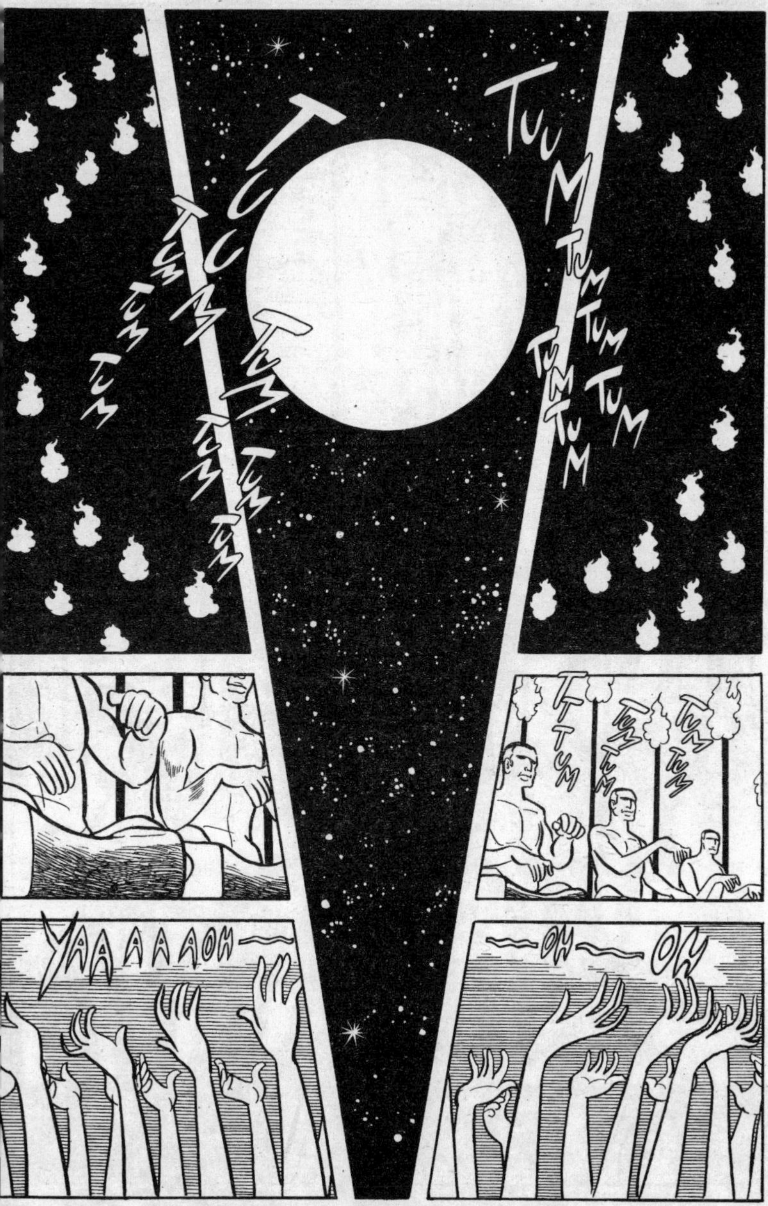
TUUM TUM TUM TUM TUM TUM
TUUM TUM TUM TUM TUM TUM TUM
TUM TUM TUM TUM
TT TUM
TUM TUM
TUM TUM
~~OH~~OH
YAAAAAOH~~

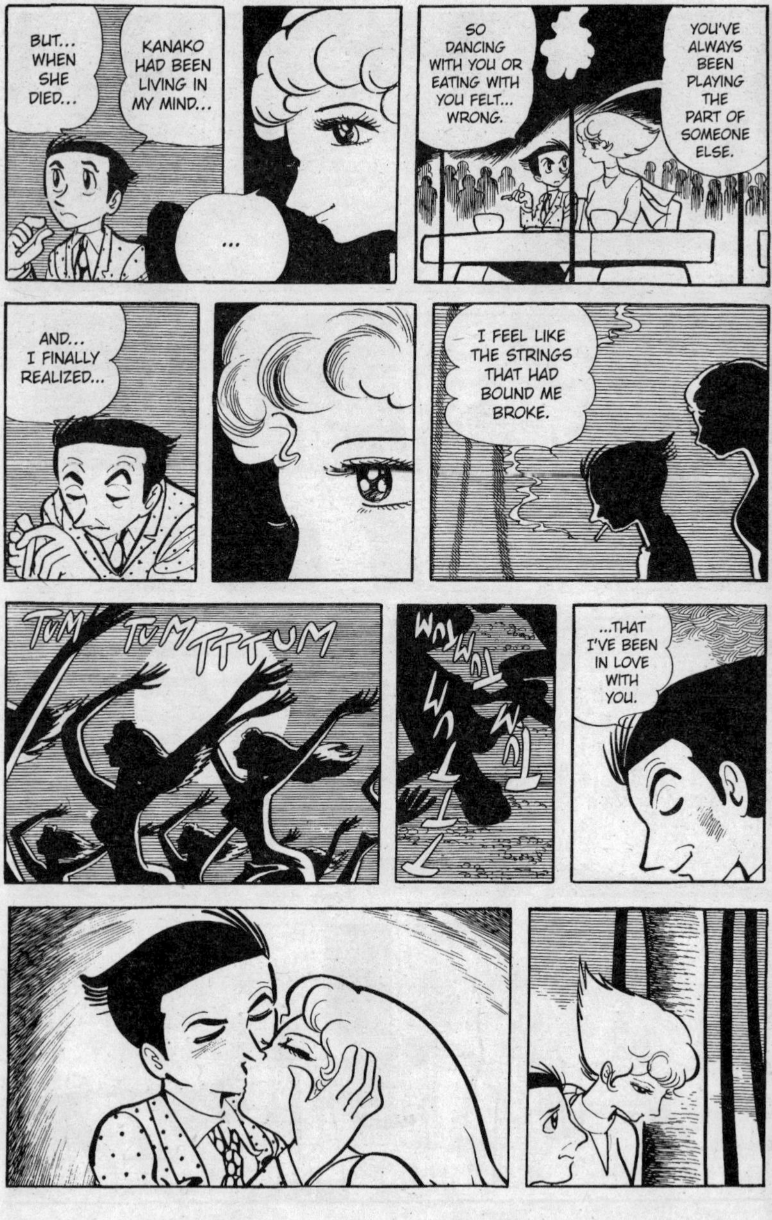
YOU'VE ALWAYS BEEN PLAYING THE PART OF SOMEONE ELSE.
SO DANCING WITH YOU OR EATING WITH YOU FELT... WRONG.
...
KANAKO HAD BEEN LIVING IN MY MIND...
BUT... WHEN SHE DIED...
I FEEL LIKE THE STRINGS THAT HAD BOUND ME BROKE.
AND... I FINALLY REALIZED...
...THAT I'VE BEEN IN LOVE WITH YOU.
TUM TUM TTTUM

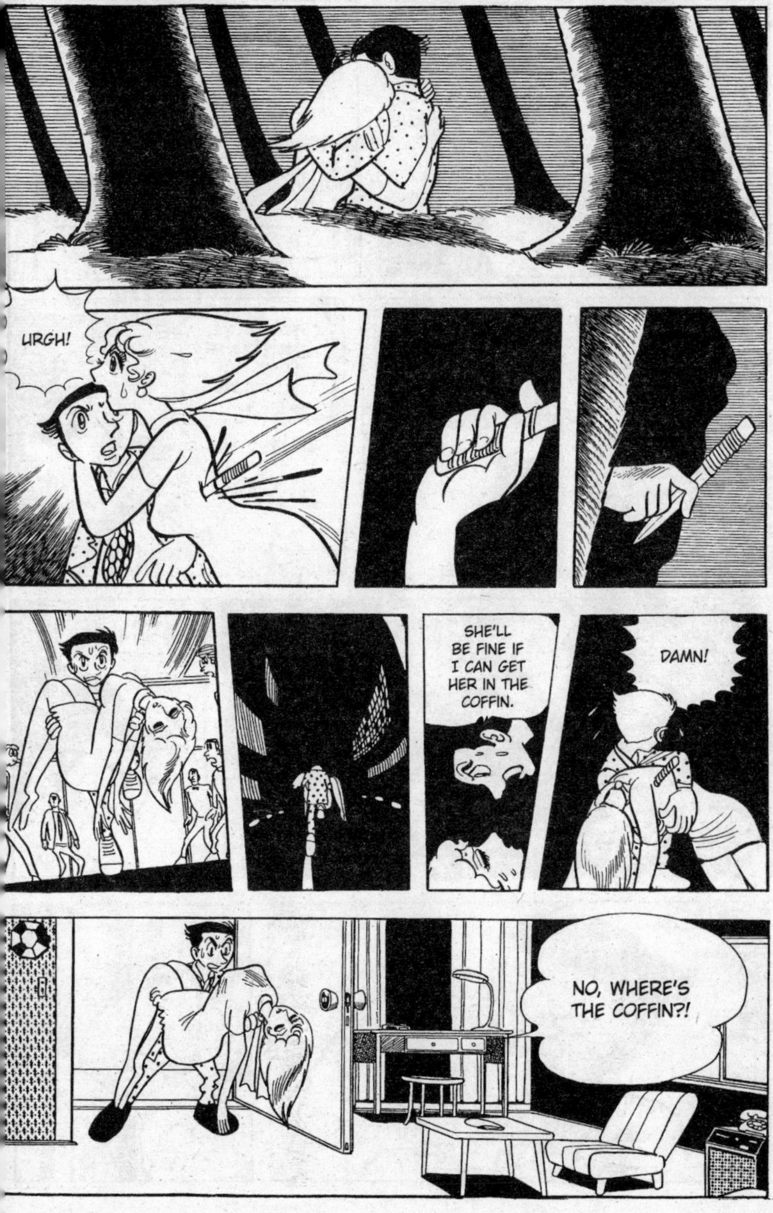
URGH!
DAMN!
SHE'LL BE FINE IF I CAN GET HER IN THE COFFIN.
NO, WHERE'S THE COFFIN?!

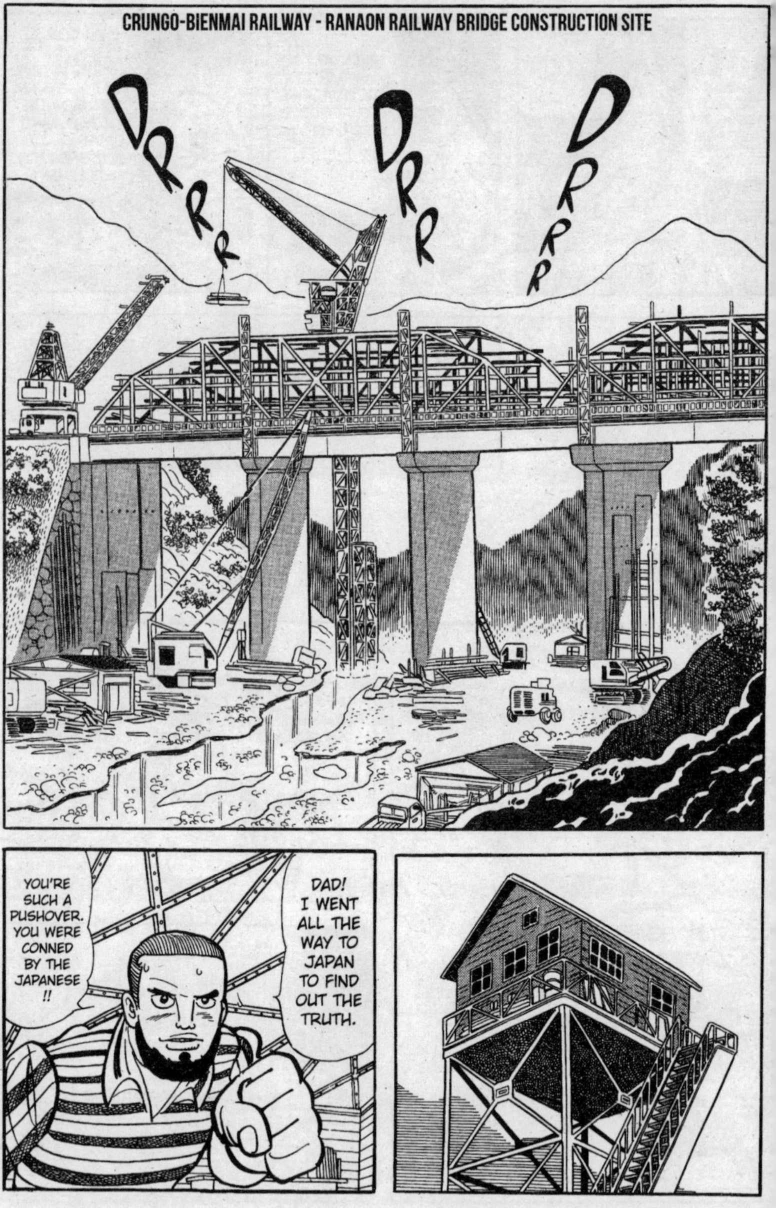
CRUNGO-BIENMAI RAILWAY - RANAON RAILWAY BRIDGE CONSTRUCTION SITE
DRRRR
DRRR
DRRR
DAD! I WENT ALL THE WAY TO JAPAN TO FIND OUT THE TRUTH.
YOU'RE SUCH A PUSHOVER. YOU WERE CONNED BY THE JAPANESE !!

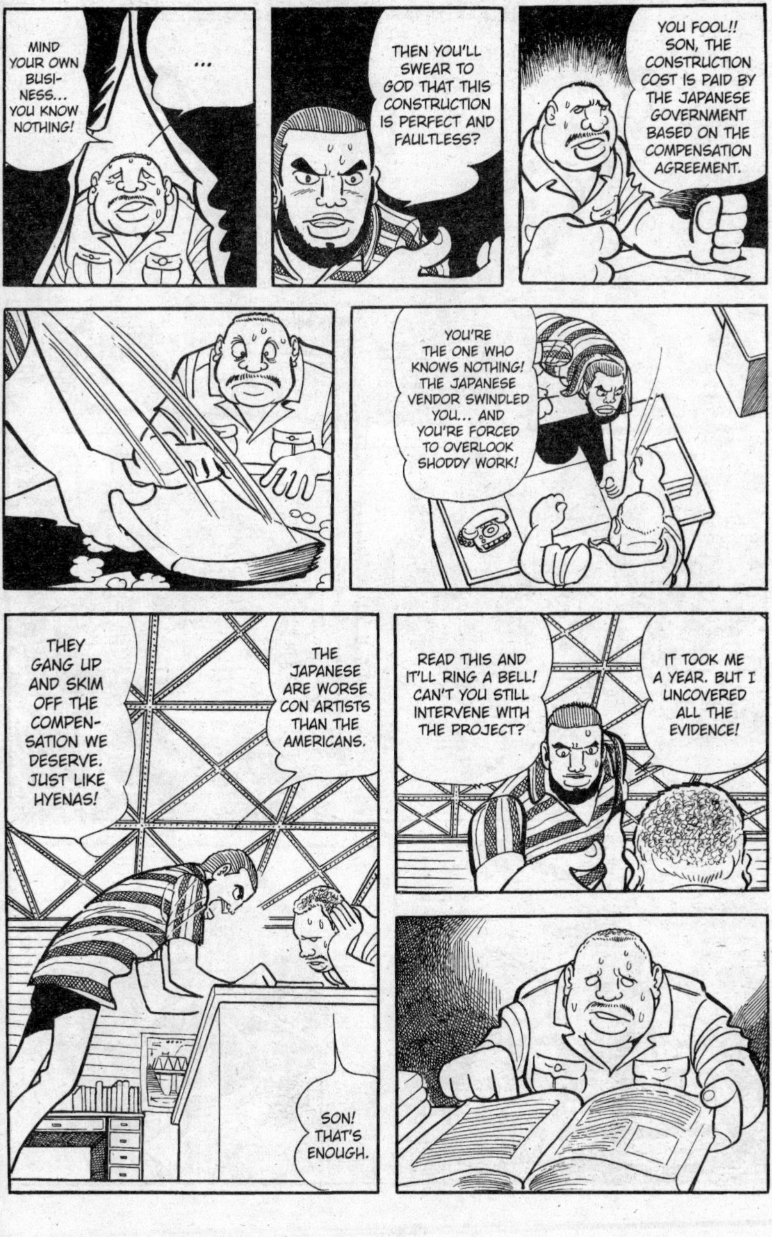
YOU FOOL!! SON, THE CONSTRUCTION COST IS PAID BY THE JAPANESE GOVERNMENT BASED ON THE COMPENSATION AGREEMENT.
THEN YOU'LL SWEAR TO GOD THAT THIS CONSTRUCTION IS PERFECT AND FAULTLESS?
...
MIND YOUR OWN BUSI-NESS... YOU KNOW NOTHING!
YOU'RE THE ONE WHO KNOWS NOTHING! THE JAPANESE VENDOR SWINDLED YOU... AND YOU'RE FORCED TO OVERLOOK SHODDY WORK!
IT TOOK ME A YEAR. BUT I UNCOVERED ALL THE EVIDENCE!
READ THIS AND IT'LL RING A BELL! CAN'T YOU STILL INTERVENE WITH THE PROJECT?
THE JAPANESE ARE WORSE CON ARTISTS THAN THE AMERICANS.
THEY GANG UP AND SKIM OFF THE COMPEN-SATION WE DESERVE. JUST LIKE HYENAS!
SON! THAT'S ENOUGH.

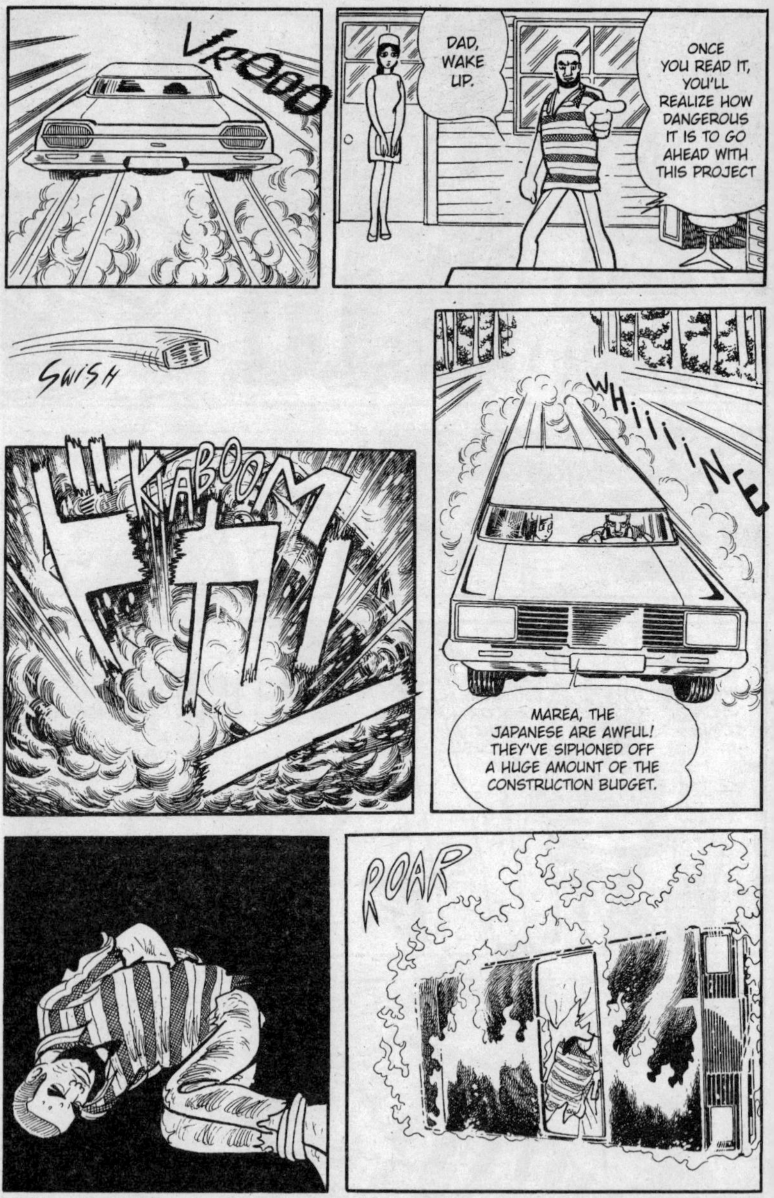
ONCE YOU READ IT, YOU'LL REALIZE HOW DANGEROUS IT IS TO GO AHEAD WITH THIS PROJECT
DAD, WAKE UP.
VROOOO
WHIIIINE
MAREA, THE JAPANESE ARE AWFUL! THEY'VE SIPHONED OFF A HUGE AMOUNT OF THE CONSTRUCTION BUDGET.
SWISH
KABOOM
ROAR

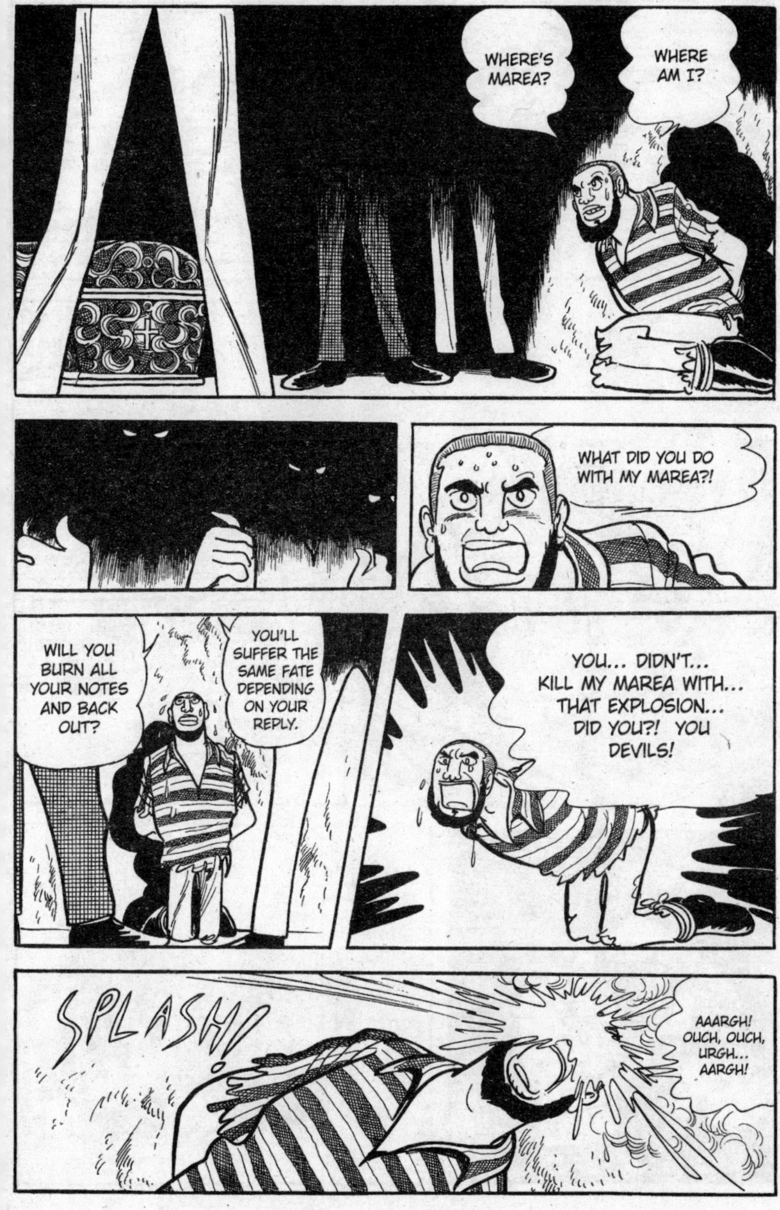
WHERE AM I?
WHERE'S MAREA?
WHAT DID YOU DO WITH MY MAREA?!
YOU... DIDN'T... KILL MY MAREA WITH... THAT EXPLOSION... DID YOU?! YOU DEVILS!
YOU'LL SUFFER THE SAME FATE DEPENDING ON YOUR REPLY.
WILL YOU BURN ALL YOUR NOTES AND BACK OUT?
AAARGH! OUCH, OUCH, URGH... AARGH!
SPLASH!

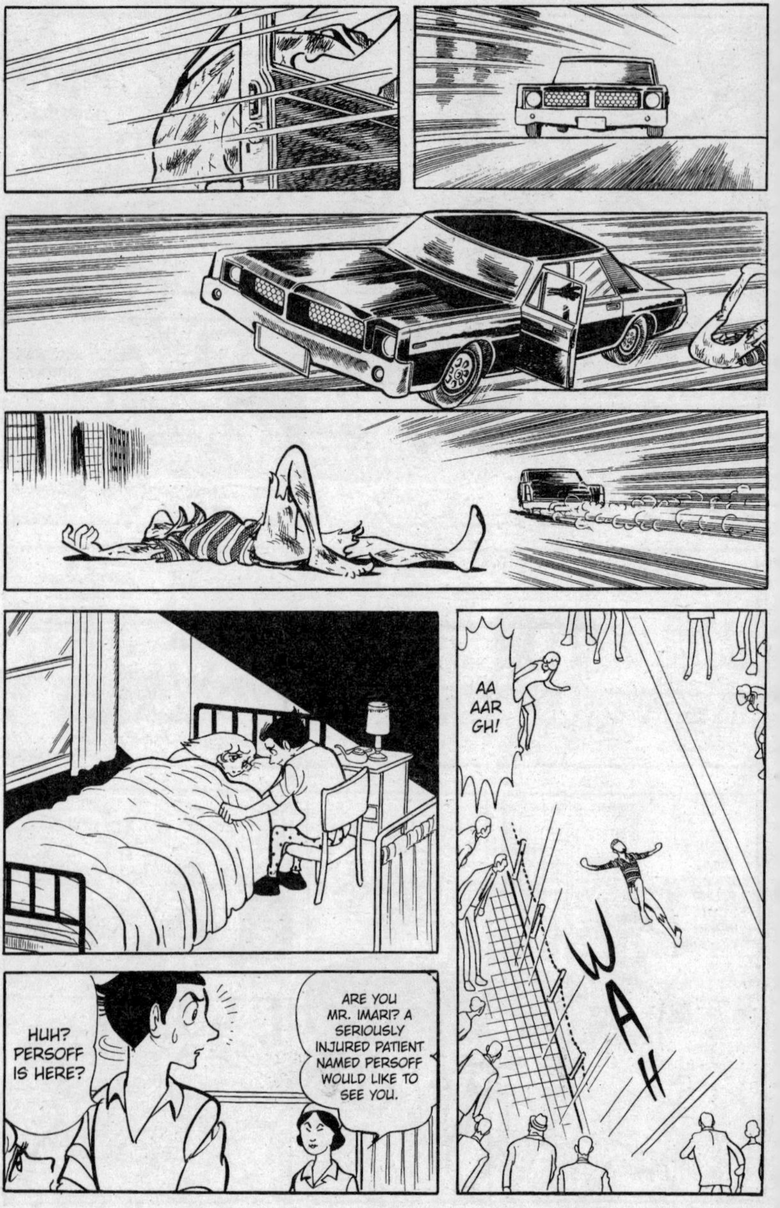
AA AAR GH!
WAH
ARE YOU MR. IMARI? A SERIOUSLY INJURED PATIENT NAMED PERSOFF WOULD LIKE TO SEE YOU.
HUH? PERSOFF IS HERE?

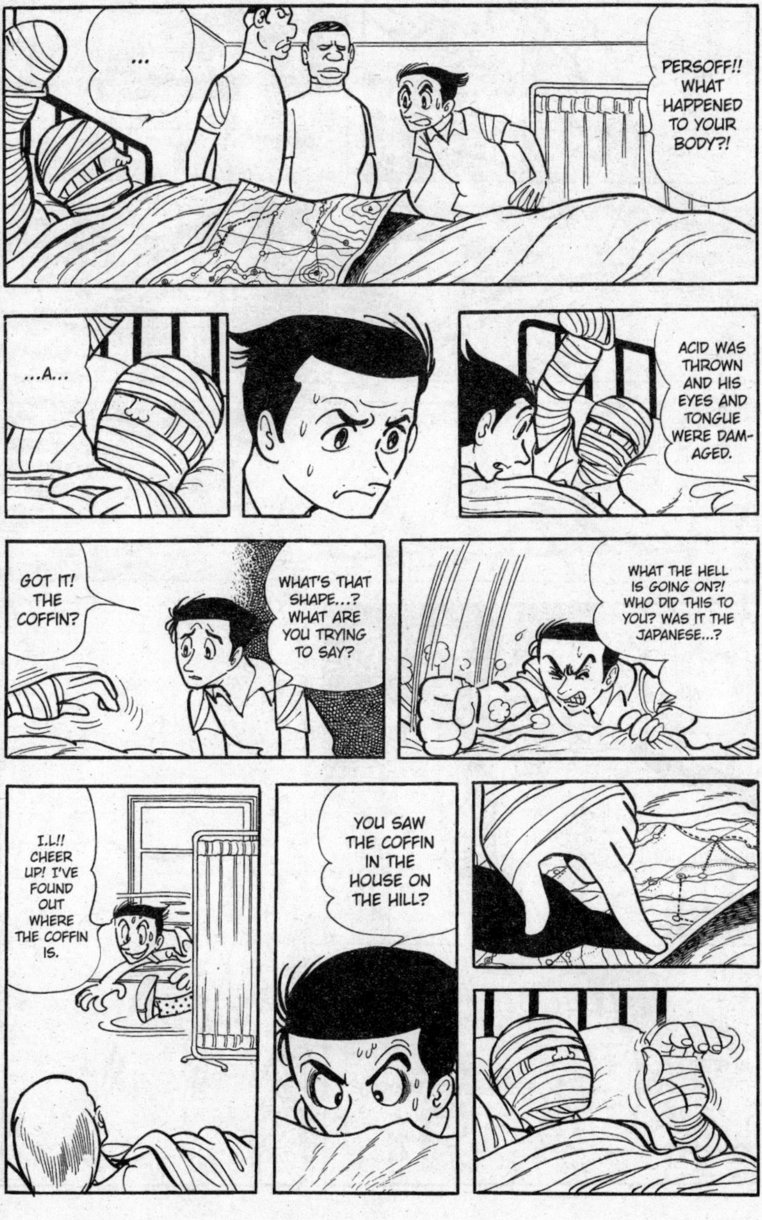
PERSOFF!! WHAT HAPPENED TO YOUR BODY?!
...
ACID WAS THROWN AND HIS EYES AND TONGUE WERE DAM-AGED.
...A...
WHAT THE HELL IS GOING ON?! WHO DID THIS TO YOU? WAS IT THE JAPANESE...?
WHAT'S THAT SHAPE...? WHAT ARE YOU TRYING TO SAY?
GOT IT! THE COFFIN?
YOU SAW THE COFFIN IN THE HOUSE ON THE HILL?
I.L!! CHEER UP! I'VE FOUND OUT WHERE THE COFFIN IS.

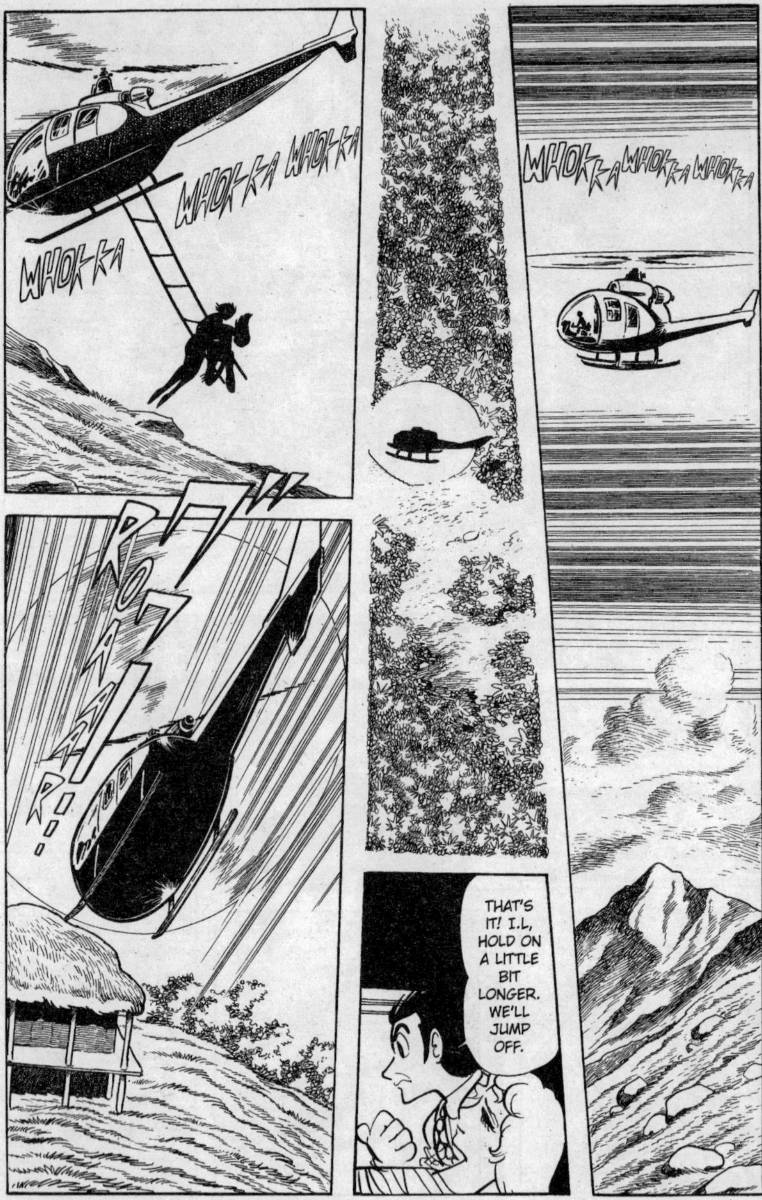
WHOKKA WHOKKA WHOKKA
THAT'S IT! I.L, HOLD ON A LITTLE BIT LONGER. WE'LL JUMP OFF.
WHOKKA WHOKKA
WHOKKA
ROAAAR!!

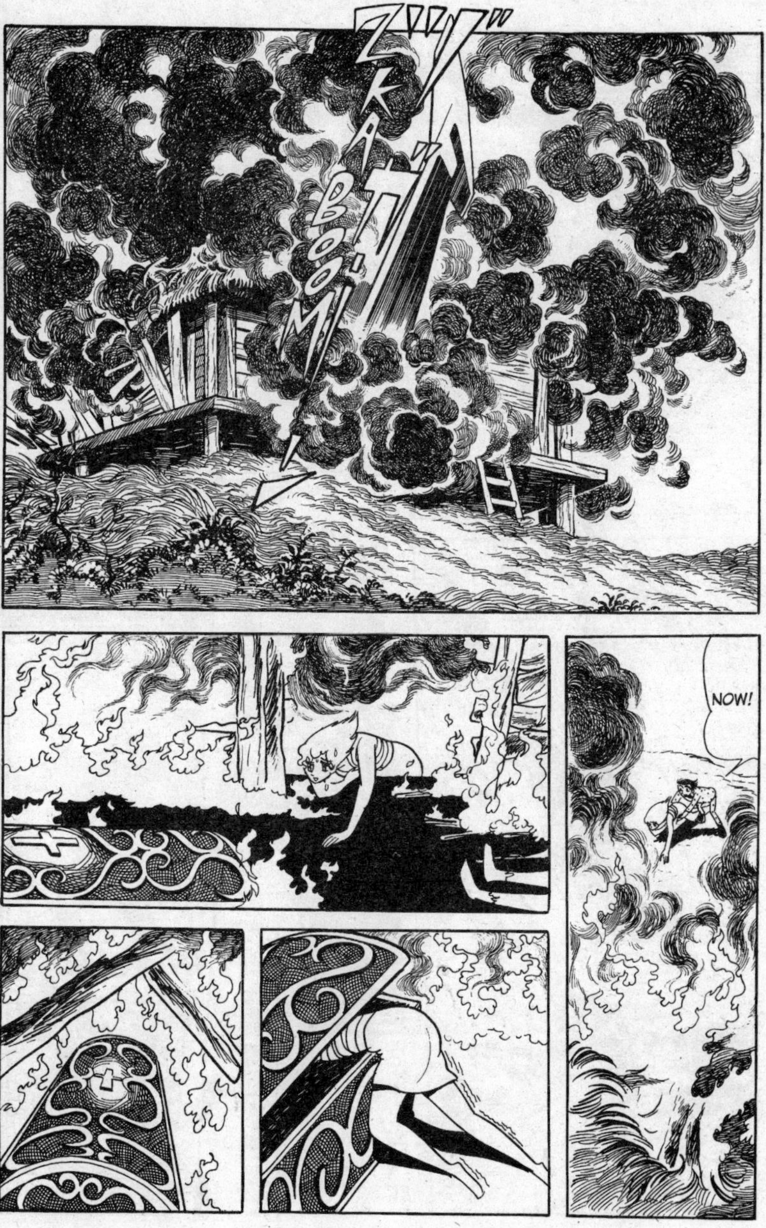
ZKA-BOOM!
NOW!

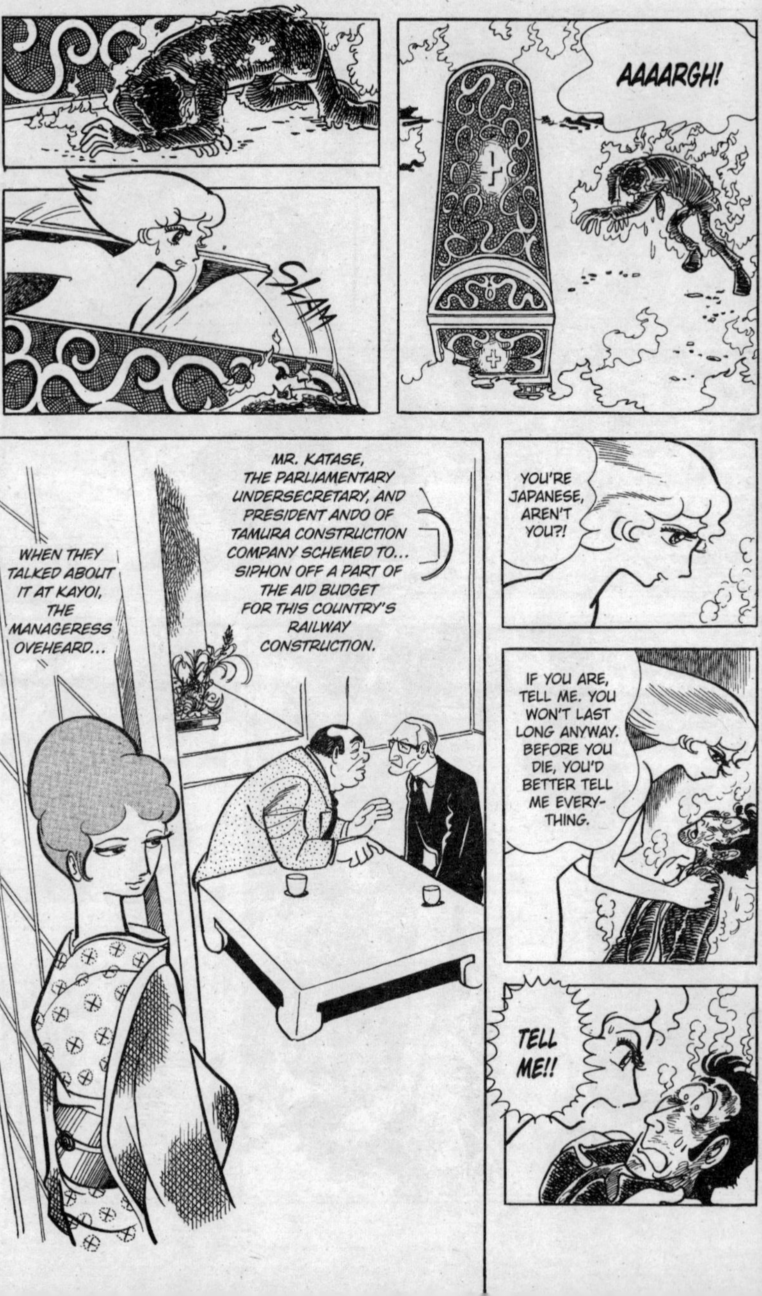
AAAARGH!
SLAM
YOU'RE JAPANESE, AREN'T YOU?!
IF YOU ARE, TELL ME. YOU WON'T LAST LONG ANYWAY. BEFORE YOU DIE, YOU'D BETTER TELL ME EVERY-THING.
TELL ME!!
MR. KATASE, THE PARLIAMENTARY UNDERSECRETARY, AND PRESIDENT ANDO OF TAMURA CONSTRUCTION COMPANY SCHEMED TO... SIPHON OFF A PART OF THE AID BUDGET FOR THIS COUNTRY'S RAILWAY CONSTRUCTION.
WHEN THEY TALKED ABOUT IT AT KAYOI, THE MANAGERESS OVEHEARD...

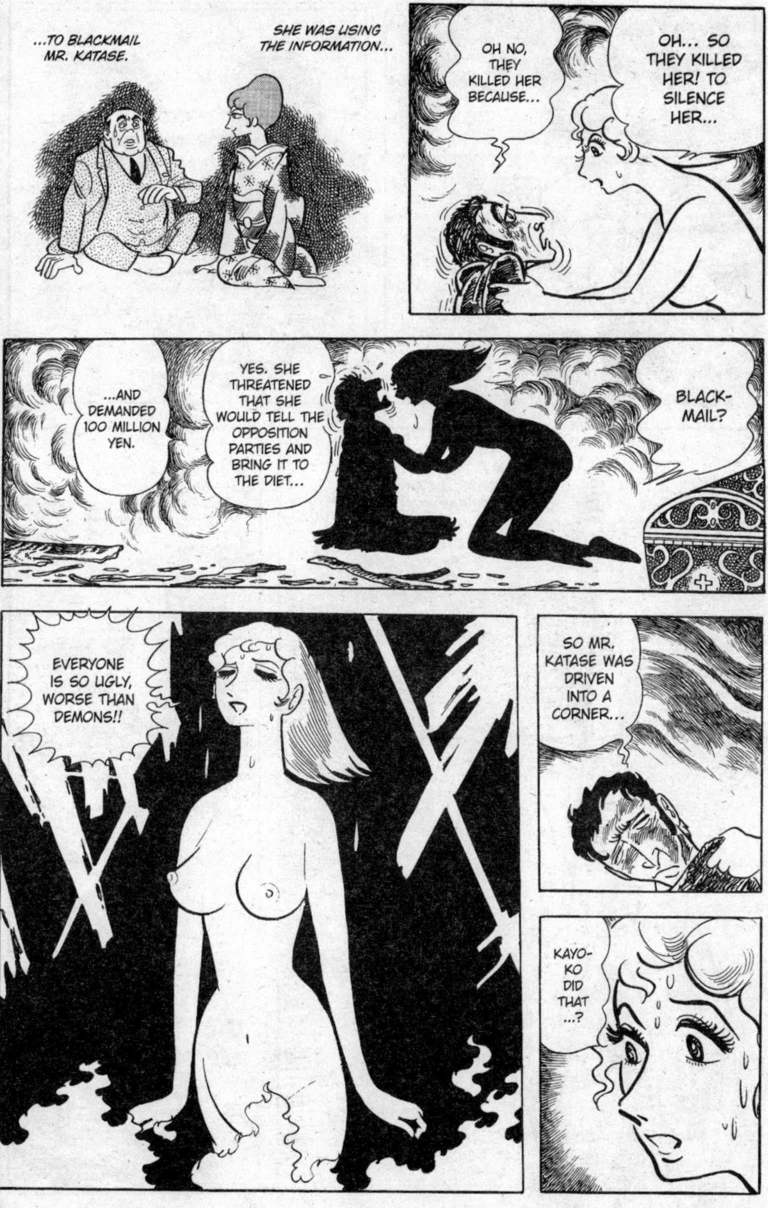
OH... SO THEY KILLED HER! TO SILENCE HER...
OH NO, THEY KILLED HER BECAUSE...
SHE WAS USING THE INFORMATION...
...TO BLACKMAIL MR. KATASE.
BLACK-MAIL?
YES. SHE THREATENED THAT SHE WOULD TELL THE OPPOSITION PARTIES AND BRING IT TO THE DIET...
...AND DEMANDED 100 MILLION YEN.
SO MR. KATASE WAS DRIVEN INTO A CORNER...
KAYO-KO DID THAT ...?
EVERYONE IS SO UGLY, WORSE THAN DEMONS!!

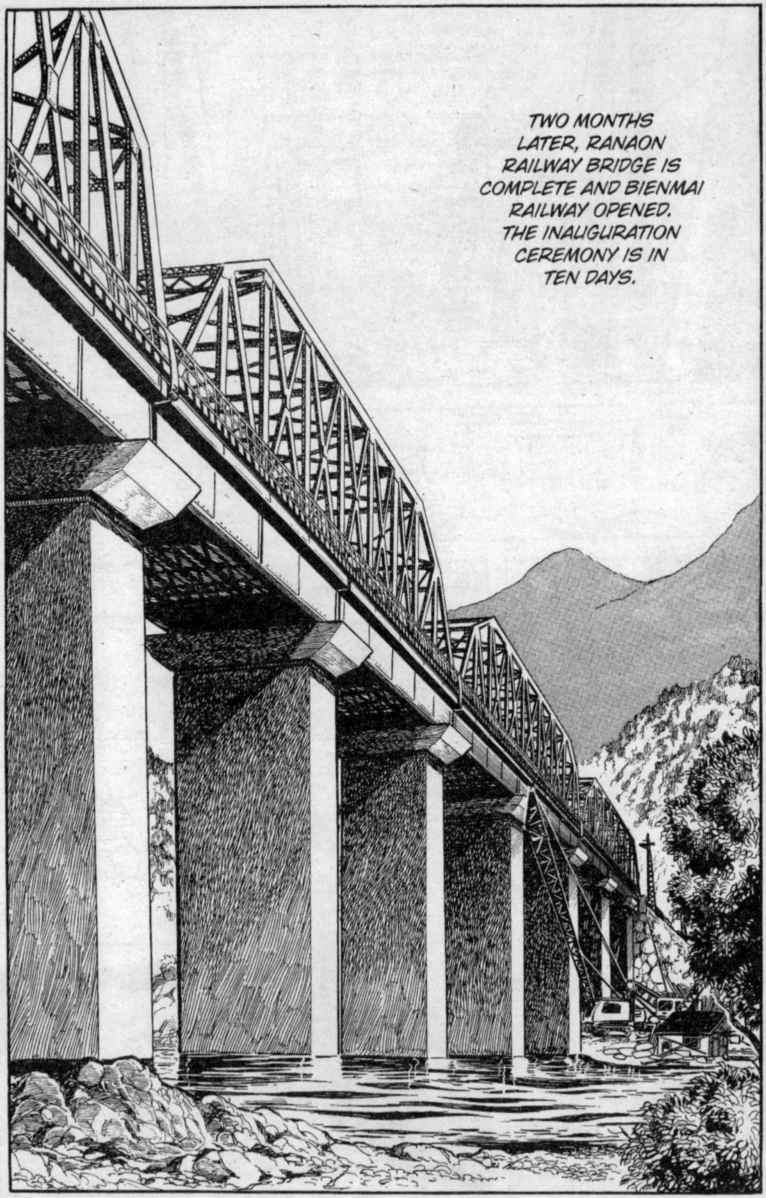
TWO MONTHS LATER, RANAON RAILWAY BRIDGE IS COMPLETE AND BIENMAI RAILWAY OPENED. THE INAUGURATION CEREMONY IS IN TEN DAYS.

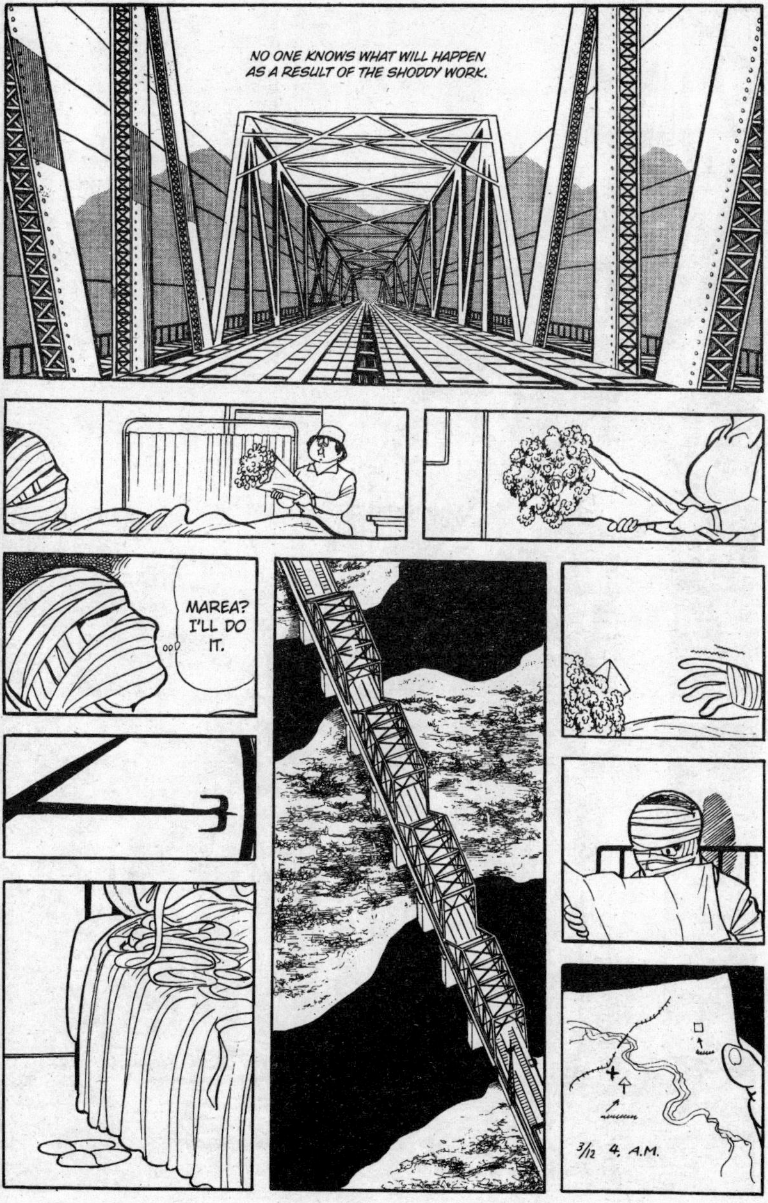
NO ONE KNOWS WHAT WILL HAPPEN AS A RESULT OF THE SHODDY WORK.
MAREA? I'LL DO IT.
3/12 4. A.M.

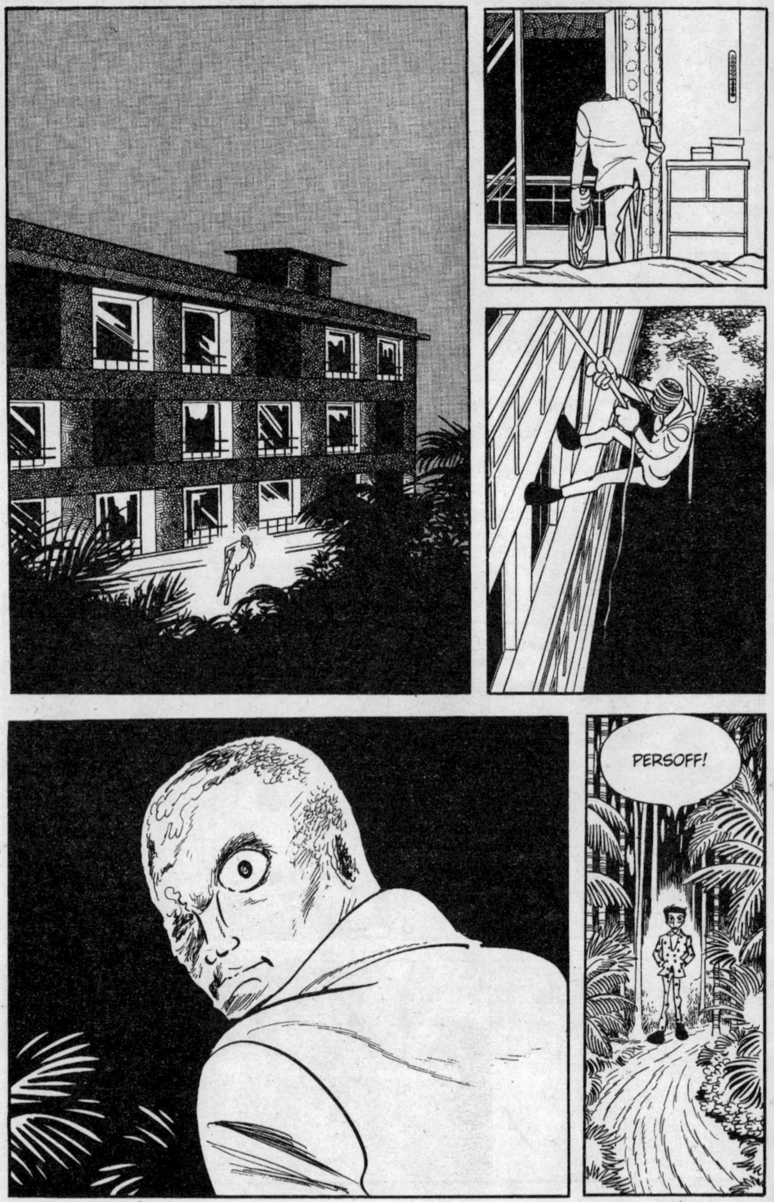
PERSOFF!

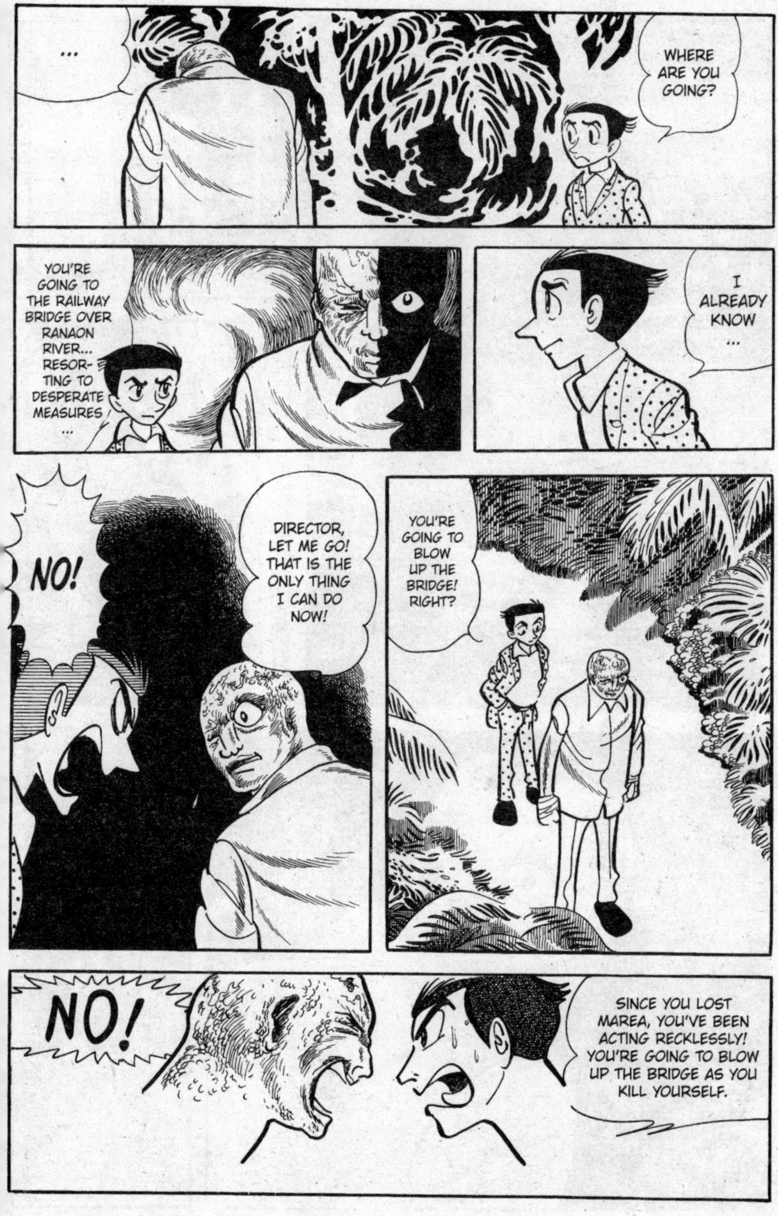
WHERE ARE YOU GOING?
...
I ALREADY KNOW ...
YOU'RE GOING TO THE RAILWAY BRIDGE OVER RANAON RIVER... RESORTING TO DESPERATE MEASURES ...
YOU'RE GOING TO BLOW UP THE BRIDGE! RIGHT?
DIRECTOR, LET ME GO! THAT IS THE ONLY THING I CAN DO NOW!
NO!
SINCE YOU LOST MAREA, YOU'VE BEEN ACTING RECKLESSLY! YOU'RE GOING TO BLOW UP THE BRIDGE AS YOU KILL YOURSELF.
NO!

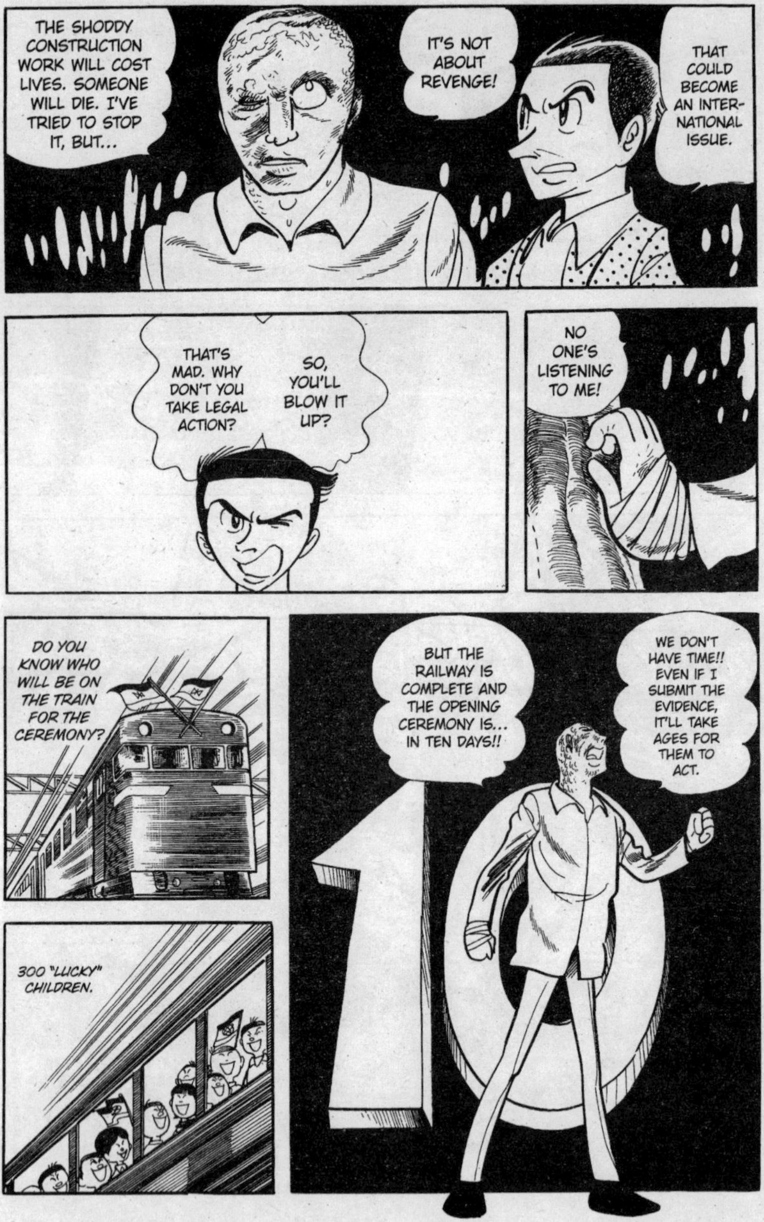
THAT COULD BECOME AN INTER-NATIONAL ISSUE.
IT'S NOT ABOUT REVENGE!
THE SHODDY CONSTRUCTION WORK WILL COST LIVES. SOMEONE WILL DIE. I'VE TRIED TO STOP IT, BUT...
NO ONE'S LISTENING TO ME!
SO, YOU'LL BLOW IT UP?
THAT'S MAD. WHY DON'T YOU TAKE LEGAL ACTION?
WE DON'T HAVE TIME!! EVEN IF I SUBMIT THE EVIDENCE, IT'LL TAKE AGES FOR THEM TO ACT.
BUT THE RAILWAY IS COMPLETE AND THE OPENING CEREMONY IS... IN TEN DAYS!!
DO YOU KNOW WHO WILL BE ON THE TRAIN FOR THE CEREMONY?
300 "LUCKY" CHILDREN.

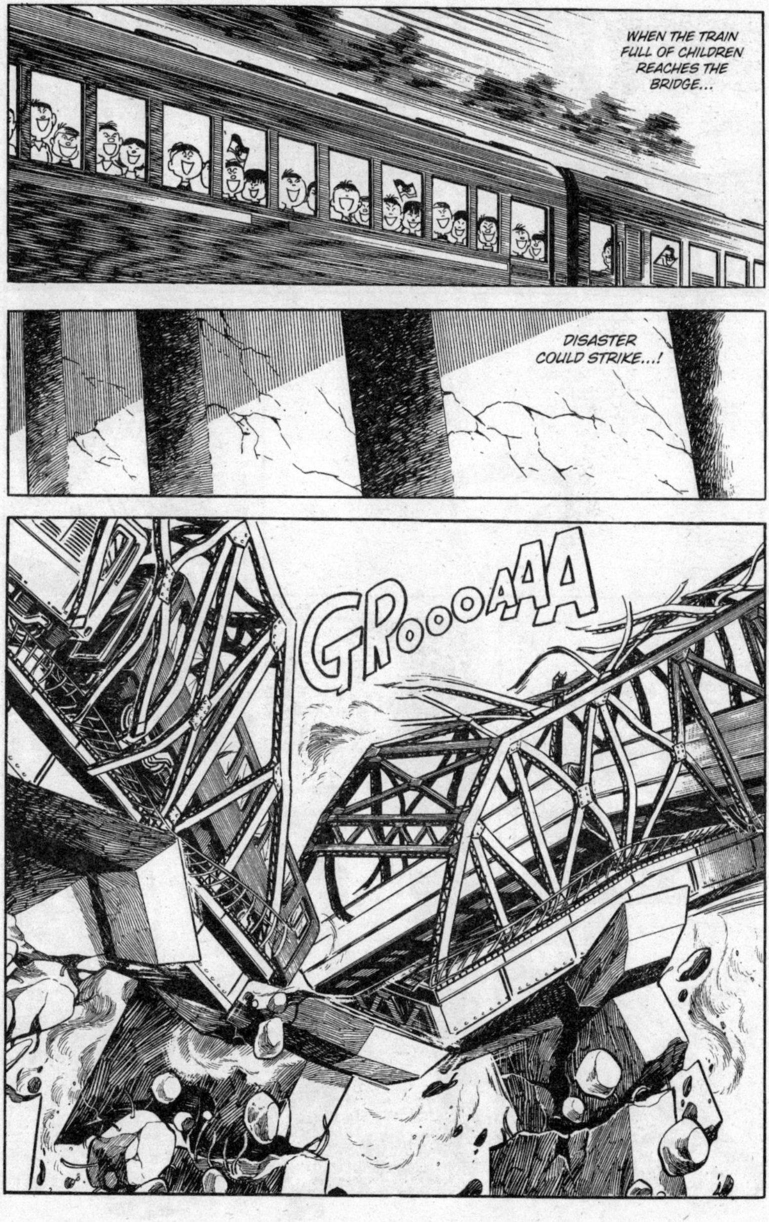
WHEN THE TRAIN FULL OF CHILDREN REACHES THE BRIDGE...
DISASTER COULD STRIKE...!
GROOOAAA

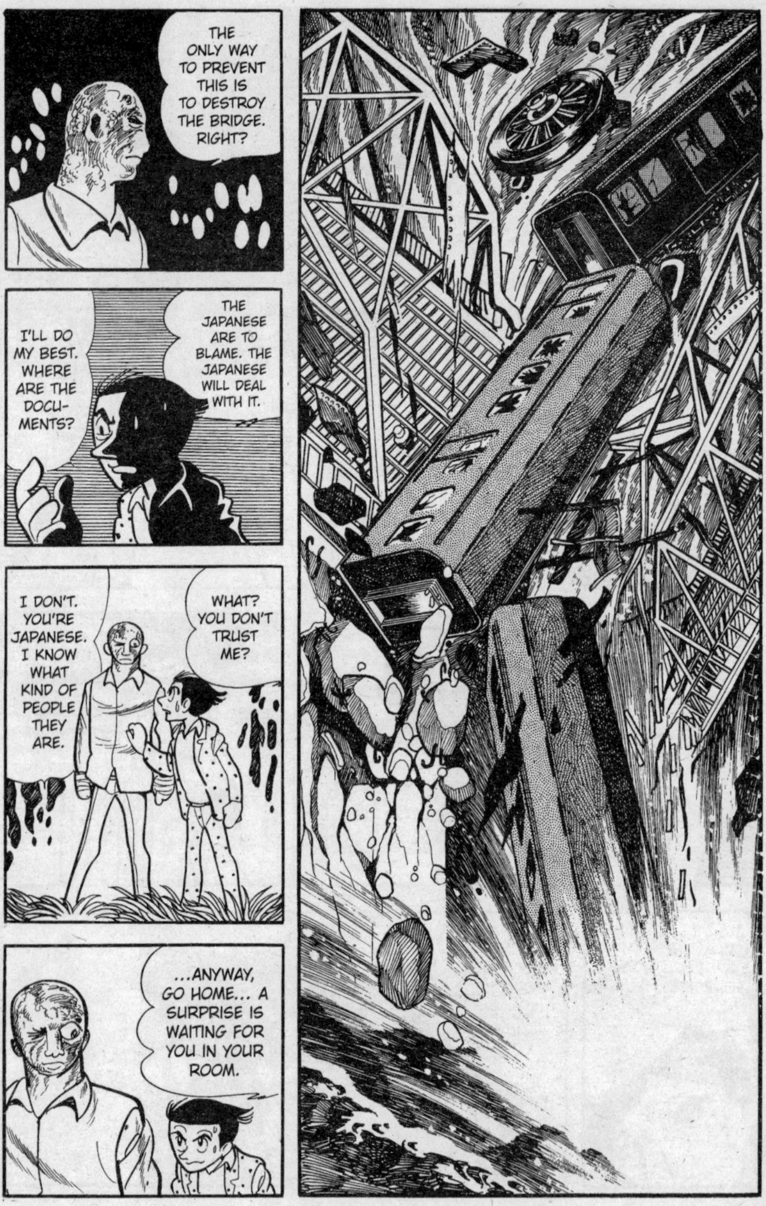
THE ONLY WAY TO PREVENT THIS IS TO DESTROY THE BRIDGE. RIGHT?
THE JAPANESE ARE TO BLAME. THE JAPANESE WILL DEAL WITH IT.
I'LL DO MY BEST. WHERE ARE THE DOCU-MENTS?
WHAT? YOU DON'T TRUST ME?
I DON'T. YOU'RE JAPANESE. I KNOW WHAT KIND OF PEOPLE THEY ARE.
...ANYWAY, GO HOME... A SURPRISE IS WAITING FOR YOU IN YOUR ROOM.

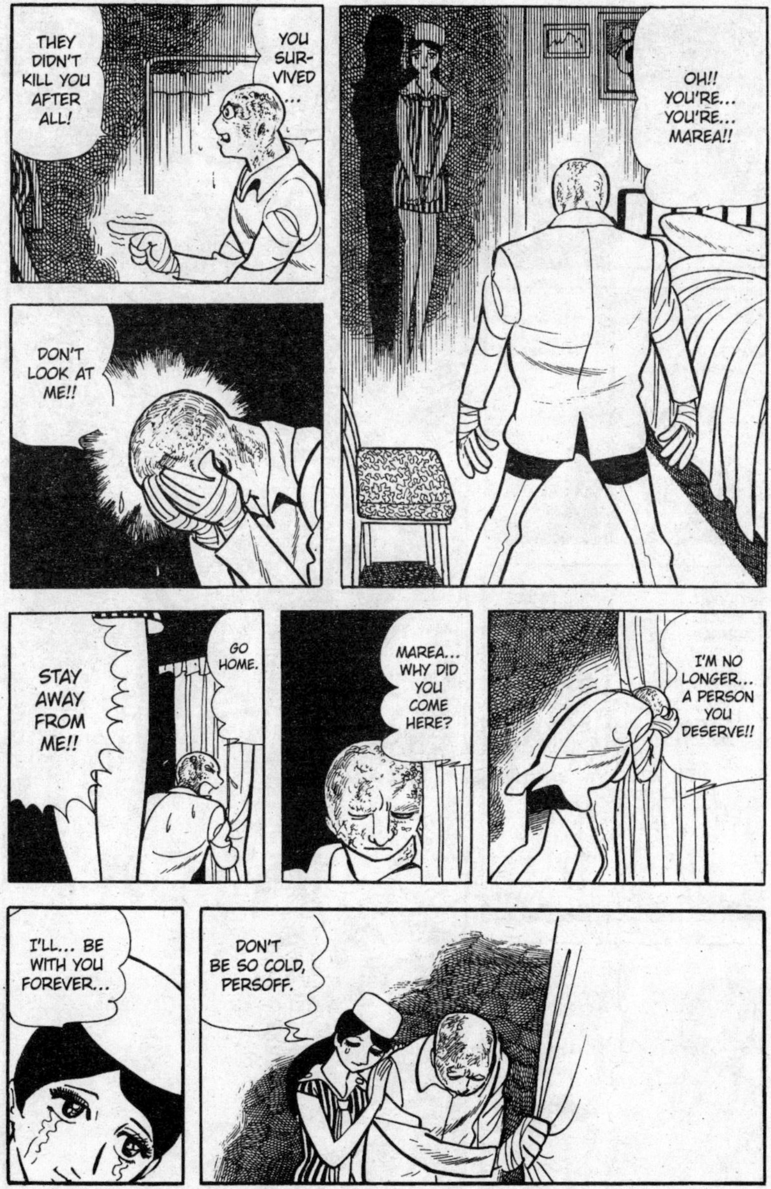
OH!! YOU'RE... YOU'RE... MAREA!!
YOU SUR-VIVED ...
THEY DIDN'T KILL YOU AFTER ALL!
DON'T LOOK AT ME!!
I'M NO LONGER... A PERSON YOU DESERVE!!
MAREA... WHY DID YOU COME HERE?
GO HOME.
STAY AWAY FROM ME!!
DON'T BE SO COLD, PERSOFF.
I'LL... BE WITH YOU FOREVER...

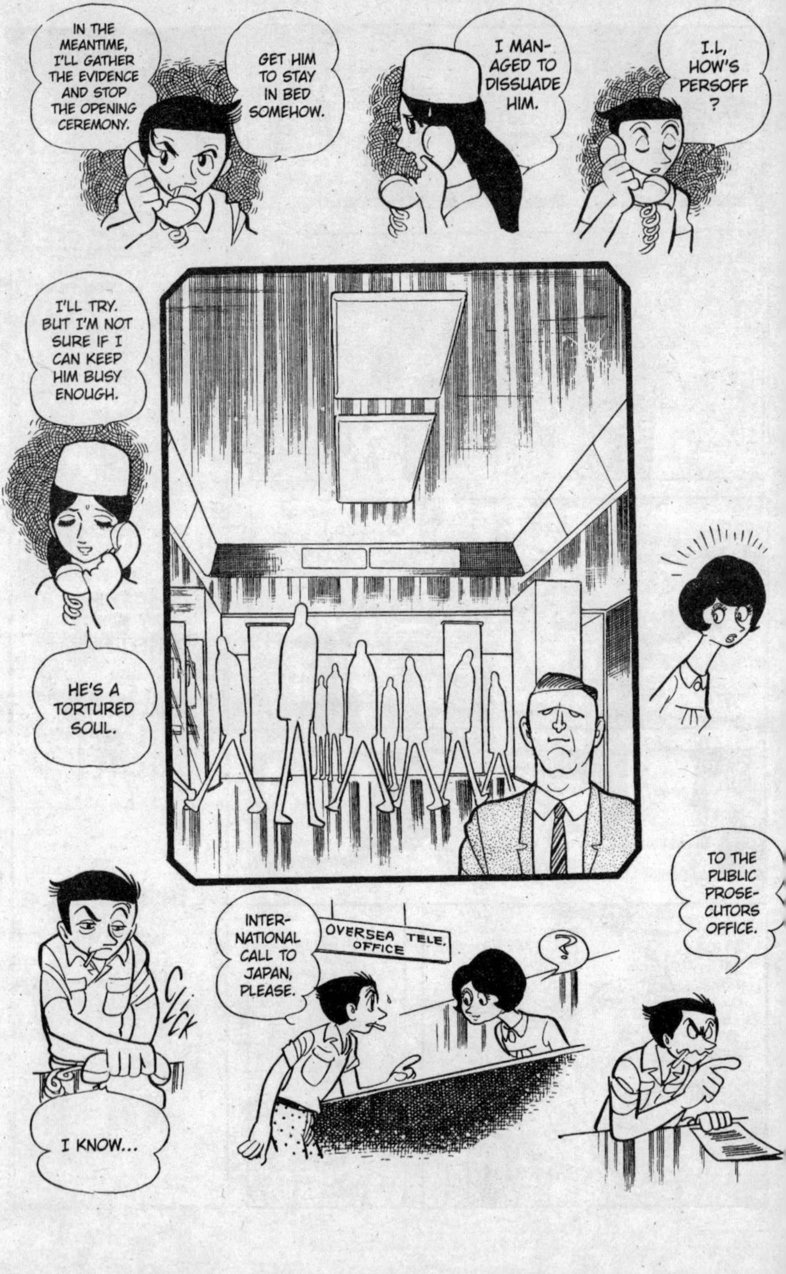
I.L, HOW'S PERSOFF ?
I MAN-AGED TO DISSUADE HIM.
GET HIM TO STAY IN BED SOMEHOW.
IN THE MEANTIME, I'LL GATHER THE EVIDENCE AND STOP THE OPENING CEREMONY.
I'LL TRY. BUT I'M NOT SURE IF I CAN KEEP HIM BUSY ENOUGH.
HE'S A TORTURED SOUL.
TO THE PUBLIC PROSE-CUTORS OFFICE.
?
OVERSEA TELE. OFFICE
INTER-NATIONAL CALL TO JAPAN, PLEASE.
CLICK
I KNOW...

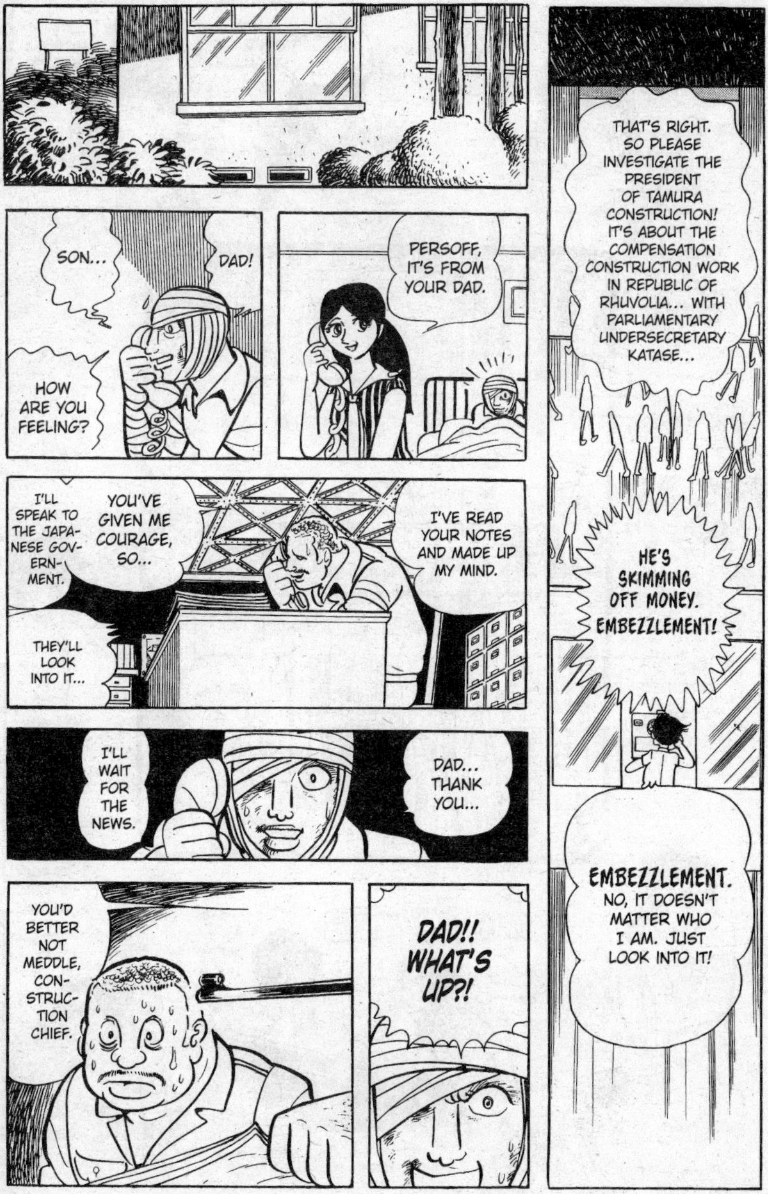
THAT'S RIGHT. SO PLEASE INVESTIGATE THE PRESIDENT OF TAMURA CONSTRUCTION! IT'S ABOUT THE COMPENSATION CONSTRUCTION WORK IN REPUBLIC OF RHUVOLIA... WITH PARLIAMENTARY UNDERSECRETARY KATASE...
HE'S SKIMMING OFF MONEY. EMBEZZLEMENT!
EMBEZZLEMENT. NO, IT DOESN'T MATTER WHO I AM. JUST LOOK INTO IT!
PERSOFF, IT'S FROM YOUR DAD.
DAD!
SON...
HOW ARE YOU FEELING?
I'VE READ YOUR NOTES AND MADE UP MY MIND.
YOU'VE GIVEN ME COURAGE, SO...
I'LL SPEAK TO THE JAPANESE GOVERNMENT.
THEY'LL LOOK INTO IT...
DAD... THANK YOU...
I'LL WAIT FOR THE NEWS.
DAD!! WHAT'S UP?!
YOU'D BETTER NOT MEDDLE, CONSTRUCTION CHIEF.

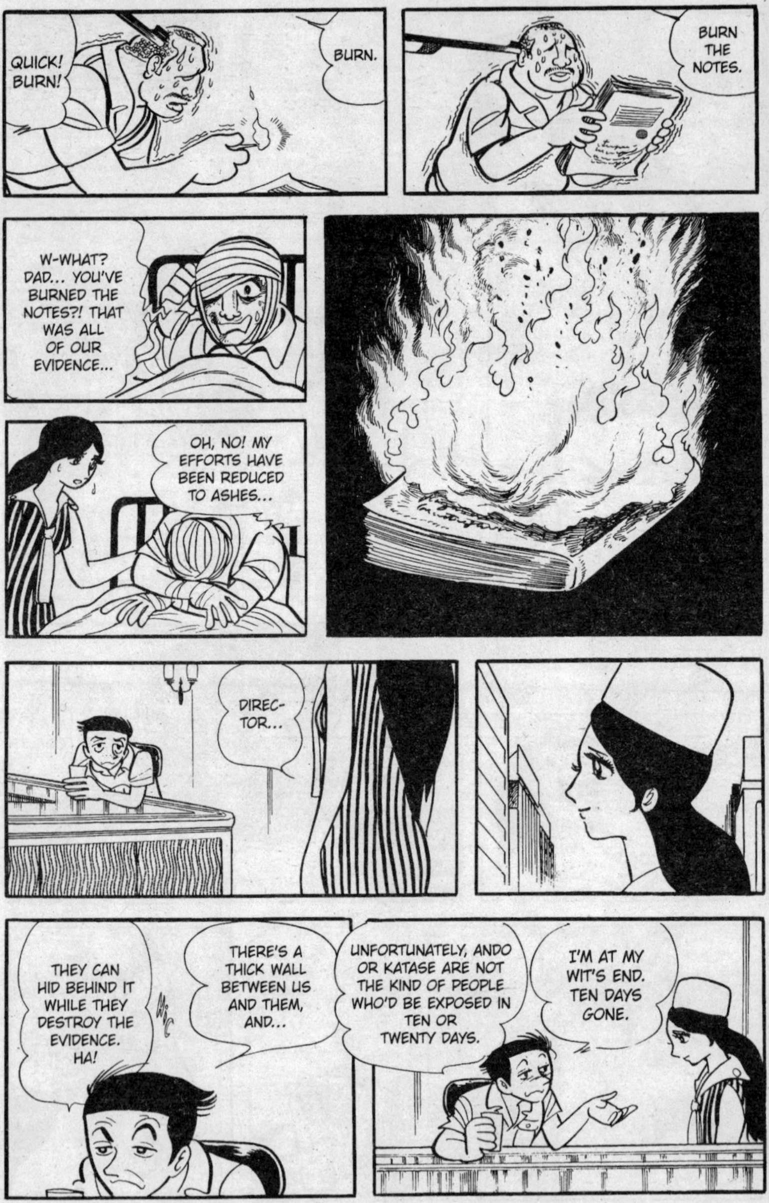
BURN THE NOTES.
BURN.
QUICK! BURN!
W-WHAT? DAD... YOU'VE BURNED THE NOTES?! THAT WAS ALL OF OUR EVIDENCE...
OH, NO! MY EFFORTS HAVE BEEN REDUCED TO ASHES...
DIREC-TOR...
I'M AT MY WIT'S END. TEN DAYS GONE.
UNFORTUNATELY, ANDO OR KATASE ARE NOT THE KIND OF PEOPLE WHO'D BE EXPOSED IN TEN OR TWENTY DAYS.
THERE'S A THICK WALL BETWEEN US AND THEM, AND...
THEY CAN HID BEHIND IT WHILE THEY DESTROY THE EVIDENCE. HA!
Hic

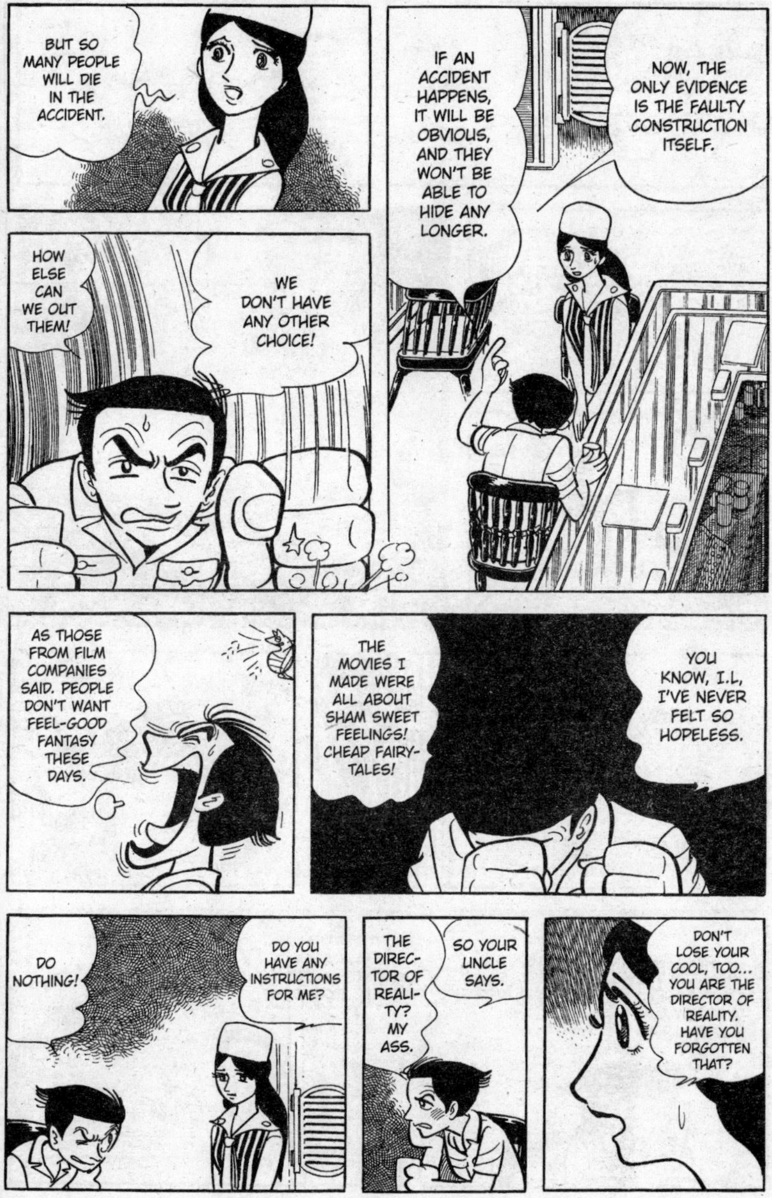
NOW, THE ONLY EVIDENCE IS THE FAULTY CONSTRUCTION ITSELF.
IF AN ACCIDENT HAPPENS, IT WILL BE OBVIOUS, AND THEY WON'T BE ABLE TO HIDE ANY LONGER.
BUT SO MANY PEOPLE WILL DIE IN THE ACCIDENT.
WE DON'T HAVE ANY OTHER CHOICE!
HOW ELSE CAN WE OUT THEM!
YOU KNOW, I.L, I'VE NEVER FELT SO HOPELESS.
THE MOVIES I MADE WERE ALL ABOUT SHAM SWEET FEELINGS! CHEAP FAIRY-TALES!
AS THOSE FROM FILM COMPANIES SAID. PEOPLE DON'T WANT FEEL-GOOD FANTASY THESE DAYS.
DON'T LOSE YOUR COOL, TOO... YOU ARE THE DIRECTOR OF REALITY. HAVE YOU FORGOTTEN THAT?
SO YOUR UNCLE SAYS.
THE DIREC-TOR OF REALI-TY? MY ASS.
DO YOU HAVE ANY INSTRUCTIONS FOR ME?
DO NOTHING!

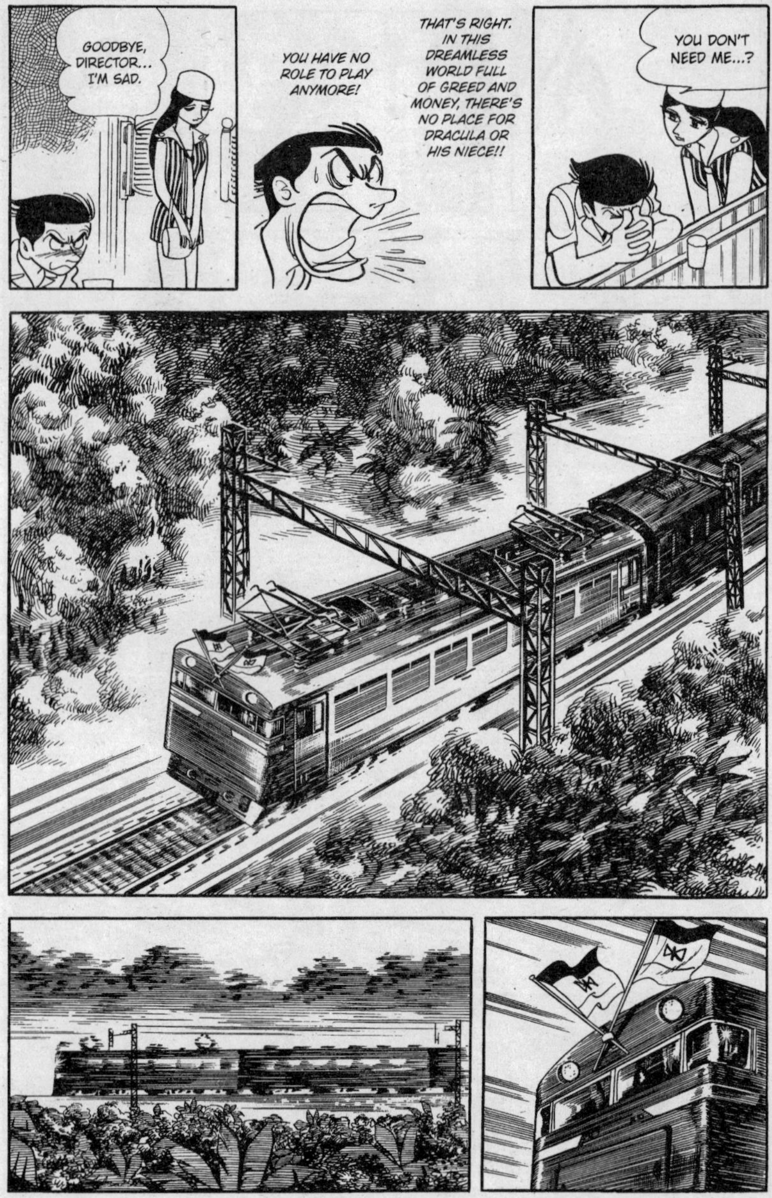
YOU DON'T NEED ME...?
THAT'S RIGHT. IN THIS DREAMLESS WORLD FULL OF GREED AND MONEY, THERE'S NO PLACE FOR DRACULA OR HIS NIECE!!
YOU HAVE NO ROLE TO PLAY ANYMORE!
GOODBYE, DIRECTOR... I'M SAD.

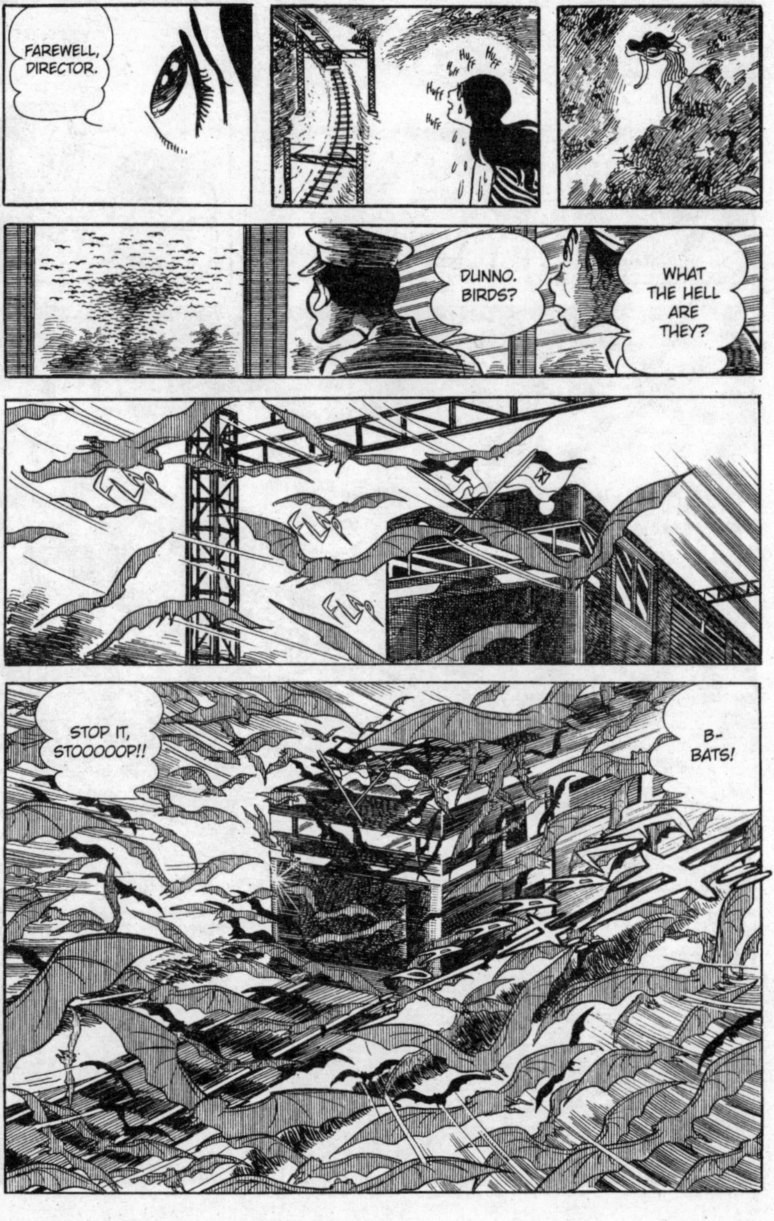
HUFF HUFF HUFF HUFF HUFF
FAREWELL, DIRECTOR.
WHAT THE HELL ARE THEY?
DUNNO. BIRDS?
B-BATS!
STOP IT, STOOOOOP!!

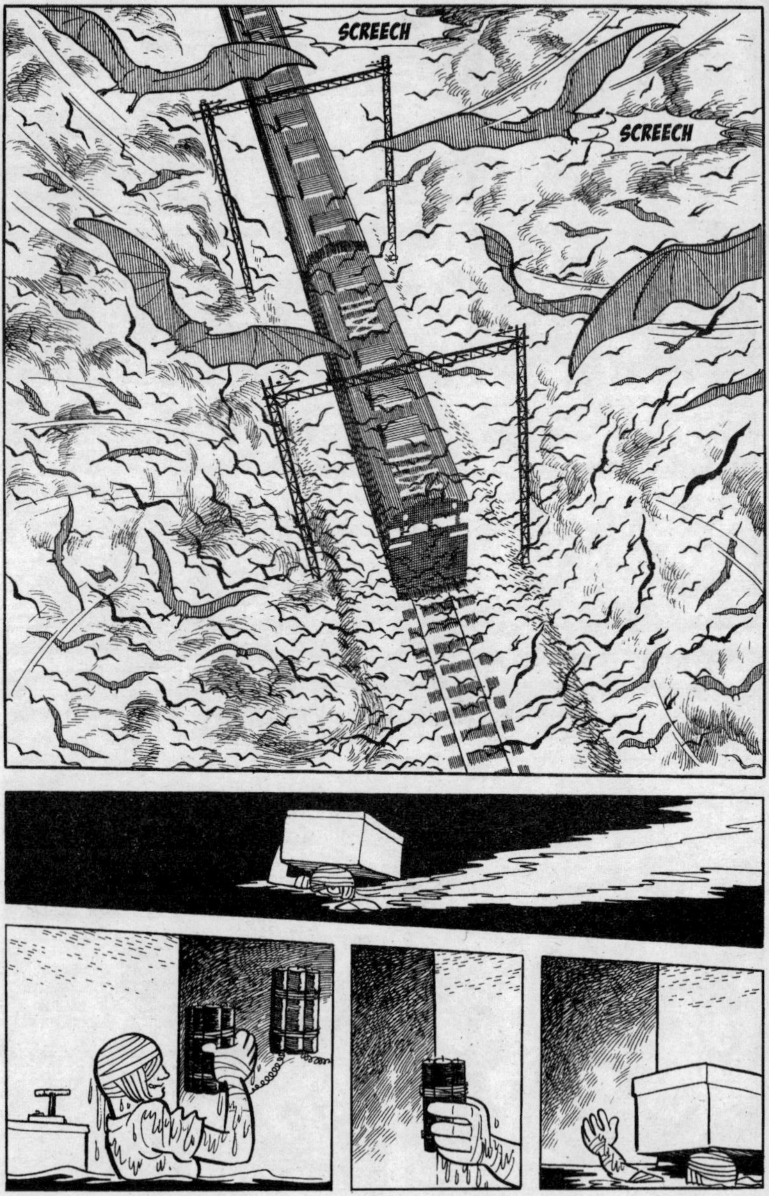
SCREECH
SCREECH

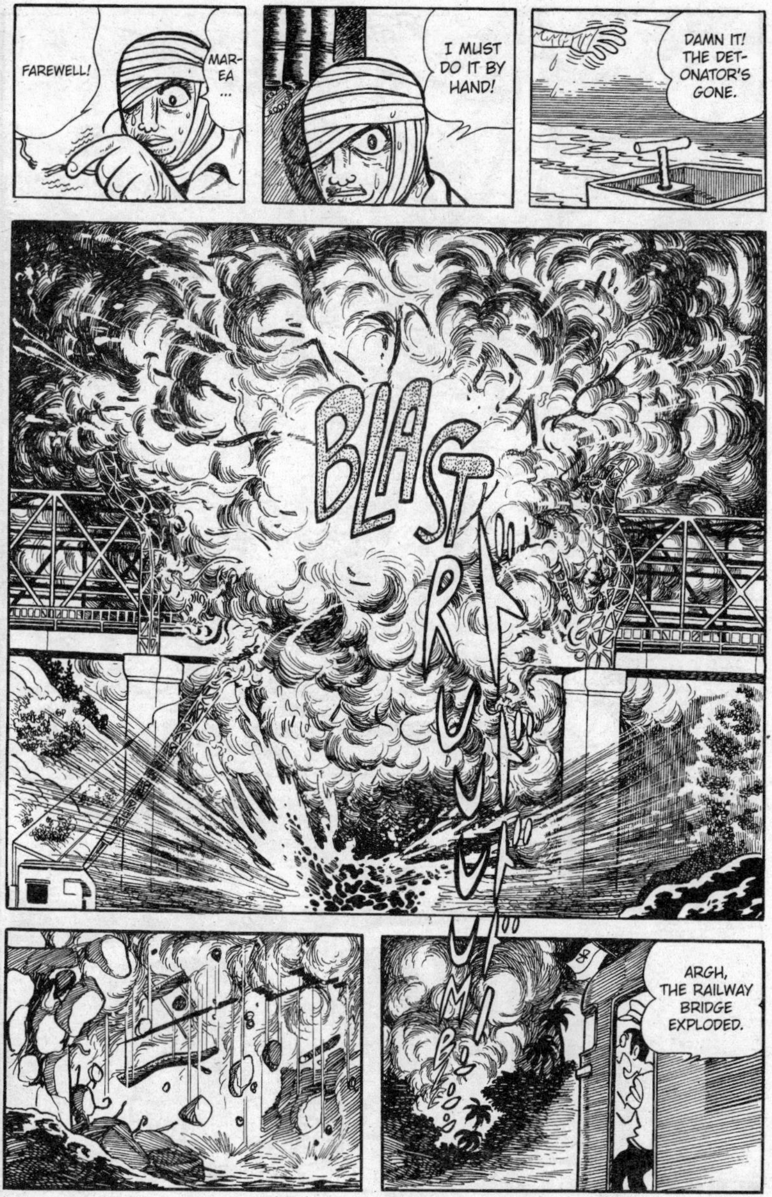
DAMN IT! THE DET-ONATOR'S GONE.
I MUST DO IT BY HAND!
MAR-EA ...
FAREWELL!
BLAST
RUUUUMB
ARGH, THE RAILWAY BRIDGE EXPLODED.

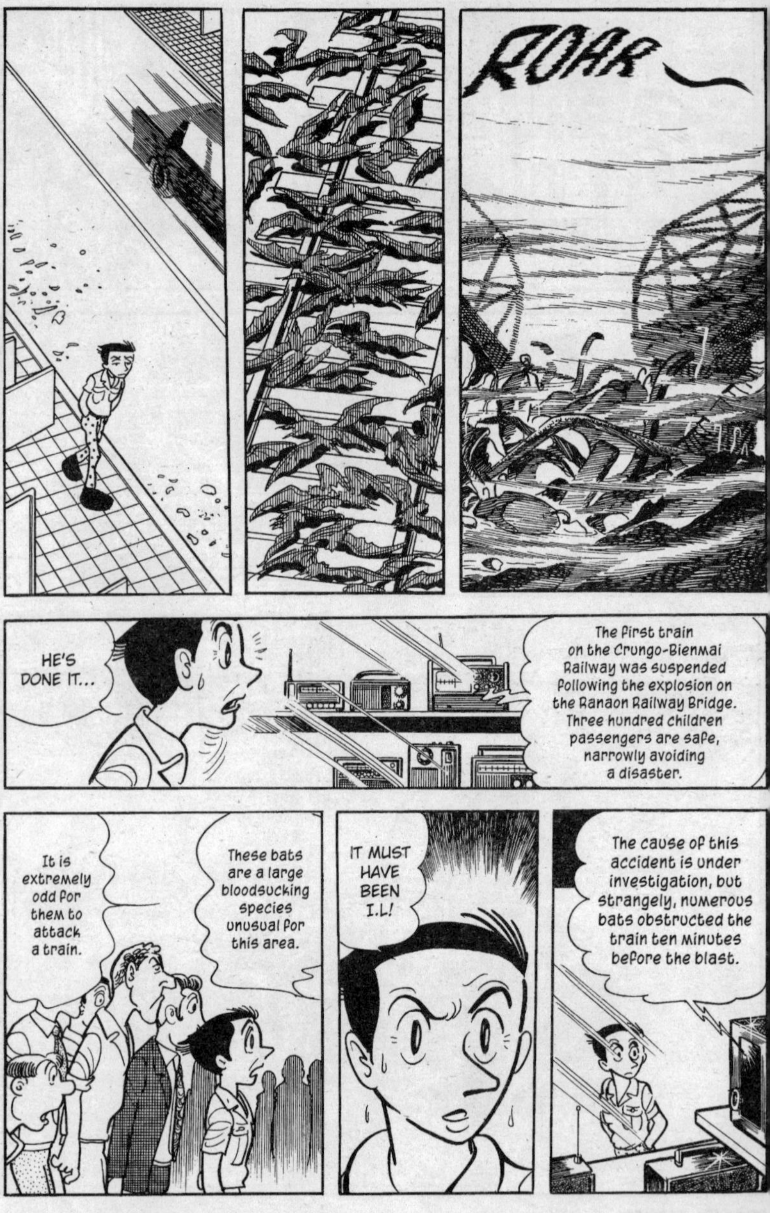
ROAR
The first train on the Crungo-Bienmai Railway was suspended following the explosion on the Ranaon Railway Bridge. Three hundred children passengers are safe, narrowly avoiding a disaster.
HE'S DONE IT...
The cause of this accident is under investigation, but strangely, numerous bats obstructed the train ten minutes before the blast.
IT MUST HAVE BEEN I.L!
These bats are a large bloodsucking species unusual for this area.
It is extremely odd for them to attack a train.

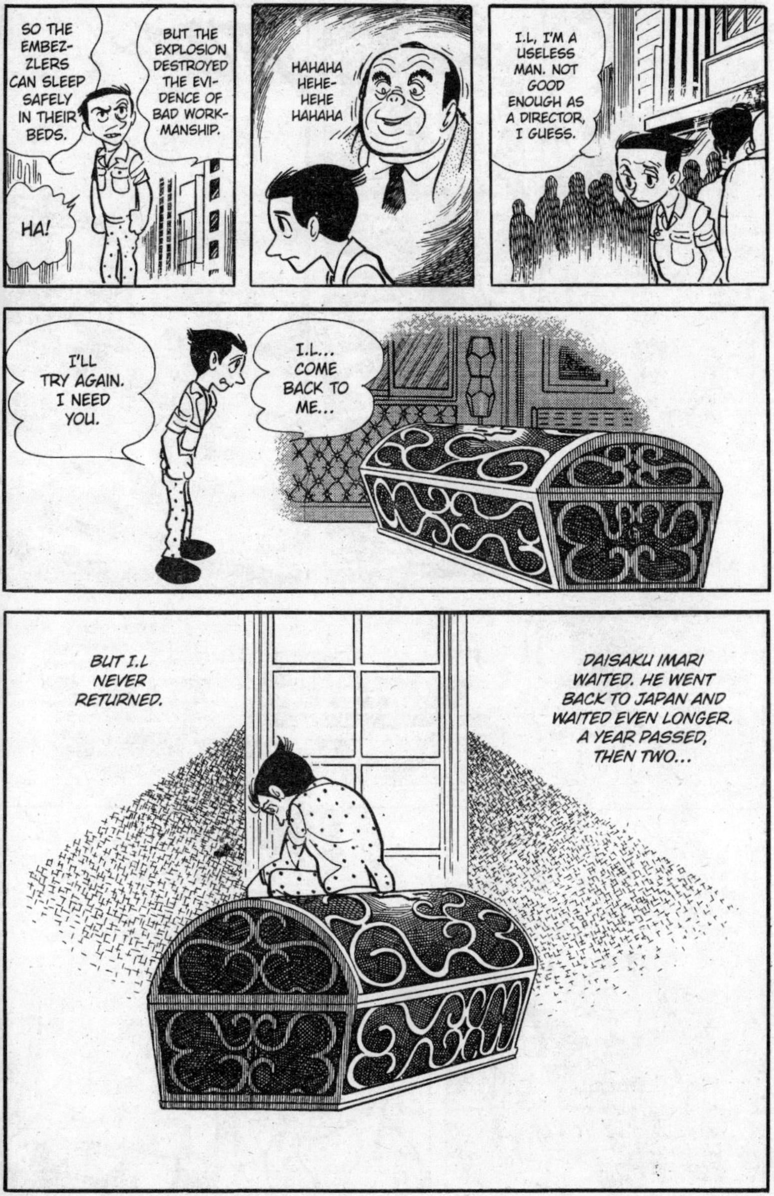
I.L, I'M A USELESS MAN. NOT GOOD ENOUGH AS A DIRECTOR, I GUESS.
HAHAHA HEHE-HEHE HAHAHA
BUT THE EXPLOSION DESTROYED THE EVI-DENCE OF BAD WORK-MANSHIP.
SO THE EMBEZ-ZLERS CAN SLEEP SAFELY IN THEIR BEDS.
HA!
I.L... COME BACK TO ME...
I'LL TRY AGAIN. I NEED YOU.
DAISAKU IMARI WAITED. HE WENT BACK TO JAPAN AND WAITED EVEN LONGER. A YEAR PASSED, THEN TWO...
BUT I.L NEVER RETURNED.

**THE END.**

# Postscript

This is the second piece I drew for Big Comic.

The first was *Swallowing the Earth*, but the story got out of hand as I was too ambitious and overenthusiastic.

At the same time, as the other artists' serialization were all one-shots, I felt each *Swallowing the Earth* episode lacked substance and that's why it wasn't as popular as other people's works.

I made the second work, *I.L*, a series, to align with the others in the magazine. Therefore, it was better received than *Swallowing the Earth*, but most of the fans who expected an epic opined that it was all small tricks and not much substance.

Because it is practically the same type of fantasy as Barbara, it may not be realistic enough.

As you know, I cannot draw women's bodies at all. Therefore, anatomically speaking, the imagery of the heroine is a mess. In preparation for publishing this piece in this collection, I was tempted to correct the awful drawings, but swallowing my pride, I left them as they were. This piece is full of things that symbolize that era, such as the Revolutionary Communist League, hippies, the Vietnam War, and absurdist cinema.

The title *I.L* was originally 'I'll', i.e. 'I will'. I knew it was an odd title, but the apostrophe became an interpunct in the magazine galleys, which made it meaningless. That is why I took the plunge and turned it into the heroine's name.

Osamu Tezuka

# ST

**This manga is prese**
**reading format.**



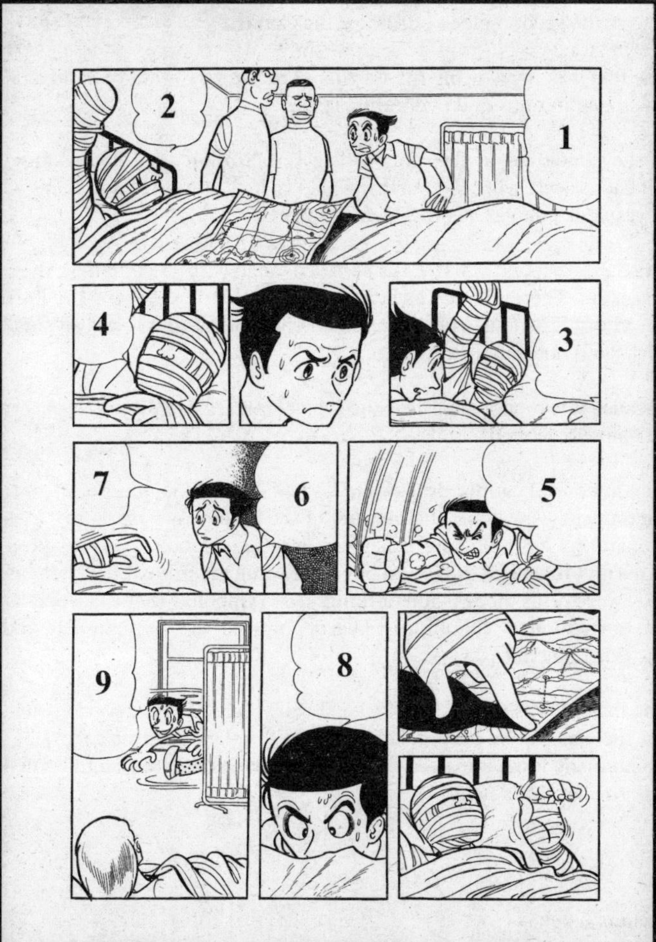
1
2
3
4
5
6
7
8
9

**Pages, panels, and speech balloons read from top right to bottom left, as shown above. SFX translations are placed adjacent to their original Japanese counterparts.**